T. W. Schultz
AF789652

CAPITAL FORMATION AND ECONOMIC GROWTH

NATIONAL BUREAU OF ECONOMIC RESEARCH

Special Conference Series

2. Conference on Business Cycles
3. Conference on Research in Business Finance
4. Regularization of Business Investment
5. Business Concentration and Price Policy
6. Capital Formation and Economic Growth

Capital Formation and Economic Growth

A CONFERENCE OF THE
UNIVERSITIES–NATIONAL BUREAU COMMITTEE
FOR ECONOMIC RESEARCH

A REPORT OF THE
NATIONAL BUREAU OF ECONOMIC RESEARCH, NEW YORK

PUBLISHED BY
PRINCETON UNIVERSITY PRESS, PRINCETON
1955

Copyright © 1955, by Princeton University Press
London: Geoffrey Cumberlege, Oxford University Press
L. C. CARD 55-6699

Printed in the United States of America
by Princeton University Press at Princeton, New Jersey

NATIONAL BUREAU OF ECONOMIC RESEARCH

OFFICERS, 1955

Harry Scherman, *Chairman*
Gottfried Haberler, *President*
George B. Roberts, *Vice-President and Treasurer*
W. J. Carson, *Executive Director*

DIRECTORS AT LARGE

Wallace J. Campbell, *Director, Cooperative League of the USA*
Solomon Fabricant, *New York University*
Albert J. Hettinger, Jr., *Lazard Frères and Company*
Oswald W. Knauth, *Beaufort, South Carolina*
H. W. Laidler, *Executive Director, League for Industrial Democracy*
Shepard Morgan, *Norfolk, Connecticut*
George B. Roberts, *Vice-President, The First National City Bank of New York*
Beardsley Ruml, *New York City*
Harry Scherman, *Chairman, Book-of-the-Month Club*
George Soule, *Bennington College*
N. I. Stone, *Consulting Economist*
J. Raymond Walsh, *New York City*
Joseph H. Willits, *Director, The Education Survey, University of Pennsylvania*
Leo Wolman, *Columbia University*
Donald B. Woodward, *Vick Chemical Company*
Theodore O. Yntema, *Vice President—Finance, Ford Motor Company*

DIRECTORS BY UNIVERSITY APPOINTMENT

E. Wight Bakke, *Yale*
Arthur F. Burns, *Columbia*
Melvin G. de Chazeau, *Cornell*
G. A. Elliott, *Toronto*
Frank W. Fetter, *Northwestern*
H. M. Groves, *Wisconsin*
Gottfried Haberler, *Harvard*
Clarence Heer, *North Carolina*
R. L. Kozelka, *Minnesota*
C. Arthur Kulp, *Pennsylvania*
T. W. Schultz, *Chicago*
Jacob Viner, *Princeton*

DIRECTORS APPOINTED BY OTHER ORGANIZATIONS

Percival F. Brundage, *American Institute of Accountants*
S. H. Ruttenberg, *Congress of Industrial Organizations*
Murray Shields, *American Management Association*
Boris Shishkin, *American Federation of Labor*
W. Allen Wallis, *American Statistical Association*
Frederick V. Waugh, *American Farm Economic Association*
John H. Williams, *American Economic Association*
Harold F. Williamson, *Economic History Association*

RESEARCH STAFF

Solomon Fabricant, *Director of Research*
Geoffrey H. Moore, *Associate Director of Research*
Moses Abramovitz
Harold Barger
Morris A. Copeland
David Durand
Milton Friedman
Raymond W. Goldsmith
Millard Hastay
W. Braddock Hickman
Daniel M. Holland
Thor Hultgren
John W. Kendrick
Simon Kuznets
Clarence D. Long
Ruth P. Mack
Ilse Mintz
G. Warren Nutter
Raymond J. Saulnier
Lawrence H. Seltzer
George J. Stigler
Leo Wolman
Herbert B. Woolley

Relation of National Bureau Directors to Publications Reporting Conference Proceedings

Since the present volume is a record of conference proceedings, it has been exempted from the rules governing submission of manuscripts to, and critical review by, the Board of Directors of the National Bureau. It has, however, been reviewed and accepted for publication by the Director of Research.

(Resolution adopted July 6, 1948 and revised November 21, 1949)

Universities–National Bureau Committee for Economic Research

This Committee is a cooperative venture of universities and the National Bureau. Its guiding objective is the encouragement of economic research on problems susceptible of objective treatment and of sufficiently broad scope to merit attention by institutions serving a scientific and public interest.

George J. Stigler, Chairman
Columbia University

G. Heberton Evans, Jr., Vice-Chairman
The Johns Hopkins University

Moses Abramovitz, *Stanford University*
Gardner Ackley, *University of Michigan*
M. A. Adelman, *Massachusetts Institute of Technology*
V Lewis Bassie, *University of Illinois*
Francis M. Boddy, *University of Minnesota*
Raymond T. Bowman, *University of Pennsylvania*
John B. Condliffe, *University of California*
James S. Earley, *University of Wisconsin*
Solomon Fabricant, *National Bureau of Economic Research*
Milton S. Heath, *University of North Carolina*
Richard B. Heflebower, *Northwestern University*
Edgar M. Hoover, *Washington, D.C.*
Elizabeth E. Hoyt, *Iowa State College of Agriculture and Mechanic Arts*
A. D. H. Kaplan, *The Brookings Institution*
Dexter M. Keezer, *McGraw-Hill Publishing Company*
M. Slade Kendrick, *Cornell University*
H. Gregg Lewis, *University of Chicago*
Adolph Lowe, *New School for Social Research*
D. C. MacGregor, *University of Toronto*
Donald Marsh, *McGill University*
Oskar Morgenstern, *Princeton University*
Eastin Nelson, *University of Texas*
William H. Nicholls, *Vanderbilt University*
Richard Ruggles, *Yale University*
Arthur Smithies, *Harvard University*
Harold M. Somers, *University of Buffalo*
Joseph J. Spengler, *Duke University*
Emanuel Stein, *New York University*
M. C. Urquhart, *Queen's University*
Rutledge Vining, *University of Virginia*

PREFACE

THIS volume contains the papers presented at the Conference on Capital Formation and Economic Growth which met in New York, November 6 to 8, 1953, under the auspices of the Universities–National Bureau Committee for Economic Research. The volume also includes discussion papers prepared at the invitation of the Conference Committee and contributions submitted by members of the Conference. The authors of the principal papers have, in a number of cases, prepared rejoinders.

The Conference Planning Committee consisted of Professors James Duesenberry, Evsey D. Domar, Alexander Gerschenkron, W. W. Rostow, and Dr. H. W. Singer. The undersigned acted as chairman of the Committee and as editor of this volume.

The book was prepared for the press by members of the editorial staff of the National Bureau of Economic Research. Their contribution is most gratefully acknowledged.

MOSES ABRAMOVITZ

CONTENTS

CAPITAL FORMATION
AND ECONOMIC GROWTH

INTRODUCTION

MOSES ABRAMOVITZ

NATIONAL BUREAU OF ECONOMIC RESEARCH
AND STANFORD UNIVERSITY

I

THE present resurgence of work on questions concerning long-period economic trends and on international differences in levels of development is a reflection of persistent and profound problems troubling the world. Within the capitalist area the decade of the thirties roused fears of economic stagnation which the turbulent experience of the forties has hardly dispelled. Stagnation apart, the increasingly articulate demands of popular electorates have fixed attention upon the very different rates of progress among countries of the Western World and stimulated scholars to measure secular rates of growth and to explore their causes. And the same stimulus, in even more intense form, is afforded by the situation in the underdeveloped countries of Asia, Africa, and South America. The growing gap between their incomes and those of the capitalist world has combined with their peoples' growing awareness of the gap to produce a tension intolerable both to their own societies and to those of the richer West. Meanwhile, West and East, the performance of enterprise economies is challenged by that of the planned economies in Soviet Russia, Eastern Europe, and, still more recently, China.

The Universities–National Bureau Committee assembled an early conference on questions of economic growth in November 1948.[1] It considered papers on the variant meanings and aspects of economic growth, on the theories and factors which have been advanced by way of explanation, and on problems of measurement involved in intertemporal, international, and interregional comparisons. The aims of this first conference were exploratory: "In view of the wide scope of the field, the relative scarcity of sustained empirical work, and the absence of an agreed upon body of theoretical hypotheses concerning factors determining economic growth, any discussion of this topic could be only in the nature of a tentative and preliminary exploration."[2]

[1] The papers submitted were published in "Problems in the Study of Economic Growth," mimeographed, National Bureau of Economic Research, July 1949.

[2] *Ibid.*, from the Foreword by Simon Kuznets.

By the end of 1951 the Universities–National Bureau Committee began to lay plans for a second meeting. It ventured to think that discussion of substantive issues would now be possible, and, in particular, that by the time of the conference the outcome of some empirical work would be ready for examination. To permit searching discussion, it seemed imperative to center attention on some single sector of the sprawling area of investigation relevant to economic growth. And among the sectors close to the center of the problem, it seemed likely that capital formation, long the object of attention for other reasons, would be found in relatively the most advanced state. The determinants of secular trends and of persistent international differences in the level of capital formation, therefore, became the specific subject of the meeting.

II

Because the theory of capital formation has been the object of study for a long time, it is not hard to fix the general outlines of the problem. The conception of the subject which helped shape our program was that the process of capital formation involves three distinct, if interdependent, activities. One is *saving*, the activity by which claims to resources, which might be exercised in favor of current consumption, are set aside and so become available for other purposes. A second is *finance*, the activity by which claims to resources are either assembled from among those released by domestic saving, or obtained from abroad, or specially created, usually as bank deposits or notes, and then placed in the hands of investors. The third is *investment* itself, the activity by which resources are actually committed to the production of capital goods. The volume of capital formation depends on the intensity and efficiency with which these activities are carried on.

So much is, of course, familiar, and the papers presented to the conference deal with some aspects of each of the activities. The matter is complicated, however, by the fact that the manner in which the activities are carried on has changed radically over time and is very different among countries. The standard theory of capital formation, on the other hand, is still heavily influenced by its origins in a particular stage of the development of capitalist economies. It is, moreover, designed to deal especially with the phenomena of interest rates and short-term investment fluctuations. The reconsideration of capital theory from the point of view of secular changes and international differences in the level of capital formation involves some formidable modifications of older views. The next sections contain some brief notes on the relation of the papers in this volume to the new conception of the subject which is slowly crystallizing.

III

The subject of saving raises two broad questions. One concerns the role of saving in the process of capital formation. Modern theory emphasizes the possibility that rates of saving and investment may be incompatible and that a level of thrift that is too high may make for lower rather than higher levels of investment. The analysis that suggests such awkward possibilities, however, is oriented to short-term phenomena and has hardly, as yet, considered the secular relations of saving and investment propensities, particularly for cyclically disturbed economies. I do no more than point to the existence of the problem since none of the papers attacks it directly.

The other great question has to do with the determinants of the supply of saving. With regard to this, our thinking has been heavily influenced by the simple view that the difference between income and "necessary expenses," which affords the power to save, is the chief determinant of the level of saving.[3] From this the easy inference is drawn that as per capita income grows, savings should increase more than proportionately. And it gives rise to the expectation that ratios between savings and national income will be higher in rich than in poor countries, and higher in a given country as its level of average income increases.

These views have received a certain support from interfamily savings comparisons and from studies of short-term savings fluctuations. But Simon Kuznets' work, the relevant results of which are presented in his paper, puts a quite fresh face on the matter. His studies, covering a number of countries, some over a considerable period of years, show: (1) that in comparisons among countries, the correlation between *per capita* income and the savings–national income ratio is far from perfect; (2) that ratios of net savings to net national product, at least for developed and semideveloped economies, fall within a limited range from somewhat over 5 to about 15 per cent; (3) that secular rises in per capita income are not generally accompanied by rises in the proportion of savings to national

[3] Cf. Alfred Marshall, *Principles of Economics*, 8th ed., London, Macmillan, 1938, p. 229.

product. With regard to the third point, the evidence rather shows that in some developed countries the savings ratio either declines slightly or is stable throughout. It also suggests, if only dimly, a long cycle in national savings ratios, ". . . its *up* phase occurring presumably some time after the rise in rates of growth of national product, and of population (in the older countries), and, perhaps, also after that in the growth of per capita product; and its *down* phase emerging at different dates in different countries, and with different degrees of abruptness associated with the disruptive effects of wars and revolutions" (page 32, below).

Although these data do not constitute direct evidence on theoretical savings supply functions, they stand as a challenge to older ideas. And Kuznets' suggestions concerning the causes of the observed savings ratios do the same. His explanation of the range within which the ratios for different countries fall places no weight on the associated range of incomes. It considers the over-all ratio to be a combination of those ruling for two groups of individuals: the rich few, who are "automatic" savers, and the poor masses, whose saving is effortful and, therefore, based on attempts at rational provision for old age. Kuznets considers that, in a progressive society, the incomes of the former group are prevented from cumulating by the economic mobility associated with progress itself. This, together with the downdrift of returns on property, prevents "automatic" saving from becoming ever larger. "Rational" saving is determined by the ratio between working life and life expectancy after retirement, by interest rates, and by the ratio between people of working age and those older. It is, therefore, dominated by demographic factors, themselves associated with economic development. Kuznets' explanation of the stability or downward drift of savings ratios in developed countries also emphasizes a set of factors intimately related to economic progress—the pressure toward higher consumption levels, urbanization, the lessening importance of the individual entrepreneur, and egalitarian legislation.

Individual saving is the typical activity by which resources are released for capital formation in capitalist countries. It is, however, but one extreme in a continuum. Even in capitalist countries the growth in the scale of investment projects has led to institutionalized saving by business enterprises out of profits and by the state out of revenues. In the United States, in the past, these sources produced some 40 per cent of all saving. As the investment projects come to be of national dimensions, there is presumably a tendency for government saving to assume greater importance, as in the development schemes of some of the poorer countries. The other extreme item in the range is provided by saving activity in a comprehensively planned state like the Soviet Union. In that country, as F. D. Holzman's paper reveals, the chief source of savings is taxation. Direct investment by individuals is insignificant. Individual saving, the retained profits of state enterprises, and even increases in currency in circulation have been relatively small.[4]

In these circumstances the level of saving depends in part on governmental policy, and in part, as Holzman argues, on the efficiency of the tax administration and on the effects of taxation on the incentive to produce. Further, since taxation must be extremely heavy in order both to cover the more common functions of government and to provide for investment, the problem of choosing forms of taxation least destructive to production incentives and to the functioning of the price mechanism as a means of allocating resources becomes crucial. According to Holzman, these considerations combine to account for Soviet emphasis on indirect taxes in spite of ideological opposition to their regressiveness. They are easier to administer, and their effect in reducing the rewards of work and of higher-paying jobs is concealed.

An interesting contrast in tax policy, therefore, emerges as we scan the spectrum from capitalism to communism. From the point of view of maximizing saving, it is a familiar maxim in capitalist countries that taxes should be light in order to provide as large a surplus for individual saving as possible.[5] As between indirect taxes and direct, especially progressive, taxes, the former are the better for saving since they protect the large income surplus of the rich and do not shrink the rewards of accumulation. In a communist country, however, taxes must be heavy to provide funds for government saving, and the yields of higher taxes need to be balanced against a possible inhibition of effort and reduction of output. But, as in capitalist countries, the indirect tax seems to be preferred—not because it protects the sources and rewards of private saving but because it protects the rewards for work, skill, and responsibility.

[4] This is not to say that inflation has not been of importance. Also, it is not possible to speak about sources of investment finance precisely because tax and other revenues of the state are not earmarked for specific purposes.

[5] This, of course, assumes that investment outlets are adequate.

IV

Financial activity arises chiefly from the fact that access to outlets for investment is confined largely to specific groups of businessmen who command the requisite technical and market information and the temperament to use it. Moreover, the scope of operations of each business group is limited geographically and industrially. Saving, on the other hand, is an activity far more widely diffused through the community and carried on by persons who generally lack the skill and personal characteristics for active investment, certainly as regards the whole of their savings. In the absence of effective financial laws, agencies, and institutions, the gap between savers and business becomes a serious block to investment, the extent of which may be roughly indicated by the gap between gilt-edge rates and the rates of interest paid by ordinary businessmen, in this country or in England, say, 150 years ago, or by the similar gap which exists in underdeveloped countries today.

In developed countries the function of finance is carried on, with varying degrees of efficiency, by an elaborate mechanism involving many agencies and institutions. Its purposes, in one way or another, are to spread information, to provide brokerage, to limit obligations, to create liquidity, and to transform the relatively risky liabilities, which are the only kind that business usually can afford to accept, into the relatively safe assets, which are the only kind that savers usually can afford to hold.

In the course of this activity, and in a degree which depends on its elaboration and efficiency, two developments take place. The first is that the real cost to business of financing its investments is reduced. The savings of the community are rendered highly mobile both industrially and geographically, less burdensome liabilities are imposed on business, and more attractive assets are acquired by savers.

At the same time the real assets of the community come to be represented by a great overlay of financial assets which reflect a tremendous quantity and variety of claims, generated by the operation of financial intermediaries, and which require for their servicing an enormous flow of money transfers. Ideally these obligations need represent no burden. If all is in order, the net cost of finance to the operating units of business is much lower than it otherwise would be. The manifold transfers and retransfers of the earnings of the underlying assets are the mechanism by which successive quantities are chipped away to pay for financial services, until at last a residual sum reaches the ultimate savers that is presumably larger than they would otherwise be able to obtain from their capital. The overlay can, however, become a burden if serious mistakes are made by business and the public either in estimating the risks involved in maintaining the flow of service charges in an unstable economy or in gauging the public's willingness, in the long run, to hold securities of different kinds. In the first event the fixed charges on business and financial institutions come to be out of proportion to earnings with obvious consequences for capital values; in the second there are readjustments in values without changes in earnings. In either event the readjustments are embarrassing or disastrous to many security holders, including intermediate financial institutions. The elaboration of financial obligations may then become a bar to current capital formation. For in the ordinary course of events, industry and finance attract savings by transforming the risk of a specific venture into a lesser risk on the general credit of the business. But when affairs are out of joint, it becomes impossible to finance even excellent risks on specific current ventures because the general credit of business and finance is prejudiced by the exaggerated claims of earlier obligations or by the evaporation of capital values.

It is to this range of issues that Raymond W. Goldsmith's paper and Edward S. Shaw's succeeding comments are especially relevant. Goldsmith presents, for the first time, long-term indexes of what he calls the financial interrelations ratio (FIR), the relation between the total volume of assets and the value of the underlying items of real capital. His series provide measures of the tendency for this ratio to rise as an economy develops and its financial activity becomes more elaborate. Goldsmith's data also show how money has declined in importance among financial assets and how banks have been supplemented and, to some degree, supplanted by other financial intermediaries. His figures suggest how the size of FIR responds to monetary fluctuations, and he considers the problem of the burden of financial claims sketched above.

Shaw's cogent discussion serves to remind us that the overlay of financial obligations represents an element of service to the economic community. He suggests how, apart from the technical innovations in financing which themselves, no doubt, stimulated economic growth and gave rise to the financial overlay, the overlay may be a response to economic development. He points out, for example, that rising real incomes generate effective demands for "savings media that do not require managerial skills, for insurance of property and life and health." This, of course, poses sharply the problem of adapting the types of securities offered to the demands of institutional investors if finance is not to be a block to investment.

Shaw also raises explicitly the question of the "burden of the debt" and suggests it may be fruitfully approached by conceiving of an equilibrium between the value of real assets and the value of the financial claims that the public wishes to hold. An equilibrium FIR, he suggests, is one appropriate to the public's demand for securities of different types, itself a product of a country's stage of economic development and institutional arrangements. He challenges us to analyze the determinants of this equilibrium in specific terms and to describe the methods by which an economy adjusts when it is out of equilibrium. His own brief notes on these questions are a stimulating beginning.

V

Investment itself is the third activity involved in capital formation. The preoccupation of economics in earlier decades with questions of income distribution gave the theory of the demand for new capital goods a particular character. It made the profitability of employing additional capital depend on the existing proportions of the factors of production—land, labor, and capital. Since the theory generally extended the operation of a law of diminishing returns from the case of changing proportions of factors to that of increasing scale of production, the inference was drawn that the demand for additional capital would tend to be high where labor and land were plentiful relative to the existing stock of capital goods.[6] Comparatively recently, the problems of business cycles and persistent depression have brought to the fore the effects of the rate of population growth and of technical progress on the demand for new capital, and studies of those questions have been valuable preparation for the longer-term issues with which we are here concerned.

It remains true, however, that the expectations that emerge from even a combination of the various causes recited above fail to square with the observed course of capital formation over time and with the variety of experience in different countries. In particular, these factors are hardly enough to explain the relative stagnation of the

[6] The present writer returns to these questions in the comment with which this volume ends.

capital-poor but population-rich or land-rich countries which failed to progress during the nineteenth century and, in many cases, remain unprogressive today. Nor do these factors seem sufficient to explain the very different times at which Great Britain, the United States, France, Germany, Italy, and Japan began their periods of rapid industrialization.

In the circumstances attention has shifted to other conditions for the productivity of capital and the demand for capital goods which, in connection with other problems, had been relegated to the background of our thought. In their most general form these conditions may be referred to as the conditions of economic leadership. For the conditions of capital productivity usually emphasized in economic theory—natural resources, population, the stock of existing capital, and the state of the arts—serve only to define a set of potentialities, of unknown character and scope, for making advantageous use of additional equipment. But when these potentialities will be seized, and the extent to which they will be seized, are matters that turn on the vigor and efficiency with which human energy is applied to finding and exploiting economic opportunities. These matters raise issues concerning human motivation and political and commercial organization, sometimes thought to be outside the scope of economics, but now clearly seen to lie near the center of the problem of economic growth. The essays below attack these questions and also those of technological progress in their bearing on investment from a number of angles.

Bert F. Hoselitz and Thomas C. Cochran contribute complementary essays on the social and political environments that shaped the origins and activities of the business classes in France, Britain, and the United States. Limited space forbids any catalogue of the many-sided contributions of these papers. I mention but two points. One is the contrast they suggest between the size, aggressiveness, and motivation of a business class in societies whose feudal traditions are relatively strong and the characteristics of the same class in countries where such traditions are weak or almost absent. The other is the evolution that both Hoselitz and Cochran find in the character of business managers and of business organization in the course of economic development, an evolution shaped apparently by the changes that emerged in the problem of obtaining finance and adapting to the requirements of large-scale production.

The same range of problems is investigated again in the essays by Henry G. Aubrey and Marion J. Levy, but this time in the quite different setting provided by underdeveloped countries. Their papers are again complementary in that Aubrey places chief emphasis upon the environmental factors limiting productive investment while Levy goes on to consider the values and motivations peculiar to a noncapitalist culture which may hinder or promote industrialization.

Aubrey directs our attention to the extremely risky character of long-term industrial investment in many countries, a riskiness arising from political instability, from the difficulty of obtaining finance in the face of chronic devaluation, and from the severity of economic fluctuations in countries dependent on one or a few exports. If, therefore, real estate and inventory speculation—the policy of "quick-in and quick-out," as it has been called—engages the energies of businessmen, this may be due in good part to a canny appreciation of the economic opportunities afforded by their national environment rather than to any peculiarities in the personal goals of investors. And Aubrey reminds us, too, that the curse of the poor is their poverty. Domestic markets are small, incapable of supporting the scale of modern establishments; transportation facilities and power are lacking or expensive; the price of capital equipment is high; skilled workers, technicians, and managers are scarce. In short, the external economies created by economic growth are still to be gained, and in their absence the immediate productivity of new capital is low.

Levy's investigation confirms many of Aubrey's findings, but he also throws light on the effects of noncapitalist motivation. In prerevolutionary China, and in some other countries, he finds that the entrepreneurial role has low prestige and that much effort is directed to getting out of occupations connected with capital formation rather than staying in them. Actions requiring the adoption of new social patterns are strongly resisted. "Otherworldly asceticism" is more highly prized than mastery over the physical facts of this world. Loyalty to family is more widely approved than calculation of economic advantage.

Business enterprises are, of course, not the only centers of economic leadership. Even in capitalist countries government constitutes a supplementary center of leadership. In communist countries it is the primary center. Gregory Grossman's article provides a description and interpretation of certain aspects of the recent history of investment in the Soviet Union. From the viewpoint of the present discussion it contributes a suggestive picture of the range of considerations which are operative in investment planning in a communist state. These, as may be imagined, are radically different from the considerations controlling the calculations of private investors in capitalist countries. This difference consists not merely in the obvious capacity of Soviet planners to choose goals for the economic system which are independent of the desires of consumers and workers. Grossman's paper is especially useful in illustrating the impact on Russian planning of cost considerations—like the need to provide education, urban housing, and community facilities—which are implicit in carrying through certain investment decisions, but which are only dimly reflected in market prices and so would affect private investment planning little, if at all.

Turning now to the last of the papers dealing with factors controlling the inducement to invest, we come to the essays by Abbott Payson Usher and W. Rupert Maclaurin on technical change and innovation. In their main outlines the two papers guide us through the successive stages of the process which, in logic, but there alone, leads from fundamental scientific progress to the commercial exploitation that is the occasion for capital investment. Both papers, however, stress that, historically, the course of events does not run invariably from general principles through engineering development to commercial application. The opposite course is also common. In the view of these writers the economic environment emerges as a great conditioning factor in the history of science, and the work of businessmen bent on exploiting that environment through the medium of technological innovation becomes crucial.

In addition to this basic theme, an important section of Usher's paper draws attention to the possibility of using the theme of technical progress to interpret the course of regional growth, rather than industrial growth, as is more commonly done. If we were to generalize the view that Usher sketches, we should recognize that some of the major trends in economic development, and in the capital formation which underlies it, are associated with the impact of technological change upon the locational advantages of different regions. These advantages, which derive from the nature and quantity of a region's resources and from their geographical position, have a value at any time that is relative to the existing state of knowledge. But technical advance makes worthless resources valuable and brings inaccessible places into the stream of trade. A combination of location theory with the history of technology and with the data of economic geography may well make an important contribution to our understanding of international differences in rates of growth during the era of rapid industrialization.[7]

VI

We take notice finally of the need to consider the three activities involved in capital formation, not in isolation, but in the light of their interrelations. These are, of course, numerous, and it would be pointless in the present context even to try to catalogue them.

If we consider the literature of recent years, the relation that has attracted most attention is that between saving and investment. With regard to nineteenth-century conditions in capitalist countries, Kuznets, in company with many others, supports the hypothesis that the availability of saving placed an effective ceiling on the level of investment. With regard to conditions between the two World Wars, many believe that the opposite was true. And, with regard to underdeveloped countries, it has often been argued that the inefficiency of financial markets has placed an effective limit on both. These hypotheses, of course, are simplifications. They may prove to be adequate theories for special circumstances. In the general case, however, it is necessary to recognize that the intensity with which each activity is carried on alters the conditions under which the others operate. All three must find their place in an adequate theoretical model applicable to secular changes and international differences in capital formation. It is hardly necessary to add that such a model will not refer to capital formation alone but will need to account for the other significant elements of economic growth.

The point of view from which such models have so far been developed has been that of the conditions of economic stability. Keynes showed that one of the conditions of stability is that the volume of saving the community desires to achieve should be equal to the volume of investment it desires to undertake. More recently, Harrod and Domar have made us aware that in a progressive economy some rate of increase in investment is required as a condition of steady growth—a rate determined by the technical capacities of capital goods and the community's propensity to save out of additional income. Adolph Lowe's paper in the present volume carries this analysis into another sphere. He points out that the conditions specified above could be sufficient only with respect to money flows. They could be sufficient in physical terms as well only in a world of

[7] Cf. the comment by Walter Isard.

utterly fluid resources. But if resources are not utterly fluid, a level of investment that adequately offsets desired saving may be out of adjustment with the capacity of the capital-goods industries in equipment and trained labor. Or the rate of increase in investment required to maintain steady growth may be out of adjustment with the capacity of the machine-tool and related industries to expand the capacity of the capital-goods industries. These states of imbalance, he shows, threaten our stability and limit our ability to progress. He therefore sets himself to analyze those conditions for steady growth that are the physical counterpart of the monetary conditions defined earlier.

VII

A reader who studies this volume with attention will, I think, be impressed with the extent to which modern studies of economic growth utilize and confirm many of the earlier insights of economic historians and theorists. It is the mark of the present revival of interest in the problems of economic growth, however, that it envisages a systematic effort to organize such comparative studies of periods and nations as may make possible the formulation and testing of widely applicable theories. As W. W. Rostow points out, a number of the essays in the present volume themselves constitute such systematic comparisons or represent work advancing toward them. Rostow's own essay may be looked on as an effort to extract common elements from the work of the various contributors and to suggest some of the problems involved in working through empirical studies to fruitful theories.

Such work, manifestly, is in its infancy. Indeed, having regard to the complexity of the problem and the need to push our studies into many distinct disciplines, few students are sanguine about our ability to achieve reliable theories of useful generality. This issue, however, will not soon be settled. For the time being, the search for general theories of economic growth serves to unify the work of many students concerned with urgent practical problems. And the scope of the work itself has its uses. Its wide range has already shaken the complacency of students with regard to the sufficiency of their own specialties. From such disturbances valuable results often emerge. In particular, it seems right to say that no other problems in recent decades have so stimulated efforts toward the unification of the social sciences as have the problems of economic growth with which this book is concerned.

PART I

SOURCES AND CHANNELS OF FINANCE IN CAPITALIST COUNTRIES

INTERNATIONAL DIFFERENCES IN CAPITAL FORMATION AND FINANCING

SIMON KUZNETS

NATIONAL BUREAU OF ECONOMIC RESEARCH
AND THE JOHNS HOPKINS UNIVERSITY

IN THIS PAPER we compare trends in capital formation and financing in a number of countries whose economies are organized as business systems. The data are scanty, particularly for periods long enough to provide historical perspective in viewing problems of economic growth. Diversity of definitions affects the comparability even of the current estimates, and the figures must be examined critically before they can be used. Under these circumstances a portion of the ensuing discussion is devoted to questions of definition, to provide unequivocal guides to the figures; and, on the principle that some rough order of magnitudes is better than complete ignorance, the qualifications detailed below are disregarded in the attempt to draw some inferences from the data.

The paper falls into three major sections. In the first we deal with the proportion of domestic capital formation to national product. We emphasize domestic capital formation first because, as historical experience suggests, domestic investment precedes foreign. We discuss the proportion to national product, an over-all measure of economic activity, to avoid complicating the comparisons by differences in absolute units.

The second section is devoted to consideration of foreign investment, i.e. the foreign-based component of *total* capital formation. From these data we can determine the shares of domestic capital formation contributed by foreign and domestic sources; or, conversely, the share of total domestic savings flowing, on net balance, abroad. By combining the data on foreign investments with those on domestic capital formation discussed in Section 1, we can derive the proportion of total capital formation to total national product.

In the third section we deal with the various sources of capital formation financing. Unlike the data on international capital movements and domestic capital formation, of which a stock, if varied and patchy, has accumulated because of long-standing interest, the data on various channels of domestic financing of capital formation are exceedingly meager. Yet the topic must be considered explicitly and available data or hints utilized, so that at least the relevant questions which may serve to guide future inquiry can be adequately formulated.

In order not to interrupt the discussion we have put all the tabular material into Appendix A. The data-minded student will probably find this appendix the most valuable and important part of the paper, and the text partly a guide to the tables and partly a tentative summary of the conclusions they suggest.

1. *Proportion of Domestic Capital Formation to National Product*

QUESTIONS OF SCOPE

Domestic capital formation as measured here comprises additions to construction (including residential), to producers' durable machinery and equipment, and to business and government inventories. Some of the available estimates exclude some of the items: e.g. most of them exclude changes in government inventories, and some of the long-term estimates also omit changes in business inventories. In some estimates the definition of producers' equipment is not explicit, and the question arises whether, for example, military tools in the hands of government and small hand tools, etc., are included. But, by and large, it is this total that, with varying degrees of grossness and netness in the additions, is approximated in the estimates of capital formation.

No *standard* definition of capital formation exists at present; and I doubt whether one is desirable now. The definition given here—which includes government capital represented by military weapons and construction, and excludes consumer durable goods other than housing—can easily be defended. On the other hand, cogent arguments can be found for the definition that excludes the former and includes the latter—which Raymond W. Goldsmith used in his recent study of saving,[1] a concept identical on a nationwide basis with capital formation.

However defined, the customary measures of capital formation tend to underestimate the true volume. They exclude most investment of resources in clearing land and in other improvements made by farmers' own labor—an important component in earlier periods—and current outlay on research and market promotion—an important component in later periods.

[1] Raymond W. Goldsmith, *A Study of Saving in the United States*, Princeton University Press, 1955.

Even more important than the differences among current definitions and the omissions just noted is the much wider range possible when the relevance of capital formation to different analytical purposes and problems is considered. If capital means tools directly employed in the economic process of production under business and even public auspices, should residential construction—quantitatively an important component of capital formation as defined here—be included? In what sense does housing help to augment the material product, except in the rather tenuous one of yielding imputed (or monetary) net rent? For a society bent on forcing the pace of its economic growth, with particular emphasis on industrialization, residential construction hardly seems to be bona fide capital, comparable with railroad equipment, blast furnaces, or even inventories. By the same rule, some additions to public capital, e.g. those designed for social services to individuals, may also seem to be more in the nature of consumption than capital formation. It is at least conceivable that under conditions of forced economic growth and industrialization, capital—and hence capital formation—may be viewed as limited to plant, equipment, and inventories that are directly serviceable as tools.

However, for some purposes neither this narrow definition of capital and of its formation nor the one used in the estimates here but a much wider one may be more pertinent. For example, if a long-term rise in national product per capita or per worker is taken to describe economic growth, it may be desirable to define capital as means, and capital formation as all uses of current product, that contribute to such rises. In other words, domestic capital formation would include not only additions to construction, equipment, and inventories within the country, but also all other expenditures except those necessary to sustain output at existing levels. It would include outlays on many items now comprised under consumption, e.g. outlays on education, recreation, and material luxuries that contribute to the greater health and productivity of individuals, and all expenditures by society that serve to raise the morale of the employed population.

This exposition of the wide scope possible for capital formation leads to two observations. First, changes in scope will yield different levels and trends in the estimates. Both the contrasting levels of the proportion of capital formation to national product in different countries and their trends based on a wide definition will be different from those based on a substantially narrower one. This will also be true of the structure of financing: the financing of capital formation more narrowly defined is distributed among various sources in an entirely different way from that of capital formation of much wider scope.

Second, the choice of a definition must obviously be guided by the major use to which the resulting measures are to be put. One can escape this choice only by preparing estimates corresponding to the widest possible definition, and by providing details on components so that narrower totals can be constructed. In this paper we do not and cannot use the widest definition, and can justify our choice merely on the grounds of practical expediency.

Our interest here is in the comparative economic growth of nations. In pursuit of that interest it would have been best to use the wider definition suggested above. The measures used here and in many other statistical studies, which correspond to the narrower definition, present an incomplete, and therefore somewhat misleading, picture of differences between developed and underdeveloped economies or between the early and later phases in the growth of developed economies. Not only capital formation, in its narrower sense, but also consumer expenditures, whose contribution to the increased productivity of the population varies as the consumption structure varies, are fundamental to the understanding of economic growth and its phases. Capital is what capital does: it raises the capacity for economic production. The minor share that capital formation as now measured constitutes of national product, particularly on a net basis, in both developed and underdeveloped countries is far from a true measure. It is hardly informative to say that net capital formation is, on the average, 10 to 15 per cent of national product in the leading industrial nations and 5 per cent or less in the underdeveloped ones. It would be more telling if we could say that the productivity-raising outlays in a developed country are about half of its national product (as they well may be) but only a few per cent in an underdeveloped country. Even more important, with the broader definition of capital we would have to examine carefully all newly produced resources and select, classify, and measure those that contribute in any way to greater productivity. We thus would get a better view of the conditions under which capital, in the narrower sense of the term, is most effectively utilized.

Unfortunately, the available data do not permit the use of the wide definition of capital formation. A narrower definition had to be employed because the whole stock of available estimates barely suffices to measure it even for enough countries and periods to permit some broad inferences—at least within the limits of time and effort that can be devoted to this paper. Thus only a part of what is wanted can be measured.

The present definition corresponds to the accepted concept of national product. Durable consumer goods other than construction are excluded because to treat such goods as a "business," and include their value under capital goods and the imputed income from them under national product, did not seem warranted. Military equipment is included because it is analogous to a variety of protective capital goods included under business capital formation: there seems to be no good reason for excluding munitions while including fences (and, for that matter, business structures which provide protection from the weather).[2]

GROSS AND NET

According to the definition used here, domestic capital formation comprises additions to the stock of goods within the country in the hands of business and government, and housing in the hands of consumers. These additions can be measured gross, i.e. as the total newly turned out, or net of current consumption. Estimates for both gross and net capital formation are used below: the former are gross of current consumption of *durable* capital (construction and equipment), the latter are net of it. Changes in inventories are taken on a net basis in *both*.

We discuss gross capital formation, in addition to net, for several reasons. First, consumption of durable capital over a year or even over a somewhat longer period is difficult to estimate. This may explain the erratic behavior of differences in the estimates of consumption among various countries. Second, the consumption estimates for the business sector are based upon depreciation allowances, and to that extent reflect a source of capital formation financing that may or may not be used, depending upon conditions. Third, individual home-owners tend to disregard the allowance for depreciation, and thus view savings as gross of that item. To the extent that such practices convert the consumption estimate into a measure of means of financing gross capital formation—means that are indissolubly

[2] This is based upon a heroically simple assumption. A more realistic alternative would have involved trying to determine how much military investment is "defensive" and how much "aggressive." Inclusion of the latter would require inclusion under national product of the yield of aggression. The difficulties of such an approach need not be stressed.

merged with "net" savings—a study of gross capital formation and its financing may be more fruitful than one of net. Finally, "replacement" of a capital good is rarely merely substituting for one tool another of the same quality: after all the price adjustments possible, $100 in 1929 prices spent in 1939 would have meant better equipment or a more suitable structure than $100 in 1929 prices spent in 1909. For all these reasons the concept of *gross* capital formation is at least as important as that of *net*, and may even be more useful for some purposes.

In discussing current capital consumption we used the term "*durable* capital assets" without defining it. Since its scope affects the magnitude of capital consumption, it should be noted that repairs and maintenance are included in some of the estimates used here and excluded from others. For the countries where these outlays are included under gross capital formation, current consumption presumably is larger relatively than for others (e.g. the United States and countries following the practice of the Organisation for European Economic Co-operation) where an attempt is made to exclude them on the grounds that they are usually treated as current expenses and are not subject to the postponable depreciation allowance.

But this item is minor compared with two questions concerning the turnover of durable capital assets: Should the gross flow of such assets include not only newly produced assets, but also those that were placed on the market and changed hands during the year? Should the study of financing include the financing not only of the new gross total of capital goods, but also of the turnover of existing ones?

The reason for these questions lies in the relation between mobility of capital and its contribution to productivity, and thus to economic growth. The ease with which existing capital goods can change hands in a better adjustment to needs is as important in many ways as the addition of newly produced capital. Such shifts of capital goods may or may not require external financing. But since we distinguish durable assets because we recognize that their current consumption is not an unequivocal act of disappearance and gives rise to sources of financing, we should be consistent and recognize that such assets—because they are durable and continue to exist as capital goods—can change hands and hence better serve their purposes. The existence or absence of financial and other facilities for such shifts is, therefore, an important matter. For this reason we repeat: Should we not deal with the gross supply on the market of at least the durable capital goods—instead of new gross capital formation alone—and search for the sources and mechanisms of the correspondingly gross savings that are employed to finance such a flow? The statistical difficulties involved here are obvious, and there is no point in dwelling on them.

The extension of gross capital formation to gross capital supply, like the wider scope of capital formation suggested earlier, may well throw more light on the problems of economic growth. For one major difference between developed and undeveloped countries, or between the early and later phases of developed countries, probably lies in the facilities provided for mobility—in its economic sense—of existing capital goods. If the data were available, it would be quite useful to gauge the volume of all durable capital goods changing hands during the year—distinguishing between those already existing and those newly produced—and to trace the flow of savings—including the proceeds of sales, just as we include the depreciation allowance under the present concept of gross savings—through the various channels in the financing of the total durable capital turnover.

But the data are even scantier for this purpose than for the analysis of consumption suggested in the preceding section. Here, as in other macro-economic measurement, we have to be satisfied with already "netted" out, comprehensive aggregates. These have their invaluable uses; but, unfortunately, they reveal little about the whole mechanism of flows and offsetting counterflows that is so important for our understanding of how the net result was effected, and why it is so different from time to time and place to place.

THE STATISTICAL EVIDENCE

Tables I-1 to I-3 in Appendix A relate to the gross and net proportions of domestic capital formation to national product. It would have been more logical to use domestic product. But total national product series are more readily available, particularly for the longer periods; and for all the countries covered in the tables the difference, in the long run, between total and domestic product was well within a few per cent of either. No sizable error is introduced, therefore, by treating the proportions as if they relate to either total or domestic product.[3]

[3] This statement would probably be much less justified if our records included truly "colonial" areas, economies in which income outflows to foreign enterprises loom large relative to total product.

Table I-1 gives, for a relatively large number of countries, the proportion of domestic capital formation to national product for a single pre-World War II year (usually 1938) and for a post-World War II period. Table I-2 shows the proportion, for a much smaller number of countries, in the 1920's. Table I-3 comprises much longer records, but for only a few countries. The evidence cannot be summarized easily, partly because of discrepancies in details of definition and treatment. A far more important limitation lies in the sensitivity of the capital formation proportion to short-term conditions, and it is difficult, therefore, to infer long-term levels from short-term data. The figures for 1938, a year marking a depression whose impact varied considerably in the several countries, are of uncertain value in determining longer-term levels of differences. Even the averages for the post-World War II period may well be atypical, since they must have been affected by the extraordinary efforts in some countries to repair war ravages and the no less extraordinary difficulties in many other countries in the way of such efforts. For the longer-term levels and trends in capital formation proportions we must rely much more on Tables I-2 and I-3, but even those must be used warily. Moreover, our conclusions may be modified when a fuller range of adequate data becomes available.

With this warning, we state what seem to be the major statistical findings suggested by the tables and comment on their rationale.

1. Except for the depressed decade of the 1930's, the long-term proportion of net domestic capital formation to net national product ranges from about 5 to about 15 per cent. The proportion for Sweden in the first decade is the only one clearly below the 5 per cent level (Table I-3, C); and there are scarcely any long periods in which the ratio is significantly in excess of 15 per cent. This range would persist if domestic net product were used as a denominator, since the latter would be smaller for those countries whose net domestic capital formation proportions are well below 15 per cent (e.g. England and France), and might be larger for those whose net domestic capital formation proportions are higher (e.g. Sweden in later decades, the United States, and Canada).

In speculating about the reasons for this range, we can assume that the lower limit of the long-term proportion of net domestic capital formation would be zero or close to it. Unless output could somehow be maintained while extraordinary economy in the use of capital was practiced, the gradual exhaustion of the domestic stock of capital would force reduction of domestic production.[4] Serious domestic capital depletion, over the long run, and a consequent long-term decline in output have occurred in history. But for those countries within the orbit of Western civilization for which we have long-term records back to the middle of the nineteenth century, the series which *exclude* the war periods do not reveal such situations.

Furthermore, given some growth of total population and some tendency toward preservation of a countrywide capital-output ratio, the lower limit of the proportion of net capital formation to net product would be significantly above zero. Assume that the country's population is growing at 1 per cent per year, that it requires a constant supply of final output per capita, and that the prevailing ratio of domestic capital stock to annual output is from 2.5 to 1, to 5 to 1. Unless this ratio can be changed significantly, the net domestic capital formation required will constitute 2.5 to 5 per cent of the national product—sufficient to increase the capital stock necessary to produce the greater *total* (but constant per capita) output required. Since residential housing and closely related facilities are a substantial part of capital formation, and since, under the assumed conditions of constant output per capita, economies in the use of capital (which would depress the capital-output ratio) are unlikely (they usually develop in a technologically progressive climate associated with *rising* per capita output), the illustration suggests that even in underdeveloped countries the mere growth of population would limit the lower level of the net capital formation proportion unless the per capita output were allowed to decline. In the countries covered in our tables both population and per capita output increased; and the low net domestic capital formation proportions are for early preindustrialization periods (Sweden), or for later periods of development when retarded growth at home permits limited use of domestic capital, and savings are in fact channeled abroad (England and France).

The upper limits on the long-term proportion of net domestic capital formation to net product can best be explained in terms of

[4] This argument should be qualified in view of the possible *omissions* in customary measures of capital formation, but such omissions are likely to be only minute fractions of national *product*. Another possible qualification—that in advanced and growing societies the mere replacement of capital increases productivity—does not apply to conditions where net capital formation is close to zero over long periods. For this occurs only in societies where economies are stagnant; and in them technical progress that explains the capacity-raising incidence of mere replacement is absent. This comment applies also to the next paragraph.

the limits on net savings proportions within a country and on the relative amount of foreign capital that the country can secure. Both groups of factors are discussed more appropriately in Section 2, "Foreign Investment and Total Capital Formation Proportions." It is sufficient to indicate here that there are obvious limits to which domestic saving for security can be rationalized and to which inequality in income distribution can originate savings beyond the "rational" security limit; and that the supply of foreign savings is affected by political conditions and by the small amount of capital available for foreign investment relative to the demand of the would-be borrowers.

2. The long-term proportion of gross domestic capital formation to gross national product ranges from about 10 to about 25 per cent. There is only one case below the lower limit (Sweden in the first decade, Table I-3, C); and the few exceptions above the upper limit are mostly in the unusual post-World War II period.

While one would assume that some relation exists between the range for the net domestic capital formation proportion and that for the gross, theoretically one could derive a markedly different set of limiting values for the latter from the former. Given a long-term proportion of net domestic capital formation to net product of 5 per cent as an observed lower limit, one must infer that the corresponding lower limit for the gross proportion is above 5 per cent. Similarly, an observed upper limit of 15 per cent for the net proportion implies a higher one for the gross proportion. One would therefore expect the long-term proportion of gross domestic capital formation to gross product to range from above 5 to above 15 per cent. But a range from 10 to 25 rather than from 7 to 75 suggests that there are certain limits upon variations in the factors that relate net and gross capital formation proportions.

These factors are the share of capital formation subject to depreciation, i.e. in the present definition the share accounted for by construction and durable equipment; the length of life of durable capital assumed in estimating depreciation; and the rate of growth of product, assuming that the proportion of capital formation to product over the past period has been constant. The role of these factors is suggested by the following equation:[5]

$$\frac{D_0}{G_0} = af\left[\frac{1-(1+r)^{-n}}{nr}\right]$$

[5] For its derivation see Appendix B—part of the analysis carried through in the National Bureau's study of capital formation and financing.

where

D_0 = depreciation during time unit 0

G_0 = gross national product during time unit 0

a = proportion of depreciable gross capital formation to total gross capital formation—assumed constant during the past

f = proportion of gross capital formation to gross national product—assumed constant in the past

r = rate of growth of gross national product, per time unit—assumed constant in the past (so that the link relative of successive annual GNP's is $[1 + r]$)

n = number of time units in life span of depreciable capital—assumed constant, with depreciation calculated along a straight line.

The constancy assumptions refer to the period included in n.

To illustrate the results one can derive from this equation, we provide a few values for the fraction that modifies af in the equation and that reflects the combined effects of the life period of durable capital and the rate of growth of gross national product (which is quite close to the rate of growth of net product).

Value of n in Years	Value of r: .01	.03	.05
20	.90	.74	.62
30	.86	.65	.51
40	.82	.58	.43

Using this table, we can easily calculate some examples. For instance, if we assume that f, the gross capital formation proportion, is .25 (i.e. at the upper limit), that a is .8 (allowing about a fifth for net changes in inventories), that r is about 3 per cent per year, and that the average life of durable capital is 40 years (a combination of a longer life for construction and a shorter one for producers' durable equipment), the ratio of capital consumption to gross national product is $.8 \times .25 \times .58$, or 11.6 per cent. The ratio of net capital formation to gross national product is then 13.4 per cent; and to net national product, 15.2 per cent. This, of course, is only one way by which an upper limit of 15 per cent for the net capital formation proportion can be translated into one of 25 per cent for the gross, although the values used in this example are, in fact, close to the United States experience (except that f is closer to 22 per cent, and n closer to 30 years, yielding a net capital formation proportion of about 12 per cent).

For a slowly growing country whose gross national product rises only 1 per cent per year and whose gross capital formation proportion is about 10 per cent (i.e. at the lower limit), if a is .8 and n is 40, the ratio of depreciation to gross national product is .0656; of net capital formation to gross national product, .0344; and of net capital formation to net national product, .037, or 3.7 per cent. A somewhat lower a, even if combined with a lower n, would yield a 5 per cent level for the proportion of net capital formation to net product.

In the above examples the upper and lower limits of the gross capital formation proportion have been connected with those of the net capital formation proportion. It would obviously be easy to link a value below the upper limit for the latter with one at the upper limit for the former, or a value above the lower limit for the latter with one at the lower limit for the former. By expanding the brief table given above to cover other values of r and n and varying a and f, we could derive various combinations of the gross and net capital formation proportions.

Such variations are of little interest since our data on the empirical values for the several constants used are so scanty; and such analysis would take us far afield anyway. But two inferences suggested by the illustrative discussion above are relevant here.

First, the lower the rate of growth of national product, the higher the relative weight of depreciation in gross capital formation and the lower that of net capital formation derived as residual. This suggests that in underdeveloped countries, where growth of national product is moderate, where the life span of durable capital assets may be short because of rapid physical deterioration even in the absence of the competitive pressure that produces obsolescence of capital goods in the more developed countries, and where the relative share of net change in inventories is not necessarily larger than in the developed countries, a fairly substantial proportion of gross capital formation to gross national product may be accompanied by an insignificant net capital formation proportion. Thus if n is 20, a is .8, and the gross capital formation proportion is 20 per cent, an r of .01 yields a net capital formation proportion of only slightly over 6 per cent; an r of about .5 per cent per year yields a net capital formation proportion, under the same conditions, of less than 5 per cent; and when r is 0, the proportion is actually .04 divided by .84, or 4.8 per cent. In that case it is limited to net additions to inventories, since there are no *net* additions to the stock of durable capital. By and large, differences in the gross capital formation proportion among developed and underdeveloped countries may be relatively much smaller than those in the net; and the former tend to underestimate the differences among countries in the share of income constituting net additions to the capital stock.

The second inference bears upon the effect of acceleration or retardation in the rate of growth of national product. With other factors constant, acceleration means a reduction in the weight of depreciation, a higher ratio of net to gross capital formation, and a higher net capital formation proportion corresponding to a given gross capital formation proportion. Retardation has the opposite effect—it increases the relative weight of depreciation and widens the gap between the gross and net capital formation proportions.

3. At some phase in the growth of a developed country within the last two centuries there must have been a substantial rise in the capital formation proportions. Given an increase, or constancy, or at least a substantial resistance to decline in the capital-output ratios, a rise in the capital formation proportions is a necessary consequence of the acceleration in the rate of population growth in the older countries, if per capita product does not decline. In fact, of course, the growth phases to which we refer are characterized by accelerated population growth (in older countries), by increases in per capita output far greater than those observed previously, and often even by rises in the capital-product ratios—all three factors implying a rise in the capital formation proportions. For reasons just suggested, the rise in the net capital formation proportion is likely to be more pronounced on a relative basis, and sometimes even on an absolute basis, than that in the gross.

Unfortunately, only the record for Sweden reaches back into the period of rising capital formation proportions; and only the gross proportion can be measured for those early decades, since the net is derived by arbitrary assumptions (which probably underestimate the true levels). But we may infer, by comparison with the current situation in underdeveloped countries, that the period of rising capital formation proportions marked the shift from the preindustrial to the modern era in all the old countries and even in some of the young, relatively "empty" countries settled by emigrants from the Western European orbit (Canada and other former British dominions, if not necessarily the United States).

What the few long series do reflect are the high capital proportion levels reached some time after the acceleration in the rate of growth occurred; and the declines, usually gradual but sometimes abrupt, from these levels. In the United States, Canada, the United Kingdom, France, and Denmark the capital formation proportions tend to decline—abruptly in the United States and Denmark after World War I. In Sweden they tend to rise during the first decades, declining toward the end of the period covered. Also in the United States and Canada the relative importance of depreciation increases, as expected, and causes a greater decline in the net capital formation proportion than in the gross. But the relation of the two series is quite different in the United Kingdom, and we are at a loss to decide whether it is because of some peculiarities of the estimating procedure or whether it reflects genuine differences in durable capital consumption practices or in the composition of the total capital stock.

One should note that, at least in the United States and Denmark, there are indications of factors other than retardation in the rate of growth of national product that explain the greater decline in the net capital formation proportion than in the gross proportion. These additional factors are the shortening of the average life of durable capital, due largely to the more rapid growth of producers' equipment than of construction, and the apparent increase in capacity to turn out more product with the same *net* stock of durable capital, a decline in the ratio of net capital stock to output. The latter trend may be explained in turn by the greater share of depreciation associated with a decline in the rate of growth of product, since "replacement" means substituting more effective equipment (even when valued in constant prices); and the growth of the share of "replacement" in total capital stock means growth of the proportion in which constancy in value is accompanied by increased efficiency.

To sum up: The preceding comments suggest a long secular swing in the capital formation proportion—its *up* phase occurring presumably some time after the rise in the rates of growth of national product and of population (in the older countries), and, perhaps, also after that in the rate of growth of per capita product; and its *down* phase emerging at different dates in different countries, and with different degrees of abruptness associated with the disruptive effects of wars and revolutions. The domestic capital formation proportions rise to upper levels of about 25 per cent for gross and 15 per cent for net (with lower ratios for the countries that channel much of their savings abroad); and the rise in the net capital formation proportion is relatively, and sometimes even absolutely, greater than that in the gross, and it may well appear earlier in the record. In the decline from the upper levels, the net capital formation proportion drops more markedly than the gross, and possibly earlier. Unfortunately, the data are not sufficient to permit us to outline this secular swing effectively or to relate it properly to similar secular swings in the growth of population and product.

2. *Foreign Investment and Total Capital Formation Proportions*

THE LINKING OF FINANCING WITH CAPITAL FORMATION

We now consider the share of domestic capital formation financed from foreign sources, and in this connection study also the proportion of total capital formation (countrywide savings) to national product. But before examining the data, we deal briefly with the major difficulties in linking any source of financing with real capital formation that must be recognized to avoid misinterpretation of the estimates.

The basic problem is that, for any active economic agent, funds from different sources are mingled in one pool out of which all activities are financed. It is, therefore, essentially arbitrary to link a specific category of funds with a specific type of use—in our case, capital formation.

This difficulty can be discerned even in the case of a person who borrows on mortgage, presumably to construct a house. On the surface there is a clear and unequivocal link between a source of finance and an item of real capital formation. But closer examination may reveal that the individual in question took a trip abroad in the same year that he borrowed the money, and spent an amount out of savings equal to his mortgage. He borrowed the money to build a house rather than to go abroad because it was easier and more "respectable" to borrow with a tangible asset as security. Can we say unequivocally that in this case capital formation was financed by borrowing rather than by savings?

If this difficulty emerges for a single economic agent, even when there is a seeming connection between an act of financing and an act of capital formation, it is much greater for the broad groups we must deal with in using the available data. The larger the group, the greater the opportunity for intermingling both sources of funds and types of uses. But this difficulty is seldom recognized. The literature and data relating to international capital flows point out the influence of a complex of both political and economic conditions on such flows but go on with misleading ease to estimate net changes in them as a "share" of capital formation. To illustrate: Before World War I, the Russian government borrowed heavily in international markets, primarily from France. Were data on real capital formation in Russia available, it would be possible to compare its net foreign borrowing with domestic capital formation and conclude that *x* per cent of the latter was "financed" from abroad. (Indeed, these are the percentages and the comparisons that are given in Appendix A.) But the Russian government may actually have spent a good part of this borrowed money on police, on the organization of pogroms, and on the state church; and the direct financing of capital formation may have been provided from other sources. The assignment of capital funds imports to capital formation within the country is thus arbitrary. To put it more precisely, it is based on the implicit assumption that, given fluidity of funds, there is a causal connection between sources of funds recognized as long-term savings and uses of resources classified as additions to stocks (i.e. capital formation). By and large, there is a closer association between capital funds and capital formation than between other funds and capital formation: inability to secure capital funds would inhibit capital formation much sooner than it would consumption. But this is a very broad association and subject to the qualification that, for any specific group of capital funds, the links with capital formation may be quite weak. In the present connection this qualification should be stressed particularly when a government borrows capital from a foreign country. For governments can obtain funds on either a short- or a long-term basis for uses that have little connection with capital formation, whereas individuals and private firms must often show some evidence of use in terms of fixed assets that may serve as security. Moreover, in foreign capital movements, government borrowing is particularly subject to political considerations that not only have little relation to capital formation, but in a sense may be inversely related to it—as the experience of foreign loans not only to Russia but to many other countries with governments inimical to economic progress testifies. Unfortunately, it is impossible to analyze here the uses to which such loans were put or to estimate the amounts that did finance capital formation within the borrowing countries. The association between flow of funds and capital formation must be made in broad terms for the larger aggregates for which data are available, with allowance for the qualification just indicated.[6]

Two other qualifications must be indicated. The first flows from the "netness" of the financing estimated in the available data. It is almost never possible to measure the gross flow of funds corresponding to the gross capital turnover suggested in Section 1. Net capital imports or exports—the only estimates we have for comparison with domestic capital formation—tend to understate greatly the importance of the flows of goods and payments across boundaries. Theoretically, it is possible to have zero or close to zero net capital

[6] The argument set forth in this and the preceding paragraph can be clarified in a restatement suggested by Moses Abramovitz, as follows:

1. In an economy in which commodity stocks are constant and savings positive, the net import of capital will simultaneously offset or "finance" all three of the following differences as aggregates: (a) value of products or resources used *minus* value of products produced domestically; (b) value of net additions to capital stock *minus* net domestic savings; (c) value of imported goods and services, including factor payments, *minus* value of exported goods and services, including factor receipts. All this is implied by the usual definitions of national income, saving, investment, and consumption.

2. Viewed as aggregates, therefore, capital imports do not finance capital formation any more than they do consumption or imports of capital goods or consumer goods. The securities against which capital is borrowed are not significant because there is no uniform connection between the form in which a loan is made and the use made of the proceeds. And even if it were true that the proceeds of foreign loans were, in the first instance, expended to purchase or produce capital, it would still be true that other resources would thereby be released for non-investment purposes.

3. Nevertheless, there is good reason to compare net capital imports with total capital formation. For when investment expenditures tend to exceed domestic savings, a number of related processes are set in motion which tend to close the investment-savings gap, some by increasing saving, but others by inhibiting investment: (a) Real income and domestic real savings tend to increase without a rise in prices. Insofar as this occurs, it implies the existence of unemployed resources easily drawn into production. (b) Money prices, money incomes, and money savings rise. In the course of this inflationary process, domestic real savings also tend to increase as a result of various expenditure lags and redistributions of income. (c) The domestic money market and the domestic commodity markets get tighter. These developments tend to check investment. (d) The tightness of the money market, however, is relieved to the extent that foreigners are induced to hold claims against the home country. The tightness of the commodity markets is relieved to the extent that an import surplus is generated, which also increases the supply of claims to be held by foreigners. In short, the check to investment is relieved to the extent that capital imports are stimulated.

4. The volume of net capital imports in a period, therefore, represents an unequivocal contribution to the increase in the supply of capital assets during the period. It is only unequivocal, however, in the sense that capital imports make *some* contribution. We cannot say how large the contribution is because we do not know how much smaller the increase in capital would have been in the absence of capital supplied from abroad.

balances, with huge volumes of international goods and payments flows. Large imports may not be possible without financing by foreign sellers, or by the financial institutions servicing them. Large exports may not be possible without financing by the domestic sellers or their financial institutions. But the destination of exports and the identity of the beneficiaries of domestic financing may be quite different from the origin of imports and the identity of the foreign creditor. It may well be that if the selling countries are not willing to finance imports, a given country cannot enjoy either the imports or the contribution which they may make to capital formation and growth. Of course, this is a corollary of the statement made earlier that "net" totals reveal neither the underlying flows and counterflows nor the importance of this mechanism to the processes of capital formation and economic growth. But it is particularly appropriate in connection with net capital imports and exports because there are so many opportunities for diverse flows and considerable offsetting in the position of any country vis-à-vis the rest of the world.

The second qualification relates to the use of total debt outstanding, either domestic or foreign, gross (i.e. with both debt and counterclaims shown separately) or net. In using such data to estimate the relative importance of the corresponding source of funds in financing past capital formation, we face a problem, because debts may be revalued through default or cancellation; and the face or market value of the debt at any given time may not reflect the actual magnitude of funds made available at the time the loans were made and the securities issued. Furthermore, even if there are no defaults, no sales of original debt issues at less than face value, etc., a cumulative total of capital formation makes sense only after its several parts have been reduced to a common price level; and that can be done if the shares per time unit of real capital formation are reflected in the data or if the total of tangible assets is revalued periodically, with the changes in bases of valuations inferred from changes in price levels. For the cumulative total of debt, no general deflation is possible: the estimates of gross and net debt issues at successive dates are indispensable. It is for this reason that the cumulative debt totals are used sparingly in the following discussion and primarily to indicate the geographical distribution of international capital lending.

THE EVIDENCE ON CAPITAL IMPORTS AND EXPORTS

In Tables II-1 to II-4 net capital imports or exports are shown as shares of net domestic capital formation, gross domestic capital formation, net national product, and gross national product. The numerator is net after capital inflows and outflows have been balanced out. For some countries and periods estimates of both inflows and outflows are available. It may seem illogical to compare a *net* capital movement with gross totals; and it is true that, theoretically, part of capital consumption, which enters gross capital formation and gross national product, must be credited to the foreign owners of capital and debited to domestic users. But in fact additions to domestic depreciation reserves or replacements of domestic capital do not add to the claims of foreign owners; and it is reasonable to include among the possible sources of financing of domestic gross capital formation the total depreciation charge, net domestic savings, and net capital imports.

The evidence on the shares of foreign investment in domestic capital formation and in national product conveys the following impressions:

1. Both net and gross domestic capital formation are sensitive to short-term changes; and the former, particularly, can drop to zero or a negative quantity in a depressed year. Hence, a fraction in which capital formation is the denominator can be quite erratic when calculated for a single year or a short period. For this reason the evidence in Table II-1, which relates to a single year and to the exceptional post-World War II period, is only of limited value. We must rely primarily on Tables II-2 and II-4, particularly the latter.

These tables show that for some creditor and some debtor countries the proportions of capital exports or imports to domestic capital formation were quite substantial. In the United Kingdom the share of net capital exports in domestic net capital formation ranged from about a third to over nine-tenths, depending upon the estimate and particularly the period; and the share in domestic gross capital formation ranged from about a fifth to three-quarters. In France, the other major creditor country, the share of capital exports in domestic net savings ranged from a sixth to three-quarters. In the Netherlands the data for the 1920's alone show that the share of capital exports was about a seventh of net domestic capital formation and about a tenth of gross, and the shares may have been appreciably higher before World War I. For some debtor countries also, the shares of capital imports in domestic capital formation were fairly substantial in the long run. In Sweden, in the early decades, the share of capital imports in domestic net capital formation ranged from a fifth to eight-tenths, and their share in gross from about a ninth to less than half (Table II-4, C); in Canada the share of capital imports in domestic net capital formation was close to a half in 1900-1920, and the share in gross from a quarter to a third (Table II-4, D); in Denmark, capital imports at their highest accounted for over a quarter of domestic net capital formation and about a sixth of gross, and for 1870-1904 were about a fifth of the former and less than a seventh of the latter (Table II-4, F). On the other hand, in the United States, capital imports did not account for sizable proportions of domestic capital formation (Table II-4, A). And, as will be indicated below, there is reason to suspect that the *available* data, because of a bias in their selection, tend to exaggerate the relative importance of capital imports and exports.

2. As indicated above, the long-term proportions of domestic net and gross capital formation to national product vary within moderate limits—from somewhat less than 5 to about 15 per cent for the former, and from somewhat less than 10 to about 25 per cent for the latter. Since capital imports and exports are in turn fractions of domestic capital formation, their long-term share in national product is small. In the 1920's, capital imports and exports ranged from less than 1 to about 2 per cent of national product (Table II-2). In the interwar period, i.e. from about 1921 to 1938, capital imports and exports ranged from less than 1 to about 2.5 per cent of national income (Table II-3). In the longer records in Table II-4, about the highest ratios shown are 6 to 7 per cent for capital exports in the United Kingdom in the decade before World War I, and over 9 per cent for capital imports in Canada in 1901-1910. But most shares in national income or gross national product are well below 5 per cent.

It should be stressed that there is no arithmetical necessity for a low ratio of capital imports or exports to either domestic capital formation or national product. Theoretically, a country could have net capital exports substantially in excess of its domestic capital formation or could import, in the long run, capital not only equal to but in excess of its domestic capital formation (implying domestic consumption larger than net national product). It is economic and related factors that limit the volume of capital movements across the boundaries to fractions of domestic capital formation and to still smaller fractions of national product.

3. The fact that the available records exaggerate the relative importance of international capital flows, when viewed against the larger canvas of the world economy, is a natural reflection of the correlation between the importance of such capital movements and the effort to collect data about them. These long-term records are either for the most prominent international creditor countries (England and France) or for the most prominent international debtor countries, in the sense that the importance of capital imports was greatest for them (Canada, Sweden, and Australia). Of the creditor countries omitted from the records, only the Netherlands, and only for limited periods, might have shown proportions of capital exports to domestic capital formation and national product as high as those for the United Kingdom; and of the debtor countries omitted, only Argentina, New Zealand, and perhaps one or two others might have shown proportions of capital imports to domestic capital formation and national product as high as those for Canada, Sweden, and Australia. Other missing creditor countries, e.g. Germany and Switzerland, would probably have shown much lower proportions of capital exports to domestic capital formation and national product than the United Kingdom and France.[7] Among the debtor countries the larger units, e.g. the United States and Japan, enjoyed capital imports that were only minor fractions of domestic capital formation and minute percentages of national product. In most of the debtor countries of any size not covered by the record, the share of capital imports—not necessarily in net capital formation but in gross and particularly in national product—must have been quite low indeed.

Another interesting aspect of the long-term record is its concentration on a period when, judging by the scanty data available for earlier and later decades, the relative importance of international capital movements may have been at its highest. From 1870 to 1914,

[7] Herbert Feis comments on Germany: "In some periods, the early seventies and middle eighties in particular, more than one-tenth, perhaps as much as one-fifth of the savings of the country made a choice of foreign employment. But that movement did not grow with the volume of savings in the nineties and after the turn of the century. From 1900 to 1914 less than one-tenth, rather than more, of current savings went abroad despite the appeal of undeveloped lands, the exertion of the Government in behalf of foreign enterprise, the great growth of the overseas banking system and commerce." *Europe, the World's Banker, 1870-1914,* Yale University Press, 1930, pp. 61-62. Quoted by permission.

particularly in the twenty years preceding the outbreak of World War I, both the phase of development of the creditor countries and international conditions seem to have been most favorable to capital exports; and the demand for foreign capital by potentially suitable debtor countries seems to have been at its strongest. At any rate, the three major creditor countries—the United Kingdom, France, and Germany—were at the height of their international lending power between 1870 and 1914; and the conditions of the would-be borrowing countries—the dominions of the British Empire, the United States, Japan, and a few Latin-American countries—warranted demand for foreign capital. The summary of the long-term record in Table II-4 is thus largely for a limited period in which the importance of international capital movement may have been greater, in relative terms, than either in the preceding or in the following decades.[8]

4. These comments suggest that international indebtedness in 1914 was the result of capital imports and exports during a period that, historically speaking, was most favorable to international capital movements. The picture, presented in *International Capital Movements during the Inter-War Period*,[9] can be introduced by a brief quotation from that source: "The chief capital exporting countries before World War I were the United Kingdom, France and Germany. At the outbreak of the war, their foreign long-term investments represented about three-fourths of all outstanding international investments. Over a period of forty years—from 1874 to 1914—the foreign long-term investments of these three countries had grown from $6,000 million to $33,000 million. Available information suggests that the total of their combined capital exports during this period slightly exceeded the difference of $27,000 million between the two estimates. Losses due to defaults and bankruptcies, particularly during the period of falling prices before the mid-1890's,

[8] Total international capital indebtedness in the early 1930's was higher than in 1913 or 1914. But this was shortly after the crest of the large capital movements of the 1920's. Table II-3 indicates that a reverse flow, from the debtor to the creditor countries, took place during the 1930's. While total international indebtedness at the end of the 1930's may have still been absolutely higher than in 1914, it is highly unlikely that its proportions to the volumes of output in current prices and to the world total of capital formation at the end of the 1930's were equal to those in 1913-1914. I am strongly inclined to believe that the relative importance of international capital was at a peak in the 1910-1913 period, and that the share of international indebtedness in the total of world real capital was significantly higher in 1913 than at any previous or subsequent time within the last two centuries.

[9] United Nations, October 1949. Quotation is from page 1.

and the probable net increase in short-term credits granted may explain this fact."

Total international long-term debt in 1913/1914 was estimated to be $44 billion, including $3.5 billion in gross credits for the United States (*ibid.*, p. 2). Excluding the latter, the sum of net credits of creditor countries amounted to $40.5 billion. In mid-1932, international debts (including political) were estimated by Julius Hirsch to be about 307 billion German marks, of which 55 billion were short-term.[10] Assuming that short-term indebtedness was the same proportion of long-term in 1913/1914 as in 1932, which may be an overestimate, we add about a fifth to $40.5 billion and get a grand total of about $49 billion for total international debt. This was the cumulative result of international capital investments over a period of at least half a century when the movement was at its height.

The relative size of this total depends upon the base with which one compares it. In 1912 the value, in current prices, of total *reproducible* wealth in one debtor country alone, the United States, was $94 billion.[11] The annual rate of net capital exports was well below $1 billion per year for the preceding half century. (Much of this, of course, was advanced when money had a higher purchasing power than in 1914.) The annual rate of domestic gross capital formation in the United States alone was, in current prices, over $3 billion from 1869 to 1914; and its national product close to $15 billion per year on the average. It is impossible to estimate the world product and capital formation over the same period; but it seems reasonable to guess that international capital movements even at their height accounted for only a limited fraction of world gross capital formation and a minor fraction of total world output.[12]

[10] Carl Iversen, *Aspects of the Theory of International Capital Movements*, London, Oxford, 1935, pp. 336-337.

[11] *Income and Wealth, Series II*, Simon Kuznets, editor, Cambridge, Eng., Bowes & Bowes for International Association for Research in Income and Wealth, 1952, Table 1, p. 306.

[12] During the period under discussion, the net capital exports were just about equal to, or not much in excess of, the income on the outstanding foreign investments. In other words, the net additions can be viewed as retention by the debtor countries of the income earned by investments extant at the beginning of each period, although, of course, funds did shift and specific debtor countries did not necessarily "retain" their earnings on borrowed capital. In this connection we quote from the United Nations report already cited: "While the growth in the investments of the three (major creditor) countries was not uniform, it was steady and, considering the three countries together, appears to have been close to the yield (interest, dividends and profits) of the investments. Over the entire period (i.e. from 1874 to 1914), the total of the estimated capital exports from the three countries practically equalled their

In addition to these limitations upon relative size, there was also the peculiar distribution of capital exports. Table II-5 shows the geographical distribution of foreign investments by the three main creditor countries on the eve of World War I. Political factors seem to have weighed heavily in determining the distribution. Of the total foreign investment by the United Kingdom, almost half was in the Empire, the largest amounts in Canada and Australia; another fifth was in the United States; and only about 5 per cent was in Asia and Africa, outside of the Empire. Of French foreign investment, about half—in Russia, Turkey, the Balkan states, Austria-Hungary, and the colonies—was dominated by political considerations. Of German foreign investment, the politically motivated share—going to Austria-Hungary, Turkey, Russia, and the Balkan states—was over a third. One could naïvely argue that, even from the viewpoint of a man living at the end of the nineteenth and the beginning of the twentieth century, a rationally conceived distribution of foreign investments would certainly have allocated larger shares to the United States, to the English-speaking colonies, to many European countries, to Japan, and to selected Latin-American countries. The rationale of large capital flows to Russia, Turkey, Austria-Hungary, and the Balkans, in view of their shaky governmental and social structures, was certainly not economic. The point is that no matter what limited international capital funds were available, only part flowed into the channels of warranted economic demand for capital formation.

5. We cannot adequately explain here why financing of capital formation out of foreign funds was so restricted in scope, even under the exceptionally favorable conditions of the half century from the 1870's to World War I. But we can say that among the forces at play, those that should be emphasized are the following: the factors that limited the proportional magnitude of savings in all countries, even in those sufficiently advanced economically to be potential capital exporters; the draft upon such savings for domestic capital formation, to provide houses for the growing population and capital to operate the domestic economy; and the general limitation of the horizon of the entrepreneur or the investing institution, which made

---

aggregate income from the investments. The average annual income—at least towards the end of the period—was about 5 per cent. . . . 'Financial' payments (capital yields and capital movements) tended to offset each other in the balance of payments of the countries, taken as a group, that were creditors on balance, and accordingly also in those which, on balance, were debtors" (p. 1).

domestic placement of funds seem preferable to the troubles and uncertainties of investment in foreign places. The limited domestic savings and the minimum demand for domestic capital formation probably explain in large part the small number of net capital creditor countries. For some of these, e.g. France, *post facto* analysis suggests that savings became available for foreign use because of limitations upon domestic investment and peculiarities of the methods of financial institutions for the mobilization and placement of savings, rather than because of any excess of domestic savings over investment opportunities at home. The latter might have developed with more dynamic entrepreneurial leadership and a better organization of apparatus for domestic financing.[13] Since in most countries, particularly those economically developed, the social order kept consumption growing *pari passu* with national output and hence kept the domestic savings proportion down, and since there was a minimum need for domestic capital formation, there were obvious limits to the total net volume of capital exports that these leading countries could generate.

True, there were factors that limited demand also. In most countries, political and social conditions were hardly conducive to the absorption of large, long-term capital imports. In these countries, economically *warranted* demand was quite limited because the political and social situation was not stable—again from the viewpoint of intelligent contemporaries.

Yet it can be argued that the limitations on demand were far less important than those on supply. By and large, the absorptive capacity of the United States and Canada and of other countries with relatively stable political and social systems and considerable opportunities for growth (Japan, Australia, New Zealand, and some Latin-American countries) would seem to have been quite sufficient to employ all the capital exports generated by the creditor countries, and probably much more. This rough judgment is supported by the rapid growth in the absolute volume of capital formation in these countries and their obvious capacity to sustain a much larger volume of payments on their international indebtedness than they actually made. To put it briefly, if perhaps too drastically: prior to World War I the volume of international capital exports was restricted primarily because the *supply* of savings available was

[13] See the stimulating discussion in Harry D. White's *The French International Accounts, 1880-1913*, Harvard University Press, 1933, particularly Chaps. XII and XIII.

limited. The situation may have changed significantly after World War I: during recent decades the limitations on the economically warranted demand for foreign capital have become more prominent, whereas, with the emergence of the United States as a potential net creditor, the limitations on the capacity to lend have become less conspicuous.

6. In the United Kingdom and France there appears to have been a rise in the proportionate importance of capital exports until the two decades before World War I. But with this war came a major break for both of these creditor countries and for Germany too. During the interwar period they recovered somewhat, only to suffer a more drastic collapse during World War II. This picture of the culmination in 1914 of the development of international capital flows, and of the sharp breaks thereafter, only strengthens the impression of the extent to which the whole network was shot through with political aspects, so that a change in the latter could produce so sharp and complete a reversal.

In the debtor countries capital imports tend to become less important as time passes and the country grows; and this trend is sharply accentuated by war whenever the debtor country is outside the area of armed conflict. In Sweden, Canada, Germany, the United States, and Australia there is a clear downward trend in the share of capital imports, pointing toward an eventual reversal of their positions from debtor to creditor nations. If data were available for the earlier decades of the nineteenth century, we would probably have found a similar process operating in some of the older European countries. We would have seen them starting as international debtors and becoming creditors by the last half or quarter of the nineteenth century.

Because of the emphasis placed on the limited magnitude of capital imports and exports and on the factors that may have caused this restriction, it may be well to repeat the qualifications on the significance of these measures. These are *net* balances and hence limited in size, and one should not infer that their significance in the development of the various countries has been correspondingly limited. The composition of foreign security and asset holdings is never the same as that of domestic security and asset holdings. The foreign investors are able to, and often do, support or complement the domestic capital market where it is weak and where, therefore, the cost of finance might become impossibly high without a foreign contribution. For several countries—primarily the smaller ones within the economic orbit of such large capital exporters as the United Kingdom, and to some extent those within the economic orbit of France—favored by political conditions, the import of such capital was of decisive significance in development. Even for the large capital-importing countries (the United States and Japan and earlier in the nineteenth century France and Germany) the receipt of goods from the economically advanced areas, financed in part by loans, provided opportunities for economic growth and prevented internal strains that might otherwise have developed. Granted the relative smallness of the share that outside funds contributed to the financing of capital formation in such large countries, the very possibility of extensive economic intercourse with the more developed economies was significant; and the net capital imports that were received were all the more valuable because they were a small balance of a much larger gross flow. It may well be that the satisfactory economic growth of underdeveloped countries of any size depends in part upon a combination of relatively small capital imports associated with much larger gross flows of commodities and services to and from developed countries. We cannot dismiss the suggestion that although the past record for the large debtor and would-be debtor countries shows relatively insignificant net capital imports, the process of which these imports were the net result was an important factor in economic growth. This statement has obvious bearing upon current discussion of the needs of underdeveloped countries for capital imports: however acute such needs may seem, the need for larger gross flows of commodities and services across the boundaries may be greater.

THE TOTAL CAPITAL FORMATION (SAVINGS) PROPORTION

By adding the share of capital imports or exports in national product to the share of domestic capital formation, we get the share of total capital formation, or of countrywide savings, in total national product. From the estimates given in Tables II-1, II-2, and II-4, three major conclusions can be reached. First, for the countries covered, which are primarily developed or semideveloped economies (although there are a few underdeveloped countries in Table II-1), the shares of net savings in net national product vary from somewhat over 5 to about 15 per cent. The corresponding range for the shares of gross savings in gross national product is from somewhat over 10 to about 25 per cent. In both cases the limits are close to those observed for the shares of net and gross domestic capital formation. The estimates for several countries omit net changes in inventories and thus understate the proportion of savings. But the adjustment for this omission is slight and would not significantly affect the limits stated.

Second, at least within the range of countries covered, a larger per capita income is not consistently accompanied by a larger proportion of long-term net capital formation or savings to national product. The United States and Canada have the highest per capita income. Yet in Table II-2 the Netherlands shows a distinctly higher ratio of net capital formation to product (17.4 per cent) than the United States (12.7 per cent). In Table II-1 the net capital formation proportions for the United States and Canada, for the post-World War II period, are 13.5 per cent and 15.2 per cent respectively. Finland, Australia, and New Zealand all have higher proportions than the United States. If we could include the major underdeveloped countries, which presumably have low net capital formation proportions, the positive association between the levels of per capita income and the savings-income proportion might be raised. Nevertheless, it is significant that the correlation between the per capita income and the savings-income ratio is not likely to be high, even if it is positive, when countries with low per capita incomes are excluded. Cross-section comparisons of the level of income and the savings proportions among countries are thus not likely to show as close a positive correlation as would similar comparisons among income groups within each country.

Third, the long-term records for several countries in Table II-4 reveal that secular rises in per capita income are *not* accompanied by rises in the proportion of net capital formation or savings to national product. In the United States, Canada, and Denmark the proportion either declines slightly or is stable throughout. In Sweden it rises until the second decade of the twentieth century, but then declines. In other words, the relation over the long period between the movements of income and of the savings-income ratio is quite different from that observed in cross-section analysis between levels of income and the proportion of savings to income within a country.

The possible reasons for the limits set to the long-term savings-income proportion and for the failure of that proportion to rise with the secular rise in real income per capita have already been discussed, in reference to the experience of the United States.[14] But

[14] Simon Kuznets, "Proportion of Capital Formation to National Product," *American Economic Review, Proceedings*, May 1952, pp. 508-526, particularly pp. 509-513 and 521-524.

we list here again the major factors involved because they may shed some light on differences in the savings-income ratio among developed and underdeveloped countries, and among the several phases in the growth of the developed countries. Also, further thought suggests the need for reformulating some of the earlier analysis of the "rational" savings of lower income groups.

The savings-income proportion of individuals is the main determinant of the ratio of net savings to net product—particularly in countries organized under the business system. In these countries, because the economic role of governments is, by definition, fairly well circumscribed, financing by governments of capital formation out of taxes or other levies is quite limited except in war years. For obvious reasons the legislative bodies will not permit the use of the compulsory apparatus of taxation to finance capital formation, except for distinctly specified and well-defined purposes; nor will they permit the executive branches to accumulate reserves that might finance capital formation independently of the periodic appropriation power of legislatures. Likewise, organized business enterprises, corporate or individual, can contribute relatively little to the *net* savings of the country because they are always under pressure to distribute a large fraction of their net earnings, and their earnings are, in the long run, a fairly limited fraction of the total net output of the nation. In the United States, for example, in "normal" periods, when government's capacity for net capital formation out of revenues was at its peak, its share in net country-wide savings was about a seventh; that of corporations and other business enterprises was about a quarter; and that of individuals was at least six-tenths of country-wide net savings. There is no reason to assume that in other business economies the proportionate importance of individuals' savings in the total of domestic savings is much lower. The major source of the limitation of the country-wide savings-product proportion therefore lies in the limits to the long-term level of the savings-income ratio for individuals.

The long-term savings-income proportion for individuals is restricted partly by factors that operate to keep down the share of total income received by the upper income groups—the "automatic" savers—and partly by those that limit the savings-income proportion for the masses of income recipients whose savings represent an effort that has to be planned on some rational considerations governing the distribution of limited income between consumption and provision for the future.

In economies that enjoy satisfactory rates of growth, the very dynamics of the growth process holds down the relative proportion of income received by the upper income groups. If we allow for no shifting and assume continuity of an initial top group (and its descendants), that group's share in country-wide income is likely to be kept down by a lower than country-wide rate of growth of service income per capita; and because of a lower rate of increase in number, the initial top group and its descendants will form, as time passes, a declining proportion of the given ordinal top group in the population. If we allow for the shifting which necessarily accompanies significant economic growth and follows from changes in the identity of industries and occupations that are growing most rapidly, we find that the identity of entrepreneurs and of others who enjoy large incomes changes from one period to the next. Such shifts in identity mean that the captains of industry, the successful practitioners of rapidly growing professions or arts, the millionaires of today, are not likely to be those of tomorrow; nor are the latter likely to be the sons of the former. This mobility prevents the cumulation of successive large gains by one group of individuals and tends to hold down the inequality in the distribution of assets and incomes.[15]

For the mass of income recipients, whose savings must be based upon a rational weighing of future security against current consumption, the limit to the savings-income ratio is imposed by this very balancing of the present versus the future. In the paper cited above, illustrative examples were given based on the assumption of a perpetual annuity yielding a consumption level upon retirement equal to half that during the twenty-five years (out of a forty-year working life) when positive savings would be made. These illustrations suggest that provision of such security calls for a savings-income ratio of from 8 to 20 per cent *over the period of working and earning life*, depending upon the assumed interest yield on savings. If we add the incomes of the retired (their savings are zero), the nationwide savings-income ratio is even lower—how much lower depends upon the proportion of retired to active income recipients and the assumed difference in their incomes.

Another simplified model worth exploring calls for enough savings to cover living expenses for the years of retirement. If annual expenses per unit are assumed to be the same for the working and retirement periods, the savings-income ratio is equal to the ratio

[15] For an exploration of the factors affecting level and trends in shares of upper income groups see Appendix C.

between years of retirement and years of work and retirement. Thus if working life is set at 45 years, and the retirement period at 15, total income earned in 45 years must be spent in 60 years, and the implied savings-income ratio for each unit *through its working life* is 33 per cent of income. If the number of working units is three times the number of units retired, the nationwide savings for the two groups combined are zero, since the gross savings of the working units are fully offset by the dissavings of the retired. But with a growing population the ratio of working population to the retired is larger than the ratio of years of work to years of retirement. Furthermore, the estimated years of retirement, underlying these full *security* calculations, is probably nearer the maximum than the average; and actual realized dissavings by the surviving retired class would thus be significantly less than those implied in the calculation. Another qualifying element is provision for an estate at death, although for the mass of income recipients this is not a major consideration. These comments suggest that savings-income ratios for the mass of income recipients are largely governed by the effects of population growth on the ratio of working units to retired, by the effects of growth in per capita income on the lag in expenditures of retired persons behind those of the younger and still active income recipients, and by the possible overestimate of the length of the retirement period. If all these considerations are valid, the savings-income ratio for the group of income recipients below the level of the "automatic" savers is not likely to be high.[16]

The two groups of factors just discussed may operate differently in underdeveloped countries. Inequality in the distribution of income may well be greater than in the developed countries, particularly those that grew rapidly in the period under observation (e.g. the United States, Canada, Australia, and Sweden). All other conditions being equal, this inequality would tend to yield a higher savings-income ratio. On the other hand, in the underdeveloped countries greater stability in the composition of upper income groups makes for a higher relative consumption level for the rich; the per capita income of the mass of the population is quite low; the rate of population growth, and hence the excess of possible savers over dissavers, is much smaller; and most important, under the family system that predominates, the older generation is supported directly by the younger. While in and of itself, the large family system theoretically

[16] In Appendix D, I have attempted to explore the implications of this model.

should not affect the relative volume of real savings in the economy, in practice it tends to "invest" any surplus resources in the younger generation rather than in some form of "capital formation" that can be entered in our statistical tables. Thus the savings for the mass of the population in the underdeveloped countries are likely to be much lower than in developed countries—even relative to income. Indeed, in these countries savings of groups below the top are probably close to zero and perhaps often negative. The depressing effects of factors determining savings of the mass of income recipients may well outweigh significantly the raising effects of the greater inequality in the size distribution of income. A large part of the savings of the upper income groups may therefore be offset by dissavings of the lower income groups, causing even greater inequality in the distribution of assets and income unless some other major factors intervene.

The savings-income ratios are somewhat higher—at least when related to per capita income—in the older developed countries (e.g. the Netherlands and the United Kingdom before World War I) than in the more rapidly growing and socially fluid countries (e.g. the United States and Australia). This difference may be due to a greater inequality in the size distribution of income in the former countries as well as a lesser internal economic mobility.

The comments above bear upon the *level* of the aggregate savings-income share, but the factors stressed concern only indirectly the long-term *trend* of such shares over time. The main factors operative in the latter connection are the ones that shape consumer responses to rises in income levels, factors which in a free and fluid society exercise pressure toward higher consumption levels. With such pressures upon the mass of income recipients, as well as upon most of the upper groups; with institutional changes that tend to reduce the saving propensities—urbanization, lessening importance of the individual entrepreneur, and the like—stability or even a slight decline in the savings-income proportion for individuals in the developed countries is hardly surprising. In recent decades egalitarian economic legislation, by reducing the share of the "automatic" savers, may also have influenced this movement. Implicit in our definition of an economy under the aegis of business enterprises are the freedom and, in a sense, the sovereignty of the ultimate consumer. It is the consumer's response to the technological changes accompanying economic growth that brings about higher levels of possible material enjoyment. It is the pacesetter in the continuous race between the rise in per capita consumption and the rise in per capita output—in which the former is not necessarily the loser.

3. *Types of Capital Formation Financing*

The various ways in which capital formation is financed are obviously important in that they determine its magnitude and structure. In some cases the stock of capital goods used by the productive enterprise is increased by the user's own efforts, e.g. a farmer who hacks out and sets up fence posts barters labor for capital. In other cases money savings are used to "finance" the acquisition of a capital good. If savings are used, the purchaser, whether an individual or a business firm, may finance the acquisition out of his own funds or may seek external sources of financing. If external financing is provided, it may take the form of a privately arranged loan between individuals or of an issue of debt or equity securities on the public investment markets, or it may involve the use of bank credit. Furthermore, external financing may be arranged either directly by the owner of funds or through an intermediate financial institution (insurance company, bank, building and loan association, etc.) to which the owner of funds has delegated responsibility for placement and management of his assets. Finally, savings motivated by security may finance only conservative investment whereas other savings may be available for venture capital financing.

Of the five dichotomies of financing suggested—money and barter, external and internal, private and public, immediate and intermediate, security and venture—some are interrelated. Obviously, barter financing as defined here can be only internal. Likewise, internal financing can be only private since it takes place within the confines of the capital-user unit. External financing, on the other hand, can be either private or public, immediate or intermediate. And both external and internal financing may be security- or venture-motivated. It is hardly necessary to dwell on these taxonomic niceties. But it is necessary to understand that these distinctions are important to the functional relation between savings, capital formation, and economic growth. Clearly, the forms of financing that function most efficiently are those that can channel savings to effect the maximum volume of real capital formation that has a structure most conducive to increased productivity of the economy. The extent to which savings flow freely or are restricted by their owners or the intermediary agents who handle them and the extent to which they are directed toward the venturesome rather than the more secure uses have great bearing on the contribution of capital formation to economic growth.

Most of the distinctions apply equally to the financing of capital imports and exports and of domestic capital. For the former, however, they cannot be used profitably because there are almost no data on the various sources of financing capital flows across boundaries and, more important, because these flows are, in large part, dictated by political considerations. We therefore omit foreign financing of domestic capital formation and confine the discussion of types of financing to domestic sources of savings, relating them to *total* net and gross capital formation (the equivalents of net and gross domestic savings).

But even for total capital formation and its counterpart, country-wide domestic savings, discussion of trends in types of financing must be conjectural for the most part. The one study I know of containing data from which long-term trends in various types of savings and financing can be derived is a recent one for the United States by Raymond W. Goldsmith.[17] The scattered data for some countries for recent years in the national accounts tables cover too short a period to be instructive and are often distorted by peculiarities of definition, particularly of government and corporate savings. Even Goldsmith's record for the United States (Table III), which covers over half a century, is so affected by war and postwar conditions that it does not reveal any clear-cut long-term trends.

As a poor substitute for the missing substantive findings we present several conclusions reached after reflection on the possible trends in the relative importance of various types of capital formation financing in developed countries with business systems. These conjectures—that is actually all they are—we attempt to keep within reasonable bounds by referring to the main institutional features of economic growth in these countries.

1. To measure capital formation produced within an enterprise by its own forces is difficult, if not impossible. Although we have no estimates for this type of activity—classified here as "barter financing"—we cannot deny that it is widespread wherever individually operated, small-scale agriculture or handicrafts prevail. In growing countries which expanded over what was virtually virgin territory (e.g. the United States, Canada, Australia, and many Latin-Amer-

[17] Goldsmith, *op. cit.*

ican countries) this type of *net* capital formation may have been quite large during the period of extensive expansion, both absolutely and relative to total capital formation. In the older underdeveloped countries, where agriculture still plays a dominant part, the maintenance of capital, and therefore barter financing of *gross* capital formation at least, may also be substantial.

It follows that in the developed countries the trend in the share of barter financing in total capital formation, gross or net, must definitely have been downward after extensive expansion had slowed down or come to an end, and after the relative shares of agriculture and other industries somewhat removed from the complex network of the money and credit system had declined. Moreover, the share of barter-financed capital formation in gross, and perhaps also in net, capital formation is probably much higher in underdeveloped than in developed countries.

2. Theoretically, barter can also be used for external financing, but this type of financing would hardly be significant. We can therefore assume that external financing can emerge only with the help of money and similar means for systematic and extended transactions among different economic units.

But if flow of money and money funds are the precondition of external financing, their very fluidity creates difficulty in properly identifying and distinguishing external and internal financing. As already indicated, to link a specific source of funds with a specific use is purely arbitrary. Thus even if, for a single enterprise, both the depreciation reserves and gross value of physical assets accounts show offsetting changes, it does not follow that an item of durable capital equipment was internally financed. In the actual transaction, the capital goods seller may have advanced credit to the firm, but the latter may have used it in turn to finance some of its customers. Only by the convention of association of long-term sources with long-lived capital can we decide that internal financing was used in this instance.

A more important point, particularly for statistical measurement, is that "internality" and "externality" are relative concepts. In the above example the question was whether financing was internal for the given firm. However, what is external to a firm may be internal to an aggregate for an industry, and what is external to an industry may be internal to a broader aggregate, and so on. For a country as a whole, only foreign sources are external; all other financing of capital formation is, by definition, internal. And for the world as a whole there can be no external financing. The basic unit used to determine internal and external financing must, therefore, be clearly stated before the differences can be discussed. For our purposes this unit is the ultimate smallest ownership unit using a specific capital good. Thus a man borrowing funds to build a house for himself is, to the extent of the loan, receiving "external" financing, although the lender may be another individual and although for individuals as a whole this transaction is internal. Likewise, a firm whose accumulated depreciation reserves are used by another firm in the same industry is treated as a lender, engaged in "external" financing. The important distinction between external and internal financing is *not* that the former involves, and the latter does not involve, extensive operations by financial institutions. (A person financing his own house internally may still need to call upon scores of financial institutions to honor his checks or claims.) The difference is rather that with internal financing the prospective user of the capital good can make all necessary decisions, whereas with external financing the approval of the lender must be obtained.

In conjecturing about the long-term trends in the distribution between internal and external financing, the residential housing component of capital formation must be distinguished from the other major component, business capital. For residential and related housing in the United States, there is some evidence that the share of *external* financing rose in the long run, say since the 1870's and even since the 1900's, and that, correspondingly, the share of internal financing declined. These trends are observed in both net and gross additions to the stock of housing. The chief reason for these movements is obvious: in the earlier decades facilities for external financing were, if not absent, so limited that individuals could not easily get long-term credit to finance the construction or purchase of homes; but with the development of financing facilities this situation was eased and credit was extended more readily. Offhand, I would expect that a similar trend developed in countries whose growth was not unlike that of the United States, e.g. Canada and perhaps Australia. For other countries I hesitate even to guess.

The trends in the financing of business capital formation may well have been different. In the early decades of the nineteenth century, before the corporate form of organization had begun to develop and before security markets with broad coverage had been established, much of the financing must have been internal. At any rate, it is difficult to envisage as large a proportion of external financing in the early decades as in the later years, which saw the development of modern methods for mobilizing large amounts of small savings and channeling them to the major capital-using enterprises. It was largely the railroads and, later, the other public utilities that provided the schools in which the methods of widespread external financing were learned (with some simpler lessons gleaned from the building of canals and turnpikes). Our supposition is, then, that the share of external financing in both net and gross business capital formation showed a secular rise, generally from the second to the last quarter of the nineteenth century (with some differences in the initial and terminal dates in the several countries).

However, this upward trend may have reached its peak in the early twentieth century when the expansion of the giant corporations may have reached its limit. The concomitant rise in the relative importance of the capital consumption allowance, a possible source of internal financing, may have prevented a possible further rise in the share of external financing in gross capital formation and may have even caused a reversal. In recent decades the share of external financing in *gross* business capital formation may have declined while its share in net capital formation may have risen.

To summarize, the rough picture suggested is a long-term swing in the share of external financing in business capital formation: for the gross ratio a sustained rise over several decades culminating early in the twentieth century, followed perhaps by a decline; for the net ratio a rise through the nineteenth century and into the twentieth, with no indication of a decline as yet. The share of undistributed profits of business enterprises in net capital formation, i.e. the share of internal financing, probably did not rise during the period studied.

Unfortunately, the data for the United States in Table III cannot be presented as evidence in support of these conjectures. All they show is that the shares of government in both net and gross savings rise somewhat and those of unincorporated enterprises decline. But the shares of savings by individuals other than farmers, which are probably the chief source of *external* financing, and the shares of savings by business, which are probably the chief source of *internal* financing, show no pronounced trends since the early twentieth century. There *is* some sign of a rise in the business share and of a decline in individuals' share in *gross* savings. But this is slight corroboration of our conjectures.

3. The distinction between private and public is applicable largely

to external financing; and there is little doubt that, in the process of economic growth, opportunities for public financing of capital formation have increased enormously and that, in consequence, the proportion of external funds that flowed through publicly organized channels must have grown at the expense of the share of flows through private channels. It seems quite likely that the proportion of publicly financed to *total* capital formation, whether for personal use (residential housing) or for business use, increased significantly in the long run. The development of the organization for the mortgage financing of residential housing and the development of the security markets for the financing of business capital formation by public utilities and large corporations both serve to strengthen this inference.

The causal relation between this trend in public external financing and the growing contribution of savings and capital formation to economic growth can hardly be exaggerated. The development of a financial organization that mobilized accumulated funds, that directed them into the channels that—against the background of the economy as a whole—seemed most promising, and, finally, that had the power—unaware though the active agents may have been of it—to create money and to generate forced savings was fundamental to economic growth in the developed countries. This extension of economic inventions, embodied in the financial system and in the legal forms of business organization and of business transactions, prevented, or at least minimized, the danger of widespread hoarding, on the one hand, and of misuse of savings, on the other. Without this organization, accumulated savings might have been misdirected, if only because the lender had to have the security of personal knowledge of the borrower or had to be near the place of investment in order to exercise some control over the use of his funds. One striking difference today between developed and underdeveloped countries is precisely in the extent to which the latter lack a well-organized, publicly established system for channeling savings into those types of capital formation that are recognized by the country-wide free market as being the most promising.

I know of no data by which the relative importance of private and public flows of savings into capital formation can be measured. Consequently, the magnitude of the trend so strongly suggested by history must also remain an unknown quantity. Nor can I say that the trend has run its course—that the proportion of external financing flowing through public channels has reached its maximum in most developed countries. It is quite possible, however, that this point has been reached in the United States.

4. The growth and relative importance of intermediate financial institutions in channeling external financing to capital-users will be discussed by Goldsmith, and there is little need to dwell upon them here. By and large, one would expect the share of these institutions in external financing, and for that matter in total financing of capital formation—certainly net and perhaps even gross—to show a definite upward trend. This appears to have been true for the United States, and may well characterize developments in other countries, particularly if financial intermediaries are defined to include governments (with their responsibility for funds of social security systems, soldiers' insurance, etc.).

From our standpoint the major significance of this trend is the transfer of responsibility for the choice of investment, and hence indirectly of capital formation, from the individual saver to an institutional agent. The extent to which it affects the type of capital formation favored could be suggested only by a careful examination of financial intermediaries—of their investment policies, of their rules and methods of operation, and of their adaptability to long-term changes in conditions. I do not feel competent to undertake such an analysis.

5. These comments obviously bear on the whole complex of problems raised by the distinction between security-motivated savings and those available for financing venture capital. The distinction is important not only for individuals' savings—those of the lower income groups are assumed to be primarily security-motivated and those of the top income groups are assumed to be more readily available for financing venture capital. It is also relevant to corporate savings; the latter are quite large, particularly if taken gross of capital consumption allowances. Without any knowledge of the investment practices of individual savers at various income levels, of business corporations in different industries, and of financial intermediaries, it is not easy even to make conjectures.

Offhand, one might argue that if, as we suggest, the shares of internal financing and of private financing declined and the share of external financing through financial intermediaries rose, the proportion of savings available for truly risky and venturesome capital formation probably declined. But it is easy to exaggerate the bearing of these trends upon the supply of funds for venture capital. In the first place, *external* financing, private or public, was rarely available for truly risky capital formation—except when the latter was supported by some public guarantee or privileged status (e.g. as in the case of railroads). The genuinely experimental ventures, the spark plugs of technological change, were financed internally. (We include here loans from relatives, friends, etc.) If external funds have never really served true venture capital, the trends in their share of financing are not relevant here; they are not necessarily less effective now than they were in the past in extensions of tested new ventures.

Second, the decline in the share of internal financing in capital formation may not have been any greater than the recession in the relative needs for venture capital formation that accompanies economic development. More important, the growth in size and economic strength of business units increased their command over internal financing (particularly if gross savings are considered) and may well have made for a greater ease in allocating a larger proportion of internal funds to exploratory and venturesome uses. It is conceivable that in many developed countries the long-term shifts from the personal and individual to the institutional type of organization were accompanied by an increase in economic power and reserves and by a growing conviction, based on past experience, of the value of exploratory and venturesome uses of funds to stimulate the improvement of old and the discovery of new methods of production, types of goods, and devices for organizing economic activity. It may therefore be misleading to translate trends in form of organization into trends in character of function discharged; a less venturesome type of organization may still operate more daringly. At any rate, this question, which has been discussed to some extent (e.g. by Schumpeter and Galbraith in connection with the effects of monopolistic organization on the performance of the capitalist system in the United States), needs further serious consideration.

The comments in this section were colored largely by the experience of the United States,[18] and my conjectures about trends were derived from general knowledge of institutional changes in the process of growth of our business economy. Some of these suppositions would probably have to be modified, perhaps not decisively,

[18] In fact, they are based partly on Goldsmith (*op. cit.*), partly on past and current studies of the National Bureau of Economic Research relating to trends in capital formation and financing in the United States.

to fit the experience of other business economies. Inferences about the structure of financing in underdeveloped countries can be made easily. One would expect to find many of the features that characterized the early phases of the trends in the developed countries: larger shares of "barter" and internal financing; and within external financing, larger shares of private than of public, of immediate than of intermediate, but not necessarily of venturesome than of security-motivated, financing. But further speculation is pointless. Our chief purpose in writing this section was to suggest plausible inferences that might indicate the directions that further thinking and exploration should take. Because data are practically nonexistent, we could not present a summary of evidence that would be acceptable, even one subject to limitations of scope and accuracy similar to those indicated in the first two sections.

APPENDIX A

Statistical Tables

TABLE I-1

Proportions of Domestic Capital Formation to National Product, Recent Years

COUNTRY	DGCF AS % OF GNP 1938	DGCF AS % OF GNP 1947-1952[a]	DNCF AS % OF NNP 1938	DNCF AS % OF NNP 1947-1952[a]
1. United States	11.3	17.9	2.2	11.6
2. Canada	14.9	22.5	4.5	15.0
3. United Kingdom	10.4	13.3	b	b
4. France	b	18.6[c]	b	9.2[c,d]
5. Germany, F.R.	19.2[e]	23.2[f]	b	b
6. Italy	18.9	20.5[g]	11.3	13.1[g]
7. Ireland	8.8	14.3	6.7	12.0
8. Netherlands	11.1	24.5[g]	1.7	15.7[g]
9. Belgium[h]	b	16.1[f]	b	b
10. Denmark	13.7	17.6	b	b
11. Norway	21.5	30.9	6.9	16.0
12. Sweden	18.8	19.6	b	b
13. Austria	b	21.1[f]	b	15.3[f]
14. Portugal[h]	12.8	13.1	b	b
15. Greece	12.7	17.0	b	b
16. Iceland[h]	b	30.5	b	b
17. Finland[h]	22.6	30.0[f]	b	22.6[f]
18. Australia	21.9	30.8	17.0	26.8
19. New Zealand	19.2	23.4	13.6	18.7
20. Philippines	b	10.6	b	6.8
21. Ceylon[h]	5.6	10.0	b	b
22. Southern Rhodesia	b	b	b	44.9
23. Chile	12.9[i]	13.2[j]	8.8[i]	10.3[j]
24. Guatemala	b	10.8	b	b
25. Honduras	8.7	13.0	3.1	8.4
26. Mexico[h]	9.7[k]	14.0[j]	3.9[k]	7.5[j]
27. Peru	b	23.1	b	10.9

[a] Percentages of totals for the period.
[b] No data.
[c] Data for 1949-1952.
[d] Unadjusted for depreciation on government capital.
[e] Data for 1936.
[f] Data for 1948-1952.
[g] Data for 1947-1951.
[h] Capital formation excludes changes in stocks.
[i] Data for 1940.
[j] Data for 1947-1950.
[k] Data for 1939.

(cont. on next page)

TABLE I-1 (cont.)

Lines	Source
1-16	*Statistics of National Product and Expenditure, 1938, 1947 to 1952,* Organisation for European Economic Co-operation, Paris, 1954.
17-27	*Statistics of National Income and Expenditure,* Statistical Paper, Series H, No. 6, United Nations, August 1954.

All underlying totals are in current prices. In this and subsequent tables:
DGCF = Domestic Gross Capital Formation
DNCF = Domestic Net Capital Formation
GNP = Gross National Product
NNP = Net National Product
NDP = Net Domestic Product

TABLE I-2

Proportions of Domestic Capital Formation to National Product, the 1920's

Country	*Period*	*DGCF as % of GNP*	*DNCF as % of NNP*
United States	1925-1930	19.8	12.0
Great Britain	1924-1930	13.0	5.4
France	1927-1930	9.8(8.4)	7.0(5.6)
Germany	1925-1930	15.5	8.2
Netherlands	1925-1930	19.4	15.3
Switzerland	1925-1930	19.3	12.7

Source: All underlying data are in current prices.

The percentages are arithmetic means of percentages for single years, except for the allowance for inventories in France, which is based on the net changes in short-term credit balances for the period as a whole. The figures in parentheses are for shares excluding inventories.

The underlying estimates of capital formation are from J. Marschak and W. Lederer, *Kapitalbildung,* London, William Hodge, 1936, supplemented for Germany by those in "Kapitalbildung und Investitionem in der deutschen Volkswirtschaft, 1924 bis 1928," *Vierteljahrshefte für Konjunkturforschung,* Sonderheft 22, Berlin, 1931. For Switzerland they are based on money flows. The underlying estimates of net national product are from Colin Clark, *Conditions of Economic Progress,* 2nd ed., London, Macmillan, 1951, except those for the Netherlands which are from *Het Nationale Inkomen van Nederland, 1921-1939,* Central Bureau of Statistics.

TABLE I-3

Proportions of Domestic Capital Formation to National Product, Long Series

A. United States

Decade	DGCF as % of GNP	DNCF as % of NNP	Depreciation as % of DGCF
1. 1869-1878	21.7	13.9	42.8
2. 1879-1888	21.0	13.8	39.7
3. 1889-1898	22.9	14.6	43.0
4. 1899-1908	21.5	12.8	46.5
5. 1909-1918	19.4	10.7	50.1
6. 1919-1928	20.6	8.8	62.4
7. 1929-1938	14.8	2.3	86.7
8. 1939-1948	28.5	11.4	67.8
Average, lines 1-4	21.8	13.8	43.0
Average, lines 5-8	20.8	8.3	66.8

Source: The percentages are based on decade estimates in current prices. These estimates, prepared by the National Bureau of Economic Research, are revisions and extensions of the series published originally in Simon Kuznets' *National Product since 1869* (National Bureau of Economic Research, 1946). The revisions and extensions were completed recently for the study of capital formation and financing, and will be published in the summary volume of that study.

B. United Kingdom

Decade	DGCF as % of GNP	DNCF as % of NNP	Depreciation as % of DGCF
1870-1879	10.5	8.7	18.8
1880-1889	9.2	7.4	21.2
1890-1899	9.7	7.9	20.5
1900-1909	10.6	8.8	18.7
1904-1913	9.4	7.6	21.0

Source: The percentages are based on decade averages in current prices. The underlying data are estimates of capital formation (excluding changes in inventories) prepared by A. K. Cairncross and cited by J. H. Lenfant in "Great Britain's Capital Formation, 1865-1914," *Economica*, May 1951, pp. 151-168; and changes in inventories estimated by E. H. Phelps Brown and S. J. Handfield-Jones in "The Climacteric of the 1890's: A Study in the Expanding Economy," *Oxford Economic Papers*, New Series, October 1952, p. 305. The national product estimates are those of A. R. Prest, "National Income of the United Kingdom, 1870-1946," *Economic Journal*, March 1948, pp. 31-62.

For 1923-1939, Colin Clark estimates *net* domestic additions to capital to be 20 billion I.U. (*The Conditions of Economic Progress*, 2nd ed., London, Macmillan, 1951, p. 494). For Great Britain, excluding Ireland, the approximate total national income for the same period is 374 billion I.U. (see *ibid.*, p. 63). The ratio of net domestic capital formation to national income for 1924-1939 is, then, about 5 per cent.

(cont. on next page)

TABLE I-3 (cont.)
C. Sweden

Decade	*DGCF as % of GNP*	*DNCF as % of NNP*	*Depreciation as % of DGCF*
1861-1870	6.3	3.8	(42)
1871-1880	9.6	5.8	(42)
1881-1890	11.6	7.1	(42)
1891-1900	14.8	8.6	45.9
1901-1910	18.7	12.2	40.0
1911-1920	21.0	14.1	38.3
1921-1930	19.7	11.9	45.2

Source: The percentages are based on decade averages in current prices. Based on estimates in Eric Lindahl, Einar Dahlgren, and Karin Kock, *National Income of Sweden, 1861-1930*, London, King, 1937, Parts One and Two, particularly the details in Part Two.

The underlying totals of capital formation exclude changes in inventories.

Depreciation was not given for the first three decades and we assumed that it formed 42 per cent of domestic gross capital formation. Net national product was adjusted to exclude the imputed income on consumers' durables other than houses. Gross national product was computed as the sum of net national product and depreciation.

A comparison of the estimates in this table (and in Table II-4,C), relating to gross domestic and total capital formation proportions, with a new set based upon recent and still unpublished work of Dr. Olof Lindahl provides fair confirmation of the levels and trends shown here. The new estimates suggest somewhat lower capital formation proportions, but the trend movements are about the same.

D. Canada

PERIOD	DGCF AS % OF GNP		DNCF AS % OF NNP		DEPRECIATION[a] AS % OF DGCF	
	Incl. Inv.	*Excl. Inv.*	*Incl. Inv.*	*Excl. Inv.*	*Incl. Inv.*	*Excl. Inv.*
Buckley						
1. 1901-1910	27.5	23.8	19.4	15.3	36.4	42.1
2. 1911-1920	22.7	19.8	14.1	10.9	44.0	50.5
3. 1921-1930	19.2	17.4	10.2	8.2	52.2	57.6
4a. 1926-1930	21.1	18.5	12.4	9.4	47.4	54.1
Firestone						
4b. 1926-1930		21.2		12.5		47.1
5. 1931-1940		13.8		4.2		72.7
6. 1941-1950		16.9		9.9		45.9

[a] Assuming that depreciation was 10 per cent of gross national product (following Buckley) for lines 1-5.

Source: Based on averages in current prices for specified periods.

Lines 1 to 4a based on estimates in K. A. H. Buckley's "Real Investment in Canada, 1900 to 1930," doctoral thesis, London School of Economics, manuscript, June 1950, pp. 119 and 178.

Lines 4b to 6 based on estimates of domestic capital formation and gross national product for 1926-1940 by O. J. Firestone in *Private and Public Investment in Canada, 1926-1951*, Ottawa, Department of Trade and Commerce, 1951. Product and depreciation estimates since 1941 are from successive publications on National Accounts of the Dominion Bureau of Statistics, particularly for 1941-1948, 1942-1949, and 1950.

(cont. on next page)

TABLE I-3 (cont.)
E. France

Period	Domestic Net Savings[a] (billions of francs)	National Income[b] (billions of francs)	DNCF as % of NNP
1853-1878	1.90	22.2	8.5
1878-1903	1.37	29.6	4.6
1903-1911	2.04	36.2	5.6

[a] René Pupin in *La Richesse de la France devant la Guerre* (Paris, Marcel Rivière, 1916), p. 111, gives estimates of average annual total savings (private, after deduction of losses) as follows: for 1853-1878, 2.20 billion francs; for 1878-1903, 2.04 billion francs; and for 1903-1911, 3.50 billion francs. From these are subtracted estimates of net foreign investment. Harry D. White in *The French International Accounts, 1880-1913* (Harvard University Press, 1933), pp. 121-122, shows net foreign investment balance at the beginning of 1880 to be 9 billion francs. On the assumption that the net outstanding balance was close to zero in 1853, the annual average of net capital exports, 1853-1880, was about 0.30 billion francs. White's estimates of net capital exports as revised by Carl Iversen in *Aspects of the Theory of International Capital Movements* (London, Oxford, 1935), p. 344, are: for 1880-1903, 0.67 billion francs, and for 1903-1911, 1.46 billion francs.

[b] Colin Clark, *The Conditions of Economic Progress*, 2nd ed., London, Macmillan, 1951, p. 80.

F. Denmark

Period	DGCF as % of GNP	DNCF as % of NDP	Depreciation as % of DGCF
1. 1870-1879	13.6	9.5	33.6
2. 1880-1889	12.1	7.9	37.4
3. 1890-1899	14.7	10.7	30.8
4. 1900-1909	15.6	10.6	36.2
5. 1905-1914	14.6	9.4	39.2
6. 1915-1920	10.3	3.2	70.8
7. 1921-1929	10.8	5.4	52.5
8. 1930-1939	13.6	8.7	39.8
9. 1940-1946	9.9	4.3	58.8
10. 1947-1952	17.0	9.7	47.6
Average, lines 1-4	14.0	9.7	34.5
Average, lines 4, 5, 7, 8	13.7	8.5	41.9

Source: All percentages are based on decade averages in current prices. Capital formation excludes net changes in inventories. The underlying estimates by Kjeld Bjerke are given in "The National Product of Denmark, 1870-1952," *Income and Wealth, Series V*, Cambridge, Eng., Bowes & Bowes for International Association for Research in Income and Wealth, in press. The ratios are to gross national product and to net domestic product. Depreciation includes the net balance of foreign factor payments.

The averages do not cover the 1915-1920 and 1940-1950 periods in order to exclude the extraordinary effect of war.

TABLE II-1

Proportions of Foreign Investment to Domestic Capital Formation and to National Product, and of Total Capital Formation to National Product, Recent Years

COUNTRY	FOREIGN INVESTMENT AS % OF DGCF		FOREIGN INVESTMENT AS % OF DNCF		FOREIGN INVESTMENT AS % OF GNP		FOREIGN INVESTMENT AS % OF NNP		GCF AS % OF GNP		NCF AS % OF NNP	
	1938	*1947-1952*[a]	*1938*	*1947-1952*[a]	*1938*	*1947-1952*[a]	*1938*	*1947-1952*[a]	*1938*	*1947-1952*[a]	*1938*	*1947-1952*[a]
1. United States	13.2	10.2	76.3	17.0	1.5	1.8	1.6	2.0	12.8	19.7	3.8	13.5
2. Canada	14.3	.8	53.6	1.3	2.1	.2	2.4	.2	17.1	22.7	6.9	15.2
3. United Kingdom	–10.4	–4.0	b	b	–1.1	–.5	b	b	9.3	12.8	b	b
4. France	b	–.6[c]	b	–1.4[c,d]	b	–.1[c]	b	–.1[c,d]	b	18.5[c]	b	9.1[c,d]
5. Germany, F.R.	0[e]	–1.0[f]	b	b	0[e]	–.2[f]	b	b	19.2[e]	22.9[f]	b	b
6. Italy	–5.2	–14.3[g]	–9.4	–24.4[g]	–1.0	–2.9[g]	–1.1	–3.2[g]	17.9	17.5[g]	10.3	9.9[g]
7. Ireland	–5.0	–64.4	–6.8	–78.6	–.4	–9.2	–.5	–9.5	8.4	5.1	6.2	2.6
8. Netherlands	27.8	–19.7[g]	204.4	–34.5[g]	3.1	–4.8[g]	3.4	–5.4[g]	14.2	19.7[g]	5.1	10.3[g]
9. Belgium[h]	b	2.2[f]	b	b	b	.4[f]	b	b	b	16.5[f]	b	b
10. Denmark	11.4	–8.9	b	b	1.6	–1.6	b	b	15.3	16.0	b	b
11. Norway	6.7	–14.2	24.7	–33.3	1.4	–4.4	1.7	–5.3	22.9	26.5	8.6	10.7
12. Sweden	–2.3	–.1	b	b	–.4	–.02	b	b	18.4	19.6	b	b
13. Austria	b	–22.6[f]	b	–33.5[f]	b	–4.8[f]	b	–5.1[f]	b	16.3[f]	b	10.2[f]
14. Portugal[h]	–51.1	–55.5	b	b	–6.5	–7.3	b	b	6.2	5.8	b	b
15. Greece	–25.3	–76.7	b	b	–3.2	–13.1	b	b	9.5	4.0	b	b
16. Iceland[h]	b	–25.6	b	b	3.6	–7.8	b	b	b	22.7	b	b
17. Finland[h]	6.1	5.8[f]	b	8.5[f]	1.4	1.7[f]	b	1.9[f]	24.0	31.8[f]	b	24.6[f]
18. Australia	–11.9	–5.7	–16.3	–6.9	–2.6	–1.8	–2.8	–1.9	19.3	29.0	14.2	24.9
19. New Zealand	–13.0	2.7	–20.7	3.0	–2.0	.6	–2.8	.7	16.6	24.0	10.7	19.4
20. Philippines	b	–35.1	b	–56.7	b	–3.7	b	–3.9	b	6.9	b	3.0

(cont. on next page)

TABLE II-1 (cont.)

COUNTRY	FOREIGN INVESTMENT AS % OF DGCF 1938	FOREIGN INVESTMENT AS % OF DGCF 1947-1952[a]	FOREIGN INVESTMENT AS % OF DNCF 1938	FOREIGN INVESTMENT AS % OF DNCF 1947-1952[a]	FOREIGN INVESTMENT AS % OF GNP 1938	FOREIGN INVESTMENT AS % OF GNP 1947-1952[a]	FOREIGN INVESTMENT AS % OF NNP 1938	FOREIGN INVESTMENT AS % OF NNP 1947-1952[a]	GCF AS % OF GNP 1938	GCF AS % OF GNP 1947-1952[a]	NCF AS % OF NNP 1938	NCF AS % OF NNP 1947-1952[a]
21. Ceylon[h]	−56.4	−12.7	b	b	−3.2	−1.3	b	b	2.4	8.7	b	b
22. Southern Rhodesia	b	b	b	−77.1	b	b	b	−34.6	b	b	b	10.3
23. Chile	−5.3[i]	−5.5[j]	−8.1[i]	−7.2[j]	−.7[i]	−.7[j]	−.7[i]	−.7[j]	12.2[i]	12.4[j]	8.1[i]	9.6[j]
24. Guatemala	b	5.4	b	b	b	.6	b	b	b	11.4	b	b
25. Honduras	16.7	−16.0	48.8	−25.8	1.4	−2.1	1.5	−2.2	10.1	10.9	4.7	6.3
26. Mexico[h]	26.2[k]	−4.1[j]	69.7[k]	−8.2[j]	2.6[k]	−.6[j]	2.7[k]	−.6[j]	12.3[k]	13.4[j]	6.6[k]	6.9[j]
27. Peru	b	−8.2	b	−20.0	b	−1.9	b	−2.2	b	21.2	b	8.7

[a] Percentages of totals for the period.
[b] No data.
[c] Data for 1949-1952.
[d] NNP and NCF unadjusted for depreciation on government capital.
[e] Data for 1936.
[f] Data for 1948-1952.
[g] Data for 1947-1951.
[h] Capital formation excludes changes in stocks.
[i] Data for 1940.
[j] Data for 1947-1950.
[k] Data for 1939.
Source: Same as for Table I-1.

TABLE II-2

Proportions of Foreign Investment to Domestic Capital Formation and to National Product, and of Total Capital Formation to National Product, the 1920's

Items	*United States, 1925-1930*	*Great Britain, 1925-1930*	*France, 1927-1930*	*Germany, 1925-1930*	*Netherlands, 1925-1930*	*Switzerland, 1925-1930*
Foreign investment as % of						
Domestic NCF	5.1	26.9	31.2	—24.3	14.4	7.7
Domestic GCF	2.8	9.7	20.8	—1.2	10.7	4.5
NNP	.7	1.3	2.0	—.8	2.0	.9
GNP	.6	1.2	2.0	—.8	2.0	.9
Total CF as % of NP						
Net, of NNP	12.7	6.6	9.0	7.4	17.4	13.6
Gross, of GNP	20.4	14.1	11.7	14.7	21.4	20.2

Source: Same as for Table I-2.

TABLE II-3

Capital Exports (+) and Imports (−)
Compared with National Income,1921-1938
(*capital movements, millions of $; national income, billions of I.U.*)

COUNTRY[a]	CAPITAL MOVEMENTS, TOTALS *1921-1929* (1)	*1930-1938* (2)	*1921-1938* (3)	CAPITAL MOVEMENTS PER YEAR *1921-1938* (4)	NATIONAL INCOME PER YEAR[b] (5)	CM PER YEAR AS % OF NI PER YEAR (6)
A. Creditors						
France	+3,037	−94	+2,943	+163.5	12.53	+1.30
Netherlands	+414	−127	+287	+15.9	2.884	+.55
Sweden	+303	+104	+407	+22.6	1.941[c]	+1.16
Switzerland	+327	−379	−52	−2.9	1.556 (1924-1938)	−.19
United Kingdom (1921)	+3,425	−893	+2,532	+148.9	23.38 (1924-1938)	+.64
United States	+5,990	−4,964	+1,026	+57.0	75.92	+.08
B. Developed & semideveloped debtors						
Argentina	−806	−272	−1,078	−59.9	3.95 (1935)	−1.52
Australia (1938)	−1,332	−58	−1,390	−81.8	3.233 (1921-1937)	−2.53
Canada	+43	+70	+113	+6.6	5.102 (1921-1937)	+.13
Czechoslovakia (1921-1924, 1938)	+208	+70	+278	+21.4	3.5 (1925, 1929, 1937)	+.61
Denmark	−112	+65	−47	−2.6	1.512 (1925-1938)	−.17
Finland (1921)	−32	+190	+158	+9.3	.711 (1924, 1926, 1929, 1938)	+1.31
Germany (1921-1923; 1936-1938)	−3,965	+460	−3,505	−292.1	19.85 (1925-1935)	−1.47
Japan (1937-1938)	−1,031	+346	−685	−42.8	8.85 (1921-1936)	−.48
Latvia (1921, 1938)	−6	+26	+20	+1.25	.361 (7 scattered years, 1925-1938)	+.35
New Zealand	−189	−13	−202	−11.2	.962 (1925-1938)	−1.16
Norway (1921-1922)	−131	+24	−107	−6.7	.731 (1923-1938)	−.92
Union of South Africa (1921-1922, 1938)	−268	−37	−305	−20.3	1.371 (1923-1937)	−1.48

(cont. on next page)

TABLE II-3 (cont.)

(*capital movements, millions of $; national income, billions of I.U.*)

COUNTRY[a]	CAPITAL MOVEMENTS, TOTALS *1921-1929* (1)	*1930-1938* (2)	*1921-1938* (3)	CAPITAL MOVEMENTS PER YEAR *1921-1938* (4)	NATIONAL INCOME PER YEAR[b] (5)	CM PER YEAR AS % OF NI PER YEAR (6)
C. Underdeveloped debtors						
Bulgaria	−48	+13	−35	−2.7		
Hungary (1921-1922, 1938)	−297	+3	−294	−19.6	1.231 (1924-1936, 1938)	−1.59
India (1921-1922)	−386	+155	−231	−14.4		
Lithuania (1921-1923, 1938)	+18	+5	+23	+1.6		
Netherlands Indies (1921-1924)	+160	+217	+377	+26.9		
Poland (1921-1922, 1938)	−332	+20	−312	−20.8	4.55 (1926, 1928, 1929, 1938)	−.46
Yugoslavia (1921-1923, 1925, 1937-1938)	−26	−82	−108	−9.0	1.48 (1925, 1929, 1938)	−.61
Recapitulation						
A countries	+13,496	−6,353	+7,143			
B countries	−7,621	+871	−6,863			
C countries	−911	+331	−600			
Sums						
All capital exports	+13,925	+1,768	+8,164			
All capital imports	−8,961	−6,919	−8,351			
Discrepancy to balance	−4,964	+5,151	+187			

[a] Years for which capital movements are not available are given in parentheses.

[b] Years included are given in parentheses.

[c] Average of real product per worker (1921-1938) multiplied by number of workers (average for 1920, 1930, and 1940).

Column	Source
1-4	Derived from *International Capital Movements during the Inter-War Period*, United Nations, October 1949, Table 1, pp. 10-12. Only those countries were included here for which at least five years out of a nine-year period were reported.
5	From Colin Clark, *The Conditions of Economic Progress*, 2nd ed., London, Macmillan, 1951.

TABLE II-4

Proportions of Foreign Investment to Domestic Capital Formation and to National Product, and of Total Capital Formation to National Product, Long Series

A. United States

DECADE	FOREIGN INVESTMENT AS % OF *DNCF*	*DGCF*	*NNP*	*GNP*	TOTAL CAPITAL FORMATION *Net as % of NNP*	*Gross as % of GNP*
1. 1869-1878	−10.7	−6.2	−1.5	−1.3	12.3	20.4
2. 1879-1888	−3.0	−1.8	−.4	−.4	13.4	20.7
3. 1889-1898	1.1	.6	.2	.1	14.7	23.1
4. 1899-1908	8.8	4.7	1.1	1.0	13.9	22.5
5. 1909-1918	25.4	12.7	2.7	2.5	13.5	21.9
6. 1919-1928	21.1	7.9	1.9	1.6	10.7	22.2
7. 1929-1938	24.6	3.3	.6	.5	2.8	15.3
8. 1939-1948	10.0	3.2	1.1	.9	12.5	29.5
Average, lines 1-4	−1.0	−.7	−.2	−.2	13.6	21.7
Average, lines 5-8	20.3	6.8	1.6	1.4	9.9	22.2

Source: Same as for Table I-3, A.

B. United Kingdom

Items	*1870-1879*	*1880-1889*	*1890-1899*	*1900-1909*	*1904-1913*
Foreign investment as % of					
Domestic NCF (I)	54.2	78.8	46.2	51.1	95.8
Domestic NCF (C-L)	34.4	51.5	29.1	38.3	84.0
Domestic GCF (I)	44.0	62.1	36.7	41.6	75.6
Domestic GCF (C-L)	27.9	40.6	23.1	31.1	66.3
NNP (I)	4.7	5.8	3.6	4.5	7.3
NNP (C-L)	3.0	3.8	2.3	3.4	6.4
GNP (I)	4.6	5.7	3.6	4.4	7.1
GNP (C-L)	2.9	3.7	2.2	3.3	6.3
Total capital formation as % of NP					
Net, of NNP (I)	13.4	13.2	11.5	13.3	14.9
Net, of NNP (C-L)	11.7	11.2	10.2	12.1	14.0
Gross, of GNP (I)	15.1	14.9	13.3	15.0	16.6
Gross, of GNP (C-L)	13.4	12.9	12.0	13.9	15.7

Source: See notes to Table I-3, B. The lines marked C-L use estimates of net capital exports shown by Cairncross-Lenfant. Those marked I are based on estimates by Albert H. Imlah, in "British Balance of Payments and Export of Capital, 1816-1913," *Economic History Review*, Vol. v (1952), No. 2, pp. 208-239.

(cont. on next page)

TABLE II-4 (cont.)

C. Sweden

DECADE	FOREIGN INVESTMENT AS % OF *DNCF*	*DGCF*	*NNP*	*GNP*	TOTAL CAPITAL FORMATION *Net as % of NNP*	*Gross as % of GNP*
1861-1870	−49.8	−28.9	−1.9	−1.8	1.9	4.5
1871-1880	−46.9	−27.2	−2.7	−2.6	3.1	7.0
1881-1890	−79.4	−46.1	−5.6	−5.4	1.5	6.3
1891-1900	−20.7	−11.2	−1.8	−1.7	6.8	13.1
1901-1910	−27.2	−16.3	−3.3	−3.1	8.9	15.7
1911-1920	9.9	6.1	1.4	1.3	15.5	22.3
1921-1930	10.8	5.9	1.3	1.2	13.2	20.9

Source: Same as for Table I-3, C.

D. Canada

PERIOD	FOREIGN INVESTMENT AS % OF *DNCF*	*DGCF*	*NNP*	*GNP*	TOTAL CAPITAL FORMATION *Net as % of NNP*	*Gross as % of GNP*
Buckley (incl. inventories)						
1901-1910	−48.2	−30.7	−9.4	−8.4	10.1	19.1
1911-1920	−43.2	−24.2	−6.1	−5.5	8.0	17.2
1921-1930	−10.7	−5.1	−1.1	−1.0	9.1	18.2
1926-1930	−18.2	−9.6	−2.2	−2.0	10.1	19.1
Firestone (excl. inventories)						
1926-1930	−17.5	−9.3	−2.2	−2.0	10.3	19.3
1931-1940	39.6	10.9	1.7	1.5	5.9	15.3
1941-1950	20.6	11.2	2.0	1.9	11.9	18.7

Source: See notes to Table I-3, D. Foreign investment, 1926-1941, from *Public Investment and Capital Formation*, Ottawa, Dominion-Provincial Conference on Reconstruction, 1945.

(cont. on next page)

TABLE II-4 (cont.)

E. France

Period	*Domestic Net Savings* (*billions of francs*)	*Net Capital Exports* (*billions of francs*)	*NCE as % of DNS*
1853-1878	1.90	.30	16
1878-1903	1.37	.67	49
1903-1911	2.04	1.46	72

Period	*National Income* (*millions of francs*)	*Capital Exports per Year* (*millions of francs*)	*CE as % of NI*
1853-1878	22,200	300.0	1.4
1880-1889	28,000	486.5	1.7
1890-1899	29,500	648.0	2.2
1900-1909	35,500	1,367.5	3.9
1910-1913	38,500 (1911)	1,329.0	3.5

Source: Same as for Table I-3, E.

F. Denmark

	FOREIGN INVESTMENT AS % OF				TOTAL CAPITAL FORMATION	
PERIOD	*DNCF*	*DGCF*	*NDP*	*GNP*	*Net as % of NDP*	*Gross as % of GNP*
1. 1870-1879	−9.3	−6.2	−.9	−.8	8.6	12.8
2. 1880-1889	−29.4	−18.4	−2.3	−2.2	5.6	9.8
3. 1890-1899	−23.5	−16.3	−2.5	−2.4	8.2	12.3
4. 1900-1909	−23.4	−14.9	−2.5	−2.3	8.1	13.3
5. 1905-1914	−8.4	−5.1	−.8	−.7	8.6	13.9
6. 1915-1920	−106.5	−31.1	−3.5	−3.2	−.2	7.1
7. 1921-1929	+7.4	+3.5	+.4	+.4	5.8	11.1
8. 1930-1939	+22.8	+13.7	+2.0	+1.9	10.7	15.5
9. 1940-1946	+218.7	+90.1	+9.5	+9.0	13.9	18.9
10. 1947-1952	−14.6	−7.7	−1.4	−1.3	8.3	15.7
Average, lines 1-4	−21.4	−13.9	−2.1	−2.0	7.6	12.1
Average, lines 4, 5, 7, 8	−.4	−.7	−.2	−.2	8.3	13.5

Source: Same as for Table I-3, F.

(cont. on next page)

TABLE II-4 (cont.)

G. Australia

Period	National Income (1) (millions of £)	Capital Imports (—) or Exports (+) per Year (2) (millions of £)	CI or CE as % of NI (3)
1. 1871-1880		—4.06	
2. 1881-1890	152 (1886)	—16.18	—10.6
3. 1891-1900	190 (1892, 1894, 1898)	—6.31	—3.3
4. 1901-1910	273	+1.75	+.6
5. 1911-1920 (10.5 years)	398	—15.74	—4.0
6. 1921-1930 (9.5 years)	732	—25.03	—3.4

Column 1 — Source

Line

4 Colin Clark, *The Conditions of Economic Progress*, 2nd ed., London, Macmillan, 1951, p. 140, average of 1901-1903 and 1913-1914.

5 *Ibid.*, 1913-1914 through 1920-1921; 1911 and 1912 assumed to be £300 million each.

6 *Ibid.*, 1921-1922 through 1929-1930.

2 & 3 Extrapolated from 1901-1903, by income in New South Wales, for 1892, 1894, and 1898 (line 3) and 1886 (line 2). Figures for New South Wales from *ibid.*, p. 145.

Column 2 Carl Iversen, *Aspects of the Theory of International Capital Movements*, London, Oxford, 1935, p. 402.

H. Japan

Period	National Income (billions of yen) (1)	Capital Imports (—) or Exports (+) per Year (millions of yen) (2)	CI or CE as % of NI (3)
1868-1895		negligible	negligible
1896-1913	2.81	—83.3	—3.0
1914-1919	7.97	+405.2	+5.1
1920-1929	11.63	—277.2	—2.4

Column — Source

1 Shigeto Tsuru, "Long-Term Changes in the National Product of Japan since 1878," in *Income and Wealth, Series III*, Milton Gilbert, editor, Cambridge, Eng., Bowes & Bowes for International Association for Research in Income and Wealth, 1953.

2 E. P. Reubens, "Foreign Capital and Domestic Development in Japan," paper presented at Social Science Research Council Conference, Spring 1952.

TABLE II-5

Geographical Distribution of Foreign Investments,
Three Main Creditor Countries,
Eve of World War I

UNITED KINGDOM	*% of Total*
Empire	47.3
Canada	13.7
Australia	11.1
South Africa	9.8
India & Ceylon	10.1
Other Europe	2.6
United States	20.0
Latin America	20.1
Argentina	8.5
Brazil	3.9
Rest	7.7
Europe	5.8
Russia	2.9
Rest	2.9
Rest of world	6.7
Total	100.0
	(£3.76 bill.)

FRANCE	*% of Total*
Colonies	8.9
Europe (incl. Asiatic Turkey)	61.1
Russia	25.1
Turkey	7.3
Balkan States	5.6
Austria-Hungary	4.9
Spain & Portugal	8.7
Rest	9.5
Latin America	13.3
Egypt, Suez, South Africa	7.3
U.S. & Canada	4.4
Asia	4.9
Total	100.0
	(45.0 bill. francs)

GERMANY	*% of Total*
Europe	53.2
Austria-Hungary	12.8
Turkey (in Asia)	7.7
Russia	7.7
Balkan States	7.2
Spain & Portugal	7.2
Rest	10.6
Latin America	16.2
U.S. & Canada	15.7
Africa (incl. German colonies)	8.5
Asia (incl. German colonies)	4.3
Rest of world	2.1
Total	100.0
	(23.5 bill. marks)

Source: Herbert Feis, *Europe, the World's Banker, 1870-1914*, Yale University Press, 1930, pp. 23, 51, and 74.

TABLE III

Distribution of Net and Gross Savings among Saver Groups, United States, Selected Periods since 1897 (*percentage shares*)

PERIOD	PERSONAL: *Nonagric. Individ.*	PERSONAL: *Farmers*	PERSONAL: *Uninc. Business*	BUSINESS CORPS.	GOVT. (INCL. NONPROFIT CORPS.)
			In Net Savings		
1897-1906	61.2	1.3	5.8	25.1	6.6
1907-1916	70.0	−5.8	3.6	23.9	8.3
1920-1929	62.8	−2.1	3.4	20.4	15.5
1920-1939	96.6	.9	−3.5	.6	5.3
1946-1949	51.8	7.2	1.4	25.3	14.3
			In Gross Savings (at Replacement Prices)		
1897-1906	43.3	8.1	8.4	33.5	6.8
1907-1916	46.1	3.8	6.0	35.6	8.4
1920-1929	40.2	4.1	6.3	36.5	12.9
1920-1939	42.8	6.6	4.9	35.8	9.9
1946-1949	36.1	8.0	4.4	36.8	14.6

Source: Based on averages of estimates (national accounting approach), in current prices, prepared by Raymond W. Goldsmith in *A Study of Saving in the United States* (Princeton University Press, 1955). Excludes savings embodied in consumer durable goods and in military goods.

APPENDIX B

Share of Depreciation in Gross Capital Formation and in Gross National Product and the Relation between Gross and Net Capital Formation Proportions

NOTATION

C_0 = net reproducible capital at beginning of time unit 0
G_0 = gross national product during time unit 0
P_0 = net national product during time unit 0
D_0 = depreciation during time unit 0
r = rate of growth of gross national product per time unit
f = proportion of gross capital formation to gross national product
a = proportion of depreciable gross capital formation to total gross capital formation
n = number of time units in life of depreciable capital

ASSUMPTIONS

We assume that:

1. The terms r, f, a, and n are constant. In calculating the stock of depreciable capital, such constancy has to be assumed for the finite period of n time units since no such capital that is older than n units survives. In calculating the stock of nondepreciable capital, the constancy must be assumed for an infinite number of time units since such capital never perishes and hence is accumulated from time immemorial.

It should be noted that the constancy assumed here is applied rigidly to facilitate the derivation of equations which are largely sums of geometric progressions. In application in empirical analysis, however, absolute invariance of these rates and proportions from one time unit to the next need not be implied: we can treat these rates and proportions as averages for the n time units (or as an average characterizing the capital stock at a given time) in which the weights have been so set as to yield a result identical with that yielded by a geometric progression applied to an invariable set of ratios or proportions.

2. The term r is positive. Unless it is, the stock of nondepreciable capital will have to be either infinitely large or determinable on grounds that cannot be defined by simple assumptions.

3. The absolute magnitudes—gross and net national product, depreciation, and capital stock—are all in constant prices.

4. Depreciation is calculated on a straight-line basis.

Derivation of Depreciable Capital Stock as a Sum of Past Depreciated Gross Capital Formation

Time Unit (1)	GCF during Time Unit (2)	Fraction of (2) Entering Capital Stock, C_0 (3)	Product of Entries in Columns 2 and 3 Unfolded as Sums (4)		(5)		(6)		.....	
$-n$	$\frac{fG_0}{(1+r)^n}$	$a \cdot \frac{1}{n}$	$\frac{fG_0}{(1+r)^n} \cdot \frac{a}{n}$							1 term
$-n+1$	$\frac{fG_0}{(1+r)^{n-1}}$	$a \cdot \frac{2}{n}$	$\frac{fG_0}{(1+r)^{n-1}} \cdot \frac{a}{n}$	+	$\frac{fG_0}{(1+r)^{n-1}} \cdot \frac{a}{n}$					2 terms
$-n+2$	$\frac{fG_0}{(1+r)^{n-2}}$	$a \cdot \frac{3}{n}$	$\frac{fG_0}{(1+r)^{n-2}} \cdot \frac{a}{n}$	+	$\frac{fG_0}{(1+r)^{n-2}} \cdot \frac{a}{n}$	+	$\frac{fG_0}{(1+r)^{n-2}} \cdot \frac{a}{n}$			3 terms
.	.	.	.		.		.			.
.	.	.	.		.		.			.
.	.	.	.		.		.			.
.	.	.	.		.		.			.
.	.	.	.		.		.			.
-2	$\frac{fG_0}{(1+r)^2}$	$a \cdot \frac{n-1}{n}$	$\frac{fG_0}{(1+r)^2} \cdot \frac{a}{n}$	+	$\frac{fG_0}{(1+r)^2} \cdot \frac{a}{n}$	+	$\frac{fG_0}{(1+r)^2} \cdot \frac{a}{n}$	+	.....	$(n-1)$ terms
-1	$\frac{fG_0}{(1+r)}$	$a \cdot \frac{n}{n}$	$\frac{fG_0}{(1+r)} \cdot \frac{a}{n}$	+	$\frac{fG_0}{(1+r)} \cdot \frac{a}{n}$	+	$\frac{fG_0}{(1+r)} \cdot \frac{a}{n}$	+	.....	n terms

Sums of columns beginning with column 4 $\frac{a}{n}\left[\frac{fG_0}{r} - \frac{fG_0}{r(1+r)^n}\right] + \frac{a}{n}\left[\frac{fG_0}{r} - \frac{fG_0}{r(1+r)^{n-1}}\right] + \frac{a}{n}\left[\frac{fG_0}{r} - \frac{fG_0}{r(1+r)^{n-2}}\right] + \cdots\cdots \frac{a}{n}\left[\frac{fG_0}{r} - \frac{fG_0}{r(1+r)}\right]$

The number of sums above is n. Their sum is

$$\sum\sum = \frac{nafG_0}{nr} - \frac{afG_0}{nr}\left[\frac{1-(1+r)^{-n}}{r}\right] = \frac{afG_0}{r}\left[\frac{nr - 1 + (1+r)^{-n}}{nr}\right]$$

EQUATIONS

The basic procedure for deriving the equations is set forth in the accompanying summary, which shows the cumulative sum of depreciated capital (the stock of depreciable capital) but which can also be used to derive the other terms in the necessary equations. The arrangement demonstrates that the stock of capital at any given time is a sum (or a sum of sums) of geometric progressions over a period of finite n units for depreciable capital or of an infinite number for nondepreciable capital.

The stock of depreciable capital at the beginning of time unit 0 is thus equal to

$$\frac{afG_0}{r} \cdot \frac{nr - 1 + (1 + r)^{-n}}{nr}$$

For n time units the accumulation of nondepreciable capital (from column 4 of the summary) is equal to

$$\frac{(1 - a)fG_0}{r} \cdot [1 - (1 + r)^{-n}]$$

But this is the cumulation of nondepreciable capital over n time units—the life of depreciable capital. At the beginning of the nth time unit preceding time unit 0 there already existed some nondepreciable capital which, by definition, persisted to time unit 0. Obviously, the cumulation of nondepreciable capital must be derived for a much larger number of time units. If for simplicity's sake we assume that this number is infinite and *provided* that r is larger than 0, i.e. positive, the stock of nondepreciable capital at the beginning of time unit 0 becomes

$$\frac{(1 - a)fG_0}{r}$$

If r is negative, the stock of nondepreciable capital would be infinitely large—since a negative r extended over an infinity of time would mean that gross national product started declining from an infinitely high level and was accompanied by an infinitely large stock of capital.

Hence, on the assumption that r is positive, we can write the equation for the stock of capital at the beginning of time unit 0 as follows:[1]

[1] It is apparent that if *all* capital is nondepreciable—which means that gross and net capital formation are identical—equation 1 becomes

$$(1) \qquad C_0 = \frac{afG_0}{r} \cdot \frac{nr - 1 + (1+r)^{-n}}{nr} + \frac{(1-a)fG_0}{r}$$

It should be noted that the tabular arrangement, and hence the resulting equation, is based on the rule that capital formation during a given time unit is not subject to depreciation until the following time unit; that such capital formation is, as it were, concentrated toward the end of the time unit. A modification to assume that capital formation during a given time unit is subject to depreciation from the beginning of that unit, rather than from the beginning of the next, could easily be introduced.

From column 4 of the tabular arrangement we can also derive the equation for depreciation or capital consumption for time unit 0, D_0, on the assumption, we repeat, that it is calculated on a straight-line basis.

$$(2) \qquad D_0 = \frac{afG_0}{nr} \cdot [1 - (1+r)^{-n}]$$

SHARE OF DEPRECIATION IN GROSS CAPITAL FORMATION

If during time unit 0 the gross capital formation proportion equals f, the constant proportion assumed for the past, the share of depreciation in gross capital formation can be defined as

$$(3) \qquad \frac{D_0}{fG_0} = \frac{a[1 - (1+r)^{-n}]}{nr}$$

$$C_0 = \frac{fG_0}{r}$$

where

$G_0 = P_0 =$ national product

$f =$ *gross* or *net* capital formation proportion

$r =$ rate of growth in gross national product or net national product;

or, to put it differently: if we assume that $b =$ net capital formation proportion and $r' =$ rate of growth in P_0,

$$C_0 = \frac{bP_0}{r'}$$

and the capital-output ratio is obviously

$$\frac{C_0}{P_0} = \frac{b}{r'}$$

directly proportional to the net capital formation proportion and inversely proportional to the rate of growth in net national product.

This is a much simpler presentation than the one followed, but we prefer the latter because it permits us to define and analyze elements in the transition from gross to net capital formation.

The following conclusions can be derived:

1. The share of depreciation in gross capital formation is not affected by the value of f as long as f is assumed constant. In other words, if all other determinants are kept constant, the share of depreciation in gross capital formation is the same whether the constant gross capital formation proportion is 10, 15, or 50 per cent.

2. The share of depreciation in gross capital formation is directly proportional to a, the ratio of depreciable to total capital formation.

3. An increase in r will lower the share of depreciation in gross capital formation, since it will increase the denominator on the right-hand side of equation 3 more than the numerator. Thus, with $a = .75$ and $n = 40$, a change in r from say .03 to .05 will lower the share of depreciation in gross capital formation from .433 to .322. Conversely, a decline in r will raise the share of depreciation in gross capital formation.

4. An increase in n will lower the share of depreciation in gross capital formation and vice versa. The increase in the denominator of the fraction on the right-hand side of equation 3 is only partly offset by the increase in the numerator. Thus, with $a = .75$ and $r = .05$, a change in n from 20 to 40 will lower the share of depreciation in gross capital formation from .467 to .322.

5. Changes in the share of depreciation in gross capital formation produced by changes in either r or n are proportionally smaller than the latter. Changes in a alone are exactly proportional to changes in the shares.

These rather simple conclusions assume considerable interest in view of the trends suggested by the empirical evidence, at least for the United States. The rate of growth in gross national product, r, tends to decline; the average life of depreciable capital, n, tends to become shorter; and the proportion of depreciable to total gross capital formation, a, tends to be constant or perhaps increase slightly. If these findings are valid, all three variables in equation 3 raise the share of depreciation in gross capital formation.

SHARE OF DEPRECIATION IN GROSS NATIONAL PRODUCT

This share is given by the following equation:

$$\frac{D_0}{G_0} = \frac{af[1 - (1 + r)^{-n}]}{nr} \tag{4}$$

All the conclusions regarding the effects of changes in a, n, and r stated above apply here. The only modification is the addition of f

to the numerator of the fraction on the right-hand side of the equation. Thus the share of depreciation in gross national product is a direct function of f and changes in the latter would result in equal proportional changes in the former.

The comment concerning the effects of the determinants, as observed in the experience of the United States, on the share of depreciation in gross capital formation applies also to their effects on the share of depreciation in gross national product. The gross capital formation proportion, f, has on the whole been constant. Consequently, the decline in r and n and the rise, if slight, in a could raise the share of depreciation in gross national product.

RELATION OF NET TO GROSS CAPITAL FORMATION PROPORTIONS

Given differences or changes in n, r, or a, there will be different and changing relations between the gross and net capital formation proportions. To derive the latter from the former, we subtract depreciation from both the numerator (gross capital formation) and the denominator (gross national product). From equations 3 and 4 it is clear that depreciation forms one fraction of gross capital formation and another of gross national product; and the difference between the two varies with the changes in a, r, n, and f. However, it is important to state the relation between gross and net capital formation proportions explicitly.

From equation 3 it is apparent that *net* capital formation is

$$(5)\quad fG_0\left\{1-\frac{a[1-(1+r)^{-n}]}{nr}\right\}=fG_0\left\{\frac{nr-a[1-(1+r)^{-n}]}{nr}\right\}$$

Since net national product, P_0, equals G_0 minus D_0,

$$(6)\quad P_0=G_0-\frac{afG_0}{nr}[1-(1+r)^{-n}]=G_0\left\{\frac{nr-af[1-(1+r)^{-n}]}{nr}\right\}$$

Hence b, the proportion of net capital formation to net national product, can be defined as

$$(7)\qquad b=f\left\{\frac{nr-a[1-(1+r)^{-n}]}{nr-af[1-(1+r)^{-n}]}\right\}$$

Equation 7 indicates clearly the relation between f and b. So long as r is positive and f is less than 1, the coefficient of f in equation 7 will be less than 1; and b will always be smaller than f.

APPENDIX C

Levels and Trends in Income Shares of Upper Income Groups

THE PROBLEM

Given top income groups, with their high savings-income ratio, would the assumption of persistent identity of the members and their descendants at the upper levels result in an upward trend in the shares of upper groups in country-wide income? Offhand, the answer might be in the affirmative, for two somewhat different reasons.

The first is the effect of concentration of savings. Since upper income groups save higher proportions of their income than lower groups, savings are more unequally distributed than income. This might mean that the upper groups accumulate income-yielding assets more rapidly than the lower groups. If so, there would be a greater concentration of such assets in the hands of a small group at the top, wider inequality in the distribution of property income, and, other conditions being equal, a rise in the shares of the given upper groups in *total* income. However, some reflection forces a modification of the argument. The distribution of income-yielding assets is already unequal at the initial date of the period for which an upward trend in upper income shares might be inferred. Since the upper income groups hold a larger than average proportion of income-yielding assets, they receive a larger than average share of property incomes. Therefore, the concentration of savings would result in an increasing concentration of income-yielding assets *only* if the inequality in the distribution of savings were wider than that in the distribution of *property* income, and, hence, wider than the inequality in the distribution of income-yielding assets.

But with this modification, the argument is valid and indeed suggests a mechanism operating to raise the income shares of upper income groups. To begin with an empirical example: during 1919-1938 the top 5 per cent of the total population in the United States accounted for 54 per cent of property income (see Simon Kuznets, *Shares of Upper Income Groups in Income and Savings*, National Bureau of Economic Research, 1953, Table 3, p. 18). If sample data permit any judgment, we can put the average share of the top 5 per cent in total savings (of individuals) during the same decades at about two-thirds (*ibid.*, Chap. 6, esp. pp. 182 ff.). If we assume these figures are continuous, the proportional additions to property holdings by the top 5 per cent group would be steadily greater than those by the income groups below the top to *their* holdings. The 5 per cent group holds only 54 per cent of assets—assumed the same as their share in property income—but accounts for two-thirds of current savings, i.e. of net *additions* to assets. Hence, the share in total wealth of the top 5 per cent would tend to increase; and, other conditions being equal, so would their share in total property income. If the country-wide proportion of property to total income does not decline, and the distribution of service income is assumed unaffected, the share of the top 5 per cent in *total* income would increase. If this share rises, the proportion of total savings accounted for by the top 5 per cent might also rise; and the chain process would start operating again—to increase the concentration of income-yielding assets, to raise the shares of the top groups in property and in total income, and so on. The process is not without limits: at some point a rise in the share of upper groups in total income may not result in further concentration of savings. But so long as inequality in the distribution of savings is *wider* than that in the distribution of property income and of income-yielding assets, there would be, unless other factors intervened, a trend toward a higher share of upper groups in property and hence in total income.

The second reason for assuming a rising trend in the income share of the top group is that its superior position enables its members, or their descendants, to occupy a continuously rising position in the ladder of *service* incomes. To the extent that high service incomes follow from long and expensive training or from a strategic ownership position—in short, from either *acquired* skill or influence—a given top income group is presumably in a position to provide, for its members and their descendants, the bases for further rises.

We find, in fact, little evidence of a secular rise in the share of upper income groups, at least in the decades covering economic growth beyond the first turbulent phases of industrialization. This appendix is devoted to the formulation of factors that offset such a trend and explain why the forces indicated above have not operated as consistently and as effectively as one would expect offhand. The offsetting factors are discussed under three heads: the demographic growth differentials that produce a situation in which the top ordinal group at the initial point in the period cannot ordinarily people, through its descendants, an identical top ordinal group a few decades later (the mixture ratio); the factors that affect the per capita income of a top group and its descendants, on the assumption of continuity; the effect of mobility, i.e. of the abandonment of the assumption of continuity that is accepted in the discussion under the first two heads.

THE MIXTURE RATIO

Assume a group in the population in year 0, at the top of the size distribution of income. If we let M stand for population and indicate the year by the subscript on the left and the percentage group from the top by the subscript on the right, total population in year 0 is ${}_0M_{100}$ and the top 5 per cent group (which we deal with here for illustrative purposes) is ${}_0M_5$.

If population grew from year 0 to year n at an annual rate, p,

$$(1) \qquad {}_nM_{100} = {}_0M_{100}(1+p)^n$$

or

$$(1a) \qquad {}_nM_5 = {}_0M_5(1+p)^n$$

An assumption crucial to the analysis in sections 2 and 3 is now introduced: that the individuals in the upper income group in year 0 and their descendants remain at their high relative position, i.e. within the top 5 per cent. On this assumption will the top 5 per cent group of year n be completely peopled by members or descendants of the top 5 per cent group of year 0?

If we designate the rate of increase of the number in the top income group of year 0 by ap, their descendants, D, can be described by the following equation:

$$(2) \qquad {}_nD_{{}_05} = {}_0M_5(1+ap)^n$$

The *mixture ratio*, i.e. the ratio to the total number in the top group of year n of the number in that group who are *not* descendants of the top group of year 0, can be defined as

$$(3) \qquad \frac{{}_nM_5 - {}_nD_{{}_05}}{{}_nM_5} = 1 - \frac{(1+ap)^n}{(1+p)^n}$$

In industrially advanced and rapidly growing countries, like the United States, a may be assumed to be much less than 1—the rate of increase of the top income group is much lower than the rate of growth of total population. Two reasons can be adduced for this. First, the rate of *natural* increase is lower for the upper income group because its birth rate is appreciably lower. Second, total population may increase because of the excess of in- over out-migration. Immigrants, however, are preponderantly in the low income groups. The first reason operates in all countries whose economic development has reached the stage of reduced death rates, differential impact of family limitation, and declining birth rates. The second operates only in countries with net immigration; the effect for countries with net emigration is the opposite.

Obtaining quantitative values for the first factor requires more knowledge than we now have concerning differences in rate of natural increase between upper and lower income groups. That these differences are pervasive and substantial can be seen from recent sample studies of income and budgets for the United States, in which a negative correlation exists between size of family and per capita income of the unit.[1] As to the immigration factor, a rough calculation shows that in the United States, of the total increase of 93.1 million in population from 38.6 million in 1870 to 131.7 million in 1940, only 68.9 million or about 70 per cent can be attributed to the natural increase of the native born of 1870.[2] The value of .5 for *a* used in the illustrative calculations of the mixture ratio is fairly realistic for a country like the United States for the period since 1870; indeed, it may be somewhat too high.

These calculations in Exhibit I show, as equation 3 indicates, that the mixture ratio is a positive function of *p* and *n* and an inverse function of *a*. For a country like the United States where *p*, on a per decade basis, varies from 10 to 30 per cent, with the average since 1870 close to 20, over a period of say 5 decades the mixture ratio can be as high as .35.

Two inferences are suggested:

1. Under the assumption of long-term continuity of the relative position of initial upper income groups and their descendants, the failure of such groups to reproduce themselves at as high a rate as total population means that the income share of an upper group will tend to decline—unless per capita incomes of the initial top groups and their descendants grow at higher rates than the per capita income of total population; or unless the new groups drawn upon attain, again under assumption of a *continuity* of standing, by a greater growth of their per capita income, a relative income excess much higher than that of their initial ancestors.

[1] Simon Kuznets, *Shares of Upper Income Groups in Income and Savings*, National Bureau of Economic Research, 1953, pp. 157-159.

[2] *Income and Wealth, Series II*, Simon Kuznets, editor, Cambridge, Eng., Bowes & Bowes for International Association for Research in Income and Wealth, 1952, Tables 44 and 45, pp. 197 and 200.

EXHIBIT I

Illustrative Calculation of Mixture Ratios
with Varying Values of p and n
Assumption: $a = .5$

	$p = .10$	$p = .20$	$p = .30$
		$n = 2$ (decades)	
1. $(1+p)^n$	1.21	1.44	1.69
2. $(1+ap)^n$	1.1025	1.21	1.3225
3. Line 2 ÷ line 1	.911	.840	.783
4. Mixture ratio (1 — line 3)	.09	.16	.22
		$n = 5$	
5. $(1+p)^n$	1.610	2.488	3.713
6. $(1+ap)^n$	1.276	1.610	2.011
7. Line 6 ÷ line 5	.793	.647	.542
8. Mixture ratio (1 — line 7)	.21	.35	.46
		$n = 10$	
9. $(1+p)^n$	2.594	6.192	13.785
10. $(1+ap)^n$	1.629	2.594	4.046
11. Line 10 ÷ line 9	.628	.419	.294
12. Mixture ratio (1 — line 11)	.37	.58	.71

2. Under the same assumption this pressure toward a decrease in the share of upper income groups will slacken as p, the rate of increase of total population, slackens and as a, which measures the relative difference between the initial top groups and total population in the rate of increase, approaches 1.

RELATIVE TRENDS IN PER CAPITA INCOME

Designate:

${}_0I$ = total income, *per capita*, of total population in year 0
${}_0I_u$ = total income, *per capita*, of upper group in year 0
${}_0W$ = service income, *per capita*, of total population in year 0
${}_0W_u$ = service income, *per capita*, of upper group in year 0
${}_0R$ = property income, *per capita*, of total population in year 0
${}_0R_u$ = property income, *per capita*, of upper group in year 0
$g, g_u, g_w, g_{wu}, g_r, g_{ru}$ = rates of growth of these magnitudes, distinguished by the subscripts; the rates apply to both initial populations and their descendants.

By definition:

$${}_0I = {}_0W + {}_0R\,;\quad {}_0I_u = {}_0W_u + {}_0R_u$$

$${}_nI = {}_0W(1+g_w)^n + {}_0R(1+g_r)^n$$

$${}_nI_u = {}_0W_u(1+g_{wu})^n + {}_0R_u(1+g_{ru})^n$$

We can express the proportional increase as a relative:

$$(4) \qquad (1+g)^n = \frac{{}_0W}{{}_0I}(1+g_w)^n + \frac{{}_0R}{{}_0I}(1+g_r)^n$$

$$(5) \qquad (1+g_u)^n = \frac{{}_0W_u}{{}_0I_u}(1+g_{wu})^n + \frac{{}_0R_u}{{}_0I_u}(1+g_{ru})^n$$

We can analyze g_r, the rate of growth of per capita property income, somewhat further:

$${}_0R = \frac{{}_0R'}{{}_0M}$$ where ${}_0R'$ is total property income, year 0
${}_0M$ is total population, year 0.

$${}_0R(1+g_r) = \frac{{}_0R'(1+g'_r)}{{}_0M(1+p)}$$ where g'_r is rate of increase in ${}_0R'$
p is rate of increase in total population.

$$= {}_0R\frac{(1+g'_r)}{(1+p)}$$

$$(6) \quad {}_0R'(1+g'_r) = {}_0R' + ({}_0I'sy)$$ where ${}_0I'$ is total income in year 0
s is savings-income proportion
y is rate of yield on savings.

Hence,

$$(7) \qquad g'_r = \frac{{}_0I'}{{}_0R'}sy = \frac{{}_0I}{{}_0R}sy$$

$$(8) \qquad (1+g_r) = \frac{1+\frac{{}_0I}{{}_0R}sy}{1+p}$$

By analogy,

$$(9) \qquad (1+g_{ru}) = \frac{1+\frac{{}_0I}{{}_0R_u}s_u y_u}{1+ap}$$

If we assume that s, y, s_u, y_u, p, and ap are constant over the period n,

$$(10) \qquad (1+g)^n = \frac{_0W}{_0I}(1+g_w)^n + \frac{_0R}{_0I}\left[\frac{1+\frac{_0I}{_0R}sy}{1+p}\right]^n$$

$$(11) \qquad (1+g_u)^n = \frac{_0W_u}{_0I_u}(1+g_{wu})^n + \frac{_0R_u}{_0I_u}\left[\frac{1+\frac{_0I_u}{_0R_u}s_u y_u}{1+ap}\right]^n$$

Before considering the trends in per capita income for initial upper groups compared with those for total population, we explore the interrelations between s and y, and g_r and g_w, for total population under different assumptions (see Exhibit II). If the rates of

EXHIBIT II

Illustrative Relations

I. Between s and y — II. Between g_r and g_w

	VALUE OF g			
	.01	*.02*	*.03*	*.04*
I. Assumptions: $p = .02$; $g = g_w = g_r$				
A. $\frac{_0R}{_0I} = .25$				
1. sy	.00755	.01010	.01265	.01520
2. s, if $y = .03$	.252	.337	.422	.507
3. s, if $y = .06$	.126	.168	.211	.253
B. $\frac{_0R}{_0I} = .20$				
4. sy	.00604	.00808	.01012	.01216
5. s, if $y = .03$	.201	.269	.337	.405
6. s, if $y = .06$	.101	.135	.169	.203
C. $\frac{_0R}{_0I} = .10$				
7. sy	.00302	.00404	.00506	.00608
8. s, if $y = .03$	.101	.135	.169	.203
9. s, if $y = .06$	.050	.067	.084	.101
II. Assumptions: $p = .02$; $s = .10$; $y = .05$				
A. $\frac{_0R}{_0I} = .25$				
10. g_r	0	0	0	0
11. g_w	.0133	.027	.040	.053
B. $\frac{_0R}{_0I} = .20$				
12. g_r	.0049	.0049	.0049	.0049
13. g_w	.011	.0238	.0363	.0488
C. $\frac{_0R}{_0I} = .10$				
14. g_r	.0294	.0294	.0294	.0294
15. g_w	.0078	.0190	.0301	.0412

growth in total, service, and property per capita income are assumed equal for a given rate of growth of population: (1) the higher the assumed rate of growth of income, the greater the implicit savings-income proportion; (2) for given rates of growth of income, the lower the rate of yield on savings, the higher the implicit savings-income proportion; (3) the greater the share of property income in total income, the higher the product of the required savings-income proportion and the rate of yield—since more is necessary to maintain such a ratio of property to total income; and (4) if we start with assumed s and y and let g_r and g_w differ, g_r will be inversely and g_w will be positively related to the initial proportion of property to total income for given values of g.

In terms of the experience of the United States, an annual p of somewhat less than .02, a g of about .03, and a ratio of property to total income of about .20 may be considered realistic; and a y of .06 may be assumed. These values in the illustrative calculations suggest a savings rate of .135. The actual value lies close to it.

We may turn now to the rates of growth of per capita income for the initial upper group and total population, as set forth in equations 10 and 11. The following relations are relevant:

${}_0W/{}_0I$ is definitely greater than ${}_0W_u/{}_0I_u$
${}_0R/{}_0I$ is definitely smaller than ${}_0R_u/{}_0I_u$
s_u is definitely greater than s

The first question is about the rates of growth of per capita service income of total population, g_w, and of the initial top group and its descendants, g_{wu}. It should be stressed that this is a ratio of total service income received by a group to *all* its numbers, including units that do not engage in service activities and their dependents. In general, g_{wu} may be assumed to be significantly smaller than g_w —for two reasons. First, the rise in per capita service incomes (wages and salaries, entrepreneurial income, etc.) is due to both inter- and intra-industry shifts—to the movement of the labor force toward the higher per capita income industries and to the rise in per capita service income within each industry. The inter-industry shift is bound to have a much larger effect on g_w than on g_{wu}: the members of the top group who derive service incomes are already likely to be in the higher paid industries. Since they are also likely to be in the higher paid positions, even the intra-industry rise may not have as great an effect on g_{wu} as on g_w.

Second, the proportion of gainfully engaged to all members of the top group is likely to decline—or at any rate fail to rise—even if the proportion for total population rises. Low reproduction rates and continuously high income position may cause a shift among the descendants of the initial top group toward women, because of their greater longevity as compared with men, which, combined with lack of pressure for gainful occupation, may result in an actual decline in the proportion of gainfully occupied. The combination of the factors just adduced may mean that the rate of increase in per capita service income of the initial top group is about half of that for total population—in the United States, inter-industry shifts alone account for about four-tenths of the over-all rise in net product per worker.[3]

The next question is about the rate of growth of per capita property income of total population, g_r, and that of the initial top group and its descendants, g_{ru} (see equations 8 and 9 in this connection). Two factors tend to make g_{ru} significantly larger than g_r : s_u, with which the rate of growth is positively related, is larger than s, and ap, with which the rate of growth is negatively related, is smaller than p. A third and important factor tends to make g_{ru} smaller than g_r : the ratio of property to total income, with which the rate of growth is negatively related, is larger for the upper group than for total population. Finally, there is the yield on accumulated savings, but no definite statement can be made whether y_u tends to be larger or smaller than y.

With this variety of factors, and one or two of them unknown, it seemed best to experiment with an illustrative calculation (see Exhibit III). The following ratios and coefficients were assumed, largely on the basis of the record for the United States from 1870 to 1940: an annual rate of growth of population of 2 per cent per year (somewhat high) and of per capita income of 1.5 per cent per year (somewhat low); an over-all savings-income proportion of 12 per cent and a yield of 6 per cent, both fairly realistic figures; a constant ratio of service to total income of 80 per cent (hence the equality of g, g_w, and g_r), which is also confirmed by whatever crude estimates of distribution of income by type we have. In addition, the following more conjectural ratios were used: $a = .5$, meaning that the rate of increase in number of the initial top group was half of the rate of increase of total

[3] *Ibid.*, p. 125.

EXHIBIT III

Illustrative Calculations in the Derivation of g_u
(Based on Equation 11)

Assumptions: $\frac{{}_0W}{{}_0I} = .80,\ p = .02,\ g = .05,\ s = .12,\ y = .06,\ g = g_w = g_r,$

$\frac{{}_0W_u}{{}_0I_u} = .60,\ ap = .01,\ g_{wu} = .5g_w$

	Assumed values of $s_u y_u$: $s_u = .30$, $y_u = .06$, .018	$s_u = .20$, $y_u = .06$, .012	$s_u = .20$, $y_u = .04$, .008	Derived $s_u y_u$
I. Derived g_u				
1. $(1 + g_{wu}) \frac{{}_0W_u}{{}_0I_u}$	.6045	.6045	.6045	.6045
2. $\frac{{}_0I_u}{{}_0R_u} s_u y_u$	.0450	.0300	.0200	
3. $(1 + \text{line } 2) \div (1 + ap)$	1.0347	1.0198	1.0099	
4. Line 3 $\times \frac{{}_0R_u}{{}_0I_u}$	.41388	.40792	.40396	
5. Line 1 + line 4	1.01838	1.01242	1.00846	
6. g_u (line 5 — 1)	.01838	.01242	.00846	
II. $s_u y_u$ needed to equalize g and g_u				
7. $(1 + g_u)$				1.015
8. Line 7 — line 1				.4105
9. Line 8 $\div \frac{{}_0R_u}{{}_0I_u}$				1.02625
10. Line 9 $\times (1 + ap)$				1.03651
11. Line 10 — 1				.03651
12. $s_u y_u$ (line 11 $\div \frac{{}_0I_u}{{}_0R_u}$)				.014604
III. g_{wu} needed to equalize g and g_u				
13. $(1 + g_u)$	1.015	1.015	1.015	
14. $(1 + g_{wu}) \frac{{}_0W_u}{{}_0I_u}$ (line 13 — line 4)	.60112	.60708	.61104	
15. $(1 + g_{wu})$	1.0019	1.0118	1.0184	
16. g_{wu}	.0019	.0118	.0184	

population, and $g_{wu} = .5g_w$, meaning that the rate of increase of per capita service income of the initial top group was half of the rate of increase of per capita service income for total population. Finally, the ratio of property to total income for the initial top group was set at 40 per cent—implying a larger group than the top 5 per cent. Within the framework set by these relatively realistic assumptions, s_u and y_u were permitted to vary.

The major conclusion suggested by these calculations is that a rate of growth of per capita income of the initial top group and its descendants *equal to or not much larger than* the rate of growth of per capita income of total population is quite likely. As line 12 in Exhibit III indicates, it would be attained with $s_u y_u$ equal to about .015. On the basis of a yield of 6 per cent this involves a savings proportion of 25 per cent; with a lower yield it means a higher savings proportion.

Two comments are pertinent here. First, the savings rate used in the first column is almost as high as that found for the top 5 per cent group in sample studies during the last two decades. But with 40 per cent of property income the group assumed here must be larger than the top 5 per cent. Furthermore, this savings rate was found for a group that includes significant proportions of recent and transitory migrants into the top group—and they are likely to save larger proportions of their income than the individuals continuously at high income levels. For a segment of the population that is assumed to be at top levels for decades, the savings-income ratio should be significantly lower than for a segment whose recent or transitory income rises result in a lagging adjustment of expenditures or in a deliberate utilization of windfall income as a reservoir against the more normal, leaner years. Hence, an s_u well below .3 is more realistic.

Second, y_u—the yield rate for the savings of the continuous initial top group and its descendants—may well be lower than, rather than equal to or higher than, the yield rate for the country's total savings. This may be due partly to the drift of such savings into more conservative investments; but it is largely due to the fact that our continuity assumption *excludes* newcomers who rise to the top because of association with new and successful industries. It is these industries that provide the source of high property income returns and have a bolstering effect on the yield rate for the total pool of country-wide savings.

THE EFFECTS OF SHIFTING

The analysis above suggests three conclusions. First, because of its lower reproduction rate, the upper income group of year 0 and its descendants will constitute only part of the upper income group of year *n*; and such admixture means, under the assumption of continuity of relative position, that the relative standing of the upper group in year *n* may be below the level ascribable to the descendants of the upper group in year 0. Second, because the per capita service income of the descendants of the upper group of year 0 is most likely to grow at appreciably lower rates than the per capita service income of total population, there is a substantial offset to any greater growth (under the assumption of continuity) of per capita property income of the descendants of the upper group of year 0. Therefore, even under the assumption of continuity, total per capita income of these descendants may not grow at a rate higher than that for total population. Third, the rate of growth of property income of the initial top group will cease exceeding the rate of growth of *total* property income as soon as the share in savings is equal to or less than the share in wealth. The combination of these three conclusions may mean a *decline*, not a rise, in the share of the given top ordinal group.

That under conditions of a progressive economy this is a likely rather than a surprising result follows from the three empirical assumptions used in the analysis: (1) service income, even for the upper income groups, was assumed to be a substantial proportion of total income; (2) the rate of reproduction of the upper income groups was assumed to be lower than that of total population; (3) the per capita service income of the upper income groups was assumed to grow at a slower rate than the per capita service income of the economy. Two of the three assumptions rest upon integral characteristics of a *growing* economy. Such growth is accompanied by substantial inter-industry shifts, which are involved in assumption 3; by a population growth pattern in which family limitation spreads from the top to the lower social groups, and in which death rates are under sufficient control so that birth rate differentials are the most important factor—both of which are involved in assumption 2. Thus the inference that, given continuity in relative position (no shifting), the share of upper income groups is likely to decline has been derived by assumptions which are characteristics of a growing and progressive economy—in which, because of that very fact, there *must* be extensive shifting in relative position, into and out of the upper income groups. For a slowly growing underdeveloped economy the assumption of continuity might produce the opposite result: with the mixture ratio quite small and the effects of inter-industry shifts on per capita service income possibly negligible, the inference might well be that the income shares of upper income groups, under the assumption of continuity, tend to rise.

Viewed against the background of a growing economy, the preceding analysis is artificial in that it combines conditions of continuity with empirical assumptions that deny them: it is hardly a surprise that allowing growth elsewhere but not in the upper income groups, *except* for the straight accumulation of savings, one concludes that the total income share of the initial upper income group and its descendants is not likely to rise but may decline. Yet such analysis has some value, because it distinguishes between the elements of continuity and shift. Of particular interest is the suggestion that it is the shift process that may account for *sustaining* the income share of the upper income groups and for keeping the share of service incomes in the total income of the upper groups as high as it is.

We have no data on this shift process, but some conjectural analysis may be useful.

1. Two obvious sources of shifting are of limited interest here. Since our distinction of upper groups at any given time is based on income size during a year or similarly short time span, purely transient elements affect the income position. Units move up into the top income groups and drop down again when these elements have passed. However, they are replaced by others, some of which may likewise be raised to high levels by transient elements. Although nothing can be said about its effect on any trends in the income shares of upper groups, such shifting is important. First, it tends to raise the income shares of the upper groups at any given time—the shares of the same ordinal top group (say of the top 5 per cent) based on an average extending over a longer period would be lower. Second, it tends to raise the savings-income proportions—not only because it increases the shares of the top group, but also because of the possible lag of expenditures under conditions of transitory rises of income. Third, like all shifts into and out of the top group, it interrupts the accumulation, in the same hands, of high income and large savings.

Likewise, cyclical elements in the shift—associated with differing sensitivity to business cycles of various industries, occupations, types of income, etc.—do not call for extended discussion. Their effects are similar to those of the more transient shifts just noted. Although they serve to maintain the high income shares and high savings proportions at any given point of time, and reduce continuity and hence the power of accumulation of assets in a few hands, they are of less interest here than the secular factors that *can* produce some long-term shifts in relative position of groups in the size distribution of income.

2. One such secular shift has been stressed in the preceding analysis. The lower reproduction rates of the upper income groups mean that for a given top group there must be inflow from below the top, i.e. from newcomers or descendants of the groups below the top in year 0. But this shift would not offset any possible decline in the shares of the top groups unless the rate of growth in per capita income of the groups drafted from below the top were very much higher than the rise in per capita income for total population—and there is no ground for this assumption. However, this shift does help to offset declines in the proportion of service to total incomes among the upper income groups.

The secular shift among industries and occupations is of greater interest. Economic growth is accompanied by continuous changes in industrial structure so that at successive points of time different industries are in the vanguard of growth. It is attachment to such industries that places people at the top of the economic ladder—as is indicated by the succession of captains of industry who are the conspicuous members of the top income group. Two aspects of such continuous inter-industry shifts are important for their effects on the top income group. First, the economic leaders of one industrial epoch cannot be identified with those of another: the descendants of the fur trade magnates are not the leading entrepreneurs in railroads and the descendants of the latter are not the leading entrepreneurs in the automobile industry. This continuous change in the family identity of successful entrepreneurs—large *and* medium—prevents the concentration of high income position associated with participation in the several leading industries over generations. Second, the entry of these units into the upper income groups when it occurs and in its early periods is via high service incomes; only at the later stages does property income become important.

One can only conjecture whether the entry of successful entrepreneurs (or other economic agents) connected with the continuously emerging successful and rapidly growing industries serves to overcome the otherwise possibly downward trend in the share of upper income groups, or even to convert it into a rising trend. That the effect is bolstering is obvious: the relative income excess (over the country-wide average) of these new entrants must be greater than that of those whom they displace. But how great the effect is, it is impossible to tell.

Two corollaries follow from this analysis. First, if the sustaining effect upon upper income shares is imparted only by new entries and new entries are associated with the emergence of new industries, there is a direct *positive* connection between the process of growth and the share of upper income groups—offsetting the possibly negative connection inferred above under the assumption of continuity. Second, the slowing down of such change, of the emergence of new industries, would, of course, tend to weaken the sustaining effect on upper income shares. However, one should define the effect properly. It may well be that, even though the rate of growth and of additions of new industries slackens, the relative income advantages grow apace. For example, if the automobile industry yielded a new group at the top of the income pyramid with a per capita income x times that of the average, whereas an earlier economic leader-industry, say the railroads, yielded a top group with a per capita income only $.8x$ times that of the average (with both top groups the same proportion of total population), the automobile industry—even if it did not boost total economic growth as much as the railroads—did have a larger sustaining effect on the shares of upper income groups.

The comments on the effect of new industries apply equally to the effect of new occupations (which often develop in connection with new industries). The one modification is that there may be greater continuity in inheritance of occupation than in inheritance of the association with the leader-industry. One can envisage a succession of surgeons, engineers, or lawyers in the family line more easily than a succession of successful entrepreneurs. But even the former is not too likely if we: (1) think of the very top ranks within one and the same occupation; and (2) consider the shifts among leader occupations and professions, so that the succession ought to be traced from the successful surgeon to the successful advertising-slogan-maker or from the popular preacher to the eminent movie comedian. Top income position in the same family line by virtue of occupation is perhaps scarcely more probable than by virtue of industry association.

CONCLUDING COMMENTS

1. The preceding analysis yields no definite conclusions concerning the factors that limit either the level of or the possible rise in

the income share of upper income groups. But it suggests that in a growing economy: (a) assumption of continuity of an initial top group and its descendants may well result in a *decline* rather than a rise of income shares of top groups; and (b) the shifting process, while interrupting the accumulation of savings and assets in the same levels, tends to *bolster* the income (and even more, the savings) share of upper income groups. In other words, the analysis casts doubt upon the possibility of rising *trends*—and hence *high* levels—of income shares of upper groups, *due to* cumulative effects of high savings rates and presumptively growing concentration of assets.

2. In the light of this summary, omissions in the analysis may well be noted. First, limited consideration was given to the inequality structure within service income distribution proper. Yet the factors that determine the range of income flowing out of active connection as an employee or entrepreneur, or any trend in that range, must also affect the income shares of upper income groups and their trends.

Second, the discussion was exclusively in terms of what happens within and to the upper income groups themselves. But their income *shares* can be moved by what happens at the low income levels. No consideration was given to any possible secular trends originating in movements endogenous to the lower income group; and it is hard to see any *long-term* factors there. But some complexes of factors can affect what might be called long swings in the upper income proportions. For example, the upper groups are largely urban. If there are protracted price level movements up or down (like the decline from the 1870's to the late 1890's), and if these movements have a greater impact on agriculture than on urban pursuits (as is usually the case), the very buoyant or depressed position of agriculture over two or three decades may be reflected in a lower or higher share of upper income groups (even in terms of constant prices—so long as there is no intra-country differential price correction). It may well be that from the 1870's to the 1890's the shares of the upper income groups in the United States increased, and possibly largely for that reason. On the other hand, during protracted war and postwar periods, reduction in unemployment and the effect of inflation on the service income differentials may raise substantially, and for long periods, the share of the lower income groups and automatically reduce that of upper income groups—the impulse coming, so to speak, from the bottom rather than from the top. Finally, there is the whole matter of government policy which can affect the shares of upper groups—not only by a progressive income tax, but also by diverting an increasing proportion of new investment into new industries under public auspices (*vide* atomic energy), leaving less for new industries under private auspices and hence reducing the bolstering effect of new industries on upper income shares.

Our interest in the shares of upper income groups in income stemmed from concern with levels and trends in the contribution of upper income groups to country-wide savings. Abstractly, it is quite possible for a low level and constancy or down-trend in the income share of upper groups to be accompanied by a high level and rise in their savings-income ratio—so that their savings, expressed as a percentage of total income, would remain constant or rise. No consideration of the levels and trends in the savings-income ratio of the upper income groups was intended here.

APPENDIX D

Analysis of Savings of Lower Income Groups

SIMPLEST MODEL: SAVINGS FOR RETIREMENT ALONE; CONSTANT POPULATION, INCOME, AND EXPENDITURES

We assume that savings are accumulated only to cover living expenses during retirement. Designate:

n = number of years in working life
K = number of years in assumed retirement
W = number of persons (units) working
O = number of persons (units) retired.

If population, age composition, age of entry into working life, and age of retirement are all constant (we assume only *one* sex), then

(1) $$\frac{W}{O} = \frac{n}{K}$$

Designate:

I = income per worker unit (including dependents)
E = expenditures per worker and per retired unit
S = savings per worker unit.

Then if I and E are constant, by assumption,

(2) $$WI = (W + O)E$$

(3) $$E = \frac{WI}{W + O} = \frac{W}{W + O} I$$

By definition,

(4) $$S = I - E$$

(5) $$\frac{S}{I} = \frac{I - E}{I} = \frac{I}{I} - \left(\frac{WI}{W + O} \div I \right) = 1 - \frac{W}{W + O} = \frac{O}{W + O}$$

Gross savings for all low income groups are, by assumption, WS. Gross dissavings for all low income groups are, by assumption,

$$O \times E = O(I - S) = OI - OS = S(W + O) - OS$$
$$= SW + OS - OS = WS$$

Net savings for all low income groups are

$$WS - WS = O$$

Note that:

1. To assume lower expenditures per retired unit than per working unit, i.e.

$$E_O < E_W \text{ or } E_O = aE_W \text{ where } a < 1$$

would mean that

(6) $$WI = WE_W + OaE_W$$

(7) $$E_W = \frac{WI}{W + Oa}$$

(8) $$\frac{S}{I} = \frac{I - E_W}{I} = 1 - \left(\frac{WI}{W + Oa} \div I \right) = \frac{Oa}{W + Oa}$$

This would mean a lower gross savings-income ratio for worker units, a smaller volume of gross savings and dissavings, and net savings still equal to zero.

2. To assume an interest return on savings in the process of their accumulation would make no difference in the analysis, since the interest would be included in I and in S. It would mean that the retired units O would be getting some income on their gradually dwindling savings balances. But this is tantamount to having a *lower* rate of expenditure per unit, and alternative interest rates could be taken into account by means of an a term similar to that given under point 1.

POPULATION GROWTH

Assume that population grows and affects W immediately and that we pass from W_0 to W_n in n years. Throughout this period, until the end of the nth year, O remains unchanged, i.e. $O_n = O_0$. But W_n is obviously larger than W_0.

Assume that W grows at the rate r. Hence,

$$W_1 = W_0 - \frac{W_0}{n} + \frac{W_0}{n}(1+r)$$

$$W_2 = W_1 - \frac{W_0}{n} + \frac{W_0}{n}(1+r)^2 = W_0 - \frac{2W_0}{n} + \frac{W_0}{n}[(1+r) + (1+r)^2]$$

$$\cdot$$

$$\cdot$$

$$\cdot$$

$$W_n = W_0 - \frac{nW_0}{n} + \frac{W_0}{n}[(1+r) + (1+r)^2 + \ldots (1+r)^n]$$

$$(9) \qquad = \frac{W_0}{n}\frac{(1+r)}{r}[(1+r)^n - 1]$$

Since, with growth in population, W will always be larger than O, by the cumulated effect of the n years between entry into O and entry into W, equation 9 combined with $O_n = O_0$ will yield the excess of W over O under conditions of constant r in W (and in O).

In year n, total gross savings will be

$$(10) \qquad W_nS = W_0S\frac{1+r}{rn}[(1+r)^n - 1]$$

Total gross dissavings will be the same as under the assumption of constant population, W_0S.

Hence, *net* total savings for all low income groups will be

$$(11) \qquad N_s = W_0S\left(\left\{\frac{1+r}{rn}[(1+r)^n - 1]\right\} - 1\right)$$

The net savings-income ratio will be

$$\frac{N_s}{W_n I} = \frac{W_0 S\left(\left\{\frac{1+r}{rn}[(1+r)^n - 1]\right\} - 1\right)}{W_0 \frac{1+r}{rn}[(1+r)^n - 1] I}$$

$$(12) \qquad = \frac{S}{I} \cdot \frac{\left(\left\{\frac{1+r}{rn}[(1+r)^n - 1]\right\} - 1\right)}{\left\{\frac{1+r}{rn}[(1+r)^n - 1]\right\}}$$

If r is larger than O, i.e. if population grows, the coefficient of S/I in equation 12 is necessarily positive and a proper fraction. Thus the proportion of total net savings to total income is a fraction of the proportion of gross savings of the W group. In other words, the lower income groups as a whole generate positive net savings.

Illustrative calculations show how the coefficient of S/I in equation 12 varies with values of r and n (see Exhibit I). Obviously, the

EXHIBIT I

Variations in the Coefficient of S/I in Equation 12 with Alternative Values of r and n

	VALUES OF r, PER YEAR		
	.01	*.02*	*—.01*
		$n = 25$	
1. rn	.25	.50	—.25
2. $(1+r)$	1.01	1.02	.99
3. $(1+r)/rn$ (line 2 ÷ line 1)	4.04	2.04	—3.96
4. $(1+r)^n$	1.282	1.640	.778
5. $(1+r)^n - 1$	.282	.640	—.222
6. $[(1+r)/rn][(1+r)^n - 1]$ (line 3 × line 5)	1.13928	1.30560	.87912
7. Coefficient of S/I [(line 6 — 1) ÷ line 6]	.122	.234	—.138
		$n = 45$	
1. rn	.45	.90	
2. $(1+r)$	1.01	1.02	
3. $(1+r)/rn$ (line 2 ÷ line 1)	2.244	1.133	
4. $(1+r)^n$	1.565	2.438	
5. $(1+r)^n - 1$	.565	1.438	
6. $[(1+r)/rn][(1+r)^n - 1]$ (line 3 × line 5)	1.2679	1.6293	
7. Coefficient of S/I [(line 6 — 1) ÷ line 6]	.211	.386	

larger r and n are, the larger the coefficient is. As a matter of curiosity we also calculate the coefficient for a negative r, i.e. on the assumption of declining population. In that case, *net* savings are negative since the declining body of workers W, saving for their own future in accordance with the ratio set by n and K, accumulate gross savings that are *smaller* than the current dissavings of the retired who originated in a larger population.

During the last century to century and a half, growth processes tended to bring about a decline in the rate of growth of population—i.e. a decline in the positive value of r—and a rise in the ratio of K, years of retirement, to n, years of work. Since these two trends have opposite effects on the net savings proportion generated by the lower income groups, their combination may have made for stability in the proportion.

Let us assume that, in the early phases, population grows 2 per cent per year; n, beginning at 15 years of age, covers 45 years; and K, starting at 60, is 10 years. The gross savings-income ratio, S/I, equals

$$\frac{O}{W} + O = \frac{K}{n} + K = \frac{10}{55} = .182$$

The coefficient of S/I, under these assumptions, is .386, and the net savings proportion for the lower income groups as a whole is .182 $\times$ .386, or .070, i.e. about 7 per cent. Now let us assume that, in later phases of development, population growth slackens to 1 per cent per year; n, beginning at 20, is cut down to 25; and K, starting at 45, is extended to 25. Under these conditions S/I is .50; the coefficient of S/I is .122; and the net savings proportion is .061. In other words, with a retardation in the rate of population growth, and with a marked reduction in years of work and a marked increase in years of retirement, the required net savings proportion for the group as a whole *declines*. With somewhat different figures, it would have been possible to show stability, or a slight rise in the net savings proportions. The major point of the illustration is the slight change in the net savings proportion, with major changes in rate of population growth and distribution of adult life between work and retirement.

Incidentally, this combination of trends increases both gross savings and dissavings. Thus, in the early phase, gross savings were 18.2 per cent of total income and dissavings were 11.2 per cent (leaving 7 per cent as the net savings residual). The gross flow of savings (savings plus dissavings, regardless of sign) was, therefore, 29.4 per cent of income. In the later phase, gross savings were 50 per cent, dissavings were 43.9 per cent, and net savings were 6.1 per cent of income. The gross flow of savings was 93.9 per cent of income, or more than triple that in the first phases. If the two trends suggested have any empirical bearing on the development of modern economies, the functions of financial institutions must have increased substantially in order to accommodate themselves to the increase in gross savings flows.

VARIATIONS IN SAVINGS PLANS AND REALIZATIONS

To the extent that we deal with security calculations, one may argue that plans are made for the accumulation of savings sufficient for the longest reasonably expected lifetime. In fact, of course, people do not live that long; and the difference between the assumed and actual lifetimes will mean *net* savings for the total of all low income groups, because *realized* dissavings will be lower than those assumed and covered by positive savings. This case is different from that mentioned at the beginning of this appendix because in the latter a lower level of expenditures upon retirement, i.e. of dissavings, was allowed for in the savings plan and *net* savings were, therefore, zero. In the present case, net savings are positive. For example, if instead of K, the number of years planned for retirement, only $K/2$ years are in fact lived through, the average number of retired units O is cut in half and net savings are generated because WS is larger than $OE/2$.

Whether this reasoning has any empirical bearing is a moot question. It is far from evident that people do overestimate length of life in making savings plans or even that they give such plans serious consideration at all. One may plausibly argue that, on the contrary, people tend to underestimate years of retirement and possible dependence. At any rate, this is not a question that can be profitably discussed in conjectural terms.

Net savings would also be realized if some provision is made for estates, i.e. if savings plans cover not only living expenses upon retirement but also some residue for survivors. The equations would have to be changed to satisfy this assumption since the yield rate on accumulations would be more important than in the present model and the net savings proportion would be determined largely by the ratio of the estate planned (or the return on it) to assumed income levels.[1]

Of somewhat greater interest in the present connection is the possibility of a systematic difference between the expenditure levels

[1] See discussion in "Proportion of Capital Formation to National Product," *American Economic Review, Proceedings*, May 1952, pp. 508-526.

per unit of the working and of the retired population, a difference associated with a growth in per unit expenditures not unlike the growth in population. Because retired units are assumed to be older than working units, the former may have established their expenditure patterns (which tend to become fixed after a certain stage in life) before the working population; and in an economy in which income and expenditures per unit are growing, expenditures per retired unit are likely to be lower than those per working unit. Incidentally, savings plans are based upon such expenditure levels because they are found satisfactory, not because of any economy pressures.

Assume, for example, that expenditure patterns become pretty well fixed by the middle of working life, and that these fixed patterns are the basis of savings and retirement plans. Assume also, for simplicity in calculation, that this level is the basis for savings throughout working life. There is, therefore, a gap of $n/2$ years between the date at which the expenditure levels that are the basis for savings plans prevail and the date when retirement begins. Assume also that per unit expenditures grow t per cent per year, reflecting a similar growth in per unit income—so that savings plans set at progressively advancing dates are based on desired expenditure levels that also grow at the rate of t per cent per year. We thus have a setup similar to that for population growth, except that the cumulation period is $n/2$ rather than n years.

We can now give the equations that take account of both population growth and growth in income and expenditures per unit.

$$(13)\quad W_nS_n = W_0S_0\left\{\frac{1+r}{rn}[(1+r)^n-1]\right\}\left\{\frac{2(1+t)}{tn}[(1+t)^{n/2}-1]\right\}$$

$$(14)\quad NS_n = W_0S_0\left(\left\{\frac{1+r}{rn}[(1+r)^n-1]\right\}\left\{\frac{2(1+t)}{tn}[(1+t)^{n/2}-1]\right\}-1\right)$$

$$(15)\quad \frac{NS_n}{W_nI_n} = \frac{S_0}{I_0}\,\frac{\left\{\frac{1+r}{rn}[(1+r)^n-1]\right\}\left\{\frac{2(1+t)}{tn}[(1+t)^{n/2}-1]\right\}-1}{\left\{\frac{1+r}{rn}[(1+r)^n-1]\right\}\left\{\frac{2(1+t)}{tn}[(1+t)^{n/2}-1]\right\}}$$

The addition of this lag of the expenditure levels that are the basis of savings plans behind those current when the plans are realized increases the possibility of net savings, and similarly to the assumption of population growth—provided, of course, that income and expenditures per unit do grow. The coefficient of S/I in equation 15 is larger than that in equation 12.

Here also we can assume two trends posited in the discussion of population growth: a decrease in n and an increase in K and a decline in the rate of growth in per unit income or expenditures, t. The former trend, of course, raises the value of S/I; both trends diminish the coefficient since n and t are reduced. The two trends combined thus have opposite effects on the *net* savings proportion that may offset each other. Their effects on the gross savings flow are the same as were indicated under "Population Growth."

EXHIBIT II

Variations in the Coefficient of S/I in Equation 15 under Alternative Values of n, r, and t

	VALUE OF t .01	VALUE OF t .02
	$n = 25$; $r = .01$	
1. tn	.25	.50
2. $2(1+t)$	2.02	2.04
3. $2(1+t)/tn$ (line 2 ÷ line 1)	8.08	4.08
4. $(1+t)^{n/2}$	1.1324	1.281
5. $(1+t)^{n/2}-1$	.1324	.281
6. $[2(1+t)/tn][(1+t)^{n/2}-1]$ (line 3 × line 5)	1.0698	1.1465
7. $[(1+r)/rn][(1+r)^{n}-1]$	1.13928	1.13928
8. $\{[2(1+t)tn][(1+t)^{n/2}-1]\}\{[(1+r)/rn][(1+r)^{n}-1]\}$ (combined with population) (line 6 × line 7)	1.2188	1.3062
9. Coefficient of S/I [(line 8 − 1) ÷ line 8]	.180	.234
	$n = 45$; $r = .01$	
1. tn	.45	.90
2. $2(1+t)$	2.02	2.04
3. $2(1+t)/tn$ (line 2 ÷ line 1)	4.49	2.27
4. $(1+t)^{n/2}$	1.2509	1.5614
5. $(1+t)^{n/2}-1$	.2509	.5614
6. $[2(1+t)/tn][(1+t)^{n/2}-1]$ (line 3 × line 5)	1.1265	1.2744
7. $[(1+r)/rn][(1+r)^{n}-1]$	1.2679	1.2679
8. $\{[2(1+t)tn][(1+t)^{n/2}-1]\}\{[(1+r)/rn][(1+r)^{n}-1]\}$ (combined with population) (line 6 × line 7)	1.4283	1.6158
9. Coefficient of S/I [(line 8 − 1) ÷ line 8]	.300	.381

EFFECT OF UNIT ORGANIZATION

We have assumed so far that working and retired units are separate. Since the large, and often joint, family structure is prevalent in underdeveloped countries and the small family predominates in the developed countries, we may ask how different assumptions concerning jointness or separateness of working and retired units would affect the analysis.

We use the simplest model here, and assume that there are *no* separate retired units—that each is joined with a working unit. The total number of units is reduced from $(W + O)$ to W since O, by assumption, is joined with W. Then, if we designate the lone working units as Y, and the joint units as Z (i.e. working plus retired), we get $Y + Z = W$.

If, for example, W is three times O, i.e. n is 45 years and K is 15 years, it follows that Z equals one-third and Y equals two-thirds of W; or Z equals one-half of Y.

For each unit under Z there is dissaving. Expenditures are 75 per cent of income for the working part and 75 per cent for the retired. Total expenditures are 150 per cent of income, and dissavings are, therefore, 50 per cent of income. For each unit under Y, savings are still 25 per cent of income. Thus gross savings, YS, are $.67WS$, gross dissavings, $2ZS$, are $.67WS$, and net savings are zero.

The reduction in the number of units by the joining of retired with working units has no effect on net savings. It could have an effect only if our assumptions concerning expenditure levels at retirement and constancy of income and numbers had been modified. However, the gross flow of savings—the total of gross savings and dissavings—is affected. In the model with separate retired units, gross savings are WS and gross dissavings are WS; and their sum, signs disregarded, is therefore $2WS$. When retired units are joined with working units, reducing the total number of units, the sum of gross savings and dissavings becomes $1.33WS$. Reduction of a third in the number of units means a reduction of a third in the gross flow of savings. The implication for the differences between underdeveloped and developed economies in the role of financial institutions handling savings flows is obvious.

The important conclusion is that, in and of themselves, the number and composition of the units can have no effect on the *net* savings proportion. Such an effect would have to be exercised through some other channel—most likely the choice, made consciously or unconsciously, between investing in more children or the younger generation and the accumulation of savings in forms that can be employed to finance capital formation (as usually defined).

COMMENT

EVSEY D. DOMAR, The Johns Hopkins University

Anyone who discusses a Kuznets paper inevitably faces a dilemma: he is presented with a wealth of material, he wants to raise a number of questions, but, alas, he is given so little time. I shall therefore take the virtues of the paper for granted and comment on a few doubtful points, concentrating not on the statistical data—this would require a paper in itself—but on questions of interpretation and concept.

The author begins with the observation that capital formation, usually defined to include expenditures on construction and on producer durables, does not include outlays on education, training, research, public health, etc., which are not less important for growth than is investment in physical capital. This is perfectly true, but must all these expenditures be squeezed into a single category? If outlays on education and training, for instance, were merged with those on physical capital, it would be necessary to allow for the depreciation or replacement of human beings as well as of physical capital. Is it not better to record such expenditures separately and then work with, and think in terms of, multiple rather than simple regression? Surely no one imagines that capital formation, even broadly defined, can be the sole explanation and cause of growth.

Kuznets would like to divide all outlays into those that raise productivity and those that do not; he suspects that the former may constitute as much as 50 per cent in developed countries, and only a few per cent in underdeveloped ones (page 22). Perhaps it would be proper to add one more category—productivity-sustaining outlays, such as necessary food and shelter, a minimum of education, and so on. In underdeveloped countries most outlays are of this nature; while a developed one devotes a good part of its resources to luxuries which neither sustain nor raise its productive capacity. A study in terms of these three categories would facilitate our understanding of the relationship between allocation of resources and growth; in particular, it would show not only the small fraction of resources devoted to an expansion of productive capacity in an underdeveloped country, but also the difficulty of raising this fraction without affecting those outlays without which the present capacity cannot be sustained.

This division of total outlays into two or three categories is, however, a task for the future, and both author and readers must be reconciled to dealing with capital formation more or less as traditionally defined, though here I do not share Kuznets' reluctance to treat residential housing equally with other forms of physical capital. In any case, capital formation as one of the determinants of growth should be expressed in real terms; it is regrettable that the author has not found it possible to take this important step. So long as we deal with gross capital formation, price deflation is less urgent because prices of capital goods usually move more or less in the same direction as do the others. But the use of net capital formation, either as an absolute magnitude or as a fraction of total output, requires estimates of depreciation of capital, and unless these estimates have been corrected for price changes the result can be quite unreliable. Net capital formation is, after all, a relatively small residual. Is it possible that the failure to deflate can account for the unexpectedly small ratio of depreciation to gross investment in the United Kingdom (Table I-3, B) as compared with this country? The ratio of depreciation to gross investment is an inverse function of the rate of growth of investment and longevity of capital; hence, with a higher American rate of growth one would expect this ratio to be lower than in Britain, unless the longevity of British capital were very much greater than ours. The deflation of output and investment series for a number of countries over a long span of time, however, is easy to suggest but difficult to construct. Let us keep the nature of the estimates in mind and be grateful to the author for what he has already done, rather than carp on that which he has not yet done.

Our next problem deals with the variables in terms of which international and intertemporal comparisons should be made. Should we take, for instance, the gross propensity to save (the ratio of gross investment to gross national product) or the net propensity to save (the ratio of net investment to net national product)? Kuznets presents both without committing himself definitely, though he seems to lean toward the net propensity to save. He introduces two other variables—the average longevity of capital and the capital coefficient—and illustrates their interactions by means of numerical examples. This presupposes, and quite correctly, that these five variables—the gross and the net propensity to save, the rate of growth, the capital coefficient, and the longevity of capital—are somehow related to one another, but I was not able to find anywhere in the paper an explicit statement of the nature of this interrelationship. And, fortunately or unfortunately, there are quite a few possibilities. One can take, for instance, the net or the gross propensity to save as well as the longevity of capital and the capital coefficient as given, and derive from them the rate of growth; or one can take the rate of growth as given, and perhaps also the capital coefficient and the longevity of capital, and derive the gross or net propensity to save. It is also possible to make some one variable (such as the capital coefficient) a function of another (the longevity of capital) or vice versa. Finally, they can all be thrown into a simultaneous system in which every variable is dependent on all the others. But unless the relationship assumed is explicitly indicated, it is difficult to understand the significance of Kuznets' numerical illustrations and to decide which variables should be used to make international or intertemporal comparisons.

Consider, for instance, the choice between the net and the gross propensity to save. If the productive capacity of capital declines more or less in accordance with the usual depreciation methods, it is the net capital coefficient (that is, the ratio between capital net of depreciation and net output, or between their respective increments) rather than the gross coefficient that is relevant. If, in addition, net savings are a function of net national product, the net propensity to save should be used. The magnitude of the gross propensity is then of little significance, though it may retain a certain statistical interest. On the other hand, if the productive capacity of capital remains relatively unimpaired until its retirement (which takes place because of technological obsolescence rather than physical deterioration), the gross capital coefficient (that is, the ratio between the stock of capital gross of depreciation and the gross national product, or between their respective increments) is relevant. If it also happens that no depreciation charges are set aside as a part of gross savings, and the latter are simply determined as some fraction of gross national product (by a planning authority, for instance), the net propensity to save has no significance as a variable and comparisons should be made in terms of gross. Finally, if the gross capital coefficient is retained as the significant variable, but gross savings consist of depreciation charges set aside, and net savings are determined independently (which, roughly speaking, is true of a capitalist economy), both the net and the gross propensity to save are significant: the net because it is an independent component of the total, and the gross because it is directly connected (via the capital coefficient) with the rate of growth. The gross propensity would of course have to be adjusted to allow for the cost of replacement.

At times one gets the impression that Kuznets is thinking in terms of a simultaneous relationship among these variables. Thus he presents a very interesting hypothesis (pages 48-50) which makes the net propensity to save a function of the rates of growth of population and income. But one cannot simply say, as he does on page 27, that the net savings are the limiting factor in growth, because a higher rate of growth might affect the propensity to save. In any case, why should a reduction in the latter over time be explained by a fall in the net capital coefficient (page 32)? Instead, wouldn't this fall increase the rate of growth? Or does the author treat the rate of growth as given (by whom?) and assume that the other variables get somehow adjusted to it?

The absence of an explicit model creates a certain lack of clarity in the author's discussion of international capital movements as well. If savings are the limiting factor in capital formation, as Kuznets states (good-bye, Keynesian economics!), capital imports can be added to domestic savings irrespective of the *direct* use to which the borrowed funds are put. Thus the old Russian government might very well have used the proceeds of its foreign loans for secret police, the state church, and pogroms, as the author suggests (page 34), but, unless these expenditures were made possible only by foreign loans (which is rather doubtful), capital imports did increase the total volume of savings available for Russian domestic investment.

The mere fact that, as Kuznets shows, international capital movements have been relatively small (and here a comparison with domestic gross or net savings should be more meaningful than with total net or gross national product) need not imply that they have been unimportant, particularly for the receiving country. Foreign capital has brought with it new techniques and new management, and has been frequently invested in highly strategic industries. This, for instance, was the case in prerevolutionary Russia.

Finally, a word about the types of financing of capital formation. This is a very important subject, and I found Kuznets' introduction to it most stimulating. Since depreciation charges are at best very approximate estimates of capital deterioration, gross capital expenditures of a firm or of an industry appear to me more significant than net; hence, a study in terms of gross expenditures will give a truer picture of the relative importance of their component parts, namely external funds, depreciation charges, and retained net earnings. Of the three, depreciation charges in this country have been, at least in recent times, by far the most important component: over the period 1929-1952 (with the exception of war years) they exceeded individual savings by a ratio of almost 3 to 1, and not all individual savings were invested in business. Together with retained net earnings, depreciation charges allow a well-established, reasonably successful, and not too rapidly growing firm to achieve practically complete independence from external financing. This, of course, is not true of new and/or rapidly growing firms; the sources of their financing are a subject certainly worth an investigation.

FINANCIAL STRUCTURE AND ECONOMIC GROWTH IN ADVANCED COUNTRIES

An Experiment in Comparative Financial Morphology

RAYMOND W. GOLDSMITH

NATIONAL BUREAU OF ECONOMIC RESEARCH

1. *What This Paper Is Not About*

THE TITLE of this conference brackets "capital formation" with "economic growth" presumably because there is a causal or functional relationship between the two concepts, more specifically because differences in levels, trends, and structure of capital formation influence the speed and character of economic growth. Similarly, the selection of "sources and channels of finance in capitalist countries" as the topic of the first group of papers presumably reflects the belief that the nature of these sources and channels has a bearing on economic growth. This paper, therefore, should deal with the effect of sources and channels of finance on the rapidity and nature of economic growth in "advanced" capitalist countries, defined as countries with a high value of real national product per head and a fully developed financial system. In particular, the paper should examine how and to what extent differences in financial structure have been responsible for differences in the rate and character of economic growth. This examination, naturally, should run in quantitative terms, i.e. it should relate certain measurable characteristics of financial structure to a quantitative expression of economic growth such as real national product per head.

The paper does not follow this straight path. Some of the reasons are accidental, such as the extreme pressure of time under which it was written. Others are more basic. First, there is no accepted and tried kit of concepts for measuring financial structure and thus distinguishing clearly and quantitatively changes in structure over time or differences in structure between countries or regions. Second, even if we hastily fashion some new tools—as will be done in section 2—there is great difficulty in finding data for different dates and different countries that are sufficiently comprehensive, detailed, and comparable to justify their application. Third, our measures of economic growth are still so crude, particularly if we go back more than a few decades, that differences—e.g. in the rate of increase of real product per head—must be pronounced and persistent to be regarded as significant. Fourth, the number of "cases" from which our generalizations would have to be drawn is woefully small—there are less than a dozen countries that can be classified as "advanced," using the two criteria of high real income per head (high by international comparison) and a well-developed financial structure; and most of these have been in this category for less than a century. Fifth—and this will be the decisive consideration for theorists—economic growth is so complex a phenomenon, obviously determined or influenced by basic factors of a physical, technological, and mass-psychological nature, that an attempt to isolate the effects of apparently secondary forces such as the character of financial institutions and the nature of credit practices does not promise success. Indeed, if differences in financial structure affect economic growth, such effects have a better chance of being identified and measured by contrasting "advanced" and "retarded," or capitalist and socialist, countries as of today; or in comparing economic growth in the now "advanced" countries before and after the industrial revolution—both subjects excluded from the assigned scope of this paper, even if I had felt bold enough to attack them. For an explanation of the differences in the speed and character of economic growth of "advanced" countries, financial factors will be, I am afraid, too weak and blunt a tool until our knowledge of both the economic growth and the financial structure of different countries is much further advanced than it is now.

This pessimistic attitude is due in part to the absence of any prima-facie evidence of a clear connection between the financial structure and the rate of economic growth in "advanced" capitalist countries during the past century.[1] In Table 1 the estimates available

[1] Abramovitz has quite correctly pointed out that this attitude, as well as the conclusions of this paper, might be different had it been possible to investigate financial structure on a broader basis than I have been able to investigate it here. This might be the case in particular if, in addition to the sample balance sheet ratios used here, consideration had been given—in quantitative terms if that were possible—to the nature of the mechanism by which funds are transferred from lenders to borrowers, following for example Abramovitz's own stimulating suggestions in *Survey of Contemporary Economics* (Bernard F. Haley, editor, Irwin, 1952, Vol. II, pp. 146 ff.). It should be clear to the reader that I am not dealing in this paper with finance or even financial structure in the broadest sense of these terms, but only with one aspect of them—the relationship between tangible and intangible assets in national and group balance sheets—that seems to lend itself well to quantitative treatment and for which the necessary basic information is available, even if only in rough form.

TABLE 1

Growth Rates of Real National Product of "Advanced" Countries, 1860-1950

(*per cent per year*)

Period	*U.S.* (1)	*Canada* (2)	*Australia* (3)	*New Zealand* (4)	*U.K.* (5)	*France* (6)	*Germany* (7)	*Nether-lands* (8)	*Belgium* (9)	*Switzer-land* (10)	*Sweden* (11)	*Norway* (12)	*Denmark* (13)
						Aggregate Real National Product							
1. 1860-1913[a]	4.3	.	3.7	.	2.4	1.1	3.0	2.3	2.2	2.6	2.0	2.3	2.8
2. 1913-1938	2.0	1.7[b]	2.1	.	1.0	1.1	1.3	2.1	1.0	1.6	1.9	1.9	2.1
3. 1938-1950	5.7	5.9	2.6	3.3[c]	1.6	.2	2.3[d]	1.8	.6	2.1	2.5	3.0	2.2
4. 1860-1950	3.8	.	3.2	.	1.8	1.1	2.4	2.2	1.7	2.1	2.0	2.3	2.5
5. 1913-1950	3.0	2.8	2.3	.	1.2	.9	1.7	1.7	.9	1.8	2.1	2.3	2.1
						Real National Product per Head							
6. 1860-1913[a]	2.3	.	1.7	.	1.5	.9	2.0	.8	1.4	1.4	1.3	1.6	1.8
7. 1913-1938	.9	.2	.4	.	.8	.9	.7	.6	.6	1.2	1.4	1.2	.8
8. 1938-1950	4.2	4.0	1.1	2.4	1.2	0	.7[d]	.6	.3	1.1	1.7	2.1	1.2
9. 1860-1950	2.2	.	1.3	.	1.2	.9	1.4	.7	1.1	1.3	1.4	1.6	1.4
10. 1913-1950	2.0	1.4	.6	.	.9	.7	.7	.6	.5	1.2	1.5	1.5	.9

[a] First period starts with years other than 1860: for U.S., 1869/1878; Australia, 1886; U.K., 1870; Netherlands, 1900; Belgium, 1846; Switzerland, 1890; Sweden, 1870; Norway, 1891; Denmark, 1870.

[b] The year 1911 instead of 1913.

[c] From 1938/1939 to 1947/1948.

[d] From 1936 to 1952.

Source: Figures in lines 3 and 8 derived from estimates of real national product given in *22nd Annual Report*, 1952, Bank for International Settlements, p. 43; and population data mostly from *Demographic Yearbook*, 1952, United Nations. Those for lines 4, 5, 9, and 10 are weighted averages of lines 1 to 3 and 6 to 8 respectively. (Values in lines 1 and 6 have been regarded as applying to full period 1860 to 1913.) Figures in lines 1, 2, 6, and 7 are based on following sources:

Column	Source
1	*Income and Wealth, Series II*, Simon Kuznets, editor, Cambridge, Eng., Bowes & Bowes for International Association for Research in Income and Wealth, 1952, p. 30, for the period 1869/1878 to 1909/1918; *National Income Supplement, 1951*, *Survey of Current Business*, Dept. of Commerce, for 1938 to 1950.
2-4, 6, 9-13	Colin Clark, *The Conditions of Economic Progress*, 2nd ed., London, Macmillan, 1951, pp. 80, 84, 85, 87, 105, 106, 108, 140, and 148, corrected by data in *Review of Economic Progress*, December 1951, for France.
5	A. R. Prest, "National Income of the United Kingdom, 1870-1946," *Economic Journal*, March 1948, pp. 58-59.
7	P. Jostock, "The Long-Term Growth of National Income in Germany," unpublished paper submitted to 1953 meeting of International Association for Research in Income and Wealth, p. 3.
8	*Statistische en Econometrische Onderzoekingen*, Centraal Bureau voor de Statistiek, Utrecht, 1950, p. 174.

in mid-1953 of growth in real national product since the middle of the nineteenth century have been brought together for all countries which can be regarded as "advanced" on the basis of the real income criterion, i.e. countries having real income per head in 1949 of over $400,[2] all of which (with the possible exception of New Zealand) also meet the second definitional criterion, that of possessing a fully developed financial system.

The outstanding—and not unexpected—feature of this table is the higher rate of growth of real national product, per head as well as in the aggregate, of the United States and Canada compared with the other "advanced" countries, most of which are situated in Western or Central Europe. Is one seriously to believe that differences in financial structure are responsible for this basic difference in the rate of economic growth which has endured for most of a century, a difference large enough to raise real income per head in the United States within one century to three times that of most of the other advanced countries? How is one to explain the fact that the country with a rate of growth nearest to the United States—Canada—has quite a different financial structure, which in several respects (e.g. concentration of commercial banking into a small number of nationwide institutions) is closer to European than American patterns? Limiting attention to "advanced" countries in Europe, is there anything in the financial structure of the Scandinavian countries or Switzerland to account for their relatively rapid economic growth, or in that of the Netherlands to explain the slow increase in national product per head? The financial systems of Germany and Great Britain have often been regarded as opposites, and much printers' ink has been spilt, particularly before World War I, in using these differences as an explanation of the two countries' relative growth. In fact, both countries show not too different rates of growth of real income, in the aggregate as well as per head, between the mid-

[2] See *National and Per Capita Incomes, Seventy Countries—1949*, United Nations, Statistical Papers, Series E J, Table 1. Germany is included because it should by 1952 have reached a per head income of over $400 and obviously belongs to this group. Luxembourg and Iceland, though meeting the income criterion, have been omitted for lack of historical data and because it is doubtful if they possess a fully developed financial system. Use of figures for one year employing official exchange rates to convert income estimates in national currencies into dollar figures is obviously open to criticism. The list of "advanced" countries would, however, be essentially the same had it been based on Clark's estimates for 1925-1934 in which an attempt is made to reduce incomes to comparable "international units" (see Colin Clark, *The Conditions of Economic Progress*, 1st ed., London, Macmillan, 1940, p. 41).

dle of the nineteenth century and 1913.[3] Finally, the rate of growth of real product per head was considerably higher from the third quarter of the nineteenth century to World War I than in the following forty years in the case of the United Kingdom, Germany, Belgium, the Netherlands, Denmark, and Australia, while the decline was small, or entirely absent, in the United States, France, Switzerland, Sweden, and Norway. Do these differences and groupings have a significant relation to financial structure?

In all these instances it can of course be argued that, while they are not decisive, differences in financial structure have been an important contributing factor in determining rate of growth of real national product, particularly if financial structure is defined more broadly than in this paper. This possibility cannot be denied or disproved. But neither can it be proven. Nor is it possible—and this is more important—to isolate and measure the contribution of financial factors. If we want to stay within the realm of measurable facts we must, therefore, give up for the time being the attempt to determine the differential effect of financial structure on economic growth among advanced capitalist countries.

Thus we must trim our sails and be content with a much more moderate contribution to the analysis of economic growth. We may first ask what, theoretically, are the characteristics of financial structure which are influenced by and in turn affect the process of economic growth? Second, we may see whether the financial structures of advanced capitalist countries show sufficient common characteristics and significant similarity in development for us to regard these financial traits as "typical" components or accompaniments of their economies and their development. It is to these two questions that the rest of this paper is directed. Naturally, it cannot treat them exhaustively or definitively. The very breadth and novelty of the questions are sufficient to dispel any illusions on these counts. All that can be done is to offer, in section 2, some suggestions of concepts that might be used in a comparative morphology of financial structure; to apply, in section 3, these concepts to changes in the financial structure of the United States during the past century; and to attempt, in section 4, a rapid glance at a few other important advanced countries—Great Britain, Germany, and the Netherlands—

[3] The advocates of the German financial system, it is true, based their arguments on differences in growth during the second half of this period. But for the years 1890-1913 the increase in real national product per head seems to have been only slightly higher in Germany (.9 per cent per year) than in Great Britain (.7 per cent).

in 1913 and at some more recent points of time, the selection of dates as well as countries depending largely on availability of data.

2. *Elements of a Comparative Financial Morphology*

A satisfactory quantitative comparison of the financial structures of different countries at rest and in motion, i.e. a comparative morphology and dynamic, requires for each of them and for a considerable period of time (1) national balance sheets with fairly detailed cross-classifications of intangible assets, liabilities, and equities by creditor (holder) and debtor (issuer) groups, and (2) use-and-source-of-funds statements, on a gross basis, for all major sectors of the economy by type of fund, thus permitting the construction of a square flow table with as many rows and columns as there are sectors to distinguish, a table which is formally quite similar to the familiar input-output matrix for interindustrial relations. This section proceeds as if such statements existed and disregards the numerous conceptual and practical problems involved in their derivation. It explores measures that could be used in such a situation to characterize financial structures and to compare them among countries over time.

One of the basic relations characterizing the financial structure on the national level is the ratio between intangible and tangible assets in the combined national balance sheet, a ratio which is equal to

$$\frac{\text{National assets}}{\text{National wealth}} - 1$$

if tangibles are regarded as including net foreign assets or obligations. It may be called the "financial interrelations ratio" because it measures the extent to which tangible assets are overlaid by a network of financial (intangible) claims, liabilities, and evidences of ownership (equities). The ratio naturally is zero when there are no intangibles, i.e. no financial interrelations, and national assets = national wealth, and is the higher the denser the net of financial interrelations.

The financial interrelations ratio (henceforth designated as FIR) is determined by the following factors:[4]

1. The definition of independent economic units each of which is supposed to have its own balance sheet. To cite only one ex-

[4] The list is not exhaustive; some of the factors could well be further subdivided.

ample: national assets, and hence FIR, are higher if unincorporated businesses are regarded as separate entities than if their assets and liabilities are treated as part of the balance sheet of proprietors, and the difference is equal to the value of the equity in unincorporated business enterprises which appears among proprietors' assets.

2. The definition of assets. Needless to say, both national assets and national wealth, and hence FIR, are affected by the scope of tangible and intangible assets included in the national balance sheet. Liberal definition of intangibles (e.g. inclusion of good will and similar assets or capitalization of claims of social security beneficiaries in excess of fund assets) will necessarily increase both national assets and FIR. Broadening of the scope of tangibles, primarily inclusion of consumer durables or of durable military assets, on the other hand, will raise national assets and national wealth by the same absolute amounts and thus will reduce FIR.

3. The valuation of assets. In periods of rising prices FIR calculated on market prices (or reproduction cost) is likely to be higher than if calculated on the basis of book values, i.e. original cost, while the opposite relationship will prevail after a prolonged fall in prices. The reason is that the book values of a large part of intangibles, particularly short-term claims, adapt themselves rather rapidly to changes in the general price level; whereas, such an adaptation takes a long time for the bulk of tangible assets, i.e. structures and equipment, though not for inventories.

4. The extent to which operation and ultimate ownership of tangible assets coincide. The greater the difference between the values of the typical ultimate unit's (household and government) tangible assets and its equity, i.e. the lower the ratio of tangible to total assets in the typical ultimate unit's balance sheet, the larger the proportion of intangible assets and liabilities necessary to bridge the gap.

5. The degree of "layering" in the economy, i.e. the number of links (independent units) in the chain between tangible assets and ultimates. Two types of layering may profitably be distinguished. The first is layering among major economic groups, i.e. the existence of nonfinancial business enterprises and of financial institutions, the former owning and operating part of tangible assets and the latter providing part of the funds with which business enterprises acquire tangible as well as intangible assets. The second is layering within major economic sectors, i.e. the fact that there are financial interrelations (creditor-debtor and owner-issuer relationships) among units

belonging to the same sector, particularly among affiliated enterprises, between suppliers and customers, and among financial institutions. The extent of this intrasectoral layering is measured by the ratio of the footings of a sector's combined and consolidated balance sheets.

6. The size of the "dead-weight debt," i.e. debt that was incurred without giving rise, as is the normal case, to assets of equal amount.[5] The classical example of dead-weight debt is government borrowing to defray military expenditures (except possibly expenditures on durable military assets, which may be regarded as part of national assets and wealth). But government or private debt incurred to cover a current deficit, i.e. consumer debt in the narrower sense of the word, belongs in the same category. Since dead-weight debt increases the assets of its holders, and hence national assets, but does not directly affect the level of national wealth, it raises FIR.[6] Indeed, the increase in national assets may easily be far in excess of the amount of dead-weight debt if part or all of the debt is bought by the central bank and thus becomes the basis of multiple expansion of assets and deposits within the banking system.

7. The extent of destruction of tangible assets by "acts of God or the King's enemies," a contingency likely to arise in significant

[5] The concept of dead-weight debt is not an easy one to handle, as Shaw's comments indicate, but I still believe that it has a place in the analysis of financial interrelations and of the connection between financial structure and economic growth. The adjective itself, which is taken from nineteenth century British financial terminology, does not, of course, imply that such debt is "dead" in the sense of being without influence on income, prices, output, and many other economically relevant factors either at the time of its creation or later. Differing from Shaw, I also believe that dead-weight debt can be defined with as much precision as other economic and financial terms. It is simply that part of liabilities which, at current valuations, is not covered by assets. Hence, there is, strictly speaking, dead-weight debt for some units in every sector. If we limit the term in statistical handling to the overindebtedness of governments, or if we equate it sometimes in further simplification with the total debt of the central government, we are applying statistical conventions whose justification depends on how closely they reflect the actual situation. Where sufficient data are available we do not have to treat the entire debt of the central government, or of other issuer groups, as dead-weight or not dead-weight, but can divide all holdings pro rata into parts that represent dead-weight debt or other debt.

[6] In real life, issuance of large amounts of dead-weight debt is invariably accompanied, sooner or later, by a rise in the price level. This rise may possibly be pronounced enough to raise the value of tangible assets so much that FIR actually declines, at least until the volume of intangibles (other than dead-weight debt) adjusts itself to the rise in price level. (In view of Shaw's comment it may be well to emphasize that such a decline in FIR is likely to be temporary and is not to be expected except during hyperinflation.)

amounts only in major wars. In such a case FIR would rise, since an unchanged volume of intangibles is compared with a shrunken tangible asset base. Actually, war-caused destruction of tangible assets (and the loss of net foreign assets, which is similar in its effects) is likely to cause an even sharper increase in FIR, as it will generally be accompanied by the creation of additional intangibles in the form of war damage compensation claims or payments. (Two examples, the British and Dutch situations after World War II, will be found in section 4.)

8. The sudden and unilateral reduction of intangibles—the modern form of *seisachtheia*—which often accompanies currency reforms and repudiations of government debt. Such actions sometimes also reduce the market value of tangibles; but generally much less than corresponds to the shrinkage of intangibles, so that FIR falls abruptly. (A classical case, the German currency reform of 1948, is illustrated in section 4.)

9. Under customary accounting conventions, following legal arrangements, rented real property does not appear in the balance sheet of the tenant but only in the balance sheet of the landlord, in which it is not distinguished from owner-operated property. As a result, the proportion of real property rented is without influence on FIR. The national balance sheet and FIR are thus invariant to shifts between owner operation and tenancy and to differences in the ratio of tenancy among countries, although such shifts and differences are of great economic significance and of importance for many aspects of financial structure. It is worth consideration whether the national balance sheet should not depart from the usual methods of business accounting by entering the value of rented property on both sides of the tenant's balance sheet, as a tangible asset on the left- and as a liability of equal size on the right-hand side, and at the same time show it in the landlord's balance sheet as a claim instead of a tangible asset. Under this treatment, spread of tenancy would increase national assets and FIR, though naturally leaving national wealth unchanged.

It may be well to illustrate these rather abstract considerations by a set of extremely simplified specimens of financial structure on the national level. They are all based on the assumptions that balance sheets exist for all economic units and that valuations are uniform. Only four sectors (groups of economic units) are distinguished: ultimates (i.e. households and private nonprofit institutions), business (nonfinancial corporations and unincorporated enterprises), financial intermediaries, and government. Business is supposed (except in Specimens 6 and 7) to be entirely financed by intermediaries. Financial intermediaries are assumed (except in Specimen 7), for the sake of simplicity, to own intangible but no tangible assets, and non-financial businesses to own tangible but no intangible assets. For the same reason ultimates are assumed (again except in Specimen 7) to be free of debt, governments to have no assets and only dead-weight debt, and financial intermediaries to be financed entirely by ultimates. Net foreign assets and liabilities are disregarded throughout.

SPECIMEN 1

No Nonfinancial Business Enterprises; No Financial Intermediaries; No Dead-Weight Debt

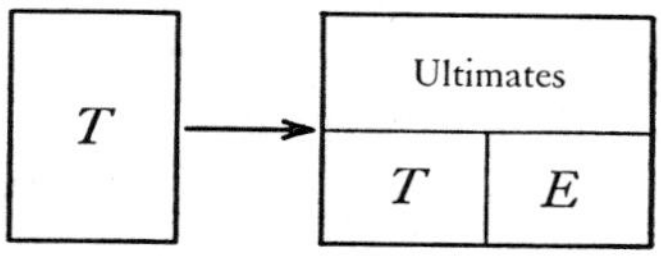

National assets = National wealth
Financial interrelations ratio = 0
Share of financial intermediaries in national assets = 0

Legend (for all specimens)

- *T* = Tangible assets
- *E* = Equity
- *L* = Liabilities
- *C* = Claims
- *S* = Stocks (i.e. equities held as assets)
- *D* = Dead-weight debt
- *O* = Surplus deficit (overindebtedness)

SPECIMEN 2

Nonfinancial Enterprises Own All Tangible Assets; No Financial Intermediaries; No Dead-Weight Debt

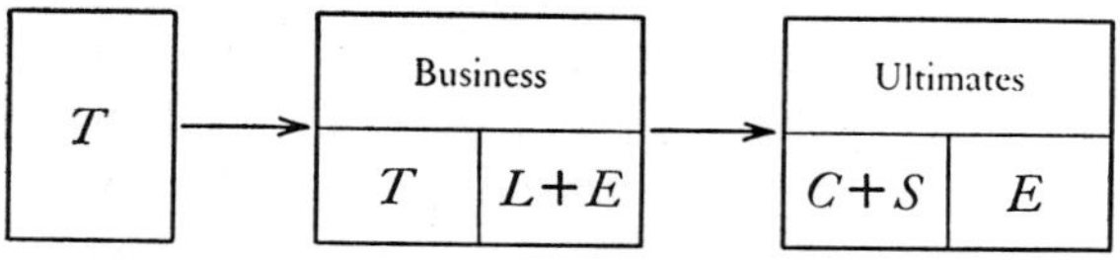

National assets = 2 × national wealth
Financial interrelations ratio = 1
Share of financial intermediaries in national assets = 0

SPECIMEN 3

Nonfinancial Enterprises Own All Tangible Assets; One Layer of Financial Intermediaries Supplies All Funds to Enterprises; No Dead-Weight Debt

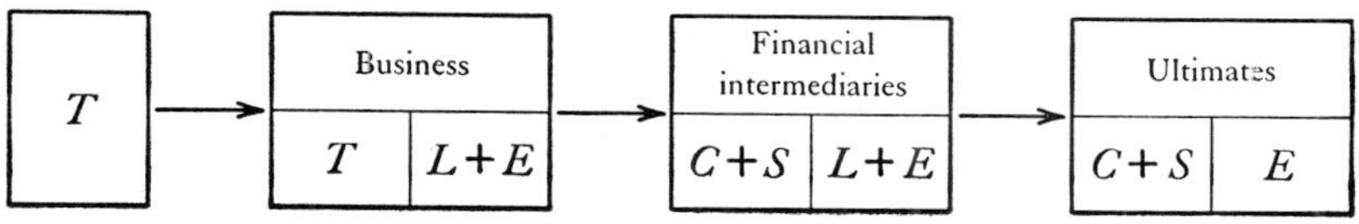

National assets	= 3 × national wealth
Financial interrelations ratio	= 2
Share of financial intermediaries in national assets	= ⅓
Layering ratio among financial intermediaries	= 1

SPECIMEN 4

Nonfinancial Enterprises Own All Tangible Assets; One Layer of Financial Intermediaries Supplies All Funds to Enterprises; Dead-Weight Debt Equal to One-Half of Value of Tangible Assets Held Half by Financial Intermediaries and Half by Ultimate Owners

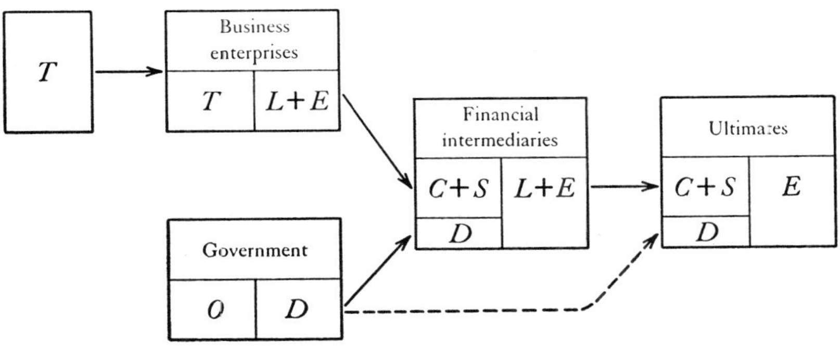

National assets	= 5 × national wealth
Financial interrelations ratio	= 4
Share of financial intermediaries in national assets	= ¼
Layering ratio among financial intermediaries	= 1

SPECIMEN 5

Nonfinancial Enterprises Own All Tangible Assets; Multi-Layered Financial Intermediaries Supply All Funds to Enterprises; No Dead-Weight Debt

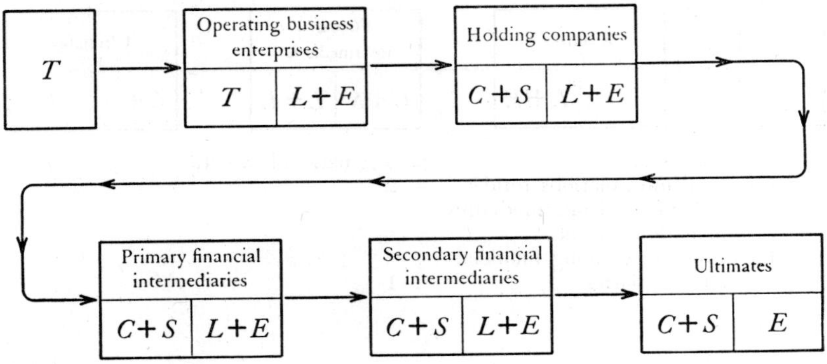

National assets	= 5 × national wealth
Financial interrelations ratio	= 4
Share of financial intermediaries in national assets	= ⅖ (⅗ including holding companies)
Layering ratio among financial intermediaries	= 2 (3 including holding companies)

SPECIMEN 6

Ultimates and Business Each Own One-Half of Tangible Assets; One Layer of Financial Intermediaries; Dead-Weight Debt Equal to One-Fourth of Tangible Assets and Held Equally by Ultimates and Financial Intermediaries

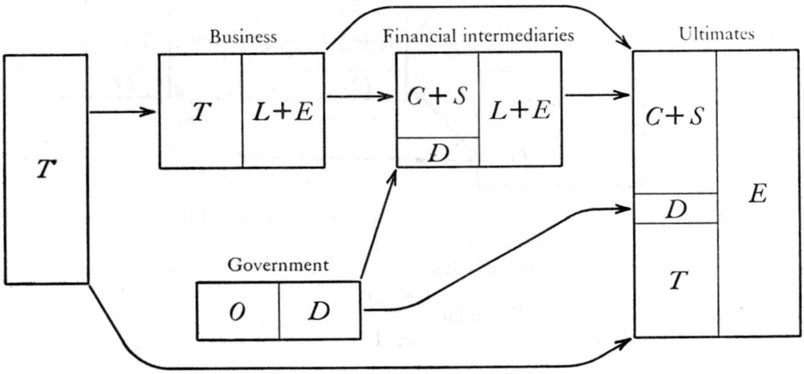

National assets	= 3⅜ × national wealth
Financial interrelations ratio	= 2⅜
Share of financial intermediaries in national assets	= ⅑ (approximately)
Layering ratio among financial intermediaries	= 1

SPECIMEN 7

Situation Similar to United States in 1949

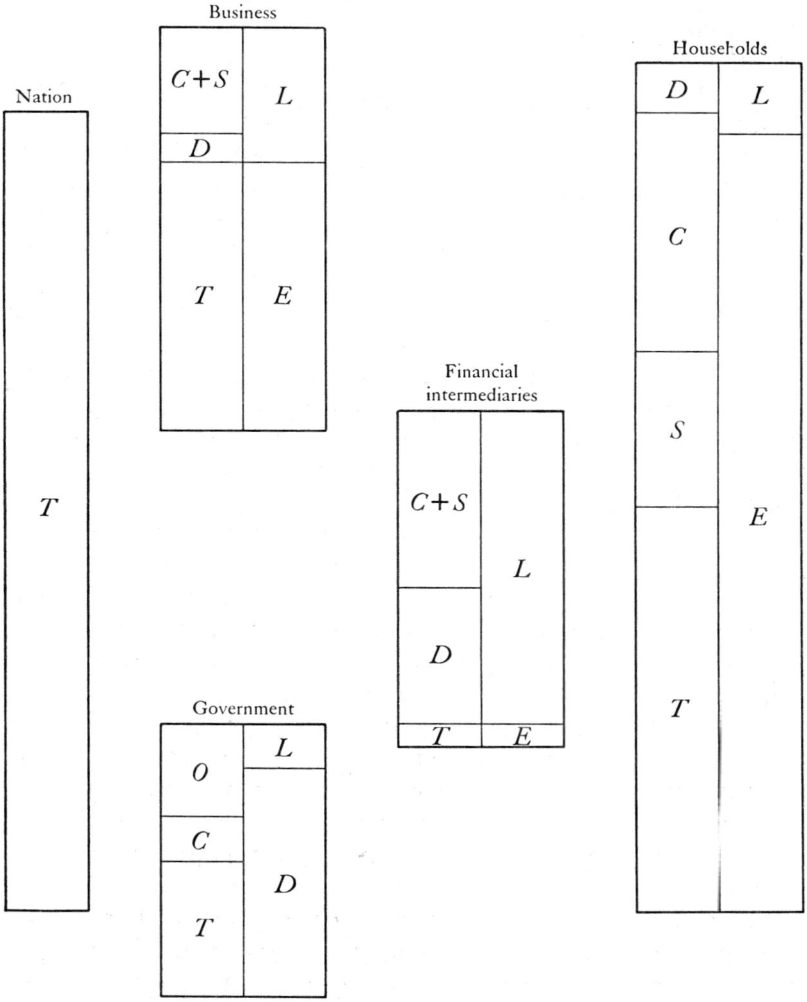

National assets	= 2 × national wealth
Financial interrelations ratio	= 1
Share of financial intermediaries in national assets	= ⅕

The only point in including these graphs is to bring home more clearly than in the text how the share of tangible assets owned by business, the extent of layering, and the size and distribution of the dead-weight debt affect FIR and the share of financial intermediaries in national assets. Specimens 1 to 5 illustrate extreme cases, not likely to be found in this pure form in actual life. Specimen 6, however, is a little more realistic, and Specimen 7, the most complicated one, is roughly modeled after the situation in the United States in 1949, the last year for which a national balance sheet is available.

It is, of course, impossible to indicate a typical or normal value for FIR. But it may be useful to show in Table 2 the values of FIR which result from certain assumptions about the value of the main determinants of the ratio, values which appear to be reasonable for modern Western-type economies.

This table shows the wide range—one-third to three—in the value of FIR that may arise without making unreasonable assumptions regarding the main determinants of the ratio. The range of FIR encountered in actual application, however, is much smaller. The share of business in tangible assets, for instance, will generally be found to lie between one-fourth and one-half, and will exceed one-half only in less-developed countries and if agriculture is regarded as part of the business sector. The share of financial intermediaries in financing business is usually of the order of one-sixth to one-third, while the layering ratios among nonfinancial business enterprises and financial intermediaries more commonly range from one and one-half to two. It is only the dead-weight debt ratio which is actually found to have a wide range from virtually zero up to one-half. FIR thus is likely to lie between one-half and one and one-half when there is no dead-weight debt. It may rise to between one and two and one-half in situations where a substantial dead-weight debt, say of up to one-half of national wealth, is present.

For the analysis of a country's financial structure, and of changes in it, there is particular interest in the relation between FIR and the assets of financial intermediaries. This can be set forth in the following formula, which also is sometimes useful as a rough estimating device when no comprehensive national balance sheet is available.[7]

[7] A stands for total assets, T and I for tangible and intangible assets. Subscripts on the right indicate holders, those on the left debtors (issuers); n stands for all groups, h for households, g for government, b for nonfinancial business, f for financial intermediaries, s for foreigners, and o for all groups except financial intermediaries.

TABLE 2

Value of Financial Interrelations Ratio under Varying Assumptions

Share of financial intermediaries in business financing (ϕ)	Layering ratio of business (λ_b)	Layering ratio of financial intermediaries (λ_f)	Share of business in tangible assets (β) .25			.50		
			Deadweight debt ratio (d)					
			0	*.25*	*.50*	*0*	*.25*	*.50*
.25								
	1.0	1.0	.31	.44	1.56	.62	1.25	1.88
		2.0	.38	1.12	1.87	.75	1.50	2.25
	2.0	1.0	.56	1.19	1.81	1.12	1.75	2.38
		2.0	.62	1.38	2.12	1.25	2.00	2.75
.50								
	1.0	1.0	.38	1.00	1.63	.75	1.38	2.00
		2.0	.50	1.25	2.00	1.00	1.75	2.50
	2.0	1.0	.62	1.25	1.88	1.25	1.88	2.50
		2.0	.75	1.50	2.25	1.50	2.25	3.00

Source: Calculated from the formula

$$\text{FIR} = \beta\lambda_b + (d\delta + \beta\phi)\lambda_f + 2d$$

where δ = proportion of dead-weight debt held by financial intermediaries. This formula considerably simplifies the actual interrelations among groups; e.g. by assuming that financial intermediaries and governments own no tangible assets, that financial intermediaries are financed entirely by households and are holding one-half of dead-weight debt, that there are no interrelations between nonfinancial business and government, and that there is no layering among households and governments.

The formula is derived by summing the assets of the four groups, which can be expressed in the terms used in Table 2 (T = tangible assets, i.e. national wealth), dividing by T, and subtracting 1 (since FIR has been defined as $[\Sigma A/T] - 1$), as follows:

Nonfinancial business	: $T + T\beta(\lambda_b - 1) = T\beta\lambda_b$
Government	: Td
Financial intermediaries	: $Td\delta + T\beta\phi + (\lambda_f - 1)(Td\delta + T\beta\phi)$ $= (Td\delta + T\beta)\lambda_f$
Households	: $T(1 - \beta) + Td(1 - \delta) + T\beta(1 - \phi) + Td\delta + T\beta\delta$ $= T(1 + d)$

$$\text{FIR} = \frac{I_n}{T_n}$$

$$= \frac{I_f + I_b + I_h + I_g}{T_n}$$

$$= \frac{A_f - T_f}{T_n} + \frac{{}_oI_b + {}_fI_b}{T_n} + \frac{{}_oI_h + {}_fI_h}{T_n} + \frac{{}_oI_g + {}_fI_g}{T_n}$$

$$= \frac{A_f - T_f}{T_n} + \frac{{}_fI_b + {}_fI_h + {}_fI_g}{T_n} + \frac{{}_oI_b + {}_oI_h + {}_oI_g}{T_n}$$

$$= \frac{{}_fI_b + {}_fI_h + {}_fI_g}{T_n} = \frac{A_f - {}_fI_f - {}_fI_s}{T_n}$$

(Holdings of claims against, and holdings of equity securities of, financial intermediaries by domestic business, households, and governments must be equal to total assets of financial intermediaries less claims, etc., of financial intermediaries and of foreigners.)

$$= \frac{A_f - T_f}{T_n} + \frac{A_f - {}_fI_f - {}_fI_s}{T_n} + \frac{{}_oI_b + {}_oI_h + {}_oI_g}{T_n}$$

$$= \frac{2A_f}{T_n} - \frac{T_f + {}_fI_f + {}_fI_s}{T_n} + \frac{{}_oI_b + {}_oI_h + {}_oI_g}{T_n}$$

$$= \frac{(2 - a)A_f}{T_n} + \frac{{}_oI_b + {}_oI_h + {}_oI_g}{T_n}$$

where

$$a = \frac{T_f + {}_fI_f + {}_fI_s}{A_f}$$

Since a is usually rather small (below .25), FIR may be said to consist of two components. The first of them is slightly below twice the ratio of financial intermediaries' assets to national wealth. The second is the ratio of intra- and intergroup claims and equities of other domestic sectors to national wealth, which consists mainly of holdings of government bonds and of corporate securities by households and nonfinancial business enterprises, of individuals' mortgage holdings, and of accounts receivable of business.[8] The advantages of this formula are that total assets of financial intermediaries are generally known or can be estimated with reasonable accuracy, and that some or most of the components of the second summand's denominator can also be estimated, even if often only rather roughly. In this way FIR can be approximated in the absence of a national balance sheet—the usual situation—when figures are available on national wealth, assets of financial intermediaries, and outstanding securities and mortgages. (In practice the item most often unavailable is business accounts receivable.)

FIR, together with its components, particularly the dead-weight debt ratio and the two layering ratios, is probably the most informative and simplest single measure of financial structure. But complementary ratios, which can generally be regarded as further subdivisions of FIR or its components, are necessary for fuller understanding of differences in financial structure between countries or over time. Among these are:

1. The share of financial intermediaries in total national assets. This is probably the best single indicator of the over-all importance of financial institutions in the national economy.[9]

2. The share of (a) note-issuing institutions (central banks) and (b) check-issuing banks in the assets of all financial intermediaries and in national assets. These ratios are of considerable theoretical importance and also turn out to be good indicators of the stage of a country's financial development. Their significance lies in the fact that they are rough measures of the share of nonmetallic money in all intangible assets. Indeed, for some purposes just this latter share may be preferable to the shares of assets of banks of issue and commercial banks in total intangibles.

3. The share of the main groups of financial intermediaries in aggregate assets of intermediaries and in total national assets. These ratios provide rough indicators of the relative importance of the different types of financial intermediaries and are therefore useful in characterizing quantitatively a country's capital market organization. The main groups to be distinguished—apart from central and commercial banks—are savings banks and similar organizations (in

[8] Accurate calculation, of course, would require some additional items such as loans among households and, if regarded as an asset, tax accruals.

[9] See Raymond W. Goldsmith, *The Share of Financial Intermediaries in National Wealth and National Assets, 1900-1949*, National Bureau of Economic Research, Occasional Paper 42, 1954.

the United States, for instance, savings and loan associations and credit unions); mortgage banks (a group poorly represented in the United States but of great importance in some other countries); insurance and pension funds, subdivided into private and government organizations; and personal trust funds insofar as they are under professional management (in the United States under the administration of personal trust departments of commercial banks and trust companies).

4. The ratio between intangible assets held by financial intermediaries and those held by all other economic groups. The function of this ratio is to indicate the degree of institutionalization of investment in intangible assets. The over-all ratio is usefully supplemented by similar ratios for the main types of intangible assets which are held in substantial amounts both by financial intermediaries and by noninstitutional investors, viz. government bonds, corporate bonds, corporate stocks, and mortgages.

5. The share of financial intermediaries in financing the different sectors of the economy. These ratios are calculated, if national balance sheets but no sources-and-uses-of-funds statements are available, as the share of a sector's borrowings from and its securities held by financial institutions to the sector's aggregate liabilities and equity. They may be regarded as a further breakdown of FIR.[10]

6. Ratio of foreign financing. This ratio has been of minor importance in the United States in the twentieth century, but in many other countries it constitutes an important characteristic of the financial structure, partly because it is the most important exogenous factor in that structure.

7. The liquid asset ratio. This ratio, which compares liquid assets, however defined, with total assets, is significant for individual economic units and groups of them up to major sectors like nonfinancial business or agriculture, but is of limited interest on a national scale. Its importance, like that of the next three ratios, lies primarily in the fact that it constitutes an important determinant of economic behavior, particularly the ability and willingness to make capital expenditures and the decisions to enlarge or curtail the scale of output.

8. The ratio of price-sensitive assets, primarily tangible assets and equity securities (including equities in unincorporated business enterprises), to total assets.

[10] Where sources-and-uses-of-funds statements are available, the ratios are calculated from total sources of funds during a given period and funds supplied by financial intermediaries, rather than from the balance sheet.

9. The ratio of indebtedness to total assets. For analytical purposes a subdivision into a short-term and a long-term debt ratio is advisable.

10. The leverage ratio, a combination of debt ratio and price-sensitive asset ratio, which measures the percentage change in equity resulting from a 1 per cent change in the level of asset prices. This ratio, which can be refined in various ways, is useful as an indicator of the effects of inflation and deflation on different sectors of the economy.

11. The self-financing ratio, which is measured when only balance sheets are available—rather unsatisfactorily if the statements are based on original cost of assets—as the ratio of earned surplus to total liabilities and equity. Calculation from a sources-and-uses-of-funds statement as the proportion between total sources of funds and retained earnings is preferable. This is one of the most important ratios characterizing financial structure, but it is not easily available because balance sheets do not often permit a comparison of earned surplus and total liabilities and equity unless calculated throughout in constant prices, and because sources-and-uses-of-funds statements are rarely available for a period long enough to permit an estimate of the contribution of internal financing to total assets or equity.

12. Concentration ratios, i.e. measures (preferably in the form of Lorenz curves) of the extent to which total assets, total equity, or other balance sheet items of the various sectors of the economy, or of the entire nation, are concentrated in a relatively small number of individual economic units. The broadest measures of this sort are distributions of national assets or national wealth by size which are familiar in the form of wealth distributions among individuals. Similar distributions, of course, can be derived, and occasionally have been, for assets or equity among corporations, among financial institutions of a certain type, or among any other group of economic units which is sufficiently homogeneous and in some sense competitive to impart economic significance to the calculation. Concentration is generally measured on a national scale, but its study is often as significant at the local level. To give only one example, the concentration of commercial banks on the national level is much more pronounced in most European countries which have nation-wide branch banking systems than in the United States. It will, however, be found that at the local level, i.e. for a given city or trade area, concentration is often higher in the United States; in

other words, the largest one, two, or three banks account for a higher proportion of total banking resources than they do in Europe.

Only FIR and a few of its components are dealt with in this paper. Hardly any use at all will be made of the other ratios, i.e. those listed under 5 to 12 above. The reason is simply that these ratios do not seem to have been calculated in a systematic and comparable way for a sufficient number of countries to permit international comparisons. On the other hand, figures for the United States, which are available at least for several of these ratios, have not been analyzed here, although they would fit into section 3, in order not to extend this paper unduly and because they have been briefly discussed elsewhere.[11]

3. *Changes in the Financial Structure of the United States*

The following summary discussion of some important measurable changes in the financial structure of the United States over the past 100 years serves three modest purposes. The first is to illustrate the application to one concrete case of the tools of financial morphology, sketched in section 2. The second is to follow the changes in financial structure that have accompanied one of the outstanding examples of economic growth of an advanced country, and certainly the most massive and enduring example: the United States since the middle of the nineteenth century. The third is to provide a standard of comparison with the much rougher measures for a few other countries to be presented in section 4.

TRENDS IN FINANCIAL INTERRELATIONS RATIO AND COMPONENTS[12]

The FIR of the American economy, as it appears in column 1 of Table 3, has shown a definite upward trend, though by no means an unbroken or regular one. Indeed, the movements of the ratio suggest a series of steps rather than a smooth curve.

The ratio was undoubtedly low in 1850, as rough as the estimates may be. It probably remained slightly below .5, indicating that

[11] For liquid asset, price-sensitive asset, and debt ratios see Raymond W. Goldsmith, *A Study of Saving in the United States*, Vol. I, Princeton University Press, 1955, Introduction, Chap. VIII; and for the share of financial intermediaries in total supply of funds, "Financial Intermediaries in the Saving and Investment Process in the American Economy, 1900-1952," National Bureau of Economic Research manuscript, Chap. VIII.

[12] This section is taken with small changes from "The National Balance Sheet of the United States," *Income and Wealth, Series IV*, Cambridge, Eng., Bowes & Bowes for International Association for Research in Income and Wealth, in press.

TABLE 3

Trends in Financial Interrelations Ratio, United States, 1850-1952

	FINANCIAL INTERRELATIONS RATIO			SHARE OF FINANCIAL INTERMEDIARIES	
		Components			
YEAR	*Total* (1)	*2 × Assets of Financial Intermediaries* (2)	*Remainder (Unadjusted)* (3)	*National Assets* (4)	*Financial Interrelations Ratio (Unadjusted) (per cent)* (5)
1850	.45	...	...	...	...
1880	.50	...	...	...	...
1900	.81	.41	.40	.11	.51
1912	.87	.48	.39	.13	.55
1922	.96	.56	.40	.15	.58
1929	1.24	.70	.54	.16	.56
1933	1.22	.81	.41	.18	.66
1939	1.21	1.00	.21	.22	.83
1945	1.73	1.36	.37	.24	.79
1949	1.24	1.00	.24	.21	.81
1952	1.08	.91	.17	.22	.84

Column		Source
1, 2	1850, 1880:	Very rough preliminary estimates.
	1900-1949 :	Raymond W. Goldsmith, *A Study of Saving in the United States*, Vol. III, Princeton University Press, 1955, Part I.
	1952 :	Rough preliminary estimates.
3	1900-1952 :	Column 1 less column 2; therefore understated by $(a/2) \times$ column 2.
4	1900-1952 :	Raymond W. Goldsmith, *The Share of Financial Intermediaries in National Wealth and National Assets, 1900-1949*, National Bureau of Economic Research, Occasional Paper 42, 1954, p. 97.
5	1900-1952 :	Column 2 divided by column 1; hence overstated by $\frac{(a/2) \times \text{column 2}}{\text{column 1}}$

intangible assets had a value of less than one-half of national wealth. This is hardly astonishing. At that time financial institutions and business corporations were still in their infancy, layering among them was almost unknown, and the dead-weight debt was negligible. It is much more remarkable—and in need of explanation—that the ratio apparently had hardly risen by 1880, although by that time commercial and savings banks had attained substantial size, railroad stocks and bonds had become common investment media, and the federal government's dead-weight debt—the legacy of the Civil War—was equal to nearly 5 per cent of national wealth.

In the last two decades of the nineteenth century the financial interrelations ratio moved to a new and considerably higher level of .8 to .9, at which it remained until the early 1920's. The rapid expansion of financial institutions in the fourth quarter of the nineteenth century and the sharp rise of security issues and security prices in its closing years, together with a slight decline in the price level of tangible assets, help to explain this increase in the financial interrelations ratio. While most of the forces raising the volume of intangible assets continued throughout the first two decades of this century, their effect on the financial interrelations ratio was now dampened by the doubling of the price level of tangible assets.[13] This rise apparently was strong enough to neutralize the sharp increase in intangibles and the creation of a dead-weight Treasury debt of nearly one-tenth of national wealth during World War I.

The second sharp upward jump, which lifted the financial interrelations ratio in a few years from 1.0 to over 1.2 in 1929, is easier to explain. It reflects primarily the "frenzied finance" of the late 1920's with its unprecedented rise in the level of stock prices, far beyond the current value of the underlying assets of corporations, and its sharp increase in the extent of layering among financial institutions and other corporations, all in the face of stability in the general price level.

The absence of movement of FIR between 1929 and 1939—even in the depth of the depression in 1933—again is a little perplexing, but probably is the result of offsetting tendencies. There was, on the side of increasing the ratio, the expansion of financial intermediaries after 1933, partly reflecting an increase in the federal government's dead-weight debt from approximately 5 to 10 per cent of national wealth. There was on the opposite side the collapse of the inflated level of stock prices as well as a considerable shrinkage in the volume of private debt. These movements in the volume of intangibles—downward from 1929 to 1933, and upward in the following six years—apparently were just of the same proportions as the decrease and recovery in the value of national wealth, which chiefly reflect changes in the price level of commodities.

[13] One might think that inflation, whether due to high dead-weight government debt or other causes, could or would produce particularly high FIR's. Their emergence, however, is prevented by the fact that open inflation also increases the current value (replacement cost) of tangible assets, and does so probably more rapidly than intangible assets grow. It is only in the case of large-scale suppressed inflation, a combination not likely to endure for long and one not yet encountered in the United States although approached in 1945, that extraordinarily high financial interrelations ratios may be expected.

Between 1939 and 1949 the financial interrelations ratio underwent the sharpest increase and the sharpest decrease of which we have knowledge. The jump from 1.2 in 1939 to a peak of 1.7 in 1945 is, of course, chiefly a reflection of war inflation, which increased the Treasury's dead-weight debt by $250 billion or 60 per cent of prewar national wealth, and increased national assets still more since a large part was placed with financial institutions and thus appears two or more times in the national balance sheet. This alone would have lifted FIR considerably. In addition, the rise in the current (replacement) value of tangible assets was held down by price controls and other devices accompanying a semisuppressed inflation. The decline in the ratio between 1945 and 1949 is to a considerable extent the effect of the belated rise in the general price level which brought it more nearly into equilibrium with the expansion of the supply of money during the preceding period. From 1945 to 1949 the volume of intangible assets expanded by only $120 billion (the dead-weight debt actually declined by about 2 per cent of national wealth), while the value of national wealth increased by $330 billion, almost one-half of which was the result of a rise in the price level.

The further, though much slower, decline in FIR for the period between 1949 and 1952, which reduces the ratio to not much more than 1 and thus brings it back to the lowest level since the mid-twenties, can probably be regarded as the tail end of the movement that started after the end of World War II. The increase in intangible assets of approximately $200 billion again was below the rise in the value of national wealth by $300 billion, but the absolute and the relative size of the difference were considerably smaller than in the 1945-1949 period.

Marginal FIR, i.e. the ratio of the increase in total assets between two bench-mark dates to the increase in national wealth, moved as follows:

1850-1880	.47	
1880-1900	1.11	1.30 (1880-1939)
1900-1912	.95	
1912-1922	1.04	
1922-1929	2.13	
1929-1933	1.28	
1933-1939	1.18	
1939-1945	2.92	1.02 (1939-1952)
1945-1949	.40	
1949-1952	.60	

Marginal FIR thus was reasonably stable at a level of slightly above 1 from 1880 to 1939 with the exception of only the late 1920's. It was at unprecedentedly high levels during World War II, the only period of suppressed large-scale inflation which this country has experienced. The low ratios of the last seven years may be nothing but the reaction to the spurt of 1935-1945, as marginal FIR for the entire period from 1939 to 1952 (or from 1929 to 1952) is on nearly the same level as the average of the preceding fifty to sixty years.

The FIR of the United States thus shows three characteristics (more intensive analysis will probably disclose others): (1) a generally rising trend over the last century; (2) movements in sharp steps rather than along a smooth curve; and (3) a tendency to remain on a level or to decline—particularly in comparison with the secular upward trend—while commodity prices rise, and to rise in periods of stable or declining prices. (The main exception to the third characteristic, the sharp rise in the ratio during World War II, reflects large-scale semisuppressed inflation.)

These characteristics will be better understood if FIR is split into two components,[14] the ratio of twice financial intermediaries' assets to national wealth and the ratio to national wealth of the inter- and intragroup intangibles of all other groups. The results are shown in columns 2 and 3 of Table 3. Two facts should be remembered: first, the ratio of financial intermediaries' assets to national wealth is less unreliable than the two other ratios, particularly than the ratio of inter- and intragroup intangibles of nonfinancial business, households, and government; second, the first of the two components into which FIR has been divided is somewhat overstated and the second understated. The overstatement of column 2 is due to its being entered at $2 \times (A_f/T_n)$, using the notation and argument of section 2, instead of at $(2 - a)(A_f/T_n)$, a generally being of the order of .2. The understatement of column 3 reflects both this omission of a from column 2 (since column 3 is the residual of columns 1 and 2) and the omission from the national balance sheet of loans among individuals and some other intangibles not involving financial institutions as holders or debtors. The effect of these two adjustments, though each of them is of moderate size, on the share of financial intermediaries in FIR is substantial. Thus the adjusted share of financial intermediaries in 1952 may be estimated at 75 per cent instead of the unadjusted value of 84 per cent, and the ratio of

[14] See page 128 above.

intangibles excluding financial intermediaries to national wealth, i.e. the second component of FIR, at .25 to .30 instead of .17. Major trends are not affected by this adjustment.

This split discloses the striking fact—which cannot be wholly or even mainly attributed to shortcomings of the figures—that the proportion of financial intermediaries' assets to national wealth has shown a pronounced upward trend since the turn of the century (a trend known also to have been present in the second half of the nineteenth century) whereas the ratio of other intangibles to national wealth has moved erratically—this may partly be due to shortcomings of the statistics—and has tended downward since the thirties. In the United States it is thus the growth of financial intermediaries' assets relative to national wealth that has dominated the movements of FIR.

There is no opportunity here to attempt an explanation of the reasons for the trends and fluctuations of shorter duration in the two components of FIR. Such an attempt will be made for the ratio of financial intermediaries' assets to national wealth in a forthcoming monograph dealing with these institutions.[15] The data are probably too scarce and as yet too little explored to do the same for the ratio of other intangibles to national wealth. Suffice it to suggest that the latter ratio is strongly influenced by the price movement of common stocks, which constitute the largest intangible asset in which financial intermediaries are not or are only little involved (see peak of the ratio in 1929); by the vagaries of individuals' holdings of dead-weight government debt (see the bulge of 1945); and by the apparently downward trend in the relative importance of business accounts receivable.

CHANGES IN RELATIVE IMPORTANCE OF DIFFERENT TYPES OF FINANCIAL INTERMEDIARIES

There are at the present time in the United States approximately two dozen reasonably distinct types of financial intermediaries, each of which can be regarded as an organized channel through which funds flow from savers to investors or among financial institutions, viz. (1) the Federal Reserve System, (2) commercial banks, (3) mutual savings banks, (4) the Postal Savings System, (5) credit unions, (6) personal trust departments (including common trust funds), (7) savings and loan associations, (8) mortgage companies and bankers, (9) land banks, (10) investment bankers and security

[15] Goldsmith, "Financial Intermediaries . . . ," as cited.

dealers, (11) life insurance companies, (12) fraternal life insurance organizations, (13) property insurance companies, (14) closed-end investment companies (including investment-holding companies), (15) open-end investment companies (so-called mutual funds), (16) federal social security funds, (17) state and local government pension and retirement funds, (18) private (self-administered) pension and retirement funds, (19) sales finance companies, (20) personal finance companies, and (21) government lending institutions.

Only very few of these channels existed, or were of substantive importance, at the beginning of the nineteenth century. An attempt to indicate the decade in which each of the now more important institutions first appeared is made in Table 4.[16] Dating of the first appearance of a new type of financial intermediary is usually definite, though abortive or insignificant first attempts have occasionally been disregarded. To assign a definite decade to "reaching maturity," in the sense of being fully developed technically and at the same time having reached a size (naturally changing over time) that lifts the institution out of the class of as yet untried experiments or of apparent failures to develop, is, on the other hand, a most difficult task, one that cannot be done without a good deal of arbitrariness, and one that however done is likely to incur the disapproval of economic historians. Yet the distinction is one that sometimes cannot be ignored because of the long interval between the first appearance of a new financial channel and its becoming a significant part of the country's financial structure. (Savings bank life insurance, though now nearly thirty years old, has not yet reached that status. Other examples of an interval of two or three decades between first appearance and maturity are provided by mutual savings banks, credit unions, life insurance companies, and personal trust departments.)

We need note here only two features of Table 4, leaving the explorations of its details to readers interested in them.

The first of these is the pronounced gap in the introduction or maturing of new financial channels in the second half of the nineteenth century. By 1850 most of the private financial institutions that are now most important in terms of resources were already well developed in the sense of operating with techniques basically comparable to, although of course much more rudimentary and much less varied than, those of today, and of covering the entire settled area within the boundaries of the United States. This applies particularly to commercial banks, life insurance companies, and prop-

[16] This table is based on data from "Financial Intermediaries. . . ."

TABLE 4

Appearance (X) of Different Types of Financial Intermediaries in the United States

	Before 1800	*1809*	*1819*	*1829*	*1839*	*1849*	*1859*	*1869*	*1879*	*1889*	*1899*	*1909*	*1919*	*1929*	*1939*	*1949*
Central bank													X			
Commercial banks	X															
Mutual savings banks			X													
Postal Savings System												X				
Credit unions												X				
Small loan companies												X				
Sales finance companies												X				
Savings and loan associations					X											
Private life insurance companies	X															
Fraternal life insurance organizations	X															
Savings bank life insurance departments													X			
Private pension funds														X		
Federal pension and social security funds														X		
State and local pension funds												X				
Investment companies																
Closed-end													X			
Open-end														X		
Land banks													X			
Mortgage companies									X							
Property insurance companies	X															
Personal trust departments			X													
Investment bankers					X											
Government lending institutions													X			

erty insurance companies. Apart from mortgage companies, which have never played a large role in the financial structure of the United States,[17] only one financial channel expanded so much during the second half of the nineteenth century that it can practically be regarded as a new one—investment banking. This evolution, however, was crucial for the changes in the country's financial structure during this period. It meant the development of corporate securities, both bonds and stocks, into one of the most important means—and strategically if not statistically the most important one—of financing economic expansion. It also meant that the bulk of the new securities were sold through the investment banking machinery to individual buyers in this country or abroad rather than to financial institutions.[18]

The second feature is the concentration of the development of new types of financial institutions in the 1920's for private and in the 1930's for governmental organizations, particularly if attention is directed toward maturation rather than experimental beginnings. The 1920's thus saw the development of investment companies, sales finance companies, personal finance companies, and private pension funds; the 1930's the rise of federal social security funds and federal lending institutions.

Table 4 is only a first step in understanding the changes in the financial structure of the United States during the past 100 years. It has two defects in particular—it is nonquantitative, each type of financial institution being implicitly treated as if it were of equal importance with the others, and it says nothing about changes in financial techniques and in functions and operations of institutions retaining their formal identity. The second defect cannot be remedied here except in issuing the warning that such changes in techniques have been common and that they have been particularly pronounced since the 1930's, when the lack of entries in Table 4 might give the erroneous impression of absence of changes in financial structure. It may suffice to point to the development of direct placement of securities, lease-back arrangements, competitive bidding for securities, government-guaranteed mortgages, and a secondary market for

[17] It may even be that these companies, or some similar organization, go back to the late eighteenth century. See H. Parker Willis and Jules I. Bogen, *Investment Banking*, Harper, 1929, p. 175.

[18] In 1900, financial institutions (excluding personal trust funds administered by banks and trust companies) held approximately 25 per cent of corporate bonds and 3 per cent of stock outstanding (*The Share of Financial Intermediaries in National Wealth and National Assets, 1900-1949*, as cited, Chap. 3, Tables 14 and 16).

mortgages to forestall such a conclusion. The lack of quantitative data on changes in financial structure in Table 4, on the other hand, can be remedied, though only to a minor extent as space is limited.[19] Indeed, all that can be done here is to look briefly at the distribution of the total assets of financial intermediaries among the main groups of institutions and at the structure of their assets and liabilities. The first set of figures will show changes in the relative importance of different financial channels, while the second set, to be discussed in subsection 3, tells us something—though far from enough—about changes in the function of the different institutions and in financial channels.

The relative importance of the main groups of financial institutions, insofar as it is measured by their total resources, has shown at least three major trends during the past century, which can be followed in Table 5:

1. The share of commercial banks has declined considerably and almost continuously. In the middle of the nineteenth century the resources of commercial banks were approximately three times as large as those of all other financial institutions put together. By 1900 commercial banks still had slightly more assets than all other financial institutions. Another half century later their share in the resources of all financial intermediaries was down to not much over one-third. Since commercial banks combine the functions of money creation (check deposits) and cloak-room banking (savings deposits), and do so to a degree varying over time, and since the share of equity in total assets decreased considerably—from over two-fifths in 1850 to less than one-tenth in 1950—it is not easy to appraise this trend. In comparison with the assets of all financial intermediaries, bank capital undoubtedly declined precipitously during the 100 years ending in 1950 (from as much as 30 per cent in 1850 to 3 per cent in 1950), savings deposits increased between 1900 and 1950 (from 6 to 9 per cent) and probably did not change much in the preceding fifty years, while demand liabilities (including circulation) declined considerably between 1900 and 1950 (from 37 to 25 per cent) after probably having slightly increased between 1850 and 1900.

2. Insurance institutions have gained in importance, particularly since the 1930's. They accounted for less than one-seventh of the

[19] The subject is dealt with more extensively in "Financial Intermediaries . . . ."

TABLE 5

Distribution of Assets of Financial Intermediaries in the United States, 1850-1949
(*per cent*)

Institution	*1850*	*1880*	*1900*	*1912*	*1929*	*1939*	*1949*
Federal Reserve banks	—	—	—	—	3.5	9.8	10.5
Commercial banks	75.0	58.0	54.5	54.9	42.9	34.0	36.4
Mutual savings banks	7.0	15.0	13.2	10.1	6.4	6.1	5.0
Banking system[a]	82.0	73.0	67.7	65.0	52.9	50.5	52.7
Life insurance companies	3.0	9.0	9.7	11.5	11.8	15.6	14.3
Property insurance companies	5.0	5.0	2.6	2.5	3.1	2.5	2.9
Private retirement and pension funds	—	—	—	—	.3	.5	1.6
Government retirement and pension funds	—	—	.1	0	.9	3.2	9.0
Insurance	8.0	14.0	12.3	14.1	16.2	21.9	27.7
Savings and loan associations	...	...	2.7	2.4	4.8	2.7	3.4
Personal trust departments	...	...	16.3	17.6	19.4	18.0	11.6
Miscellaneous private[b]	...	...	1.0	.9	6.5	3.2	1.9
Government lending institutions	—	—	—	0	.2	3.8	2.8
Miscellaneous	10.0	13.0	19.9	20.9	30.9	27.7	19.7
Total	100.0	100.0	100.0	100.0	100.0	100.0	100.0

[a] Includes postal saving.
[b] Includes investment and investment holding companies, mortgage companies, land banks, and credit unions.
Source: 1850, 1880: Extremely rough estimates; 1900-1949: Raymond W. Goldsmith, *The Share of Financial Intermediaries in National Wealth and National Assets, 1900-1949*, National Bureau of Economic Research, Occasional Paper 42, 1954, p. 39.

assets of all financial intermediaries in 1912, but are now approaching one-third.

3. Public financial intermediaries have likewise risen in importance, particularly if the Federal Reserve banks are put in this category. Their share in total assets of financial intermediaries was insignificant until World War I, but now amounts to almost one-eighth excluding and over one-fifth including the Federal Reserve banks. These figures, of course, are not adequate indicators of the impact of government on the financial structure since they cannot take account of the effect of government guarantees, particularly of the guaranteeing of a large fraction of all mortgage loans outstanding; or of government regulation of many features of financial transactions, e.g. through the rules governing the investment of the funds of most types of financial institutions and many aspects of corporation finance and trading in securities.

CHANGES IN FINANCIAL CHANNELS

1. *Changes in Sources and Uses of Funds by Financial Intermediaries.* The structure of assets and liabilities of all financial

intermediaries taken together, which gives a clue to the sectors from which they draw funds and the sectors to which they make funds available, is shown in Table 6, though only for the past fifty years.

TABLE 6

Structure of Assets and Liabilities of Financial Intermediaries, United States, 1900-1949
(*per cent*)

	1900	*1912*	*1929*	*1939*	*1949*
Cash	15	13	11	22	16
U.S. government securities	4	2	6	20	41
State and local government securities	6	5	5	6	4
Corporate bonds (including foreign bonds)	13	16	14	12	9
Corporate stock	5	8	14	10	7
Mortgage loans	20	20	20	14	11
Short-term loans	28	29	23	10	9
Tangible assets	5	4	3	4	1
Other assets	4	2	5	2	2
Total assets	100	100	100	100	100
Equity	18	18	20	13	13
Liabilities to households	55	57	54	56	59
Liabilities to business	11	11	7	7	7
Liabilities to government	1	2	2	3	3
Liabilities to banks	7	7	5	10	7
Unclassified liabilities	8	5	12	11	11
Total liabilities and net worth	100	100	100	100	100

Source: Raymond W. Goldsmith, *The Share of Financial Intermediaries in National Wealth and National Assets, 1900-1949*, National Bureau of Economic Research, Occasional Paper 42, 1954, Table 8, p. 45.

Several changes in financial channels can be inferred with reasonable confidence from these figures:

a. An increasing proportion of total funds of financial intermediaries has been channeled to the federal government. This trend reached its peak in 1945 when one-half of the assets of financial intermediaries consisted of United States government securities. Seven years later the share had fallen back to not much over one-third.[20]

b. Mortgage loans, mostly made available to finance urban residential construction, have accounted for a declining share of all funds supplied by financial institutions—one-fifth from 1900 to 1930, but not much over one-tenth in 1949.

[20] Figures for 1945 and 1952, not shown in Table 6, will be found in "Financial Intermediaries. . . ."

c. The most pronounced relative decline has occurred in the financing of business, the share falling from approximately one-half of total assets of financial intermediaries in 1900 to one-fourth in 1949. The decline in funds made available directly to business, however, has been much sharper in short-term loans than in purchase of business securities in the open market or through direct placement.

d. Most of the funds with which financial intermediaries operate have always been supplied by domestic households. The share of business has shown a slightly declining trend from fully one-tenth in 1900 to 7 per cent in 1949.

These trends are the results of a combination of the accounts of more than a dozen different types of financial intermediaries, some of which have shown considerable variations in behavior. More adequate inferences on changes in financial channels from the balance sheets of financial intermediaries would require separate treatment of the main intermediaries, which is out of the question in a short paper like this.[21]

2. *Changes in Distribution of Intangible Assets between Financial Intermediaries and Other Groups.* A more significant indication of the nature of financial channels and changes in them is given by the proportion of the main types of intangible assets held by financial intermediaries. These figures, summarized in Table 7, indicate the division of holdings of these assets between financial intermediaries and all other groups taken together—i.e. in the case of securities and mortgage loans, primarily nonfarm households. They do not by themselves measure, or even approximate, the share of intermediaries in financing the various sectors of the economy. To do so sources-and-uses-of-funds statements would have to be available for protracted periods. What little information is now available on this point will be reviewed below.

The outstanding feature of Table 7 is the increasing share of financial intermediaries in almost all important types of intangible assets since at least 1900, and probably since the middle of the nineteenth century, though detailed quantitative evidence has not yet been worked up for the period from 1850 to 1900. This increase is most pronounced in the case of corporate bonds. By 1900, financial intermediaries had provided only one-third of this form of financing for corporations. Fifty years later their share approached seven-eighths. Combining all financing through securities and mortgages,

[21] For basic data and some discussion see "Financial Intermediaries . . . ," Chap. IV.

TABLE 7

Share of Financial Intermediaries in Selected Intangible Assets, United States, 1900-1949
(*per cent*)

	1900	*1912*	*1929*	*1939*	*1949*
A. Including Personal Trust Departments					
Bonds	42	41	50	73	72
United States government	54	67	52	80	69
State and local governments	60	54	54	69	77
Corporate (including foreign)	35	36	48	66	86
Stocks	8	10	14	23	24
Preferred	7	10	19	33	37
Common	8	9	14	22	22
Mortgage loans	55	66	67	70	72
Farm	37	47	59	76	67
Nonfarm	65	78	69	69	72
Short-term loans	35	45	45	.	40
Short-term business loans	27	35	27	.	30
B. Excluding Personal Trust Departments					
Bonds	34	33	36	59	64
United States government	54	67	47	73	63
State and local governments	51	45	34	46	53
Corporate (including foreign)	26	28	33	46	77
Stocks	3	2	6	8	9
Preferred	1	1	6	16	20
Common	3	2	6	6	7
Mortgage loans	37	53	61	64	70
Farm	19	34	53	69	66
Nonfarm	47	65	63	63	71
Short-term loans	35	45	45	.	40
Short-term business loans	27	35	27	.	30

Source: Raymond W. Goldsmith, *The Share of Financial Intermediaries in National Wealth and National Assets, 1900-1949*, National Bureau of Economic Research, Occasional Paper, 42, 1954, p. 51, and worksheet data.

which together account for the bulk of all long-term financing, the share of financial intermediaries increases from less than one-third from 1900 to 1929 (not much over one-fourth if personal trust departments are excluded, as the trustees have only limited control over the funds) to three-fifths in 1949 and to still well over one-half without personal trust departments. The institutionalization of financial channels which these figures reflect and measure is one of the outstanding characteristics of the changes in this country's financial structure over the past century.

3. *Sources of Financing of Main Sectors.* Probably the most important single characteristic of financial channels is the distribution of total sources of funds among internal funds and external funds

with the latter subdivided into institutional and other funds.[22] It is this subdivision which determines, or reflects, the demand for funds that appears in the market—internal financing obviously generates no such demand, but quite on the contrary may increase the supply of funds unless fully invested in tangible assets—and which also indicates to what extent external funds have taken the detour through financial intermediaries in reaching borrowers and issuers of securities.

If the first half of this century is taken as a whole—a procedure permissible only provisionally because of the great differences in the economic character of subperiods—it appears that less than one-fifth of the total net asset expansion of farm and nonfarm households, less than one-third of that of state and local governments and of unincorporated business enterprises, but three-fifths of the net asset expansion of nonfinancial corporations required external funds, i.e. had to go through financial channels (Table 8). In the case of the federal government the excess of current expenditures over current income has been so great, i.e. internal financing has been negative to such an extent, that external financing through the sale of government securities is almost four times as large as total financing. Combining these six sectors, it appears that saving (retained net income) has financed a little less and external financing a little more than one-half of net asset expansion; and that slightly more than one-half of external financing or approximately 30 per cent of net asset expansion has been provided by financial intermediaries. These are the relations shown in Table 8; like all calculations of this type, they are only rough approximations.[23] Table 8, however, also provides a comparable breakdown of the sources of financing for seven periods of five to twelve years' duration. It will immediately be seen that there have been considerable changes in sources of financing from period to period, some of which are

[22] The calculation can be performed on a gross or a net basis, i.e. internal funds may include or exclude capital consumption allowances. If the financing of gross capital expenditures is under study, the gross approach is the one to be used. In an analysis of net asset changes, however, net expenditure figures are appropriate.

[23] It should be noted that Table 8 eliminates capital gains and losses from income and hence from internal financing, and is based on replacement cost depreciation allowances which in this period are higher than the customary original cost allowances so that internal financing represents a smaller proportion of net asset expansion (which, of course, excludes revaluations) than it would if the conventional treatment had been followed.

TABLE 8

Sources of Financing of Main Sectors of United States Economy, 1901-1949
(*per cent*)

SECTOR	INTERNAL FINANCING (1)	EXTERNAL FINANCING: *Total* (2)	EXTERNAL FINANCING: *By Financial Intermediaries* (3)	EXTERNAL FINANCING: *By Others* (4)	TOTAL FINANCING (5)
		A. 1901-1949			
Nonfinancial corporations	38	62	23	39	100
Unincorporated business	70	30	12	18	100
Agriculture	85	15	7	8	100
State and local governments	71	29	21	8	100
Federal government	—264	364	228	136	100
Nonfarm households	86	14	8	6	100
All sectors	47	53	29	24	100
		B. 1901-1912			
Nonfinancial corporations	33	67	24	43	100
Unincorporated business	67	33	53	—20	100
Agriculture	43	57	24	33	100
State and local governments	49	51	21	30	100
Federal government	50	50	6	44	100
Nonfarm households	88	12	9	3	100
All sectors	61	39	18	21	100
		C. 1913-1922			
Nonfinancial corporations	40	60	18	42	100
Unincorporated business	78	22	22	0	100
Agriculture	7	93	43	50	100
State and local governments	37	63	28	35	100
Federal government	—349	449	145	304	100
Nonfarm households	86	14	7	7	100
All sectors	51	49	19	30	100
		D. 1923-1929			
Nonfinancial corporations	28	72	29	43	100
Unincorporated business	31	69	21	48	100
Agriculture	110	—10	1	—11	100
State and local governments	60	40	20	20	100
Federal government	528	—428	—14	—414	100
Nonfarm households	73	27	15	12	100
All sectors	62	38	19	19	100
		E. 1930-1933			
Nonfinancial corporations	78	22	13	9	100
Unincorporated business	166	—66	47	—113	100
Agriculture	51	49	28	21	100
State and local governments	4	96	67	29	100
Federal government	—126	226	232	—6	100
Nonfarm households	—767	867	645	222	100

(cont. on next page)

TABLE 8 (cont.)
(*per cent*)

SECTOR	INTERNAL FINANCING (1)	EXTERNAL FINANCING Total (2)	By Financial Intermediaries (3)	By Others (4)	TOTAL FINANCING (5)
All sectors	94	6	13	−7	100
		F. 1934-1939			
Nonfinancial corporations	128	−28	36	−64	100
Unincorporated business	143	−43	−48	5	100
Agriculture	106	−6	6	−12	100
State and local governments	129	−29	22	−51	100
Federal government	−55	155	96	59	100
Nonfarm households	78	22	0	22	100
All sectors	42	58	38	20	100
		G. 1940-1945			
Nonfinancial corporations	62	38	6	32	100
Unincorporated business	97	3	4	−1	100
Agriculture	108	−8	−6	−2	100
State and local governments	129	−29	8	−37	100
Federal government	−351	451	289	162	100
Nonfarm households	98	2	1	1	100
All sectors	16	84	52	32	100
		H. 1946-1949			
Nonfinancial corporations	49	51	27	24	100
Unincorporated business	75	25	34	−9	100
Agriculture	84	16	8	8	100
State and local governments	64	36	26	10	100
Federal government	−81	181	132	49	100
Nonfarm households	78	22	15	7	100
All sectors	76	24	14	10	100

Source: Raymond W. Goldsmith, "Financial Intermediaries in the Saving and Investment Process in the American Economy, 1900-1952," National Bureau of Economic Research manuscript.

rather erratic. The main trends stand out more clearly if we disregard the periods affected by wars and the Great Depression.

Column 3, the share of intermediaries in total financing, is possibly the ratio of most interest for a study of the capital market. In what might be called "normal" periods (1901-1912, 1923-1929, 1934-1939, 1946-1949) financial intermediaries have provided between one-fourth and one-third of total net financing of nonfinancial corporations. Their share has been somewhat lower, but also fairly regular, in providing funds to state and local governments. Fluctuations are too wide and irregular to show anything like a normal level or a trend for the other groups, except possibly for nonfarm households, for which the increasing recourse to institutions in financing the acquisition of houses and consumer durables has led to a rise from less than one-tenth before 1922 to one-seventh in the 1920's and after World War II.

4. *International Sidelights*

This section, I am aware, should discuss statistical measures of financial structure in other advanced countries in a manner similar to the treatment accorded to the United States in the preceding section. That, alas, has been impossible, partly for lack of data and partly for lack of time. There is only one country—the Netherlands—for which a national balance sheet comparable in approach and in detail to that constructed for the United States exists, but it is available for only two recent dates (1939 and 1947-1948). For Great Britain there are the somewhat rougher statements which Professor Hicks has put together for 1932-1934 and 1947-1949. For all other countries one would have to start practically from scratch with occasional estimates of national wealth as the only substantial help. In this situation it is entirely out of the question to present a systematic comparison of measures of financial structure of the main advanced countries over the last 50 to 100 years. It is not even possible as yet to calculate FIR and its main components for all or most advanced countries at any one recent date, though approximations could in most cases be made if one were willing to devote the necessary time to the task. But such comprehensive coverage is probably not required to obtain a preliminary picture of the quantitative characteristics of differences in financial structure among advanced countries and the main changes in such structures since the end of the nineteenth century. It may suffice for that purpose to look at a few examples which, it is hoped, on the one hand will illustrate situations of long-term economic equilibrium, using the years 1913 and 1938 as the last instances of an approach to such a state of affairs in the Western World; and on the other will demonstrate the effects of "abnormal" situations such as inflation followed by currency reform (Germany in 1925-1929 and 1948-1951) or of war losses and war debts without monetary reform (Great Britain and the Netherlands in the late 1940's).

Because I regard whatever figures I shall use in this section as purely illustrative I do not feel called upon to indicate in detail the sources and methods from and by which they have been derived as I would if I intended to make a contribution to the financial history of the various countries used as examples. I hope, nevertheless, that the order of absolute and relative magnitudes of the figures is correct, and that they are sufficiently reliable for the limited use that is made of them. If nothing else, the attempt to do work of this type to a little more exacting standard for one country would keep me from making any further-reaching claims for what follows.

AVANT LE DELUGE (THE WORLD OF 1913)

For many people, including I should think not a few economists, the world of 1913 has the attraction that always attaches to a "Golden Age"—an attraction that grows the further that age recedes into the past. Standing at the end of what was truly *saeculum mirabile*, if economic progress is the test, the years immediately before 1914 represent possibly the last period in which something like long-term equilibrium prevailed. At the same time the period is close to the earliest date at which the system of check deposits and multiple credit expansion, corporate predominance in major industries, and large-scale investment banking, the triad which characterizes finance or security capitalism, had been fully developed for a sufficiently long time—in most countries for one or two generations—to be "mature."[24] It is, therefore, doubly interesting to see how the financial structure of the advanced countries looked in 1913, even if this can be done at the moment only in a superficial and in some respects an impressionistic way.

What Table 9 provides is indeed only a rough and unduly simplified picture, but I doubt whether better basic data—for which there is a crying need—would invalidate the conclusion that the level of FIR was approximately the same for the United Kingdom and Germany, viz. a little below 1, and was only slightly lower for the United States and lower still for France. Similar rough estimates could probably be prepared for a few other advanced countries for which estimates of national wealth are available, but I have not had the time to examine the relevant financial statistics.

Among components of FIR, one was reasonably similar among countries—the share of the assets of the banking system in national

[24] The word is used here not in the derogatory sense of stagnation and senescence that has recently been attached to it by politicians but simply in the sense of an economic society which has passed the experimental stage and has reached a stable institutional pattern.

TABLE 9

The Financial Interrelations Ratio and Its Components before World War I, Selected Countries
(*as ratio of national wealth*)

	United States (1912)	*United Kingdom (1913)*	*Germany (1913)*	*France (1913)*
1. Intangible assets (FIR)[a]	.82	.95	.95	.70
2. Assets of banking system[b]	.16	.12	.14	.10
3. Assets of other financial institutions	.04	.08	.15	.05
4. Government debt outside financial institutions	.02[c]	.04	.07	.10
5. Domestic business securities outside financial institutions	.28	.18	.09	...
6. Mortgages outside financial institutions	.04	...	.08	...
7. Foreign investments (gross)[d]	.04	.26	.09	.16

[a] Includes other intangibles not covered in lines 2 through 7, particularly business receivables. Does not include proprietors' equity in unincorporated business; hence differs for United States from Table 3.

[b] Central, commercial, and savings banks.

[c] Government securities alone are zero.

[d] Includes gold, direct foreign investments, and foreign investments held by financial institutions.

wealth and assets.[25] France again showed the lowest ratio.[26] On the other hand, differences were pronounced in the absolute level and the relationships of the shares of other financial institutions, government debt held outside of financial institutions, business securities, mortgages, and foreign investments. It is, of course, just these differences that reflect the variations of financial structure among the four countries.

The share of financial institutions other than banks varied from approximately .05 in the United States and France to .08 in the United Kingdom and .15 in Germany. The particularly high German ratio was due to the existence of a well-developed system of mortgage banks and credit unions—two types of institutions which are virtually unknown in the Anglo-Saxon countries, where some of their functions are discharged by commercial and savings banks, and are of considerably smaller relative size in France. Differences in the share of life insurance companies tended in the opposite

[25] It will be remembered that this ratio (as does line 3) enters FIR at nearly twice the value shown in line 2.

[26] The differences are considerably smaller if national assets rather than national wealth are used as denominator. In that case the ratios are .06 for France against .06 for the United Kingdom, .07 for Germany, and .08 for the United States.

direction. Their share was relatively high in the United States and the United Kingdom and relatively low in Germany and France.[27]

The differences are easiest to explain in the case of holdings of government securities outside of financial institutions, primarily holdings by individuals. Here the contrast is between the United States, with only very small intangible assets of this type, and the three European countries, with ratios varying from approximately .04 (United Kingdom) to .10 (France). This difference reflects primarily variations in the ratio of total government debt to national wealth or assets[28] since at that time only a minority of that debt was held by financial institutions. One must be careful, however, in drawing inferences from the figures as they stand. The British and French government debts had been incurred mainly by the central government and were largely the result of military expenditures. Most of the German government debt, on the other hand, had been contracted by the Laender and much of it had been used to finance the acquisition and expansion of the country's government-owned railway system.

Differences were apparently marked and significant in the share of domestic business securities (primarily corporate stocks and bonds), but the estimates for this component of national assets unfortunately are particularly precarious, subject to incomparabilities among countries,[29] and missing for France. It is nevertheless unlikely that better figures would basically modify the conclusion to be drawn from Table 9 that the importance of domestic business securities among national assets and in relation to national wealth was higher in the United States than in Europe, and among the three European countries was much higher in the United Kingdom than in Germany, France probably ranking last. One reason for these differences is the larger share of business done by corporations in the United Kingdom and particularly in the United States compared with the Continent, but if the figures are even roughly cor-

[27] It amounted to approximately .04 (of national wealth) in the United Kingdom, .03 in the United States, .02 in Germany (.03 including social insurance organizations), and not much over .01 in France.

[28] The share of total government debt in national assets was less than .03 in the United Kingdom, .05 in Germany, and .08 in France.

[29] The American ratio is based on the market value of corporate securities and the face value of corporate bonds; the German one on the market value of corporate stock and the face value of corporate bonds and capital of G.m.b.H.'s (organizations similar to British private companies); the British ratio is based on the face value (rather than the market value) of capital of public and private companies, and thus is too low.

rect other factors must have been at work which I have not had an opportunity to examine.[30]

The largest differences, finally, appear in the share of foreign investments and they are certainly not due to a statistical mirage, rough as the figures are. The ratio of foreign investments (gross, including gold) to national wealth was only .04 in the United States against ratios of approximately .09 in Germany, .16 in France, and .26 in the United Kingdom. These figures cannot be used as measures of the contribution of foreign investments to FIR without some downward adjustment since some foreign investments are held by financial institutions (and hence are already included in lines 2 or 3 of Table 9) and others consist of tangible rather than intangible assets. But even after such adjustments the differences among countries would still be very great and the relations among the ratios for various countries would probably not be much different from those shown in Table 9.

Finally, to show how large differences in financial structure may hide behind the same FIR, and to warn about the indiscriminate use of the ratio, a comparison will be made between the United Kingdom and Germany, using aggregate FIR as the basis:

	United Kingdom	*Germany*	*Difference*
Total	.95	.95	—
Banking system (2 ×)	.25	.29	−.04
Life insurance (2 ×)	.07	.04	+.03
Other financial institutions (2 ×)	.10	.28	−.18
Government debt	.04	.07	−.03
Mortgages	small	.08	(−.05)
Domestic business securities	.19	.09	+.10
Foreign investments	.27	.10	+.17

GREAT BRITAIN

Up to World War I, or at least until close to the end of the nineteenth century, Great Britain occupied in the world of finance a position similar to the one held by the United States since the end of World War II, and possibly since as early as the 1920's—that of the leading financial power, whose methods to a considerable extent set the tone and the standard. It is, therefore, very regrettable that we are not yet in a position to provide an adequate quantitative

[30] The share of agriculture in total national assets is a factor obviously negatively related to FIR since agriculture is only rarely conducted in corporate form except in colonial areas. This factor helps to explain the low FIR for France and the United States in comparison with the United Kingdom, but makes the high FIR of Germany more remarkable.

picture of the financial structure of Great Britain at its zenith. However, Hicks' statements of national assets and wealth, available for 1932-1934 and 1947-1949,[31] provide a starting point for a picture of the British financial structure under the influence of the Great Depression and World War II and permit useful comparisons with the United States.

TABLE 10

Selected Characteristics of Financial Structure, United Kingdom and United States, Selected Years (*as ratio of national wealth*)[a]

	UNITED KINGDOM			UNITED STATES		
	1913	*1932-1934*	*1947-1949*	*1912*	*1933*	*1949*
1. Intangible assets (FIR)[b]	.95	1.45	2.60	.82	1.20	1.22
2. Assets of banking system[c]	.12	.25	.60	.16	.20	.25
3. Assets of insurance organizations	.04	.10	.16	.03	.09	.12
4. Assets of financial institutions (2 ×)	.40	.80	1.60	.40	.66	.90
5. Government debt outside financial institutions	.04	.16	.50	.02[d]	.07	.11
6. Domestic business securities outside financial institutions	.18	.30	.30	.28	.36	.18
7. Total government debt	.05	.41	1.20	.04	.13	.33
8. Foreign investments (gross)[e]	.26	.21	.11	.04	.06	.07
9. Share of financial institutions in FIR	.42	.55	.62	.49	.56	.73

[a] Except for line 9.
[b] Does not include proprietors' equity in unincorporated business; hence differs for United States from Table 3.
[c] Central, commercial, and savings banks.
[d] U.S. government securities alone are zero.
[e] Includes gold, direct foreign investments, and foreign investments held by financial institutions.

The figures, as they are arranged in Table 10, seem to be good enough, notwithstanding their numerous and all too obvious shortcomings—not Hicks' fault—to justify the following conclusions:

1. Both in 1913 and in 1933 the FIR of the United Kingdom was only slightly above that of the United States. In 1949, however, the British FIR was more than twice as high as the American, and this was the result exclusively of a rise in the British ratio.

2. The rise in the British FIR between 1933 and 1948—as well as the smaller advance from 1913 to 1933—is due primarily to a sharp increase in the dead-weight debt ratio coupled with a moderate increase in national wealth (which would be transformed into a decline if account were taken of the rise in the price level), an in-

[31] J. R. Hicks, *The Social Framework*, Oxford, Clarendon Press, 1942, p. 103; 1952, p. 109.

crease which in turn reflects the effects of two World Wars on domestic tangible assets and particularly on net foreign assets.

3. The components of FIR that have increased most in both countries, though much more so in the United Kingdom, are bank assets and government securities held outside financial institutions, both reflections of the growth of dead-weight government debt.

4. The share of all financial intermediaries in FIR has increased in both countries, and virtually to the same extent—rising from slightly less than one-half in 1913 to two-thirds in the late 1940's.

5. In both countries the share of assets of insurance organizations has increased steadily and strongly. It is now four times as high as in 1913 both in the United Kingdom and in the United States.

6. Foreign assets (including gold) have contributed a declining component of FIR in the United Kingdom, but constitute a rising though still very small share in the United States.

FINANCIAL STRUCTURE, INFLATION, AND CURRENCY REFORM—THE GERMAN CASE

Changes in the financial structure of Germany over the last half century are of particular interest because they show more clearly than developments in any other advanced country the effects of inflation and of currency reform accompanied by a radical *seisachtheia*, and not once but twice. Again although the figures that can be hastily put together from outside the country are very approximate, Table 11 suggests the following conclusions:

1. In 1913, after half a century of rapid economic development, Germany's FIR was quite similar to those of the United States and the United Kingdom at slightly less than 1, but the share of financial intermediaries in FIR was considerably higher.

2. Two years after the first currency reform, i.e. at the end of 1925, FIR at .35 was abnormally low for an advanced country. However, it was even lower at the end of 1948, half a year after the second and still more radical currency reform. At that time FIR was only slightly above .20, and a large part of this small ratio was attributable to the assets of the central bank, reflecting essentially the provision of the economy with a new currency.

3. Both post-reform levels of FIR were obviously not compatible in the long run with the operation of an advanced economy. Hence in both cases a rapid increase in FIR occurred. However, the ratio was still far below the 1913 level six years after the first and four years after the second currency reform when the economy had been

TABLE 11

Selected Characteristics of Financial Structure, Germany, 1913-1951
(*as ratio of national wealth*)[a]

	1913	*1925*	*1929*	*1938*	*1948*	*1951*
1. Intangible assets (FIR)	.95	.35	.65	.80	.22	.40
2. Assets of banking system[b]	.14	.06	.12	.17	.06	.09
3. Assets of insurance organizations	.03	.01	.02	.04	.01	.01
4. Assets of financial institutions (2 ×)	.57	.20	.45	.60	.16	.28
5. Government debt outside financial institutions	.07	.02	.04	.03	.01	.02
6. Domestic business securities outside financial institutions	.09	.06	.09	.07	.02	.04
7. Mortgages outside financial institutions	.08	.01	.02	.02	.01	.01
8. Total government debt	.10	.05	.07	.07	.05	.05
9. Share of financial institutions in FIR	.60	.57	.69	.75	.73	.70

[a] Except for line 9.
[b] Central, commercial, and savings banks.

fairly completely restored in a physical sense. Indeed, notwithstanding considerable further expansion of the financial network after the Great Depression, FIR in 1938, i.e. fifteen years after the first currency reform, was still slightly lower than before World War I.

4. As in the United States and in the United Kingdom, the share of financial intermediaries in FIR increased from 1913 to the present time, but much less pronouncedly. Although the 1913 share was higher than in the United States or in the United Kingdom, the present share is on the same level as in the two other countries.

5. The effects of the two inflations are particularly visible in the ratio of the assets of insurance organizations. The long-term trend toward an increase in the ratio was obviously also at work in Germany, but it was sharply interrupted twice by inflation and currency reform. As a result, the ratio at the middle of the century was still well below the 1913 level.

6. The sharp expansion in the proportion of dead-weight government debt to national wealth and national assets, which is characteristic of developments in the United States and the United Kingdom in the twentieth century—as well as in most other advanced countries—and which is largely responsible for the rise in FIR and the increase of the share of financial intermediaries in it, is entirely absent in Germany. Twice a very heavy national debt was piled up, but twice it was almost entirely eliminated.

THE NETHERLANDS

This short list of "case studies" in national financial structure may be brought to a close with the Netherlands for the reason, already mentioned, that even though it is not as large or typical an economy as the United States, Great Britain, Germany, or France, it is the only country which seems to have a national balance sheet very close in concept and detail to that used in section 3 for the United States. The comparison, unfortunately, must be limited to the late 1930's and 1940's as no attempt seems to have been made to draw up a comparable statement for the Dutch economy at an earlier date. Table 12 shows the relevant figures.

TABLE 12

Selected Characteristics of Financial Structure, Netherlands and United States, 1939 and 1947-1949
(*as ratio of national wealth*)

	NETHERLANDS		UNITED STATES	
	1939[a]	*1947*[b]	*1939*	*1949*
1. Intangible assets (FIR)[c]	1.00	1.60	1.20	1.22
2. Assets of banking system[d]	.10	.35	.25	.25
3. Assets of insurance organizations	.06	.12	.09	.12
4. Assets of financial institutions (2 ×)	.32	.94	.82	.90
5. Government debt outside financial institutions	.10	.29	.07	.11
6. Domestic business securities outside financial institutions	.14	.17	.28	.18
7. Mortgages outside financial institutions	.11	.05	.04	.03
8. Total government debt	.13	.64	.17	.33
9. Foreign investments (gross)[e]	.30	.28	.10	.07

[a] Based on J. B. D. Derksen, *A System of National Book-keeping Illustrated by the Experience of the Netherlands Economy*, National Institute of Economic and Social Research, Occasional Paper x, 1946, p. 19.

[b] Based on *Statistische en Econometrische Onderzoekingen*, 1949, pp. 9 ff.

[c] Does not include proprietors' equity in unincorporated business; hence differs for United States from Table 3.

[d] Central, commercial, and savings banks.

[e] Includes gold, direct foreign investments, and foreign investments held by financial institutions.

In 1939, FIR was slightly lower for the Netherlands than for the United States, due chiefly to the relatively smaller size of assets of the banking system. Claims against insurance organizations and corporate securities (chiefly stocks) held outside financial institutions were also of less importance in the Netherlands. Foreign investments, as well as mortgages and government debt held by individuals, on the other hand, bulked considerably larger.

At the end of 1947, in the midst of the reconstruction following World War II, FIR for the Netherlands had sharply risen to approximately 1.60, well above the United States ratio for 1949 of 1.22. The higher value of FIR is due primarily to the higher dead-weight debt ratio in the Netherlands, which in turn is partly attributable to heavy war damage compensation claims accounting for 12 per cent of tangible assets. The relatively heavy weight of government debt affects FIR twice: first, by raising the holdings of government debt by households and business (Table 12, line 5); and second, by increasing the assets and deposits of the banking system (line 2). Of the other components of FIR two, business securities held outside financial institutions and the assets of insurance institutions, are practically equal in both countries. The third and smallest component, mortgages held by households and business, is considerably more important in the Netherlands than in this country, because in the Netherlands most mortgages are still held by individuals, while they are found mostly in institutional portfolios in the United States.[32, 33]

If allowance is made for this greater dead-weight debt, which is largely a legacy of World War II, the national financial structure of the Netherlands is thus seen to be essentially similar to that of the United States with one important exception—foreign investments constituted only a very small proportion of national assets or national wealth in the United States, but were of great importance in the Netherlands.

5. *In Place of a Conclusion*

This paper, it must be admitted, has not shed much light on the influence of financial structure on economic growth. All that we can possibly derive from the cursory review of changes in financial structure of the leading "advanced" countries reflected in certain ratios derived from national balance sheets are suggestions of a few trends in finance that have accompanied economic growth in Western communities since the industrial revolution:

1. The financial interrelations ratio, i.e. the ratio of intangible assets to national wealth, has shown a secular tendency to rise.

[32] Total mortgages are of equal importance in both countries—7 per cent of national wealth.

[33] Another item of considerably larger weight in the Netherlands in 1949 is tax accruals, which are estimated at 13 per cent of national wealth (3 per cent for business and 10 per cent for households) against only 2 per cent in the United States. This item reflects extraordinary tax arrears and unpaid installments on two capital levies.

2. Advanced countries since the turn of the century rarely have shown FIR of substantially less than 1.

3. A high FIR—say, in excess of 1½—has been found only in connection with a large dead-weight government debt, i.e. after prolonged and expensive wars.[34]

4. Before the Industrial Revolution, intangibles took the form predominantly of loans among individuals, unincorporated business enterprises, and governments. Financial intermediaries were almost entirely absent. The first intermediaries to acquire substantive importance—measured by their assets in comparison with national assets—were banks of issue. Commercial banks (banks of deposit) followed. In the first century after the Industrial Revolution—i.e. in Western Europe and North America until approximately the middle of the nineteenth century—financial intermediaries other than banks remained small and played only a subsidiary role in the financial structure.

5. Since statistics have been available, i.e. since late in the nineteenth century, the share of the banking system in national assets and its contribution to FIR have had a tendency to decline.

6. Within the banking system the proportion of assets held by the central bank of issue generally shows a declining trend. Both this trend and the decline in the share of the banking system in national assets mean that the same monetary base has come to support a larger financial superstructure. They also mean that money creation through the banking system has lost in importance as a method of financing. These tendencies, however, have been reversed during wars.

7. The share of insurance organizations, both private and public, in FIR has tended to rise.

8. The status of an "advanced" country is compatible with quite different financial structures in the sense of differences in the ratio (to national wealth or national assets) of the assets of financial in-

[34] The rise in prices of tangible assets that generally accompanies large-scale war expenditures might be thought to prevent a substantial increase in FIR. It should be remembered, however, that an increase in government debt held by financial institutions leads to at least twice as large an increase in the absolute value of national assets, and that usually part of the total government debt during a war is absorbed outside of the banking system and does not result in an increase in the money supply. Indeed, it would be only if the money supply were increased by the full amount of the government debt that, abstracting from changes in velocity of circulation and volume of real output, the value of tangible assets could be assumed to increase in the same proportion as the money supply with the result that the increase in dead-weight debt would not lift FIR.

stitutions and of government debt, business securities, and mortgages held outside financial institutions. Apparently, however, no country has moved into the "advanced" category without a banking system of substantial size (say, with assets of at least one-tenth of national wealth), without corporations' accounting for a large part of all business done, with a high level of interest rates (say, in excess of 5 or 6 per cent for high-grade bonds), while it was undergoing secular inflation, without a substantial ratio of national saving and capital formation (say, at least one-tenth), and unless a substantial proportion of business expansion has been financed out of retained earnings.[35]

Even if it should turn out that all or virtually all advanced countries have, during the twentieth century, actually met the tests set forth above, it still would have to be established that the same tests have not also been met by less advanced or "underdeveloped" countries.

COMMENT

EDWARD S. SHAW, Stanford University

The general subject of Goldsmith's paper is the connection between the level of capital formation and the channels and practices by which investors obtain access to financial resources. The initial question posed is the connection between physical assets and the debts and claims to which the accumulation of physical capital (and other activities) has given rise. The principal measure of this relationship, which the author considers an index of financial maturity, is the financial interrelations ratio and certain of its statistical components. These indexes express the national net accumulation of debts as a ratio of the value of physical assets. They pertain exclusively to the structure of balance sheets, bypassing both flow patterns and price relationships, two varieties of index which, we all know, have been used more commonly to measure financial maturity.

Goldsmith's second objective is to show that a country which is relatively mature in its accumulation of physical assets is also

[35] The last four characteristics have not been substantiated in this paper. Evidence on interest rates is hardly required; that on the national saving and capital formation ratio will be found in Kuznets' paper. There really is not enough material for a considered statement on the share of self-financing for more than a few advanced countries and for more than a few periods, or on the share of corporations in business done.

mature in its financial accumulation, in the sense that its FIR is relatively high and that at least some of its components tend to fall into a distinct pattern. One of his results is that "Since the turn of the century, advanced countries rarely have shown FIR of substantially less than 1"; another is that in advanced countries financial intermediaries other than banks tend to gain an increasing share of total financial assets. Goldsmith does not indicate whether and, if so, how physical maturing and financial maturing are mutually stimulative.

The study is rewarding to the rest of us in various ways. It is a prime example of empiricism, based on the premise that "naturally" an examination of the links between finance and growth "should run in quantitative terms." It provides ingenious indexes for measuring financial development both aggregatively and partially. It suggests fascinating new insights into economic history and historical methodology. It pinpoints important instances in which long-run and short-run analysis must be concurrent. While its own objective is limited, references to the larger work indicate that important analytical developments are under way there.

The first issue on which one might attempt constructive criticism is dead-weight debt. Goldsmith's general definition is this: dead-weight debt increases national assets in a combined balance sheet, but does not directly affect the level of national wealth in a consolidated balance sheet. The statistical definition is more restricted, apparently including only the outstanding debt of national governments. His central conclusions regarding dead-weight debt are that it bears a high proportion to national assets and national wealth in most advanced countries and that it is largely responsible for the complex and powerful network of financial intermediaries in advanced countries.

May I suggest, first, that "dead-weight debt" is an ambiguous category of debt. It is always perilous analytically to try to match increments in specific debt forms with increments in specific assets. Moreover, any of the usual definitions of dead-weight debt leaves one at a loss as to how to classify debt in many specific cases. What of private debt incurred in hyperinflation that results only in price advances rather than in increases in the substance of wealth? What of private debt incurred simply to improve liquidity? My question is whether dead-weight debt is really identifiable for quantitative analysis.

Is dead-weight debt really dead? It is arguable that the existence of government securities in some circumstances relieves private borrowers of the need to issue their own securities for the purchase of physical assets. If public debt were not as high as it is, private debt might be higher. Is the public debt dead if it displaces live private debt?

In other cases outstanding public debt provides collateral or secondary reserve without which private debt would not be issuable for financing tangible assets. If it were not for the "dead" debt, there could not be as much "live" debt. I doubt whether conceptually or statistically securities can be put into two boxes marked dead and alive.

In his present paper Goldsmith indicates some uncertainty in the theoretical aspects of public debt. At one point (footnote 6) he suggests that the issue of public debt in large amounts is invariably accompanied by inflation, with or without lag, possibly in sufficient degree to lower FIR—the ratio of financial assets to tangible assets. At a later point (page 3, especially footnote 34) he concludes that high FIR's are found only in connection with large public debt, and denies that government borrowing is likely to bring inflation adequate to stabilize or lower FIR. A country becomes financially "advanced" if it has had heavy public borrowing and if the effect of this dead-weight debt on FIR is not erased by inflation in commodity prices. We are told that the demand for government securities at a stable price level is both a function of the stock of real wealth and not such a function.

These issues of dead-weight debt seem to call for theoretical meditation before statistical measurement. Although I have not meditated seriously about debt theory, I recommend discarding the "dead-weight" concept in favor of some other way of classifying securities.

I am confident that in his larger work Goldsmith will infuse some of the life of demand and supply analysis into his study of financial growth processes. It is interesting to speculate about, and even to examine empirically, the needs and desires of both buyers and sellers that have created markets for the accumulating mass of securities. Goldsmith tells us that securities do accumulate; that they are diversified in changing patterns and dispersed in changing proportions among various holders; that the accumulation, diversification, and dispersion can be measured; and that these measures can be put alongside those of physical accumulation. He has taken this mechanical step so expertly that one anticipates keenly what he will have to say about the economics of financial accumulation.

Financial assets would not accumulate in real-value terms if there were not willing holders. Financial intermediaries would not multiply if there were not a real demand for their services. They are not simply layers in a pyramid of security issuers and owners; they have distinctive services to sell. Where does the demand for these services come from, and is their emergence a part of the growth process? Accumulating securities are in effect the capital equipment, or part of it, for certain service industries. How do profitable opportunities arise for these industries?

To begin with, one may speculate that physical accumulation and rising real income per capita generate effective demands for money balance in notes and deposits, for savings media that do not require managerial skills, for insurance of property and life and health. In other words, rising real income generates demand for services of such financial intermediaries as commercial banks, savings banks, and insurance companies. Equalization in income distribution may tend to shift the balance of personal demand for savings media away from stocks and bonds and mortgages to, say, insurance policies, government securities, and savings and loan shares. Thus the general public releases stocks and bonds to insurance companies and savings banks so that the latter can provide savings media that cater to the popular taste. Again, cyclical instability may intensify the public's demand for security in the form of unemployment insurance or gilt-edge vehicles for saving, opening market opportunities for insurance companies, pension funds, and savings banks.

Rising FIR and a proliferation of financial layers, then, are partly a response to real demands for new services. These demands are generated in the growth process. To a degree they may develop comparably in different countries, but one should also expect their complex and changing pattern to reflect peculiar aspects of the growth process country by country. My impression is that an early effort to incorporate them in a tentative theory of growth would lead to some interesting experiments in assembling and manipulating statistics.

Here and there in Goldsmith's paper one finds tantalizing suggestions that there are equilibrium levels and disequilibrium levels for his financial ratios. There are hints that forces can be identified which tend to restore an equilibrium once disturbed. Thus he speaks of FIR ratios that are not "compatible in the long run with the operation of an advanced economy." He refers to "situations of long-term economic equilibrium" in which presumably FIR's are not distorted by recent spurts in dead-weight debt. One has the impression that Goldsmith may have thought more than he admits of economic forces that are somehow regulated by the reserve ratio of real assets to paper assets. In his present paper, analysis of equilibria and disequilibria seems to be inhibited by the working principle that investigation of the role of finance in growth "naturally should run in quantitative terms. . . ."

Experimentally, one might hypothesize that at any given stage of development in per capita real income in any given institutional setting there is a normal FIR. At any higher stage of development this same FIR would be too low—below equilibrium. At any lower state of development it would be too high—above equilibrium. Goldsmith warns us that these normal levels cannot be identified, except possibly for 1913 and 1938, but he seems to feel that they may exist.

What happens in disequilibrium? How, for example, is a subnormal FIR corrected and with what consequences for both the real rate of growth and the financial rate of growth? This may be a matter of pressing interest, since in Goldsmith's tables 1952 seems to be a subnormal year in the United States. A subnormal FIR can be raised by a flurry of security issues, by a boom in security prices, or by a fall in reproduction costs of real assets—i.e. by an inflation of financial assets or a deflation of real assets. To put it another way, either interest rates can be forced down to inflate security prices and stimulate security issues, or interest rates can be put high and commodity prices forced down to deflate real production costs and retard the rate of real accumulation. Goldsmith's data seem to say that 1880 and 1922 as well as 1952 were years of subequilibrium FIR's. After 1880, security issues and prices rose notably. The sequel was repeated in the 1920's. Let us hope that the possible imbalance of 1952 will be corrected in the same way rather than by a goods deflation. The present Treasury view in this country appears to prefer the latter solution.

An excessively high FIR may indicate a complex imbalance that induces debtors and creditors to adjust debt and asset positions. The correction comes, as Goldsmith illustrates, by debt cancellations, by deflation of security prices, by inflation of commodity prices. Given time, such an imbalance might be corrected by the relatively slow processes of real economic growth. That is, an economic system might grow up to a high FIR. The likelihood is, though, that inflation would have to be held in check during the growing-up period by price controls and allied devices.

As a minor aside, reasoning about the equilibrium value of FIR might help to solve an old puzzler, When is a debt a burden? The answer may be that debt is burdensome when it is either too large or too small in relation to the value of real assets. It is not burdensome when FIR is at equilibrium level for the given stage of development. If an equilibrium level of FIR is conducive to economic growth, society may tolerate, even need, not only a rising total of debt but a rising ratio of debt to wealth and income.

Goldsmith comments that FIR has risen not continuously but by jumps. There may be something in the physiology of growth that requires this; or there may be some discontinuities in Goldsmith's statistics; or the considerable variation in the length of intervals in his table may be responsible for it. But the explanation could also be that some of the FIR values are close to the equilibrium trend line and others are more or less remote from it. A time series including disequilibrium values should hardly be expected to cling closely to a smooth trend curve. The values of FIR for 1880, 1922, 1945, and 1952 might well be significant deviations from equilibrium values.

I have been suggesting that one way to think about the role of finance in economic growth would be to define the implications of an equilibrium level of FIR, to study the sources of disequilibrium, and to work out the nature of adjustments that restore equilibrium. Monetary theory, as we know it, may have been a rather good approximation of this kind of analysis when money constituted a larger proportion of outstanding securities and when banks were relatively more important as sources of finance than they are now. Goldsmith's data bring out the relative decline of money among financial assets and of banks among financial institutions. I take this to mean that traditional monetary theory is in need of reorientation. Perhaps it should be renamed "debt theory" or "financial theory," taking for its area of competence supply and demand functions for all securities including money. Its responsibility would be to examine the nature of market equilibrium and the processes of adjustment to disequilibrium for financial assets generally.

We may take it for granted that Goldsmith will devise other measures of financial structure and development than he presents in this fragment of his work. These particular ones, and especially FIR, are not very sensitive to the forces, perhaps some of them financial, which account for wide differences in per capita income between, say, the United States and the United Kingdom or Germany. Moreover, the differentials in income suggest that among the several countries there are significant differences in demand for the services of financial intermediaries. If this is so, there should be more evidence of it than one finds in Goldsmith's data.

A supplementary measure would be an incremental FIR. Existing aggregates of securities and of real assets are so very large that, in an average FIR, they conceal degrees of difference in rates of financial and physical accumulation. I would think, too, that some explicit use should be made of the structure and level of interest rates as a measure of financial development. On his final page, Goldsmith comments that a high level of interest rates is not congenial to financial or physical maturing. Income measurements would not be superfluous—income originating in financial activity, the relative importance of income of independent proprietors as against interest and dividends, the distribution of interest and dividends between foreign and domestic recipients, the ratio between gross and net interest, etc. One may hazard the guess that some of these measures would bring out more clearly the relative roles of finance in advanced countries. Until they have been explored, I would hesitate to accept Goldsmith's doubts concerning the role of finance in stimulating a comparatively high rate of growth in this country.

Reply by the Author

I have taken account of some of Shaw's very helpful comments quite inadequately by means of a few minor changes in the text and a couple of footnotes. Unfortunately, I cannot do anything at this time about his basic suggestion of a closer tie between the analysis of financial growth and standard demand and supply theory, e.g. by defining equilibrium levels of FIR or by connecting the level of FIR with the character of the demand for the services of financial intermediaries. Such a tie is certainly desirable, but it would call for a far-reaching expansion, rearrangement, and revision of the entire paper. This leaves just one or two comments or interpretations of Shaw's that I would not accept, although my formulation in the original draft may have been responsible for his making them.

FIR and the other measures used in the paper are at this stage quite empirical. There is no implication that a rising FIR necessarily measures the approach to financial maturity. Nor is there intention of establishing, or even asserting, that maturity in a country's accumulation of physical assets and maturity in its financial structure go together. (Indeed, I would not know how to define the former.) Similarly, there is no implication that financial maturity is necessarily connected with the existence of a large dead-weight debt. Maybe Shaw was misled as to my stand by the fact that all the advanced countries I used by way of example have at one time or another had a large dead-weight debt. But such a debt is not part of the definition of a financially advanced country. There certainly are cases of financially advanced countries having only a very small government debt, dead-weight or productive—for example, before World War I, the United States, Switzerland, and the Netherlands.

PART II

SAVINGS AND FINANCE IN THE SOVIET UNION

SOME CURRENT TRENDS IN SOVIET CAPITAL FORMATION

GREGORY GROSSMAN

UNIVERSITY OF CALIFORNIA

1. *Introduction*

THIS CONFERENCE meets thirteen months after the adoption of the *Directives on the Fifth Five-Year Plan* by the Nineteenth Congress of the Communist Party of the Soviet Union, and in the middle of the time span covered by the Plan (1951-1955).[1] Several commentaries on this and attendant documents have already appeared in Western literature.[2] It is indicative of the paucity of our information that we must inquire at the outset whether the plan is still an operational order to those who manage the Soviet economy. The stroke of fate which carried away Stalin's life early in March 1953 has reverberated to upset established balances within the Soviet polity, and to reshape the course of history on both sides of the Iron Curtain. It is inconceivable that this shock could have left the rigid structure of Soviet plans, annual and quinquennial, without need of substantial repair and overhaul.[3] It is therefore safer to view the *Directives* not as a blueprint of the impending development of the Soviet economy through 1955, but as a clue to the Soviet government's estimate, *in mid-1952*, of the possibilities of development in the *then* desired direction. The word "clue" is used advisedly, for the published document is only a brief summary of the Five-Year Plan (FYP). Considering the authorship of the document and the circumstances under which it was issued, we should

The author acknowledges gratefully the support and assistance extended by the Russian Research Center, Harvard University, to this study. Thanks are also due D. B. Shimkin for many valuable comments.

[1] The text of the *Directives* and of the report on it by M. Z. Saburov (the then chairman of the Gosplan) appear in *Pravda*, October 12 and 10, 1952, respectively. English translations in *Current Digest of the Soviet Press*, January 10, 1953, pp. 3-10, and December 6, 1952, pp. 3-8. References to the Fifth Five-Year Plan will be hereafter cited by part and section, thus: *Directives* I, 5.

[2] Among those in English see: "Moscow Has a Plan," *Twentieth Century*, November 1952; *Economic Survey of Europe since the War*, Geneva, United Nations Economic Commission for Europe, 1953, Chap. IV; "The Kremlin's Plan V," *Fortune*, February 1953, pp. 113 ff.; Maurice Dobb, "Rates of Growth under the Five-Year Plans," *Soviet Studies*, April 1953, pp. 364-386; and Peter Wiles, "The Soviet Economy Outpaces Ours," *Foreign Affairs*, July 1953, pp. 566-580.

[3] See the Postscript to this paper.

not assume that it necessarily represents an accurate and faithful summary of the complete Plan.

A third area of doubt is the "realism" of the Plan, or at least of those portions which have been revealed to us. The attainment of the targets for 1955 is predicated on great increases in the productivity of labor and equipment in industry and construction, and of labor and land in agriculture. For instance, labor productivity in industry is to rise by 50 per cent between 1950 and 1955, though this is not inconsistent with the claimed rise of 18 per cent through 1952.[4] While bearing in mind the large program for irrigation and melioration, we may be even more skeptical of the projected increases in the per hectare yields of agricultural crops: about 50 per cent for grains, potatoes, and sunflower seed, and about 25 per cent for cotton, sugar beet, and flax.[5] Since the crop targets are fully dependent on these yields, the opinion that of all portions of the Plan "the agricultural production program is the least likely to materialize" seems reasonable.[6]

With these doubts in mind, I shall discuss the implications of the Plan with respect to capital formation, emphasizing especially the trend toward much greater capital-intensity of investment. Some explanations of this trend will be offered as tentative hypotheses.

2. *Manpower and Investment in the Fifth Five-Year Plan*

One of the most interesting figures in the Fifth FYP is the projected increase of only 15 per cent in the number of workers and employees, or roughly speaking, in the non-agricultural labor force.[7] This amounts to an average annual increase of 2.8 per cent (Table 1). For industry[8] alone, the projected rate of growth in employment is apparently even lower, and can be estimated on the basis of output and productivity targets to be 13 per cent, or 2.5 per cent per year. Contrast the rates of growth of employment in the Fifth FYP with the actual record of the first two Plans taken to-

[4] *Directives*, concluding part, and *Pravda*, January 29, 1952 and January 23, 1953.

[5] See *Economic Survey of Europe since the War*, as cited, Table 19, p. 45, which is based on the *Directives* and other Soviet sources. In the case of grain the yield in 1952 was no higher than in 1950.

[6] "Moscow Has a Plan," as cited, p. 389.

[7] *Directives* IV, 1. The term "workers and employees" in Soviet usage includes a few million employed in agriculture (at state farms and machine tractor stations), but excludes nearly the same number of handicraftsmen; it also presumably excludes forced labor in camps.

[8] For the definition of industry see note a to Table 1.

TABLE 1

Workers and Employees in the U.S.S.R., Selected Years, 1928-1955

YEAR	TOTAL	INDUSTRY[a]	
		Total	*Workers Only*
	Yearly Average (*millions*)		
1928	11.6	3.87[b]	3.36[c]
1932	22.9	8.0[d]	5.76[c]
1937	27.0	10.1[e]	8.05[e]
1940	31.2	10.9[f]	8.38[g]
1941 annual plan	(32.4)[h]	(11.4)[i]	(8.81)[i]
1942 plan	(32.0)[e]	(11.8)[e]	(9.2)[e]
1945	27.3	n.e.	n.e.
1946	31.0	9.9[j]	7.6[j]
1947	32.2	10.7[j]	8.2[j]
1948	34.2	11.8[j]	9.1[j]
1949	36.0	12.6[j]	9.6[j]
1950 plan	(33.5)[k]	(11.9)[j]	(9.1)[j]
1950	38.2	13.8[j]	10.6[j]
1951	39.8	14.7[j]	11.2[j]
1952	40.7	15.1[j]	11.6[j]
1955 plan	(43.9)[l]	(15.6)[j]	(12.0)[j]
	Average Annual Rate of Increase[m] (*per cent*)		
1928-1937 (1st and 2nd FYP's)	9.8	11.2	n.e.
1937-1942 plan (3rd FYP)	3.5	3.2	2.6
1937-1940	5.0[n]	2.6[n]	1.3[n]
1945-1950 (4th FYP)	7.0	n.e.	n.e.
1947-1951	5.4	7.9	
1950-1955 plan (5th FYP)	2.8	2.5	

[a] By Soviet definition includes manufacturing, mining, electric power generation, forestry, and fishing.

[b] *Trud v S.S.S.R.* (*Labor in the U.S.S.R.*), Moscow, Tsentral'noe upravlenie narodnokhoziaistvennogo ucheta (TsUNKhU) Gosplan S.S.S.R. (Central Administration for Economic Accounting, Gosplan, U.S.S.R.), 1936, p. 11. Indicated figure is the sum of figures for large-scale and small-scale industry, forestry, and fishing, and is presumably comparable with data for subsequent years.

[c] Estimated by applying ratio of workers to all personnel in large-scale industry to employment in all industry (*Trud v S.S.S.R.*, as cited, p. 11 and Table 23, p. 93). The 1928 figure includes apprentices; hence rate of growth from 1928 to 1937 not computed.

[d] *Sotsialisticheskoe stroitel'stvo Soiuza S.S.R.* (*Socialist Construction of the U.S.S.R.*), Moscow-Leningrad, 1939, p. 138.

[e] *Tretii piatiletnii plan razvitiia narodnogo khoziaistva Soiuza S.S.R.* (*Third*

(cont. on next page)

TABLE 1 (cont.)

FYP for the Development of the Economy of the U.S.S.R.), Moscow, Gosudarstvennaia planovaia komissiia (State Planning Commission), 1939.

[f] Industry accounted for 35 per cent of all workers and employees in 1940. N. Voznesensky, *Voennaia ekonomika S.S.S.R. v period Otechestvennoi voiny* (*The War Economy of the U.S.S.R. during the Patriotic War*), Moscow, 1948, p. 109.

[g] Computed from employment, output, and productivity data in the 1941 Plan. *Gosudarstvennyi plan razvitiia narodnogo khoziaistva S.S.S.R. na 1941 god* (*State Plan for the Development of the Economy of the U.S.S.R. for 1941*), reprinted by the American Council of Learned Societies, pp. 3, 512, and 513, and adjusted as under note h.

[h] Adjusted by Eason (see the Source) for consistency with published revision of 1940 figure.

[i] *Gosudarstvennyi plan razvitiia narodnogo khoziaistva S.S.S.R. na 1941 god*, as cited, p. 512. Adjusted by the present author as in note h. The figure for "workers only" obtained by applying the same ratio of workers to total personnel in industry as indicated for a somewhat smaller coverage in the Source.

[j] Computed on the basis of scattered statements on changes in industrial output and labor productivity, ultimately linked to the 1940 figure. Productivity changes presumably refer to workers only. Total employment in industry arbitrarily assumed to move proportionately with the number of workers.

[k] *Zakon o piatiletnem plan vosstanovleniia i razvitiia narodnogo khoziaistva S.S.S.R. na 1946-1950 gg.* (*Law on the FYP for the Reconstruction and Development of the Economy of the U.S.S.R. for 1946-1950*), sec. III, 2.

[l] *Directives* IV, 1.

[m] Computed from year preceding inauguration of FYP to last year of Plan.

[n] Not adjusted for intervening changes in territory and length of work-week.

n.e. = no estimate.

Source: Warren W. Eason, "Population and Labor Force," in *Soviet Economic Growth*, Abram Bergson, editor, Row, Peterson, 1953, Table 3.3, p. 110, except as indicated by footnotes. Eason's figures are from official Soviet sources, adjusted to an annual average basis from 1945 on.

gether: 9.8 per cent per year for the whole economy and 11.2 per cent yearly for industry.[9] The Fifth FYP rates are unprecedentedly low except in relation to those of the Third FYP as originally projected and those actually achieved from 1937 to 1940, at least in the case of industry. But this latter comparison must be interpreted with caution because of the specific events which occurred in the 1937-1940 period: the territorial expansion during 1939 and 1940, the rapid conversion to munitions production during those years, and

[9] Were the First FYP taken alone, the rates would have been even higher, but it is combined with the Second FYP because the huge inflow of labor into non-agricultural employment between 1928 and 1932 was not really assimiliated and absorbed until the following quinquennium, while recruitment for non-agricultural employment during the Second FYP was accordingly lower because of this "internal" reserve of manpower. Similiarly, the increase in non-agricultural employment during the Fourth FYP was probably considerably affected in its earlier years by demobilization. Therefore, an alternative calculation covering the later years 1947-1951 is presented in Table 1.

the extension of working hours by some 17 per cent in mid-1940. However, the similarity between the planned growth over 1937-1942 and that over 1950-1955 is of some significance, especially since it extends beyond mere employment data.

The slowness of the increase in non-agricultural employment during the Fifth FYP, relative to past peacetime experience, cannot be explained by a compensating lengthening of the work-week, for no such provision appears in the *Directives*, nor is a lengthening likely, considering that the forty-eight-hour week is still in effect.[10] The question is doubly challenging because the slow rise in non-agricultural employment is to be associated with an unprecedentedly large volume of investment. Evidently, each recruit to employment outside of agriculture will be accompanied by much more new capital than during previous peacetime periods, or even than was planned for the unrealized Third FYP. Unfortunately, although the general picture is fairly clear, it is difficult to give faithful quantitative expression to this phenomenon, not only because of the usual conceptual and theoretical obstacles to the "physical" measurement of investment, but also (and especially) because of the scarcity and unreliability of Soviet data. Hence the cryptic official statements on the volume of investment will have to be supplemented by several indirect real indicators of capital formation.

The Fifth FYP explicitly calls for an increase of 90 per cent in the volume of gross fixed capital investment by the state over the five years, as compared with the preceding quinquennium, and an increase of 110 per cent in agriculture alone.[11] Since it is unlikely that in the Fourth FYP agriculture received more than a fifth of all fixed investment,[12] and an even smaller fraction of fixed investment *by the state*, presumably the increase in fixed investment outside of agriculture for the Fifth FYP period, over the preceding period, has been planned at just under 90 per cent. This seems to check with a scheduled doubling of (gross) investment in industry alone,[13] and with these planned outputs of investment goods in 1955, expressed as ratios of the respective outputs in 1950: cement, 2.2; bricks, 2.3; slate, 2.6; all building materials, "not under" 2.0; output of the machine-building and metal-working industries (proba-

[10] That is, barring the outbreak of war, in which case the Plan as revealed would be scrapped anyway.

[11] *Directives*, concluding part and II, 12.

[12] Cf. Norman M. Kaplan, "Capital Formation and Allocation," in *Soviet Economic Growth*, Abram Bergson, editor, Row, Peterson, 1953, Table 2.7, p. 52.

[13] *Directives* I, 3.

bly including munitions), 2.0; large metal-cutting tools, 2.6; equipment for iron and steel mills, 1.85; and chemical equipment, 3.3. A corollary of these figures is that by 1955 the rate of gross investment (in all forms) out of the gross national product will probably be substantially higher than it was in 1950, when it had already reached, by our very crude estimate, about 25 per cent (factor cost basis, adjusted *à la* Bergson).[14]

At the same time, the *absolute* increase in the number of workers and employees during the Fifth FYP is to be only slightly more than one-half that during the Fourth Plan period, and an even smaller fraction for industry alone.[15] Thus if the investment data are to be taken seriously and the employment targets are not understated, the (gross) "incremental" *capital-intensity* in the non-agricultural sector—defined as the volume of (gross) fixed capital investment divided by the increment in the number of workers and employees—is to be nearly four times as high during the current Plan as in the Fourth FYP period. For industry alone, the incremental capital-intensity seems to increase even more in the present period. It is likely that adjustment to a *net* investment basis, which is not attempted here, would not greatly alter the picture. The relative quality, or relative potential productivity, of an average "unit" of fixed investment in the two quinquennia should of course also be considered. It is not clear to what extent the Soviet index takes account of this element, if at all. The likelihood that an average "unit" of investment increases in its potential productivity over time thanks to the progress of technology in general, and Soviet technology in particular, must be—at least in some part—balanced against the probability of diminishing returns to capital and the depletion of some natural resources.

But comparisons with the Fourth Plan period, so greatly dominated by reconstruction, are perhaps of limited significance for a longer-run view of Soviet capital formation. Consequently, an attempt has been made to construct indicators of the capital-intensity of Soviet investment by selected periods over the whole span of time since the beginning of the Plan Era—that is, for 1928-1955. The calculations and results appear in Table 2. Aggregative ruble figures would have been of very questionable use for this purpose. Un-

[14] Cf. Abram Bergson, *Soviet National Income and Product in 1937*, Columbia University Press, 1953.

[15] Underlying data in Table 1; the exact fraction for industry is not known for lack of an employment estimate for 1945.

fortunately, physical indicators of investment common to all the periods are very scarce. Indeed, the only two series which seem to be more or less usable for the purpose are employed in the table, namely: (1) the consumption of cement during the *whole* period in question, and (2) the absolute *increase* in electric power output (or, alternatively, electric power consumption in industry) between the year preceding the period in question and the terminal year of the period. The rationale of the procedure is that cement consumption is highly correlated with total construction, which in turn is highly correlated with the "physical volume" of investment. (For the Third and Fifth FYP periods estimates of planned cement *output* are substituted for consumption, but the distortion is probably slight.) Furthermore, since the bulk of Soviet power output is consumed by producers, rather than by ultimate consumers, and since at least the share taken by industry is quite stable, the increment in electric power output can be taken as a measure of the increase in power available to the non-agricultural labor force over the period. Analogously, the increase in power consumption by industry is taken as an indicator of the power available to workers employed in industry.

On the surface it would seem that each of these two indicators contains an upward bias. The great jump in cement consumption in the current quinquennium is undoubtedly connected with the large "cement-intensive" projects of the first half of the 1950's—dams, canals, and probably airfields. In addition, housing and road construction may demand an unusually large amount of cement in the present period. The rate of growth of power output also probably exceeds the rate of growth of physical capital due to the trend toward greater electrification of production in general, and the rapid growth of electricity-using industries (e.g. aluminum). On the other hand, it is likely that, with time, cement tends to be "combined" with more productive equipment, and electric power is used to run more productive machinery (in the sense of more final goods produced by it per kilowatt-hour consumed), so that the upward bias just mentioned may be offset to an unknown degree. Note that while all gross fixed investment is supposed to increase 1.9-fold during the Fifth Plan as compared with the Fourth Plan period, cement consumption (output) is to rise 2.6-fold, and the increment in power output is to rise 1.8-fold.[16]

[16] Lines 1 and 2, columns 3 and 5, of Table 2.

TABLE 2

Indicators of Capital-Intensity of Investment, Selected Years, U.S.S.R., 1928-1955

	1929-1937 (1st and 2nd FYP's) (1)	*1938-1942 (3rd FYP) plan* (2)	*1946-1950 (4th FYP)* (3)	*1948-1951* (4)	*1950-1955 (5th FYP) plan* (5)
1. Cement consumption (or output) (millions of metric tons)	33.65[a]	(40.9)[b]	33.1	38.0	(85.9)[c]
2. Increase in total electric power output (billions of kw-h)	31.4	38.6	40.8	47.1	72.2
3. Increase in electric power consumption by industry (billions of kw-h)	21.7	26.4	n.e.	n.e.	60.0
4. Increase in total number of workers and employees (millions)	15.4	5.01	11.0	6.0	5.7
5. Increase in line 4 corrected for lengthening of work-week in 1940[d] (millions)	15.4	5.01	12.9	7.0	6.7
6. Increase in number of workers and employees in industry[e] (millions)	6.23	1.7	n.e.	4.0	1.8
7. Increase in line 6 corrected as in line 5[d]	6.23	1.7	n.e.	4.7	2.1
8. Cement consumption (output) per added worker or employee, corrected; line 1 ÷ line 5; col. 1 = 100.	100	373	117	249	587
9. Increase in power output per worker or employee, corrected; line 2 ÷ line 5; col. 1 = 100.	100	378	155	330	529
10. Increase in power consumption per worker or employee, corrected, in industry only; line 3 ÷ line 6; col. 1 = 100.	100	445	n.e.	n.e.	821

(cont. on next page)

TABLE 2 (cont.)

[a] Output minus exports.

[b] Output; figures for 1938 through 1941 obtained by straight-line interpolation.

[c] Output; 1953 and 1954 figures obtained by straight-line interpolation.

[d] Employment for years after 1940 multiplied by 1.17.

[e] By definition Soviet industry includes manufacturing, mining, electric power generation, forestry, and fishing.

n.e. = no estimate.

Note: All increases are differences between figures for last year of given period and last year of preceding period.

Source: For cement and power: *Narodnoe khoziaistvo S.S.S.R., Statisticheskii spravochnik* (*The Economy of the U.S.S.R., Statistical Manual*), Moscow, TsUNKhU S.S.S.R., 1932, p. xxxiv; *Sotsialisticheskoe stroitel'stvo S.S.S.R.* (*Socialist Construction of the U.S.S.R.*), Moscow, TsUNKhU S.S.S.R., 1936, pp. 19, 22, and 183; *Tretii piatiletnii plan razvitiia narodnogo khoziaistva Soiuza S.S.R.* (*Third FYP for the Development of the Economy of the U.S.S.R.*), Moscow, Gosudarstvennaia planovaia komissiia (State Planning Commission), 1939, pp. 202 and 205; Demitri B. Shimkin, *Minerals—A Key to Soviet Power*, Harvard University Press, 1953, Tables 95 and 100; *Economic Survey of Europe in 1951*, Geneva, United Nations Economic Commission for Europe, 1952, Table 58; and *Economic Survey of Europe since the War*, Geneva, United Nations Economic Commission for Europe, 1953, Table 17. For power consumption by industry: Table 4. For employment: Table 1.

These series are divided by the *increase* in the total number of workers and employees in the whole economy to obtain indicators of incremental capital-intensity in the non-agricultural sector. However, since the concept of capital-intensity as here used refers in some sense to the combination of the factor "labor" with the factor "capital," a further adjustment is necessary to allow for the lengthening of the work-week by the decree of June 26, 1940. The adjustment factor, applicable only to columns 3 to 5, is 1.17. Other variations in the work-week are disregarded, and it is also assumed that the Third FYP did not contemplate any change in this respect.

The ratios in question are shown in lines 8, 9, and 10 of Table 2. As has been suspected, the figures for the Fourth Plan period turn out to be unrepresentative of the trend and fall much below it, reflecting both the rapid expansion of non-agricultural employment and the setback during the war. But the years 1948-1951 already show a marked turn toward the late prewar situation, as exemplified by the unrealized Third FYP. The upward trend is resumed in the current Plan. Lines 8 and 9 suggest that each *additional* worker or employee is to be accompanied (with adjustment for working hours) during the Fifth FYP period by five to six times as great a volume of investment in fixed capital as was true during the first two Plan periods. Obviously, this is only a very rough and tentative indication of the rise in the incremental capital-intensity incidental to Soviet economic growth, though the fact of a very marked rise is hardly to be doubted. As may be expected, capital-intensity in industry alone, as suggested by increments in power consumption in industry (line 10), shows an even steeper rise from 1929-1937 to 1950-1955.

3. *Growth of the Capital Stock, 1928-1955*

The effect of a rising incremental capital-intensity in the Soviet economy is, of course, to increase with time the ratio of the *stock* of fixed capital to the amount of labor working with it. Again, satisfactory data are lacking, but some rather indirect evidence of this process may be obtained from the computations presented in Tables 3 and 4, where the consumption of power is used as a rough indi-

TABLE 3
Estimated Supply of Mineral and Hydroelectric Energy, Selected Years, U.S.S.R., 1928-1955
(*per cent; 1928 = 100*)

Year	*Total*	*Per Capita*	*Per Worker or Employee*	*Per Worker or Employee, Adjusted for Lengthening of Work-week*[a]
1928	100	100	100	100
1932	184	n.e.	93	93
1937	352	322	151	151
1940	442	348	164	152
1942 plan	650[b]	n.e.	236[b]	236[b]
1946	407[c]	n.e.	152[c]	n.e.
1950	672	510	204	173
1955 plan	998[b]	700[b]	264[b]	224[b]

[a] 1940 multiplied by .925; 1950 and 1955 multiplied by .85. No adjustment made for 1946, as the statutory work-week was probably significantly exceeded in that year.
[b] Based on planned *output* of energy, rather than on consumption.
[c] Hydroelectric power omitted in both numerator and denominator for lack of data for 1946; indexes probably slightly understated thereby.
n.e. = no estimate.
Source: Appendix Table.

cator of the capital stock on hand. Table 3 shows in index form the total energy available to the Soviet economy from mineral fuels and hydroelectric power in selected years from 1928 through 1955, figures for the latter year being planned targets. The underlying data were obtained chiefly from Shimkin's estimates of mineral consumption, converted to conventional coal units as indicated in my Appendix Table. It must be noted that not all sources of energy are comprised in the index. Fuelwood and horses (as well as other animals) are notable omissions;[17] consequently, the indices in Table 3 exaggerate somewhat the increase in the energy available to the Soviet economy. On the other hand, the omissions may be justified on the ground that our interest in energy is chiefly in its capacity as an indicator of the capital stock assisting the "workers and employees" in production. In this respect the relative importance of fuelwood and animal power is, and has been, probably quite small. Since the personnel of the machine-tractor stations and of the state farms, the "energy-using" parts of agriculture, are subsumed under the category of workers and employees, this category contains virtually all the labor force engaged in lines of activity with a substantial use of power, with the significant exception of the military.

The results of rapid economic development, as well as the setbacks caused by the war, are vividly reflected in the table. By 1950 the index of total energy consumption reached 672 (1928 = 100); and on a per capita basis, 510. However, the intervening influx of labor into "worker and employee" status has been large and the workweek lengthened somewhat, so that the annual amount of energy consumed per worker or employee only doubled, and rose by only 73 per cent on a man-hour basis. Moreover, the levels of energy consumption planned for 1942, whether per capita (insofar as they can be inferred), or per worker or employee, or per man-hour, which were implicit in the Third FYP, were reached in 1950, although total energy consumption was slightly higher. In the case of the supply of energy per man-hour the deficiency is quite large—173 versus 236. Significantly, even by 1955 the supply of energy per man-hour will not yet quite attain the level planned for 1942, if our calculations are without major error.

How faithfully do the data in Table 3 represent the "true" growth of the stock of fixed capital of the Soviet economy? Will the capital stock in 1955 (if the Plan is realized), in some meaningful sense, be in fact ten times as large as in 1928? These questions must be left open. It is curious, though, to note the close agreement between the

[17] In 1937 these two sources accounted for 11.7 and 2.9 per cent, respectively, of total energy production in the Soviet Union. Chauncey D. Harris, "Industrial Resources," in *Soviet Economic Growth*, as cited, Table 5.2, p. 169.

series in column 1 and the data given by Voznesenskii[18]—namely, that the value of fixed capital of the "socialist enterprises" of the U.S.S.R., exclusive of the value of livestock, rose as follows:

Year	*Billions of 1945 Rubles*	*Index Numbers (1928 = 100)*
1928	140	100
1932	285	203
1937	564	403
1940	709	506

For years after 1928, these index numbers are uniformly 10 to 12 per cent above the indexes of total energy supply in Table 3. If Voznesenskii's coverage were extended to include enterprises of all kinds as well as the value of livestock, this gap would probably vanish, and possibly even turn into a difference in the other direction. Unfortunately, his figures are of unknown reliability, and of course do not refer to any year more recent than 1940.

Last, Table 4 presents estimates of electric power consumption per worker in Soviet industry, with a rough correction to a man-hour basis. As may be expected, the series rise much more rapidly than those in Table 3, and, for reasons already intimated, they probably greatly exaggerate the growth of the volume of fixed capital in Soviet industry. For instance, total consumption of electric power in industry rose nineteenfold between 1928 and 1950, though it does not seem plausible that the capital stock of industry increased in a comparable ratio. But whatever the precise magnitudes involved, there is a clear suggestion in Table 4 of a rapid rise in total capital, and capital per worker, in Soviet industry.[19]

4. *Factors behind Capital-Intensity*

The preceding sections have attempted to show that the "incremental" capital-intensity, at least in the non-agricultural sector, is planned to be unprecedentedly high in the current FYP; and that at

[18] N. Voznesensky, *Voennaia ekonomika S.S.S.R. v period otechestvennoi voiny* (*The War Economy of the U.S.S.R. during the Patriotic War*), Moscow, 1948, p. 12.

[19] Contrast the data on electric power use by Soviet industry (Table 4) with the following information on the number of electric motors and their capacity "at work" in Soviet agriculture in 1950: in all agriculture, "over" 75,000 motors, 400,000 kilowatts (*Elektrichestvo*, No. 11, 1952, p. 9); on collective farms, "over" 36,000 motors, 215,000 kilowatts (*ibid.*, No. 10, 1950, p. 8). In that year there were 254,000 collective farms before their amalgamation into 97,000 larger units, and the labor force in *all* agriculture was probably over 40 million.

TABLE 4

Electric Power Consumption per Worker in Soviet Industry, Selected Years, 1928-1955

Year	*Electric Power Consumed by Industry*[a] *(billions of kw-h)* (1)	*Number of Workers in Industry*[a] *(millions)* (2)	*Power per Worker (kw-h)* *(1) ÷ (2)* (3)	*Power per Worker, Adjusted for Lengthening of Work-week* (4)
1928	3.38	3.36[b]	1,006[b]	1,006[b]
1932	8.88	5.76	1,540	1,540
1937	25.1	8.05	3,120	3,120
1940	33.4	8.38	4,000	3,690
1942 plan	51.5	9.18	5,610	4,770
1950	64.5	10.6	6,080	5,170
1952	83.2	11.6	7,170	6,090
1955 plan	124.6	12.0	10,340	8,790

[a] Industry includes manufacturing, mining, electric power generation, forestry, and fishing.

[b] Number of workers indicated for 1928 includes apprentices; thus power per worker is correspondingly understated for this year by an unknown amount, probably in the order of 10 per cent.

Column

1 For 1928 and 1932, *Sots. stroi.*, 1936, p. 28; for 1937 and 1942, *Tretii piatiletnii plan razvitiia narodnogo khoziaistva Soiuza S.S.R.* (*Third FYP for the Development of the Economy of the U.S.S.R.*), Moscow, Gosudarstvennaia planovaia komissiia (State Planning Commission), 1939, p. 43; for 1940, power consumed by industry assumed to have been the same percentage (69) of total power output as in 1937, and total output (48.3 billion kilowatt-hours) from *Economic Survey of Europe since the War*, Geneva, United Nations, Economic Commission for Europe, 1953, Table 17; for 1950 and 1952, total output from *ibid.*, share consumed by industry taken for both years as five-sevenths, as given in *Elektrichestvo*, No. 10, 1952, p. 93; and for 1955, product of columns 2 and 3.

2 From Table 1.

3 For 1955, consumption in industry per worker is planned to be 1.7 times the 1950 figure, from M. Z. Saburov in *Pravda*, October 12 and 10, 1952, English translations in *Current Digest of the Soviet Press*, January 10, 1953 and December 6, 1952.

4 1940 multiplied by .925; subsequent years multiplied by .85. Note that the increase in power consumption per worker (Column 3) from 1940 to 1955 plan checks very closely with Saburov's assertion of a planned 2.6-fold increase (*loc. cit.*); 4,000 × 2.6 = 10,400.

the end of the period, in 1955, the average Soviet worker (or worker-employee) will presumably have the benefit of a considerably larger amount of productive capital than ever before in Russian experience, as indicated by the projected consumption of electric power in industry and of mineral energy in the whole economy. This development is due not only to the large and rapidly growing volume of investment, but also (at least in part) to the retardation in the growth of the non-agricultural labor force in general, and of industrial employment in particular. In fact, it is very likely that the whole increase in the category of workers and employees is to be drawn from the natural increase in the population, and that the agricultural population is planned to remain virtually unchanged in number during the quinquennium. If so, this is apparently a new phase in Soviet planning, approximated in the past only by the provisions of the Third FYP.

To facilitate treatment, it may be postulated, probably with little violence to Soviet reality, that the decision on the share of the national product to be allocated to investment over a prospective planning period is most fundamental and has priority over all but a few of the other major planning decisions. It may be further assumed that the posited production targets in the two major sectors, agriculture, and outside of agriculture, can be achieved by a series of alternative combinations of labor and capital. An isoquant may be visualized for each of the two major sectors, with labor and capital along the two coordinates of the plane. The constraints are (1) the total amount of capital for use in both sectors (equal to the stock at the beginning of the period plus additions to it from current investment), and (2) the total labor for distribution between the two sectors. Thus choice of a position on one of the isoquants (say, the combination of capital and labor with which the non-agricultural output target is to be produced) uniquely determines the position on the other isoquant. Moreover, the same decision obviously also determines the capital-intensity, "incremental" and "average," in each sector. This is the highly schematized conceptual framework within which the subsequent discussion will proceed.

Although the distribution of investment and that of labor between the sectors of the economy are in this view mutually determined and of equal significance, the remainder of this article will discuss chiefly the problems of labor transfer within the Soviet economy, since these are probably more complex and more intractable than those of the allocation of investment funds between sectors. In particular, the possible reasons for the retardation in the growth of the non-agricultural labor force will be explored. They will be distinguished according to whether they tend to detain (or even retain) labor in uses other than non-agricultural employment—hereafter referred to as the *detentive* factors—or to deter labor from being advantageously absorbed in non-agricultural employment—hereafter called the *deterrent* factors.

5. *Detentive Factors*

The detentive factors are (1) the high goals and composition of the present labor supply in the agricultural sector, (2) the effects of the educational goals, (3) the expected reduction in the proportion of women in the labor force, and (4) the maintenance of the strength of the armed forces.

AGRICULTURE

The ambitious nature of the agricultural part of the Fifth FYP has already been noted. It is apparently planned that the gross output of agriculture will rise by something like 50 per cent over the quinquennium, based on very large expected increases in yields per hectare and per animal, and labor productivity in agriculture is accordingly scheduled to rise by 40 per cent. Although there may be serious doubt whether these goals can be attained and therefore whether the consumption targets of the plan are realistic, the regime's concern over the fulfillment of the latter may have militated against any substantial reduction in the agricultural population over these five years. It must be remembered that, under present circumstances, even a stable agricultural population implies an improvement in the labor supply in this sector. First, at present there is an exceedingly high ratio of women to men in agricultural work and especially among those actually performing field tasks. This is a result of male losses in past wars, military service, transfer to non-agricultural employment, and detention in forced labor camps. While some of these causes will presumably continue to withdraw men from agricultural employment, distortions from other causes, especially war losses, are likely to be gradually rectified with time, thus leading to a slow improvement in the "quality" of agricultural labor. Second, the large age-group born during the second half of the 1930's, between the demographic disasters of collectivization and those of World War II, will be reaching working age in the middle 1950's, thus raising the ratio of workers to dependents. But both of these factors will probably have only a limited effect within the time span of the current Plan, i.e. through 1955.

The extent to which manpower needs in Soviet agriculture at the present time retard the growth of the rest of the economy depends in part on the possibility of replacing labor by capital in this sector. The very low labor productivity in Soviet collective and state farms, as compared with productivity in American farming, for example, also suggests an extremely low marginal productivity, and therefore ample possibility for such replacement in the *long run*. Thus on examining the ratio of tractors to total *arable* area in the U.S.S.R. and other countries Dobb thinks that "there does not seem to be much sign of an early limit being reached to labor-saving improvement in agriculture" in the former, though he adds that "it is possible, however, that some slackening in the proportional (as distinct from the absolute) growth of the industrial labor-force may have to be allowed for inside the present decade" on this score.[20] He might also have pointed, in this connection, to the remaining vast potential for rural electrification.[21] But other careful students would probably attribute the low productivity largely to the specific organizational forms of Soviet agriculture, which tend to be wasteful of human and material resources and injurious to incentives,[22] and would therefore presumably be skeptical of the possibilities of releasing much agricultural labor through further mechanization.

The whole problem of the transfer of underemployed manpower from agriculture into other sectors of the economy is, of course, not independent of the costs of retraining, moving, and urbanization, as well as the actual opportunities for the substitution of labor for capital in *non*-agricultural employment. This is an extremely complex economic calculation even for a Gosplan; outside observers can do no more than raise questions.

Before leaving the consideration of agriculture as a detentive factor, it should be noted that the regime may have other than strictly economic reasons for not reducing the size of the rural population, such as maintenance of the birth rate, political (and police) control, etc.

EDUCATION

By 1955, enrollment in full-time educational institutions may cut appreciably into the labor force, and may be responsible in considerable measure for the retardation in non-agricultural employment. Most important here is the projected expansion in attendance in the last three grades of secondary education, the so-called grades eight to ten, corresponding roughly to the ages fourteen-fifteen to

[20] *Op. cit.*, p. 372. [21] See footnote 19.

[22] Cf. Naum Jasny, *The Socialized Agriculture of the USSR*, Stanford University Press, 1949, esp. Chaps. XVII and XVIII.

sixteen-seventeen. It is planned to extend education through the tenth grade to all children in the more important cities and towns, and to increase enrollment in the upper grades elsewhere as well. This is to increase total enrollment in the last three grades by 1955 to 4-fold the number in urban centers, and to 4.5-fold in rural areas, as compared with 1950.[23] The absolute numbers involved are not known, but on the basis of prewar school statistics and postwar data on total enrollment the planned *increase* of the number attending the three grades may be about 5 to 7 million.[24] In addition, enrollment in secondary *technical* schools and in institutions of higher learning is apparently scheduled to rise, judging by references to future graduations. Perhaps an increase of several hundred thousand may be anticipated on this account.

However, some of these increases may be at the expense of enrollment in the labor reserve schools for industrial training, and, of course, not all of the pupils and students in question would be in the non-agricultural labor force if not in school. Thus the net impact on employment is likely to be smaller than the above figures suggest, but still probably in the millions. This impact is greatest during the initial years, while the "stock" of pupils and students is being built up. In later years graduations and releases will presumably catch up with admissions, except for the normal growth in the school population, and the retarding effect of this factor will disappear.

HOUSEKEEPING

A very gradual drop in the proportion of women in the non-agricultural labor force may be expected in the foreseeable future. This proportion (related to the total number of workers and employees in the economy) rose during the 1930's to 40 per cent just before the war, then jumped for obvious reasons to 53 per cent in 1942, and fell only to 47 per cent in 1947. Since then there has been a slight reduction to 45.7 per cent for 1950; later postwar data are apparently not available.[25]

The expectation of a further reduction in the proportion of women

[23] *Directives* IV, 5, and Saburov, *op. cit.*, IV.

[24] In 1952 alone, it is claimed, enrollment in grades eight to ten increased by 1 million pupils, as compared with 1951. *Pravda*, January 23, 1953.

[25] All figures are taken from Warren W. Eason, "Population and Labor Force," in *Soviet Economic Growth*, as cited, Table 3.3, p. 110; they were obtained by him from Soviet sources. There may have been a temporary rise in the proportion in 1948, immediately after the currency reform.

in the non-agricultural labor force rests on a priori grounds. The most important of these is the continuous improvement in real wages and consumption standards, which may be expected to reduce the pressure for housewives to seek active employment. A gradual return of the sex ratio among adults to a more normal level is likely to have the same effect, though probably on a smaller scale.

MILITARY SERVICE

An important rival to non-agricultural employment with respect to manpower and the most uncertain and indefinite element from the point of view of an outside analyst is, of course, military service. But two factors point to *at least* a maintenance of the armed forces in a constant ratio to the total population through the current quinquennium. First, the new military classes in the middle 1950's will be larger than at the beginning of that decade, for the reason already mentioned. Second, the Fifth FYP seems to imply an expansion of the military effort[26] and may, therefore, divert at least the same amount of manpower to this use.

6. *Deterrent Factors*

The deterrent factors which tend to keep labor from being advantageously absorbed in non-agricultural employment are (1) the initial cost of transferring workers to urban communities, (2) the goal of maintaining or increasing consumption standards, (3) considerations of military strategy, and (4) the technological bias inherent in Soviet ideology. Working *within* the non-agricultural sector, these factors militate for a lesser use of labor in production, and therefore call for a higher capital-intensity in this sector in order to achieve the desired output. The non-agricultural sector is understood here in a broad sense, including, but not limited to, the urban economy in general. In fact most of the problems discussed under this rubric arise out of the costs and hazards of urbanization, rather than out of the characteristics of the production processes as such.

COST OF URBANIZATION

It seems quite possible that the initial cost of "urbanizing" workers and their families causes Soviet planners to minimize the transfer of manpower from agricultural employment to industrial and other

[26] Consider the increases in the output of aluminum, petroleum products, and other products of military significance. Cf. "The Kremlin's Plan V," as cited.

urban pursuits, and therefore to press for the substitution of capital for labor in the non-agricultural sector.

A major handicap to further industrialization seems to be the severe shortage of urban housing. In the earlier phase of its economic development the Soviet Union had been able to draw on the urban capital (chiefly housing) which it inherited from the past to an extent that was probably not fully appreciated by contemporary observers. Thus, while the urban population increased from 26.3 million at the end of 1926 to 55.9 million at the beginning of 1939, or by 112 per cent, the available urban dwelling space rose only by about 50 per cent. As a result, the urban space per capita fell from 6 square meters to just over 4 square meters, on the average. Some housing slack was acquired with the territorial annexations of 1939-1940, though it was inconveniently localized. Then came the war losses. However, by 1950 not only were these apparently made good (at least in quantity if not in quality) but enough additional space was built to keep pace with the growth of the urban population. Thus approximately the same amount as before the war, 4 square meters per capita, seems to have been available at the beginning of the Fifth FYP.[27] With this figure as an average, the situation must be considerably worse for large parts of the urban population. The regime is, by all indications, seriously concerned with the housing shortage and is making an unusually determined effort to alleviate it. But whether the current Plan in fact provides for a substantial housing improvement is not clear, for the conclusion depends on one's interpretation of the construction provisions of the Plan, and on one's estimate of the growth of the urban population to 1955.[28]

[27] The space estimates are by Timothy Sosnovy, prepared for his forthcoming book, *The Housing Problem in the Soviet Union*, and here used with the author's kind permission. The Soviet concept of dwelling space (*zhilaia ploshchad'*) excludes secondary space such as hallways, kitchens, lavatories, and closets.

[28] The Plan calls for 105 million square meters to be placed in use by the state, and an undetermined, but undoubtedly much smaller, amount by individuals (*Directives* IV, 3). However, there is evidence to the effect that the measure of space was redefined in 1948, resulting in an inflation of new construction figures. (I owe this observation to Carolyn Recht of the Russian Research Center, Harvard University, who is making a careful study of Soviet housing.) The actual increase in urban dwelling space may altogether be under 30 per cent, if the Plan materializes fully. Compare this with the scheduled increase of 15 per cent in the number of workers and employees, with probably an appreciable increase in the number of dependents (students, housewives, etc.) per gainfully employed person, as discussed in the preceding section. Hence the impression that the Plan envisages only a modest improvement in per capita urban housing space at best.

At any rate, it seems quite safe to assume that the regime rules out a further deterioration of the severe housing situation, even if greater overcrowding under peacetime conditions were thinkable. The resource has been depleted. Presumably, new migrants to the cities and towns have to be supplied with at least the existing average housing ration. This space must be newly constructed, with a corresponding claim on the state's investment resources. But capital needs do not stop here. If the already low standards of urban conveniences and necessities are not to be further diluted, additional capital has to be concomitantly invested in such facilities as streets, urban transportation, some public utilities, schools, retail outlets, and so forth. Moreover, the transfer of a given "primary" number of persons to cities or towns requires the transfer of others to service the primary migrants, and still others to service the second group, and so forth in a convergent series. The "secondary" migrants—that is, all those who "follow" the primary—will be engaged in such occupations as retail trade, urban and interurban transportation, municipal services and administration, and education. Finally, if all these people are to be recruited chiefly from among the peasants, a capital outlay by the state is also necessary at the outset to train them in their new functions and to underwrite their low productivity. Very likely also some investment is necessary in agriculture to compensate for the withdrawal of manpower from that sector.

The investment i' by the economy—that is, by the state—occasioned by the movement of an additional person to an urban location can be expressed as follows:

$$i' = [(h + f)(1 + d) + t + a](1 + s)$$

where h = capital cost of housing per person
f = capital cost of other urban facilities per person
d = number of dependents per gainfully employed
t = cost of retraining a migrant, and similar expenses
a = compensating capital investment in agriculture per worker withdrawn
s = number of "secondary" migrants per "primary" migrant.

It must be noted that in the industrialization of typical capitalist countries the capital requirement to the potential employer of raw labor did not, and does not, amount to the full extent designated by i'. True, the private employer may undertake the cost of training or retraining, and not infrequently may find it necessary or expedient to invest in housing for his personnel, and sometimes even in certain other facilities of an urban character. But he will rarely be concerned with providing the same for the "secondary" labor force, and will never be required to furnish capital to the agricultural sector in order to compensate for his recruitment of manpower. To the planners of the all-embracing Soviet state, all these are, or should be, costs of equal concern; moreover, there is reason to believe that the planners in fact do take such considerations into account.

But there is another quantity of capital, i'', which, if invested in labor-saving equipment in the non-agricultural sector, would completely dispense with the transfer of the worker from the village into the city. In an optimal situation it is the marginal rate of substitution between capital and labor along the isoquants standing for total non-agricultural output. But under actual conditions, and especially with the Soviet distinction between "leading" and other branches of the economy, the value of i'' may be expected to vary widely from one branch to another. If i'' is lower than i' in any particular line of activity, there is patently an economic case for choosing a more labor-saving, i.e. a more capital-intensive, method of producing a given output. Certain preliminary calculations made by Carolyn Recht of the Russian Research Center, Harvard University, point to a strong likelihood that in at least some instances this is the case at the present time in the Soviet economy. Unfortunately, the pertinent quantitative information is scarce, and the whole question is further clouded by uncertainty as to how meaningful Soviet accounting prices are.[29]

Considerations of this sort have apparently figured in the recent thinking of Soviet planners and economists. On the operational side much of the present expansion in the non-agricultural sector, especially in industry, seems to be taking place through the release of manpower from established production units to expanded or newly created ones, thanks to the replacement of labor by capital in the former. Malenkov specifically brought up this point in his report to the Nineteenth Party Congress.[30]

Theoretically, his question was treated in the context of optimum allocation of investment funds by P. Mstislavskii.[31] True, these

[29] Miss Recht's calculations were made for her doctoral dissertation on Soviet housing problems, in progress, and are here mentioned with her kind permission. This whole section owes much to her comments.

[30] *Pravda*, October 6, 1952, and *Current Digest of the Soviet Press*, November 8, 1952, p. 5.

[31] "Nekotorye voprosy effektivnosti kapitalovlozhenii v sovetskom khoziaistve"

sources do not discuss the relative magnitudes of i' and i'', in our symbols, but the preference for the more capital-intensive solution as against a greater influx of manpower from agriculture is perhaps implicit.

In this connection, the efforts of the Soviet Union to mechanize "labor-intensive" processes, and further to automatize production, must be noted. After the initial postwar reconstruction job was largely completed, a vigorous campaign was launched to mechanize the labor-intensive processes in industry, construction, and other branches outside of agriculture. These traditional areas of very low labor productivity in the Soviet economy—e.g. handling of materials, warehousing, inspection, and many construction jobs—are now being mechanized, or in some instances rationalized in other ways, such as through the introduction of statistical quality control.[32]

Automation, a much more ambitious undertaking than the mechanization of labor-intensive processes, is also by all evidence receiving very serious attention. The Soviet interest in automatics and allied problems dates back at least to 1934, when a Committee (later Institute) on Automatics and Remote Control (*Telemekhanika*) was established at the Academy of Sciences. The journal *Avtomatika i Telemekhanika* has appeared since 1936. The Third FYP and the resolutions of the Eighteenth Party Congress (1939) gave political significance to the development of automatics, but apparently very little was done before the war. Since the war the subject has been seriously pursued, and it is very prominent in the *Directives* for the Fifth FYP. Some results have already been accomplished, notably in hydroelectric generation (a minor field for labor-saving) and a few machining operations. But the scope of true automation so far attained is probably small, and the results likely to accrue by 1955 cannot be determined without an intensive examination of the

("Certain Questions of the Effectiveness of Capital Investment in the Soviet Economy"), *Voprosy ekonomiki* (*Problems of Economics*), No. 6, 1949, pp. 96-115; condensed English translation in *Current Digest of the Soviet Press*, March 4, 1950, pp. 12-19. Mstislavskii's contribution pertained to the quarter-century-old, and as yet unresolved, Soviet controversy on the theory and practice of choice of investment variant to achieve a desired fixed output, and the related problem of the place of interest in Soviet economic calculations. See my "Scarce Capital and Soviet Doctrine," *Quarterly Journal of Economics*, August 1953, pp. 311-343, and the bibliographical references therein.

[32] This is not the place to appraise the success of the campaign up to now. Undoubtedly, some advance has been registered in the last five or six years. What I should like to stress is the direction and earnestness of the planners' thinking.

available literature, which is not attempted here. It is quite likely that the successes to date have been chiefly of an experimental and pilot nature, so far of little impact on labor requirements. Nevertheless, the direction of thought and the intensity of interest must be noted. With time, this field may affect considerably the character of Soviet industrialization and may conceivably upset the still rather close relationship between industrialization and urbanization.[33]

A corollary of the emphasis on capital-intensive (i.e. labor-saving) modes of production, to which the cost of urbanization under present Soviet conditions may be contributing, is a more rapid rise in the productivity of labor, especially in industry. This is not to say that rising labor productivity is not a target per se, independent of the pressure of urbanization costs, but it must also be seen in the broader context of the allocation of the economy's investment resources between "overhead" and "production" capital. For this reason, as well as for many others, some of the recent appraisals of the prospects of labor productivity in the Soviet Union may turn out to be unduly negative.[34]

SUPPLY OF CONSUMERS' GOODS

The burden of maintaining desired consumption standards, or desired rates in their improvement, may also cause Soviet planners to hold down the transfer of agricultural manpower to non-agricultural, especially urban, employment. The consumption levels of the non-agricultural population (excluding, of course, inmates of concentration camps) are probably at this point (1953) appreciably higher than those of the peasants. This is probably particularly true of the per capita purchases of manufactured consumers' goods. What is more, the gap between the two has been, by all indications, steadily widening over the last few years, and will probably continue to widen, considering the doubt as to the attainability of the agricultural goals of the Fifth FYP. Given the gap, the smaller the move-

[33] In this connection, I found stimulating an unpublished paper by Richard L. Meier of the University of Chicago, entitled "Automatism in the Early Stages of Economic Development" (February 1953). Meier sees the advent of automation in industry as ushering in new opportunities for industrialization in hitherto backward areas with a minimum of social dislocation and with large savings in investment in social overhead capital. Much of his thinking is relevant to the Soviet situation. Cf. John T. Diebold, *Automation*, Van Nostrand, 1952, *passim.*

[34] E.g. Irving H. Siegel, "Labor Productivity in the Soviet Union," *Journal of the American Statistical Association*, March 1953, pp. 74 ff.

ment out of agriculture into other employment, the more consumption standards can be raised in *each* sector, other things being equal. This may correspond to the political aims of the regime, and thus may argue against a rapid increase in the category of workers and employees.

CONSIDERATIONS OF MILITARY STRATEGY

The hazard of aerial bombing in the event of war reinforces the other considerations against rapid urban agglomeration, and perhaps lends an aspect of imperativeness to them. But if industrialization goals are not to be sacrificed while the size of the urban population is held down, additional capital equipment, often expensive and complex, must replace labor. This makes the physical plant a more rewarding target to the attacker, and renders repair more difficult and more protracted in case of damage. It is hard to say where the balance is struck in the minds of Soviet planners.

However, labor-saving variants of production processes, and especially automatic processes, also have the advantage that they are less likely to be disrupted by a withdrawal of manpower during a mobilization. This holds especially true, of course, for industries of strategic importance, the "leading" branches of the economy and of industry in Soviet parlance. The preference enjoyed by these industries in the U.S.S.R. in terms of allocation of capital, modern equipment, skilled labor, etc., is perhaps understandable for this reason. Although in general the economic effect would be greatest if capital were so allocated as to equalize its marginal productivity of the factor in all uses, in the "leading" as well as in the other branches, actual Soviet practice becomes more rational than may seem the case at first glance if a correction factor, representing the probability of the particular enterprise not being operated at all in the event of war, is introduced into the calculation. Whether Soviet planners reason in these terms or not, their practice seems to produce such an effect.

TECHNOLOGICAL BIAS

The several deterrent factors discussed above militate against the transfer of manpower from agriculture into industrial and urban employment, with the implication that the productivity of labor in industry and other branches (except agriculture) must be raised by means of a greater capital-intensity of production to the levels required to achieve the desired outputs. But high labor productivity and its concomitant, advanced technical design, may be desirable in themselves or as manifestations of the technological and political achievements of the regime. Technological supremacy and high labor productivity have been an integral part of the ideology of Soviet communism since Lenin's day and have been continuously regarded as prime political goals. Moreover, individual achievements in the technical field, or even mere intentions of achievement, have been adroitly used for whipping up enthusiasm at home and earning good will abroad. Despite the condemnation of "gigantomania" in the late 1930's, there has constantly been a preference for the grandiose project and for the most advanced technical design, sometimes at excessive economic cost. Even on more modest levels economic calculation often yields to technological criteria, at least in the "leading" branches and "leading" enterprises (which are fortunate enough to be allotted the necessary means).[35] Is it not possible, therefore, that the combination of a low rate of absorption of labor into non-agricultural employment, and especially into industry, with the large volume of investment in this sector is viewed with favor because it harmonizes with the technological bias of the Soviet regime, quite apart from strictly economic calculations?

7. *Concluding Remarks*

I shall not try to divine the relative importance of the several factors, detentive and deterrent, enumerated in the last two sections. The list is undoubtedly incomplete anyway. But there is no doubt that one of the outstanding features of the Fifth FYP is a significant retardation in the rate of growth of non-agricultural employment. In this respect it is reminiscent of the Third FYP (see Table 1), which, of course, was never fully realized. There are other interesting similarities between the two Plans: in projected rates of growth of the output of all industry and of many individual commodities, in the relationship between the planned increases in the output of producers' goods and of consumers' goods, in the growth of agricultural output and of railroad traffic, and in rates of increase in labor productivity.[36]

Good reasons can be found for these similarities. In the fall of 1952 as well as in the spring of 1939—the times of adoption of the Plans—the U.S.S.R. found itself in an uneasy peace. Military needs

[35] Cf. "Scarce Capital and Soviet Doctrine," as cited.

[36] The two Plans are conveniently compared in *Economic Survey of Europe since the War*, as cited, pp. 39 and 41.

claimed much of the national product at both times (although the size and character of the military establishment were considerably different in 1952 from what they were in 1939). Each Plan was adopted six to seven years after the passing of a major disaster and after a feverish period of construction or reconstruction, marked by an unforeseeably large expansion of the non-agricultural labor force. The task of assimilating and absorbing this labor faced each of the two Plans (though the Second FYP had already done some of this for the Third). Urban consumption levels were, I believe, approximately the same in 1952 and in 1939; so was urban housing space—about 4 square meters per person. But the peasants were probably worse off in the later period. Finally, the rates of investment out of the national product were about the same at the start of each Plan; whatever advantage now accrues to the Soviet economy from a larger total product is largely offset by the heavier military burden and by the larger number of mouths to feed. But the similarity should not be pressed too far, for the absolute goals of the Fifth Plan are much larger than those of the Third FYP, the volume of investment much greater, the industrial base much broader, and the levels of technological skill higher. The figures in Tables 2 through 4 reflect some of these differences.

At the present time there is not only unprecedentedly high average capital-intensity (for the U.S.S.R.), but also extreme unevenness in technological advance and in labor productivity. Within certain limited areas of the "leading" branches of the Soviet economy, labor productivity is probably quite comparable with, and sometimes possibly even exceeds, the accepted levels in the United States, thanks to modern equipment, mass production, incentive pay, sufficient training, and pressure from all the agencies of the state. Moreover, in these limited areas Soviet technologists and scientists are undoubtedly pushing against the frontiers of knowledge, with the aid of Western achievements, largely available to them, and of their own not inconsiderable talents. It would be wrong in my estimation, however, to view these areas as typical of the Soviet economy, however much Soviet propaganda would so desire. Walter Galenson's computations of productivity relative to American levels show a wide difference between individual industries, with machine-building and iron-and-steel industries yielding the highest, and consumers' goods industries the lowest, ratios.[37] These computations pertain to

[37] "Industrial Labor Productivity," in *Soviet Economic Growth*, as cited, pp. 202 ff., esp. Table 6.8.

the late 1930's. If an analogous investigation were possible for the present, Soviet industries would probably show a similarly wide range of labor productivities relative to the American.[38] Moreover, smaller organizational units—individual shops or operations—would exhibit an even greater variation in the relative levels of labor productivity. Greater contrasts than those within Soviet industry can hardly be found, and, for that matter, the same is true for contrasts between industry and agriculture in the U.S.S.R.

The regime is well aware of this general picture,[39] and, like any inefficiency, low labor productivity presents a challenge and a potential for improvement—the inefficient group "hiding" a "reserve" in Soviet parlance. Moreover, this reserve has a considerable advantage over a pool of underemployed manpower in agriculture inasmuch as it is already within the urban environment, is presumably provided with housing and other facilities at the existing norms, and has been exposed to techniques. It is made up mainly of workers who are now being supplied with additional capital equipment and are gradually being reshuffled over the non-agricultural sector.

However, the consequences of a high planned incremental capital-intensity are not limited to a beneficial effect on labor productivity. Other problems arise simultaneously, such as the creation of a spectrum of skills required by the higher level of mechanization, and an appropriate replacement policy for equipment. To date, the prevalent attitude of Soviet writers (though less of engineers than of economists) has been to deny the existence of an obsolescence problem in the Soviet economy. The position has been dogmatic, but perhaps not without some merit under conditions of extreme shortage of equipment in relation to the demands of the Plans. However, if the stress is now about to shift to modernization, in order to permit the release of labor with low productivity to man the new production lines, a more flexible attitude on replacement will undoubtedly be required. It will be interesting to watch the Soviet response and, especially, its theoretical underpinnings.

The discussion so far has assumed that both the volume of investment and the desired bill of goods for the prospective period are given, and has revolved essentially around the question of the optimum capital-intensity (ratio of capital to labor) in each sector,

38 *Ibid.*, pp. 207-210.

39 Cf. Malenkov's complaint of the low productivity in certain areas of industry at the Nineteenth Party Congress. *Pravda*, October 6, 1952, and *Current Digest of the Soviet Press*, November 8, 1952.

i.e. of the best allocation and distribution of the available investment resources and labor over the economy. It has been suggested that problems of labor transfer are more difficult and complex than those of the distribution of investment funds, and the possible reasons behind the provisions of the Fifth FYP has been therefore treated primarily from the side of labor allocation. However, the available volume of investment resources and the production targets are of course not independent postulates for planning, but are mutually defined in their broader outlines. Thus it is quite possible that the retardation in the expansion of non-agricultural employment, and the rising capital needs required to assist the transfer of manpower and to replace labor, might explain the small but perceptible retardation in the rate of growth of industrial output indicated by the Fifth Five-Year Plan. The average yearly rate for *all* industry called for by the Plan is 12 per cent. The rates already realized within this period are, by Soviet claim:

Period	*Per Cent Increase*
1950-1951	16
1951-1952	11
1952-1953 (first halves)	10

Compare these rates with past rates as recomputed by Hodgman:[40]

Period	*Per Cent Increase per Year*
1927/1928-1932	14.5
1932-1937	16.6
1927/1928-1937	15.7
1946-1950	20.5

(The rate of growth during 1946-1950 was, of course, favorably affected by the reconstruction character of most of the period.) Other reasons for the slowing down of industrial expansion can be adduced, and Dobb in his analysis of this question does not assign causal significance to the small increase in non-agricultural employment.[41]

Furthermore, the element of rationality in Soviet economic development should not be overstressed. Not all the major decisions are

[40] D. R. Hodgman, "Industrial Production," in *Soviet Economic Growth*, as cited, p. 242. Hodgman's index is essentially one of *large-scale industry*; extension to *all* industry would somewhat lower his figures. The official claims of industrial growth have of course been very much higher and are generally considered by American students to be inflated. However, the new Soviet index, in effect apparently since 1950, may contain little upward bias, if any (cf. Alexander Gerschenkron, "Reliability of Soviet Industrial and National Income Statistics," *The American Statistician*, April-May 1953, p. 19).

[41] *Op. cit.*, pp. 376 ff.

the result of "scientific social engineering"; ideological constraints and technological biases play their part. To put it another way, not everything is calculated with paper and pencil in hand. To a large extent the Fifth Five-Year Plan is probably a resultant of numerous autonomous forces, a compromise between several political factions and scores of bureaucratic leviathans within the body of the regime. These forces have a dynamic of their own, and a full understanding of the Plan requires the knowledge of this dynamic, which is unfortunately denied the outside observer.

Postscript

The preceding lines were written in July 1953. It is known now (March 1955) that productivity in industry and construction has not advanced at the pace foreseen in the Fifth FYP, though claims are made that industrial production targets have been met on the whole. Accordingly, the number of workers and employees by the end of 1954 already exceeded the goal for the end of 1955, and the urban population is probably growing more rapidly than anticipated. These developments must be seen in the context of the far-reaching measures, especially with regard to agriculture, that have been introduced since Stalin's death.

As a result of these changes, the Fifth FYP—in the sense of a definite and detailed document—may be pronounced dead, though its demise has not been officially subscribed. The new measures are too far-reaching not to affect significantly every major part of the Plan for the remainder of its life span. However, it would be easy to overrate the deflection in the economic course which has taken place since March 1953. There is no evidence that the larger trends have already suffered significant reversal or change. The Soviet Union is apparently continuing to invest at a very high rate in relation to its product and in very large absolute volume, to raise rapidly the amount of capital supplied to each industrial worker, to press for large technological gains, and to push up labor productivity with all the means at its command. In these respects, as in most others, the same range of means is employed as heretofore, and the institutional structure has hardly been affected. More fundamentally, the potentials for development and the limitational factors inherent in the Soviet economy must have outlived Stalin, and are now guiding the thought and shaping the actions of his successors. Hence, although this paper may now pertain to a historical rather than a living and operational document, its relevance to an analysis

APPENDIX TABLE

Supply of Mineral and Hydroelectric Energy, U.S.S.R., Selected Years, 1928-1955
(*millions of metric tons, except as indicated*)

	1928 (1)	*1932* (2)	*1937* (3)	*1940* (4)	*1942 Plan* (5)	*1946* (6)	*1950* (7)	*1955 Plan* (8)	*Factor to Convert into 1 Million Tons of Conventional Coal* (9)
				In Natural Units					
1. Coal, bituminous and anthracite	31.9	55.7	108.3	142.5	230.0	124.0	215.0	372	.907
2. Lignite	3.05	6.91	17.6	23.5		48.0	62.7		.486
3. Peat	5.32	14.79	23.8	32.1	49.0	28	42.4	53.8	.41
4. Petroleum	8.60	15.24	26.57	28.50	49.5	23.7	35.0	69.9	1.4
5. Natural gas (billions of cubit meters)	.27	.905	1.98	2.0	5.5	1.7	2.6	4.7	1.3
6. Hydroelectric power (billions of kw-h)	.36[a]	.70[a]	4.0	5.1	9.2	n.e.	12.7	35.0	.6
			In Conventional Coal Units of 7,000 Calories per Kilogram						
7. Coal	28.9	50.5	98.2	129.2	191	112.5	195.0	303	
8. Lignite	1.5	3.4	8.5	11.4		23.3	30.5		
9. Peat	2.2	6.1	9.8	13.2	20.1	11.5	17.4	22.1	
10. Petroleum	12.0	21.3	37.2	39.9	69.3	33.2	49.0	97.9	
11. Natural gas	.3	1.2	2.6	2.6	7.2	2.2	3.4	6.1	
12. Hydroelectric power	.2[a]	.4[a]	2.4	3.1	5.5	n.e.	7.6	21.0	
13. Total, lines 7-12	45.1	82.9	158.7	199.4	293.1	182.7[b]	302.9	450.1	
14. Population, approximate annual average (millions)[c]	152	n.e.	166	193	n.e.	n.e.	200	217	
15. Workers and employees (annual average, millions)[d]	11.6	22.9	27.0	31.2	32.0	31.0	38.2	43.9	
16. Supply of mineral and hydroelectric energy (kg. of conventional coal per capita)[e]	297	n.e.	955	1,030	n.e.	n.e.	1,510	2,070	
17. Supply of mineral and hydroelectric energy (kg. of conventional coal per worker or employee)[e]	3,890	3,620	5,880	6,390	9,160	5,890[b]	7,930	10,250	

(cont. on next page)

APPENDIX TABLE (cont.)

[a] Regional hydraulic stations only, but exclusion of other hydraulic stations not significant for these years.

[b] Exclusive of hydroelectric power.

[c] Population figures are approximate estimates by the author.

[d] Number of workers and employees as in Table 1.

[e] Rounded.

n.e. = no estimate.

Source: All fuel and power data in natural units are estimates of *consumption*, except the following, which are output data: all figures for peat and hydroelectric power and all figures for 1942 (plan) and 1955 (plan). All consumption estimates are from Demitri B. Shimkin, *Minerals—A Key to Soviet Power*, Harvard University Press, 1953, Table 100, p. 391. Output targets for 1942 are from *Tretii piatiletnii plan razvitiia narodnogo khoziaistva Soiuza S.S.R.* (*Third FYP for the Development of the Economy of the U.S.S.R.*), Moscow, Gosudarstvennaia planovaia komissiia (State Planning Commission), 1939, pp. 44 and 202. Conversion of natural gas into cubic meters is from Shimkin, *op. cit.*, p. 198. Output targets for 1955 are from *Economic Survey of Europe since the War*, Geneva, United Nations Economic Commission for Europe, 1953, Table 17, pp. 42-43, except that the 1955 target for natural gas was obtained by applying ratio of increase in the *Directives*, i.e. 1.8, to Shimkin's estimate. Peat output: for 1928 and 1932 from *Sots. stroi.*, 1936, p. 130; for 1937, 1940, 1946, 1950, and 1955 (plan) from *Economic Survey of Europe since the War*, as cited, Table 17, pp. 42-43; and for 1942 (plan) from *Tretii piatiletnii plan . . .*, as cited, pp. 44 and 202. Hydroelectric power output: for 1928 and 1932 from *Sots. stroi.*, 1936, p. 90 (refers to regional stations only); for 1937 from Chauncey D. Harris, "Industrial Resources," in *Soviet Economic Growth*, Abram Bergson, editor, Row, Peterson, 1953, p. 169; for 1940, 1950, and 1955 (plan) from *Economic Survey of Europe since the War*, as cited, Table 18, p. 44; and for 1942 (plan) from *Tretii piatiletnii plan . . .*, as cited, pp. 44 and 202.

Conversion to conventional coal units: For coal and lignite through 1940 at 6,350 and 3,400 calories per kilogram, respectively, which are the approximate rates implicit in Shimkin, *op. cit.*, Tables 49 and 50, pp. 176-177; for 1942 (plan) at 5,800 calories per kilogram for coal and lignite together (cf. *ibid.*); and for 1950 and 1955 (plan) at 5,700 calories per kilogram for coal and lignite together (cf. *ibid.*). For other sources of energy, rates as given by Harris, *op. cit.*, Table 5.2, note j, p. 169, based chiefly on Soviet sources.

and evaluation of current problems of Soviet economic development has not seriously suffered from the recent turn of events.

COMMENT

NORMAN M. KAPLAN, Rand Corporation[1]

Grossman has presented an able, thoughtful, and very interesting analysis of the growth of the Soviet labor force. Observing an un-

[1] I am indebted to my colleague Gershon Cooper for helpful discussions during the preparation of these comments.

precedentedly low rate of increase in the non-agricultural labor force planned for 1951-1955, he states and explores a number of hypotheses as possible explanations. Though this discussion is inconclusive, though the hypotheses are neither accepted nor rejected, the paper brings forcibly to our attention possible perspectives in Soviet economic development. Indeed, one of these—an unprecedented emphasis on the growth of agriculture—has had rather dramatic verification in recent months.

The intent of the paper, however, is more ambitious than the achievements just described. The analysis of changes in the non-agricultural labor force is part of a larger argument which, to put it baldly, goes as follows: The basic empirical observation is that in the non-agricultural sector of the economy "incremental capital-intensity," defined as the ratio of investment to the absolute increase in the labor force, is planned to be unprecedentedly high in 1951-1955. This increase in incremental capital-intensity is due to an increase in investment and a decrease in the increment to the non-agricultural labor force. If investment and labor increments are regarded as substitutes in the process of economic growth, the decrease in the increment to the non-agricultural labor force is itself an explanation of the increase in non-agricultural investment and incremental capital-intensity. Furthermore, when the retardation in the growth of the non-agricultural labor force is analyzed, the labor-saving explanation for the increase in incremental capital-intensity is reinforced by the discovery of factors which suggest a desire or a necessity to substitute capital for labor in the non-agricultural sector of the economy. Thus the conclusion seems to be that non-agricultural incremental capital-intensity is unprecedentedly high because capital is being substituted for labor.

Because I have reservations about the relevance of the argument to trends or policy in capital formation and because these reservations do not depreciate the analysis of labor force changes, I wish to discuss separately and in turn: (1) the trends in capital-intensity, (2) the meaning of capital-intensity, and (3) the demand for, and supply of, non-agricultural labor.

1. *Trends in Capital-Intensity.* The basic quantity which Grossman seeks to measure is the incremental capital-intensity, i.e. the ratio of investment to the increment in the labor force, in the non-agricultural sector of the economy. In the absence of investment data at constant prices for the entire period of interest, two series are used as indicators of investment: cement output (where possible,

less exports) and the absolute *increase* in electric power output. The results of the calculation show a very large increase in the incremental capital-intensity of the non-agricultural sector, especially for the Fifth FYP (1951-1955). Depending upon which of the two series is used as the investment indicator (see Grossman, Table 2), the incremental intensities turn out to be as follows (1929-1937 = 100):

1938-1942 plan	373-378
1946-1950	117-155
1948-1951	249-330
1951-1955	529-587

The rationale for the indicator series is that: (1) cement consumption and new construction are correlated; (2) the absolute increase in electric power output and that in producers' durables are correlated; and (3) new construction and investment are correlated, as are producers' durables and investment.[2] Except for a comparison of the increase in investment, cement output, and the increment in electric power output between 1946-1950 and plan 1951-1955, the hypothesized relationships among the series are not tested. I have attempted to show the comparison, with the limited data available, in Table 1. Since the use which Grossman makes of the indicator series requires not only that investment be correlated with cement output or the increment in electric power output but that the *percentage changes* in the series be *equal*, Table 1 compares for various time periods the percentage changes in investment with the percentage changes in cement output and the increment in electric power output.[3]

The results provide small comfort.[4] *Within* each of the time seg-

[2] I have improvised somewhat on Grossman's statement of the rationale: see Grossman, pages 176, 177 above.

[3] There are a number of ambiguities in the postwar data which I have not taken the space to discuss.

[4] I have also looked into the relationships between cement output and new construction and between the increment in electric power consumption and producers' durables in the United States, with the following data and results emerging:

a. For new construction I used the sum of private and public construction in 1945-1949 prices (*Construction and Building Materials, Statistical Supplement*, Dept. of Commerce, May 1953, pp. 40 and 42). For cement output I used the Federal Reserve Board index of cement production. I compared the two series for 1920 to 1929, 1935 to 1950, and 1946 to 1952 separately. For each of the periods as a whole the percentage increase in cement output was appreciably *less* than the percentage increase in new construction. Within each of the periods cement output became a substantially better indicator of new construction whenever the ratio of public to private investment increased substantially.

b. The comparison between incremental electric power consumption and

TABLE 1

Investment, Cement Output, and the Increment in Electric Power Output, U.S.S.R., Selected Time Periods from 1933 to 1955
(*in percentages with the first year of each time period equal to 100*)

Time Period	*Investment*	*Cement Output*	*Increment in Electric Power Output*
1933 plan	100[a]	100[a]	100[a]
1934 plan	140[a]	158[a]	128[a]
1935 plan	156[a]	182[a]	203[a]
1936 plan	168[a]	218[a]	243[a]
1937 plan	178[a]	273[a]	325[a]
1937	100[b]	100[b]	100[c]
1942 plan	166[b]	178[b]	226[c]
1946	100[d]	100[e]	100[e]
1947	110[d]	139[e]	161[e]
1948	135[d]	194[e]	198[e]
1949	162[d]	245[e]	261[e]
1949	100[d]	100[e]	100[e]
1950	123[d]	127[e]	103[e]
1951	138[d]	152[e]	106[e]
1952	153[d]	174[e]	112[e]
1946-1950	100[f]	100[f]	100[f]
1951-1955 plan	190[f]	263[f]	177[f]
1950	100[g]	100[h]	100[h]
1955 plan	160-180[g]	220[h]	117[h]

[a] Calculated from data in State Planning Commission of the U.S.S.R., *The Second Five Year Plan for the Development of the National Economy of the USSR (1933-1937)*, London, Lawrence, pp. 560-561, 577, and 581. The investment data are in 1933 plan prices.

[b] Calculated from data in *Tretii piatiletnii plan razvitiia narodnogo khoziaistva Soiuza S.S.R. (1938-1942 gg.)*, Moscow, Gosudarstvennaia planovaia komissiia, 1939, p. 26. The 1937 investment figure is in 1937 prices, and the 1942 plan figure in December 1936 prices; consequently, the percentage change in investment is somewhat understated.

[c] The figures for 1937 and 1942 plan electric power output are from *Tretii piatiletnii plan . . . ,* as cited, p. 213. The 1936 figure is from *Narodno-khoziaistvennyi plan Soiuza S.S.R. na 1937 god*, Moscow, Gosudarstvennaia planovaia komisssiia, 1937, pp. 64-65. The 1941 plan figure is obtained by linear interpolation between the 1937 and 1942 plan figures. The percentages are then calculated from the increments in electric power output.

[d] Annual investment for 1947 through 1950 is obtained from I. Kuz'minov, "Nepreryvnyi pod'em narodnogo khoziaistva S.S.S.R.—zakon sotsializma," *Voprosy ekonomiki*, 1951, No. 6, p. 33. The 1951 and 1952 figures are from *Pravda*, January 29, 1952, p. 2 and January 23, 1953, p. 2, respectively. Each of these figures is stated as a percentage of the figure for the preceding year and is in comparable prices. I have chained the percentages.

[e] Calculated from data in *Economic Survey of Europe in 1951*, Geneva, United Nations Economic Commission for Europe, 1952, pp. 127 and 128;

(cont. on next page)

TABLE 1 (cont.)

Economic Survey of Europe since the War, Geneva, United Nations Economic Commission for Europe, 1953, pp. 42 and 43; and Kuz'minov, *op. cit.*, p. 30.

[f] Grossman, pp. 178-180 above.

[g] If 1951-1955 plan investment is 190 per cent of 1946-1950 investment, 1955 plan investment is less than 190 per cent of 1950 investment because of the very rapid increase in investment from the low of 1945 to 1950. On the basis of 1951 and 1952 investment figures I would judge that 1955 plan investment is to be about 160 per cent of 1950 investment. To take account of possible underfulfillment of the 1951 and 1952 investment figures, I have set a range with an upper limit of 180 per cent for the ratio between 1955 plan investment and 1950 investment.

[h] Calculated from data in *Economic Survey of Europe in 1951*, as cited, p. 127, and *Economic Survey of Europe since the War*, as cited, pp. 42 and 43. Electric power output for 1954 plan was obtained by linear interpolation between the 1950 and 1955 plan figures.

ments examined, except for the most recent years, both cement output and incremental electric power output increase by larger percentages than investment; in the years since 1949, cement output leads, but incremental electric power output lags behind, investment in percentage increases. There may very well be relationships over time between investment, on the one hand, and cement or incremental electric power output, on the other, but the data seem to deny equality in percentage increase over time. The hypothesized relationships may be adequate to yield what Grossman requires—namely, an indication of *increasing* incremental capital-intensity—but as indicators in a more accurate sense they seem to fail.

Although incremental capital-intensity in conceived as a measure of the additional capital available per additional worker, it is defined in terms of *gross* investment and the difference between net and

producers' durables was made separately for two periods, 1923 to 1929 and 1947 to 1951. For the 1923-to-1929 period, I used Shaw's series on total producers' durables in 1913 prices (William H. Shaw, *Value of Commodity Output since 1869*, National Bureau of Economic Research, 1947, p. 77). For the same period I used alternatively two electric power series: electric energy used in manufacturing and extracting, and sales of power in kilowatt-hours by electric utilities to non-residential consumers (*Historical Statistics of the United States, 1789-1945*, Bureau of the Census, 1949, pp. 157 and 159). For the period from 1947 to 1951, only the second electric power series was available to me (in the *Statistical Abstract of the United States*, Bureau of the Census, for the relevant years). For the 1947-to-1951 period, I used producers' durables in 1929 dollars from the GNP accounts. In both the 1923-to-1929 and 1947-to-1951 periods the percentage changes in incremental electric power output behaved in an extremely erratic fashion vis-à-vis the percentage changes in producers' durables: for some years the percentage change in electric power output was far below, and for other years far above, the percentage change in producers' durables.

gross investment in the numerator is ignored.[5] In the Fifth FYP as against prewar periods, I suspect the difference is appreciable. For example, capital repairs as a percentage of total investment (inclusive of capital repairs) were 18 per cent in 1951 plan as against 13 per cent in the Plan for 1938-1942, 11 per cent in 1937, and less than 10 per cent in 1933-1937.[6] After twenty years of economic growth and five years of war (1928-1953) the arithmetic aspects of the matter suggest a ratio of capital consumption to gross investment which is appreciably greater at the end of the period than in the early years of the period.[7] Accordingly, if the incremental capital-intensity series are accurate as defined, I would suspect an overstatement of the trend in additional capital per additional worker due to time changes in the ratio of capital consumption to gross investment.

In addition to incremental capital-intensity, Grossman seeks to measure trends in average non-agricultural capital-intensity, i.e. the ratio of capital to labor in the non-agricultural sector of the economy. In this calculation the total supply of mineral and hydroelectric energy (in conventional coal units) is used as the indicator of capital. The results of the calculation show a large increase in average capital-intensity between 1928 and 1955 plan, interrupted en route by declines between 1928 and 1932 and between 1940 and 1946; in 1955 plan, average capital-intensity, however, is to be less than that foreseen for 1942 by the Third FYP (Grossman, Table 3). For the prewar years the percentage increases in energy supply and the percentage increases in capital at constant prices correspond very closely; for the postwar years no capital series is available for comparison.[8]

[5] A statement that adjustment to *net* investment "would not greatly alter the picture" apparently refers to the comparison between 1951-1955 plan and 1946-1950 capital-intensities only.

[6] For the underlying data see A. Zverev, "Biudzhet mirnogo khoziaistvennogo i kultur'nogo stroitel'stva," *Planovoe khoziaistovo*, 1952, No. 1, pp. 29 and 30; *Tretii piatiletnii plan razvitiia narodnogo khoziaistva Soiuza S.S.R. (1938-1942 gg.)*, Moscow, Gosudarstvennaia planovaia komissiia, 1939, pp. 26, 115, 116, and 225; *Sotsialisticheskoe stroitel'stvo Soiuza S.S.R. (1933-1938 gg.)*, Moscow-Leningrad, Tsentral'noe upravlenie narodnokhoziaistvennogo ucheta, 1939, pp. 113 and 115; and E. Granovskii and B. Markus, *Ekonomika sotsialisticheskoe promyshlennosti*, Moscow, 1940, p. 533.

[7] See Evsey Domar, "Depreciation, Replacement and Growth," *Economic Journal*, March 1953, pp. 1 ff., for an analysis of the relationships between capital consumption and gross investment and for illustrative calculations (p. 3) of the ratio of depreciation to gross investment as a function of time, the rate of increase of gross investment, and the average life span of capital.

[8] See Grossman, pages 180-182, where the correspondence between percentage increases in total capital and in energy supply is noted. A similar cor-

Thus the trends noted are (1) an unprecedentedly high incremental capital-intensity projected by the Fifth FYP in comparison with earlier periods and (2) increasing average capital-intensity over time. In one sense there is nothing inherently surprising, i.e. demanding explanation, about such trends. Similar trends have occurred elsewhere in growing economies. In the United States, for example, average capital-intensity in the non-agricultural sector of the economy was, with 1880 = 100, 130 in 1890, 143 in 1900, and 166 in 1912.[9] In manufacturing, incremental capital-intensity was, with 1899-1904 = 100, 105 in 1904-1909, 115 in 1909-1913, and 186 in 1913-1920.[10]

2. *The Meaning of Capital-Intensity.* Why measure capital-intensity, incremental or average? What do such measures signify?

Average capital-intensity, as a measure of the stock of capital available per worker, is certainly relevant to problems of economic growth. If by economic growth we mean an increase in aggregate and per capita output, probably the two most important determinants of growth are technological advance and increased average capital-intensity. Emphasis on average capital-intensity is further warranted by the absence of aggregate measures of technological advance, and by the reflection in increased average capital-intensity of significant aspects of technological advance, i.e. the industrialization of productive processes.

From the relevance of average capital-intensity, however, that of incremental capital-intensity does not follow. Incremental and average capital-intensities are not so related that inferences about one can be drawn from observations of the other. Increasing incre-

---

respondence can be obtained for percentage increases in non-agricultural capital or in non-agricultural productive capital and percentage increases in energy supply. For the capital series see Norman M. Kaplan, "Capital Formation and Allocation," in *Soviet Economic Growth*, Abram Bergson, editor, Row, Peterson, 1953, Appendix Table v (Appendix distributed separately).

[9] For non-agricultural capital in 1929 prices see Simon Kuznets, *National Product since 1869*, National Bureau of Economic Research, 1946, pp. 218 and 219. For the non-agricultural labor force see *Historical Statistics of the United States, 1789-1945*, as cited, pp. 63 and 65. The increase in average capital-intensity is understated by being unadjusted for the decrease in hours worked per week (*ibid.*, pp. 66-67).

The same data indicate the following changes in incremental capital-intensity, with 1880-1890 = 100: 94 in 1890-1900, 111 in 1900-1912.

[10] See Paul H. Douglas, *The Theory of Wages*, Macmillan, 1934, Tables 6, 8, and 9, pp. 121, 125, and 126. The same data indicate the following changes in average capital-intensity, with 1899 = 100: 119 in 1904, 143 in 1909, 154 in 1913, and 213 in 1920 (*ibid.*, Table 12, p. 129).

mental capital-intensity does not imply increasing average capital-intensity; increasing average capital-intensity does not imply increasing incremental capital-intensity.[11] Therefore, inferences about

[11] Let $K=$ capital; $L=$ labor; $t=$ time; $\dot{K}$ and $\ddot{K}=$ the first and second derivatives, respectively, of capital with respect to time; and $\dot{L}$ and $\ddot{L}=$ the first and second derivatives, respectively, of labor with respect to time. For the present purposes K and L are each regarded as functions of time alone. By definition, average capital-intensity is K/L and incremental capital-intensity is $\dot{K}/\dot{L}$. What does increasing average capital-intensity imply? If

$$\frac{d\left(\frac{K}{L}\right)}{dt} > 0$$

then

$$\frac{L\dot{K} - K\dot{L}}{L^2} > 0 \text{ or } \frac{\dot{K}}{\dot{L}} > \frac{K}{L}$$

What does increasing incremental capital-intensity imply?
If

$$\frac{d\left(\frac{\dot{K}}{\dot{L}}\right)}{dt} > 0$$

then

$$\frac{\dot{L}\ddot{K} - \dot{K}\ddot{L}}{\dot{L}^2} > 0 \text{ or } \frac{\ddot{K}}{\ddot{L}} > \frac{\dot{K}}{\dot{L}}$$

Since

$$\frac{\dot{K}}{\dot{L}} > \frac{K}{L}$$

does not imply

$$\frac{\ddot{K}}{\ddot{L}} > \frac{\dot{K}}{\dot{L}}$$

and

$$\frac{\ddot{K}}{\ddot{L}} > \frac{\dot{K}}{\dot{L}}$$

does not imply

$$\frac{\dot{K}}{\dot{L}} > \frac{K}{L}$$

average capital-intensity may be increasing with either increasing or decreasing incremental capital-intensity, and incremental capital-intensity may be increasing with either increasing or decreasing average capital-intensity.

There is, however, one set of circumstances in which an observation of increasing incremental capital-intensity adds information about the change in average capital-intensity. Suppose that for $t = t_0$,

$$\frac{\dot{K}}{\dot{L}} > \frac{K}{L}$$

changes in the stock of capital per worker cannot be drawn from observations of incremental capital-intensity. The justification for measuring incremental capital-intensity must lie elsewhere.

Grossman relates increasing incremental and average capital-intensity to the substitution of capital for labor in investment alternatives. His problem is, Why are the non-agricultural capital-intensities (incremental and average) provided for by the Fifth FYP (1951-1955) so unprecedentedly high? The problem is approached as an allocation problem, i.e. What determines the distribution of capital and labor between the agricultural and non-agricultural sectors, given the total output of each sector and the total capital and labor force for the economy?[12] Moreover, the only problem explicitly discussed is, Why is the rate of growth of the non-agricultural labor force foreseen by the Fifth FYP so unprecedentedly low?

To pursue the conceptual framework employed by Grossman, suppose we postulate a production function for the non-agricultural sector of the economy in which output X is a function of labor L and capital K, a function which is different for different points in time. Suppose, further, we date the variables by using the subscripts 0, 1, and 2 to represent the values of the variables at the successive points in time 0, 1, and 2, respectively. Thus we have observable values of output, labor, and capital for each of three points in time. In addition, for each of the three outputs we have, at least conceptually, an isoquant which represents alternative combinations of capital and labor yielding the given output. Chart 1 presents (1) the isoquants for $X = X_0$, $X = X_1$, and $X = X_2$; (2) three points A, B, and C, the coordinates of which represent observed capital and labor for $X = X_0$, $X = X_1$, and $X = X_2$; and (3) for expository purposes, point D, an alternative (and unobserved) combination of labor and capital on the isoquant for $X = X_2$. If we connect the points A, B, and C by straight lines, the slopes of the lines represent observed incremental capital-intensities, e.g.

$$\frac{K_1 - K_0}{L_1 - L_0}$$

---

and that for $t \geqq t_0$, $\dot{K}$ and $\dot{L}$ are positive. Then if $\dot{K}/\dot{L}$ is a monotonically increasing function of time for $t \geqq t_0$, K/L is also a monotonically increasing function of time for $t \geqq t_0$.

[12] For a closer examination of Grossman's conceptual framework see my footnote 15.

CHART 1

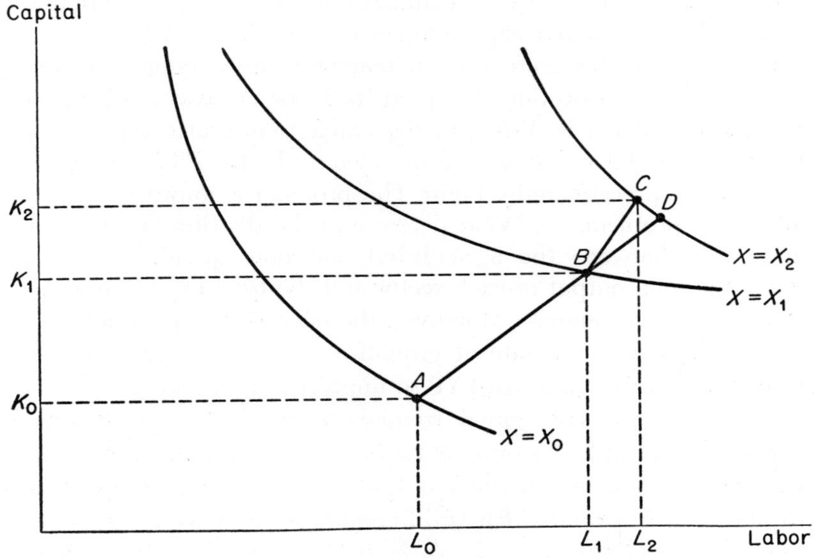

The ratios of each pair of coordinates of points *A*, *B*, and *C* represent observed average capital-intensities, e.g. K_0/L_0. I have selected the points so that incremental and average capital-intensities increase with time.[13]

In a static sense the alternative implied by capital-labor substitution is a movement along an isoquant, e.g. a movement from point *C* to point *D*. In a dynamic sense the alternative implied by capital-labor substitution is a movement from one to another time path of investment and additions to the labor force by which a later (and higher) output is achieved, e.g. a movement from *BC* to *BD*. Is there in either sense a relationship between capital-intensities, as time series, and substitution between capital and labor?

In the static sense the marginal rate of substitution between capital and labor is the slope of the isoquant (and is negative). Thus conceptually associated with points *A*, *B*, and *C* are three such marginal rates of substitution—the tangents to each of the isoquants at points *A*, *B*, and *C*. What Grossman has measured, however, are the (positive) slopes of *AB* and *BC* and the ratios of each pair of

[13] I.e. the slope of *BC* exceeds the slope of *AB*, point *C* is above the straight line drawn through *B* from the origin, and point *B* is above the straight line drawn through *A* from the origin.

coordinates for points *A*, *B*, and *C*. It is clear that neither the marginal rate of substitution nor changes therein are measured by incremental or average capital-intensities. Moreover, without permissive information about the production functions, one cannot infer from increasing average capital-intensity that the marginal rate of substitution is numerically larger at point *C* that at point *B*; nor can one make the converse inference.[14] Finally, it is clear from Chart 1 that incremental capital-intensity per se is irrelevant to this class of inferences.

In a dynamic sense the substitution of capital for labor can be interpreted to mean that in the movement from one isoquant to a later (and higher) one a time path is followed which has a larger ratio of investment to the increment in the labor force than an alternative time path, e.g. in Chart 1 that the slope of *BC* is greater than that of *BD*. Within Grossman's conceptual framework, however, there is in one sense no alternative time path. If total output in each of the agricultural and non-agricultural sectors of the economy is given, if total capital and labor for the economy are given, and if the allocation of resources is (or is planned to be) efficient in the sense that no reallocation of resources can increase one of the outputs without decreasing the other, the distribution of capital and labor between sectors is uniquely determined by the given outputs and the given capital and labor totals.[15] To avoid this,

[14] There is a special case in which increasing average capital-intensity implies increasing marginal rates of substitution at the observed points, and conversely—namely, a production function which is invariant with time and homogeneous of degree 1. This case, however, is certainly not applicable to Soviet economic development.

[15] Grossman's conceptual framework for the analysis of capital-intensity in the Fifth FYP, adopted to "facilitate treatment," is as follows (pp. 182-185): In each of the agricultural and non-agricultural sectors of the economy, output is given by the plan and there is an isoquant which states the alternative (minimum) combinations of capital and labor by which the given output can be produced. Given also are total capital (the sum of beginning capital and net investment during the plan) and total labor. The problem is, What determines the unknowns, the distribution of capital and labor between the sectors? The system is stated to have the property that choice of a point on one isoquant "uniquely determines" the point on the other and also determines average and incremental capital-intensity in each sector.

It seems to me that these simplifying assumptions have all but simplified the problem out of existence. If the isoquants in each of the sectors have the usual properties of negative slope and convexity to the origin, i.e. if the marginal rate of substitution of capital for labor increases as the quantity of capital increases relative to that of labor, there is no factor distribution problem within the framework stated except in the special sense of a choice between two inefficient allocations. Suppose we draw the usual Edgeworth diagram in which the two sectors of the economy are related through their common use of capital and labor, from given totals, to produce agricultural output Y and non-agricultural output X. Of the infinite number of isoquants in each sector

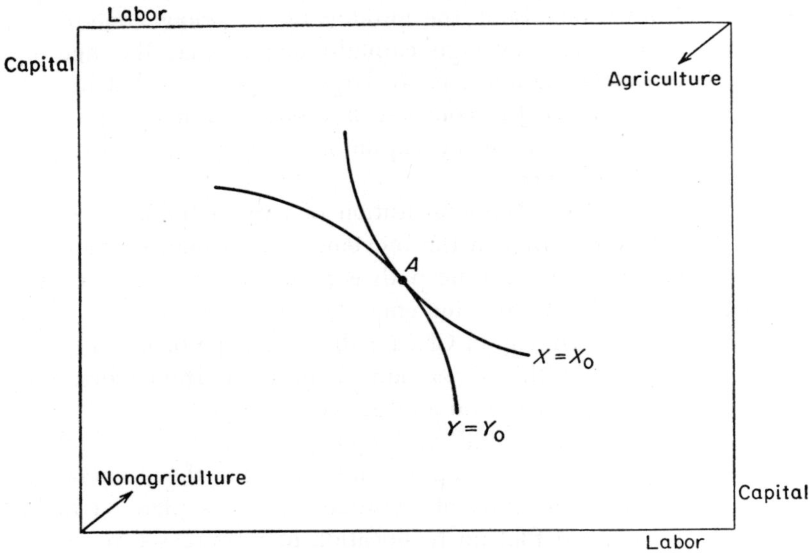

associated with the infinite number of outputs in each, only the pair for the given outputs ($Y = Y_0$ and $X = X_0$) is presented. If the two isoquants touch (but do not intersect) as in the diagram at point A, there is only *one* distribution of capital and labor consistent with the given outputs and the given total capital and labor. That is to say, the distribution of capital and labor between sectors is uniquely determined by the given outputs and the given total capital and labor. If the isoquants intersect, there are *two* distributions of capital and labor between the sectors which will produce *exactly* the outputs given with full employment of total capital and labor. Both points of intersection, however, represent inefficient allocations of resources in the sense that reallocations of capital and labor between the sectors can increase one of the outputs without decreasing the other. There are an infinite number of such possible reallocations, represented by all points in the area bounded by the intersecting isoquants. For any pair of given outputs in this area, however, there is only *one* distribution of capital and labor consistent with the given total capital and labor. Thus either (1) the problem is a choice between two, and only two, inefficient allocations in the face of unambiguously preferable allocations; or (2) the assumption of given outputs must be relaxed and the problem cannot be conceived as a choice among points on a given isoquant; or (3) the assumption of full employment of total capital and labor must be relaxed, in which case choice of a point on one isoquant does *not* determine the point on the other.

If *within* either the non-agricultural sectors or the agricultural sectors the ratio of the marginal physical productivities of capital and labor is not uniform in all uses, the entire conceptual apparatus collapses because the allocation of resources cannot be described as a point on an isoquant.

let us treat the output of the agricultural sector as a residual and consider the non-agricultural sector of the economy alone.

In Chart 1, then, there are an infinite number of alternative paths from, say, X_1 to X_2 : some will have slopes greater than the slope of *BC* and others like *BD* will have slopes less than *BC*. All, moreover, are in the nature of the case unobserved. If it is held that, in the dynamic sense, *BC* substitutes capital for labor, the alternative and unobserved time path (say, *BD*) with which *BC* is compared must somehow be specified. Two possible specifications come to mind from Grossman's paper: an optimal time path with a slope less than that of the observed path,[16] and an extrapolation of previous trends. It is possible that *BC* substitutes capital for labor is an uneconomic way, i.e. that there is an alternative path, *BD*, which in some sense is optimal. But the optimal time path, however defined, is not relevant to *observed trends* in capital-intensities because the implication of an optimal, less capital-intensive time path is only that incremental and average capital-intensities, whether increasing or decreasing, are larger than they *should* be.

To infer from increasing incremental capital-intensity that capital is being substituted for labor might also mean that, apart from the choice among investment alternatives which yield identical outputs, incremental capital-intensity is (or should be) invariant with time. That is to say, *BC* is held to substitute capital for labor because its slope is greater than that of *BD*, derived from a continuation of *AB*. I see no reason, and Grossman advances none, to expect a continuation of past trends. The variables omitted are the increment in output[17] and technological change: the ratio of investment to the increment in the labor force depends not only on capital-labor substitutions but also on the increment of output, in kind and quantity, and on the range of technologically possible

[16] As a possible explanatory factor in the retardation of the rate of growth of non-agricultural labor, Grossman mentions a technological bias on the part of Soviet planners in favor of "the grandiose project and . . . the most advanced technical design" in non-agricultural production, a bias which originates in ideological affection for high labor productivity and uneconomic criteria for investment choice (page 195).

It should also be noted that Grossman regards his discussion as one of "optimum capital-intensity" (page 197).

[17] In a concluding paragraph Grossman relaxes his assumption of given output but only to point out the possibility "that the retardation in the expansion of non-agricultural employment, and the rising capital needs required to assist the transfer of manpower and to replace labor, might explain the small but perceptible retardation in the rate of growth of industrial output indicated by the Fifth Five-Year Plan" (page 198).

capital and labor coefficients associated with the increment of output and feasible capital-labor substitutions. I see no reason to believe that the influence of output increments and technological change is (or should be) neutral with respect to capital-labor ratios, incremental or average. Accordingly, I see no reason to infer from increasing incremental capital-intensity, from the fact that the slope of *BC* exceeds the slope of *AB* (or *BD*), that capital is being substituted for labor.

Where does all this lead? My original question was, Why measure incremental or average capital-intensity? By way of summary, I am led to the following conclusions: (1) Though the stock of capital available per worker is a relevant quantity from the viewpoint of economic growth, no justification for the measurement of incremental capital-intensity can be derived thereby. Incremental and average capital-intensities, as defined, are not so related that an increase in one implies an increase in the other. (2) In the structure of Grossman's argument, increasing incremental and average capital-intensities are related to the substitution of capital for labor in investment alternatives. No connection between the quantities measured and the concept suggested is successfully established in the paper, nor am I able to establish one. If a connection cannot be established, Grossman's analysis of the retardation in the rate of growth of the non-agricultural labor force—interesting enough in itself—bears no systematic relationship to the observed trends in capital formation. In my opinion his conceptual framework fails to unify the empirical observations of increasing capital-intensities and the explanatory analysis which follows.

3. *The Non-agricultural Labor Force, Demand and Supply.* Apart from its implications with respect to Soviet capital formation, Grossman's analysis of recent trends in the non-agricultural labor force commands attention on its own merits. The basic observation is that, as foreseen in the Fifth FYP, the 1951-1955 percentage increase in the non-agricultural labor force is to be unprecedentedly low.[18] The problem is to explain the retardation in the rate of growth.

[18] It should be noted that this retardation is especially striking in comparison with previously realized increases (Grossman, Table 1). Both the Third and the Fourth FYP (1938-1942 and 1946-1950) provided for rates of growth which were not substantially larger than that in the Fifth FYP and for absolute increases which were about the same as that in the Fifth FYP. Thus the average annual rate of growth of the non-agricultural labor force was 3.5 per cent from 1937 to 1942 plan, 3.8 per cent from 1945 to 1950 plan, and 2.8 per cent from 1950 to 1955 plan; the absolute increments were about 5.0 million "workers and employees" from 1937 to 1942 plan, about 6.3 million from 1945 to 1950

Grossman states and explores a number of hypotheses as possible explanations. They are classified into *detentive* factors, i.e. those which tend to detain labor in uses other than non-agricultural employment, and *deterrent* factors, i.e. those which tend to deter labor from use in non-agricultural employment. More conventionally, the classification separates the factors which influence the supply of non-agricultural labor from the factors which influence the demand for it. It would be difficult to think of hypotheses which are important possibilities and which are excluded from consideration. It is impossible to disqualify any considered.

Among the most interesting of the possible explanatory factors is the cost of urbanization. The hypothesis is that the capital cost of urbanization is sufficiently high to deter the transfer of labor from agriculture and to promote the substitution of capital for labor in non-agricultural sectors (Grossman, pages 188-193). The calculus suggested is as follows: Given outputs in the agricultural and non-agricultural sectors, there is a capital cost to the economy (i') involved in the transfer of an additional worker from agriculture to another sector. In somewhat simplified form,

$$i' = h(1 + d) + t + a$$

where $h =$ the capital cost of housing and other urban facilities per person

$d =$ the number of dependents per wage earner

$t =$ the cost of training an agricultural worker in non-agricultural work

$a =$ the investment in agriculture necessary to replace the transferred worker and maintain output.

Under the same assumptions there is an alternative capital cost to the economy (i'') which is the equipment expenditure in non-agricultural sectors necessary to maintain output in lieu of the use of

plan, and about 5.7 million from 1950 to 1955 plan. The Third FYP was, of course, interrupted by the war: the average annual rate of growth from 1937 to 1940 was 5.0 per cent, though this partly reflects the territorial additions in 1939-1940. The increases foreseen by the Fourth FYP were vastly overfulfilled. Thus the query arises, Will the Fifth FYP increases in the non-agricultural labor force be significantly overfulfilled? The data available in November 1953, when this comment was written, suggested a negative answer (see *Pravda*, January 29, 1952 and January 23, 1953, and *Vestnik statistiki*, 1953, No. 4, p. 8). However, as Grossman's postscript indicates, recent data reveal that in 1954 the number of "workers and employees" was already in excess of that originally planned for 1955 (see *Pravda*, January 21, 1955).

an additional worker. If $i' < i''$, the worker will be transferred; if $i' > i''$, the worker will be retained in agriculture. Grossman mentions some preliminary calculations which suggest that for some branches of the non-agricultural economy, $i' > i''$. Needless to say, when these calculations appear they will be received with great interest.

A few comments, however, are in order here.

1. Population growth in the U.S.S.R. implies expenditures on housing, consumer facilities, and training whether or not there is a transfer of labor from agriculture to the non-agricultural economy. In the decision to transfer or not to transfer labor, only the difference in such expenditure is relevant. Thus if i' and i'' are calculated literally as defined, i' will be overstated in relation to i'' because the capital cost of rural housing and other rural facilities has been ignored in h and the cost of training agricultural labor has been ignored in t.

2. If there is surplus labor in agriculture, as Grossman elsewhere suggests (page 186), this may imply zero or negative marginal productivity in agriculture and, therefore, a zero value for a.

3. The need to compensate agriculture with capital for its loss of labor derives from the assumption that (planned) outputs in agriculture and the non-agricultural sectors are given. Under less restrictive assumptions, whether agriculture should be so compensated depends upon the marginal productivities of capital in agriculture and other sectors, made commensurate by the planners' preference function. Though there is certainly an allocation problem posed by possible capital-labor substitutions, it would be irrational for Gosplan to think in terms of the calculus suggested, *given* the output of both sectors. There is also a marginal rate of substitution between agricultural output and non-agricultural output which cannot be ignored.

4. It seems to me that Grossman overstates the failure of a market economy, in comparison with an all-embracing planned economy, to take into account the social costs of urbanization. There may be many such social costs which do not enter the private cost function of the entrepreneur. However, the costs of housing and urban facilities would seem to enter the cost functions via the wages found necessary to attract labor.

5. In connection with the data on capital-intensity, it should be noted that a larger increase in the non-agricultural labor force might increase observed incremental capital-intensity via the impact on

observed investment of increased expenditures on housing and other urban facilities. Unless the numerator of incremental capital-intensity is restricted to certain kinds of investment, it is not clear to me that a decrease in the incremental labor force means an increase in investment, even abstracting from the considerations previously mentioned.

With respect to the other hypotheses listed by Grossman I have only a few scattered comments:

1. Grossman's remarks on the Soviet bias in favor of advanced technology (pages 194-195) and on the Soviet interest in mechanization and automation (pages 192-193) whet my appetite for more. I would like to know how advanced Soviet technology is, how uneven their advances are, what opportunities exist for further technological imitation of advanced economies, what modifications they have made in borrowed processes and products, what capital-labor substitutions they make in detail, which inputs they economize relative to United States practices, etc. It seems to me that a comparative study, combining engineering and economic talents, of U.S.-U.S.S.R. technology, manufacturing processes, and product design is long overdue.

2. Grossman expects a reduction in the proportion of females in the non-agricultural labor force largely on the grounds of the continuous improvement in real wages and consumption standards (page 187). An increase in real wages, however, has both an income effect and a substitution effect on the choice between housekeeping (leisure?) and gainful employment.[19] It is not clear, therefore, whether an increase in real wages deters or encourages participation of females in gainful employment.

3. Grossman notes a planned increase, from 1950 to 1955, of 5 to 7 million students in the last three grades of secondary school and of possibly several hundred thousand in secondary *technical* schools and in institutions of higher learning. Of course, not all these students would be in the *non-agricultural* labor force were they not in school, but many would be and those that would have been in the agricultural labor force might have permitted additional transfers of labor from agriculture to other sectors. If, in the absence of the increased educational program, the planned 1955 non-agricultural labor force would have been 4 million more than presently planned for 1955, the absolute increase in the non-agricultural labor force

[19] See Gershon Cooper, "Taxation and Incentive in Mobilization," *Quarterly Journal of Economics*, February 1952, pp. 43 ff.

would have been almost 10 million from 1950 to 1955 plan as against 11 million between 1945 and 1950 and the average annual rate of increase would have been 4.7 per cent as against 5.4 per cent between 1947 and 1951, 5.0 per cent between 1937 and 1940, and 3.5 per cent between 1937 and 1942 plan (Grossman, page 193). Thus the increased educational program might well be the entire explanation for the *unprecedented* lowness of the Fifth FYP rate of increase. In any case, the increased educational program certainly represents, in a real and important sense, a substitution of capital for labor via investment-in-self.

4. Among the factors mentioned as possible explanations for the retardation in the rate of growth of the non-agricultural labor force is the ambitious nature of the Fifth FYP agricultural output goals. The suggestion of an increased concern on the part of Soviet authorities for future agricultural development is of particular interest because of its rather dramatic verification in recent events.[20]

Achievements recorded by the end of 1952 must have made it clear to Soviet authorities that, without extraordinary measures, the announced goals for 1955 plan agriculture and consumers' goods were unattainable. In an August 1953 speech Malenkov sounded a new note of urgent concern for the Soviet consumer. The newness of the note consisted in: (1) repetition of a two- to three-year time horizon within which a sharp rise in consumers' goods output is to be effected, (2) admission that the current level of consumers' goods output is unsatisfactory and the diagnosis that this is due to past emphasis on heavy industry and transport in capital formation, and (3) admission that agricultural output has lagged seriously and that it is necessary "first of all" to develop agriculture if consumption increases are to be attained. Though various measures were more or less vaguely described, even less than usual was to be learned about resource allocation from the 1953 Soviet budget, presented in August 1953, because of unusually large unexplained residuals on both the revenue and expenditure sides. Consequently, in the absence of further revelations of intentions, reservations about possible shifts in the pattern of Soviet economic development seemed prudent.

The new note continued in the Soviet press during August and

[20] These remarks were written in November 1953 and are based on *Pravda* issues from August through October. The decrees referred to on agriculture, retail trade, and consumers' goods are in *Pravda*, September 26, September 29, October 1, October 23, October 28, and October 30, 1953.

September 1953. Finally, there appeared a series of speeches, reports, and *decrees* which add up to quite impressive *plans* for large and short-run consumption increases and agricultural improvements. There is not space to discuss these developments in detail. Suffice it to note here that: (1) despite failures in 1951 and 1952, many of the ambitious goals set by the Fifth FYP for 1955 plan agriculture and consumption are now to be achieved in 1954; (2) investment in agriculture, trade, and consumers' goods industries is to be increased markedly: (3) little is now being said about the "Great Stalin construction projects" and nothing about the most ambitious of them (e.g. the Turkmenian project); (4) there is little indication of a problem with respect to the agricultural labor force except in the case of specialists, of whom 100,000 are to be sent to machine and tractor stations from ministries and local authorities in 1954 plan; (5) there are suggestions of the use of international trade to provide consumers' goods imports in exchange for producers' goods exports.

So far, of course, these are just plans. But if fulfilled, the plans will mean rapid increases in living standards. If not fulfilled by significant margins, I feel from the way in which the changes have been stated that serious internal problems may ensue. Future developments in these sectors must be watched with care.

Alexander Erlich, Russian Research Center, Harvard University; and National Bureau of Economic Research

Grossman has marshaled impressive evidence in support of his thesis. The increase in capital-labor ratios in Soviet industry as shown by his figures is striking indeed; and while I have no quarrel with his interpretation of this trend, I would like to contribute a very tentative additional suggestion. It seems not unreasonable to surmise that the Soviet economy may now be experiencing a delayed "replacement echo" of the great investment boom which began in the late 1920's and continued unabatedly until the German invasion of 1941. There can be no doubt that a good deal of equipment built in the period of the First and Second FYP's is now ready for retirement. True, in earlier years the presence of large blocks of worn-out and antiquated equipment would by no means have justified the conclusion that this equipment would actually be scrapped: the Soviet writings of the 1930's and 1940's bear eloquent testimony to the fact that the Soviet economic administration consistently adhered to the policy of working the old equipment to death. In view of the very substantial expansion of the Soviet capital-making capacity in the postwar period, however, a guess could be ventured that the Soviet economy could now afford to retire the still serviceable old plant and replace it with the new, rather than to let the latter come, as it were, on the top of the first.

Should such a change in policy have actually taken place (and this is for the time being, to repeat, merely a not implausible hypothesis), the increase in the *net* investment per industrial worker would be, in all probability, considerably smaller than Grossman's figures would indicate. It should be noted, however, that his two indicators of the capital-labor ratio would not be affected by this to the same degree. Since the cement series reflects the behavior of *total* constructional activity over time, the increase of the share of replacement in the gross investment should correspondingly reduce the net portion of this series for the relevant years. The situation is different with regard to the power consumption series, which measures *increments* and not totals: the figures it contains should be taken to represent net magnitudes even under assumption of a change in replacement policy, since the part of the newly installed plant which represents the replacement of the retired units would now be consuming the power supply set free after the scrapping of the old plant. The figures in the relevant part of line 10 in Grossman's Table 2 would still tend to overstate the incremental capital ÷ labor ratio to the extent to which the increased power consumption per worker would be paralleled by a less-than-proportional increase (or by an actual decline) in the use of non-electrical energy per worker. But this qualification raises no new points because the possibility of such upward bias was explicitly recognized by Grossman.

Abram Bergson, Columbia University

In his illuminating essay Grossman describes and explains recent trends in the allocation of labor and capital between the agricultural and non-agricultural sectors of the Soviet economy. This is a topic that might be examined from more than one standpoint, but interest here revolves chiefly around the recurring problem of the efficiency of resource allocation. In the present context what is in question particularly is the extent to which the Russians tend to realize their "production possibilities" in the allocation of labor and capital between the agricultural and non-agricultural sectors. In studying the trends in this allocation, one is interested in variations in this tendency over time. The realization of production possibilities, it will be recalled, is a desideratum that is entirely independent of the Soviet authorities' preferences regarding the bill of goods. If production possibilities are not attained, a suitable reallocation affords an opportunity to increase the output of either agricultural or non-agricultural goods, or, if it is so desired, both of these products.

While it has seemed desirable to state this problem somewhat more explicitly than Grossman does, I must leave to the reader a review, in the light of my remarks, of the interesting facts and arguments he sets forth. I will comment here on only one or two aspects of the problem.

Grossman cites a number of factors which may tend to limit Soviet transfers of labor from agriculture to industry. One is the "technological bias" of the Soviet planners which leads them to seek continually to raise the productivity of labor in industry. A review of Soviet writings would undoubtedly yield a good deal of support for the view that such a bias actually operates in the U.S.S.R. Moreover, it is a familiar notion that in a country such as Russia, where a vast population has been and still is engaged in agriculture, the bias might lead to economic waste. The precise sense in which a waste results, however, is not always made clear, so it may deserve underlining that the diseconomy takes the form of a failure to realize the theoretic desideratum, the community's production possibilities. Thus if the Russians are to achieve this goal, sizable transfers of labor from agriculture to industry may have to be carried out year after year. These transfers would proceed simultaneously with an allocation of investments which would both assure the release of workers from agriculture and equip them for work in industry.

Insofar as a country attains its production possibilities, the total output of both industrial and agricultural products is greater than it would be otherwise. But with the indicated allocation of labor and capital the productivity of labor in industry may nevertheless rise only slowly. If an allocation in accord with production possibilities were instituted in circumstances where previously it had not been realized, it might even lead to a drop in labor productivity. This is to say that with a bias in favor of labor productivity such as that in the U.S.S.R., an efficient allocation might never be realized at all. Moreover, the barrier to its full-scale introduction would grow ever greater, the higher the level of industrial productivity actually attained.

While Russia has a vast agricultural population, the question involved here is the extent to which it is economically surplus, in the sense that labor may be released from the agricultural sector at the price of relatively limited investments or loss in output. Grossman comments only briefly on this question. For reasons which I have set forth elsewhere,[1] my own inclination is to think of larger possibilities of further labor economies than he does.

Grossman points out that the transfer of labor from agriculture to industry may be limited also by superior urban living standards. Given this superiority, the transfers are costly in terms of consumers' goods. I have no question to raise on this score, but account should be taken also of the further problem of transferring food from the country to the city. The transfer of workers does not lead automatically to a release of the agricultural produce needed to support the migrants; somehow the government must extract the produce from the peasantry. This problem of the "marketed share" of agricultural produce has long been central in the government's relations with agriculture. While the government's control of agriculture through the collective farm system has enabled it to raise the marketed share far above the low levels attained under peasant agriculture in the late 1920's, the government must hesitate to increase still further such exactions. This would be an additional factor tending to limit transfers of labor. Moreover, as will readily be seen, this would also tend to cause further deviations from production possibilities.

In his discussion of recent trends in the allocation of labor and capital, Grossman focuses attention especially on the low rate of growth (2.8 per cent per year) projected for the non-agricultural labor force under the Fifth FYP (1951-1955). He views this as marking a new phase in Soviet planning. On the face of it this development also emphasizes the question of the degree to which Soviet resource allocation realizes production possibilities. But I do not wish to pursue this aspect further here. Rather, my concern is a limited factual one. In my opinion Grossman is undoubtedly right in thinking that the low rate of growth projected in the current plan sets a precedent, but in appraising its extent I would like to emphasize a few matters which he may not have stressed sufficiently.

[1] See my discussion in *Soviet Economic Growth*, Abram Bergson, editor, Row, Peterson, 1953, pp. 308-310.

While I agree with Grossman in assuming that the Fifth FYP still warrants careful study despite the important economic events since Stalin's death, a question is in order concerning the "realism" of the Plan at the time of its promulgation. One inevitably wonders in particular how seriously to take the feature which occupies a central place in the discussion: the rate of growth projected for the non-agricultural labor force. Some interest may attach, then, to the following tabulation of the Russians' record of fulfillment of the labor force goals of their Five-Year Plans to date:[2]

	Workers and Employees[a] *(millions)*
Actual, 1927/1928	11.3
1st FYP goal, 1932/1933	
Minimal variant	14.8
Optimal variant	15.8
Actual, 1932	22.9
2nd FYP goal, 1937	28.9
Actual, 1937	27.0
3rd FYP goal, 1942	32.0
Actual, 1940	31.2
Actual, 1945	27.3
4th FYP goal, 1950	33.5
Actual, 1950	38.2
5th FYP goal, 1955	43.9
Actual, 1951	39.8
Actual, 1952	40.7

[a] Strictly speaking, these Soviet official data refer to all hired labor, including not only non-agricultural but also several million agricultural wage earners.

Evidently, the four previous Plans were unevenly fulfilled. Since the First and Fourth Plans were greatly overfulfilled, one is impelled to question the "realism" of the goal of the current Plan. However, it will be noted too that during the first two years of the present Plan, 1951-1952, the Russians managed to keep more or less within the framework of their current long-term goal; very possibly the present plan will turn out to be operational after all.

[2] On the scope of the figures see Grossman's essay, notes to Table 1. The figures on actual employment are from *Trud v S.S.S.R.*, Moscow, TsUNKhU, 1936, pp. 10 ff.; Warren W. Eason, "Population and Labor Force," in *Soviet Economic Growth*, as cited, p. 110; and Grossman's essay, Table 1. The Plan goals are from Grossman's essay; *Piatiletnii plan narodno-khoziaistvennogo stroitel'stva S.S.S.R.*, Tom I, Moscow, Gosplan S.S.S.R., 1929, p. 127; and State Planning Commission of the U.S.S.R., *The Second Five Year Plan for the Development of the National Economy of the USSR (1933-1937)*, London, Lawrence, p. 545.

In considering to what extent the present Plan represents a break with past experience, two other matters must be examined. First, as Grossman explains, the rate of growth projected under the Fifth FYP (2.8 per cent per year) is actually only a little lower than the one that was projected under the Third (3.5 per cent per year). The rate actually realized under the latter Plan prior to the German attack, i.e. in the period 1937-1940, was 5.0 per cent, but the 1940 employment figure on which this growth rate is based reflects the expansion in Soviet territory during 1939-1940. However, it does not take into account an increase in working hours from an average of about forty-one to forty-eight per calendar week in June 1940.

Second, the actual rate of growth under the Second FYP was but 3.3 per cent. Grossman apparently feels that for his purposes the Second FYP ought to be lumped with the First. This is on the plausible ground that many of the workers recruited under the First FYP were not really assimilated until the following quinquennium. It should be observed, however, that the current Plan may in some measure be similiarly related to its predecessor, which witnessed a major expansion in the labor force not only during but after demobilization.

Reply by the Author

My appreciation to the three commentators for lighting their lamps in the dark alley into which I have lured them! I find myself in sympathy with all of Bergson's and Erlich's remarks, and so, after a nod in their direction, I turn to Kaplan's comments. Kaplan has paid me the high compliment of studying my paper carefully, and preparing a most patient and valuable critique of it. I am in accord with him on some of his points; with regard to some others our differences are slight. My rejoinder is therefore addressed only to the major issues between us.

Do my indicators—cement consumption and the increment in electric power output—indicate anything? Kaplan has constructed his Table 1 to show the relationship between annual movements in investment (at stable prices) and in these two series[1] during selected periods in Soviet experience. The investment series are from Soviet sources and their exact derivation is not always clear, but they may be provisionally accepted in the absence of more reliable data. The

[1] The fact that he uses cement *output* while I refer to cement consumption where possible should not make much difference.

three series show far from identical annual changes, the correspondence between investment and increment in power being poorer than that between investment and cement output. Better correspondence would probably be found if blocks of years (as in my Table 2) rather than individual years were the basis of comparison; but the nature of the data prevents this.

Kaplan is probably right that "as indicators in a more accurate sense" my two series "seem to fail." But I was not so hopeful as to demand this of them. My purpose has not been to draw exact inferences with regard to the relative volume of investment during the various periods, but rather to sketch the major outline of the rise in incremental capital-intensity in the non-agricultural sector of the Soviet economy. I regarded the two series as a "very rough and tentative indication," and Kaplan's Table 1 seems to support me in this view, for it does show that on the whole the order of magnitude of the volume of investment is preserved in one or both of the other series. In Kaplan's own words (italics his), "The hypothesized relationships may be adequate to yield what Grossman requires—namely, an indication of *increasing* incremental capital-intensity. . . ."

Kaplan's section on "The Meaning of Capital-Intensity" is most stimulating. He is quite right, of course, about the mathematics. Increasing incremental capital-intensity does not imply increasing average capital-intensity. If in the paper I appear to assume so, it is only because the suggested magnitudes are such that the incremental capital-intensity in the U.S.S.R. during the Fifth FYP must almost certainly have exceeded the average capital-intensity, and therefore the latter must have been rising as well. The contrary possibility is hardly worth attention in this instance. Further, he is correct in that the marginal rate of substitution between capital and labor is not measured by the incremental or average capital-intensities. (Nor have I tried to use them in this way.) Now he asks: (1) Since the stock of capital per worker, i.e. the average ratio, is the relevant quantity from the viewpoint of economic growth, why introduce the incremental concept? and (2) What is the relation between a rising incremental capital-intensity and a notion of substitution of capital for labor (which can be read into my approach)?

1. I would answer that the incremental ratio is relevant to the *process* of economic growth, and hence to planning for it, quite apart from its impact on the average. The characteristic features of an economy derive not only from the capital-labor ratio at some

point in time, but also from the slope of the path traversed to get there, i.e. from the incremental ratio. This indeed is implicit in much of the contemporary discussion of the "advantages" of economic backwardness. Average capital-intensity is an inadequate tool for a dynamic analysis of the process of growth, in part because of such well-known phenomena as the limited economic mobility of capital after it has been embodied in capital goods and the poor reversibility of certain socio-economic processes such as urbanization.

Perhaps an appeal to extreme cases will help to emphasize my point. Surely the process of growth is different if capital is the only factor whose supply increases significantly while the supply of other factors remains constant (incremental capital-intensity equals infinity), or if it is labor which alone increases (incremental capital-intensity equals zero). Numerous important variables are affected thereby, such as the technology of new investment projects, extent of obsolescence and replacement of existing capital equipment, transfer of labor within the economy to achieve its better combination with capital, urbanization, and so forth. (Given the target isoquant, the marginal rate of substitution is affected thereby, though we cannot a priori tell more than the direction of the difference.) This range of problems overlaps those discussed in my paper in connection with labor allocation, thus showing the presence, if not of a "systematic relationship" between the two parts of my paper (which Kaplan fails to find), at least of a logical nexus between them.

It has been pointed out[2] with good reason that by comparison with average capital-intensity, incremental capital-intensity will fluctuate violently and so give an exaggerated picture of policy changes. This difficulty can be avoided in part by comparing groups of years instead of individual years, as is done in the paper. But in this instance we may be particularly fortunate in that erratic fluctuations in the incremental ratio are presumably kept down, thanks to full employment of labor and capacity in the non-agricultural sector in all periods, consistently high rates of investment out of national product, and constant pressure to expand output.

2. Inquiring into the existence of a logical connection between incremental capital-intensity and the notion of substitution of capital for labor, Kaplan fails to find it established in my paper, nor can he establish one for a dynamic context. His critique is illuminating, but his search is unnecessary. Insofar as a notion of substitution underlies

[2] E.g. by Moses Abramovitz in a private communication to the author.

my discussion, it is substitution *along* the target isoquant, i.e. in a static and not in a dynamic sense. (Substitution of capital for labor does have an unambiguous meaning in the former sense, as Kaplan agrees.) Incremental capital-intensities enter only as alternative paths traversed to reach the target isoquant. The substitution in question is therefore not a dynamic concept, but a description of the difference between points on the same isoquant.

Perhaps if the phrase is to have a useful connotation in a dynamic picture at all, it should be defined operationally: we can call it a significant replacement of labor by capital in *existing* enterprises so as to release all or part of the manpower required to operate the newly created production facilities. The reshuffle of labor would presumably be based on efficiency considerations, i.e. on a comparison of the marginal rates of substitution between capital and labor in the old and in the projected production facilities. It is clear that incremental capital-intensity would have to be above a certain value in order for this, and not the reverse, movement of labor to take place; and the higher the incremental ratio, the more labor has to be so transferred (given the target isoquant of the sector within which the reshuffling takes place). A large reshuffle of this sort is an important aspect of the economy's growth process—hence perhaps a justification of the use of the incremental concept. As mentioned in the paper, the Soviet economy seems now to be experiencing such labor transfer within the non-agricultural sector.

Kaplan correctly points out[3] that under my "simplifying assumption" of the whole economy's being represented by two isoquants, and fixed supplies of two factors, the choice of a position on one of them does not uniquely determine the position on the other, as I stated, except at the optimum for the whole system.

The last section of Kaplan's comments deals with numerous points in relation to my detentive and deterrent factors. I reply selectively.

I omitted the cost of training agricultural labor and of providing rural housing from the definition of i' because these, under Soviet conditions, are typically not costs to the state, and it is the state's computations that we are trying to reconstruct. I would not expect Soviet planners to be especially concerned with them in choosing between investment alternatives.

Kaplan's case "that a larger increase in the non-agricultural labor force might increase observed incremental capital-intensity via the

[3] His footnote 15.

impact on observed investment of increased expenditures on housing and other urban facilities," assuming (I take it) an invariant non-agricultural output, is not a possibility that would be knowingly and rationally chosen by the planners. It requires more of *each* factor of production to achieve the same output. It is, of course, just with reference to Soviet attempts to get away from this inefficiency that I try to explain the small planned increase in non-agricultural employment during the Fifth FYP.

I expect a reduction in the proportion of women in the non-agricultural labor force as a result of a future rise in real wages. Kaplan points out, correctly, that "An increase in real wages . . . has both an income effect and a substitution effect on the choice between housekeeping (leisure?) and gainful employment." He concludes, "It is not clear, therefore, whether an increase in real wages deters or encourages participation of females in gainful employment." Prediction in this case is no less hazardous than in so many others, but perhaps past experience tips the scales in favor of the attitude taken in my paper. I refer to the increase in the proportion of women in the non-agricultural labor force coincident with the decline in real wages after 1928, and the small reduction in this proportion since 1947.[4] True, the proportion continued to rise even in the late 1930's, i.e. after real wages had substantially recovered from their lows in the first half of the decade. But it must be remembered that these years also witnessed a sharply accelerated withdrawal of males from the non-agricultural labor force into military service and forced labor camps.

I should like to conclude by reiterating Kaplan's plea for a thorough and competent study of the various facets of Soviet technology. The results should be most relevant to an understanding of past Soviet development, the potential for growth in the near future which the economy contains, and the dynamics of the growth process itself.

[4] Cf. Warren W. Eason, "Population and Labor Force," in *Soviet Economic Growth*, Abram Bergson, editor, Row, Peterson, 1953.

FINANCING SOVIET ECONOMIC DEVELOPMENT

F. D. HOLZMAN

UNIVERSITY OF WASHINGTON

THE PURPOSE OF THIS PAPER is threefold: to explain Soviet choice among sources of finance, to present and analyze the relevant data, and to evaluate the fiscal and monetary policies pursued. It should be stated at the outset that the sum of amounts collected from the various sources of finance always substantially exceeds the value of gross national investment. This is because from the same pools of funds the Soviet government finances not only investment in fixed and working capital, but government stockpiles of strategic materials, expenditures of the Ministry of Armed Forces for defense, administrative activities of the various departments of the government, expenditures on health and education, transfer payments, subsidies to state enterprises which sell their output at below-cost prices, and gross expenditures of the machine tractor station complex.[1] Since budgetary receipts, the largest single source of funds, are not earmarked for specific expenditures, there is no way of determining how the one category of expenditures which is directly relevant to economic development, viz. gross investment, was financed. We are limited to discussing the sources of finance of the whole of the "nonconsumption" activities of the Soviet state, loosely defining "nonconsumption" as the sum of goods and services purchased by the state plus transfer payments to the household. Because of our interest in how the state planned its economic expansion, investment from private profits and private depreciation funds will not be considered; private investment expenditures were, however, insignificant in all but the first year or two of the period under review. Discussion will center around the first three Five-Year Plan periods, i.e. from 1928/1929, when the first Plan went into operation, until 1940, the third and last completed year of the Third Plan (which was truncated by World War II). This period is adequate

Part of the research for this paper was accomplished while I was attached to the Russian Research Center, Harvard University. The financial assistance of that organization is gratefully acknowledged, as are the critical comments of Mathilda Holzman and Gregory Grossman.

[1] Before 1930 the transportation and communications systems were included in the budget on a gross basis; this was true of almost all state enterprises during War Communism (1918-1921).

to illustrate the problems faced and policies adopted by Soviet planners.

Before turning to the sources of finance, a few words will be devoted to a consideration of the significance of money and finance for the functioning of the Soviet economy. Those unfamiliar with the Soviet economy may be misled by the emphasis on the words "planning" and "controls" into thinking that money is not important in the Soviet economy. While the Soviets rely more on direct economic controls than any other nation in the world today, and while such controls, where they are used, substitute for money and the market mechanism as the allocator of scarce resources, money has not been replaced by direct controls. There are no direct controls in large sectors of the Soviet economy. Consumer goods, for example, are distributed at present by the market mechanism; the amount of consumer goods which any household can purchase is determined by its current and accumulated earnings. The labor market, though less free than it was in the 1930's, still depends primarily on differential wage payments for the allocation of labor. Other markets (raw materials and producer goods), though on the whole more subject to direct controls, do nevertheless contain substantial areas in which free market forces are still allowed to operate. Even where allocation is accomplished directly, to the extent that prices provide the planners with a basis for allocation, money functions as a standard of value, if not as a medium of exchange.[2] Failure by the Soviets to keep their financial house in order will have a deleterious effect on the economy (through reduced incentives, misallocation of resources, etc.) so long as markets and prices are used by them to perform economic functions.

1. *Choice among Sources of Finance*

A listing of the major Soviet sources of finance has a conventional ring: direct taxation of the population, sales taxes, profits taxes, sales of government bonds to the population and to state institutions, retained profits of enterprises, depreciation reserves, bank credit, household savings. While there are many real similarities between the above categories and their Western counterparts, closer examination reveals substantial differences both of an institutional nature and in their relative importance. A cursory glance at Table 1 reveals

[2] Money continues to flow, of course, but the possessor of money has so little option as to its use that the role of money in the transaction must be considered trivial.

TABLE 1

Sources of Soviet Finance as Percentages of Adjusted Total, 1937

Major indirect or commodity taxes	71.9
Direct taxes	3.8
Sales of government bonds to population	4.1
Miscellaneous budgetary receipts	7.3
Retained profits of state enterprises	4.6
Indivisible fund of collective farms	1.7
Depreciation reserves	5.4
Voluntary household savings	1.0
Increase of currency in circulation	1.4

Source: Taken from Tables 3 and 4 below. The above items total to more than 100 per cent for reasons discussed in the notes to Tables 3 and 4.

that the financial path followed by the Soviet Union differs in several significant respects from the paths followed by many Western nations.

FOREIGN BORROWING

Outstanding for its absence from Table 1 is foreign borrowing. I do not think it would be possible to single out over the past 150 years many nations which have industrialized, especially in the early stages, without some foreign aid. The Soviets industrialized without any significant foreign aid, not because they wanted to—they did not—but because the Western World was hostile to them[3] and they, in turn, were hostile to and distrustful of Western nations. This was not a climate in which international capital was likely to flow freely and abundantly. With some minor exceptions, the Soviets paid in gold, commodities, and in imperial crown jewels for all goods purchased from other nations in the interwar period. In recent years the situation has changed somewhat. During the war, of course, the Russians received considerable help from the United States in the form of lend-lease shipments; and since the war reparations have contributed, in some years, respectable sums to budget receipts.[4] Finally, there may be considerable capital flow between the Soviet Union and the countries within its political orbit, but on this there is very little reliable information as to either amount or direction.

[3] And not only for ideological reasons. Remember that Western investors took a heavy loss when the Bolsheviks refused to honor the very large foreign debts of the Russian imperial government.

[4] Amounting to as much as 3 to 4 per cent of total budget receipts.

VOLUNTARY SAVINGS

The Soviets have always encouraged voluntary saving by the population. A large network of banks in both urban and rural areas has been developed to foster the saving habit; the 5 per cent interest on time deposits (six months or more) is the highest obtainable in the Soviet Union;[5] the Currency Reform of December 1947 applied a much more favorable conversion rate to savings deposits than to either cash or government bonds. Nevertheless, understandably enough, savings have never amounted to much in the Soviet Union. The annual increment to savings deposits is only a fraction of 1 per cent of total household money income.[6] The average Soviet citizen is in much too great need of current goods and services to put aside large sums of money to meet future needs. And those future needs which induce the greatest amount of saving in Western nations (e.g. provision against sickness, accidents, old age, unemployment, etc.) are relatively well provided for in the Soviet Union by a comprehensive social security system. Furthermore, the incentive to save must certainly have been vitiated by twenty years of rapidly rising prices in the consumer goods markets, not ending until the currency reform of 1947.[7] Finally, of course, the state imposes upon the population such a high rate of compulsory saving that little is left to individual initiative.[8]

COMMODITY TAXES

Most of the compulsory savings of the economy are collected by the state in the form of taxes and are reflected in the budget accounts;[9] and indirect or commodity taxes are responsible for from two-thirds to three-fourths of budgetary receipts. The three principal commodity taxes are the turnover tax, deductions from the

[5] Demand deposits pay only 3 per cent.

[6] Cf. F. D. Holzman, "The Burden of Soviet Taxation," *American Economic Review*, September 1953, Table 1.

[7] Since the currency reform, consumer goods prices have declined steadily; this may eventually have a positive effect on the incentive to save. From 1928 to 1947, consumer goods prices increased, on the average, about twentyfold. Cf. Naum Jasny, *The Soviet Price System*, Stanford University Press, 1951, Chap. 2.

[8] Perhaps it should also be noted that the Soviet rural population appears to have the usual peasant distrust of banks and prefers to hold a large part of its savings in the form of cash.

[9] The Soviet state budget is a consolidated budget consisting of the all-Union, republican, and local budgets. It is equivalent to the sum of the federal, state, and local budgets in the United States.

profits of state enterprises (profits tax), and the social insurance markup. The turnover tax is essentially a sales tax levied, at present, exclusively on consumer goods—except for petroleum and petroleum products, where the tax substitutes for explicit rent payments. Before 1949 it was levied on producer goods as well, but for fiscal control of the tax-paying enterprises rather than for revenue. The rates on consumer goods are highly differentiated, varying from 1 per cent of the *selling price* on some commodities to as much as 90 per cent on others.[10]

The deduction from profits is correctly not called a tax on enterprise[11] by the Soviets because it applies to nationalized industries. The state does not tax the profits of its own industries; it simply transfers money from one state account to another. From a fiscal point of view the deduction from profits, as part of profits, adds to the price paid by the consumer; in this respect it does not differ from the turnover tax and can properly be considered a commodity tax on the household. Every enterprise pays a minimum 10 per cent tax on profits for purposes of fiscal control. The remaining profits are used as needed to finance investment planned for the enterprise and to make payments into the Directors' Fund.[12] Any surplus above these needs is *deducted* into the budget.

The social insurance markup is a form of payroll tax, and for our purposes can be looked upon as adding to the price of commodities bought by the household, just like the turnover and profits taxes. The receipts from this tax are derived as additions to the wage funds of enterprises, the percentage varying from 3.7 to 10.7, depending on conditions of employment and other factors in the separate branches of the economy. It is claimed that part of the receipts from this tax are earmarked for sickness and old age insurance.[13]

Why is commodity taxation the dominant method of extracting

[10] Looked upon as a markup over cost, as is customary in the West, the tax rates are much higher, of course. A 50 per cent tax becomes one of 100 per cent; a 90 per cent tax becomes one of 900 per cent.

[11] Although for convenience it will be referred to as a profits tax.

[12] For incentive reasons from 1 to 5 per cent of planned profits and 15 to 45 per cent of overplan profits are deducted into the Directors' Fund. These amounts are disbursed as bonuses to workers and managers, for workers' housing, for cultural projects, and for extra-plan investment in the enterprises.

[13] We might also have included in the category of taxes which enter the commodity price structure the incomes of economic organizations which are allocated "to the trade unions and special funds for workers' training and education" (cf. Abram Bergson, "Soviet National Income and Product," *Quarterly Journal of Economics,* May 1950, p. 288).

savings from the population in the Soviet Union? Conversely, why is little reliance placed upon income (direct) taxation, the form of levy preferred in the United States and in many other Western nations?[14] Soviet preference for commodity taxation is certainly not to be explained on ideological grounds. In fact, the predominance of the turnover tax among Soviet taxes has proved embarrassing to Soviet economists. Marxist writers consistently attacked indirect taxes as socially inequitable and regressive; bad associations also stem from the reliance of the tsars on highly regressive excise taxes (especially on alcoholic beverages) for the bulk of their revenue. That the Soviets rely on commodity taxation in spite of their "ideological" bias attests to its superiority for their purposes.[15]

Soviet preference for commodity taxation appears to rest primarily on three considerations. First, there is the "money illusion," which has it that workers are more conscious of the impact on their economic position of changes in wages than of the impact produced by changes in prices. A corollary to this is the hypothesis that workers are more sensitive to changes in direct taxes (and thus in take-home pay) than to changes in indirect taxes (reflected in commodity prices). The money illusion, therefore, would cause commodity and income taxes of equal size to have different impacts on work incentives. This is particularly important in the Soviet Union, where almost all income is earned income. Analytically, it is possible to separate the impact of taxes on incentives into at least two categories: the effect on the work-leisure ratio and the effect on differential wages as a factor in choosing between jobs. Most writers dealing with this subject concentrate on the work-leisure ratio, arguing that high taxes, and particularly high marginal rates of tax, reduce the incentive to work, and that indirect taxes, as a consequence of the

[14] The Soviet income tax on the urban population does not differ substantially from the income taxes in other countries except that different social and economic classes pay according to different rate schedules in application of Soviet "class policy." Thus workers, artists, professionals with private practices (e.g. lawyers and doctors), and private shopkeepers pay at rapidly ascending rates (on identical money incomes) from left to right. The rural population pays a very different sort of tax (called the agricultural tax) because the bulk of peasant income is in kind. This necessitates, among other things, fairly cumbersome methods of assessing personal income and estimating the amount of tax to be paid. The agricultural tax discriminates in favor of the collective farmer and against the private peasant.

[15] In fact, for about twenty years they have not referred to it as a tax on the population, but rather as "accumulation of socialized industry," implying that the amounts returned to the budget are a result solely of great increases in productivity.

illusion, minimize the disincentive effects of taxes. This line of reasoning ignores the income effect of taxation,[16] or at least assumes that the substitution effect between work and leisure is more important than the income effect. There is no empirical evidence, to my knowledge, to support this assumption, and, in fact, the income effect may actually be strong enough to induce Soviet workers to greater effort. If this were the case, it could not be argued that the Soviet choice of commodity taxation preserves work incentives.

It can be argued, without equivocation, that the Soviets took advantage of the money illusion effects of commodity taxation to preserve the effectiveness of their differential wage structure as an incentive mechanism for allocating labor. In order to attract workers, Soviet policy has been to pay higher wages to persons in jobs requiring greater skills, in expanding industries, and in jobs or areas where work conditions are undesirable. Up until the late 1920's or early 1930's this policy had not been implemented successfully, hampered to a considerable extent as it was by the hangovers of an earlier "equalitarian" philosophy regarding wage differentials.[17] An attempt was made to improve the situation; in 1931 Stalin intervened and, in a speech calling for greater wage differentials, set the new policy. He said: "In a number of our factories, wage scales are drawn up in such a way as to practically wipe out the difference between skilled labour and unskilled labour, between heavy work and light work. The consequence of wage equalization is that the unskilled worker lacks the incentive to become a skilled worker and is thus deprived of the prospect of advancement; . . . in order to get skilled workers we must give the unskilled worker a stimulus and prospect of advancement, of rising to a higher position. . . ."[18] Bergson's wage study indicates that wage differentials in the Soviet Union in 1934 were about as great as those in the United States at a comparable stage (1904) of economic development.[19]

In the late 1920's and early 1930's, at the same time that Soviet wage differentials were being increased for incentive reasons, taxes were also being increased. The average rate of taxation about doubled from 1926 to 1936, increasing by substantial amounts al-

[16] That persons having their incomes reduced by taxes would tend to work harder.

[17] Cf. Abram Bergson, *The Structure of Soviet Wages*, Harvard University Press, 1946, Chaps. 13 and 14.

[18] Joseph Stalin, *Problems of Leninism*, Moscow, Foreign Languages Publishing House, 1940, pp. 371-373.

[19] Bergson, *The Structure of Soviet Wages*, as cited.

most every year of the period;[20] by 1930 it amounted to about 50 per cent of household income.[21] Clearly, Soviet differential wage policy was in danger of being weakened by Soviet tax policy. Reliance upon income taxation under these circumstances would have had a much more adverse impact on the incentive-wage system than commodity taxation for at least two reasons. First, under the Soviet pay-as-you-earn system of income taxation, workers are as likely to base job decisions on differential take-home pay as on gross wage differentials. On the other hand, if no income tax were levied, gross wage differentials would probably retain much of their incentive effect, even with high levels of commodity taxation. Second, for political reasons income taxation would almost necessarily have to be progressive, or at least proportional, thereby reducing wage differentials relatively as well as absolutely; this would not necessarily be so for sales taxation, especially when the tax is hidden, and when it has a highly differentiated rate structure, as is the case in the Soviet Union.[22] This facet of the money illusion is undoubtedly an important reason for Soviet use of commodity taxation.

A second factor explaining Soviet reliance on commodity taxation is administrative in nature. The turnover tax, particularly in the early stages of its development, was levied on and collected from state industrial enterprises (procurement agencies in agriculture) and wholesale organizations. This provided the cheapest and least evadable method of collecting money taxes from the population since the number of industrial enterprises and wholesale organizations was not large and they maintained relatively good money accounts; it also provided a continuous source of funds—the larger enterprises made daily payments to the budget. These considerations were quite crucial in the late 1920's and the early 1930's, before the administrative apparatus of the state had achieved anything like its present-day efficiency. Reliance upon income taxation would have meant levying and collecting taxes from 30 to 40 million householders, many of whom were still illiterate. Furthermore, at that time a large segment of the peasant population still had not been herded into col-

[20] Cf. Holzman, *op. cit.*, Table 3. [21] *Ibid.*, Table 3.

[22] The Soviet turnover tax appears to have had a somewhat regressive rate structure in the prewar period; the postwar structure seems to be considerably less regressive and may be roughly proportional. The rate structure is much too complex, and the information on income-expenditure patterns much too limited, for us to come to any but the most tentative conclusions on this matter, however. Cf. F. D. Holzman, *Soviet Taxation: The Fiscal and Monetary Problems of a Planned Economy*, Harvard University Press, 1955, Chap. 6.

lective farms, where it could be reached without excessive costs by tax collectors.

A third consideration, and one which is stressed by Soviet economists, is the use of the turnover tax to facilitate price planning. The Soviets have attempted to maintain a market for consumer goods in which free choice prevails. Prices are not set freely by decentralized agents as is usually the case in Western nations; rather, prices are centrally administered and the state is responsible for adjusting relative prices. Maintenance of appropriate price flexibility is, for obvious reasons, facilitated by the existence of a large element of tax in the cost-price structure. In fact, without either a commodity tax or a subsidy (which can be considered a negative commodity tax in this case) it would not be possible to alter relative prices much faster than relative changes in productivity would permit[23] (i.e. prices would approximate long-run cost).

INCOME TAXATION

In spite of the advantages and magnitude of Soviet commodity taxation, the population is also required to pay an income tax. The only significant function which this tax seems to serve is to discourage private practice by professionals[24] (e.g. doctors and lawyers) and other "nonworker" elements in the urban population. These groups pay a discriminatorily high tax, which reaches 55 and 65 per cent, respectively, on incomes in excess of 70,000 rubles; workers and salaried employees, who comprise 90 per cent or more of the nonagricultural labor force, pay according to a schedule which reaches a maximum rate of 13 per cent on all income over 12,000 rubles annually. While the "class policy" feature of the income tax may have been important twenty years ago, before the private sector of the economy had been thoroughly squelched, it can hardly be considered so any more. Moreover, the tax certainly has little fiscal importance.[25] It is difficult to understand why the Soviets continue to use direct levies on income when they could be replaced very easily by a small increase in commodity taxation. Perhaps they are continued through inertia, or because the Soviets wish to maintain intact the direct tax apparatus for possible future use.

[23] This is especially true since the Soviets have virtually no explicit rent payments but include them implicitly in the turnover tax.

[24] Also perhaps to extract the "economic rent" from such practices.

[25] What we have said of the urban income tax applies also to the agricultural tax. The agricultural tax discriminates against the private farmer and in favor of the collective farmer.

SALES OF GOVERNMENT BONDS

Sales of government bonds constitute, in effect, another form of direct levy on the Soviet population. Similarity of these bond sales to taxation rests on the following characteristics: considerable social pressure is brought to bear upon the population to subscribe from two to four weeks' wages a year; these amounts are deducted from workers' wages every month just as direct taxes are; most bonds are not redeemable until the full term has expired;[26] a series of conversions (1930, 1936, 1938) and the 1947 Currency Reform have together resulted in extended maturities, reduced interest rates, and a reduction by two-thirds, in 1947, of the value of all outstanding obligations; rapidly rising prices have steadily reduced the real value of these highly illiquid assets. The disadvantages of direct taxes, in general, seem to apply to sales of bonds also, although bond sales in the late 1920's may have been more "voluntary" in nature. To the extent that they were (are) voluntary, disincentive effects would, of course, have been (be) reduced.

Since the Currency Reform of 1947, consumer goods prices have declined steadily. If this trend should be continued, the usefulness of bonds as a form of taxation will have been substantially reduced. On the one hand, falling price levels will cause the real rate of interest on the bonds to exceed the nominal rate so that, in time, repayment may become a real burden on the current Soviet budget. Before 1947 the real rate of interest was undoubtedly negative due to continuous inflation—the burden of repayment was insignificant.[27] On the other hand, it seems doubtful that price levels will fall rapidly enough to increase voluntary savings, especially in the form of illiquid bonds, to the amount of the annual issue of bonds. Thus, as prices fall the disadvantage of larger "real" repayments would seem to more than offset the advantage of smaller disincentive effects as the bonds become a slightly less unattractive form of investment.

[26] Lottery winners have their bonds redeemed at the same time they receive their lottery prizes. At present, one-third of the subscribers to a bond issue eventually win lottery prizes.

[27] Of course, very few bonds were ever actually paid off: the conversions put off repayments in the 1930's and the currency reform of 1947 eliminated the need for repayment on two-thirds of all outstanding obligations. However, even if there had been no conversions, the real value of ten-year bonds at maturity could hardly ever have amounted to more than about one-quarter of original value, so rapid was the rise in consumer goods prices in the pre-1948 period. Cf. Naum Jasny, *The Soviet Economy during the Plan Era*, Stanford University Press, 1951, p. 58.

RETAINED PROFITS

Funds for investment are also available in the form of retained profits accumulated by both state enterprises and collective farms.[28] The annual plans usually call for a substantial part of the investment in the fixed and working capital of established state enterprises to come out of the retained profits of these enterprises. State enterprises also receive grants from the budget for the same purpose. It is difficult to understand what difference, if any, there is between these two methods of finance, and why the Soviets do not concentrate on either one or the other. It is frequently contended that managerial incentives are sharpened if managers are allowed to finance investment from retained profits rather than by budget subsidy. There is the implication in the case of retained profits that, if the manager is more (less) efficient, he may have more (less) funds to invest because profits will be larger (smaller). This implication does not square with the usual conception of an enterprise's fulfilling its investment plan from retained profits and then automatically transferring the remainder, after deductions into the Directors' Fund, into the budget.[29] Part of the Directors' Fund is, of course, used for extra-plan investment; but the incentive to increase profits by reducing costs and increasing output exists regardless of whether the enterprise has its own profits to begin with or receives a budget subsidy.[30] Soviet preference for budget-financed investment probably lies in the greater administrative flexibility which this method *may* confer; it is, undoubtedly, simpler to alter investment plans in the short run if funds are doled out from the budget than if they are accumulated by enterprises in which the investment is planned.

The collective farms (and other cooperatives) not nationalized and the property of the state (though under strict state control, of course) must meet the bulk of their investment requirements from their own resources. The farms are required by law to withhold

[28] This is also true of the consumer and producer cooperatives, but the amounts have never been significant.

[29] More often than not, the retained profit of a group of enterprises has been redistributed among them for investment purposes by the administrative head of the group (or *glavk*, translated "chief administration"). Recently, the power of the *glavk* to do this was reduced. Cf. *New York Times*, August 14, 1952, article by Harry Schwartz.

[30] This is because the bulk of the deduction into the Directors' Fund is based on overplan profits, and a firm which reduced planned losses by a certain amount would be considered to have exceeded the plan in the same direction as one which increased positive profits.

from 12 to 20 per cent of their total net money income (after meeting costs of production, excluding payments to labor) in a so-called "indivisible fund" which is to be used for capital investment.[31] Most of the current money income of the collectives is, of course, distributed among the collective farmers in payment for their labor. Investment by the collective farms (except in kind) has never amounted to much because most of their machinery requirements (tractors, combines, etc.) are met, for a price, by the state-owned machine tractor stations (MTS). The MTS have been since 1938 included in the budget on a gross basis; all of their expenditures, including new investment, are financed by budget subsidy. Collective farms with insufficient funds to finance their investment requirements can borrow small sums from the Agricultural Bank.

FUND FOR AMORTIZATION

Most economic organizations which use capital equipment are required to consider depreciation a cost of production and to maintain depreciation reserves. Western economists generally consider that these reserves understate depreciation in view of the extensive Soviet cost inflation, because of the fact that original rather than replacement cost is used in computing depreciation, and because inexpert handling of equipment appears to be widespread and may have had the effect of reducing the physical life of much equipment. Originally, the reserves were devoted exclusively to replacing old, and constructing new, equipment. Since 1938, part of these funds have been made available for capital repair.

MINOR SOURCES OF BUDGET RECEIPTS

The more important sources of budget revenue have already been noted: turnover tax, deductions from profits of state enterprises, the social insurance markup, direct taxes on the population, and sales of government bonds. The budget derives revenue from many other sources. Customs are, perhaps, the most important of these. In the prewar period they amounted to as much as 2 per cent of total budget receipts in some years. During the war, receipts from tariffs on regular imports were strongly supplemented by local currency resulting from lend-lease sales; since the war, regular receipts have

[31] Receipts from sale of surplus property or livestock are also deposited in the "indivisible fund." Initially, this fund is based on the value of the property and money payments of the collective farmers to the collective farm at the time the farm is organized.

been supplemented by reparations. Other sources are an inheritance tax which at present is simply a fee for the processing of legal documents, fees for commercial forestry and fishing, fines, licenses, the *gross* receipts of the machine tractor stations, and taxes on the profits of the collective farms and other cooperatives. Taken individually, these items do not generally provide much revenue; in the aggregate, however, their contribution is not insubstantial.

THE STATE BANK: CHANGES IN CURRENCY IN CIRCULATION

A substantial share of the working capital requirements of the economy are financed by the State Bank (Gosbank) in the form of short-term loans. In the early 1930's, when the basis of the present Soviet banking system was established, the Bank was given authority to extend short-term credit to finance goods in transit, seasonal production processes and expenses, and other temporary working capital needs connected with the production and turnover of goods.[32] Permanent working capital was to be furnished to new enterprises needing it by the budget in the form of interest-free grants; additions to permanent working capital were to be financed either by the budget or out of the retained profits of the enterprises. If the working capital needs of enterprises had been seasonally stable, there would have been no necessity, in the original Soviet scheme of things, for the short-term credit operations of the State Bank. "The function of short-term credit in the Soviet economy . . . [was], broadly speaking, to level out fluctuation in the flow of materials and goods."[33] The functions of the State Bank were extended in the mid-1930's, however, when it was authorized to finance a large percentage of the *permanent* working capital requirements of trade organizations; and again in 1939 when it was assigned the task of regularly financing part of the *permanent* working capital needs of heavy industry. This deviation from the original principle which guided the granting of short-term credit was introduced with the purpose of giving the State Bank control over the activities of enterprises in these sectors.[34] Apparently, these enterprises "experi-

[32] Cf. Alexander Baykov, *The Development of the Soviet Economic System*, London, Cambridge University Press, 1946, p. 404.

[33] L. E. Hubbard, *Soviet Money and Finance*, London, Macmillan, 1936, p. 228.

[34] This refers to the well-known "control by the ruble." That is to say, by making state enterprises dependent upon the State Bank for funds, the Bank is placed in a position in which it can supervise and check the progress of enterprises, and put pressure on enterprises which are not operating satisfactorily or according to plan.

enced little variation in working capital requirements, and thus were able to escape the control and supervisory functions of the Gosbank."[35] This is the situation at present; it should be noted, however, that during the war the Bank was authorized to advance large credits for the reconstruction of enterprises in liberated areas, to make payments to military personnel under certain special conditions, to facilitate the evacuation of industries eastward during the German advance, and to meet other extraordinary needs. Presumably, credit is no longer granted for these special purposes.

It is important to note that the State Bank is, in normal times, the *only* source of currency issue in the U.S.S.R. With the exception of the years 1941-1943—years of great internal disruption, when the budget ran deficits which were financed by currency issue—short-term loans to finance the above-noted working capital needs of enterprise have been the sole source of new currency in circulation. The extension of new short-term loans does not always, or usually, lead to a currency increment, however. New currency is issued to finance short-term loans only if no currency is returned by the population from other sources. Other sources of funds are excesses of budget receipts over budget expenditures, of retained profits over investment financed from retained profits, of depreciation reserves over expenditures from depreciation reserves, etc. These funds and others mentioned above are all reflected in the accounts of the State Bank either by direct deposit or indirectly through the deposit in the State Bank of the reserves of the special banks for long-term investment (see below). To the extent that currency receipts in the State Bank are greater than expenditures (including long-term loans) from these receipts, new short-term credit can be extended without the issuance of currency; in fact, if there should be a surplus of deposits over expenditures, including short-term loans, currency will be withdrawn from circulation. If, on the other hand, expenditures, including short-term loans, exceed receipts, new currency is circulated. If, therefore, we were interested in measuring the amount of Soviet nonconsumption expenditures (as we are below) from sources of finance, we would not include gross changes in the amount of short-term credit outstanding; this would involve a double count because bank loans are an expenditure item in the national financial accounts. We simply add (subtract) increases (decreases) in cur-

[35] Gregory Grossman, "The Union of Soviet Socialist Republics," in *Comparative Banking Systems*, B. H. Beckhart, editor, Columbia University Press, 1954, pp. 733-768.

rency in circulation. To clarify this point, an estimate of Soviet financial accounts for 1936 is presented in Table 2.

TABLE 2

Estimate of Soviet National Financial Accounts, 1936
(*billions of rubles*)

Receipts		*Expenditures*	
1. Budget receipts (including bonds)	94.4	1. Budget expenditures	92.5[a]
2. Retained profits		2. Investment and other expenditures financed outside budget	
a. State enterprises	8.9	a. From retained profits	
b. Collective farms	1.5	i. State enterprises	8.9[b]
c. Others	?	ii. Others	2.6[c]
3. Depreciation reserves	4.9	b. Depreciation	?
		c. Net increase in short-term credit (State Bank)	8.1
		d. Long-term loans to collective farms and farmers	1.5[d]
Subtotal	109.7	Subtotal	113.6
4. Currency issue	1.6	3. Currency withdrawal	0
5. Discrepancy	2.3		
Total	113.6	Total	113.6

Figures for which sources are not cited were taken from tables later in this chapter.

[a] Same source as budget receipts.

[b] Planned investment in fixed capital from S. N. Prokopovich, *Biulleten'*, March 1936, No. 127, p. 30. Planned investment in working capital from G. F. Grinko, *Financial Program of the U.S.S.R. for 1936*, Moscow, Foreign Languages Publishing House, 1936, p. 15.

[c] At least 2.6 billion rubles of other investment from profits can be estimated from A. Smilga, "Finansy sotsialisticheskogo gosudarstvo" ("Finances of Socialist State"), *Problemy ekonomiki* (*Problems of Economics*), 1937, No. 2, p. 115.

[d] K. Plotnikov, *Biudzhet sotsialisticheskogo gosudarstva* (*Budget of the Socialist States*), Moscow, p. 140.

It would hardly be necessary to discuss the special banks for long-term investment had they not been misnamed banks. Their primary function is to disburse and supervise the use of funds previously collected rather than to create new credit. The bulk of these funds are budgetary grants to enterprises in the national economy for investment in plant and equipment and working capital. Other funds held and disbursed by these banks are retained profits of state enterprises, the indivisible fund, retained profits of other cooperatives, and that part of the reserves for depreciation used to finance new investment.[36] Apparently, the special banks "lend" to both individuals and enterprises, but the amounts involved are

[36] The part used for capital repair is deposited in the State Bank.

not significant and will be ignored here except for long-term loans by the Agriculture Bank to collective farms. The special banks keep their excess funds on deposit with the State Bank; thus the State Bank is seen to be the custodian of excess investment funds for virtually the whole Soviet economy. Long-term loans of the special banks, like short-term loans, are expenditure, not receipt, items in Soviet financial accounts; they are reflected in "sources of finance" only insofar as they affect the amount of currency which has to be circulated by the State Bank to finance its short-term credit operations.

TAXATION IN KIND

No mention has been made so far of taxation in kind of agriculture because it does not *directly* provide the state with monetary reserves for financing nonconsumption expenditures; indirectly, however, it does. The tax in kind takes the form of compulsory deliveries of agricultural products by collective farms and peasant farmers to state and cooperative procurement agencies. While the farms and peasants are not uncompensated for their deliveries, the price paid by the state (called procurement price) is usually far from sufficient to cover costs of production; and, of course, it is only a fraction of the retail price (minus processing and distribution costs) at which the state resells these items to the population. The high retail price is achieved by superimposing a turnover tax on procurement price plus costs of processing and distribution. The portion of the turnover tax collected by virtue of the below-cost procurement price is the monetary equivalent of the tax in kind on that part of the compulsory deliveries sold to the household.[37] Delivered produce not sold back to the household (e.g. stockpiled or used in the production of final products not sold to the household) is not reflected in the budget and may be classified as "investment in kind" by the state.

This classification holds in all circumstances in which producing agents are directly paid less than cost of production or less than the value of their product (or not at all). A major case in point is, of course, that of unfree labor in the Soviet Union. The evidence indicates that workers in this category are remunerated at less than

[37] If the procurement price of a bushel of grain which cost 40 rubles to produce were only 20 rubles and the state resold the grain (as bread) for 100 rubles, the turnover tax on a bushel would be 80 rubles, of which it could be said that 20 rubles (40 minus 20) was paid by the producer and 60 (100 minus 40) by the consumer.

the free market wage for comparable performance.[38] To the extent that the products of unfree labor are sold to the population at high prices and add to the receipts of the turnover tax, the tax in kind on unfree labor (in the form of below-market wage payments) is reflected in budgetary receipts. To the extent that the services of these laborers are directed into nonconsumption activities such as gold mining, construction, irrigation projects, and the building of dams and roads (and these are the sorts of activities typically handled by the MVD), they may be classed as investment in kind by the state.

It should be noted that there is still another important source of investment in kind in the Soviet Union. We refer to that part of the income in kind of the agricultural sector of the economy which is neither taxed away by the state nor consumed by peasant households, but which is devoted to the following years' production (e.g. seed, feed, stockpiles, increasing livestock herds). Needless to say, none of the above categories of investment in kind are readily susceptible to measurement; nor can we, for that matter, even say what part of the turnover tax is a tax on the consumer and what part is a tax on the agricultural producer.[39]

How is Soviet preference for taxation in kind of agriculture to be explained? Basically, the difference between taxation of industrial income and taxation of agricultural income stems from the fact that industry and the output of industry are almost 100 per cent state-owned, while agriculture consists primarily of collective farms, which are not owned by the state, and of individual peasant farmers.[40] This form of organization of agriculture, rather than state-owned farms with the farmers receiving wages, creates two serious problems for the state. First, the state must secure by some means a substantial share of the output of the agricultural sector to be transferred to the city for personal and industrial consumption and for export. Taxation of the money incomes of agricultural producers would not necessarily secure this result: if the amount of the tax were calculated on the basis of actual money income, the peasants

[38] Bergson, in his famous study of Soviet wages, demonstrated that relative wages in the Soviet Union appear to reflect relative differences in productivity (cf. Bergson, *The Structure of Soviet Wages*, as cited, pp. 207-209). On this basis one can take the free-market wage for a particular job as a rough measure of the value of the job performance to the state.

[39] This separation is attempted for grains, on the basis of heroic assumptions, in Holzman, *Soviet Taxation*, as cited, Chap. 7.

[40] The *sovkhozy*, or state farms, are owned by the state but produce a very small percentage of total agricultural output.

could reduce their money income, hence tax payments, by cutting down sales of agricultural output; even if taxable income were based on production, the peasants could, by cutting back on their consumption of industrial consumer goods, still avoid the necessity of having to sell as much agricultural output as the state needed to meet its requirements. These are not idle possibilities in a country where adequately feeding the population has been—and will continue to be, barring unforeseen developments—a very serious economic problem. By means of money taxation, alone, it might prove impossible to reduce the food consumption of the peasants below a level consistent with the needs of the nation as a whole for food. Second, as we have seen, for incentive and other reasons the state collects most of its budget receipts in the form of indirect taxes. Since the bulk of the turnover tax, the major indirect tax, is collected in the form of a markup on agricultural products (because food is the principal item of personal consumption in the Soviet Union), the incidence of the turnover tax on the agricultural population considered as consumers is relatively small because a large part of its income takes the form of consumption of home-produced food. Another form of tax on the peasantry must be substituted for indirect money taxation if a high rate of saving for the economy as a whole is to be maintained. The tax in kind solves these two problems at once for the state: it insures state procurement of the required amount of agricultural produce, and it forces a high level of savings upon the agricultural population.

2. *Trends in Sources of Finance*

Financial data covering the first three Five-Year Plan periods (1928/1929-1940) are presented in Table 3. Before analyzing the data, three explanatory (methodological) comments are in order.

COMMENTS ON METHODOLOGY

First, the various indirect taxes and retained profits of state enterprises, as presented by Soviet sources, must be adjusted because a part of these taxes are levied on commodities which are not purchased by the population (e.g. tanks and food purchased by the armed forces) but are purchased by state enterprises and organizations for final use. To the extent that taxes levied by the state serve simply to pay other taxes levied by the state, the transaction is appropriately viewed as a pure transfer payment within the state sector, and not as a purchase of goods or services. The turnover tax requires relatively little adjustment because it is levied primarily on goods purchased by the household. The profits tax, social insurance markup, other indirect taxes, and retained profits of enterprises require a more substantial reduction because the incidence of these categories on producer goods and raw materials is somewhat heavier. No precision can be claimed for this adjustment, though breakdowns of some of the above taxes by ministries (commissariats) and in some cases by commodities facilitated the estimates.[41] The deduction of indirect taxes from the value of goods and services purchased by the state yields results which approximate factor cost rather than market price valuation.[42]

Second, an important expenditure on budget account is subsidies. For our purposes, subsidies can be classified under two headings: payments to enterprises in the national economy which operate at a loss, primarily those in the extractive and producer goods industries, and payments to the machine tractor stations, which, at least since 1938 when they were placed in the budget on a gross basis, have not earned enough to pay their way.[43] To the extent that subsidies serve to lower the price of goods purchased for final consumption by the state, they do not affect the validity of our figures. True, the state pays a below-cost price for commodities purchased —but the reduced price is largely offset by the subsidy payment. As in the case of commodity taxes on producer goods, mentioned above, these subsidies represent a transfer within the state sector of the economy. To the extent, however, that subsidies reduce the cost of consumer goods and services, they affect the validity of our data as a measure of the funds available for investment because they reduce the amount of taxes (as shown by the budget) actually available to finance nonconsumption expenditures. That is to say, subsidies which lower the cost of consumer goods can be looked upon, for our purposes, as a reduction in the net taxes on the population.

Most of the consumer subsidies are a result of the subsidy to the

41 Cf. Appendix, notes to Table 3.

42 There are still many deviations from factor cost valuation, however, although indirect taxes are the worst offenders. There are also subsidies (to be mentioned below) and valuation of the tax in kind (see above), to list but two of the most important.

43 This is due primarily to the fact that their receipts in kind (and most of the payments for services rendered to collective farms are in kind) are valued, for budgetary accounting purposes, at the very low procurement prices —the same prices the peasants themselves receive from the state in return for obligatory deliveries. If these deliveries were valued at cost, or at retail price, the MTS might turn out to be going concerns.

TABLE 3

Sources of Soviet Finance, 1928/1929-1940
(*billions of rubles except as indicated*)

	1928/1929	1929/1930	1931	1932	1933	1934	1935	1936	1937	1938	1939	1940
Budget receipts												
Major indirect taxes												
Turnover tax	3.1	5.4	11.7	19.6	27.0	37.6	52.2	65.8	75.9	80.4	96.9	105.9
Profits tax	.6	1.6	2.2	2.0	3.4	3.1	3.3	5.3	9.4	10.5	15.8	21.7
Social insurance	1.2	1.4	2.2	3.6	4.3	5.7	7.0	8.9	6.6	7.2	7.6	8.5
Total	4.9	8.4	16.1	25.2	34.7	46.4	62.5	80.0	91.9	98.1	120.3	136.1
Adjusted total	3.7	6.3	12.4	19.6	27.2	36.9	52.5	64.0	74.7	79.7	99.3	111.5
Direct taxes	1.1	1.1	1.6	2.4	3.5	3.8	3.2	3.8	4.0	5.1	7.0	9.4
Gross sales of bonds	.7	1.3	3.3	3.9	4.4	4.3	4.9	4.9	5.9	7.6	8.4	11.5
To population	.1	.7	1.6	2.4	3.2	3.4	3.8	3.5	4.3	6.1[b]	6.7[b]	9.2[b]
Other receipts	2.1	3.1	4.2	6.5	3.8	3.9	4.4	5.7	7.6	16.7	20.3	23.2
Total budget receipts	8.8	12.9	25.2	38.0	46.4	58.4	75.0	94.4	109.3	127.5	156.0	180.2
Adjusted budget receipts	7.6	11.8	21.5	32.4	38.9	48.9	65.0	78.4	91.1	109.1	135.0	155.6
Retained profits of state enterprises	2.7	3.8	3.8[b]	4.6	4.6	3.3	4.5	8.9	7.6	5.2	10.5[c]	10.3
Adjusted retained profits	2.0	3.0	2.6	3.2	3.4	2.2	2.9	6.3	4.8	3.2	6.6	6.0
Indivisible fund of collective farms	0	.2	.4	.5	1.3	1.5	1.3	1.5[b]	1.8	2.5	2.9[b]	3.3
Voluntary household savings[a]	.2	.2	0	.2	.2	.5	.8	1.1	1.0	2.0	.6	.2
Depreciation reserves	1.0[b]	1.1[b]	1.6[b]	2.0	2.6	3.3[b]	3.9[c]	4.9	5.7	6.8[b]	7.9	9.0[b]
Increase in currency circulation	.7	1.7	1.3	2.7	−1.6	.9	2.0	1.6	1.5[b]	1.6[b]	1.6[b]	0
Unadjusted total	13.2	20.7	32.3	47.8	53.3	67.4	86.7	111.3	125.9	143.6	178.9	202.8
Deduct: adjustment	1.9	2.9	4.9	7.0	8.7	10.5	11.6	18.6	22.0	20.4	24.9	28.9
Adjusted total	11.3	17.8	27.4	40.8	44.6	56.9	75.1	92.7	103.9	123.2	154.0	173.9
Per cent increase in adjusted total		57.5	53.9	48.9	9.3	27.6	32.0	23.4	12.1	18.6	25.0	29.2
Expenditures												
Increase in State Bank loans[a]	.7	2.3	7.9	1.9	3.7	3.1	9.5	8.1	5.9	4.2	3.0	7.1
Long-term loans to collective farms[a]	n.a.	n.a.	.6	.4	.2	.4	.5	.8	1.1	n.a.	n.a.	n.a.

TABLE 3 (cont.)

[a] Not included in totals.
[b] Estimate.
[c] Planned figure.
n.a. = not available.
Source: See Appendix, Notes to Table 3.

machine tractor stations, although part of this subsidy, no doubt, also affects the price of goods purchased by the state. The cost of consumer goods is also reduced by subsidies to the producer goods and extractive industries, insofar as the products of these industries (e.g. fuel) are used eventually in the production of consumer goods; but the subsidy to the consumer from this source is not likely to amount to much.

No adjustment for the subsidy to consumer goods products will be made here, however, for three reasons: the adjustment is not very large; the data are sufficient to make rough estimates for only the last three years of the period under observation; undervaluation of MTS receipts in kind, mentioned in the preceding footnote, may all but eliminate the subsidy, in real terms, to the MTS.[44]

Third, the Soviets do not have explicit cost categories which correspond to the Western categories of interest as the cost of capital, rent as the return to land, and profits as the return for exceptional entrepreneurial ability.[45] Furthermore, as we have noted, depreciation is understated; and neither depletion nor obsolescence is explicitly considered a cost. In some cases Soviet economists have indicated that these costs are *implicitly* covered by commodity tax payments. Thus the large turnover tax on petroleum and petroleum products is considered by Soviet economists to reflect the large differential rent earned by the industry and to substitute for explicit rent payments.[46] In general, however, the missing factor costs are not earmarked at all and there does not appear to be any

[44] For those interested the adjustment has been attempted elsewhere: cf. Holzman, "The Burden of Soviet Taxation," as cited.

[45] Some exceptions are the following: persons living in apartment houses in the cities pay nominal rent; interest is charged on short-term loans from the State Bank; and some payments for exceptional entrepreneurial ability are made out of the Directors' Fund and in the form of premiums for managers whose plants fulfill or overfulfill output plans.

[46] "To the extent that differential rent does not receive independent expression in all branches of the national economy . . . rent is paid in the form of the turnover tax." A. Gordin, "Ekonomicheskoe znachenie sistemy oblozheniia po oborotu" ("Economic Significance of the Turnover Tax System"), *Sovetskie finansy* (*Soviet Finance*), 1947, No. 8, p. 12.

satisfactory way of estimating them.[47] Our estimates (below) of the "true" value (in the Western sense) of Soviet nonconsumption expenditures are for this reason understated. It appears unlikely, however, that the understatement is large[48] or that it seriously affects the estimates in this paper.

TRENDS IN SOURCES OF FINANCE

Let us turn now to an examination of the data. From 1928/1929 to 1940, the twelve years under consideration, the total funds raised for expenditures on investment, defense, health, education, transfer payments, etc., rose from 11.3 billion rubles to 173.9 billion rubles—a fifteenfold increase. With the exception of the years 1933 and 1939, the annual percentage increases fall into three groups: roughly 50 per cent from 1928/1929 to 1932, 25 per cent from 1933 to 1936, and about 15 per cent from 1936 to 1940. The increases in each period reflect three factors: growth of national output, cost (price) inflation, and growth of the state industrial and collective farm economies at the expense of the private enterprise economy. The exceptional increase in the years of the first Five-Year Plan is probably largely a result of the swift "liquidation" of the private economy in those years. Cost inflation, which plagued the Soviets unremittingly from 1928 to 1936, appears to have slackened somewhat from 1937 to 1940; this may explain the dampened increase in total sources of finance in this latter period. As a very rough approximation, the inflationary element in the increase in Soviet sources of finance can be eliminated by using the average wage rate as a deflator.[49] The results indicate that the "real" increase in nonconsumption expenditures by the state, due to liquidation of the private economy and to the real growth of national output, was, as a *minimum*, about 100 per cent in the first FYP period and 200 per cent

[47] Some writers assume that these factor costs are represented by profits of state enterprises (e.g. Paul Baran, "National Income and Product of the U.S.S.R. in 1940," *Review of Economic Statistics*, November 1947, pp. 226-233). There is no indication that retained profits are of the correct magnitude to represent the missing factor costs; and although the magnitude may be appropriate for a given year, by coincidence, its arbitrary variation over time would cast doubt upon its usefulness for a series of years.

[48] Cf. D. R. Hodgman, "A New Index of Soviet Industrial Production," *Review of Economics and Statistics*, November 1950, p. 335.

[49] This would only account for expenditures on industrial commodities. The cost to the state of agricultural commodities is the "procurement price"—and we have no index of such prices. The average wage rate actually gives us a *minimum* deflator for industrial goods because to the extent that productivity increased, the wage rate is too large a deflator (cf. footnote 50).

from 1928/1929 to 1940.[50] The estimated increase from 1932 to 1936 is amazingly small, about 15 per cent; this undoubtedly reflects the inadequacies of our deflator, however—Soviet increases in industrial productivity in this period are generally believed to have been quite large.[51]

The various sources of finance are presented in Table 4 as percentages of the total.[52] The outstanding trend here is the rapid growth of the major indirect taxes. In a period of five or six years these taxes double in relative importance and bear about two-thirds of the burden of the state's financial requirements. The trends in direct taxes on the population and retained profits of state enterprises are in the opposite direction. In absolute figures, direct taxes do not decline—in fact, they increase slightly. But with total financial requirements increasing rapidly and being satisfied from other sources, the relative importance of direct taxes is reduced.

The decline in the relative importance of profits of state enterprises from 1928/1929 to 1935 is somewhat more dramatic. My guess is that with the beginning of the First FYP and the greater centralization of decision-making which this entailed, it was decided that funds for investment in industry would be more fluid and more easily controlled if first deducted into the budget and then

[50] These are the figures:

	1928/1929 or 1929	*1932*	*1936*	*1940*
1. Source of finance, index	100	361	820	1,539
2. Average annual wage, index	100	178	357	509
Line 1 ÷ line 2	100	203	230	302

Source of wage figures: For 1929 and 1932, *Socialist Construction of the U.S.S.R.*, Moscow, 1936, pp. 368-369; and for 1936 and 1940, Abram Bergson, "A Problem in Soviet Statistics," *Review of Economic Statistics*, November 1947, p. 236.

To adjust for changes in productivity, it would be necessary to deflate the wage index by the increase in productivity. Thus if productivity had doubled by 1940 in all of the activities financed by the Soviet government, then the adjusted deflator for 1940 would be 509 ÷ 2, or 255; the real increase in government activity would correspondingly rise from 302 to 604. For an indication of the increase in Soviet industrial productivity in the prewar period see Walter Galenson, "Industrial Labor Productivity," in *Soviet Economic Growth*, Abram Bergson, editor, Row, Peterson, 1953. See also comments by Joseph Berliner regarding overhead personnel, *ibid.*, pp. 215-221.

[51] See Galenson, *op. cit.*, pp. 195 and 196.

[52] The various items do not add up to 100 per cent, however. For reasons mentioned earlier, the total is obtained by including only Bank loans financed by new currency; here we included the total of new loans by the banks regardless of whether they were financed by new currency, budgetary surplus, or some other source of excess funds because of our interest in the extent of the banks' participation in economic activity.

TABLE 4
Sources of Soviet Finance as Percentages of Adjusted Total, 1928/1929-1940

	1928/ 1929	*1929/ 1930*	*1931*	*1932*	*1933*	*1934*	*1935*	*1936*	*1937*	*1938*	*1939*	*1940*
Receipts												
Major indirect taxes (adjusted)	32.7	35.4	45.3	48.0	61.0	64.9	69.9	69.0	71.9	64.7	64.5	64.1
Direct taxes	9.7	6.2	5.8	5.9	7.9	6.6	4.2	4.1	3.8	4.1	4.5	5.4
Sales of bonds to population	.9	3.9	5.8	5.9	7.2	5.9	5.0	3.7	4.1	4.9	4.3	5.3
Total budget receipts (adjusted)	67.3	66.3	78.5	79.4	87.2	85.9	86.6	84.6	87.7	88.6	87.7	89.5
Retained profits of state enterprises (adjusted)	17.6	16.9	9.5	7.9	7.6	3.8	3.8	6.7	4.6	2.8	4.2	3.4
Indivisible fund of collective farms	0	1.1	1.4	1.2	2.9	2.6	1.7	1.6	1.7	2.0	1.9	1.9
Voluntary household savings	1.8	1.1	0	.5	.4	.9	1.1	1.2	1.0	1.6	.4	.1
Depreciation reserves	9.8	6.2	5.8	4.9	5.8	5.8	5.2	5.2	5.4	5.5	5.1	5.1
Increase in currency in circulation	6.2	9.6	4.7	6.6	—3.6	1.6	2.7	1.7	1.4	1.3	1.0	0
Expenditures												
State Bank loans	6.2	12.9	28.3	4.6	8.3	5.4	12.7	8.8	5.6	3.4	1.9	4.1
Long-term loans to collective farms	n.a.	n.a.	2.1	1.0	.4	.7	.7	.9	1.0	n.a.	n.a.	n.a.

The percentages add up to more than 100 per cent because the adjusted total includes only currency-financed bank loans, while here we are interested in all State Bank loans and long-term loans to the collective farms.

n.a. = not available.

Source: Same as for Table 3.

redirected in the economy, than if invested directly by enterprises earning profits.[53] In 1936, retained profits almost doubled in relative importance as the Soviets reduced subsidies to industry and increased the amount to be invested from retained profits with the avowed purpose of improving managerial incentives. This effort appears to have lost momentum in the years immediately following.[54]

The trend in bond sales to the population parallels that of direct taxation with the exception of 1928/1929 and 1929/1930, when the Soviets first began to tap this source of revenue.

The short-term working capital loans of the State Bank follow a more erratic course than any other category listed. The direction of change is altered seven times in twelve years, and most of the changes are large and involve either a "doubling" or a "halving" in the relative importance of these loans from one year to the next. The only consistent trend is the downward swing from 1935 to 1939, and this may be explained as part of the general anti-inflationary policy followed in those years. The increase in 1940, however, was probably due to the decision in 1939 to finance with State Bank credit part of the permanent working capital needs of heavy industry. No explanation is offered for the zigzag path of State Bank loans from 1931 to 1935. The increase from 1928/1929 to 1931 reflects the pursuance of a relatively wide-open credit policy; in fact, so leniently was credit granted in these years that state enterprises were forced to default in 1931 and 1932 on the repayment of more than one-third of the outstanding short-term debt.[55]

Not only was short-term credit on the increase during the First Five-Year Plan period, but it was to a considerable extent financed by increases in cash currency. In fact, the total increase in currency

[53] During and shortly after World War II, retained profits declined to virtually nothing, presumably for the same reason. In 1947, retained profits totaled 1.5 billion rubles, which was less than .5 per cent of the budget receipts for that year.

[54] Another attempt at reducing subsidies and increasing investment from retained profits was made in 1949.

[55] This problem was solved by converting the short-term debt to long-term debt (see Appendix, notes to Table 3).

The rapid increase in credit has been ascribed by Hubbard to failure to carry out the spirit of the credit reform of January 1930. This neglect "led to the automatic issue of bank credit and relieved state enterprises of any urgent necessity to regulate their finances, with the result that the Gosbank practically went over from a system of granting credits repayable at a fixed maturity to granting nonrepayable loans. Enterprises, therefore, ignored their financial position and that of their own clients, and undertook liabilities which they had little or no prospect of meeting." Cf. Hubbard, *op. cit.*, p. 18. Quoted by permission.

in circulation for the years 1928/1929, 1929/1930, and 1932 was 5.1 billion rubles while the total increase in short-term credit outstanding was only 4.9 billion rubles (see Table 3); the increase in currency in circulation in 1931 was also large, though not comparable to the increase in short-term credit in that year. New currency in circulation constituted between 5 and 10 per cent of total sources of finance from 1928/1929 to 1932, a very large amount indeed. Thereafter the importance of new currency declined. In 1933 the amount of currency in circulation actually declined by almost 25 per cent, the result of a very large budget surplus in that year. As one would expect, 1933 was a relatively deflationary year: wage inflation slowed from a gallop to a trot (see Table 6) and repressed inflation was substantially reduced. From 1934 to 1939, currency in circulation continued to increase but occupied a relatively minor role among total sources of finance.[56]

Of the remaining sources of finance, the depreciation reserve is the only one which is important. With the exception of 1928/1929, this reserve remained a fairly constant percentage of total sources of finance in the prewar period. Voluntary household savings pursued an erratic course and, on the average, amounted to only about 1 per cent of the total savings of the economy. Funds for investment in the collective farms (both sources) were likewise small; because the machine tractor stations were owned and financed by the state, the investment requirements of the collectives were not very great. Furthermore, part of their investment requirements are met "in kind" in the form of so-called "seed funds" and "feed funds" and of collective farm labor mobilized to perform special tasks.

It would have been a large gap indeed if in this paper the estimates of Soviet sources of finance could *not* have been related to the total income (output) of the nation. To draw up a reliable estimate of Soviet national income even for one year, however, is a major task in itself; to draw up reliable estimates for every year of the period under discussion would have required years of research. For purposes of this paper a compromise is offered: a rather *crude* "modified" gross national product series is estimated for the years 1928/1929 to 1940. Gross national product is calculated as the sum of two major components—government (plus collective farm) ex-

[56] The velocity of circulation was increasing in this period so that given increments to currency in circulation were becoming more and more inflationary. For data on velocity see Raymond P. Powell, "Soviet Monetary Policy," doctoral dissertation, University of California, 1952, p. 193.

penditures and household expenditures—and all estimates are net of indirect taxes.[57]

Our modified gross national product series is presented in Table 5. Two versions of the breakdown between government and household are presented. In the first, government *expenditures* include expenditures on health and education—the bulk of these are, in fact, purchased by the government and made available to the household as free services. Since, however, the household (*qua* household) actually consumes these services,[58] a second breakdown (between government consumption and household consumption) is presented, in which expenditures on health and education are deducted from government expenditures and added to household expenditures.[59]

The importance of the government sector in the Soviet economy is strikingly established by the percentage relationship between government expenditures and gross national output. With the exception of the first year of the industrialization drive, 1928/1929, when economic mobilization had not yet attained full momentum, and the year 1933, when a strong attempt was made to stem the rising tide of inflation, government expenditures consistently totaled from 60 to 65 per cent of gross national product. Government consumption, though a somewhat smaller percentage of total product than government expenditures, is, nevertheless, also very impressive. On the average it amounted to about 50 per cent of GNP, household consumption constituting the other 50 per cent. In the year 1929/1930, however, households consumed only 44 per cent of a rather small national product; in the "good" years 1937 and 1938 households were allocated 55 per cent of the marketed national output. Threat of war was no doubt largely responsible for the decline in the share of household consumption in 1939 and 1940.

[57] The methods used to estimate Soviet gross national product and the serious limitations of these estimates are set forth in detail in the Appendix, Notes to Table 5. See also Table 5, footnote e.

[58] While it may be true that expenditures on education may include communist propaganda, scientific research (including atomic research), and other things not consumed by the population, for reasons noted elsewhere (Holzman, "The Burden of Soviet Taxation," as cited) I feel that these items do not constitute a large part of the total. Expenditures on education and health also include capital expenditures, but these are a small part of the total.

[59] Military subsistence might also have been added to household consumption, but reasonably reliable data were not available for most years. With the exception of 1939-1940, this item was probably not very large. The term consumption is here taken to mean the use or consumption of both consumption and investment goods.

TABLE 5

Modified Gross National Product,[e] U.S.S.R., 1928/1929-1940

	1928/ 1929	*1929/ 1930*	*1931*[a]	*1932*	*1933*	*1934*	*1935*	*1936*	*1937*	*1938*	*1939*	*1940*
1. Total sources of government funds[b]	11.3	17.8	27.4	40.8	44.6	56.9	75.1	92.7	103.9	123.2	154.0	173.9
a. Deduct: transfer payments	1.5	1.7	2.4	4.1	4.7	5.5	5.7	7.5	11.0	10.9	12.6	14.6
2. Government expenditures on goods and services valued net of indirect taxes	9.8	16.1	25.0	36.7	39.9	51.4	69.4	85.2	92.9	112.3	141.4	159.3
a. Deduct: expenditures on health and education	1.4	2.1	3.4	4.6	5.9	8.1	12.8	19.5	23.4	26.3	28.5	31.5
3. Government consumption[c]	8.4	14.0	21.6	32.1	34.0	43.4	56.6	65.7	69.5	85.0	112.9	127.8
4. Total household money income[d]	19.3	22.7	32.7	56.3	67.8	85.8	107.4	133.6	155.6	180.0	210.1	236.0
a. Deduct: taxes on household (incl. indirect)	7.5	11.6	18.7	28.7	37.9	47.9	64.5	80.3	89.0	97.9	124.2	141.5
savings, cash holdings, trade union dues	1.1	2.3	1.6	3.3	.9	2.0	3.5	3.6	3.6	4.8	3.6	1.8
5. Household purchases of goods and services valued net of indirect taxes	10.7	8.8	12.4	24.3	30.8	35.9	39.4	49.7	63.0	77.3	82.3	92.7
6. Household consumption[c] (line 5 + line 2a)	12.1	10.9	15.8[a]	28.9	36.7	44.0	52.2	69.2	86.4	103.6	110.8	124.2
7. Modified gross national product[e] (line 3 + line 6 or line 2 + line 5)	20.5	24.9	37.4	61.0	70.7	87.3	108.8	134.9	155.9	189.6	223.7	252.0
8. Proportion of government expenditures to GNP (line 2 ÷ line 7)	47.8	64.7	66.8[a]	60.2	56.4	58.9	63.8	63.2	59.6	59.2	63.2	63.2
9. Proportion of government consumption to GNP (line 3 ÷ line 7)	41.0	56.2	57.8[a]	52.6	48.1	49.7	52.0	48.7	44.6	44.8	50.5	50.7

[a] Estimates of household income believed to be sharply understated for 1931. Cf. F. D. Holzman, "The Burden of Soviet Taxation," *American Economic Review*, September 1953.

[b] Includes funds for investment on collective farms.

[c] Consumption is here taken to mean the use of both consumption and investment goods.

[d] See Holzman, *op. cit.*

[e] Gross national product is designated "modified" because it does not include private investment expenditures, certain implicit factor costs (mentioned above), and consumption and investment in kind in agriculture. For discussion, as well as for sources and methodology, see Appendix, Notes to Table 5.

3. *Evaluation of Soviet Financial Policies*

Three basic objectives of Soviet fiscal policy in the prewar period were the following:

1. A falling price level in the market for consumers' goods. This objective was included in each of the first three Five-Year Plans.

2. Maintenance of free choice in the market for consumers' goods. This required, of course, the avoidance (elimination) of repressed inflation since equitable distribution is impossible where "too much money chases too few goods."[60] Ever since the disastrous attempts during War Communism (1918-1921) to do away with the use of money, the Soviets have recognized and striven for free market distribution of consumers' goods.

3. Maintenance of relatively stable or declining producer goods prices. To this end, a system of subsidies was introduced to keep down the prices of newly introduced producer goods until such time as new techniques of production had been mastered and economies of scale achieved. Accomplishment of this objective required accomplishment of a subsidiary objective: that increases in the remuneration of factors of production (in this case, labor) not exceed, by much, increases in productivity. Comparison of Soviet wage and productivity targets bears this out.[61] Stability of producer goods and raw materials prices obviously simplifies the planning process, and this appears to have been the main reason for this Soviet objective.

A brief look at the economic history of the prewar period indicates that, for the most part, the Soviets were unsuccessful in achieving these financial goals. Consumer goods prices rose rapidly and steadily throughout the entire period. Jasny estimates the cost of living of urban workers to have risen 750 per cent from 1928 to 1937, and 1,100 per cent by 1940.[62] This is indeed rampant inflation. Pro-

[60] Equitable distribution is used here to mean distribution in accordance with differential earnings ("to each according to his labor"); and distribution in accordance with differential earnings is an essential condition for the successful operation of a labor market in which wage incentives are depended upon for the economic allocation of labor. Economic allocation of labor by market forces can be considered an aspect of objective 2 above.

[61] In the First FYP, for example, wages in large-scale industry were to increase from 40.7 to 46.9 per cent while productivity (for a slightly different coverage of industry—so-called VSNKh industry) was to increase from 85 to 110 per cent. Cf. *Piatiletnii plan narodno—khoziaistvennogo stroitel'stva S.S.S.R.* (*Five-Year Plan of National Economic Development*), Moscow, 1930, pp. 190 and 192.

[62] Jasny, *The Soviet Economy during the Plan Era*, as cited, p. 69.

ducer goods prices also rose, though much less rapidly than those of consumer goods for three reasons: the prices of producer goods were not inflated by the imposition of large (increasingly large) commodity taxes, loss-covering subsidies were disbursed on a profligate scale, and productivity was increasing relatively rapidly. Nevertheless, by 1940, producer goods prices had risen, according to Jasny, to about 250 to 350 per cent of the 1928 level.[63] The annual wage rate rose on the average, as we have already noted, by about 500 per cent from 1928 to 1940; not even *Soviet* productivity estimates, which are afflicted with the same upward bias as the industrial production index, show a comparable increase over the same period. Soviet performance was, perhaps, best in the case of repressed inflation. While repressed inflation was on the rise[64] from 1928 to 1932, it declined steadily from 1933 to 1937;[65] rationing was discontinued in 1935-1936, and roughly uniform prices prevailed in all markets in 1937 and 1938. There is evidence to indicate that some repressed inflation developed again during the year 1940.[66]

Thus we have seen that while Soviet financial objectives were, on the whole, noninflationary, inflation did, in fact, pervade the Soviet economy in the prewar period. What does this imply about the Soviet sources of finance analyzed in the previous sections? It implies that Soviet financial policy was inflationary: that either the short-term credit operations of the State Bank were too large, *or*, if not too large, they were financed too little by budgetary and other surpluses of receipts over expenditures and too much by the printing of new currency. The amount of currency in circulation increased from about 2 billion rubles in January 1929 to an estimated 16 billion in January 1941[67]—an eightfold increase in twelve years.[68] Sophisticated analysis is hardly required to indicate that this is a very large increase and would, under most circumstances, be incompatible with monetary stability. That it was incompatible with Soviet

[63] Jasny, *The Soviet Price System*, as cited, Chap. 2.

[64] As measured by the spread between the prices in state stores and on the free collective farm markets.

[65] For citations see Holzman, "The Burden of Soviet Taxation," as cited.

[66] Irving B. Kravis and Joseph Mintzes report that shortages of many commodities developed in 1940 in government stores. See their "Food Prices in the Soviet Union, 1936-50," *Review of Economics and Statistics*, May 1950, pp. 165-166.

[67] For sources and methods see Appendix, Notes to Table 3.

[68] Velocity of circulation was also increasing in this period. Cf. Powell, *op. cit.*, p. 193.

monetary stability has been very ably demonstrated by Raymond Powell in his doctoral dissertation.[69]

It is useful, in analyzing Soviet inflation, to begin at the enterprise level because excess liquidity first expresses itself in the Soviet economy in the form of excess deposit balances available to managers of enterprises. From their behavior it is quite clear that managers of Soviet enterprises had available to them funds which were more than adequate to meet their needs in the prewar period, in terms of labor, raw materials, and other inputs at planned prices. Responsibility for this high degree of liquidity must be attributed largely to the disproportion mentioned above, between taxes and bank credit. The effect of this excess liquidity was different in the markets for industrial raw materials and equipment, on the one hand, and the labor market, on the other. Inflation in the raw materials and equipment markets has always been repressed because prices are quite rigidly controlled, as are allocations of important commodities. Repressed inflation was manifest, as is typical in such situations, in the hoarding by Soviet enterprises of everything they could get their hands on which might be useful at some later date. To paraphrase a Soviet economist: enterprises will refrain from using surplus funds to buy supplies only when they are already "clearly and significantly oversatiated."[70]

The labor market in the 1930's constituted an important leak in the system of direct controls over inflation in the enterprise sector. The market for labor was relatively free, i.e. there was very little direct allocation of labor and the wage rate was not very effectively controlled. Managers used excess funds to compete for workers, and this resulted in a rapid and continuous increase in wage rates throughout the prewar period.[71] The increases, it should be noted (Table 6), were considerably over and above those planned by the Soviet authorities.[72]

[69] *Ibid.*

[70] V. Batyrev, "Voprosy planirovaniia privlechennykh resursov gosudarstvennogo banka" ("Problems of Planning the Liabilities of the State Bank"), *Dengi i kredit* (*Money and Credit*), 1941, No. 1-2, p. 37.

[71] It also resulted in a level of labor turnover in industry which averaged about 100 per cent annually during the first two Five-Year Plan periods. See *Sotsialisticheskoe stroitel'stvo S.S.S.R.* (*Socialist Construction of the U.S.S.R.*), as cited, p. 531.

[72] The various techniques used by managers to avoid wage controls and the unsuccessful attempts by the authorities (in the prewar period at least) to prevent a bidding up of wage rates by State Bank control over the disbursal of enterprise payroll funds are both described in detail elsewhere. Cf. Holzman, *Soviet Taxation*, as cited, Chap. 2.

TABLE 6

Average Annual Wage Rate, Planned and Realized, U.S.S.R., 1928-1942

Year	*Planned (rubles)*	*Realized (rubles)*	*Planned Increase*[a] *(per cent)*	*Unplanned Increase*[b] *(per cent)*	*Total Increase*[c] *(per cent)*
1928	690[d]	703		2	
1929		800			14
1930		936(879)[e]			17
1931	941	1,127	7.1[e]	20[f]	20
1932		1,427			27
1932 FYP[g]	(994)[g]				
1933	1,523	1,566	6.7	3	10
1934	1,625	1,858	3.8	14	19
1935	2,031	2,269	9.3	12	22
1936	2,465	2,856	8.6	16	26
1937	2,978	3,038	4.3	2	6
1937 FYP[g]	(1,755)[g]				
1938		3,467			14
1939		[3,867][h]			[11][h]
1940		4,069			[5][h]
1942 FYP[g]	(4,100)[g]				

[a] The percentage increase from the realized wage of one year to the planned wage for the subsequent year.

[b] The increase of realized over planned wages for the same year.

[c] The increase from the realized figure of one year to the realized figure for the subsequent year.

[d] This figure is for the year ending October 1, 1928.

[e] The planned wage rate for 1931 is coupled (in the source) with a realized figure for 1930 which differs from other realized figures in our series. Nevertheless, it is meaningful to use the figures which have been coupled, and this has been done.

[f] The unplanned increase may be too high because of the discrepancy mentioned in note e. That is to say, 941 rubles may be a somewhat low wage rate because it is based on a preliminary realized wage for 1930 which is too low. Hence, the increase from 941 to 1,127 may be too high.

[g] These are the figures contained in each Five-Year Plan for the last year of the Plan period.

[h] Average wage was unavailable for 1939. Interpolation was used to obtain the figure entered. The basis for the interpolation was the total wage bill figures for 1938-1940 presented in Holzman, *Soviet Taxation*, as cited, Table 4.

Source: See Appendix, Notes to Table 6.

At the risk of considerably oversimplifying a very complex problem, I think it could be stated, as a first approximation, that the wage inflation and the credit policy which permitted it can be used to explain Soviet failure to achieve all three financial objectives listed above. We have already pointed out how wage inflation pushed up the prices of producer goods by increasing money costs of production. Part of the increase in consumer goods prices was similarly due to rising wages.[73] In the case of consumer goods, of course, causation operated through both supply and demand: consumer goods prices were increased not only because of the increase in money costs of production (this applied particularly to industrial consumer goods) but also because household incomes were rising much faster than the output of consumer goods. Finally, *unplanned* increases in wage rates contributed to repressed inflation. For to the extent that the household sector earned more income than the fiscal authorities had anticipated, with no compensating increases in output, tax revenues tended to fall short of the amounts needed to prevent repressed inflation in the consumer goods markets.[74] Greater reliance on income taxation would have provided the Soviets with some built-in flexibility against wage inflation; unfortunately for them, commodity taxation, which was preferred for other reasons, does not have this property.

Because this paper is concerned primarily with Soviet finance, the explanation of the failure of the state to achieve its financial objectives has been couched, so far, entirely in terms of Soviet monetary and fiscal policy. The analysis must be carried one step further. For while the appropriate monetary conditions may be *necessary* for the development of an inflation, they are not *sufficient*, as the old quantity theorists would have had us believe. Not only must managers of Soviet enterprises have had excess funds at their disposal; they must also have had an incentive to spend them. The incentive in the case under discussion must have been strong because, in both bidding up wages and hoarding materials, managers were defying Soviet law. Why were managers willing to engage in these unlawful activities? Primarily because the labor and materials they were attempting to secure were essential to fulfillment of the tasks assigned to them by the Plan; and the risks attached to underfulfillment of planned output, together with the rewards for over-

[73] Until 1935-1936 the percentage of commodity tax in the consumer goods price structure was increasing rapidly and these taxes may have been the most important factor in the rapid rise of consumer goods prices. After 1936, however, the percentage remained relatively stable; from 1936 to 1940 and thereafter, almost the entire increase in consumer goods prices can be attributed to wage inflation.

[74] Repressed inflation is generated by other factors also, of course: simple failure to plan adequate taxes, reduction (either planned or unplanned) in the percentage of national output available for consumer goods production (e.g. due to crop failure), and failure to achieve productivity goals in the production of consumer goods. (Soviet productivity goals were *typically* unfulfilled in the prewar period.)

fulfillment, were apparently sufficient to overcome the fear of penalties connected with overspending the payroll and with commodity hoarding.[75]

The Soviets plan for full employment of labor and important resources; this is assured in theory, by their method of balanced estimates.[76] In practice it appears that little or no slack is allowed to take care of unforeseen contingencies (e.g. crop failure, failure of productivity to increase as planned, industrial breakdowns of one sort or another). How else could one explain the use of the "leading link" in Soviet planning?[77] The substantial underfulfillment of output plans in the prewar period also suggests that the Soviets plan to do too much with their resources, although here other factors may also have played a part. Moreover, underfulfillment of the output plan for any intermediate products means, of course, that some enterprise further along the line is unable to obtain all of the inputs to which it is entitled under the plan; the output of the second enterprise is thereby reduced and third enterprises are adversely affected; and so on. Under these conditions full employment planning is tantamount to overfull employment planning.[78] The real demand for labor and resources, as set forth by the economic plan, exceeds the physical supply which becomes available in the course of executing the plan. Soviet credit policy translates this real demand into effective demand, and the inflation described above is the result.

To facilitate an assessment of the relative importance for Soviet inflation of fiscal and monetary policies and overfull employment planning, respectively, the following four situations are distin-

[75] Cf. the interesting discussion by Joseph Berliner entitled "The Informal Organization of the Soviet Firm," *Quarterly Journal of Economics*, August 1952, esp. pp. 356 ff.

[76] For the most important commodities and for labor the Soviets draw up balance sheets which contain, on one side, the total supply of the commodity (by source) and, on the other side, the total demand or uses to which the commodity is to be put.

[77] The leading link is the industry or sector whose development is considered most crucial during a planning period (usually a year). Provision is made, in case shortages develop (and they always do), for the leading link industry to get highest priority in the allocation of scarce materials. In fact, an elaborate system of rationing important commodities among enterprises is always in use (see Gregory Bienstock, Solomon M. Schwarz, and Aaron Yugow, in *Management in Russian Industry and Agriculture*, Arthur Feiler and Jacob Marschak, editors, Oxford, 1944, pp. 58 ff.).

[78] A high level of investment, it should be noted, is not a prerequisite of overfull employment planning, as many seem to assume. All that is necessary is that targets be set higher than availabilities—this can happen with a zero rate of investment in a planned economy.

guished: (1) inflationary credit policy and overfull employment planning, (2) disinflationary credit policy and overfull employment planning, (3) inflationary credit policy and underemployment planning, and (4) disinflationary credit policy and underemployment planning. The results in (1) and (4) are ambiguous: inflation in the former and absence of inflation in the latter.

With respect to (3), the experience of capitalist nations in an analogous situation (depression and liberal credit policy) has been that unless the "real" conditions (e.g. expectations and investment opportunities) are favorable, liberal credit policy is not likely to touch off an expansion. The same appears to be true in the Soviet Union. Managers of Soviet enterprises gear their activities quite closely to the plan,[79] and there is reason to believe that if Soviet planning were less frenzied, Soviet managers would cease hoarding materials, bidding up wages, and so forth. In fact, there is evidence that managers of Soviet enterprises attempt to keep the plan from being set so high in the first place.[80] Thus it appears reasonable to argue that an inflationary credit policy might not lead to inflation in the U.S.S.R. if overfull employment planning were not practiced.

With respect to (2), capitalist experience suggests that expansions *may* be brought to an end by credit stringency (e.g. Hawtrey's theory). But many of the factors which are crucial in the capitalist case would not operate in the Soviet case or in any situation in which government investment plays a significant role. For example, in the Soviet Union, credit stringency would not lead to rising interest rates and expectations of reduced profits and thence to a lower level of business activity; rather, the objectives of enterprises, as set by the plan, would remain undisturbed by monetary phenomena. This leads us to believe that while prices of the factors of production might not be bid up in terms of money because of credit stringency, possibly some nonmonetary manifestations of inflation would develop: nonpecuniary rewards would be stressed and would be used to bid for labor; commodity hoarding would continue to occur; labor hoarding would develop; more extensive barter

[79] Cf. Berliner, *op. cit.*, p. 349, where he discusses *shturmovshchina*. *Shturmovshchina* refers to the ". . . typical breakneck pace of work toward the end of the month . . . in order to meet the monthly plan." During the first three weeks of the month the pace is much slower.

[80] *Ibid.*, pp. 353-355, refers to what Soviet managers call *strakhovka*, or the "safety factor." One of the principal manifestations of the "safety factor is the striving to have the firm's output plan set at a level well below capacity. . . ."

would take place and the prices of scarce goods would tend to be bid up in terms of other goods.

To summarize: The Soviets followed fiscal and monetary policies in the 1930's which, under Soviet conditions, proved to be basically inflationary. These policies would not have led to inflation, we believe, had the Soviets not simultaneously pursued an overfull employment planning policy which was inflationary in "real" terms. Soviet planning policy is believed to have been basically responsible for the Soviet inflation of the interwar period, though it was, no doubt, aided and abetted by the pursuance of an inflationary credit policy.

CONQUEST OF INFLATION IN THE POSTWAR PERIOD?

In the postwar years the Soviets appear to have achieved most of the financial objectives which they espoused but failed to achieve before the war. The period of financial stability began after the Currency Reform of December 1947, which wiped out the tremendous repressed inflation generated during the war years. Since the Reform there has been neither open nor repressed inflation in the market for consumer goods. In fact, prices in state and cooperative stores have been reduced every year for six successive years—the dream of the 1930's come true. Prices in the free collective farm markets have declined commensurately and are reported to be very little above state prices, indicating an absence of repressed inflation. Producer goods prices were raised sharply in 1949 with the express purpose of eliminating subsidies. Since then they have declined on three separate occasions: January and July 1950 and January 1952.[81] Finally, wages, which as we have seen are the real devil in the piece, appear to be rising much less rapidly than in the prewar period (if at all).[82]

[81] The real situation on producer goods is not crystal clear. Jasny (*The Soviet Price System*, as cited, pp. 38 ff.) claims that the price increase in 1949 was far too large and that the successive price cuts represent not reductions in money costs but simply compensation for the earlier "blunder." It should also be noted that analysis of the budgetary data indicates that subsidies are probably still being paid to enterprises in the national economy, and these could conceivably be responsible for the price cuts. These factors notwithstanding, it seems fairly certain that costs of producer goods are not rising as rapidly as they did in the prewar period.

[82] Schwartz estimates a 4 per cent increase in the average wage rate from 1947 to 1948 (Harry Schwartz, "Soviet Labor Policy, 1945-49," *The Annals of the American Academy*, May 1949, pp. 81-82). Barker estimates 3 per cent increases in both 1949 and 1950 (G. R. Barker, "Soviet Labor," *Bulletins on Soviet Economic Development*, June 1951, p. 21). Other less direct indicators, e.g. correlation of average wage rate with bond sales and direct taxes, lead

It is difficult to say which factor or factors have been decisive in controlling inflation in the postwar period. It is also almost impossible to determine whether financial policy is less inflationary now than in the prewar period. True, budgetary surpluses since 1946 have been much larger than ever before;[83] but we have little information on the amount of credit extended in this period or on the extent to which other sources of funds have been utilized. And there *is* evidence to indicate that the larger budget surpluses are being matched by greater extensions of short-term credit.[84]

It is even more difficult to say whether or not Soviet physical planning techniques have been altered so as to bring real demand and supply into closer alignment. Soviet literature in this field, particularly the recent articles, is not very informative. To my knowledge, no basic changes have been introduced, but I confess to incomplete knowledge of these matters.[85]

Assuming that the combination of Soviet financial and planning policies is presently as inflationary as it was in the prewar period, two factors now operate to prevent these policies from having as inflationary consequences for the labor market (thence the consumer and producer goods markets) as they had in the 1930's. These are direct controls over labor mobility and State Bank control over wage expenditures by enterprises and organizations. Several types of direct controls over labor were introduced in the year or two before the Soviets entered World War II; these controls were strengthened during the war years and have remained in force since

---

to similar conclusions. There has been no *direct information* in the postwar period on Soviet average wage rates.

83 Budgetary surpluses as a percentage of total budgetary receipts have been as follows: 1946, 5.5; 1947, 6.4; 1948, 9.7; 1949, 5.7; 1950, 2.2; 1951, 5.7; and 1952 plan, 6.2. In contrast, surpluses in the prewar period exceeded 5 per cent only twice (1933, 9.3, and 1934, 5.1) and 3 per cent only four times out of twelve years. Cf. Holzman, *Soviet Taxation*, as cited, Chap. 9; also "The Soviet Budget, 1928-1952," *National Tax Journal*, September 1953.

84 "In the postwar years, even more than before the war, temporarily free funds of the budget are used to extend *short*-term credit to the economy. The 1949 budget provides for an excess of receipts over expenditures of 30.7 billion rubles. This not only strengthens monetary circulation but serves as a most important source of extension of short-term credit to the economy." K. N. Plotnikov in *Pravda*, May 18, 1949.

85 One change which has been made is a vast extension in the number of commodities which are directly allocated and for which "balances" are constructed. Cf. E. Lokshin, "Voprosy planirovaniia material' po-tekhnicheskogo snabzheniia narodnogo khoziaistva S.S.S.R." ("Problems of Planning Material-Technical Supplies of the National Economy"), *Planovoe khoziaistvo*, 1950, No. 2, p. 46.

the end of the war. The most important of these controls from our point of view is the regulation which requires every worker to carry a labor book (which contains his occupational history) and to hand this book over to his employer (manager of an enterprise) as a condition of employment; the employer is not required to give the book back to the worker, except under special circumstances. This can be used fairly effectively to prevent workers from leaving a job—or to prevent other employers from pirating one's employees by offering higher wages or other inducements. Although the Soviet press gives many indications that in some areas excessive labor mobility is still a problem, the introduction of labor books must have helped reduce Soviet wage inflation.[86]

Throughout the 1930's the Soviets attempted, with apparently no success, to repress inflation in the labor market by State Bank control over expenditures for wages. In September 1939, however, a law was passed which, though it contains some loopholes, has been fairly effective in reducing these overexpenditures. This law allows only minor deviations from the principle that the State Bank disburses cash for overexpenditures on wages only to those enterprises which exceed their gross output targets.[87] Immediately after the decree was introduced, overexpenditures declined sharply,[88] and they continued to decrease every year until 1945, excepting 1942; in 1945, overexpenditures of industrial enterprises, as a percentage of the authorized wage fund, were "one and one-half times lower" than in 1939.[89] On the basis of these quantitative statements and numerous qualitative statements, I consider it probable that considerable headway has been made toward controlling open inflation

[86] Other controls over labor mobility are the labor draft for boys of fourteen to seventeen years of age, which is designed to teach them certain trades and compel them to work at the trades for a specific number of years, and a regulation which allows the government to transfer skilled workers anywhere in the U.S.S.R. without regard to their own wishes. Neither of these can be considered as being as generally significant for wage inflation as the use of the labor books.

[87] The text of this decree and related decrees is contained in I. L. Kukulevich and M. A. Rubin, *Planirovanie i analiz trudovykh pokazatelei* (*Planning and Analysis of Labor Indicators*), Moscow, 1948, pp. 235-249. A history of control over expenditures from the wage fund is contained in *Kreditnoe i kassovoe planirovanie* (*Credit and Cash Planning*), V. M. Batyrev, editor, Moscow, 1947, pp. 61 ff., and Holzman, *Soviet Taxation*, as cited, Chap. 2.

[88] N. Sokolov, "Gosbank v bor'be za ekonomiiu v narodnom khoziaistve" ("The State Bank in the Struggle for Economies in the National Economy"), *Planovoe khoziaistvo*, 1940, No. 3, p. 40.

[89] N. Zabozlaev, "Kontrol' gosbanka nad raskhodovaniem fondov zarabotnoi platu" ("State Bank Control over Wage Fund Expenditures"), *Den'gi i kredit*, 1946, No. 6-7, p. 8.

in the labor market by Bank control over wage expenditures. Since hardly a month goes by, however, without some Soviet economist calling for greater Bank supervision over the wage fund, we can assume that this form of control has not reached its ultimate stringency.

The continued occurrence of overexpenditures of the wage fund, as well as the need for Bank controls over wages and for labor books,[90] are evidence that Soviet financial and planning policies are still inflationary. Repression of inflation at the enterprise level does, of course, largely eliminate rising prices in both the producer and consumer goods markets, in addition to contributing to the avoidance of repressed inflation in the consumer goods markets. While this should make the performance of the Soviet economy more efficient, it does not eliminate all of the unnecessary evils associated with overfull employment planning. Thus the existence of repressed inflation at the enterprise level means that the associated problems of bottlenecks and commodity hoarding will continue to be present; and the introduction of controls over labor mobility and over wage levels, if successful, may eventually induce labor hoarding.[91] There is even evidence that the managerial incentive to produce efficiently and to earn large profits tends to be vitiated by repressed inflation in the factor markets. Finally, under many circumstances direct controls may be less effective in allocating resources than the market mechanism, and they are costly to operate. These difficulties are not likely to be eliminated by further multiplication of direct controls over economic activity. Rather, a basic revision of the Soviet theory and practice of both physical and financial planning would be required. Whether or not the Soviets ever undertake such a revision would seem to depend on two factors: first, on their comprehension of the cause of their difficulties; second, on losses to the national output of sufficient magnitude (by their measurement) to merit a revision.

[90] The labor book system would probably be retained for other reasons than controlling inflation. It would, for example, be useful in reducing labor turnover even in noninflationary periods, and as a general instrument of control over the working force.

[91] I hesitate to say which would constitute a more serious problem for the planners: labor hoarding or the excessive labor turnover which characterized the 1930's.

APPENDIX

NOTES TO TABLE 3

Turnover tax:

1928/1929 and 1929/1930: Sum of figures for excise, draft, and other minor taxes later combined into the turnover tax. *Sotsialisticheskoe stroitel'stvo S.S.S.R.* (*Socialist Construction of the U.S.S.R.*), Moscow, TsUNKhU, 1934, p. 493.

1931-1940: K. N. Plotnikov, *Biudzhet sotsialisticheskogo gosudarstva* (*Budget of a Socialist State*), Moscow, 1948, pp. 17, 102, and 181.

Profits tax: *Ibid.*, pp. 17, 102, and 181.

Direct taxes: *Ibid.*, pp. 21, 44, 102, and 181.

Social insurance: *Ibid.*, pp. 17, 102, and 181.

Sales of government bonds:

1928/1929-1932: *Socialist Construction of USSR*, Moscow, Foreign Languages Publishing House, 1936, p. 514.

1933-1937: *Gosudarstvennyi biudzhet S.S.S.R. za vtoriiu piatiletku, 1933-37* (*State Budget of the U.S.S.R. in the Second Five-Year Plan*), Leningrad, 1939, pp. 8-10.

1938-1940: Plotnikov, *op. cit.*, p. 181 gives only total bonds sold. Assumption is made that 80 per cent are sold to the population and 20 per cent to institutions; this ratio held in the years previous.

Total budget receipts: Plotnikov, *op. cit.*, pp. 17, 102, and 181.

Increment to savings deposits:

1928/1929-1932: *Sotsialisticheskoe stroitel'stvo S.S.S.R.*, as cited, p. 502.

1933-1940: Alexander Baykov and G. R. Barker, "Financial Developments in the U.S.S.R.," *Bulletins on Soviet Economic Development*, No. 3, University of Birmingham, August 1950, p. 18. Savings are not counted directly in estimating total sources of finance, but are counted indirectly as part of government bond sales since the reserves of savings banks are invested in government bonds.

Increment to currency in circulation:

1928/1929 and 1929/1930: A. Z. Arnold, *Banks, Credit, and Money in Soviet Russia*, Columbia University Press, 1937, pp. 257 and 412.

1931-1936: *Money and Banking*, II, Geneva, League of Nations, 1938, p. 183.

1940: N. Voznesensky, *The Economy of the USSR during World War II*, Public Affairs Press, 1948, p. 81.

1937-1939: Currency in circulation is observed to bear a relationship to size of the wage bill (payroll), wage rate, and value of retail sales (retail trade turnover). Using these relationships, estimated for previous years, estimates were made for 1937-1939. The results were hardly different from those which would have been obtained by simple extrapolation.

Increment to short-term loans:

1928/1929-1932: Arnold, *op. cit.*, pp. 271 and 372.

1933-1940: Gregory Grossman, "The Union of Soviet Socialist Republics," in *Comparative Banking Systems*, B. H. Beckhardt, editor, Columbia University Press, 1954; in 1931 and 1932, state enterprises, which were unable to repay up to 6 billion rubles in short-term loans, were relieved of these debts. In their place, government long-term securities were substituted. This operation technically reduced the amount of short-term credit outstanding by calling part of the amount by another name. For this reason we are interested in the total of short-term loans and government securities. In the late 1930's these securities were retired by the budget. This operation was purely a bookkeeping transaction and had no impact on the economy. Therefore, the retirement of the securities is not considered to have reduced the total of short-term credit at the time.

Total sources of finance include only short-term credit financed by increments to currency in circulation for reasons mentioned in the text.

Retained profits of state enterprises: These figures are obtained by deducting the profits tax (above) from total profits. Sources for total profits are:

1928/1929 and 1929/1930: K. Shmelev, "K edinom finplanu na 1930/31 g." ("Toward a Unified Financial Plan for 1930/31"), *Finansovye problemy planovo go khoziaistva* (*Financial Problems of a Planned Economy*), 1930, No. 6, p. 19.

1931: Interpolation of 1929/1930 and 1932.

1932: A. K. Suchkov, *Gosudarstvennye dokhody S.S.S.R.* (*Government Revenue of the U.S.S.R.*), Moscow, 1949, p. 131.

1933: I. Konovalov, "Finansovyi plan na 1934 g." ("Financial Plan of 1934"), *Planovoe khoziaistvo*, 1934. It should be noted that a figure of 7.3 billion rubles, in contrast to the figure of 8 billion rubles used here, is cited by *Biulleten'*, March 1936, No. 127, p. 28, edited by S. N. Prokopovich.

1934: *Ibid.*, p. 28.

1935: G. F. Grinko, *Financial Program of the U.S.S.R. for 1936*, Moscow, Foreign Languages Publishing House, 1936, p. 15.

1936: *Finansy i kredit S.S.S.R.* (*Finance and Credit*), V. P. D'iachenko, editor, Moscow-Leningrad, 1940, p. 292.

1937-1940: Suchkov, *op.cit.*, p. 131.

1938/1939: A. G. Zverev, *Gosudarstvennye biudzhety soiuza S.S.R., 1938-1945 gg.* (*State Budgets of the U.S.S.R.*), Moscow, 1946, p. 42 (1939 is plan).

Indivisible fund of collective farms:

1928/1929-1934: *Socialist Construction of U.S.S.R.*, as cited, pp. 346-347. Figures for 1928/1929 and 1929/1930 were given as for the years 1929 and 1930. These figures also include some (unknown amount of) investment in kind by the collective farms.

1935: According to Grinko, *op. cit.*, p. 9, the money income of the collective farms in 1935 was 9 billion rubles. According to S. Nosyrev, "Ustav sel'skhokhoziaistvennoi arteli i finansovoe khoziaistve kolkhozov" ("Statutes of Agricultural Artels and Finances of Collective Farm Economies"), *Sovetksie finansy* (*Soviet Finance*), 1947, No. 1, p. 21, 14.7 per cent of collective farm money income was deposited in the indivisible fund in 1935.

1937: According to *ibid.*, 12.4 per cent of collective farm money income was deposited in the indivisible fund in 1937. According to S. Nosyrev, "Ukrepliat' finansovuiu ditsiplinu v kolkhozakh" ("Strengthen the Financial Discipline in the Collective Farms"), *Sovetskie finansy*, 1945, No. 11, p. 20, the money income of collective farms in 1937 was 14,180 million rubles.

1938: Nosyrev, "Urekpliat' finansovuiu ditsiplinu v kolkhozakh," as cited, p. 20.

1940: Nosyrev, "Ustav sel'skhokhoziaistvennoi arteli i finansovoe khoziaistvo kolkhozov," as cited, p. 24.

1936 and 1939: Interpolation.

Depreciation reserves (amortization fund):

1932: *Vtoroi piatiletnii plan razvitiia narodnogo khoziaistva S.S.S.R.* (*Second Five-Year Plan for the Development of the National Economy*), Gosplan, Moscow, 1934, Vol. I, p. 420.

1933: Konovalov, *op. cit.*, pp. 177-181.

1935 (plan): *Narodno-khoziaistvennyi plan na 1935 god* (*National Economic Plan for 1935*), Moscow, 1935, p. 408.

1936: G. F. Grinko, *Finansovaia programma Soiuzu S.S.R. na 1937 god* (*Financial Program of the U.S.S.R. for 1937*), Moscow, 1937.

1937: Abram Bergson, "Soviet National Income and Product," *Quarterly Journal of Economics*, May 1950, p. 216.

1939: Zverev, *op. cit.*, p. 49. This is the planned figure.

1928/1929-1931 and 1934: E. L. Granovskii and B. L. Markus, *Ekonomika sotsialisticheskoi promyshlennosti* (*Economics of Socialist Industry*), Moscow, 1940, p. 517, give amortization figures for large-scale industry for 1926-1936. In the years 1932, 1933, 1935, and 1936, for which we have amortization figures for the whole economy, the total figures are consistently 1.9 times as large as those for large-scale industry. This enables us to estimate the missing years.

1938 and 1940: Interpolation and extrapolation.

Long-term loans by Agriculture Bank to collective farms:

1931-1932: V. P. D'iachenko, "Finansovaia pomoshch' Sovetskogo gosudarstva kolkhoznomu stroiu" ("Financial Aid of the Soviet State to Kolkhoz Construction"), *Voprosu kolkhoznogo stroitel'stva S.S.S.R.*, Moscow, 1951, p. 255.

1933-1937: Plotnikov, *op. cit.*, p. 140. (Plotnikov also lists loans to collective farmers for purchase of cattle.)

Adjustment for indirect taxes and profits of state enterprises: It was pointed out in the text that the indirect taxes as they are listed in the budget include taxes paid within the government sector of the economy by one organization or enterprise to another, the incidence of which is never on the household. It is impossible to adjust indirect taxes precisely to take account of this because the distribution of these taxes between the household and government sectors is not published. For some years now, turnover tax and profits figures have been published broken down by commissariat. It is possible to make rough guesses, on the basis of these breakdowns, as to the percentage of the tax paid by the consumer and the part paid by government organizations. For example, it was assumed that all profits and turnover taxes originating in the commissariat of heavy industry were paid by government enterprises or organizations; on the other hand, almost all of the taxes and profits originating in the commissariats of food and procurement were assumed to have been paid by households, although some allowance was made, for example, for purchases of goods by the Ministry of the Armed Forces; it was guessed that about 75 per cent of the turnover tax originating in light industries was paid by households; and so forth.

Turnover tax data are available by commissariat for 1934-1937 and 1939-1941, and by commodity for 1936. The sources are:

Year	Source
1934 and 1935 plan	S. N. Prokopovich, *Biulleten'*, March 1935, No. 120, p. 25.
1936	A. Smilga, "Finansy sotsialisticheskogo gosudarstva" ("Finances of a Socialist State"), *Problemy ekonomiki* (*Problems of Economics*), 1937, No. 2, p. 114.
1936	By commodity: Grinko, *op. cit.*, p. 64.
1937 plan	Same as for 1936.
1939 plan	*Tretiia sessiia verkhovnogo soveta S.S.S.R.: stenograficheskii otchet* (*Third Session of Supreme Soviet: Stenographic Report*), May 1939, pp. 328-329.
1940 plan	*Shestaia sessiia verkhovnogo soveta S.S.S.R.: stenograficheskii otchet* (*Sixth Session . . .*), April 1940, p. 232.

Year	Source
1941 plan	*Vosmaia sessiia verkhovnogo soveta S.S.S.R.: stenograficheskii otchet* (*Eighth Session . . .*), February 1941, pp. 498-499.

The deductions for the turnover tax varied from about one-sixth to one-ninth.

The adjustment for profits was much more tenuous. Breakdown for total profits by ministry was only available to me for 1935 (Grinko, *op. cit.*, p. 16) and 1936 (Smilga, *op. cit.*, p. 112). Deductions from profits are available in breakdown form for many other years and these aided in making judgments (this was especially true of the stenographic reports). It was finally decided to adjust profits downward by one-third for all years; this fraction seemed appropriate in the years for which data were available. It should be remembered that many taxes (profits) levied originally on producer goods are eventually included in the cost of consumer goods.

This ratio (one-third) was also used for social insurance and other indirect taxes. The social insurance estimate was based on data presented by Bergson ("Soviet National Income and Product," as cited, Appendix, p. 19) and is admittedly very rough; the same ratio was used for other minor indirect taxes for lack of a better expedient. These items are not very large, and unless the one-third estimate is very far off the final results will not be significantly affected.

NOTES TO TABLE 5

The following budget expenditure figures were used for this table (in billions of rubles):

	1928-1929	*1929-1930*	*1931*	*1932*	*1933*	*1934*	*1935*	*1936*	*1937*	*1938*	*1939*	*1940*
Education	1.1	1.7	2.8	3.8	4.9	6.3	8.8	13.9	16.5	18.7	20.3	22.5
Health	.3	.4	.6	.8	1.0	1.8	4.0	5.6	6.9	7.6	8.2	9.0
Social insurance	1.1	1.2	1.9	2.9	3.2	3.4	3.7	5.0	5.2	6.0	7.2	[7.8]
Social security	.1	.1	.1	.2	.2	.2	.2	.2	1.3	2.0	[2.3]	3.1
Subsidies to mothers								.1	1.0	.9	1.1	1.2
Debt service	.3	.4	.4	1.0	1.3	1.9	1.8	2.2	3.5	2.0	2.0	[2.5]

Year	Source
1928/1929 to 1937	All figures except debt service from N. Rovinski, "Sovetskie finansy i kulturnaia revoliutsiia" ("Soviet Finances and the Cultural Revolution"), *Finansy S.S.S.R. za XXX let* (*Soviet Finances for Thirty Years*), Moscow, 1947, pp. 209 and 218. Debt service for 1928/1929 to 1932 from Plotnikov, *op. cit.*, p. 52, and for 1933-1937 from *Gosudarstvennyi biudzhet S.S.S.R. za vtoruiu piatiletkii,* as cited, p. 10.
1928-1940	Education, health, and subsidies to mothers from Plotnikov, *op. cit.*, pp. 220, 223, and 225. Social insurance: for 1938 from *ibid.*, p. 219, and for 1939 and 1940 (plan) from Zverev, *Gosudarstvennyi biudzhety soiuza S.S.R., 1938-1945 gg.*, as cited, p. 83. Social security: for 1938 and 1939 (plan) from *ibid.*, p. 56, and for 1940 from Plotnikov, *op. cit.*, p. 329. Debt service from D'iachenko, *Finansy i kredit, S.S.S.R.*, as cited, p. 280 (1940 is plan).

Methods and Limitations. Gross national product is calculated as the sum of two major components: government (plus collective farm) expenditures and household expenditures. The sum of total expenditures by the government and investment expenditures by the collective farms is equal to the sum of the sources of finance presented in Table 3. (This is because the total of sources of finance includes a balancing item, currency in circulation, rather than the total loans of the banking system.) To the extent that any source of finance is left unspent (e.g. budget surplus), this fact is reflected in the amount (reduction in this case) of currency required to finance the loans of the State Bank.[1] Expenditures by the government and collective farms on goods and services for final use are obtained by deducting from total sources of finance the transfer payments to the household sector. Indirect taxes have also been removed by an adjustment noted in the text.

Expenditures by households for final goods and services are obtained by deducting from total household money income the total of taxes on households (including indirect taxes) and all household outlays other than those for goods and services (e.g. increments to savings deposits and to cash hoards, and trade union dues).[2] The sum of expenditures by households and by the government for final goods and services is equivalent to a "modified" gross national product, net of indirect taxes.[3]

In addition to the crudity of some of the estimates, gross national product thus obtained suffers the following three defects: First, investment by industry from private profits and private depreciation funds has not been included. While this exclusion will not significantly affect the totals after, say, 1932, those for 1928/1929 to 1931 may be moderately understated and the proportion of consumption expenditures to national product correspondingly overstated. Second, as already noted, some real costs of production are not explicitly recognized and paid for by the Soviets (e.g. rent and long-term interest) and are therefore omitted from the present estimates. This leads to an understatement of gross national product; it should *not* affect the proportions between government and household expenditures, however. Some writers have imputed these costs to profits of state enterprises.[4] While this procedure may be satisfactory for any single year, profits vary too arbitrarily in amount to be used for a whole series of years. Third, neither consumption nor investment in kind is included in the estimates presented. The omission of these figures results in an understatement of gross national product and an understatement of the percentage of household consumption to gross national product (since consumption in kind is undoubtedly greater than investment in kind). Baran and

[1] Cf. discussion on page 242 above.

[2] These data are available in F. D. Holzman, "The Burden of Soviet Taxation," *American Economic Review*, September 1953, Tables 1 and 2.

[3] Net of indirect taxes does not imply factor cost, however. Consumer purchases include, for example, expenditures on the collective farm markets at prices which, in many years, were considerably higher than the prices (including indirect taxes) of the same commodities sold by the state. Some deviation from factor cost also exists because of subsidies, although, for reasons mentioned above, it is believed that this is not serious. To summarize: we have considerable doubt that ostensible subsidies to the consumer, via subsidies to the machine tractor stations, are, in fact, real subsidies because the receipts in kind of the machine tractor stations are accounted for at the very low obligatory delivery prices. Moreover, the low cost to the state of subsidized producer goods is offset, at least in part, by current budgeted subsidies to producer goods enterprises operating at a loss.

[4] E.g. Paul Baran, "Soviet National Income and Product for 1940," *Review of Economic Statistics*, November 1947, p. 230.

Bergson[5] have made estimates of agricultural income in kind for 1940 and 1937, respectively; the effect of taking these figures into account in our estimates will be indicated below. It is not feasible to estimate income in kind for other years; nor can the Bergson and Baran estimates, for that matter, be considered much more than statistical expedients.

Some idea of the modifications required in the ratio of government to household consumption by inclusion of income in kind is indicated in Table A-1, which incorporates the Bergson and Baran estimates. The inclusion of income in kind in the years 1937 and 1940 increases the share in national output of households by about 6 percentage points:[6] to 60.5 per cent in 1937 and 54.3 per cent in 1940. These percentages, it should be noted, are considerably higher than Jasny's for both 1937 and 1940 (51.2 and 45.5 per cent),[7] but slightly less than Bergson's for 1937 (64.2 per cent). The gross national product total is about 10 per cent less than Bergson's estimate of 221.9 billion rubles for 1937, and about 5 per cent less than the comparable Baran figure for 1940.[8] The discrepancies are believed to be attributable primarily to the expedient employed by both Baran and Bergson of imputing missing factor costs. Reconciliation with Jasny's work is impossible because of differences in methodologies employed.

TABLE A-1

Rough Estimate of Gross National Product, Including Income in Kind, 1937 and 1940

	1937		1940	
	Billions of Rubles	*Per Cent of Total*	*Billions of Rubles*	*Per Cent of Total*
Government consumption, market[a]	69.5		127.8	
Government consumption, kind[a]	8.0[b]		10.0[b]	
Total government	77.5	39.5	137.8	45.7
Household consumption, market[a]	86.4		124.2	
Household consumption, kind[a]	30.0[c]		34.7[d]	
Add: Military subsistence	2.5[c]		5.0[e]	
Total household	118.9	60.5	163.9	54.3
Gross national output	196.4	100.0	301.7	100.0

[a] Consumption is here taken to mean the use of both consumption and investment goods.

[b] *Guess* as to the amount of investment in kind for purely illustrative purposes.

[c] Abram Bergson, "Soviet National Income and Product," *Quarterly Journal*

[5] Abram Bergson, "Soviet National Income and Product," *Quarterly Journal of Economics*, May 1950, p. 214.

[6] If Jasny's estimates are to be trusted, income in kind is much smaller than is indicated by Bergson or Baran. His estimates show income in kind to be less than 15 per cent of total household consumption (cf. Naum Jasny, *The Soviet Economy during the Plan Era*, Stanford University Press, 1951, p. 66).

[7] *Ibid.*, Error and Omission Sheet (dated June 20, 1952).

[8] The comparable figure would be Baran's national income of 302.38 billion rubles plus his depreciation allowance of 15.5 billion rubles.

TABLE A-1 (cont.)

of Economics, May 1950, p. 214. This includes an unspecified amount of investment in kind of agriculture.

[d] P. Baran, "Soviet National Income and Product for 1940," *Review of Economic Statistics*, November 1949, p. 229.

[e] Estimate based on Bergson's current figure for 1937, and Jasny's estimate for 1937 and 1940 in 1926/1927 prices (see Naum Jasny, *The Soviet Economy during the Plan Era*, Stanford University Press, 1951, p. 66).

NOTES TO TABLE 6

This table was compiled jointly by Raymond P. Powell and myself.

Source:

Planned figures:

1928: *Piatiletnii plan narodno-khoziaistvennogo stroitel'stva S.S.S.R.* (*Five-Year Plan of National Economic Construction*), Moscow, Gosplan, 1929, Vol. 2, pp. 208-209.

1931, 1934, and 1936: *Planovoe khoziaistve*, 1930, No. 12, p. 369; 1934, No. 5-6, p. 199; 1936, No. 2, p. 281.

1933, 1935, and 1937: Charles Bettelheim, *La planification soviétique*, Paris, Marcel Rivière, 1945, 2nd ed., p. 306.

1932 FYP: *Summary of the Fulfillment of the First Five Year Plan*, International Publishers, no date, p. 296.

1937 FYP: *The Second Five Year Plan*, translated by I. B. Lasker and John Swift, International Publishers, pp. 624-625.

1942 FYP: *Tretii piatiletnii plan razvitiia narodnogo khoziaistva Soiuza S.S.R.* (*Third Five-Year Plan for the Development of the National Economy of the U.S.S.R.*), Moscow, Gosplan, 1939, pp. 228-229.

Realized figures:

1928: K. N. Plotnikov, *Biudzhet sotsialisticheskogo gosudarstva* (*Budget of a Socialist State*), Moscow, 1948, p. 72.

1929-1935: *Socialist Construction in the U.S.S.R.*, Moscow, State Planning Commission, 1936, pp. 368-369.

1936-1940: Abram Bergson, "A Problem in Soviet Statistics," *Review of Economic Statistics*, November 1947, p. 236.

COMMENT

RAYMOND P. POWELL, Yale University

Mr. Holzman has provided us with both a statistical record of the sources of Soviet finance and an appraisal of the consequences of financial policy for Soviet economic development. Those who themselves have done battle with Soviet materials will recognize the expenditure of energy and ingenuity which his paper represents.

(*1*) The usefulness of the paper's statistical data seems to me to be impaired somewhat by an apparent confusion over the meaning of the term "sources of finance." Since this is not an uncommon confusion in discussions of the financing of economic development, and since it here gives the Soviet accounts an unnecessarily exotic character, an attempted clarification may be in order.

To put it crudely, one may ask either, Where did the *money* come from? or, Where did the *saving* come from? Statistically, the two answers may be similar, depending upon the structure of financial institutions. Analytically, the two are distinct. In the paper at hand, the tables appear to be answers to the second question; the text for the most part, but with frequent exceptions, is in terms of the first.

The distinction could be made more precise in the following way: We could conceivably record the total of money flows, on current and capital account, among the several sectors of the Soviet economy: let us say, households, enterprises, the budget, and the banks.[1] Making the same simplifying assumptions as Holzman apparently makes—that all charges accruing are paid, that sales equal output for each enterprise (to avoid investments "in kind"), and that omitted transactions are zero—we could construct for each sector an equation of this form: money receipts plus increases in monetary liabilities equal money expenditures plus increases in monetary assets.

Given sufficient data, we would probably be wise to stop at this point. We could bypass such problems as the meaning of "sources of finance" and move directly to an analysis of *particular* money flows. Lacking the necessary data, we must somehow consolidate the sector accounts.

Two consolidations, which are conventional and which yield familiar results, are immediately suggested. We could, on the one hand, deduct current expenditures (wages and taxes) from both sides of the equation for the enterprise sector and obtain the counterpart of our own sources-and-uses-of-corporate-funds account. Since Holzman has found it advisable to eliminate the transactions between budget and enterprises, we could consolidate the accounts of these two sectors, with this result:

(1) Taxes + retained profits + depreciation + State Bank and Savings Bank loans = budget purchases of goods and services and transfers to households + gross investment[2] + increases in the money balances of budget and enterprises

[1] This can be done for 1937 by combining banking data for that year with the data given in Abram Bergson's *Soviet National Income and Product in 1937*, Columbia University Press, 1953.

[2] Investment is used here in the usual sense of additions to plant, equipment, and inventories, with capital gains excluded from both sides of the equation. In reality, inventory gains and losses are known to have been large in the

This is still analogous to a sources-and-uses account, allowance being made for the inclusion of budget transactions. Total loans appear on the receipt side, increases in money holdings on the expenditure side. It answers the question, Where did the money come from? i.e. What were the money receipts from which budget and (noncurrent) enterprise expenditures were made? It records what I should judge is most commonly meant by "sources of finance."

It serves, moreover, a familiar and useful analytical purpose. We would like to know what determined the supply of funds available for developmental purposes and what determined the uses to which they were put. Were the two equated by variations in interest rates, by rationing on the supply side, by profit considerations on the demand side, or in some other way?

We could, on the other hand, deduct current expenditures from both enterprise and household accounts and consolidate all four sector accounts. The result would be this:

(2) Personal saving + taxes + retained profits + depreciation = budget purchases of goods and services and transfers to households + gross investment

This is the equally familiar gross saving and investment account. Both bank loans and money balances here disappear. Total receipts and expenditures, given our present simplifying assumptions, are less than those in the first equation by the amount of additions to the money balances of the budget and enterprises. This answers the question, Where did the saving come from? i.e. How was the income arising out of current production disposed of? This too serves a familiar purpose, in analysis of the determinants of the level of income, employment, and prices.

I do not suggest that these two equations are independent of one another. Our central problem is to determine how changes in the variables of one impinge upon those of the other. I argue only that we have two distinct questions with equally distinct answers.[3]

There is, finally, a third possible consolidation of our total money-flow accounts, though one which is less conventional. We could

---

Soviet Union, but I am uncertain of their treatment in profit and investment figures as recorded both in Soviet sources and in Holzman's tables.

[3] In a more familiar institutional setting the same contrast could be drawn in terms of the market for securities (or loanable funds, or "money") and the market for goods and services.

consolidate the *three* sectors—enterprises, budget, and banks—with this result:

(3) Taxes + retained profits + depreciation + increases in the money balances of households = budget purchases of goods and services and transfers to households + gross investment

This is identical with the second equation, except that additions to the money holdings of households have been substituted for personal saving, to which, again on present assumptions, they are equal. As in the second equation, bank loans do not appear among receipts nor money balances of enterprises and the budget among expenditures. This can best be regarded as a variant of the saving-investment account, and would appear to serve much the same analytical purpose. It has the advantage of specifying the assets in which personal saving eventuates.

In Holzman's paper the data on "sources of Soviet finance" are provided in Tables 2 and 3, both of which are constructed in the same way. The receipt side in both is clearly the receipt side of our third equation, i.e. a saving-plus-taxes total, personal saving having been replaced by additions to households' money balances. The expenditure side, which is complete only in Table 2, is less obvious, but would appear (unless the footnotes indicate something different) to approximate the receipt side of a sources-and-uses account. That is to say, in Table 2 "saving and taxes" appear to have been equated to "investment and government purchases of goods and services," but the latter has been classified not by kind of expenditure (plant, equipment, etc.) but by the *sources* from which those expenditures were financed (budgetary funds, retained profits, and bank loans). This would, at any rate, explain the otherwise paradoxical treatment of bank loans as "expenditures" (Table 3).

It follows, incidentally, that if this is the proper interpretation, Table 2 (and Table 3, if completed) ought not to balance. Total "sources" exceed "saving plus taxes" by the increase in money balances of enterprises and the budget. In Table 2 the budget's balances have been deducted from the "sources" account. Enterprise balances have not, so an equivalent discrepancy ought to remain and, perhaps coincidentally, in fact does remain: in 1936, enterprise bank balances increased by about 2.3 billion rubles,[4] the amount of the discrepancy shown in the table.

[4] See Table II in my dissertation, *Soviet Monetary Policy*, University of California, 1952.

Otherwise, the meaning of these two tables is clear, though one might question (see Table 3 and also pages 232 and 254) in what sense savings bank deposits are any more voluntary or any more "savings" than are additions to the currency holdings of households.

I have belabored these obvious and perhaps trivial issues with the aim of establishing, first, that when Holzman speaks (pages 242, 248, 253 and Table 3) of currency issue, or of a total of which it is a component, as a "source of finance" he is using the term in a different sense from that which it has (pages 230, 253, and, at least implicitly, throughout section 3) when bank loans are treated as a "source of finance." Second, the fact that a consolidation such as my third equation or Holzman's tables eliminates bank loans and the money balances of the budget and enterprises from the account in no way implies that these are insignificant variables. That they are significant is apparent from what Holzman says in his concluding section. It would have been helpful to have had a record of their behavior, i.e. an ordinary sources-and-uses account. (We do, of course, have bank loans appended to Table 3, as "expenditures.") Finally, that the same consolidation retains currency issue in the accounts in no way implies that this is the relevant variable for monetary policy or that it properly measures the inflationary impact of the Bank's operations, which are the apparent inferences of the statements made on page 242 and page 258. The Soviet State Bank no more controls (or controlled) the volume of currency in circulation than does our banking system, and its currency emission is no better a measure of its contribution to Soviet inflation than would a similar record be of inflation in the U.S. economy.

With respect to Table 5, which represents an interesting attempt to calculate nonconsumption uses of output from the total of saving and taxes, I would raise two questions. First, when the problems at hand are financial, is anything gained by adjusting the value of transactions from a market price to what approximates a factor cost valuation—particularly when such adjustments inevitably add an uncertain error to figures which are already of questionable reliability? And second, is a total of nonconsumption expenditures, inclusive of the current costs of the machine-tractor stations, of the operating costs of government, and of military outlays, a satisfactory measure of "developmental" expenditures? The answer to the latter depends in part, of course, upon the availability of data on the relevant expenditures.

(2) In the concluding section of his paper Holzman undertakes to analyze the consequences of the choice of financial sources (in the sense of my first equation) for the course of Soviet development. This is nearly synonymous with attempting to answer the question of the causes of the Soviet inflation of 1928-1941. For the latter, Holzman offers *two* explanations, which, however, are meant to be not so much competitive as proceeding at different levels of abstraction.

The first of these is a "real" theory which attributes Soviet inflation, ultimately, to an "overfull employment planning policy." On the face of it, this, or some other "real" explanation, is certainly more plausible than any explanation running in monetary terms. The Soviet Union experienced real changes of such magnitude in these years that inflation appears to have been an inevitable result.

Nevertheless, this strikes me as being neither a testable hypothesis nor, for that matter, an inflation hypothesis. It is untestable because we have no way of determining how full employment plans in any year would have looked, or of measuring the divergence of actual plans from that hypothetical norm. We do not know how far plans served the purpose of targets, and thus how far realizations were a function of plans. Holzman, moreover, is more confident than I am that the inflationary pressure from Soviet enterprises ceases when plans have been fulfilled.

Other "real" theories of Soviet inflation are testable but do not fit the facts well. The most common of these is the argument, never to my knowledge worked out in detail,[5] that inflation was produced by the high rate of investment, by the allocation of a very large proportion of current output to nonconsumption uses. Holzman rejects this (see footnote 78) and I think rightly. The great hurdle for any such explanation is the extremely *erratic* path of Soviet inflation. Average wage rates rose by more than 25 per cent in 1932 and 1936, by less than 10 per cent in 1933, 1937, and, evidently, 1940,[6] and there is no apparent correspondence between fluctuations in wages and fluctuations in the level of investment.

Holzman's particular "real" theory, on the other hand, does not seem to have much to do with inflation, unless that elastic word

[5] It seems to be implicit, for example, in Alexander Gerschenkron's remarks in *Soviet Economic Growth*, Abram Bergson, editor, Row, Peterson, 1953, pp. 30-31. ("The high rate of nonconsumption is closely connected with inflationary pressures and the specific inefficiencies which attach themselves to inflationary processes.")

[6] See Holzman's Table 6.

is to be stretched inordinately. I am not sure in what kind of inflation "prices of the factors of production might not be bid up in terms of money" but "possibly some nonmonetary manifestations of inflation would develop" (page 263), or what is meant by a policy "which was inflationary in 'real' terms" (page 264). Certainly, no one has supposed that the path of Soviet development would have been smooth in the absence of an excess of monetary demand. Indeed, I would doubt that the rate of Soviet growth would have been significantly accelerated or decelerated by any conceivable behavior of the prices of inputs and products.[7] But this does not require that we enter all strains and stresses in the Soviet economy under the category of inflation.

The monetary explanation offered here seems to me, on the other hand, to fit reasonably well what we know of Soviet institutions and the available statistical data. Though I shall not attempt it here, I think it can be shown:[8]

1. That the highly variable "source of finance," State Bank loans, was in fact a relatively stable function of the value of working capital stocks—and as the result of a deliberate but mechanical banking policy. This was an economy of "rationed credit," where the ration was inflexible but exceedingly liberal.

2. That the equally variable "use" of funds, additions to money balances of the Soviet state budget (the reported budget surplus), tended to offset the Bank's operations, but did so erratically and inadequately.

3. That, as Holzman shows, given this net injection of money (bank loans minus budget surplus), households and enterprises had the motivation and the opportunity to increase their rates of expenditure to a multiple of the initial injection.

4. That the rise in these rates of expenditure produced, with varying lags, rises in commodity prices, which in turn increased the value of working capital stocks—which induced a rise in bank loans, and so on. There was, in effect, a built-in mechanism of cumulative inflation.

In this process the decision to rely chiefly upon indirect taxes played a strategic role. Given this decision, and given the supply of goods to be made available to consumers, the Soviet authorities could forestall or reduce suppressed inflation only by resorting to

[7] Because of the dominance of direct physical controls in the system.

[8] Data supporting these assertions can be found in my *Soviet Monetary Policy*, as cited.

open inflation, by raising the prices of consumer goods. Moreover, given the decision to impose the turnover tax, for the most part, as goods entered the distribution network (for agricultural goods, as they were transferred from procurement to processing organs) rather than at the point of final sale, any rise in consumers' prices was reflected back in the value of inventories, and thus in bank loans, regardless of the behavior of costs.

This process, finally, was no more *wholly* independent of "real" forces than was any other inflation of which we have knowledge. Real forces in the sense of psychological motivations were clearly crucial for the behavior of households and enterprises and probably crucial for that of the central authorities themselves. Real forces in the sense of physical ones came into play at a number of points, most obviously in determination of the price level which would clear the market for consumer goods. But there was no simple and direct dependence of monetary upon real variables, nor is there any obvious covariation of the two. To an exceptionally large degree, Soviet economic development and Soviet inflation may be regarded as independent phenomena.

As Holzman points out, the evidence is insufficient for judging whether the postwar decline of prices and apparent stabilization of wages are attributable to the restraining of monetary demand or to the tightening of direct wage controls. It is worth noting, however, that whereas in the prewar period Soviet managers showed an amazing capacity for evading wage controls, the rate of inflation (as measured by the total wage bill) nevertheless progressively declined. From 1929 to 1932 the wage bill quadrupled, from 1933 to 1936 it more than doubled, from 1937 to 1940 it rose by less than 75 per cent. In the same three time intervals the surpluses accumulated by the budget (and usually immobilized as deposits at the State Bank) rose from 6 to 40 to 75 per cent of the total loans issued by the State Bank. Such evidence as we have suggests that in the postwar period this ratio has been still higher and for the entire period from 1941 to 1952 may approach 100 per cent.[9] The obvious inference is that the budget has finally attained sufficiently large

[9] It would be more accurate to relate the budget surplus to the total money stock, which is usually greater than State Bank loans. Loans are used here because money stock figures are unavailable for the postwar period. The ratios given are reliable only as rough indices of the change over time in budget offsets to bank lending, not as measures of the absolute size of the offset. Data for the calculations are taken from Tables II, XXIV, and XXVI in *Soviet Monetary Policy*, as cited, and from *Pravda*, August 6, 1953, p. 2.

surpluses to more than offset the inflationary impact of bank lending, but this is an unverifiable hypothesis in the present state of our knowledge.

(3) I would like to conclude by recurring to the theme of my opening remarks, the meaning of "sources of finance," but only with respect to an odd detail.

I have said that one meaning of the term is the source of "money" and have indicated that this single meaning covers two different processes. For enterprises, households, and the budget, "sources" in this sense are money receipts from other sectors. For banks, "sources" are monetary liabilities incurred, which is a shorthand way of saying money which they have received from no one but which they themselves have created—this, after all, is what distinguishes them as banks. But there is nothing improper in speaking of currency emission and deposits as the sources which "finance" bank loans (see page 251, for example) so long as the process involved is not misunderstood.

It should be noted, however, that the Soviet view of banking is not ours, though it is a familiar one. In the standard Soviet view,[10] banks are (except for currency emission) simply financial intermediaries, paying out the deposits of one client (budget or enterprise) in loans to others, the volume of loans being determined by the volume of deposits, and not, as we would have it, the other way around. Therefore, when a Soviet economist states, as in the quotation in footnote 84, that "In the postwar years, even more than before the war, temporarily free funds of the budget are used to extend *short*-term credit to the economy" (italics in the original), this is not to be read to mean that "larger budget surpluses are being matched by greater extensions of short-term credit" (Holzman, same page) but rather that short-term credit is being matched by larger budget surpluses. This statement, incidentally, substantiates the conclusion I have suggested above.

Reply by the Author

I am indebted to Powell for his comments on my paper. In particular, the methodological discussion of the first half of his com-

[10] Cf., for instance, A. M. Aleksandrov, *Finansy i kredit S.S.S.R.*, Moscow, 1948, pp. 251 and 255; Z. V. Atlas and E. Ia. Breg'l, *Denezhnoe obraschenie i kredit S.S.S.R.*, Moscow, 1947, p. 46; G. A. Kozlov, *Sovetskie den'gi*, Moscow, 1939, p. 227; and M. Usoskin, *Osnovye kreditnogo dela*, Moscow, 1946, p. 94.

ments places my statistical estimates in a more appropriate analytical framework. My remarks will be confined to the major points raised in the remainder of Powell's comments which deal with the causes of Soviet inflation. I think it is quite clear that our differences are differences in emphasis rather than in choice of basic variables. However, for purposes of this conference, the topic is of sufficient importance to warrant some additional remarks. Soviet industrialization provides an example of large-scale capital accumulation by a nation with a very low standard of living. This experience is relevant in thinking about the industrialization of backward areas. An important problem faced by the Soviets and one likely to be faced by any backward nation (or advanced nation, for that matter) attempting rapid capital formation and economic development is that of coping with inflationary pressures. Unless we are quite clear about the relative importance of the various factors which have contributed to Soviet inflation, the lessons inherent in the Soviet experience may go unlearned.

(*1*) Powell feels that my overfull employment planning hypothesis of Soviet inflation is not testable. He says (page 279): ". . . we have no way of determining how full employment plans in any year would have looked, or of measuring the divergence of actual plans from that hypothetical norm. We do not know how far plans served the purpose of targets, and thus how far realizations were a function of plans." But are such direct observations necessarily required to prove that the Soviets planned to do more with their resources than availabilities permitted? I would maintain that the existence of overfull employment plans in the prewar period can be inferred from three other observations: there were (1) powerful incentives of both the carrot and the stick variety designed to insure plan fulfillment and (2) substantial areas in which output plans were underfulfilled as indicated by Soviet figures, at the same time that there was (3) a scarcity of both labor and nonlabor inputs in industry as indicated by frequent references in Soviet literature to bottlenecks, commodity hoarding, and intense competition for workers on the labor market. The occurrence of this scarcity (3) is strong evidence that underfulfillment (2) was not caused by a failure of incentives (1) to operate. When Powell argues that "We do not know how far plans served the purpose of targets" he is ignoring the material of Berliner's which I presented on page 261.

This, incidentally, does not exhaust the evidence presented by Berliner in support of this point.[1]

Powell is correct, of course, in suggesting that inflationary pressures originating in the enterprise sector may continue even after plans have been fulfilled. There are several reasons for believing, however, that such pressures would tend to subside after the plan has been achieved. First, as Berliner has demonstrated, the marginal output premiums connected with the achievement of the plan are much larger than those for subsequent overfulfillment. Second, although the reverse is true in the case of Directors' Fund bonuses, these have a much smaller incentive effect than the output premiums for reasons discussed elsewhere.[2] Third, Berliner's "safety factor" would act as a strong disincentive factor once the plan had been fulfilled. Finally, the incentive which arises from fear of punishment or of demotion because of poor performance would also cease to operate after the plan had been fulfilled.

(2) A substantial part of Powell's argument against my position seems to be based on a confusion about my "real" theory of Soviet inflation. Having argued against my overfull employment planning hypotheses, he proceeds to write as though I had also proposed the high rate of investment as an explanation of Soviet inflation. These arguments are presented in spite of his explicit recognition (page 279) that I have rejected this explanation; reference is made to my footnote 78, where the opinion is expressed that overfull employment planning may be practiced though the rate of investment (and of economic development) is small or even zero.[3] But then on the next page, as part of his refutation of my position, Powell says: "Certainly, no one has supposed that the path of Soviet development would have been smooth in the absence of an excess of monetary demand. Indeed, I would doubt that the rate of Soviet growth would have been significantly accelerated or decelerated by

[1] Berliner, of course, is concerned with the monthly, quarterly, and annual plans of *enterprises*. When we spoke earlier in the paragraph of plan fulfillment, we were referring to the quarterly and annual plans of *industries* and *commissariats*, i.e. the aggregates of the enterprise plans. The Five-Year Plans are to be viewed as more in the nature of general policy goals than in the nature of operational targets.

[2] Joseph Berliner, "The Informal Organization of the Soviet Firm," *Quarterly Journal of Economics*, August 1952, and F. D. Holzman, "The Profit-Output Relationship of the Soviet Firm: Comment," *Canadian Journal of Economics and Political Science*, November 1953, pp. 523-533.

[3] I would admit, of course, that in a situation which called for a zero rate of net investment, the chances are the tempo of planning would probably be much slower.

any conceivable behavior of the prices of inputs and products. But this does not require that we enter all strains and stresses in the Soviet economy under the category of inflation." A similar argument is presented at the middle of page 281. These arguments are clearly based on a misunderstanding of my position. Powell is in error when he asserts that I "enter all strains and stresses in the Soviet economy under the category of inflation." My position is simply that "real" inflationary pressures are generated in the factor markets by the Soviet practice of setting output targets too high to be achieved with available supplies of raw materials, equipment, and labor, and in view of projected productivity levels. The Soviet system of rewards and penalties ensures that serious attempts will be made to achieve these targets. This creates a very specific type of inflationary impulse which, as noted above, is neither directly nor necessarily associated with the rapid rate of Soviet economic growth. Presumably, this source of inflationary pressure could be removed by setting targets at levels consistent with the supply of the factors of production; at the same time, investment and economic growth could be maintained unchanged at current high rates[4] since production cannot, after all, exceed the limits set upon it by the supply of the factors of production, despite Soviet overfull employment plans.

(3) Powell presents some interesting material in support of a monetary explanation of Soviet inflation. He shows that changes in the Soviet inflationary process were correlated with changes in the relationship between the budgetary surplus and State Bank loans. It hardly seems necessary to point out that this correlation cannot be taken to ascribe a *causative* role to the monetary factor, as Powell *implies*.[5] That the tail follows the dog certainly does not prove the tail is pushing the dog. From a theory of inflation which assigns (as I have done) a permissive rather than a causative role to money, one would also predict a close relationship between the financial variables and the level of costs and prices (open inflation).

The crucial question in my opinion, and one to which Powell has not addressed himself, is, Why did the managers of Soviet enterprises compete so strongly for both workers and nonlabor factors of production? The money created by the banking system must, after all, be spent by managers of enterprises before it can have an inflation-

[4] See preceding footnote.

[5] Though he asserts more than once in his comments the importance of "real" factors.

ary effect. Powell admits that "Real forces in the sense of psychological motivations were clearly crucial for the behavior of households and enterprises and probably crucial for that of the central authorities themselves" (page 281). In view of this admission, and the evidence which I presented to indicate that plant managers gear themselves fairly closely to plan (pages 261 and 263), it seems to me that it was up to Powell to demonstrate that the *availability of funds, per se,* was the driving force behind the observed inflationary process. For to demonstrate anything less than this is to admit in effect that the monetary factor played a permissive rather than causative role, the position which I took in my paper.

(*4*) Though Powell and I are in agreement that the postwar "deflation" may have been due either to "the restraining of monetary demand or to the tightening up of direct wage controls," he emphasizes the former, and I the latter, explanation. The basic difficulty with the monetary explanation, it seems to me, is that it implies the elimination of repressed inflation in the factor markets. That is to say, the stability of prices cannot be attributed at the same time to both fiscal and direct controls: if fiscal policy has been successful in reducing excess liquidity in the factor markets, direct controls are redundant; if direct controls are responsible, excess liquidity must still be present. If Powell were right, one would expect a relaxation of direct controls and an end to commodity hoarding in the postwar Soviet Union. There is no evidence that these have occurred; direct allocation of producers' goods and raw materials has been substantially extended (cf. my footnote 85), the Soviet journals continue to inveigh against commodity hoarding, direct controls over labor mobility (the passbook system) have never been relaxed, and State Bank controls over wage fund expenditures are more stringent than before the war and the cry is for still greater stringency. In view of these facts, I cannot believe that a more judicious budget surplus–bank credit policy was responsible in any causal sense for the Soviet price decline. The increased use of direct controls, on the other hand, seems to me a much more plausible explanation. In my opinion, these controls would not be pursued with such vigor were they not still needed to repress inflation. As a matter of fact, the success of the Soviets in *repressing* inflation in the labor market by use of direct controls has been, no doubt, a *contributing* factor to the size of the budget surpluses realized in the postwar period. Soviet law provides that excess funds (working capital) held by enterprises shall be automatically deducted into the budget. To the extent that enterprises have funds in their deposit accounts with which to bid up wages (due to the large amount of short-term credit outstanding) but cannot do so because of direct controls over labor mobility and over wage-fund expenditures, the budget is regularly provided with a source of revenue not otherwise available. And, of course, to the extent that inflation in the labor market is repressed, budget expenditures for wages are held down below what they would otherwise be. Unfortunately, there is no way, to my knowledge, of ascertaining the relative contributions of these factors to the large budgetary surpluses of the postwar period.

PART III

THE INFLUENCE OF ENTERPRISE AND BUSINESS ORGANIZATION IN ADVANCED COUNTRIES

ENTREPRENEURSHIP AND CAPITAL FORMATION IN FRANCE AND BRITAIN SINCE 1700

BERT F. HOSELITZ

RESEARCH CENTER IN ECONOMIC DEVELOPMENT AND CULTURAL CHANGE, UNIVERSITY OF CHICAGO

1. *Introduction*

From the end of the seventeenth to the end of the nineteenth century the economic structure of Western Europe underwent a profound change. Gross national income grew at an accelerated rate, and the center of gravity of the economy shifted from primary to secondary and later to tertiary industries. The Industrial Revolution reached its peak in the first quarter of the nineteenth century in England and in the third quarter in France. After that, rates of growth declined in both countries, but the trend proceeded along paths whose basic contours had been traced in the decades preceding the turning point. In order to understand fully the role of entrepreneurship in Britain and France, and its relationship to capital formation and economic development, its place and function must be examined in the period when modern industrialism was ushered into these two countries.[1]

Unfortunately, we lack reliable data which describe precisely the magnitude of growth rates and concomitant changes in the economic structure of the two countries during the period in which modern industrialism was born. We are fortunate, however, that there were several acute observers who had a predilection for "political arithmetic" and who have left us computations of national

[1] Although the approach in this paper is "genetic" in the sense that emphasis will be placed upon tracing the evolution of entrepreneurship and its relation to capital formation over time, I shall not discuss the wider problem of the "origin" of capitalism, or its earlier roots in late medieval and early modern economies. Also, I am aware that some writers, among them notably John U. Nef (e.g. "The Industrial Revolution Reconsidered," *Journal of Economic History*, May 1943, pp. 1-31), have stressed the development of industry in Britain and France in the period preceding the middle of the seventeenth century. The facts cited by this group of scholars are, of course, not disputed. But as I shall try to show, in spite of the presence of quite sizable industrial and commercial enterprises in this period, the economic center of gravity was still very firmly in agriculture and the techniques and organization of agricultural production underwent far-reaching changes only after the middle of the eighteenth century.

income and wealth at different crucial periods in the growth process. Recognizing the many shortcomings of even the best and most reliable of these estimates, we may, nevertheless, use them as bench marks which indicate (within tolerable limits) the order of magnitude of over-all output and the shifting composition of national gross product.

For Britain a very useful series marking the historical trend of national income and its composition has been published by Colin Clark. His figures for France, especially for the earlier years, are derived from less trustworthy estimates and he has subjected them to less rigorous analysis. However, some fairly reliable recomputations of French national income in the period from the end of the *ancien régime* to the end of the Napoleonic period have been published by A. Chabert, and these data, together with figures derived from Simiand's *Le Salaire*, and Clark's data for the more recent years also yield a useful and tolerably accurate series ranging over a long period of time.[2] On the basis of these sources Table 1 has been constructed to provide a general survey of the long-run growth of British and French national income and to indicate the gradual shift of the economic center of gravity from primary to secondary and tertiary industries. This shift may be measured either by the share of the national product due to primary as against nonprimary production, or by the distribution of the labor force among different branches of economic activity.

The most striking difference in the growth patterns of the two countries is in the over-all rate and the timing. In Britain the level of income began to grow noticeably during the eighteenth century and made rapid strides forward during the early nineteenth century. In France it remained fairly level from the end of the *ancien régime* to the end of the Napoleonic period, then advanced slowly during the next thirty years until it entered a period of more rapid growth in the second half of the nineteenth century.[3]

[2] For specific references see the Sources to Table 1.

[3] This point is confirmed also by a new "preliminary" analysis of the historical development of French national income by members of the Institut de Science Economique Appliquée, "La croissance économique française," in *Income and Wealth, Series III*, Milton Gilbert, editor, Cambridge, Eng., Bowes & Bowes for International Association for Research in Income and Wealth, 1953, pp. 45-100. According to this analysis the annual growth rate of French national income in the period from 1780 to 1914 was 1.81 per cent, but the estimates of Dutens and Dupin for the period before 1840 yield rates between 1.20 and 1.61 per cent, whereas those of Simiand, Froment, and Pupin for the second half of the century show rates between 1.56 and 2.01 per cent.

TABLE 1

National Income and Its Distribution in France and Britain, Selected Years
(for Great Britain all absolute figures are in millions of pounds; for France in billions of francs)

YEAR	NATIONAL INCOME *In Current Prices* (1)	NATIONAL INCOME *In Constant Prices* (2)	PROPORTION OF INCOME EARNED IN PRIMARY INDUSTRY (3)	PERCENTAGE DISTRIBUTION OF LABOR FORCE IN: *Primary Industry* (4)	*Secondary Industry* (5)	*Tertiary Industry* (6)	INDEX (7)
			Great Britain				
1688	50.8	56.4	48 (41)				90
1770	127.8	126.5	(46)				101
1797/1800	217.5	171.3	(46)				126.9
1812	290.0	177.2	37	46			163.7
1847	370.0	381.2		21.9	47.9	30.2	96.8
1868	753.0	767.7	20	14.8	48.8	36.4	98.1
1883	1,120.0	953.0		12.8	49.8	37.4	117.5
1913	2,013.0	2,013.0		8.0	46.0	46.0	100
			France				
1789/1790	4.65	7.05	68.1				66
1810	6.27	8.47					74
1820	7.86	9.83	64.9	63			80
1850	9.7	11.35		43	38	19	85.5
1880	22.7	20.64					110.0
1910	33.5	32.21		33.0	46.6	20.3	104
1930	243.0	30.42		24.5	40.0	35.4	711

Figures for Great Britain for 1688 and 1770 are for England and Wales only; figures for all other years include Scotland.

Figures for France in columns 1 and 2 pertain to national income less indirect taxes.

Figures in columns 4, 5, and 6 do not refer in all cases to the year listed but sometimes to the year closest to it.

Source: All data are taken from Colin Clark, *The Conditions of Economic Progress*, 2nd ed., London, Macmillan, 1951, except as indicated below:

For Great Britain: Data in parentheses in column 3 were computed by the writer. Clark's estimate of the proportion of national income earned in primary industry in 1688 seems too high, and recomputation of Gregory King's data yields the lower figure in parentheses. All data for 1770 were computed from the following three works of Arthur Young: *A Six Months Tour through the North of England*, London, Strahan, 1770, Vol. IV; *The Farmer's Tour through the East of England*, London, Strahan, 1771, Vol. IV; and *Political Arithmetic, Part II*, London, Cadell, 1779. The figures in columns 2 and 7 for 1770-1847 were recomputed according to the data in Arthur D. Gayer, W. W. Rostow, and Anna Jacobson Schwartz, *The Growth and Fluctuation of the British Economy, 1790-1850*, Oxford, Clarendon Press, 1953, Vol. I, pp. 468-470.

For France: The data in columns 1 and 3 were obtained chiefly from Alexandre Chabert, *Essai sur le mouvement des revenus et de l'activité économique en France de 1789 à 1820*, Paris, Librairie de Médicis, 1949, and François Simiand, *Le Salaire*, Paris, F. Alcan, 1932, Vol. III. Some alterations were made in index numbers for the early part of the nineteenth century on the basis of the discussion by Chabert.

These differential rates of growth are also correlated with the movement among industrial branches. In Britain, agriculture was the predominant form of economic activity until the late eighteenth century. After 1800 its relative importance declined and by the middle of the nineteenth century only about a fifth of the total national product was due to primary production. In France a similar process occurred, but the shift from primary production to manufacturing and service industries occurred only during the reign of Louis Philippe and proceeded from then on at an accelerated rate. While Britain's secondary and tertiary industries made up a large part of the national product by the middle of the nineteenth century, France attained a similar position only shortly before the outbreak of World War I.

Compared with Britain, France exhibits a pattern of retarded economic growth and industrialization. Yet in the history of the two countries there was a time when there were few apparent differences in the over-all productivity of the various factors, and when technological procedures and general economic organization appear to have been on a fairly even level. In fact, in the sixteenth century, France probably was slightly ahead of England in the distribution of technical skills, and perhaps even in the general level of welfare. It is important, therefore, to look for explanations which account for these differences in the growth rates of the two countries, whose over-all cultural, political, and economic situation did not differ very profoundly in the early sixteenth century; and to explore the lasting effects of the differential rates and timing of economic growth and the special features of the present economic conditions which can be attributed to the differences in the time lag of the main economic advances.

Among the explanations of Britain's forging ahead of the rest of Europe has been one which has stressed her natural endowments, notably her position as an outpost of Europe in the North Atlantic and her favorable balance of raw materials. This theory has commonly been associated with Henry Thomas Buckle, but parts of it have appeared in later accounts of British commercial and economic supremacy.[4] Although it is plausible that these environmental factors played a significant role, the theory cannot be taken as a full explanation of the differential growth of national outputs. The

[4] See, for example, William Cunningham, *Outlines of English Industrial History*, Macmillan, 1895, pp. 17-27, and Abbott Payson Usher, *Industrial History of England*, Houghton Mifflin, 1920, pp. 262 ff.

voyage from the North Atlantic coast of France to the New World is not much longer than that from England. Moreover, the two countries have fairly similar endowments of basic resources, which, considering the magnitudes of output of various industries in the eighteenth century, were ample in both countries. Britain attained its early industrial growth in the production of woolen textiles and of iron products and hardware. Even though Britain rather than France was the homeland of sheep herding, France had access to sufficient quantities of the raw material from domestic sources and, if necessary, from imports from Spain. France's iron ores were as rich and as abundant as England's, and for a significant period in the development of this industry Britain was dependent on importing large quantities of Swedish and Russian iron and even some American iron.[5]

Neither geographical position nor the endowment of agricultural or mineral resources can thus fully account for the differences in economic advancement in the two countries during the eighteenth and early nineteenth centuries. In my opinion, the decisive factors have to be sought rather in their respective social environments. Here again, explanations for England's primacy have not been lacking. Max Weber's thesis of the influence of the Protestant ethic on the spirit of capitalism and hence indirectly on economic practice is too well known to require extensive reiteration. But this thesis provides only an explanation of the general framework for these differential growth processes rather than an analysis of the detailed mechanisms involved. In order to obtain clearer insight it is necessary to study the groups of persons who were the chief instrumentalities

[5] According to the statistics on the British foreign trade in iron published by Harry Scrivenor (*History of the Iron Trade*, London, Longman, Brown, Green & Longmans, 1854, pp. 58 and 137), imports of bar iron rose from an average of 15,642 tons annually in the period 1711-1718 to an annual average of 51,716 tons in 1786-1792 and 48,780 tons in 1793-1799. By the end of the Napoleonic wars annual imports of bar iron had fallen to an average of 13,995 tons. British iron exports showed a steady increase from an annual average of 4,365 tons in 1711-1718 to one of 29,446 tons in 1796-1805, and to one of 91,772 tons in 1815-1822. Hence, the net import surplus of bar iron amounted to 11,277 tons annually in 1711-1718, and 19,334 tons annually in the last years of the eighteenth century. By about 1805-1810 Britain became a net exporter of bar iron and in the period 1815-1822 showed an annual export surplus of 77,777 tons. Most of the British iron imports came from the Baltic area, and some allegedly even from Siberia (see the anonymous pamphlet *The Interest of Great Britain in Supplying Herself with Iron Impartially Considered*, London, ca. 1750; see also the discussion of British iron imports in Ephraim Lipson, *The Economic History of England*, London, A. & C. Black, 1931, Vol. II, pp. 160-162).

of this growth process, whose economic decisions were crucial to it, and who bore the major risks of the advances and deserve the major credit for them. Since the process of accelerated growth was associated with a gradual transformation of the economy from dependence chiefly on agriculture to dependence on industry, mining, transportation, and commerce, we must look to these groups as the main agencies of economic change. Furthermore, we should expect that the role performed by such persons included not merely the accumulation of capital and redirection of economic activity, but also the introduction of technological and organizational innovations. The innovating function is associated with entrepreneurial behavior, and considerable light may be shed on our problem by a careful examination of entrepreneurship and its relation to capital mobilization in Britain and France in the crucial two centuries from about 1700 to 1900. The question may also be stated in another form: What were the significant aspects of entrepreneurship in the two countries? What impact did entrepreneurs (i.e. innovators) exert on the general growth process of the economy? Finally, what traditions of entrepreneurship which continued to affect innovation and economic advancement even after the peak growth rates had been passed were evolved in the two countries?

Although in the further course of this paper primary emphasis will be laid on the role of entrepreneurs, the conditions under which they acted, and the influences to which they were subjected, this should not be interpreted to mean that entrepreneurship is to be regarded as the sole significant variable in capital formation. Certainly, in the face of the economic advance of the Soviet Union and of governmental attempts at induced development in many so-called backward countries, it cannot be maintained that economic growth without entrepreneurs is impossible or that the main impetus to economic progress always comes from private profit-seeking individuals. The experience of Britain and France is, therefore, not universally applicable. It is not a part of the general social theory but a description of particular historical processes.

Nevertheless, the stress on entrepreneurship and the comparison of the processes and results of entrepreneurial activity in France and Britain are valid because, within the capitalist society of Western Europe, private entrepreneurs were regarded as the main carriers of innovations in productive techniques and forms of business organization and the chief determinants in the use and allocation of investment. Especially in the nineteenth century, when the greatest forward steps were taken in both countries, the position of entrepreneurs as an economic elite was undisputed.

The attempt to deal with these questions stresses the appearance in the unfolding industries of "new men" whose outlook and actions were decisive in determining the nature of economic progress in England and France. But the men themselves were influenced by already existing traditions. They were born into a social order in which behavior patterns in the economic field, as in others, were relatively fixed, and, above all, in which considerations of social prestige and even economic advantages were dependent upon specific political and legal institutions. These traditions, shaped especially in France by the impact of government, provide an important clue to the relative backwardness of France in comparison with England. They appear to explain why French entrepreneurship in the eighteenth and even the early nineteenth century did not develop as rapidly and as freely as in Britain, and why in the late nineteenth century, when rapid strides forward were made in gross national output, there evolved in France forms of entrepreneurship different from those in Britain.

2. *The Development of French Entrepreneurship up to the End of the* Ancien Régime

In a short but brilliant article Henri Hauser has tried to interpret the conditions which influenced French economic development under the *ancien régime*.[6] Although he does not explicitly discuss entrepreneurship, his essay not only presents an explanation of the patterns of French business behavior under the *ancien régime* but also points to the sources of some of the rigidities which have persisted in French entrepreneurial practice. Hauser thinks the financial crisis of 1559, in which the Lyons credit market collapsed, was profoundly important. The consequences of the crisis were aggravated because price stability did not follow it. This resulted partly from the impact of American specie which for the first time exerted a strong influence on France and partly from the outbreak of the religious wars which flared up and lasted for thirty years. A period of unrest, monetary instability, and internal devastation ensued which lasted three or four decades and which seriously unsettled the French economy; it was probably of a magnitude comparable with

[6] "The Characteristic Features of French Economic History from the Middle of the Sixteenth to the Middle of the Eighteenth Century," *The Economic History Review*, October 1933, pp. 257-272.

that of the period in modern Germany comprising the inflation, the Hitler regime, and the war. Entire social classes were deprived of their substance; the small nobility witnessed the disappearance of its money rents, on which it lived; the peasants, whose debt burden would have been lightened in real terms by the inflation, were the heaviest losers from the often wholesale destruction of fields, flocks, and even villages. Such workers as there were fell victim to the inflation, since money wages proved to be sticky and trade union organization was absent. Many emigrated to escape their misery.

In view of the terrible economic devastation which occurred, it is no wonder that when peace was finally made during the reign of Henry IV the institutions then created were influenced by the recent violence. They also proved to be extremely hardy and durable—most of them persisted all through the *ancien régime,* and some even beyond. They were based on the assumption that France needed not only a strong central government with the political function of maintaining internal peace and securing the nation against the outside, but also a strong and thriving economy, necessary for internal stability and external power.

However, if the government was to fulfill its role adequately it had to replenish the badly depleted exchequer and to assure an efficient and flexible system of collecting revenues. Since almost all of the taxes in force were excise and other indirect taxes (a situation not uncommon in underdeveloped countries), the farming out of taxes was considered, in the short run, to be the most effective way of filling and periodically replenishing the exchequer. Thus the financiers who advanced money to the government and recouped their advances by collecting taxes on their own account formed an important group in the country. Their political and economic significance began to increase when municipalities adopted the same system of tax collection. Extraordinary impositions by the crown and other taxing bodies were continually growing; as a result, the financiers increased in number, prestige, and power. They acquired wealth in order to buy government posts for their descendants. In this way not only would they become lenders to the state and recoup their loans from tax revenue, but if they could acquire a title of nobility they would be exempt from most or all of the most onerous taxes.

Thus tax farming became a very remunerative and desired business career, which attracted a good part of the available entrepreneurial talent. But since the net profits from this profession were constantly reinvested in titles of nobility or the purchase of government posts, or spent in conspicuous consumption, bribes, and other forms of nonproductive outlays, considerable portions of the national savings which flowed through the hands of the tax farmers were never converted into productive investment. That part which reached the government was spent for maintenance of the monarch, for war, or for the many favorites in the royal bureaucracy. Only a small part was actually put into schemes of amelioration, notably transportation facilities, some land reclamation, and encouragement and general subsidization of industry.

But not all Frenchmen could choose this relatively safe and remunerative way of making money through public service. Although the Edict of Nantes gave Protestants theoretically equal rights in government service, they were actually discriminated against and were only reluctantly, and often with difficulty, admitted to government positions. Moreover, after 1661 they were formally excluded from admission to public service. Thus the large families in the Protestant centers had no incentive to invest their capital in public posts. For this reason Protestant rather than Catholic families tended to build family businesses, to train their sons for business careers, and to expand their business interests by prudent intermarriage. Since the Huguenots formed the leading elite in French business, it can easily be understood what a terrible blow was dealt to French economic growth and to French entrepreneurship by the revocation of the Edict of Nantes and the accompanying mass emigration of French Protestants.

By the time of the Glorious Revolution, which in Britain saw the mercantile class firmly seated in the saddle, the flower of French entrepreneurship was destroyed. In the subsequent crisis Louis XIV had to apply to foreigners or emigrated Protestants for many of the financial and entrepreneurial services he needed.

Although the French Protestants formed the main group from which the entrepreneurial class was drawn before their exile, the political insecurity in which they lived made them look with favor on certain types of investment and disparage and even avoid others. They preferred investment in financial and commercial enterprises to investment in manufacturing, especially in those industries—like mining or iron smelting—in which capital requirements were high. However, this does not mean that Protestants shied away from manufacturing altogether. It was well known that they excelled in several industries and that, with emigration, their industrial talents were transferred to Britain, Holland, and other countries where they were eagerly accepted. But the insecurity of their position and the likelihood that without notice they might lose the product of many years of saving and work made them invest their capital in the most mobile and most liquid forms. Thus where large capital accumulated in French Protestant hands it was usually invested in financial and commercial enterprises. Most of the Huguenot manufacturing enterprises were small artisanlike shops.[7]

These conditions account for the fact that private sources supplied capital for industrial development only in small quantities. They help to explain why the government, in true mercantilist fashion, stimulated industrial development indirectly by subsidies and directly by the establishment of royal manufactures. The groundwork for this policy had also been laid under Henry IV, whose councilor Barthélemy de Laffemas was the paragon of a mercantilist statesman. Although Sully and even Richelieu favored a greater degree of freedom of enterprise, Colbert was firmly convinced that the promotion of industry and the provision of employment were properly within the province of royal power. Thus the system of royal manufactures was supplemented by a policy of public subsidization of industry; this was an important avenue by which a portion of the nation's savings found its way into industrial investment. The intervention of the government in economic affairs in general, and in the development of industry in particular, was so prominent that the system has been called one of "state socialism."[8]

The interrelations of these factors account for the characteristics of French entrepreneurship that appeared toward the end of the *ancien régime*. The emigration of the Huguenots in the late seventeenth century and the many fateful wars of Louis XIV had been blows which the country did not overcome until well after the middle of the eighteenth century. Industrial development doubtless picked up and grew at a more rapid pace afterward. But the sociopolitical system remained fixed. Most of the accumulated capital

[7] The excellence of the Huguenots in certain industrial fields and the benefits derived by the countries to which they migrated have already been commented upon by Samuel Smiles (*The Huguenots*, Harper, 1868, pp. 132-133). See also Henry Sée, *L'évolution commerciale et industrielle de la France sous l'ancien régime*, Paris, M. Giard, 1925, pp. 148-150.

[8] See Prosper Boissonade, *Le socialisme d'état*, Paris, H. Champion, 1927, which contains copious examples of public subsidization and guidance of industry. There exist several monographs on various royal manufactures and privileged industries in France under the *ancien régime*. A good bibliography is contained in *ibid.*, pp. 337 ff.

was concentrated in the hands of financiers or merchants who invested it, if at all, in the expansion of their own enterprises and in land. Enterprising individuals who might have struck out on their own were seriously impeded, partly by the restrictions imposed and tenaciously enforced by the artisans' corporations, and partly by insufficient capital. Thus even after 1750, industrial development depended to a large extent on securing government subsidies in the form of loans, exemption from certain kinds of taxation, or a guaranteed income for the entrepreneur, all of them expedients which had been practiced under Colbert.

Henri Sée sums up the privileges which were extended to these entrepreneurs by saying that "manufacturers were conferred titles of nobility sometimes" but that "most often they were granted interest-free loans for their first plant, or even given workshops, or the construction of machines was paid for." Similarly, workers in privileged industries were exempted from certain taxes and other burdens; in this way their living costs were reduced and entrepreneurs were permitted to pay them lower wages.[9] With varying emphasis this remained the pattern all through the *ancien régime*. An interesting example of it is afforded by the introduction of spinning and carding machines in France by the English Milne family. Not only were the Milnes enabled by a royal grant to establish their textile machinery factory, but after it had been in operation for four years the Duke of Orleans contracted with them to supply him exclusively with their machines and put John Milne in charge of his spinning factory at Montargis and the Englishman Foxlow in charge of his other factory, at Orleans. This laid the groundwork for the prosperity of the Milnes, who after the outbreak of the revolution became large entrepreneurs in the French spinning industry.[10]

In the iron industry royal subsidies played a similar role. The establishment of the foundry at Indret, near Nantes, where cannon were produced for the French navy, began through the collaboration of La Houlière and the English ironmaster John Wilkinson. Wilkinson's original gratuity from the crown was 12,000 livres per year, which later was raised to 50,000. His real rise began after he came to know Ignace de Wendel, the founder of Le Creusot. Wendel had

[9] Sée, *op. cit.*, p. 134.

[10] Charles Ballot, *L'introduction du machinisme dans l'industrie française*, Paris, F. Rieder, 1923, pp. 64-75. The royal subsidy to the Milnes consisted of a lump sum of 60,000 livres (part of which was destined to repay the advances made by their French sponsor), an annual gratuity of 6,000 livres, and a premium of 1,200 livres for each device which they turned out.

already obtained 600,000 livres for the construction of a large smelter and foundry; when this establishment was finally built through the joint planning of Wilkinson and Wendel in 1787, the stock company of Le Creusot was formed. It had a total capital of 10 million livres, and the king participated in it.[11]

This pattern of industrial development was quite usual during the second half of the eighteenth century in France. In southern France the provincial estates and some members of the clerical hierarchy were especially energetic in fostering industrialization, and even small quasi-artisan workshops were not beneath their benevolent notice. For example, in 1751 in the Provence the king granted an annual subsidy of 12,000 livres for six years for the encouragement of silk-spinners. At the end of this period, in 1757, an *Arrêt du conseil d'état* ordered the imposition of an annual sum of 6,000 livres, for six years, on the towns of Marseille and Arles and surrounding communities for the subsidization of silk-throwers. After another six years, in 1763, this *Arrêt* was renewed.[12] Royal encouragement was apparently contagious; the pressure of silk workers who came to depend on these subsidies supported local authorities in a movement to extend subsidization. In 1756 on the initiative of the Diocese of Lavour and the Estates of Languedoc a factory producing silk stuffs was erected and the Avignon merchant Jacques Reboul put in charge. This activity of the provincial government tended to grow. A commission of manufactures was set up which annually screened large numbers of applications for subsidies. In 1759, for example, 3,000 livres was given to a manufacturer of Nîmes, another 3,000 livres to the dyer Eyman, 800 livres to the Sieur Gily "for having set an example in using coal in the burning of lime," etc.[13]

These examples could be multiplied in great number. Whether the field is surveyed by industries or by geographical areas, the crown's subsidization of industry was imitated by provincial estates and sometimes by local aristocrats and members of the high clergy. At the same time there was a growing acknowledgment of the tech-

[11] See Bertrand Gille, *Les origines de la grande industrie métallurgique en France*, Paris, Editions Domat Montchrestien, 1947, pp. 193-199, and Sée, *op. cit.*, p. 292.

[12] See Emile Isnard, "L'industrie de la soie en Provence au XVIIIe siècle," in *Mémoires et documents pour servir à l'histoire du commerce et de l'industrie en France*, Julien Hayem, editor, Paris, Hachette, 1917, Vol. II, p. 21.

[13] See Leon Dutil, *L'état économique du Languedoc à la fin de l'ancien régime*, Paris, Hachette, 1911, pp. 331-332 and 469.

nological superiority of Britain. Prizes were given to those who either succeeded in imitating British methods of production or surpassed British skill by better methods, and British engineers and technicians found France a fruitful and profitable field for their talents. In addition to John and James Milne and John Wilkinson, other English entrepreneurs, especially technicians, were attracted to France by special favors bestowed on them by the king's ministers. The jenny for the spinning of wool was introduced principally by English mechanics.[14] Englishmen like Michael Alcock were active in the metal trades; he set up a plant producing small metalware at Charité-sur-Loire. Another Englishman, Terry, founded an engraving plant at Paris, and two Sheffield silver-platers, Rothelham and Drellat, set up a plant in Paris in 1790. Even John Kay, the inventor of the flying shuttle, spent several years in France, where he attempted to sell his inventions of a lace-making machine and a leather-stamping machine to the government. His efforts failed and he returned home disappointed.[15]

But the traffic in men also went on in the opposite direction. Frenchmen went to England to learn secrets of many trades and brought innovations back with them. One of them was the "projector" Leturc who was sent to England virtually under government orders as an industrial spy. He took a false name and carried on his correspondence in code. Another was Gabriel Jars, who traveled openly and collected and published a series of valuable accounts of mining and metal production[16] In addition, there were many small artisans and workmen who spent some time in England studying the new techniques in engineering, the metal trades, and textile-manufacturing.[17]

The general picture of French entrepreneurship and capital formation under the *ancien régime* may therefore be summarized in these terms: Industrial development, to a large extent, was under the tutelage of the state. While British mercantilism consisted primarily of the regulation of foreign trade and shipping, and the control of

[14] Ballot, *op. cit.*, p. 178.

[15] *Ibid.*, pp. 480-487.

[16] On Leturc see *ibid.*, pp. 273-277; also Gabriel Jars, *Voyages métallurgiques*, 3 vols., Lyon, G. Regnault, 1774-1781.

[17] For example, a certain Gaulard-Desaudray visited Boulton and Watt in Birmingham, a certain Lecour also spent some time at Birmingham to learn the manufacture of polished steel objects, and there were many others. Ballot (*op. cit., passim*) lists many engineers and workmen who traveled in both directions to impart the more advanced techniques of Britain to France.

foreign exchanges, in France the general supervision and control of technological and industrial development were added to these other features. In addition to the king and his ministers, a number of aristocrats and high functionaries of the church showed their interest in industrial development either by subsidizing existing firms or by participating in newly established enterprises. Although a certain amount of private initiative was evident, the role of the government always remained paramount, and even continued in influence after 1789, especially under Napoleon. The government not only initiated new projects and imported engineering talent from abroad, but also stood ready on many occasions to bail out enterprises which had incurred losses and to subsidize by various means (e.g. exemption from certain types of taxation) enterprises which could not otherwise have survived. French entrepreneurs came to look upon the government as a force of central importance in the national economy. The government and its appendages thus became the most important institution through which the savings of the nation were collected and mobilized for new investment.

This central role of the government doubtless enhanced the feeling of dependence on government service and government subsidies for new enterprises and contributed to the well-known aspiration to attain a *rentier* status, which was, and still is, so typical of the French middle class. The role of the government had yet another fateful consequence. Since it tended to encourage industries whose products found a relatively good market in France, and since in the royal manufactures it placed primary emphasis on output which was distinguished by superior quality and taste, it encouraged two other traditions which still play an important part in France. Instead of looking for large but yet unknown markets and instead of maximizing total profits by mass sales with little unit profit, French entrepreneurs came to seek earlier and more assiduously than British or American entrepreneurs the relatively safe shelter of monopoly.

3. *More Recent Developments in Entrepreneurship and Capital Formation in France*

At the end of the *ancien régime*, when French industrial development was profoundly affected by government regulation and subsidization and by importation of foreign technologies, the first steps toward the evolution of factory organization were taken. Under Napoleon these trends continued, on the whole, unabated. Napoleon's reign may be regarded as the last stage in French mercantilism. The radical individualism proclaimed by the Revolution was repudiated, and protectionism, even a species of bullionism, was the basic principle on which the economy was built.[18] Although the First Empire formed an ideological anticlimax to the democratic radicalism of the First Republic, the middle classes had freed themselves from many of the oppressive fetters with which they had been burdened in the *ancien régime*. Thus they found a potentially more profitable field open for their economic activity. Nevertheless, we should not be misled into believing that Jean Baptiste Say, who translated the principles of Adam Smith to accord with French conditions, correctly represented the dominant ideology of the French industrial entrepreneurial class. Now as before, the latter submitted willingly to the guidance and general supervision of the government, which accepted these "responsibilities" as a matter of course. The crowning act in this policy was the decree of June 26, 1810, in which a Council of Factories and Manufactures was established and a large inquiry into the state of French manufactures ordered. To be sure, many of the members of the Council were large manufacturers—in fact, its membership was a roster of the largest and most successful entrepreneurs of that day. But apart from producers of textiles, chiefly cotton textiles, and a few metallurgical entrepreneurs, most of the big business leaders were merchants and financiers. Industrialists continued to look to the government to bail them out in periods of difficulty, and after the crises of 1806 and 1810-1812 the government responded fully to these expectations. In both instances Napoleon tried to meet the crisis by more stringently enforced protectionist measures, by loans or gift-loans of several millions of francs to manufacturers, a large portion of which went to the largest firms, and by the establishment of preferential market outlays for French industry.[19]

After the downfall of Napoleon the situation changed profoundly. The governments of the Restoration were politically much weaker than those of the *ancien régime* and of Napoleon. This is clearly

[18] Alexandre Chabert, *Essai sur le mouvement des revenus et de l'activité économique en France de 1789 à 1820*, Paris, Librairie de Médicis, 1949. On the bullionist inclinations of Napoleon see Eli Heckscher, *The Continental System*, Oxford, Clarendon Press, 1922, pp. 71-73.

[19] Chabert, *op. cit.*, pp. 333-342 and 361-384. One of the sales privileges established for French industry was, for example, the decree of December 28, 1807, which prohibited the importation of cotton goods of other than French origin into Italy (*ibid.*, p. 368).

shown by their sensitivity to the revolutionary movements of 1830 and 1848. Moreover, industrialism in France had reached a stage at which it could not be expected to submit passively to government regulation. Entrepreneurs were still willing to accept bounties and subsidies from the state, but they wished to receive these benefits in a form similar to that demanded by their British counterparts. Low wages, government prohibition of labor unions, and a system of taxation which interfered as little as possible with the development of industry and yet provided sufficient protection for the domestic market were the desiderata of the entrepreneurial class. But although the government tried to meet these demands, French industry, which was at an awkward stage of development, could not make much use of the results. It had grown too big to be placed under the full tutelage of the state, and at the same time it had not developed sufficient traditions of independent initiative to forge ahead rapidly and vigorously. Moreover, it was at this stage that the disadvantages of industrial backwardness were felt most strongly. Industrial technology in Britain had advanced to such a degree that in many industries transfer of the most up-to-date technology required the mobilization of relatively large sums of capital. This was a task to which French entrepreneurs had never been accustomed and which they were unable to meet. While in Britain the initial stages in the development of the iron and cotton industries had preceded the railway boom, in France the building up of the entire complex of basic industries in metallurgy, textiles, food-processing, and chemicals and the provision of more modern transportation facilities had to be accomplished simultaneously.

At this point, only an innovation of grandiose proportions could have met the challenge, and by a strange accident, or perhaps by the logic of historical necessity, the men to make this innovation were found. Grounded in the field of entrepreneurship with the longest and most deeply rooted traditions in France, that of financial manipulations, and inspired by a philosophy which extolled the advantages and progressive character of a system of capitalist industrialism, a new form of banking was evolved; this, more than any other event, cut the Gordian knot binding the forces of industrial progress. I refer to the formation by the brothers Péreire of the Crédit Mobilier, the first industrial investment bank in France and in the world. This epoch-making innovation and its meaning for French economic development has recently been brilliantly described by Gerschenkron, and all I can do here is paraphrase his words.[20]

The investment bank of the Crédit Mobilier type circumvented several bottlenecks simultaneously. Above all, it succeeded in mobilizing large amounts of capital for industrial development in a form acceptable to French savers. Second, it overcame the shortage of creative entrepreneurs, by undertaking the entrepreneurial functions itself and reducing many of the actual managers of industrial firms to executors of policies. Third, it introduced a method of mobilizing investment which fitted smoothly into the prevailing patterns of economic organization in France: it permitted the persons who were supplying capital for the financing of industrial development to perform *rentier* roles to which they were accustomed. Fourth, it maintained the symbol of financial supremacy over the growing power of industrial entrepreneurship by placing a credit institution in the position of industrial planner and developer and reducing the industrialists to a rank of secondary importance. Finally, it filled a painfully felt vacuum which had developed since the fall of Napoleon by performing a function which before had been performed by government. In doing all this it came into harsh conflict with the representatives of "old wealth," the Rothschilds and the Lafittes, who had followed on the whole the traditional financial policies of being bankers to the government and profiting from the financing of commercial and exchange transactions. Although, as Gerschenkron points out, this conflict probably caused the ultimate downfall of the Crédit Mobilier, the victory for the representatives of "old wealth" was worse than Pyrrhic. They gained because they became converted and adopted the methods of industrial investment financing which the Crédit Mobilier had introduced.[21]

The formula discovered by the brothers Péreire provided the solution to the chief problems which had prevented more rapid economic development not merely in France, but on the entire continent of Europe. In order to explore the consequences which an institution like the Crédit Mobilier had for the further development of entrepreneurship in France, let us look at the general views on industrialization and its relation to credit operations which the founders of the Crédit Mobilier held.

[20] See Alexander Gerschenkron, "Economic Backwardness in Historical Perspective," in *The Progress of Underdeveloped Areas*, Bert F. Hoselitz, editor, University of Chicago Press, 1952, pp. 10 ff.

[21] *Ibid.*, p. 11.

Emile and Isaac Péreire were Saint-Simonians, and their intellectual membership in this school of social thought is, I believe, of fundamental importance for the understanding not only of their own life work, but also of the nature of the impact which the Crédit Mobilier exerted on industrial entrepreneurship in France.

Saint-Simon is commonly regarded as a "socialist forerunner," an interpretation which is too simple and ambiguous and does not explain his position in the intellectual history of France. Nevertheless, it is a bitterly ironical trait of French intellectual history—and perhaps an additional symptom of France's economic backwardness, as compared with her intellectual maturity—that the Physiocrats, the group of thinkers who extolled the sole productivity of agriculture, were to become the apostles of capitalism, and that a man who is generally typed as a "socialist forerunner" should have inspired ideas which led to the development of institutions making possible the realization of industrial capitalism in France.

But we are concerned here with Saint-Simon's ideas on industrialism and on the relation of credit to industry. The industrial system, which was a somewhat idealized description of industrial capitalism, was in his view the only one which would lead at the same time to the physical and spiritual happiness of the masses of the people. At the very center of this new industrial system stood the institutions which provided credit. Money or money's worth was the measure of all things, and, depending upon whose interests were served by the existing monetary and credit institutions, Saint-Simon stipulated two opposing systems: the old system in which credit was in the service of a centralized arbitrary anti-industrialist government, and the new system in which credit was fully and exclusively used to support the productive forces of society. However ambiguous Saint-Simon may have been on many points—and there are harsh contradictions even in some of his most fundamental definitions—his doctrine of the place of credit was sharply and clearly defined.[22] And Saint-Simon knew what he was talking about. His acquaintances included the banker Lafitte, and his close friends included Lafitte's associate Perregaux. Among his chief disciples were Enfantin, son of a banker; Olinde Rodrigues, the director of the Caisse Hypothécaire; Duveyrier, son of a bank director and later editor of the

[22] A convenient summary of the relevant theories of Saint-Simon on the two systems and on the place of credit in relation to each may be found in *L'oeuvre d'Henri de Saint-Simon*, Célestin Bouglé, editor, Paris, F. Alcan, 1925, pp. 136-173.

journal *Crédit*; and d'Eichthal, who also came from a prominent banking family. These were the men with whom the brothers Péreire associated in their youth and with whom they discussed the role of banking and credit institutions in the new society.[23]

Here, then, must be sought the origin of the conceptions which the Péreires formed about the place of an industrial investment bank, and which they later realized in the Crédit Mobilier. But it is important to note that in the Saint-Simonian system the superiority and very central position of the banker are emphasized. Although the professions of the merchant and manufacturer were older, after the "banking industry" appeared in the plans it soon took on the unquestioned role of leader. These ideas were also reflected in the procedures developed by the Péreires for their investment bank. Industrial and commercial entrepreneurship were subordinate so long as the unquestioned leadership of the captains of industry who controlled the banks was assured. From the tutelage of the crown, French industry—after an uneasy interval—had passed into the tutelage of credit institutions. Again the financier was on top and again the industrial entrepreneur was subordinate; again the latter was looking for stimulation and, when things went badly, for support from someone else. Again industry was made dependent upon an organization which was more powerful and controlled more wealth, which was more flexible and, because of its varied investments, more farsighted than the industrial entrepreneur.

And just as in Britain the early joint stock companies had been favored by the trend of the time into which they had been born, and hence could fulfill the expectations held for them, the new system of investment banking in France fulfilled the promises its inventors had made. It was the new type of banking which made possible the construction of a railway network not only in France, but also in Spain, Austria, and Russia; it facilitated the urban redevelopment of cities and the grandiose replanning of Paris under Haussman; it helped domesticate industries in France which had languished before or been beset by shortages of capital; it contributed to make the fifty years in which it flowered the period of the most rapid economic development which France ever witnessed.

But the fact that the brothers Péreire and the Crédit Mobilier lost out to the representatives of "old wealth," even though the

[23] For Saint-Simon's associations with bankers and members of bankers' families see Johann Plenge, *Die erste Anlagebank: Gründung und Geschichte des Crédit Mobilier*, Essen, Baldeker, 1921, pp. 16-17.

latter adopted their principles of banking, had an important influence on the future development of French entrepreneurship. The experiment in banking represented by the Crédit Mobilier may be regarded as having exerted a double impact. On the one hand, it was an innovation in the field of organization; on the other, it was the carrier of a new expansionist ideology. Whereas the financiers of long standing—Rothschild, Lafitte, and their ilk—adopted the organizational form ushered in by the Crédit Mobilier, they did not also adopt its spirit, which still had a strong Saint-Simonian flavor. It was inevitable that the new form of credit organization should demand the extension of investment in industry, transportation facilities, public utilities, and urban construction. The very momentum imparted by the new banking organization carried its reformatory effects beyond its own existence. But although the new practice of investment banking demanded a constant accumulation of real capital financed through the agency of the banks, the conservative spirit of the representatives of "old wealth" gradually led to a reduction in the rate of capital formation and to an increasing prevalence of portfolio investments. For example, the French banks participated in the financing of Russian railway expansion, but they did this by lending money to the Russian government, which in turn built the railways.

As a result, during the last 350 years French industrial entrepreneurship, except in special cases, has never escaped entirely the tutelage of either the state or large finance. I do not mean that French industrialists developed no initiative on their own—a few French industrial entrepreneurs could be cited who displayed a spirit of venturesomeness which compares not unfavorably with that of British businessmen of the Industrial Revolution or American businessmen of the last three generations, who are customarily believed to represent the best traditions of entrepreneurship. But not only were these men exceptional; they also had to operate in a social environment in which imaginative venturesomeness was not supported by general tradition and by institutions facilitating this type of social action. These factors seem to explain quite adequately the rather stagnant situation of French entrepreneurship in the nineteenth and twentieth centuries, which David Landes has so brilliantly described.[24]

[24] See the following of his works: "French Entrepreneurship and Industrial Growth in the Nineteenth Century," *Journal of Economic History*, May 1949, pp. 45-61; "Business and Businessmen in France," in *Modern France*, Edward

More recent evidence of this attitude is reflected in the complaint of American observers about the relative lack of success of the Mutual Security Administration in France. American cost-saving techniques are freely adopted by French industrialists, but often output is not expanded and the savings not passed on to consumers. The lowering of costs through the adoption of new techniques, on the contrary, often results in the layoff of workers and the maintenance of a given, relatively rigidly limited output, with an accompanying increase in unit profits. At the same time, inventiveness and technical ingenuity are concentrated on the production of qualitatively better and artistically more tasteful products rather than on the lowering of costs and the development of sales methods which will insure mass sales.

In his analysis of the decline of classical capitalism, Sombart has drawn attention to what he considers to be the paramount tension in the economic ethic characteristic of the "spirit of capitalism." This tension consists in the contrast between "rationalism and irrationalism, between calculation and speculation, between the bourgeois spirit and the robber spirit, between prudence and venturesomeness."[25] France, beginning with the *ancien régime,* abounded in entrepreneurs who exhibited the first of these contrasting pairs of attitudes. The French middle classes were rational, calculating, and prudent, and they still form the archetype of the bourgeois. However soaring may have been French imagination in the fields of literature and the arts, it remained close to earth in the field of entrepreneurship. By contrast, however pedestrian the British, especially the Victorians, in the more exalted realms of human culture, in economic matters they exhibited an astoundingly vigorous spirit of venturesomeness, daring, and "irrationality" in Sombart's sense. I will not judge whether these differences are the cause, or merely symptoms, of the more rapid and farther-reaching economic advance in Britain. But whichever they are, these differences are part of general attitudes toward entrepreneurship and capital formation which have deep traditional roots in the histories of the two countries, and which continued for a long time to impinge upon the speed and direction of their economic development.

M. Earle, editor, Princeton University Press, 1951; and "Entrepreneurial Research in France," *Explorations in Entrepreneurial History,* October 1950, pp. 35-43. See also John McDonald, "French Business Talks Back," *Fortune,* April 1952, pp. 120-121 and 178-188.

[25] Werner Sombart, *Die Zukunft des Kapitalismus,* Berlin, Buchholz & Weisswange, 1932, p. 8.

4. *Characteristics of British Entrepreneurship and Capital Formation*

In Great Britain the 200 years from the Glorious Revolution to the end of the nineteenth century saw the formation of entrepreneurial traditions and attitudes which were in sharp contrast to those of France. Not only did genuine private entrepreneurship develop in Britain on a large scale, but the mobilization of capital for industrial development was channeled through private rather than public institutions. This should not be interpreted to imply that the British government in the seventeenth and eighteenth centuries was not mercantilistic and jealous of its right to regulate economic life. But regulation in Britain was confined chiefly to international trade and those branches of the national economy which were of overwhelming importance for the political fate of the country, notably shipping and the provision of armaments and other war material.

While the British government closely supervised and participated in industrial development only in rare and specially selected circumstances, perferring to guide the economy by indirect means, the general socio-economic situation in Britain also differed from that of France in two other aspects. British guilds and corporations were relatively weaker than their French counterparts, and the internal mobility of the population was much higher than in France. Moreover, the crown depended for its fiscal needs less on internal excises and more on revenue from international trade and the granting of commercial and industrial monopolies. The institution of tax-farming did not develop in Britain. One of the chief factors which prevented such a development was the growing power of the middle class in the British Parliament. It is a difficult historical task to disentangle the reciprocal causal chains between the forms of taxation and methods of tax collection, on the one hand, and the growth of middle class wealth and political power, on the other. British merchants and industrialists could control the forms and burden of taxation to which they were subject through their parliamentary institutions. At the same time they could maintain the supremacy of Parliament, and its right to control the revenue demands of the government, because they occupied positions of economic power and the crown therefore could not dispense with their collaboration or acquiesence with impunity. The English revolutions of the 1640's and 1688 conclusively established the stability of this internal balance of power.

The role of the British government, however, took another direction. As in many countries with a young and growing industry, entrepreneurs relied chiefly on two markets where an effective demand, backed by readily available cash, appeared to exist. One of these was the export market, the other the government's need for supplies. The large companies selling British products abroad were organizations through which British producers could readily dispose of all or part of their output. The knowledge of the availability of such (monopsonistic or oligopsonistic) demand conditions was conducive, at least in part, to the development of certain industries, notably textiles, certain chemical and metal products, and those producing commodities demanded by the government. For example, some of the most successful iron enterprises achieved their important position in the industry because of contacts which they, or certain partners in these firms, maintained with government officials engaged in the purchase of cannon and other war material.

These influences, which are generally similar to tendencies existing in currently underdeveloped countries, had an important bearing on the industrial development of England chiefly because they favored the development of certain industries as against others. They account in large part for the relatively early development of the textile and iron industries in Britain, and of "luxury" industries in France. But this industrial development in Britain led to geographical decentralization and a shift of the center of gravity of the population from the South and East of England to the North and Northwest. One aspect of British economic development in the eighteenth century was an extension of the internal geographical frontier into new areas of settlement and the growth of new agglomerations of population. The process was not merely one of progressive growth of already existing urban centers. The towns which at the end of the seventeenth century had been largest and most important grew also, but at a much smaller rate than the new towns.

The movement and geographical redistribution of the British population before and during the Industrial Revolution have often been described and need no repetition here.[26] The point I wish to stress, however, is that this internal reallocation of population meant that industrial development proceeded on two fronts. In part, in-

[26] See esp. Arthur Redford, *Labour Migration in England, 1800-50*, Manchester, The University Press, 1926, pp. 8-17, 32-37, 48-53, and 175 ff., and maps in Appendix.

dustry expanded in the old centers, where it built on already existing capital markets, on families already entrenched in certain trades and on traditions of production and marketing, not to speak of the guilds. At the same time industry developed in new areas, into which entrepreneurs and workers poured from various parts of Britain: these were areas into which large quantities of capital had to be brought from the outside, and where new forms of enterprise and new marketing relations could develop more easily and with fewer impediments from traditional patterns and vested interests.

The development of the British iron industry is a good example in point. The main center of iron production in the early eighteenth century was the Black Country in the Midlands. The Weald (Sussex and Kent) and the Forest of Dean (Gloucestershire) had already passed their peak period. The forests were exhausted, and the furnaces in these counties were smaller than the newer ones which had been constructed in Staffordshire and Shropshire. In 1717, of a total production of about 18,600 tons of iron, roughly 6,000 tons were produced in the Midlands region (including North Wales), about 5,500 tons in the Weald and the Forest of Dean combined, 2,100 tons in the East of England (notably Yorkshire and Derbyshire), and 1,900 tons in South Wales. The remainder was produced in scattered furnaces located in various parts of the country. Scotland produced only negligible amounts of iron.[27]

The three regions which showed the greatest advance in iron production in the following 120 years were the Midlands, South Wales, and Scotland. The industrial weight of the Midlands as a center of the iron industry was founded on their importance as a fabricating rather than a raw materials center. During most of the eighteenth century, Britain was a net importer of raw iron, and only around 1805 did she become a net exporter of the crude product. The chief consuming region of imported iron—most of which came from the Baltic area—was the Black Country. For example, much of the activity of Sir Ambrose Crowley, one of the pioneers of the iron industry, consisted in trading raw iron to the Midlands area, and Knight, one of the members of the Stour partnership, imported American raw iron into the region as early as 1728.[28]

[27] This distribution is based on the information listed in E. W. Hulme, "Statistical History of the Iron Trade of England and Wales, 1717-1750," *Transactions of the Newcomen Society*, Vol. IX (1928-1929), p. 13.

[28] See Michael W. Flinn, "Sir Ambrose Crowley, Ironmonger, 1658-1713," *Explorations in Entrepreneurial History*, March 1953, p. 169, and R. L. Downes,

Britain's dependence on imported iron was regarded with alarm by many mercantilist writers, who proposed a series of remedies. Although early in the eighteenth century Abraham Darby of Colebrookdale had invented a process by means of which coke rather than charcoal could be used in the production of pig iron, this process spread slowly and did not gain general acceptance until the third quarter of the century. Even before that time the main remedy for the dependence on imported iron, and for the need to extend the production of domestic raw iron, consisted in the construction of new furnaces in relatively underdeveloped ore-rich areas where there was also an abundance of water and forests. The early movement of the iron industry to South Wales was motivated chiefly by the relative lack of industrialization in the region, supported by its favorable location and resource endowment.

Later, when the main problem of the iron industry was to have coal readily available, the abundance of rich coal seams in South Wales enhanced its value as an iron-producing region. Since further technological development emphasized even more the need for coal, the rise of the Welsh iron industry was assured. The abundance of coal in the Midlands had similar effects. It is not surprising that by 1823 South Wales and the Midlands together produced 374,000 tons of pig iron out of a total production in all of Great Britain of 455,000 tons.[29]

The great upsurge of British iron production began in the last quarter of the eighteenth century. In the nine years between 1788 and 1796 the total output of pig iron almost doubled (from 68,300 tons to 125,100 tons); in the succeeding decade it doubled again (to 252,800 tons); in the next nineteen years it almost doubled once more; and by 1839 it amounted to 1,248,800 tons, almost twenty times the output of fifty years earlier. This great increase in iron production was due to the rapid development of iron-producing facilities in South Wales and the Midlands, and only toward the end of this period did Scotland and Northeast England contribute significant portions of the total production.

Although the general trends of growth of productive facilities for the raw material were parallel in South Wales and the Midlands, they exhibited one significant difference: the production of raw iron

---

"The Stour Partnership, 1726-36: A Note on Landed Capital in the Iron Industry," *Economic History Review*, New Series, Vol. III (1950-1951), No. 1, p. 93.

[29] See Scrivenor, *op. cit.*, p. 135.

in the Midlands was largely an appendage of the already established fabricating plants. Productive facilities for the turning out of pig iron were established and owned by individuals or partnerships whose main interest lay in their control of iron-fabricating establishments. It was the engineering and hardware firms and the owners of foundries and wire, nail, and plate factories who acquired control over pig-iron-producing facilities. In South Wales, on the other hand, fabricating was much less important. Its convenient location permitted the easy transportation of the bulky raw product, and the relative scarcity of skilled labor made the establishment of fabricating plants unattractive. To be sure, there were quite a few forges and other plants there, but the major portion of investment in South Wales was in production of the raw iron.

If we may use an analogy from the present, South Wales—a region which, during this period at least, depended upon the exportation of one or two raw, or at best semifinished, products—may be regarded as a "one-crop economy," and because of the relative recency of its development, as compared with the older manufacturing centers of Britain, it exhibited some of the characteristics of a newly developed country. It depended upon the rest of Britain for a part of its manpower and for most of its capital and entrepreneurship. Although there was mobility also into the Midlands, Yorkshire, and elsewhere, the economic history of South Wales in the 100 years between 1750 and 1850 may be regarded as typical of the process of extending the internal frontier to new and relatively virgin territories within Great Britain.

Another factor, the magnitude of the initial investment required, makes the development of pig iron production in the period of the Industrial Revolution a good example of the forms of capital formation and entrepreneurial recruitment in Britain. The English iron industry was organized along capitalistic lines rather early, certainly beginning with the quite general adoption in the sixteenth century of Continental techniques of blast furnaces and water-powered machinery by English ironmasters. This was true of all stages of the production process prior to fabrication.[30] Even before the adoption of Cort's techniques, the production of raw iron required relatively large capital investments. The introduction of Cort's process was of great importance to the growth of the industry because it reduced costs markedly and permitted the substitution of coke-smelted iron

[30] T. S. Ashton, *Iron and Steel in the Industrial Revolution*, London, Longmans, 1924, p. 4.

for the charcoal product. But this new process required the erection of puddling furnaces and rolling mills and the use of more powerful and complex engines, which in turn required more reliable sources of power than could be afforded by waterwheels. Thus the most up-to-date production methods of bar iron in the late eighteenth century called for steam engines which found an ever-widening acceptance in the industry.[31]

In addition to the increase in capital requirements necessary for an efficient plant using the then most recent available technology, the cost of mineral leases rose considerably. Since South Wales had been a relatively unexploited region in the early eighteenth century, the price rises for leases over time were especially great there. But the rapid increase of iron production in other parts of Britain produced similar effects everywhere.[32]

Because the capital needs of the iron industry were relatively large, its growth shows perhaps better than that of any other industry the methods of capital accumulation and especially its concentrated mobilization for the economic development of a relatively underdeveloped area, such as South Wales. Some of the figures of the capital needs of the iron industry even in its very early stages show the magnitude of the capitalization required. The most important partnership of the Midlands iron industry in 1692, composed of five men, owned four active and one defunct furnace, six forges, three slitting mills, and a storehouse at Bedley. The total capital contributed to the partnership was £36,277. In 1700 another partnership, associated with it, operated two furnaces, three forges, and a plating mill. The partners were credited on the books of the company with a "stock" of £21,426.[33]

[31] Between 1775 and 1800 Boulton and Watt erected 325 steam engines, of which 37 were in foundries and forges. The engines in iron works were larger, on the average, than those in other types of production. While the average horsepower of all machines erected by Boulton and Watt in this period was slightly above 16.5, those in the iron industry had an average of 28 horsepower. Some of the largest among them had close to 50 horsepower. Cf. John Lord, *Capital and Steam Power*, London, P. S. King, 1923, pp. 172-175.

[32] For example, the annual rent of the lands on which the Plymouth furnace (in South Wales) was eventually to be established was £60 in 1765. In 1786 this rental had risen to £268 for a slightly larger piece of land. Similarly, the rent for the land at Ynyscedwyn on which a furnace and two forges had been established in 1723 amounted to £7 per annum. Thirty years later the leases were renewed at an annual rent of £30. Cf. John Lloyd, *The Early History of the Old South Wales Iron Works, 1760-1840*, London, Bedford Press, 1906, pp. 5-6 and 75.

[33] See B. L. C. Johnson, "The Foley Partnerships: The Iron Industry at the

But during the ensuing fifty years the costs of erecting and putting an iron works into operation with furnaces, smelters, and forges increased considerably. In 1812 Thomas Attwood testified that a complete iron works could not be constructed for less than £50,000. In 1789 the Bleanavon iron works were established in South Wales with three furnaces at an actual cost of £40,000, and the two furnaces which were erected in 1794 at the Nantyglo works (South Wales) cost £27,316.[34]

If we consider that the number of furnaces in South Wales increased from 14 in 1788 to 197 in 1852 and that the number in the Midlands in the same period rose from 33 to 220, we can gauge the magnitude of the capital accumulation process concentrated in this short period. Furnaces were not all. They had to be supplemented by forges, by slitting and rolling mills; and costly mineral rights and leases on land had to be acquired. To this should be added investment in transport facilities such as canals and roads, a portion of which was borne by the entrepreneurs in the iron industry.

These considerations raise two important questions. How was such a vast amount of capital mobilized and what people were entrusted, or found themselves, with its control? Mechanisms for the raising of large quantities of capital were, of course, not unknown in Britain at that time. The overdrafts allowed to the East India Co. by the Bank of England at the beginning of the eighteenth century amounted to £20,000; by the 1760's they had risen to £200,000 and even £300,000. Similarly, the South Sea Co. was allowed an overdraft of £150,000 in 1726, and even in the 1750's when its mercantile activities had declined to a shadow and the company had become a "mere handler of annuities" its drawing right with the Bank of England amounted to £50,000.[35] These credits were given, it should be noted, only to companies, and even among these only to the strongest and most powerful ones. At the time the East India Co. obtained the right of overdraft exceeding £200,000 it had gained political supremacy in India, and for all practical purposes performed the functions of political government as well as trade.

End of the Charcoal Era," *Economic History Review*, New Series, Vol. IV (1951-1952), No. 3, pp. 326 and 329.

[34] See Ashton, *op. cit.*, p. 163; Lloyd, *op. cit.*, p. 160; and A. H. John, *The Industrial Development of South Wales, 1750-1850*, Cardiff, University of Wales Press, 1950, p. 25.

[35] See J. H. Clapham, *The Bank of England: A History*, Cambridge, Eng., The University Press, 1945, Vol. I, pp. 117-121.

But apart from the experience of the great and powerful companies, the credit market for merchants was, on the whole, much better developed than that for fixed investment in industry. In part this was due to the fact that as long as most industrial investment was rather small, the actual demand of merchants for capital to finance their inventories was larger than the demand of small industrialists for fixed capital. This appears quite clearly in many sources originating in the eighteenth century. For example, in an anonymous little book which appeared in 1747 describing the various trades, the differences in the requirements of capital between a working jeweler and a trading jeweler is indicated in the following words: "To set up a Master, who only works for others, will want no more than £20, but a Dealer in Diamonds, etc. must have Cash in proportion to his stock."[36] This observation of our anonymous author appears to hold for the majority of industries of the time. Heaton explains the rarity of factories in the earlier stages of the Yorkshire woolen industry, in part, by the absence of large sums of capital available for industry, and by the fact that whatever capital was available in northern England usually would be invested in commerce.[37]

During this period a large part of English industry was still in a quasi-artisan stage. If we scan the list of occupations and the capital investment needed which the anonymous author of *A General Description of All Trades* gives, we find that in many industries between £50 and £200 is all that is required to set a person up in business. In some exceptional cases as much as £500 may be required. However, the writer of the booklet points out that "those who keep Forges or Foundries, deal in Bar-iron, and export and import much, employ thousands [of pounds]."[38]

[36] *A General Description of All Trades Digested in Alphabetical Order, Etc.*, London, T. Waller, 1747, pp. 122-123. Similar differences in capital requirements are also indicated for button-makers and button-sellers (p. 48), upholsterers who only fabricate and those who also engage in trade (p. 215), and many other trades. That the capital requirements of traders as compared with manufacturers were generally much larger is confirmed also by R. Campbell, *The London Tradesman*, London, T. Gardner, 1747, and by R. B. Westerfield, "Middlemen in English Business, 1660-1760," *Transactions of the Connecticut Academy of Arts and Sciences*, Vol. 19 (1915), pp. 111-445.

[37] Herbert Heaton, *The Yorkshire Woollen and Worsted Industries*, Oxford, Clarendon Press, 1920, p. 90.

[38] *A General Description . . .*, as cited, p. 126. Apart from persons engaged in trade, who usually are considered to need a minimum of £500 and more often £1,000 to set themselves up in business, the only industries with capital requirements of a magnitude comparable to that of the iron industry and other forms of the metal trades are brewing ("many Thousands"), distilling ("£500 at least"), printing ("from £1000 to £5000"), dyeing ("from £500 to

Thus only few manufactures at that time had passed from an artisan-type scale of organization to a factory scale. The iron industry and, closely following it, the manufacture of cotton textiles were paving the way for the advance of large-scale industrialism in Britain. In fact, the very extension of the internal economic frontier, coupled with the development of capital-intensive industries at the geographical margin (iron in Wales, Scotland, and North England; cotton in Lancashire and later in Scotland), seems to have facilitated the introduction of factory production. Here industrial production was so undeveloped that no local traditions, local guilds, and craft groups stood in the way of the factory. Here experimentation with large-scale production was easier than in the older industrial centers, where traditional industrial techniques were more firmly established.

The technological innovations in the iron and cotton industries also made necessary the introduction of factory methods in establishments located in the older industrial centers. While the transition from small-scale handicraft and the putting-out system to the factory system was slower in these older areas, the new form of industrial organization was gradually transmitted from the geographically marginal parts, where the Industrial Revolution took place more abruptly, to the older industrial areas around London, Birmingham, Sheffield, Bristol, Nottingham, Coventry, and elsewhere.

Simultaneously with the development of large-scale investment in the geographically marginal areas there occurred an innovation in the financing of industry. The partnership had been an early form of mobilizing large amounts of capital in the iron industry and of minimizing the risk of any one participator. Elaborate descriptions of the Stour partnership, the Foley partnerships, and the partnership operating iron works in the Furness district show that this form was applied early in the iron industry, primarily because of the vertical organization prevailing there. Although some of these early partnerships owned and operated more than one works, the typical arrangement of assets was the ownership of furnaces, smelters, forges, warehouses, and often various types of fabricating plants.[39] This

£2000"), shipbuilding ("generally a large Undertaking, for which Reason it is fittest for Money's men to engage in"), soap-boiling (£2,000), and one or two others (from *ibid.*, pp. 35, 80, 29, 83, 189, and 196, respectively). On capital required in industry see also J. H. Clapham, *An Economic History of Modern Britain*, Cambridge, Eng., The University Press, 1926, Vol. I, p. 68.

[39] See Johnson, *op. cit.*; Downes, *op. cit.*; A. Fell, *The Early Iron Industry of Furness and District*, Ulverston, H. Kitchin, 1908; Arthur Raistrick and E.

pattern of establishing partnerships was extended to South Wales. But since there was little opportunity for vertical organization of the industry, partnerships soon acquired several works located near one another, and some had holdings comprising works not merely in the South Wales area, but also in the Midlands, Yorkshire, and elsewhere. The development of this type of control is exhibited by the fact that in 1788 there were 14 works with 17 furnaces and with 25 persons in entrepreneurial positions in South Wales. In 1806 there were 24 works with 48 furnaces and with 47 persons in entrepreneurial roles, and in 1823, 19 works with 72 furnaces and with 35 entrepreneurs. After 1823, joint stock companies were organized in the iron industry and the old pattern of partnerships receded. By the middle of the nineteenth century the partnership in this industry was, on the whole, a thing of the past.

The development of partnerships and horizontal combination in the industry facilitated and indeed suggested the formation of joint stock companies, which up to 1825 had been absent from the iron industry and had prevailed chiefly in commercial, canal, and other transportation companies. Today a primary distinguishing feature of joint stock companies is the limited liability of their shareholders. But this was not always the case in Britain. In fact, the right of limited liability of registered stock companies was established universally only by an act of 1885. The main differences between the partnership and stock company were the greater number of partners in a stock company and the fact that the members of a partnership were usually more actively engaged in administering the business of their firm than were the members of a stock company. The stock company permitted the accumulation of larger amounts of capital and drew moneys into fixed industrial investment from persons who had neither the interest nor the inclination to engage actively in managerial roles, but who sought chiefly a profitable return on their capital.[40]

The industrial joint stock company in its pre-1885 form in Britain represented, therefore, an organization appropriate to a system in

---

Allen, "The South Yorkshire Ironmasters, 1690-1750," *Economic History Review*, May 1939, pp. 168-185; and, summarizing this trend, Ashton, *op. cit.*, pp. 48 ff. and Chap. VII, *passim*.

[40] A good short description of the nature of stock companies in the nineteenth century in Britain and the trends leading to the further development of a joint stock company structure is given by Geoffrey Todd, "Some Aspects of Joint Stock Companies, 1844-1900," *Economic History Review*, October 1932, pp. 46-71.

which risk-taking as a social function had become institutionalized. The earlier partnerships, made up entirely of private individuals and financed by the capital of these same individuals, were the first institutions in this process which necessitated the concentration of relatively large amounts of capital.

The mobilization of large quantities of capital in the form of fixed assets in industry differs profoundly from an accumulation of capital of similar magnitude in trade or finance. In the latter much of the capital is invested in assets with a relatively quick turnover, and although the total risk may be high, the degree of liquidity is also relatively high. Moreover, the economic horizon of persons investing in commerce or finance usually is narrower than that of persons who sink large sums into the construction of such relatively durable assets as furnaces, forges, puddling and rolling mills, and mines. The large-scale industrial entrepreneur and later the industrial stock company committed themselves more fully to an uncertainty-bearing function than did the investor in a commercial partnership or company.

It is no wonder, therefore, that the great entrepreneurs of the Welsh iron industry of the late eighteenth century—the period when rapid development on a vast scale occurred in that part of Britain—were individuals who possessed most clearly the characteristics of the risk-taking, innovating entrepreneur of the textbooks. Although as prudent men they avoided overly great gambles—a factor which accounts, for example, for their preference for lease rights to coal- and ore-bearing land as against outright purchase of the land—they were obviously taking immense risks, and they understood, and apparently were fully conscious of, this role. The absence of local financial institutions which could have supplied the necessary loan funds for industrial development and the apparent unwillingness of metropolitan bankers to venture their funds in the risky iron enterprises in South Wales enhanced the sentiment of self-reliance and individualism of these pioneers. How else can we interpret the statement of one of the most successful South Wales ironmasters, Richard Crawshay, the "Iron King," when he said, "I shall not take any partners as long as I live."[41] Samuel Homfray, another pioneer in the South Wales iron industry, apparently was a gambler on occasion; after having helped finance the locomotive of the Cornish engineer and investor Trevithick, he bet Crawshay £1,000 that it

[41] John, *op. cit.*, p. 57. Similar statements of individualist confidence and optimism are cited there.

could convey a load of iron by steam power from the Pennydarren iron works to the Glamorganshire Canal, nine miles away. He won the bet.[42] The career of Samuel Homfray's brother, who was knighted in 1810, bankrupt in 1813, and a coal magnate prior to his death, bespeaks no risk shyness.[43] But not only were these entrepreneurs willing to take financial risks; they constantly adopted technical innovations and were prepared to reinvest profits. Scrivenor wrote of the extension of the South Wales industry in the first half of the nineteenth century that the speculative mania and extravagant establishment and extension of plant, notably by the joint stock companies, would bring about the ruin of the industry.[44]

The most successful and at the same time the most typical of all these men was Anthony Bacon, who began as a coal merchant in Whitehaven, emigrated to Maryland, returned to London to become a merchant, contracted with the government to supply British garrisons in Africa, entered Parliament when American affairs were under discussion, furnished African Negroes to the government in the West Indies, acquired a small fleet of ships, and started coal-mining in South Wales. The outbreak of the American Revolution gave him an opportunity to supply cannon to the British army, which in turn spurred on his efforts to establish himself more firmly in the iron industry. His business interests included grants of coal mines in Cape Breton, estates and fisheries in the colonies, and a series of partnerships and other connections with politically influential people, which made it possible for him to obtain repeated orders from the government for supplies of food, war material, coal, and other things. Bacon was a captain of industry *par excellence*. He, more than anyone, must be credited with having opened the Rhondda Valley to economic exploitation.[45]

Men like Bacon, Crawshay, and the Homfrays set the pace. They formed the backbone of the industrial partnerships which developed the iron industry in an outlying, relatively undeveloped region. They were the people who were willing to take great risks, but whose expectations of profit were self-confirming in an age in which the

[42] See Lloyd, *op. cit.*, p. 88, and C. Wilkens, *The History of the Iron, Steel, Tinplate, and Other Trades of Wales*, Merthyr Tydfil, J. Williams, 1903.

[43] See John, *op. cit.*, p. 34.

[44] Scrivenor, *op. cit.*, pp. 280-283.

[45] See the stimulating sketch of Bacon's life by L. B. Namier, "Anthony Bacon, M.P., an Eighteenth-Century Merchant," *Journal of Economic and Business History*, November 1929, pp. 20-70.

entire economy experienced rapid growth. There were setbacks and occasional bankruptcies; but, on the whole, the expectations of large profits materialized, and this encouraged others—lawyers, merchants, and even clergymen—to entrust their funds to these industrial pioneers. The supply of capital funds became so great after the first important successes in the Welsh iron industry that the result was the development of the joint stock companies and lavish extension of plant, which, as we have seen, was regarded with some misgivings by Scrivenor.

The most adequate characterization of the shifts in the type of entrepreneurship developed in this industry can be gauged by a comparison of the occupational backgrounds and geographical origins of Welsh ironmasters at different periods of time. As long as the industry was small, local people—landlords and artisans—predominated. When the merchants from the old commercial centers became attracted to the industry it started its period of phenomenal growth. Of seven persons who were known to have held entrepreneurial positions in the Welsh iron industry in 1723, four were landowners, one a merchant, and two ironmasters. Of the twenty-five persons in entrepreneurial positions in 1788, nine were merchants, thirteen ironmasters, two entrepreneurs in other industries, and one a manager in iron works. Not one was a landlord. The occupational characteristics of 1788 remained fairly stable throughout the rest of the eighteenth and the first half of the nineteenth century. Half of the entrepreneurs had started as merchants, and the other half as engineers, small masters, or managers in the iron industry or related industries (such as copper, brass, tin plate manufacture, or engineering).

As to their geographical origin, five of the seven entrepreneurs in South Wales iron works in 1723 were natives of South Wales, one came from London, and one from the Midlands. Of the thirty-five entrepreneurs in the South Wales iron industry in 1796, ten were natives of South Wales, four came from Bristol, six from London, ten from the Midlands, and five from elsewhere. If we combine the two classifications we find that most of the local entrepreneurs in the early period were landlords, but that by the end of the eighteenth century most of the South Wales natives were ironmasters. Of the persons coming from outside the area, most of the immigrants from London and Bristol were merchants, and so were a few from the Midlands. But the bulk of the persons originating in the Midlands were ironmasters who transferred their field of activity to the newly developing region.[46]

This provides a fairly clear clue to the origin of the capital which flowed into the industry. The land was supplied by local landlords, who also contributed capital for the construction of canals and other means of transportation to make the region more accessible. Since little fabricating was carried on in South Wales, and since it developed into one of the major exporting areas of coal and of bar iron, facilities for out-shipment were of the utmost importance. Most of the capital for investment in furnaces, forges, and other plant equipment was supplied by merchants (many of them iron or coal merchants, but some cloth merchants and others) from London and Bristol. Of special importance were some Bristol Quakers whose business connections reached not only into the South Wales iron industry, but also into the Midlands and North Wales iron industry. The famous Darby family which set up the works at Coalbrookdale originated in Bristol, and many other well-known Midlands Quakers in the iron trade had close connections with their coreligionists among the Bristol merchants.[47] As the eighteenth century drew to an end, the Bristol merchants began to be eclipsed by London merchants who eventually came to dominate the industry financially. Technical and engineering talent was supplied chiefly from the Midlands, but after the industry had been domiciled for some time in South Wales, native engineers and ironmasters tended to reach entrepreneurial positions in it.

What general conclusions can be drawn from this account of the development of the iron industry in a region which early in the eighteenth century was "underdeveloped" and which in the course of some 120 years became one of the most highly capitalized manufacturing regions of Britain? Most of the capital—apart from land—which was needed to develop the industrial complex had to be supplied from the outside, and by the nature of the factory type of enterprise, large individual chunks of capital were needed. These could only come from the government, the aristocracy, or already wealthy merchants. It was the latter who provided the bulk of the needed

[46] These data, as well as other information contained in this essay on entrepreneurship in the South Wales iron industry, are drawn from an as yet unpublished paper, "The Geographical and Occupational Origin of South Wales Ironmasters, 1717-1839," which is being prepared by Marshall Kolin.

[47] See two works by Arthur Raistrick: *Dynasty of Iron Founders: The Darbys and Coalbrookdale*, London, Longmans, 1953, pp. vii-viii and 83-85, and *Quakers in Science and Industry*, London, Bannisdale Press, 1950, *passim.*

funds, in a surge of innovating and enterprising spirit whose origins are somewhat of a mystery. Once the early ventures proved successful, the flood of capital offered for investment increased, and at times even led to perhaps untimely expansion of the industry. But, on the whole, the steadily increasing demand for iron and steel products created by the railway age confirmed the expectations of the profitability of such investment and produced recurring waves of new capital.

Most of the early entrepreneurial talent also came from outside the region. The merchants stepped into financial, organizational, and managerial positions, and the ironmasters who had gained their early experience elsewhere filled the leading technical and supervisory posts. Although many of these men started from fairly small beginnings, few actually rose from the very bottom of the social scale. Most of the Welsh ironmasters came from merchant families or were sons of small manufacturers; only a few had yeoman or peasant parents, and hardly any came from working class families. Nevertheless, the recruitment of entrepreneurial talent for the industry suggests the persistence of a degree of geographical and social mobility of a substantially higher order than was the case in France at that time and even later.

This picture of the development of entrepreneurship and formation of capital in the South Wales iron industry resembles analogous contemporary processes elsewhere in the industrially undeveloped parts of Britain. The growth of the Scotch iron industry, which did not start on a significant scale until after the middle of the eighteenth century, followed similar lines, and a superficial survey of the evolution of cotton-spinning and -weaving in Lancashire and elsewhere in North Britain appears to show similar characteristics.

In the other industrial centers economic development showed some contrast to this pattern notably with respect to the source of capital and the rapidity of factory development. In 1926 Sir John Clapham wrote of London that "to this day [it] is the home of small businesses," and of Birmingham it was said in 1799 that, comparing its manufactures with those of Leeds and Manchester, "there are very few that may be called large capitals. There are many manufactories in Birmingham which do not employ £100; some about £1,000, and, speaking in general of the higher descriptions of manufactures, about 6 or £7,000."[48] Similar observations can be made about other older

[48] Clapham, *An Economic History of Modern Britain*, as cited, Vol. I, p. 68; and *Reports from Committees of the House of Commons*, London, 1803, Vol. x, Miscellaneous Subjects: 1785-1801, p. 663.

centers of industrial production, such as Sheffield, Bristol, Coventry, and Norwich. In these places a substantial portion of industry developed more or less gradually out of the earlier artisan-type organizations. The capital needs for enterprises on such a relatively small scale could often be met out of the earnings of the masters themselves. This facilitated upward movement in the social scale, and since the rigid social structure characteristic of medieval society had broken down in Britain long before the Reformation, a large amount of vertical social movement actually occurred. Hence, in the early stages of British industrial development many factory masters started as artisans or workmen and in the course of their lives changed from that status to one of industrialists or masters. For example, William Hutton says of Birmingham that in 1793 there were 94 persons in that town who possessed more than £5,000, 80 who had £10,000, 17 with £20,000, 8 with £30,000, 7 with £50,000 and 3 with upwards of £100,000. He adds that out of these 209, "103 began the world with nothing but their own prudence; 35 more had fortunes added to their prudence, but too small to be brought into account; and 71 persons were favoured with a larger, which, in many instances, is much improved."[49] Similarly, Boulton said that "all the great manufacturers that I have ever known have begun the world with very little capitals."[50]

The life histories of most of these entrepreneurs are, of course, very difficult to reconstruct in sufficient detail to account for the degree of vertical mobility that existed. The South Wales ironmasters, whose early origins I have tried to ascertain, started from somewhat more affluent circumstances than was often believed or granted. That myth sometimes intervenes to make a dramatic story even more dramatic is evidenced by the way some of the most distinguished historians treat the career of some spectacular figure who has risen decisively in the social scale. The career of Ambrose Crowley may serve as an illustration. Lipson writes of Crowley that he "began his career as a working blacksmith and ended it as a knight, an alderman and sheriff of London, and a member of Parliament."[51] The implication of this statement is clear. We are presented

[49] *History of Birmingham*, 4th ed., 1809, pp. 136-137, cited in Henry Hamilton, *The English Brass and Copper Industries to 1800*, London, Longmans, 1926, p. 271.

[50] Cited in Hamilton, *op. cit.*, p. 271, note. Hamilton lists still other opinions in the same vein and some further evidence on both the smallness of many of the Birmingham enterprises around 1800 and the fact that their owners had risen from lowly status and accumulated all or most of the capital by their own thrift.

[51] Lipson, *op. cit.*, Vol. II, p. 176.

with a man who started as a simple small artisan and became one of the greatest merchants and ironmasters of his day. But Michael W. Flinn, who has more recently studied the career of Crowley, contradicts Lipson's statement about Crowley's origins. In fact, he explicitly says that Crowley's "origins were by no means as obscure as has been suggested; he did not began his working life as a common smith. He was born . . . the son of a prosperous ironmonger of the same name."[52] We would find, I trust, many other life histories which have been somewhat overdrawn in a similar manner, and I believe it would not be too far wrong to regard the statements of Hutton and Boulton as somewhat exaggerated. They were expressing as fact what in their day was widely believed. Even if these accounts of the lowly beginnings of many men who became captains of industry are perhaps not fully accurate in all details, they nevertheless provide evidence that the rise of men from poverty to great riches was considered quite possible and indeed a not infrequent occurrence, and that vertical social mobility was common and accepted without question.

Vertical mobility in the recruitment of entrepreneurs seems to have been a characteristic of British industry which never fully died out and which to this day has been an essential force in providing industry with vigorous new blood. In an investigation undertaken shortly before the outbreak of World War I on the social origins of directors and managers in the cotton industry, Chapman found that a large percentage of entrepreneurial and managerial personnel both in manufacturing and spinning establishments rose from the position of operative or clerk. In about 1911 he sent out 248 questionnaires asking for the occupational origin of entrepreneurial personnel in the cotton-manufacturing, cotton-spinning, and doubling industry. He received 179 replies. Among those replying, 141, or 79 per cent, indicated that they had risen from low positions to those of manager, owner, or member of the board of directors. This study exhibits such an astounding degree of vertical mobility that its findings must be accepted with great caution.[53]

Chapman's study is more important for its ideology than for its facts. This same belief in the necessity of an open social order is revealed in a recent account of British entrepreneurship by

[52] Flinn, *op. cit.*, p. 163.

[53] See S. J. Chapman and F. J. Marquis, "The Recruitment of the Employing Classes from the Ranks of the Wage-Earners in the Cotton Industry," *Journal of the Royal Statistical Society*, February 1912, pp. 293-313.

Richard Fry, financial editor of the *Manchester Guardian.* Fry may certainly be regarded as a witness who expresses the predominant sentiment of British entrepreneurs about their own social role, their function, and the ladder of ascent leading to positions occupied by business leaders. Although he did not make a statistical study, as Chapman did, providing us instead with impressionistic glimpses of the social milieu of modern British entrepreneurs, he appears to be a strong adherent of the rags-to-riches story. He begins his account by picking out four "typical" successes of the interwar period. These four are Lord Nuffield, who before World War I "had a bicycle shop in Oxford"; Bernard Westfall, "a parson's son" who studied at Cambridge on a scholarship and "in 1922 went as a factory clerk" to a printing firm; William Butlin, who at fifteen went to Canada as a drummer boy and when he was twenty-one "worked his way across, arriving with £5 in his pocket"; and Jack Billmeir, who "started work at 14 (in 1914) in a shipbroker's office at 8 s. a week." Elsewhere in his article he mentions other "typical" cases, such as that of Arthur John White, whose life story also falls in the rags-to-riches class.[54]

I do not imply that Fry's facts are wrong. I wish to stress, however, that since the stories he relates are regarded by him as "typical," it appears that there is widespread unquestioning acceptance of the tradition that many of the most successful entrepreneurs were bootblacks, newsboys, or close to that status at some time early in their careers and that they rose from the very bottom of the social scale to the very top. I am not aware that a careful study of the social and occupational origins of British entrepreneurs has ever been undertaken. Chapman's essay, although conceived in the true scientific spirit, is too limited in scope and is methodologically too defective to count. Haxey's book[55] provides some interesting source material of a gossipy kind, but cannot be regarded as a serious study of the social characteristics of British entrepreneurs as a class. In any case, from the works of Taussig and Joslyn, William Miller,[56] and others on the characteristics of the American business elite, we have reason

[54] See Richard Fry, "The British Business Man: 1900-1949," *Explorations in Entrepreneurial History*, November 1949, pp. 35-43.

[55] See Simon Haxey, *Tory M.P.*, London, Gollancz, 1939.

[56] F. W. Taussig and C. S. Joslyn, *American Business Leaders: A Study in Social Origins and Social Stratification*, Macmillan, 1932, and William Miller, "American Historians and the Business Elite," *Journal of Economic History*, November 1949, pp. 184-208.

to doubt that the instances that Fry reports are "typical" of British entrepreneurs as a whole.

Nevertheless, as long as enterprises were small, mobility upward from the position of operative or journeyman to that of master or even owner-entrepreneur meant mobility for a relatively short distance, and was encountered probably not infrequently. This degree of mobility was sufficient to create the belief in the power and in the possibilities of ascent; its importance was overstressed and its prevalence exaggerated. It became and remains an important myth of British entrepreneurial circles. A piece of social reality from the days when industrial enterprises were scarcely larger than handicraft shops has lived on to become perhaps the most powerful buttress of independent entrepreneurship in contemporary Britain.[57]

5. *Recent Changes in Entrepreneurship in Britain*

Bank credit played an increasingly important role in Britain as the nineteenth century wore on, but it was chiefly used for working capital. Most of the fixed capital in British industry was supplied out of savings of private individuals and reinvested profits and earnings of going enterprises. Perhaps the best summary of this situation is provided by Sir John Clapham, who writes that the London money market "was important mainly as a furnisher and economiser of circulating capital. . . . It was of more immediate importance to the merchant than to the manufacturer, because the circulating element dominates commerce. . . . The provincial banker gave every assistance to men he trusted, allowing them ample overdrafts at all times; but even he regarded plant, machinery 'or works of any description' as ideally bad security for loans. Almost all the fixed capital of manufacturing industry, as it existed in 1850, and the overwhelmingly greater part of the additions and renewals made during the next thirty-six years, came from what the economists of the age called—with more reason than their critics have sometimes allowed—the abstinence of those steady manufacturers whom the provincial bankers trusted."[58]

Here was a characteristic mode of supplying industry with capital

[57] A book-length study on the role of the rags-to-riches story in the United States, which shows how important was and is the belief in the possibilities of social mobility upward over often large distances, will, I hope, soon be published by my colleague and friend R. Richard Wohl. Its tentative title is *Onward and Upward: American Ideologies of Success.*

[58] Clapham, *An Economic History of Modern Britain,* as cited, Vol. II, pp. 355-356.

for its fixed assets which differed profoundly from the pattern which developed in France and other parts of the Continent.

These methods of supplying industrial fixed capital contributed in Britain to the prevalence, even today, of small and medium-sized plants in many industries which in the United States, and even Germany, are normally considered to require large corporate organization. In part this explains why in many branches of engineering, food-processing, construction, and other fields, British industry is less productive than German or American industry. In part it also appears to confirm Schumpeter's thesis that most conspicuous economic progress is made not in those industries in which competition by many small firms prevails, but in those in which large concerns abound. If the problem is looked at from Schumpeter's viewpoint that economic progress is served by what he calls "creative destruction" of capital, it is easy to see that in a small enterprise, in which the horizon of the owner is circumscribed by considerations of his nearest of kin, destruction of capital, even if it be creative destruction, will be engaged in at best hesitatingly and gingerly.[59] The very smallness of enterprise militates against grand and widespread introduction of innovations in either technology or industrial organization.

Moreover, the very fact that Britain became an industrial country earlier than her main competitors now imposes a serious disadvantage on her. Her capital equipment is older and more obsolete as is her form of industrial organization. Gerschenkron has reminded us that for long France and Germany bore the burden of backwardness. We can turn his observation around and find that Britain is weighed down by the burden of too early industrialization.[60] This situation

[59] Joseph A. Schumpeter, *Capitalism, Socialism, and Democracy*, Harper, 1942, Chap. VII.

[60] See Gerschenkron, *op. cit.*, pp. 4-7. Thorstein Veblen saw and evaluated clearly the "penalty" which England had to pay for "having been thrown into the lead and so having shown the way." The entire fourth chapter of his *Imperial Germany and the Industrial Revolution* (new ed., Viking, 1939) is devoted to this issue. Veblen stresses especially the fact that the earlier creation of real capital in Britain burdened her with a technology which tended to become outdated, but which was difficult to change, since this would require a complete replacement of large chunks of technologically inefficient plant by new plant. (E.g. the narrow-gauge railroads of Britain would have to be replaced by broader-gauge railroads. This would require not merely the creation of new, admittedly more efficient freight cars, but also the rebuilding of stations and shunting and switching yards—in fact, of almost the entire existing plant. This is clearly impossible.) Veblen also draws attention to the fact that "the system which the English . . . worked out into its farther consequences was the system of handicraft and petty trade, and the frame of mind native or normal

was not counteracted to any large extent by flexible adjustment to newly arising demand patterns or to the competition of the newer industrial nations. In design and general execution British products remained, on the whole, conservative, though qualitatively superior. As other countries became more and more formidable competitors in industrial products, British entrepreneurs tried to take primarily defensive measures. Control of the international financial markets, gentlemen's agreements forming quasi cartels, the buttressing of the bonds of Empire, and, finally, protective tariffs and exchange control were the chief measures taken to provide some degree of security and stability for British industry. These measures are symptomatic of the loss of much of the earlier spirit of ebullient venturesomeness and creative entrepreneurship.

But this change of heart was not confined to the small industrial entrepreneur, whose base of operations remained strictly limited in a world in which he had to compete with giant firms controlling vast arrays of sales forces, modern research laboratories, and the most up-to-date technological and organizational equipment. The spirit of prudence, caution, and conservatism was catching. Combined with Britain's political decline and the loss of many of her foreign markets to younger and more vigorous competitors, it affected all layers of British entrepreneurship. Although a portion of British industry remained relatively small, it was only a portion, and, as was shown earlier in this essay, the most spectacular advances in technology and most decisive victories in creative entrepreneurship had been won in the fields in which large-scale enterprises developed. In these fields, however, the general adoption of the joint stock company form contributed to the decline of venturesomeness.

The joint stock company became the vehicle for large-scale industrial organization soon after 1825. It experienced rapid extension in the succeeding twenty-five years, chiefly because of its use in the financing of railways. In the early stages of railway-building and of factory industry, only minute amounts of capital were supplied by banks. Just as in the earlier case of canal-building, a considerable portion of the capital needed for the construction of early railways was raised in the various localities which were connected by them. Tooke waxes quite indignant when he discusses this terrible "passion

to this industrial system is that which stands for self-help and an equal chance" (*ibid.*, pp. 99-100). This is a highly abbreviated statement of a point which is discussed at considerably greater length in the text.

for Railway Gambling [which] had penetrated the upper and middle classes. . . . In every street of every town persons were to be found who were holders of Railway Shares."[61] Now it is true that many people borrowed from the banks in order to raise capital for the purchase of railroad shares, a practice which in Tooke's view had such nefarious aspects. But the important thing is that banking capital for railway construction became available only indirectly; that is, not the banks, but private individuals, undertook to gamble. Here is another instance which shows how the early nineteenth century stock company represented a means by which the by now institutionalized roles of risk-taking could be exercised.

Joint stock company ownership made possible consolidation of railroads, and, with the general applicability of limited liability for all registered stock companies, these large organizations became by the turn of the century administrators of funds which were supplied to them by persons filled not with the "passion for Railway Gambling" or, for that matter, any other kind of gambling, but progressively more with a *rentier* outlook.[62] Thus by the beginning of the twentieth century, the evolution of entrepreneurship in Britain had come full circle. From small beginnings the British middle classes rose to become one of the chief factors contributing to making Britain the leading industrial nation in the world for some 200 years and at the same time the most important political power in Europe. With the decline of Britain's economic and political leadership came the decline in the enterprising spirit of her business leaders. The traditions of individualism and radicalism in the British middle classes were not strong enough to overcome the forces which, in the new

[61] Thomas Tooke and Henry Newmarch, *A History of Prices*, London, Longman, Orme, Brown, Green & Longmans, 1857, Vol. v, p. 234. On the financing of the earlier British railways see Leland H. Jenks, *The Migration of British Capital to 1875*, Knopf, 1927, pp. 130 ff.

[62] Unfortunately, there is little evidence available in printed sources on the prevalence of this attitude in present-day Britain. Most of the liberal economists who opposed the "socialism" of the Labor government were chiefly concerned with the evils of planning and did not discuss the shortcomings of entrepreneurs, or, if they did, they attributed the loss of entrepreneurial spirit to the increased vexations placed upon businessmen by the various forms of government regulation and interference. One factor strengthening the *rentier* outlook of British entrepreneurs, and of the British public in general, has been mentioned by Jenks. He suggests that the growth of British foreign investment in the third quarter of the nineteenth century had two concomitant effects. First, the paramount place in the investment market was secured by banks, and, second, this "fostered the growth of a rentier governing class, whose economic interests lay outside the community in which they lived and exerted influence." *Op. cit.*, p. 334.

environment, tended to exert a paralyzing influence on the old spirit of speculativeness and venturesomeness. The small man found safety in withdrawing into a hard shell of a narrow market, using time-tested procedures and technologies and serving a range of known and faithful customers. The large firms appeared to conform to that law of capitalistic development which Sombart stated when he said that in the age of corporate enterprise "even a rationalization of entrepreneurship has taken place, so to speak. We can pursue this change in detail. We see how the importance of specific entrepreneurial activity, or intuition, of a 'sixth sense' diminishes. The number of knowable, predictable circumstances increases and the inclination of business leaders grows to base their enterprises on a foundation of knowledge. *Enterprises thus attain the character of administrations, their leaders the character of bureaucrats,* and the gigantic size of the apparatus contributes to this development."[63] Sombart might have added that the people holding the stock of these enterprises progressively acquire the character of *rentiers.*

6. *Summary*

In this paper an attempt has been made to provide a partial explanation of the differences in the timing and rate of growth of the French and British economies since the coming to power of a capitalist social order in the two countries. The chief variables which were selected for study were the forms of entrepreneurship and the source and magnitude of capital supplied for fixed investment in secondary production. While the two variables are correlated with one another, they may be discussed separately. Industrial entrepreneurs may come from families which already hold positions of economic power, or they may originate in the lower social strata and succeed in moving upward to positions of business leadership. Capital may be supplied by the state, by persons holding accumulated wealth, or by the rising entrepreneurs who may come into possession of some small initial sum through luck, accident, or hard work, but who continue to increase the capital at their disposal through abstinence and "inner-worldly asceticism."

In France the chief characteristic of industrial growth under the *ancien régime* was the predominance of government as initiator of a large portion of industrial expansion and as supplier of capital for industry. Industrial entrepreneurs, as such, played a secondary role.

[63] Italics added. Sombart, *op. cit.*, pp. 8-9.

Their prestige and political power were subordinated to those of officials and large financiers, a pattern which remained characteristic of later French economic development. Reinvestment of profits, although not uncommon, never took on great significance because businesses were run on a family basis and the status and consumption needs of the family members competed with the needs of the business for new capital. Moreover, since industry developed under an umbrella of state regulation and protection, many industrial entrepreneurs tended to be overly cautious when the economy had grown to be too large for the state to take all industry under its tutelage. Hence, expansion was often kept back, new investment delayed, and a policy of risk-taking avoided. A recent indication of this attitude toward investment is provided in a book by Jacques Lacour-Gayet which appeared in the spring of 1953. Although it is devoted chiefly to a restatement of the principles of classical nineteenth century liberalism, Lacour-Gayet discusses in one chapter what French industry must do to become as successful as American industry. His main emphasis is on the expansion of sales and on technical and organizational improvement of the distributive apparatus. Only very scanty attention is given to the cheapening of production and the general improvement of company management.[64] The efficiency of the American self-service supermarket could not be overlooked, but the less obvious complements of American industrial success remained closed to this Frenchman, in spite of his penetrating mind and his attempt to see the American picture as a whole. Similarly, the accounts published of that French "maverick" entrepreneur Marcel Boussac stress his emphasis on expansion of sales. But at the same time they relate that the organization of his cotton "empire" is as centralized as that of any other French firm, his heirs apparent in the business are his son-in-law and his brother, he makes all important decisions himself, and the magnitude and structure of the managerial staff of his enterprises are quite unlike those of any American counterpart.[65]

The point I wish to stress is not that an aggressive sales policy is unimportant, but that it is a *result* rather than a *cause* of development. Sales are necessary because mass production of cheap articles has been made possible through investment. The force pushing an economy forward is not the attempt to expand sales; it is the willing-

[64] See *Nouveaux propos d'un liberal*, Paris, S.P.I.D., 1953, esp. pp. 95 ff.

[65] See John McDonald, "Marcel Boussac: Tycoon," *Fortune*, September 1952, pp. 107-109 and 198-206.

ness to risk the investment of fixed capital with the expectation, perhaps even the gamble, of conquering a market. What Lacour-Gayet preaches and what Boussac practices is an imitation not of American methods and practice, but of the methods and practice of the merchant adventurers of 400 years ago.

The crucial difference between French and British entrepreneurship is the attitude toward investment of risk-bearing fixed capital. In France the bulk of this capital was supplied first by the state and later by the investment banks. The state could and did minimize the risks by concentrating on the subsidization of those industries whose products enjoyed a well-defined effective demand, and by recouping losses from general tax revenue. The investment bank minimized risk either by spreading its investments over different industrial branches, so that losses in one would be counterbalanced by gains in another, or, if it chose to concentrate its investments in one industry alone—as tended to be the case in pre-World War I Germany—by attempting to acquire a monopoly position and to minimize risks by the monopolistic exploitation of consumers.

It is not surprising that the theory of "finance capitalism" which seemed to fit conditions of post-1871 Germany and France so well had only a very uneasy applicability to Britain and the United States. In fact, one of the criticisms leveled against Hilferding's book on the subject[66] is that he draws his examples exclusively from Continental experience and omits almost completely any reference to the "classical country of capitalism," Great Britain.

The reason for this inapplicability of an important portion of Hilferding's thesis to British conditions lies in the different nature of entrepreneurship and capital mobilization in that country. In Britain capital was supplied by individual merchants, industrialists, and, after the generalization of the joint stock company, the public at large. Investment in risk-bearing industrial fixed capital became a socially accepted function which could be exercised by anyone who had liquid funds or access to them through borrowing. In the classical period of British industrial development, from about 1775 to that triumphant symbol of British preeminence, the Great Exhibition of 1851, this was the characteristic pattern of industrial investment. That the joint stock company later came to push the individual industrial entrepreneur and even the partnership into the

[66] Rudolf Hilferding, *Das Finanzkapital*, Wien, Wiener Volksbuchhandlung, 1923, esp. Chaps. IV and V.

background is not surprising, for it could muster amounts of such magnitude as fully to overwhelm the small men.

But the patterns of social action developed in the Industrial Revolution in Great Britain had two important, lasting consequences. The social order was shaken up and movement upward became not only possible, but even a matter of quite common occurrence. This possibility of rising in the social scale became surrounded with an almost legendary aura; the belief in its importance has contributed in no small measure to the existence of greater economic opportunities in Britain for the common man even today. Second, the impetus imparted to British entrepreneurship in its most vigorous period resulted in a rapid advance of national output and productivity, so that at the present Britishers, in spite of setbacks and a gradual stagnation of the rate of economic progress, have a higher average real income than Frenchmen or other peoples on the European continent. However high or low one may estimate social equality and a more elevated level of material living standards, the "heroic" period of British economic development made these things possible. In the last analysis they belong to the characteristics which form the distinguishing marks of a nation.

THE ENTREPRENEUR IN AMERICAN CAPITAL FORMATION

THOMAS C. COCHRAN

UNIVERSITY OF PENNSYLVANIA

ON THE BASIS of present historical materials, it is impossible to treat statistically the historical effect of entrepreneurs on capital formation in the United States. The most that the historian can do is to indicate some of the general outlines of entrepreneurial development, call attention to additional material that might be investigated more carefully, and suggest some relevant factors that have not in the past been much considered by theoretical economists.

Problems regarding the entrepreneur in capital formation do not differ greatly from those in general economic growth. This statement rests upon a definition of the entrepreneur as one who makes the sequence of decisions necessary for organizing and carrying on the supply of goods or services for profit. Such a definition may include members of boards of directors, salaried managers, and nonemploying business proprietors. It conceives of entrepreneurs as a broad social group employed in administering business, most of whose basic decisions are concerned with the allocation and use of capital. As generally defined in terms of increasing national product or real per capita income, economic growth also depends largely upon allocation and use of capital.

Kuznets has suggested six major questions around which the historico-statistical record of economic growth can be analyzed.[1] Four of his categories are concerned with (1) the precise composition of the industrial process, (2) the adjustment of the labor force, (3) the obtaining of requisite material and technological means, and (4) the disposition of the industrial products. The present discussion will be focused on the areas indicated in his two remaining questions: (5) "How was the expansion financed?—with particular reference to the sources of savings that financed accumulation of capital and the mechanisms that were evolved both to mobilize savings and to direct them into proper investment channels"; and

The author is indebted for suggestions and criticisms to Arthur H. Cole, Leland H. Jenks, and others at the Research Center for Entrepreneurial History at Harvard; Moses Abramovitz; Simon Kuznets; and Harold F. Williamson.

[1] *Problems in the Study of Economic Growth*, National Bureau of Economic Research, Special Conference Series, No. 1, mimeographed, 1949, p. 12.

(6) "Who were the active agents of industrialization—the carriers of technological change and the spearheads in the institutional and economic breaks that were the indispensable prerequisite and accompaniment of the industrial process—and what was their role in the conflicts that the impact of industrialization created within the economy?"

As Kuznets goes on to say, "Clearly each of the broad questions comprises a host of others." Leland Jenks holds that a general theory of society—specifically, some sort of sociology of change—is necessary to account for economic development. The role of the entrepreneur in capital formation and other activities is shaped by a combination of factors involving personality types, cultural attitudes, technological knowledge, and available physical resources. Merely to list these factors calls attention to the intangible character of all but one of them. The personality-culture complex may someday be segmented into measurable factors, but that achievement still appears to be far in the future. It may be easier, in fact, to find some measures or uniform aspects of the entrepreneurial role as a whole. But so far no indexes have met with any wide acceptance.

Turning to the supply side of the relationship, the amount of new capital available from either domestic or foreign sources may vary greatly in relation to national income. This subject has, of course, been pursued recently by many able scholars, and the model proposed here will no doubt seem oversimple. To try to distinguish the element of entrepreneurship or enterprise, however, it may be permissible to divide the factors that produce commercially usable credit into those dependent on the general culture and those directly responsive to entrepreneurial activity. Such a division must be seen simply as a heuristic device, since entrepreneurship itself is part of the general culture and habits of saving are no doubt altered by the returns on investment. But from the standpoint of this artificial division we may say that Americans had certain propensities to save, not directly the product of contemporary entrepreneurial activity, and that the creative role of the entrepreneur in capital formation was to mobilize existing savings, supply incentives for a higher rate of saving, utilize credit mechanisms that could lead to forced saving, and achieve productivity from the use of capital that would add to the national income and particularly to the supply of business savings. There are at least two types of entrepreneurial functions involved in the performance of this highly generalized role: those of the entrepreneur who acquires, allocates, and manages capital for actual production; and those of the financial agent who develops ways of raising capital for the use of others.

If history is to make its maximum contribution to any current problem it is usually necessary to go back to proximate origins and see existing institutions in earlier and simpler forms. The historian sees the activities of the big business manager of the twentieth century emerging from those of the industrial entrepreneur of the nineteenth, and these in turn against the background of earlier American agricultural and commercial culture. The historical technique gains in utility for present world problems from the fact that in relation to Great Britain the United States up to about 1850 was an underdeveloped area.

This continued colonial relationship in ideas, technology, and in most other aspects of the culture presents a case study, interesting because it differs so markedly from the relationship of advanced industrial and underdeveloped areas at the present day. Since American development has seldom been seen in terms of this analogy, there is probably something to be learned from looking at it this way.

1. *The Entrepreneur in Early America*

It is obvious from a cursory view of United States history that the nineteenth century entrepreneurs represented a high level of business energy. Statistical series document the rapid growth of American business and productivity, particularly during the period from about 1830 to the end of the nineteenth century. Of fundamental importance to an understanding of this period of tremendous growth is the fact that potential entrepreneurs came from the already economically well-developed nations of Western Europe. The immigrants to America were from Great Britain, Holland, Germany, France, and Sweden, where, either in rural or urban areas, they had in general been in contact with fairly advanced stages of trade and handicraft. The natives of America, the Indians, were slow in adopting capitalist culture patterns. But the immigrants, unlike the people of most underdeveloped areas today, had value systems already adjusted to capitalist needs and goals. The fact that the two early American colonizing agencies were companies designed to return profits to stockholders gave a business atmosphere to problems of settlement.[2]

To a greater degree than the European population as a whole, the

[2] See Wesley F. Craven, *Dissolution of the Virginia Company*, Oxford, 1932.

migrants represented heterodox minorities conditioned to searching for new ways of coping with their social and physical environment. In this country, Europeans found communities with relatively low man-land ratios and almost unlimited opportunity for increasing returns from the application of labor. As a result, a premium was placed on putting to use devices or methods that would save man-hours, regardless of their efficiency in relation to physical resources.

To some extent colonial society reproduced European feudal patterns and recognized class distinctions, but barriers to social mobility were relatively weak. The early comers, who presumably did much to set colonial culture patterns, were conditioned by the needs of relatively open-class pioneer communities. There was no great difficulty in achieving high social prestige through the acquisition of property within a man's own lifetime.[3] This raises the question of the extent to which this conditioning created an attitude of competitiveness, or what has later been called a class-status-prestige complex, stronger than that of the nonmigrating English or Continental peoples. Aside from business, including farming, the avenues for social prestige were relatively few and unrewarding. The salaried positions in the army and navy were held by British officers merely stationed here for a brief period. Similarly the highest offices of government were of British appointment and the church had no colonial hierarchy that led to such posts as canon, dean, and bishop. In the later years of colonial development there were relatively few opportunities to gain rapid wealth from the land. Thus trade and manufacturing necessarily became chosen avenues for social mobility.

Elements favorable to entrepreneurial activity appear to have resulted from the loose integration of American culture. Patterns disrupted by transplantation and to a lesser extent by competition with those of other cultures did not resume their old depth or fixity. This meant that the entrepreneur could restructure the culture more nearly to suit his ends. Ralph Linton, for example, has written of the innovator as a deviant personality in terms of deeply patterned cultures.[4] This was not necessarily the case in the United States. Since new environments and new possibilities in transportation con-

[3] See W. T. Baxter, *The House of Hancock*, Harvard University Press, 1945, and James B. Hedges, *The Browns of Providence Plantations*, Harvard University Press, 1952. Although Baxter is a professor of accounting, neither book has a satisfactory analysis of capital accounts. Merchants did not balance their books with a view to determining net worth.

[4] In *The Progress of Underdeveloped Areas*, Bert F. Hoselitz, editor, University of Chicago Press, 1952, p. 75.

tinuously forced change, innovators may well have had personalities that could be called normal to the culture.[5] In fact, if one uses the term broadly to indicate new methods not previously practiced by the particular group, innovation must have been frequent, once a certain stage of development was reached in the new American areas.[6]

Another factor favorable to the prestige and success of the entrepreneur was the lack of established leadership in new communities. The local merchant or manufacturer might readily occupy the power vacuum which existed because of the lack of well-established leading landowners and politically prominent families, such as characterized old settlements.

As business success came increasingly to be the avenue to social prestige, a large supply of men was available for entrepreneurial pursuits. In addition, many occupations that in a foreign nation would not have been regarded as entrepreneurial or conducive to innovation or expansion in capital investment turned out to be such in the United States. For example, an able man keeping a general store in a growing part of the United States usually had an eye on every local opportunity. As soon as he made a little money in the store, he spread out into other local enterprises and became, in a sense, a small-scale general entrepreneur. In good times, college professors, doctors, and lawyers all joined in the scramble for wealth —for the profitable allocation of capital.

Lewis Atherton's studies indicate the high social prestige and the subsidiary enterprises of general storekeepers even in the relatively static Deep South.

"Here," he writes, "there was a tendency to develop a position of great influence. While this was primarily economic in nature, it also frequently expressed itself in political terms. Membership on the local city council was quite common, an indication of mercentile influence in the rise of interior towns and villages. At least one storekeeper was generally to be found on city councils, and frequently the majority came from that occupation. Self-interest of course made the work attractive. When municipal ordinances covered

[5] There has been no historical study of personality types per se. This supposition might be tested from the many biographies, collected letters, and autobiographies of businessmen of the early nineteenth century. See Henrietta M. Larson, *Guide to Business History*, Harvard University Press, 1948.

[6] Modifying this is the fact that frontier communities with their cooperative labor practices tended to standardize procedures. See Donald McConnell, *Economic Virtues in the United States*, published by author, 1930, pp. 12 ff.

mercantile and peddling licenses, rates of drayage and the speed at which drays could travel, business hours, rules for the city market, inspection of weights and measures, fire regulations, and similar subjects, it behooved a storekeeper to exert himself to obtain an opportunity to participate in making the decisions. . . .

"Obviously the storekeeper devoted his attention primarily to his immediate business functions. As emphasized throughout this study, he provided the dry goods, groceries, and tools necessary for the operation of farmers throughout the South. In doing this, he served as a middleman between seaboard wholesalers and southern farmers, thus handling the generous and long-range credit which characterized the system. He bartered merchandise for farm crops, and by marketing the latter offered an outlet for southern farms.

"In the process of providing these basic economic services the storekeeper naturally contributed to other economic and social activities as well. In processing farm crops for market he provided an elementary type of manufacturing by operating subsidiary enterprises such as sawmills and gristmills. Banking, farming, transportation, and land speculation were all so closely related to his scheme of operation that he had to deal with the problems involved in each. Moreover, storekeepers constituted the central group in the development of interior villages and towns in the ante-bellum period."[7]

There are no equally comprehensive studies of small mill, shop, and financial enterprises in the more rapidly growing regions.

Eighteenth and nineteenth century America had subcultures with differing sets of values. These ranged all the way from that of back-country people who had much of the cultural outlook of the Middle Ages still intact to the progressive business culture of Puritans and Quakers along the northeastern seaboard. In this latter culture frugality and saving were seen not only as manifestations of a proper life, but also as a means for acquiring more economic power that could be used for God's work. A foreigner viewing this segment of the culture in 1836 wrote, "There is, probably, no people on earth with whom business constitutes pleasure, and industry amusement, in an equal degree with the inhabitants of the United States of America."[8] These were the proper values for entrepreneurship and

[7] Lewis E. Atherton, *The Southern Country Store*, Louisiana State University Press, 1949, pp. 191-193. Quoted by permission. See also his *The Pioneer Merchant in Mid-America*, University of Missouri Press, 1939.

[8] F. J. Grund, *The Americans*, London, 1837, Vol. 2, p. 202. There is a voluminous literature of accounts by foreign travelers from which the char-

rapid capital formation. When carried westward by merchants, teachers, skilled workers, and transportation executives this "puritan" subculture came to dominate most of the nation.[9]

Another set of general conditioning factors is connected with the rapid geographical and demographical expansion in the eighteenth and nineteenth centuries. A high reproduction rate insured an expanding local population in almost every settled area. In addition to this, immigration was rapid after about 1845. These factors meant that, aside from a few declining agricultural areas in the East, a business started in almost any community would grow if it merely held its competitive position. The usual western promoter would have agreed with J. W. Smith of Hudson, Ohio that it was safe continually to add new business ventures, since as the town grew each would "support the other."[10]

2. *Capital Formation in the Nineteenth Century*

In the early phase of industrialization most initial financing was of local origin and there was an intimate relation between entrepreneurs and investors. Expansion of the business was usually financed by reinvesting profits. In this way the efficiency of the entrepreneur as a manager had a direct bearing upon the rate of capital formation. Harold F. Williamson has suggested that the desire to keep control of invested capital may have led entrepreneurs to favor reinvestment of earnings in their own firms rather than in more productive outside activities.

The rise of large-scale transportation and public utility enterprises from about 1820 on emphasized new methods of finance: widespread sale of securities and creation of bank credit. The first method raised the problems of entrepreneurial capital obtained from investors, without intimate knowledge of the properties named on their cer-

---

acteristics of American culture might be reconstructed in a systematic way. Hunt's *Merchants Magazine, De Bow's Review,* and the *Bankers' Magazine* also contain articles on American business practices written by foreign (usually British) businessmen.

[9] McConnell's *Economic Virtues in the United States,* as cited, repays reading in this connection.

[10] This situation is indicated in the early pages of city and county histories. I found it to be the case with most successful local brewers. It is indicated in my *The Pabst Brewing Company* (New York University Press, 1948), but since Pabst was selling in the national market, expansion by reinvestment in the company was more attractive than in the case of the local brewery. Therefore, general investment activity came at a later stage in the career of Frederick Pabst.

tificates of ownership, and by impersonal appeals in one section of the country for capital to be invested in another.

Much ingenuity was required to raise enough capital to build cities and railroads at the rates that prevailed from 1830 to 1860. The population in cities over 8,000 increased from 4.9 per cent of the total in 1820 to 16.1 per cent in 1860, and the number of such cities from 13 to 141. From 1836 until the late 1840's, depression and debt repudiations retarded the raising of capital for railroad construction, but in the decade of the 1850's the United States laid down more than 20,000 miles of track.

Capital for these ventures was raised by a series of devices in which the role of entrepreneurship is often hard to distinguish from that of government responding to public pressure. The means represented a mixture of techniques both borrowed from Europe and originated in the United States: (1) Commercial banks bought stocks for their portfolios.[11] On occasion, states forced banks to invest in internal improvements in order to gain renewal of their charters. (2) Commercial banks extended renewable loans or demand loans secured by stock to various business enterprises, particularly railroads. These loans became in effect a part of the capital structure of the road, and were ultimately paid off from the sale of securities. (3) Development banks were chartered by the states for the express purpose of issuing notes that could be used to build internal improvements. Occasionally, railroad companies were granted banking privileges to enable them to issue their own notes. (4) Real estate companies were associated regularly with the construction of railroads and often with the starting of factories.[12] Since the improvement projected promised an almost certain rise in surrounding land values, large investors could be forced to buy stock in the railroad or manufacturing company in order to be included in the land company.[13] (5) Construction companies, again

[11] For material on this and other aspects of the mechanics of investment in the nineteenth century see Fritz Redlich, *The Moulding of American Banking*, Hafner, 1951, Vol. 2. His book contains the only adequate account of the rise of investment banking.

[12] For examples of real estate companies in manufacturing finance see George S. Gibb, *The Whitesmiths of Taunton*, Harvard University Press, 1943, and Charles W. Moore, *Timing a Century*, Harvard University Press, 1945, both in the Harvard Studies in Business History.

[13] There is plenty of material on railroad finance and promotion and the early history of railroad companies; for an introduction see Frederick A. Cleveland and Fred W. Powell, *Railroad Promotion and Capitalization in the United States*, Longmans, 1909.

promising a more certain and immediate return than the improvement that was being constructed, could often raise equity capital or loans when the transportation company could not. (6) State and local governments put up large sums for the purchase of railroad and canal securities, generally through the sale of their own bonds, and insofar as these investments were not serviced by the improvement company the burden was borne by taxation.[14] (7) Entrepreneurs also persuaded some of the states, such as Georgia, Pennsylvania, and New York, to build major railroads or canals at state expense.[15]

In this broad capital-raising process the difficulty in distinguishing between general cultural factors and those specifically connected with the pattern of entrepreneurship becomes obvious. One might say it was an entrepreneurial culture. In fact, it is hard to distinguish between entrepreneurs and the rest of the population. From the demands of their function, the entrepreneurs were presumably the men of energy and imagination, along these material lines, and they educated the rest. The rise of a belief in material progress and of a willingness to make present sacrifices for future material rewards had been going on since the colonial period.

The economic returns from improved transportation were so high and widespread, particularly in interior communities previously cut off from markets, that such improvements became a major goal.[16] Local people were ready to make sacrifices to secure transportation and unquestionably dreamed of benefits that exceeded the ultimate reality. The people of Oswego, New York, for example, were said to be "unanimous for anything in the form of a railroad whether it goes crooked or straight they seem to have no care."[17] When the capital required exceeded that which could be raised by local

[14] Harry M. Pierce contends that when governments invested in railroad securities at prices that could not have been obtained in the open market, the difference between the government and the market price was a subsidy. *Railroads of New York: A Study of Government Aid, 1826-1875*, Harvard University Press, 1953, pp. 20-21.

See also Carter Goodrich and Harvey H. Segal, "Baltimore's Aid to Railroads," *Journal of Economic History*, Winter 1953, pp. 2-35, and Milton Heath, "State Aid to Railroads in the South," *Journal of Economic History*, Supplement x, 1950, pp. 40-52.

[15] There was also some financing of internal improvements by lotteries. See H. J. G. Aitken, "Yates and McIntyre: Lottery Managers," *Journal of Economic History*, Winter 1953, pp. 36-57.

[16] See Leland H. Jenks, "Railroads as an Economic Force," *Journal of Economic History*, May 1944, pp. 1-21.

[17] Pierce, *op. cit.*, p. 42.

entrepreneurs, they joined with investors in efforts to secure state aid.

Between 1835 and 1840 Illinois illustrated the excessive public investment in a frontier area produced by a combination of popular demand, persuasive entrepreneurs, and a great boom period.[18] Encouraged by a federal land grant of 290,914 acres, the legislature in 1835 authorized a $500,000 bond issue to finance a canal between Lake Michigan and the Illinois River. As security for the bonds, the state pledged the federal land and the canal tolls.

But this was only a beginning. The full force of the boom psychology struck the state in 1836 and 1837. Land near the Chicago end of the canal which had remained unsold at $1.25 an acre less than ten years before now sold as high as $20,000 for a building lot. Caught in the excitement of the early months of 1837, the legislature established a comprehensive system of internal improvements. Seven railroads were to be built at once, each starting from an intersection with a navigable river, and construction work was to progress simultaneously in both directions! Navigation of the major rivers within the state was to be improved, and $200,000 was earmarked for compensation to counties in which no railroad or river improvements took place. An issue of $8,000,000 in 6 per cent bonds, salable only at par or above, was provided to pay for the state system. Needless to add, the depression which commenced in mid-1837 resulted in abandonment of most of the work and default on the bonds.

Each new tier of western states went through such periods of overoptimism and overinvestment, in either the 1830's, the 1850's, the 1870's, or the 1880's, and private enterprise followed the same pattern. R. Richard Wohl has written a case history showing a boom-time pattern of mid-nineteenth century private investment.[19] His account is especially interesting because it illustrates the tendency of the optimistic business atmosphere to turn American professional men into entrepreneurs. Wohl's leading figure, Henry Noble Day, was a professor in the Western Reserve Theological Department at Hudson, Ohio to whom the boom of the early 1850's brought dreams that his village would become a great railroad center. Day's conversion to business life was aided by the fact that education did not share in the flush times. The closing of the Theological Depart-

[18] See Reginald C. McGrane, *Foreign Bondholders and American State Debts*, Macmillan, 1935, pp. 102 ff.

[19] R. Richard Wohl, "Henry Noble Day," in *Men in Business*, William Miller, editor, Harvard University Press, 1952, pp. 178-188, *passim*. Quoted by permission.

ment in 1850 just as the railroad from Cleveland was nearing Hudson ended Day's teaching. He justified his transition to full-time entrepreneur in Calvinistic terms: "The characteristics which Christianity in its present stage seems to require are chiefly vigor of invention, skill in execution and subscribing to the true end of industrial arts—utility."

As in most western towns the railroad seemed the key to unlimited prosperity. Before the Cleveland and Pittsburgh even reached Hudson and years before any through connection to the East, Day was chartering branch lines and planning a transcontinental system through the town.

"But for Henry Day himself the dream he had for Hudson had become a sacred reality. He was able to anticipate its completion when the first few spadefuls of earth were taken out for grading. He proceeded therefore to enact the logic of his expectations. He began to create a network of businesses in Hudson to service the demands arising out of the railroad building boom and to cash in on the enlarged market which would result once the roads were completed. . . .

"In 1849, Henry Day began what was to be the seat of nearly a dozen separate businesses. That year he approached Western Reserve College for a loan of $1,500 with which he would undertake to construct a large commercial building. Since the railroad was to come shortly to Hudson, there would be a great demand for business floor space, of which there was hardly any available in the town. Against the loan he would pledge the lot on which he intended to erect the structure. In addition, he would pay the going rate of interest and retire the loan as rapidly as he could.

"No sooner had he begun the actual building when his plans for the structure were enlarged into something far grander. Less than a year later, the [un]completed building had exceeded its planned cost of $3,000. . . . Before the structure was completed to his satisfaction it had swallowed up $18,000, although the source of this capital remains to this day a mystery which cannot be solved from the tangled, incestuous financing which prevailed in Henry Day's enterprises.

"The structure was a magnificent aberration, entirely out of scale with the relatively small, low buildings which filled the rest of the village. It was a five-sided, three-story edifice—an earlier Pentagon—and was soon packed full of a collection of businesses at the bottom of each of which was Henry Day, impartially providing capital, plans, and enthusiasm. . . .

"In the meantime the projected railroads brought a great stream of cash and hundreds of workers into Hudson. Of the $200,000 pledged for the Clinton Railroad, $18,000 was expended within Hudson itself, a proportion far greater than it appears, since many of the subscriptions to stock were made in the form of lands, not cash. The numerical expansion of the population also created a host of new problems which boomed business. The greatest demand was for shelter and Henry Day proposed to meet it with a vertically integrated scheme for new housing.

"One of the greatest benefits of the railroad boom, its protagonist argued, was to be the enhancement of local land values. Hence Henry Day, associating himself with the most powerful elements in the community, purchased—on credit, of course—large tracts of land outside the main area of settlement in the town, but immediately adjacent to it. Here—in what he labeled 'Day's Addition'—he proposed to rear the housing which was to accommodate the present increase in population as well as the further additions which would surely come after the railroads were fully built. To finance construction and sale of his houses, Day conceived a special kind of banking organization, the 'Hudson Society for Savings.'"

The main sources of capital for the Day companies were the enterprises of his relatives. He drew on the working capital of New York and southern trading and banking companies and on family wealth accumulated from earlier mercantile ventures in the East. In this way eastern credit was stretched to the utmost for Ohio improvements. The result, as in many similar instances, was collapse of the whole structure in the business recession of 1854.

In Day's case and many others, including state-financed ventures, most or a large part of the capital prematurely invested was lost. The railroad culverts melted away as farmers "borrowed" the stones, and the grading reverted to humps in the pastureland. But there were nearly similar cases where the bad initial estimates, the "entrepreneurial errors," as John E. Sawyer has called them, led to the construction of ultimately valuable works that would not have been undertaken or continued had the true costs and difficulties been known in advance or at an early stage. Sawyer writes that "Once in operation, to fit our conditions the project must have proved to be such—according to the definition chosen, such a contribution to the economic development of the community or such a source of profits to its owners—as to have more than justified the total cost. That it paid off in any form means, of course, that the error in estimating costs was at least offset by a corresponding error in the estimation of demand."[20]

He cites as well-known instances the Welland and Middlesex Canals, the Hoosac Tunnel, and the building of Sault Ste. Marie, Michigan. In the latter case Francis H. Clergue built an industrial community with power, pulp and other mills, machine shops, foundries, nickel mines, iron mines, railroads, charcoal kilns, and finally a large-scale steel industry in advance of any local or otherwise established demand. Sawyer concludes: "Here capital was progressively, and more and more unwillingly, poured into a lasting exercise in economic development that proved a near miss from the point of view of its investors; but which was then so far under way that the 'high social cost of abandonment' enabled it to command transitional public funds when crisis came to the over-extended empire."

As the foregoing examples have illustrated, acute scarcity of local capital in western communities did not prevent the coming into being of an excess of capital equipment. In the upswings of the business cycle there was a continuous trend toward overexpansion. Business buildings were bigger and more numerous than the trade warranted, railroads were built ahead of traffic, and factories were started before there was an adequate market. The successful local man would likely engage in more enterprises than he could effectively manage. But such excessive activity led to a continuous movement of workers, either manual or white-collar, into the entrepreneurial ranks. This, in turn, meant that entrepreneurs were recruited from a very large percentage of the total population and that there was a good deal of movement into and out of entrepreneurial activities.

Vigorous individual entrepreneurship may necessarily have a high ratio of miscalculation and failure, a high ratio of entries and exits. American entrepreneurs like R. H. Macy and Cyrus McCormick failed in their early ventures, and many successful companies have been through one or more bankruptcies. Managerial know-how, essential to ultimate capital formation, was learned at the expense of empty-handed creditors.

3. *General Entrepreneurs in the Nineteenth Century*

It has seemed convenient to refer to the men who organized and controlled multifarious enterprises as general entrepreneurs. The

[20] John E. Sawyer, "Entrepreneurial Error and Economic Growth," in *Explorations in Economic History*, May 1952, pp. 200 and 203-204. Quoted by permission.

criteria of general entrepreneurship is that the man should not immerse himself in the details of management in any single enterprise, but that alone or in cooperation with similar operators he should control a number of enterprises in diverse, but not necessarily unrelated, lines of business. A man like Erastus Corning of Albany traded in hardware, manufactured iron, controlled railroads, and was president of a bank that supplied credit for such enterprises.[21]

General entrepreneurs operating regionally or locally formed an important link between the creation of credit and productive enterprise. As presidents or directors of banks they were in favored positions for negotiating loans. Sometimes "secured" by the stock of the enterprise involved, more often merely by one- or two-name paper, bank loans were frequently the source of both fixed and working capital. During boom periods the imaginative ventures of these entrepreneurs, such as Henry Day, undoubtedly drew bank credit far in excess of local savings into long-term construction[22] and by the resulting inflation taxed the rest of the community for the benefit of faster capital formation.

By the same mixture of enthusiasm and ability, entrepreneurs in control of large ventures drew upon the capital resources of Europe. This took place in two ways. First, since men like Cornelius Vanderbilt, Henry Villard, Nathaniel Thayer, or John Murray Forbes were known to foreign bankers, their participation in a venture was a sufficient guarantee to attract foreign capital.[23] Second, these men and their companies advertised the West and its farming land. This attracted immigrants with capital in cash or skill.[24] At the least, the economy gained an able-bodied adult worker without having to pay for his upbringing. At the most, the economy might gain the transplantation of a going enterprise, either agricultural or industrial, from Europe to America. For example, the Bests who started the Pabst Brewery moved their business from Mettenheim in the Rhenish Palatinate by selling their brewery and building a new one with the proceeds in Milwaukee, Wisconsin.[25]

[21] Irene Neu, thesis on Erastus Corning, Cornell University, 1948.

[22] Jenks, *op. cit.* See also his *The Migration of British Capital to 1875*, Knopf, 1927.

[23] See Thomas C. Cochran, "The Legend of the Robber Barons," *Pennsylvania Magazine of History and Biography*, July 1950, pp. 311 ff.

[24] Charlotte Erickson is working on a thesis at Cornell on the recruitment of labor from foreign countries in the nineteenth century.

[25] Cochran, *The Pabst Brewing Company*, as cited, pp. 1 ff.

The general entrepreneurs played a major role in reshaping the American environment to fit their needs. Small groups of them in Boston, New York, and Philadelphia promoted and organized most of the large privately owned transportation and public utility enterprises. They saw the possibilities, and paid the lobbyists needed to secure charters for the major company and for attendant development and construction companies.[26] Their subscriptions to stock and bonds, in either the main company or the construction company, provided a considerable part of the initial funds and gave the banks with which they were connected the confidence to extend loans.

It seems probable that the eastern groups of general entrepreneurs, with their relatively good command of capital and their over-all view of situations, undertook long-range development more rapidly than institutional or local interests would have. For example, before the Michigan Central reached Chicago the Boston and New York entrepreneurs responsible for its finance were already planning for a western connection; and before the western connection, the Chicago, Burlington, & Quincy, reached the Mississippi the same entrepreneurs were projecting an extension across Iowa.

Entrepreneurs interested in politics, like Stephen A. Douglas, secured a policy of assisting railroads by federal land grants, delivered through the states from 1850 to 1860 and directly from the federal government to projected transcontinental lines from 1862 to 1871. These aided greatly in attracting domestic and foreign capital to railroad construction.[27] Investors who might be skeptical about the immediate earning power of a railroad across the prairies had faith in the ultimate value of the farming land. This seemed particularly true of foreign investors. The land grants undoubtedly drew otherwise unavailable money from England and Continental Europe into projects like the Illinois Central and the Northern Pacific.[28]

State and local credit also played a major part in starting the canal and railroad transportation system. With considerable oversimplification, one might distinguish two stages in the early development of both finance and transportation: a first stage in which finan-

[26] Thomas C. Cochran, *Railroad Leaders, 1845-1890*, Harvard University Press, 1953, p. 194.

[27] Thomas C. Cochran, "Land Grants and Railroad Entrepreneurship," *Journal of Economic History*, Supplement x, 1950, p. 62.

[28] See Paul W. Gates, *The Illinois Central Railroad and Its Colonization Work*, Harvard University Press, 1934, and James B. Hedges, *Henry Villard and the Railways of the Northwest*, Yale University Press, 1930.

cially weak entrepreneurs sought the aid of the state and local governments and welcomed state-owned enterprise as a needed supplement; and a second stage in which stronger general entrepreneurs bought out the government-owned enterprises, retired government-owned securities, and proceeded on a private enterprise basis. The dividing line between these stages depended largely upon the sums required by the projected enterprises in relation to the local supply of capital and the probability of immediate returns. In the East there were few new state activities after 1850, although local subscription to stocks and bonds continued into the 1870's.[29] In the Mississippi Valley state enterprise continued through the 1850's and farther west, state and federal aid was common until the panic of 1873.

The greatest demands for capital between 1850 and 1890 came in connection with railroad construction. According to the admittedly inaccurate capital estimates of the federal census there was $533 million invested in manufacturing (including hand and neighborhood industries) in 1849 and only $318 million in railroads. By 1889 the two sums were $6,525 million in manufacturing and $9,680 million in railroads. Henry Adams said, "My generation was mortgaged to the railroads and nobody knew it better than that generation itself."[30] Negotiating and servicing this mortgage constituted the greatest achievement of nineteenth century American entrepreneurs in the field of capital formation.

The feat of assembling nearly $10 billion in capital, largely through the security markets, should not obscure the fact that some of this capital and much of the $6.5 billion credited to manufacturing were the result of reinvested earnings. In industry, marketing, and agriculture, entrepreneurs created capital through successful management that brought in large earnings, coupled with low salary levels and small allocations to dividends or paid-out profits. During the first twenty years of the corporate history of the Pabst Brewing Co., for example, over 75 per cent of net earnings were reinvested and less than 25 per cent paid out in dividends. Up to 1889 the president and vice-president of this company, which was by then worth $5,000,000, drew salaries of $2,500 a year.[31] Other studies in

[29] See Pierce, *op. cit.*, Chap. I.

[30] Henry Adams, *The Education of Henry Adams*, Houghton Mifflin, 1930, p. 240.

[31] Cochran, *The Pabst Brewing Company*, as cited, pp. 84 and 94.

company history indicate that this picture is probably representative of family and other closely owned companies.

4. *Entrepreneurs in Banking*

So far the emphasis has been on the promoters and managers of enterprise, but the supply of capital for internal improvements was also a function of entrepreneurship in the field of banking, a product of manipulation and innovation in the mechanics of money and credit.

Redlich has covered the development of entrepreneurship in United States banking so throughly in his *Moulding of American Banking* that it is necessary only to summarize his findings here.[32] Between 1800 and 1850, American financial entrepreneurs developed institutions to encourage saving and to collect such funds in usable pools. Chartered commercial banks, which had first appeared in 1780, spread rapidly during this period, and savings banks, building and loan associations, and life insurance companies were started. While most of the investment from the latter three types of pooled savings was in urban mortgages, this in turn released other credit for manufacturing and transportation investment.[33]

Laws against branch banking in many states, and the willingness of state legislatures after 1815 to charter banks, led to a great spread of small banking units run on an experimental basis by local entrepreneurs. In 1840 there were 900 banks; by 1861 the number reached 1,600. While there were various state stipulations regarding reserves, taken as a whole the system was capable of expanding credit both rapidly and unwisely. The unwise advances, in turn, led to bank failures and the temporary prostration of local business. Whether a few large banks with branches, such as exist in most European nations, would have produced a more rapid economic growth can probably never be decided. These thousands of banking entrepreneurs lacked expert skill in assessing risks and were therefore likely to be bound by custom in extending credit, but they were close to the needs of their local communities, and they were no doubt influenced by the risk-taking spirit of the local businessmen.

The other major development of this period was the beginning of specialized investment banking. In the early nineteenth century

[32] The Redlich work has been cited. See also Ralph W. Hidy, *The House of Baring in American Trade and Finance*, Harvard University Press, 1949, and Jenks, *The Migration of British Capital to 1875*, as cited.

[33] Roy A. Foulke, *Sinews of American Commerce*, Dun & Bradstreet, 1941, pp. 89-150.

the American agencies for selling securities were numerous and unspecialized. Securities might be contracted or negotiated for by incorporated commercial banks, private banks, general enterpreneurs, foreign bankers or their agents, brokers, or traveling salesmen. Most of these middlemen hoped to sell all or a large part of the securities abroad. The close connections between American and British financial markets gave investment in the United States a different aspect from the buying of securities in other underdeveloped areas. The chief British houses, such as Baring Brothers, Thomas Wilson, or the Rothschilds, had either trusted correspondents or agents in this country. Englishmen were used to appraising American commercial risks and readily shifted to appraising the risks of publicly or privately financed transportation.

The good standing of American state securities in the British market, prior to the defaults of 1841, was one reason for the extensive use of state credit for financing banking and transportation. By 1847, state debts, largely contracted in aid of transportation, totaled $224 million.[34] From about this time on, London provided a fair market for issues of the larger American railroads, while the standing of state securities was still depressed by defaults. As a result, well-sponsored railroads found their own bonds more salable than those of most of the states.

But the foreign market was not available to small transportation companies and public utilities or to American manufacturing enterprises. Local money-raisers resorted to many devices. Lotteries, improvement banks, building and loan companies, and mortgage banks all appeared within the first two decades of the nineteenth century. Some of these, such as western improvement or mortgage banks, were schemes for monetizing debt and then gradually passing the obligations eastward. Underlying this ingeniousness in creating credit were a faith in the immediate profitability of applying capital to many processes and a confidence in the general devotion to the goal of money-making.

Throughout the period before the Civil War, commercial banks were both buyers and middlemen in the investment security business. The Bank of the United States of Pennsylvania, during its brief career following the end of the federal charter in 1836, took a leading part in security negotiations. The companies chartered under various state "free banking" acts also participated in investment business, particularly in state and municipal securities.

[34] Redlich, *op. cit.*, p. 344.

With the rapid spread of railroads and gas and water companies, private bankers found their investment business becoming more important in relation to the old stand-bys of note brokerage and foreign and domestic exchange. August Belmont, as American agent for the Rothschilds; Prime Ward & King; George Peabody; Drexel; Brown Brothers; E. W. Clark; Corcoran & Riggs; and Vermilye were among the houses that became sufficiently specialized to be called investment bankers in the years before the Civil War.

The federal flotations of $2.5 billion in public debt during the Civil War resulted in a new maturity for American financial markets. The handling of the contracting, selling, and refunding of these issues built up a few specialized houses that, with the exception of Jay Cooke & Co., were to dominate the security markets in the United States for the next sixty years. In the post-Civil War period, as in earlier years, the strength of houses such as Drexel-Morgan, J. & W. Seligman, or Kidder, Peabody lay largely in good foreign connections, while the fatal weakness of Jay Cooke was his failure to establish real strength in London, Paris, Berlin, or Frankfurt.

Between 1865 and 1880, American investment banking entrepreneurs developed the underwriting and selling syndicate and the practices of banker leadership and responsibility in the affairs of their major clients. It is hard to estimate the effect of these practices on capital formation. Cooperation in selling syndicates probably mobilized more of the nation's savings for large-scale projects than might have been reached through the earlier, less highly organized efforts, but research would be needed to demonstrate this.

Still harder to judge is the effect of banker leadership, as illustrated by J. Pierpont Morgan. From the late 1870's on, Morgan asked for and received representation on the boards of certain railroads that he financed; by the middle 1880's he insisted on companies retaining the services of the syndicate leaders responsible for outstanding issues, at least in the case of his own clients;[35] and by the 1890's he was initiating reorganizations and mergers of railroads and industrial companies. Morgan's efforts probably drew more foreign capital into the United States than would have come otherwise, but the effect of his plans was often to check the rate of expansion of a road or an industry so that new commitments would not endanger the servicing of senior securities. Other leaders in the investment banking field operated in much the same fashion. These bankers also tended to share the view that monopoly created stability and a

[35] Cochran, *Railroad Leaders, 1845-1890*, as cited, p. 71.

well-ordered economy, whereas competition was upsetting and dangerous.

5. *Factors Retarding Capital Formation in the Nineteenth Century*

While nineteenth century American culture appears to have been one of the most favorable in world history for entrepreneurial activity, there were certain negative elements stemming either from the general environment or from the attitude of certain groups of entrepreneurs. Insofar as these elements curtailed or reduced the vigor of creative entrepreneurial activity, they may be assumed to have hindered capital formation.

One type of hindrance to effective entrepreneurial action was maladjustment between labor supply and demand. With the shifting of industry resulting from technological change, adjustment in the case of labor presumably never approaches close to perfection, but the process of internal westward growth and European immigration to the eastern seaboard imposed unusual difficulties on the United States. The decline of agricultural activities after about 1830 in parts of the Northeast and an already large population tended to produce a regional surplus of native-born labor. From the 1840's on, immigrants arrived in the eastern ports at a rate generally in excess of the growth of opportunities for local employment. How to draw effectively upon these pools of labor was an entrepreneurial challenge throughout the last half of the nineteenth century. Entrepreneurs tried a number of expedients. Associations were formed in the 1850's to move labor westward, chiefly at the expense of employers interested in western ventures. The difficulty with this device was lack of any guarantee that the laborer would arrive and work satisfactorily to repay the cost of his transportation. Some samples of the numbers actually moved make it appear that most entrepreneurs regarded the risk as too great. Railroad entrepreneurs made arrangements to move workers westward for their own purposes, often with land as an ultimate reward for fulfillment of the labor contract. Western states and territories, anxious to gain population, established eastern and European agencies to encourage migration. From the Civil War on, some companies made a business of importing Asiatic or European workers under contract, but the practice was prohibited by acts of Congress in 1882 and 1885, respectively. The extent to which these devices equated supply and demand has still to be investigated.

A second set of possible retarding factors stemmed from sectional and local rivalries and ambitions that led entrepreneurs or their political representatives to sacrifice the general to what seemed the special welfare. Part of the division of opinion came from geographical position, and part from differing types of entrepreneurship. The large export agriculturist thought in terms, and had real economic interests, different from those of the protected small manufacturer. Geographical-occupational cleavages led not only to conflicts over national policy, but also to a rather general preference for locally instead of centrally controlled activities. Sometimes Congress was swayed by local interests from all parts of the nation, as in state banker opposition to central banking; at other times the interest represented might be more strictly sectional, as illustrated in the New England fear of loss of labor due to more liberal land laws.

Here again the effects of these pressures on capital formation have never been determined. Although central banking, for example, would have given businessmen a uniform currency and solved some domestic exchange problems, it would also have tended to curtail credit inflation, which was one of the important factors in capital formation during the sharp upswings of the business cycle. It is hard to tell whether the entrepreneurial pressure that contributed to the writing of federal land laws in 1785 and 1796, under which very little land was sold, had any considerable effect on the westward movement, since the surrounding states had ample land for sale on favorable terms. If the laws did check migration, it is also hard to tell what effect this had on economic growth.[36] The eastern business argument that labor was needed there for commerce and industry and that western investment under existing conditions of transportation was lost to the national economy undoubtedly had some truth.

The planter-entrepreneurs who represented the slave plantation system in Washington on many occasions blocked policies that might have aided industrial capital formation. The most obvious issue involved was the protective tariff. Except in 1816, the South was opposed to protection, and, aided by northern railroad and commercial interests, it managed to prevent or modify tariff increases prior to 1861. The probable effect on the United States of a moderate rather than a high tariff policy prior to the Civil War is a question that

[36] For discussion of the land laws see Fred H. Harrington, Merle Curti, Richard H. Shryock, and Thomas C. Cochran, *An American History*, Harper, 1949, Vol. I, pp. 221-223.

has occupied economic thinkers for more than a century without a conclusive answer being produced.

The planters came to fear the social effect of creating an urban Negro working population, and, after a brief period of encouragement to local industry from 1815 on, southern investors put their capital to other use, often outside their own region. There has not been sufficient study of southern investment to tell how much of the planters' savings went abroad.

The South, to some extent, had cultural patterns common in underdeveloped agricultural regions in the twentieth century. There was high concentration of income, a general estimate for 1860 being that three-quarters of the export income was distributed to about 8,000 families. But in spite of concentration of income, luxurious living standards seemed to prevent the planter elite from promoting a high rate of capital growth.

The problem of the internal efficiency of the specialized slave plantation system is too complex to discuss here.[37] But there is at least a possibility that the planter-entrepreneurs, with their semi-feudal cultural values, stood in the way of more rapid capital growth both in their own section and in the nation as a whole.

The southern influence in Washington was hostile to many policies of the entrepreneurs interested in developing the West. Not only did the westward movement draw population away from the old South, but the slave system could not readily be transplanted to many new territories. While it has been noted that eastern businessmen also were doubtful of the value to them of rapid western growth, after the middle 1840's the combination of heavy immigration and increasing western investment opportunities won many of them over to an expansionist policy. Hence, by the 1850's it was chiefly southern influence that blocked federal subsidies for a centrally located transcontinental railroad, freer disposal of western land, river and harbor development, and other internal improvements. Whether more lavish federal aid in the West at an earlier period would in the long run have contributed to capital growth remains a moot point.

A deterrent to capital investment similar to the rivalry of sectional entrepreneurs in national politics was the power of local or special interests in state legislatures. Businessmen and other citizens of the

[37] See Emery Q. Hawk, *Economic History of the South*, Prentice-Hall, 1934, pp. 271-273, and John S. Spratt, "The Cotton Miner," *American Quarterly*, Fall 1952, pp. 214-235.

counties that benefited from the Erie Canal system in New York State, for example, were able up until 1851 to get the legislature to place clauses in railroad charters either prohibiting the carriage of freight or forcing the payment of canal tolls on railroad shipments.[38] The Camden & Amboy Railroad in New Jersey was able through special charter provisions and political influence to prevent for thirty years the chartering of any competing New York–Philadelphia line.[39]

A third type of deterrent to entrepreneurial activity and capital growth was the depression phase of business cycles. Fluctuations in prices, business activity, and employment seem to have been more severe than in the nations of Western Europe. As already illustrated, American entrepreneurs appear to have reached greater heights of incautious optimism during booms than did their European counterparts, and consequently the ensuing debacles were more prostrating. On the one hand, the price inflations that usually accompanied upswings undoubtedly led to diminished consumption by receivers of fixed incomes and larger entrepreneurial profits, both of which stimulated capital investment. But the relatively prolonged stagnation in new investment during the major depressions to some extent offset the capital gains of the boom.

Many leading entrepreneurs and some economic writers were aware of a general cyclical movement and understood the merits of countercyclical investment. But to raise capital by security flotation in a depression was extremely difficult. This is abundantly illustrated in the letters of nineteenth century railroad presidents. Even the minor recession of 1848 led John Murray Forbes to write, "At this moment it is impossible to get subscriptions to any Rail Road however promising." Ten years later he counselled, "We [should] let our Stockholders recover from the depression of the past year and regain confidence before we plunge into anything *however* good." In 1874 John W. Brooks wrote, "The bare idea, even of discussing a new project, would injure one's reputation for sanity." And looking back on these years, Frederick W. Kimball noted that "During the recent depression nobody would even listen to the establishment of a new enterprise."[40]

[38] Frank W. Stevens, *The Beginnings of the New York Central Railroad*, Putnam, 1926, pp. 267-273.

[39] John W. Cadman, Jr., *The Corporation in New Jersey*, Harvard University Press, 1949, pp. 54-59.

[40] Quoted in Cochran, *Railroad Leaders, 1845-1890*, as cited, pp. 105 and 106.

A fourth set of deterrents to entrepreneurial action might be put under the heading of insufficient security. This had many forms. The most routine commercial transactions involved risks when conducted across state lines and at a distance. Prior to the spread of the railroad, inland transportation and transfer agents were unreliable. To be sure of receiving his goods intact and on time, the inland merchant had to travel with them.[41] Before the beginning of credit agencies in the 1830's, it was difficult to know who could be trusted in distant cities, and unfamiliar bank notes might prove to be depreciated or counterfeit. State courts could impede collection of debts by "foreigners," and the status of corporations doing business outside the state of their incorporation was questionable prior to the 1880's. While the United States was nominally one country, the difficulties of doing some kinds of interstate business in the first half of the nineteenth century were almost as great as though the boundary lines were those of independent nations.

Added to these insecurities arising from poor trade facilities and discriminatory local statutes was a lack of the police protection necessary for maintaining orderly markets. Robbery by stealth or violence was frequent, particularly in the newer regions. Only a few cities had organized police protection.

The low business ethics of many American entrepreneurs were a hindrance both to business efficiency and to the raising of capital. Confidence men selling shares or lots were abundant. Bankruptcy with concealed assets was a common recourse for avoiding embarrassing obligations. Capital was frequently squandered in ways that made it hard to draw the line between overoptimism and outright dishonesty. In building the western railroads, for example, construction was often managed and partly financed by local entrepreneurs who were, at the least, somewhat careless in handling easterners' money. Forbes wrote, "My feeling . . . is . . . that Landowners and R. Road contractors are the ones who too often get the whole benefit of the money that capitalists put into the West."[42] But corporate stockholders were also defrauded by eastern operators of apparently high standing. Railroads were gutted by construction companies controlled by the railroad officers. Presidents of corporations printed fake stock certificates and sold them on the exchanges. Contracts were freely broken when it was inconvenient to live up to them.

[41] See Atherton, *The Pioneer Merchant in Mid-America*, as cited.

[42] Quoted in Cochran, *Railroad Leaders, 1845-1890*, as cited, p. 100.

The result of such entrepreneurial practices was unquestionably to discourage investment in the common stock of corporations.

A related deterrent to investment in stock was the lack of regulation of security exchanges and original prospectuses. Let the buyer beware was completely the rule up until the late 1860's. Then after Drew, Fiske, and Gould had swindled Commodore Vanderbilt by wholesale printing of stock certificates, the New York Stock Exchange regulated itself to the extent of demanding information on the total number of shares issued by a company whose stock was traded on the Exchange. But the states and the federal government continued their laissez-faire attitude. The effect was to increase the preference of the conservative investor for mortgages or other forms of local investment where he could keep watch on the entrepreneurs who had his money.

6. *Factors Retarding Capital Formation in the Late Nineteenth and the Twentieth Century*

By the end of the nineteenth century the rate of net capital formation was declining slightly in comparison with the rate of increase in either national income or gross national product, and the latter two series in turn were advancing at a less rapid rate than in earlier decades. The apparent turn of the curve was undoubtedly affected by changing cultural factors that have not been subjected to analysis sufficient to support generalizations. The effect of the West as a promised land and a stimulant to saving and investment was probably lessening. The problems of urban industrial society were emphasizing security and deemphasizing individual initiative, risk-taking, and the "puritan" attitude. The confidence that change meant progress was probably less than in earlier years. A doctrine of consumption was threatening the doctrine of frugality and thrift. But in addition to these and similar deterrents to capital formation, the changing character of entrepreneurship played a part.

A number of important changes in entrepreneurial roles were unfavorable to capital formation: the increase in the size of companies, with an attendant bureaucratization of entrepreneurial functions; the substitution of professional executives for owner-managers; the greater persistence of monopolies and other large organizations regardless of economic efficiency; the inheritance of managerial functions by less able heirs; the supersedure of the influence of general entrepreneurs by that of investment banking houses and other financial institutions; and the deterring effect of taxes and government regulation.

In the large companies that appeared rapidly beginning in the 1880's, the chief executives frequently rose through the ranks. They succeeded by being "good organization men" with a proper regard for loyalties and morale. A study by Mabel Newcomer of the careers of the top executives of the largest nonfinancial corporations for 1899, 1923, and 1948 shows the increasing trend away from independent business backgrounds. Including in her "entrepreneur-capitalist" group (those who have run their own business) "bankers, brokers, and those engineers and lawyers who had a hand in organizing the corporation which they head," she finds that three-fifths of the 1899 group fall in this category, one-third of the 1923 group, and only one-quarter of the 1948 group.[43] The attitude of these professional entrepreneurs toward liquidation or serious risk-taking was likely, to say the least, to be more conservative than that of the owner-manager (owning entrepreneur) or the general entrepreneur.

Not only was the salaried professional disinclined to pursue policies that might eliminate his job, regardless of the profitability of these policies to the stockholders, but he might also be loath to recommend investments that would upset personal relations within the organization. For example, the assets of a steamship company became almost completely liquid during World War II through the sinking of its vessels and resulting insurance payments. There was little prospect that the company's normal trade would be profitable for new vessels in time of peace. The chairman of the board, a large stockholder, and an independent capitalist played with the idea of liquidating the operating end of the business and investing the capital in more promising enterprises. Profit considerations pointed overwhelmingly in that direction. But none of the professional managers in the company, whose jobs would disappear, favored such a plan. In the end the company decided to continue its customary type of operations. The pressures of personal relations and the momentum of a going concern won out over what appeared to promise maximization of profit for the stockholders.

These considerations plus that of size alone, and threatened government prosecution under the antitrust laws, tended to make big-

[43] "The Chief Executive of Large Business Corporations," *Explorations in Entrepreneurial History*, October 1952, pp. 13-14. See also the articles by Winifred Gregory and Irene Neu and by William Miller in *Men in Business*, as cited.

company entrepreneurs think more in terms of maintaining a given market position and stabilizing sales than in terms of continued technological innovation and expansion at the expense of competitors. Furthermore, if one or a limited number of companies controlled production in an industry, it was possible for entrepreneurs to slow down the pace of innovation in the interest of reducing risk and lengthening the period of utilization of existing equipment—a process that might increase immediate purchasing power but slow down capital formation and future production. Well-known illustrations of the slowing down of innovation in the interests of more complete utilization of existing equipment are the American Telephone & Telegraph Co.'s treatment of the hand-set phone after 1907, and General Electric's and Westinghouse's relatively slow response to the possibilities of fluorescent lighting between 1896 and 1938.[44]

If complete figures could be assembled, it might turn out that, other things being equal, the larger a firm the longer its life expectancy. Sampling studies point in this direction. But if the longevity is because of size rather than economic efficiency, the prolongation of the large unit presumably hinders new capital investment and ultimately retards the increase of productivity in the industry. Looked at from the standpoint of the present discussion, this is another example of diminished entrepreneurial efficiency in capital allocation resulting from bigness.

There have been no quantitative studies of the qualitatively recognized shift in entrepreneurship from the founding generation in medium and big business to the sons and heirs of the founders. The period 1880 to 1910 would appear to embrace many such shifts. It seems likely, from isolated case studies, that the second generation tended to be both less able and less interested in expansion than its predecessors.[45]

During the same period the increasing size of security flotations, the better organization of the American money market, and the rise

[44] See N. R. Danielian, *A.T.&T.*, Vanguard, 1939, pp. 102-103, and Arthur A. Bright, Jr., *The Electric-Lamp Industry*, Macmillan, 1949, pp. 384-391. Paul G. Clark in *The Structure of American Economy, 1919-1939* (Wassily Leontief, editor, 2nd ed., Oxford, 1951) pictures the investment policy of AT&T as a kind of automatic adjustment to new demand on a basis worked out by engineers. Entrepreneurial decisions do not appear explicitly.

[45] A number of business histories illustrate this point. Among them see Harold F. Williamson, *Winchester*, Combat Forces Press, 1952; C. W. Moore, *Timing a Century*, Harvard University Press, 1945; Thomas Navin, *The Whitin Machine Works since 1831*, Harvard University Press, 1950; and Cochran, *The Pabst Brewing Company*, as cited.

of strong American investment banks and insurance and trust companies all deprived the general entrepreneur of his control over capital and thereby weakened his authority. The bankers institutionalized general entrepreneurial functions, and the representatives of banking houses took the independent financier's place of authority on boards of directors. The effect seems to have some similarity to that of the replacement of owner-managers by professionals. The investment bankers were interested in stability and "sound" financial practices which would tend to insure the servicing of bonds. They were often unwilling to agree to new investments requiring security issues unless these fitted in with the anticipated movements of the stock market or their general financial plans.

Some new industries, when they reached the point of needing large capital issues, were held back by the conservatism of institutionalized financial entrepreneurship. The automobile and moving picture industries offer illustrations. In automobiles, investment bankers refused to back W. C. Durant's original organization of General Motors. When this company finally secured banker aid in 1910 the conditions were onerous financially and involved effective banker control of the company during the lifetime of the loan. Under this system, for the next five years, General Motors sales increased less rapidly than those of the industry as a whole.[46] In motion pictures Fox and Loew's both encountered Wall Street indifference or hostility. In other words, the bankers represented conservative elements generally opposed to taking new types of risk, even though the latter might promise considerable economic gain if successful.

The deterring effect of tax and regulatory policies on entrepreneurial capital formation has been written about extensively. For instance, the relative failure of the railroads to improve their capital structure and equipment between 1910 and 1918 is blamed by competent scholars on the psychologically discouraging effect of overzealous regulation by the Interstate Commerce Commission. The failure to achieve any net private capital formation during the 1930's has frequently been blamed on the effect of New Deal regulations on entrepreneurial initiative.

The diversion of capital into enterprises lacking comparative advantage by tariffs and subsidies is another example of government "interference." Entrepreneurs would not have invested in new American merchant ships from 1936 on, save for large-scale government subsidy. Insofar as the economy had unemployed resources in this

[46] Ralph Epstein, *The Automobile Industry*, A. W. Shaw, 1928, p. 221.

period, such allocation of capital may have cost nothing, but in principle it produced facilities available more cheaply from foreign nations.

It seems likely that the direct effect of regulation is always adverse to entrepreneurial initiative, but rate-fixing, for example, may have an indirect stimulating effect on technological innovation. An ex-president of a telephone company remarked in conversation that AT&T had to depend on research and resulting improvements in order to make the profits necessary for dividends and expansion under a system of government-controlled rates.

Against this list of possible deterrents to active and intelligent entrepreneurial risk-taking arising from twentieth century conditions should be set some favorable factors: increasing public willingness to invest in stock exchange securities; the accumulation of large pools of small savings by banks and insurance companies; the employment of specialists, such as industrial engineers, economists, and accountants, who, aided by business periodicals and special reports, tended to produce more calculated and presumably more efficient investment policies; the persistence of small business; and direct government aids to, and tax incentives for, investment.

Increasing public familiarity with security investment arose from many sources. Urban middle and upper class income-receivers were getting a larger percentage of the total income as urban population became larger in relation to rural, and as entrepreneurial, managerial, and professional occupations increased. This group was, presumably, more likely to invest in securities than was the farm or small-town population. As business units grew larger, more were publicly financed and the securities of old, well-established companies offered reasonably safe investments. In addition, increasingly active security-selling by banks and brokerage houses from 1897 to 1929 and the government bond-selling campaigns of World War I undoubtedly swelled the ranks of security-holders. Hence, entrepreneurs could undertake large ventures with more assurance of adequate and economical financing.

In this connection it may be noted that as successful companies came to provide more of their working capital from profits or security issues, the demand for short-term, renewable loans began to fall, particularly in the major metropolitan areas. As a result, banker-entrepreneurs in the 1920's were forced to do more of their lending with securities as collateral, and to buy more securities for bank portfolios than in previous decades. This transferred much of the strain of the 1929-1933 decline from other enterprises to the banks themselves. Whereas short-term loans had in general been collectable, the banks were now left holding securities that in some cases declined to a fraction of their former value. However, the problems of banker entrepreneurship in the 1920's and 1930's have been so thoroughly discussed and investigated that nothing can be added here.

The accumulation of vast capital pools from insurance policy premiums and bank deposits went on rapidly from the 1890's, partly as a result of aggressive selling campaigns by insurance and banking entrepreneurs. The life insurance companies granted large areas to central agents, to be exploited on a commission basis. Banks fought for deposits by sending salesmen to call on the more substantial businessmen and by advertising extensively to attract small depositors.[47] Investment trusts also drew the savings of small investors into large pools. After World War II, pension funds became an important form of pooled savings, amounting by 1952 to over $2 billion a year.[48] In addition, corporate savings in the form of reserves against depreciation or depletion represented large blocks of capital available for investment.

Looked at broadly, the increasing emphasis on both personal and corporate financial security was putting the disposition of a large portion of savings into the hands of professional entrepreneurs. Unquestionably, these pooled resources offered an increasingly good market for securities regarded as safe investments. Between 1947 and 1951 about 40 per cent by value of the new security issues were sold privately to other companies. In the case of large corporate issuers and large buyers, investment bankers had no entrepreneurial role in the proceedings. But the bankers could still put small issuers in touch with small insurance companies and collect a "finders fee."

The entrepreneurs of commercial banks and insurance companies also took a direct part in allocating capital for long-run uses through

[47] For insurance see Shepard B. Clough, *A Century of American Life Insurance*, Columbia University Press, 1946, pp. 158-172 and 239-243; Marquis James, *The Metropolitan Life*, Viking, 1947, pp. 340-345; and Owen J. Stalson, *Marketing Life Insurance*, Harvard University Press, 1942, pp. 508-648. There is no adequate history of the entrepreneurial and marketing aspects of banking in the twentieth century. I have made certain studies for a large New York bank, which have some manuscript discussion of the pre-World War I operation of New York banking, but all of this material is treated as confidential.

[48] For more on these new forms of savings and investment see Donald L. Kemmerer, "The Marketing of Securities, 1930-1952," *Journal of Economic History*, Fall 1952, pp. 454-468.

term loans. To improve their languishing business in the middle 1930's, banks started lending funds to selected customers on a periodic amortization basis for as long as ten years. After World War II, bank terms were generally cut to five years, but insurance companies were often prepared to assume such a loan for ten years more. Through amendment of state laws, life insurance companies and trustees were permitted to invest limited amounts in equities. In this way insurance executives in the 1930's became entrepreneurs of housing development. At this same time the taking over of collateral forced banker-entrepreneurs, temporarily at least, into equity ownership.

As with most of the twentieth century changes discussed here, the effect of this minor revolution in financial practices on net capital formation seems ambiguous. A much larger proportion of total savings than ever before was automatically mobilized and put in the hands of entrepreneurs. Or conversely, the private investor had relatively less to say about the formation of capital. But the professional entrepreneurs who control the funds have to view them in general as reserves whose value must be protected rather than as capital that can properly be put into high-risk, high-profit enterprises. On this basis small businessmen claim to be largely prevented from drawing upon these corporate funds, while the local man of large income, with his savings cut by insurance, pensions, and taxes, cannot perform his historical role of risk-taking investor.

The spread of business information firms, expert consultants, and other special services, leading presumably to what Arthur H. Cole has called a more cognitive type of entrepreneurship, went on rapidly around the turn of the century. Companies set up legal departments, authorized shop procedure analyses, introduced cost accounting, and made more use of forecasting.[49] Insofar as these expedients increased the efficiency of production, they added to the value of already-invested capital, and thereby increased total capital. But the battle was far from one-sided. As studies of the relative efficiency of large and medium-sized business have indicated, some of these special services, at least, scarcely compensate for the problems in forecasting and operation introduced by the increasing size of companies.

Over the last 150 years management has been hard pressed to keep pace with the changes introduced by new technology. It does

[49] The Research Center in Entrepreneurial History at Harvard is studying the impact of Taylorism on American business.

not seem a foregone conclusion that the large-company entrepreneur of today, with a high percentage of specialized staff among his employees, is necessarily better able to cope with his particular environment than was the owner-manager of the early nineteenth century selling in local or regional markets. It is possible that the "revolution in transportation" and the rapid growth of a competitive national market outdistanced the devices of management in the mid-nineteenth century and produced a period of relatively poorly informed entrepreneurship for which this later flowering of special services offered a cure.[50]

The rise of large bureaucratic organizations in which decisions were made by professional administrators should not obscure the fact that a great part of the capital allocation in the economy has remained in the hands of small enterprisers. According to both the Commerce Department and Dun & Bradstreet's listings of firms, the number of enterprises has somewhat more than kept pace with United States population increase during the twentieth century.[51] Including the policy-making officials of large companies, therefore, the percentage of Americans engaged in entrepreneurial activity other than agriculture has substantially increased. Many of these smaller firms, to be sure, are not in a position to seek more of the market by reducing prices, although almost any of them may grow by offering better service. Many operate in specialized markets that do not encourage expansion through additional capital investment in that particular business. But in general it may be assumed that in this small-industry, -transportation, and -service area of the economy, many of the entrepreneurial culture patterns of the nineteenth century still persist.

There are also substantial regions of the United States that still are underdeveloped areas. Large parts of the South and Southwest have lacked the managerial and labor skills necessary to establish a broad pattern of industrialization. In West Texas, for example, entrepreneurs interested in investing in new types of industry often find the banks ready to finance only cattle, oil, crops, and a few other old lines of activity.[52] Furthermore, the federal tax law allowing a large deduction for depletion encourages further investment in oil,

[50] For criticism of the general inefficiency of iron and steel entrepreneurs in the 1870's see Andrew Carnegie, *Autobiography*, Doubleday, 1923, pp. 129 ff.

[51] Rudolph Jones, *The Relative Position of Small Business in the American Economy*, Catholic University of America Press, 1952, pp. 34-35.

[52] Based on interviews with selected Texas entrepreneurs, summer 1950.

and the price support program reinforces cultural leanings toward investment in agricultural land.

Therefore, while it may be affirmed that these underdeveloped areas foster a relatively high degree of entrepreneurial energy in capital allocation, this is expressed in specialized and limited ways. Both the Texas and southern California bankers and businessmen interviewed presumed that the general level of assessment of industrial risk and wise allocation of capital were highest in the old centers of the East and Middle West.

For these reasons, and because of the high stage of development of big companies in the older industrial areas, much of the new development of the resources of the Gulf Coast, the Rocky Mountain states, and even the Pacific Coast is being carried on by branches of established national concerns.

While in certain lines of business the entrepreneur may have his range of choice curtailed by bureaucratic or monopolistic arrangements, government has provided him with increasing facilities and safeguards for conducting his operations. Highway and bridge construction in conjunction with the motor vehicle have made major investments possible in new areas and have encouraged entrepreneurs to relocate plants.[53] Improved police and fire protection and more uniform state laws have all encouraged investment in new areas. Only in the twentieth century have some parts of the United States become sufficiently regulated to permit the easy conduct of business. There has been too little historical study of twentieth century business, and of the service group in particular, to estimate the stimulating effect of these factors on entrepreneurship.

Finally, the allocation of capital by entrepreneurs has been profoundly influenced since 1940 by government military policy. Entrepreneurs have been partially relieved of the necessity of deciding what forms new investment should take. The nineteenth century situation of obvious needs in excess of capital resources has been largely recreated. Under these circumstances it is difficult to estimate the role of the entrepreneur in capital formation under conditions of stabilized government demand and fewer shortages in productive resources.

7. *Conclusion*

A survey of the history of American capital formation, which prior to 1940 was directed to a large extent by the imagination of

[53] See K. William Kapp, *The Social Costs of Private Enterprise*, Harvard University Press, 1950.

entrepreneurs, supports the hypothesis that growth depended more on where and how capital was invested than on the absolute quantity of voluntary savings, that well-managed capital increased rapidly from the reinvestment of earnings. In good times entrepreneurs, largely through the mechanisms of banking, drew on credit in excess of savings—in fact, without much regard for the immediate level of domestic saving. Resulting inflations forced involuntary saving on those receiving fixed incomes.

A very large part of the capital goods created by these entrepreneurs had ultimate economic value, even though the original promoters may have failed to produce early profits. Capital invested in transportation paid enormous economic returns through the opening up of natural resources, which included coal in close proximity to iron ore. Similarly, investment in manufacturing brought ultimate profits because of cheap fuel and raw materials and the large home market made available by transportation. But if the resources in agricultural land or minerals had been less, the same quantity of initial capital and the same diligence in operation would not have produced the same end results or given the same incentives to further effort. Entrepreneurial activity is seen, therefore, as related to the utilization of resources, and to an initially low man-land ratio and a rapid increase in population.

The precise influence of the entrepreneur in this capital growth is as difficult to measure as is the influence of any single factor mentioned above. It seems probable that such social complexes cannot be broken down into measurable factors, and must, for the present at least, be treated as Gestalts. The whole process of which entrepreneurial energy was a part changed significantly over time. To men of the nineteenth century brought up in Western European traditions it was obvious that America needed transportation, and that transportation would eventually pay for itself. To say the same thing in general economic terms, there were valuable resources that could be exploited by the existing technology. The cost of railroads or canals over long distances was very high; for sixty years after 1830 there was this major industrial use for capital. Large additional sums were necessary to bring high-grade mines into effective production. With abundant materials, simple machines promised good returns from mass production. In this complex, rewards for individual success were high. All that was needed for rapid growth was for entrepreneurial imagination to proceed in the routine patterns of the culture.

The ending of what may very tentatively be called the early or pioneer stage of industrial economy and the rise of large corporate business units changed the character of the complex leading to growth. Judging by Kuznets' figures on the declining rate of net capital formation and by the increasing percentage of non-agricultural businessmen in the population, the change appears, up to 1940 at least, to have retarded activities leading to capital formation by entrepreneurs. The superseding of independent financiers (general entrepreneurs) by investment bankers, the rise of professional, salaried managers, the growing complexity of the industrial economy, and the increase of government taxation and controls all appear to have worked against imaginative risk-taking.

Some leading scholars of the subject have been led to the belief that private entrepreneurship is destroying itself by its own creations of bigness and planning.[54] Whether or not this view is correct, there seems no doubt that the entrepreneur of the mid-twentieth century operates in a different cultural setting and responds to different motivations than did his predecessor of 1850. Meanwhile, the large-scale entrance of the federal government as a user of capital equipment tends to obscure the underlying economic trends in entrepreneurial risk-taking or capital allocation and use. Under these circumstances, with the entrepreneur hemmed in by bureaucracy, complexity, and political action, it is hard to forecast his role in capital formation.

COMMENT

ALEXANDER GERSCHENKRON, Harvard University

I agree with much of what Hoselitz has said in his very interesting paper. It is primarily my need to conform to "role expectation" as a discussant that has caused me to put down on paper a few comments on points where some disagreement exists.

Hoselitz has attempted to place the treatment of entrepreneurship and capital formation in France and England against the background of the respective rates of economic development in the two countries. Although this is a fruitful approach, some critical remarks may be in order.

Hoselitz says that in the sixteenth century the two countries were

[54] See Joseph A. Schumpeter, *Capitalism, Socialism and Democracy*, Harper, 1942, and Fritz Redlich, "The Business Leader as a 'Daimonic' Figure, II," *American Journal of Economics and Sociology*, April 1953, pp. 289-299.

approximately equal with regard to productivity and technology, with France probably having a slight edge. We cannot be absolutely sure, but this seems a very plausible statement. Presumably, the rate of growth was faster in England during the sixteenth century, partly because of internal disturbances in France (as is generally recognized) and partly because of the greater backwardness of England at the beginning of the century (a fact less generally admitted). In this respect the penetration of German technological progress into English metallurgy and mining was of central relevance.

Furthermore, Hoselitz introduces a table which indicates that the rates of economic growth during the first half of the nineteenth century were much higher in England than in France. Even if expressing national income in constant 1913 prices raises frightening index number problems, it is perhaps plausible to assume that the main point the comparison is designed to convey is well taken. But why is Hoselitz concerned with the sixteenth century at all? This is not entirely clear to me. Is it because he asserts that the rate of growth in France has been lower than in England ever since the near equality in productivity levels in the sixteenth century? There is at least such a hint in the paper. But if we are allowed to play a little with the figures in his table, the result would seem to corroborate this writer's previously formed impressions, namely, that per capita income in England in 1800 may have been about 10 per cent higher than in France, but not much higher.

Hoselitz speaks at length of the terrible effects on France of the financial crisis of 1559; he places much emphasis on the devastating effect of the religious wars that followed that crisis; he cites in the same connection the dire effects of the price revolution and, in fine, of the expulsion of the Huguenots. I find it difficult to agree that the effects of the price revolution upon French economic development were as unmitigatedly unfavorable as Hoselitz makes them out to be. But this is beside the point. The point rather is that if there had been such "terrible economic devastation" in France as is described by Hoselitz (page 298), the closeness of the per capita levels of output in the two countries at the end of the eighteenth century is rather surprising. Moreover, if despite all the disabilities France succeeded in maintaining or nearly maintaining her position vis-à-vis England, the French economy must have done very well in the intervening period. And the proper question to ask should refer to the reasons for such an astonishing performance.

Hoselitz does not ask the question explicitly, but it seems that his reference to the industrialization policies of the mercantilistically oriented governments in France is designed to provide an answer to the tacit question, and the same answer is intended to serve as an explanation for the discrepancies in the rates of growth as between the two countries in the first half of the nineteenth century. In other words, the industrialization policies of the French government succeeded in keeping up the rate of growth till the end of the eighteenth century, but at the same time they prevented the emergence of a self-reliant entrepreneurial group interested in risk-taking and ready to commit itself to the policy of long-term investment in fixed capital.

This, of course, is a possible answer if one is willing to accept the particular sociology and reading of history implicit in it. The government performs wonders for industry by providing entrepreneurs with multifarious grants, interest-free loans, tax reductions, etc. But the result is the *rentier* psychology of the French entrepreneur. "This central role of the government doubtless enhanced the feeling of dependence on government service and government subsidies for new enterprises and contributed to the well-known aspiration to attain a *rentier* status, which was and still is so typical of the French middle class" (page 304). Is this not too sweeping? Not that it is necessarily incorrect. But I should want some more specific evidence as to the plausibility of that sequence.

Surely, the Russian state of the 1890's did a great deal to encourage entrepreneurial activities, and by devices that were not dissimilar from those used by the French government. But if one considers the very great changes that took place within the entrepreneurial classes between, say, 1885 and 1910, it is very difficult to argue that state aid had resulted in the destruction of entrepreneurial initiative. In fact, everything we know points in the opposite direction. It can be argued, of course, that the Russian state of 1885-1900 did not exercise any regimentation of production comparable to that of Colbertian or post-Colbertian France. This is true. But I still feel that Hoselitz's history, like his sociology, may be a little too sweeping. He says: "Although a certain amount of private initiative was evident, the role of the government always remained paramount, and even continued in influence after 1789, especially under Napoleon" (page 304). Surely, this is a patently inadequate description of France in the second half of the eighteenth century, when there was a great decline in the degree of economic regimentation and the economy seemed to grow at a fast clip.

Hoselitz is quite right in referring to Napoleon. But Napoleon was in many respects a return rather than a link in an unbroken chain. It is perfectly true, I think, that the policies during the Continental blockade created complex problems which the weak Restoration governments could not readily solve, and the commercial policies of the Bourbons were to some extent dictated by the legacy of the industrial hothouse inherited from the Napoleonic period. Still, much more important than that legacy were the political necessities of the Bourbons, that is, their need to find support within specific narrow groups. This need resulted in the toleration of the solidarity bloc and the imposition of a tariff policy which isolated France economically and accounted more than anything else for the relative economic stagnation in France in the first half of the nineteenth century. I believe at any rate that it is possible to explain that stagnation without much recourse to such deficiencies in entrepreneurial vigor as may have existed in France. But was France really lacking in entrepreneurial vigor?

How was the period of stagnation broken? By the appearance of a group of great entrepreneurs, many of them belonging to the Saint-Simonian group, as is so well described in Hoselitz's paper. But what caused the sudden appearance of those men? Hoselitz is not quite sure. He speaks of "a strange accident, or perhaps . . . the logic of historical necessity." I do not quite know what the latter means and I should have preferred to be led across Buridan's bridge more gently and more slowly. But I can see that it is difficult for Hoselitz to perceive in that event more than a strange accident. After having shown how government policies in France ruined the French entrepreneur and after having explained the low rate of growth before 1850 in terms of lack of entrepreneurial spirit, he was indeed entitled to expect that the last sparks of entrepreneurial strength had been successfully extinguished between 1815 and 1850. That the actual outcome was very different is certainly strange but only in the light of the somewhat unguarded generalizations that have been made earlier.

I feel it is much more natural to explain the change by reference to the liberalizing influence of Napoleonic policies, which broke up the solidarity bloc and created a climate within which entrepreneurial activity could successfully unfold and be applied to the great innovations of the period. Seen in this light, the appearance of the Saint-Simonian group is neither a strange accident nor the result of some iron law of historical development, but a rather natural consequence of the very nature of entrepreneurship. I doubt very much that a group which by definition constitutes an elite group, a group of uprooted men who have forsworn tradition and allegiance to the dominant value system of the community (Schumpeter), can be said to be lastingly influenced by extraneous unfavorable conditions. The Saint-Simonian episode shows that with particular clarity. It reveals the suddenness with which entrepreneurs appear and are ready for constructive action once a favorable conjuncture of circumstances has developed. Let me add that the history of Russian entrepreneurship after the emancipation of the peasantry seems to point to the same conclusions. There is, of course, no doubt that the entrepreneur provides a powerful dynamic force in economic development. But in attempts to construct models of economic development which deal with sudden initial spurts of economic growth, it is not at all paradoxical to say that just because the entrepreneurs are an active individualistic group composed of independent men, in a certain sense, they are likely to play the role of the dependent rather than the independent variable. (This, of course, does not mean that for other purposes and in other contexts it is not most profitable and illuminating to focus attention upon changes in entrepreneurial attitudes and behavior. Quite the contrary is true. It is, for instance, perfectly clear that changes with regard to standards of honesty and time horizons may be of the greatest possible importance for the understanding of the changing nature of economic development.)

Similarly, the role played by the banks in the industrial development of France is explicable much less by the scarcity of entrepreneurial talent than by the scarcity of capital under specific conditions of backwardness; that is to say, in conditions where capital-intensity of output has increased as compared with what it had been in an advanced country. It does make some difference whether the industrialization spurt occurs during the "textile age" or the "railroad age." In addition, in a backward country the very breadth of the industrialization effort calls for a much larger supply of capital than was the case with the more gradual development in the advanced country. I agree with the author that the banks in fact did perform entrepreneurial functions. But in general, with regard to the banks as in so many other respects, there is much similarity between the economic history of France and that of Germany. It is not obvious at all that there were significant basic differences with regard to the entrepreneurial element in the two economies. In particular, one might think of Hoselitz's statement that the French entrepreneur came to seek earlier and more assiduously than the British or the American entrepreneur the relatively safe shelter of monopoly (page 304). Surely, German entrepreneurs were at least as eager to enter into monopolistic compacts as their *confrères* in the West. And yet the fact remains that the Germany economy had been able to sustain a high rate of industrial growth while the magnificent initial effort in France, though not leading to stagnation at all, failed to produce an equal rate. In any attempt to explain the slow rate of growth in France comparisons with Germany present themselves almost inescapably. Once such comparisons are admitted, it is not too difficult to draw up a list of accelerating factors that existed in Germany but could not be found in France to any comparable extent, or, obversely, a list of retarding factors in France that did not exist in Germany. I doubt very much that differences in entrepreneurial behavior would deserve a high rank on such a list, and I doubt even more that such differences in entrepreneurial behavior as can be found are not fairly explicable as the result of other differences, more fundamental and much less volatile, between the two economies.

Just because I believe that the entrepreneurial approach to economic history has opened up new and profitable areas of research I am fearful of attempts to overstress the role of the entrepreneurial factor. It would be unfortunate if grave doubts were to be cast upon the validity of the approach because it has proved unable to support a weight of emphasis for which it was never designed.

Perhaps one final remark is in order. While the foregoing remarks suggest the existence of some disagreement between Hoselitz and myself, its extent should not be exaggerated. I feel that essentially it is a question of a different distribution of emphasis. I fully appreciate the fact that Hoselitz has written his paper within a framework given by an assigned topic which in itself has forced him to stress certain aspects of the development at the expense of others.

E. P. Reubens, The City College of New York

In his explanation of the differential growth of the British and French economies, Hoselitz lays great stress on the different degrees of economic intervention by the state in those two countries. He presents France as a case of nearly arrested development involving a paternalistic government and a persistently adolescent business class; while laissez-faire Britain is a picture of energetic, self-reliant entrepreneurs turning the economic wheels faster and faster.

The conclusions drawn from these facts seem rather dubious. There is much evidence that the contribution of the state to economic growth may frequently be positive and even essential, and that in any particular case the actual results depend very largely upon the form and direction of state action.

Japan is an example of state promotion of economic growth, along lines which appear to have been indispensable under then-existing conditions and which certainly were crowned with substantial success. The government pioneered industrial innovations, subsidized some private ventures in the earliest stages of a new industry (but only in high-cost industries of strategic importance were subsidies substantial and persistent), placed armament orders, provided social-overhead capital, curtailed consumption by taxation, promoted private saving and channeled that saving into industrial investment, secured capital from abroad at a time when both direct investments and private loans were virtually unobtainable, promoted and supervised industrial combinations, explored foreign markets, and so forth. Not only did this paternalism succeed, but the system actually was increasingly "privatized" as time went on (except in a few fields, such as railways and steel). The kind of action the Japanese government did *not* take was the primarily "protective" type: sustained high tariffs, long-run domestic monopolies, extensive subsidization. This is to say that the Japanese government avoided most of the devices whose main effect is to protect inefficiency or to raise prices without justification.

A somewhat similar record is revealed in the rise of modern Germany. Even in the New World we must recognize the important role of governments—especially state and local authorities—in providing social-overhead capital.

To explain Britain's rapid progress during the nineteenth century without much government participation in economic activities—i.e. at home, ignoring the vast colonial activities—more emphasis might be placed on her head start, backed up by her favorable situation in the circumstances of that era and stimulated by the profit inflations flowing from wars and monetary expansion. The growth of France, in contrast, seems to have been held back in considerable degree by the difficulties of following closely behind the leader without an equally favorable geographical and cultural environment, and also by a concern for preserving a broad agricultural sector in the economy as well as an excessive reliance upon various forms of protection for the new industrial sector.

Indeed, I would directly question Hoselitz's assumption that the existence of an active government tends to produce passivity among businessmen. In France it may have done so; but the causation may have run partly the other way: in the absence of an aggressive entrepreneurial class the French government more and more had to take over the functions of that class.

Under different circumstances the role of government may be equally vital without moving in the same direction. Both Germany and Japan indicate how an active, fostering governmental role is conducive to rapid growth and a gradually widening sphere for private business. Underdeveloped economies today, which appear to need the fostering role of the state to a greater degree than was usually the case in the past, face a choice not between state action or none, but rather between the constructive and obstructive lines of state action, in various degrees of collaboration with private enterprise.

Harold F. Williamson, Northwestern University

In setting out to answer the questions of how economic expansion was financed in an underdeveloped United States and who were the active agents in industrialization, Cochran has made a significant contribution to the field of economic history. The part played by American entrepreneurs in capital formation and economic growth has been discussed piecemeal in a wide variety of publications, but this represents a pioneer attempt to treat American economic development around this central theme.

As a generalization the author suggests that "The role of the entrepreneur . . . is shaped by a combination of factors involving personality types, cultural attitudes, technological knowledge, and available physical resources" (page 340). The interrelations of these four factors form the basis for his study of the role of American entrepreneurs in capital development.

There is no question that at the beginning of the colonial period the North American continent between the 25th and 49th parallels offered abundant opportunities for economic development. As a "backward area" vis-à-vis Western Europe the colonies had access to the accumulated technical knowledge of an advanced economy. While these characteristics were not to be found generally in other parts of the world, they were not unique and in themselves do not account for the remarkable economic expansion which followed. It was their combination with particular personality types and cultural attitudes that gave the American economy its distinguishing features.

In many respects the most interesting and significant part of the paper reveals how personality types and cultural attitudes favorable to active entrepreneurial participation in the economy emerged early in the colonial period. A background and training in Europe had prepared even the first colonizing adventurers to look for effective ways of exploiting the resources of the New World. A selective process which determined the types of individuals who migrated brought a high percentage of actual or potential entrepreneurs to the American colonies. Positions with the church, the government, or the military which carried high prestige in the mother country were largely absent from the colonial setting. The result was the development of a cultural environment that not only accepted but put a premium on "wealth-getting" as a means of acquiring social status. In such an environment the entrepreneur, in contrast with his position in many societies, was not considered a deviant personality. In other words, there was "built into" the American society a set of institutions or cultural values that accepted change as normal and rewarded the individuals who brought it about.

Given these conditions, the stage was set for the remarkable economic growth that followed. Cochran illustrates in some detail how extraordinarily ingenious successive generations of American businessmen were in expanding the supplies of capital funds by adapting old institutions or evolving new types. He calls attention in passing to several questions, as yet unanswered, regarding certain elements of the American scene that may have retarded capital accumulation. The concluding section deals with a number of recent changes in the environment that may have weakened the position of the entrepreneur in the economy.

The only serious omission in this otherwise excellent description and analysis of the motives for and methods employed in expanding capital funds has to do with the reinvestment of earnings by American business. It is true that the growth of railroads and public utilities in the nineteenth century required investment funds beyond the amounts that could be generated within individual concerns, and that the growth of corporations in these fields began to change the role of the entrepreneurs by the introduction of professional managers and large groups of stockholders who had little, if any, influence on management policies. It would be a mistake, however, to become too preoccupied with this segment of the economy. In the fields of manufacturing, distribution, and marketing (not to mention agriculture) the family-owned or closely held company was predominant throughout the greater part of our history. The nature and circumstance that prompted the great majority of these organizations to meet their capital requirements out of earnings should receive careful attention, not only for historical reasons but also because much the same psychology seems to influence investment decisions in these fields even when stock ownership is widely distributed and professional management is introduced.

As a matter of practical necessity Cochran confined his attention largely to an analysis of the forces that affected the supply of capital. In terms of economic growth, however, the question of the efficient allocation of capital funds is of considerable significance. By raising the questions regarding the effect on the supply of capital of maladjustments between the demand for and supply of labor, sectional and local rivalries, and the lack of security associated with certain types of investments and particular regions, the author gives evidence of imperfections in the organization of the capital markets. But this topic should be developed further. More needs to be known about the extent to which mobility of capital was affected by ignorance and by barriers that were deliberately introduced. For example, was the secrecy that surrounded business operations down to recent times a factor that led to a large amount of reinvestment in firms when capital might have been more productive elsewhere? How much were banks influenced in their lending operations by tradition which made it difficult for different types of business to secure accommodation? Answers to these and similar inquiries would give a better understanding of how effectively capital funds were allocated historically in the American economy.

These comments do not detract from the fact that insofar as the economic historian fulfills his function as "handmaiden" to the economic theorist by presenting a careful and accurate account of the evolution of a particular set of institutions, Cochran has discharged his obligations in a highly competent fashion. But if the purpose of this conference is to contribute to theoretical generalizations about capital formation, it is pertinent to ask what conclusions may be drawn at this level from his paper. Why, for example, was he assigned a topic which carries the implication, in its title at least, that the entrepreneur was important in American capital formation?

Perhaps the key to any broad conclusion that may be drawn from the paper lies in the generalization advanced regarding the factors that combine to affect the role of the entrepreneur. It may be assumed from the examination of the American experience that there are four "necessary" (but not sufficient, each by itself) conditions if entrepreneurs are to play an active role in capital formation and economic growth. These are the "right kind" of personality types, the right kind of cultural attitudes, technological knowledge, and access to physical resources, all of which were coexistent in the American scene from early in the colonial period.

The very juxtaposition of these factors makes it difficult, however, to evaluate the role of the entrepreneur in American development. To the extent that the social environment imposed few obstacles to change, his role was much less significant than if resistance had been strong. In fact, given this kind of an environment, it would not be important to study the entrepreneur except as an agent in the mechanism that resulted in change. The opposite point of view would assume that the entrepreneur was a positive force, constantly struggling to introduce new production functions and attempting to modify institutions in the face of inertia or active opposition. He would thus assume the key role in bringing about economic development.

To pose the problem in this fashion comes dangerously close to asking whether the social environment creates the entrepreneurs or the entrepreneurs create the social environment. The purpose is not to push the argument to such extremes. It is rather to call attention to the importance of determining the relative independence and dependence of each of these two factors in economic growth. A satisfactory answer would go a long way toward establishing a basis for an acceptable theory of capital formation and economic development.

LELAND H. JENKS, Wellesley College

It is significant, I think, that both Hoselitz's and Cochran's papers have a good deal more to say about entrepreneurs and their social milieus than about capital formation. There is a good deal in Cochran's about factors affecting capital *allocation*, but that is not necessarily the same thing as capital formation. This emphasis may be inherent in the entrepreneurial approach to long-run economic changes. As I see it, the greatest common factor unifying such an inquiry is the assumption that a general theory of society—specifically, some sort of sociology of change—is necessary to account for economic development. The economic data alone do not enable us to understand how people can respond differently to identical stimuli. Accordingly, "entrepreneurship" symbolizes a good deal more than the actions of one or more businessmen. It symbolizes an undetermined range of considerations—largely outside the purview of static models—which also impinge on the decisions of businessmen, including their decisions to be businessmen.

Cochran explicitly assumes a Schumpeterian entrepreneur who introduces innovations in the production function, which involve (in Schumpeter's words) "a non-negligible outlay of capital." The essential function of entrepreneurship, then, is capital allocation along lines involving novelty (hence also "uncertainty"?). But I think that Cochran should make clear that this sort of operation does not *determine* unambiguously either the direction or the amount of economic change for a given society. It should be pointed out frankly to a group interested in measurement that in terms of an entrepreneurial approach there is nothing remotely resembling equivalence between inputs and outputs. For the economy as a whole, for instance, innovation may emerge as capital-saving. Thus our explanatory schemes must not be thought of, even surreptitiously, as introducing a principle of conservation of effort; neither should they be criticized or apologized for as falling short of such a standard in their demonstrations.

Doubtless I was supposed to make reference to capital migration. In Cochran's paper British capital figures as a means employed by financial entrepreneurs in the United States to enable them to carry forward new enterprises. At least in this context a restricted meaning for capital is used—something like monetary capital or purchasing power.

I am not so sure of Hoselitz's position. As a matter of fact, he virtually ignores these same railroad bonds and their counterparts in fifty other countries in speaking of *British* growth. Hoselitz defines economic growth in terms of national income and seeks in entrepreneurship an explanation of the fact that Great Britain has outrun France. Now we know that in the generation before World War I—to go no further—a substantial part of British investment income was derived from such things as American railroad bonds, rubber plantations in Malaya, and so on. (There had been prior capital allocation to these countries, by financial, commercial, or industrial entrepreneurs, or all three, almost always resident in Great Britain.) There was simply nothing comparable in the case of France. The dimensions of this overseas activity were such that it cannot be regarded as irrelevant to any measure of British economic growth, but especially not to national income.

We might ask, Without her overseas economic empire would Britain have run ahead of France? So stated, an answer would have to be speculative. What we can be sure of is that only analytically, not historically, can British economic growth in the nineteenth century be limited to the British Isles. Even if we were to include what has been passed over (for of course Hoselitz is not ignorant of these matters), we could still look for differences between France and Great Britain in entrepreneurship. But the factors which Hoselitz stresses so heavily to account for French backwardness—government patronage and powerful financial sponsorship—are elements which have also been conspicuous in British enterprise overseas. It is curious that Hoselitz notes capital migration when he is talking about France and the British who helped start things there, but omits it in discussing British economic growth.

One could move on from here to comment on a strain of nostalgia in both papers, and their marked ambivalence as to the consequences of bigness. But this is enough to suggest that we are still a long way in this entrepreneurial approach from being sure that some of our statements will not be as true if we turn them upside down.

I must say that I concur wholly with Cochran's suggestion that we think of entrepreneurship as part of a process which itself undergoes change in time, and with his further suggestion that "growth depended more on where and how capital was invested than on the absolute quantity of voluntary savings . . ." (page 372).

Reply by Bert F. Hoselitz

I wish to express my appreciation for the very penetrating critical comments by Gerschenkron, Reubens, and Jenks. In part they place emphasis on points insufficiently underlined or entirely omitted in my paper, and in part they direct attention to portions of the argument which need to be sharpened or further elaborated. Above all, I must thank Gerschenkron for having supplied a number of facts which were badly neglected in my paper. I want to support fully his emphasis on the noticeable decline in economic regimentation during the last few decades of the *ancien régime*; on the fact that Napoleon's policies, and even those of the Directoire, represent a return to much earlier practice; on the constraints imposed on the Restoration government due to its political weakness; and on the strong impetus given to French economic development through the liberalizing tendencies of the government of Napoleon III.

The most rapid advances in French industrial history were probably made in the last halves of the eighteenth and nineteenth centuries, periods in which liberal tendencies were relatively strongest in France. But even in these periods French growth rates do not seem to have reached those of Britain in its best decades. Although "the scarcity of capital under specific conditions of backwardness" (another factor stressed by Gerschenkron) can be made accountable for this failure, France did engage in large-scale financing of foreign governments and enterprises at a time when—measured by British standards—considerable expansion of the domestic capital plant would have been possible. Even if great weight can be attributed to the factors mentioned by Gerschenkron, there is need to explain why repeated relapses into relative stagnation occurred in France and why a sustained period of growth commensurate with that in Britain, Germany, or the United States is absent.[1]

[1] There is only one factual point raised by Gerschenkron with which I cannot agree, and that is the difference in per capita incomes in England and France at the end of the eighteenth century. I believe England's superiority to have been substantially greater than 10 per cent. In support of this view I cite three pieces of evidence: (1) Colin Clark (*The Conditions of Economic Progress*, 2nd ed., London, Macmillan, 1951, pp. 71 and 80) computed British and French annual incomes per head of working population and expressed them in International Units. For the first decade of the nineteenth century he obtains an annual income per worker of 566 to 584 I.U. in Britain and of 248 I.U. in France. (2) Arthur Young, who was an acute and experienced observer, declared that in France "those who lived on agricultural labor, and they were the greatest number, were 76 per cent as well off as in England" (cited in Eugène Gaudemet, *L'abbé Galiani et la question du commerce des blés à la fin du règne de Louis XV*, Paris, Arthur Rousseau, 1899, p. 75). (3) If we convert Henry Beeke's estimate (*Observations on the Product of the Income Tax*, etc., London, J. Wright, 1800, pp. 126 and 136) of approximately £170 million into francs, we obtain (at the rate of 21 francs per pound) an English national income in 1798/1799 equal to approximately 3,570 million francs, whereas, in 1800, French national income was estimated at 5,402 million francs (cited in *Income and Wealth, Series III*, Milton Gilbert, editor, Cambridge, Eng., Bowes & Bowes for International Association for Research in Income and Wealth, 1953, p. 53). With a population in England of approximately 9.5 million and a population in France of about 27 million, these figures yield an average income of 375 francs in England and of 200 francs in France.

In addition to rectifying the factual historical record, Gerschenkron also touches upon a fundamental sociological problem, the place of the factor of entrepreneurship in a historical explanation of economic processes. It is extremely tempting to engage in a full-scale examination of this question, but its magnitude would require a full-length paper, at least. Nevertheless, because of its central importance, and because some of Jenks' and Reubens' remarks deal with this problem, I shall explain the sociological assumptions on which my paper is based. Gerschenkron expresses the view that entrepreneurs are likely to play the role of the dependent rather than the independent variable in attempts to construct models of economic development (page 376). I fully agree with this viewpoint, and I believe that close reading of my paper will reveal that it was written with this conception in mind. At the end of the introductory section I point to the influence exerted by legal and political institutions on entrepreneurial activity. In discussing the development of entrepreneurship in Britain, I stress the nature of the internal political balance in seventeenth century England, the fact that certain important developments affecting capital mobilization and technical guidance of new enterprises became possible because these enterprises developed on the periphery. Again, I show how the openness of the social structure in Britain was a determining factor in entrepreneurship and how later, through the influence of rich returns from overseas investment and the accumulation of large amounts of capital, the original vigor of British entrepreneurs appears to have subsided.

If I understand my critics correctly, the problems at issue are essentially two: (1) Granted that entrepreneurship is a dependent variable, what is the precise nature of its relation to other variables that exert an influence on the pace of development? and (2) What influence do various forms of government control and guidance of industry exert on the number, independence, and self-assertiveness of entrepreneurs?

I shall take up the second point first. Although some views on this, as well as on the first question, are implicit in my paper, I did not intend to provide a full answer for either. Above all, I did not intend to compare the relative efficacy of government action and action by private individuals in achieving a high level of economic development. What I did mean to show was how certain forms of government regulation tend to retard rather than further economic growth in an institutional environment in which primary reliance for the guidance of investment is placed on private entrepreneurs. The examples of Russian, Japanese, and German experience, therefore, do not disprove my contention but point to the need of distinguishing between types of government intervention which impede the development of private enterprise, which do not impede it, and which are neutral. Let us consider, for example, the case of Imperial Germany, which is cited by Gerschenkron and Reubens as an example in contradiction of my general viewpoint.

Our appraisal of the influence which the German government exerted on German industry may be somewhat colored by our interpretation of the over-all character of its politics. There is no doubt that of all modern capitalist governments the German, and before it the Prussian, were the most authoritarian and the most paternalistic in relation to the individual citizen. On the surface this would lead one to assume that the German government also exerted the strongest regulatory influence on industry. But I believe that this was by no means the case. There is no necessary connection between absolutism in the exercise of political power and full-scale government control of economic affairs. The governments of Prussia and pre-1914 Germany were, on the whole, rather liberal in economic affairs and, so far as I can see, interfered little to prevent the full development and aggressive assertion of private entrepreneurship. The German government tried, of course, to carry out an economic policy. Bismarck even passed labor and social insurance laws which were regarded as anathema by the more doctrinaire liberals of the time. But there is a vast difference between a set of economic policies which merely determine the external framework within which private entrepreneurial action is possible and the more direct intervention in industrialization processes which was characteristic of pre-revolutionary France. Unlike the latter, the German government supplied rules for the game but did not take the cards away from the players in order to deal its own hand.

There are still other factors in the socio-economic picture of pre-1914 Germany which exerted an influence on entrepreneurial action, chief among them the somewhat ambiguous social position of businessmen between a landholding but largely impoverished aristocracy and a professional lower-middle class with status aspirations far beyond its economic importance. It would lead us too far astray to discuss these factors in detail. But the fact that their presence in Germany cannot be disputed makes me wonder whether analogous variables may not be discernible in Russia and Japan.[2]

The problem of the precise nature of the relation between the variable "entrepreneurship" and other variables which exert an influence on the pace and direction of economic growth seems to be central to Gerschenkron's remarks. He thinks that I overstressed the role of the entrepreneurial factor and underemphasized other factors. In particular he cites the example of pre-1914 Germany and the emergence of the Saint-Simonian entrepreneurs around the middle of the nineteenth century in France.

Gerschenkron and I are agreed that this emergence constitutes a break with the past. The main issue is the explanation of the sudden appearance of these men. Gerschenkron finds my explanation inadequate. His criticism, however, attributes a view to me which I do not hold. He says that I was "entitled to expect that the last sparks of entrepreneurial strength had been successfully extinguished between 1815 and 1850" (page 376), and that, on the basis of this assumption, the emergence of the Saint-Simonians was indeed a "strange accident." Apparently, I expressed myself so clumsily that even as acute and well-informed a reader as Gerschenkron could be misled. I did not say, nor did I imply, that entrepreneurship was killed under Napoleon I and his Bourbon successors. In particular, I believe that it could be shown that in the field of financial talent there was an unbroken line from Jacques Coeur and the moneymen of the Lyons exchange in the sixteenth century, via the more eminent tax-farmers and men like Law and Necker, to the bankers of the "old school," and finally to the brothers Pereire. And I referred to "historical necessity" because I felt that the new impetus in the 1850's came from the money side rather than from industry, and that this was quite in the line of French entrepreneurial traditions and in profound contrast to those of Britain.

But in order to supply a fuller explanation of the problem, of which the Saint-Simonian episode is merely an example, and in order to purge myself of Gerschenkron's complaint that the sociological theory underlying my exposition is too simple, I wish to add a few remarks on two socio-psychological generalizations, which should,

[2] This fact also makes me suspect that the "privatization" of the Japanese economy did not proceed so smoothly or, indeed, so far as Reubens claims. I base this opinion too on a recently published paper by Marion J. Levy, Jr., "Contrasting Factors in the Modernization of China and Japan," *Economic Development and Cultural Change*, October 1953, pp. 161-197.

perhaps, have been stated explicitly in my paper in order to avoid misunderstandings. I will state them rather categorically since a full discussion of these complex relations would lead far beyond the space at my disposal. Some further elucidation of these thoughts may be found in my paper on "Entrepreneurship and Economic Growth."[3]

The first proposition is that it is probably incorrect to speak of entrepreneurship as a homogeneous phenomenon. One must distinguish different forms of entrepreneurship depending upon the general institutional environment—notably, the degree of governmental guidance of and interference in the economy—and upon the nature of the business in which entrepreneurs are engaged. I believe that an important difference exists between industrial entrepreneurs, on the one hand, and financial and commercial entrepreneurs, on the other. The differences between the groups of entrepreneurs is due mainly to three factors, two of which have general applicability and the third of which has special relevance for Western European countries. The first is that, *ceteris paribus*, investment in industry is riskier than investment in finance or trade, since the invested capital turns over more slowly and is more specifically tied to supplying a particular market. Second, the industrial entrepreneur, at least in the early stages of industrialization, must possess not only talent for business but often also technological knowledge and skills and a greater genius for leading men in a joint task than a merchant or financier. And finally, in the countries of Western Europe entrepreneurship in trade and finance has much deeper roots and longer-lasting traditions than that in industry. This means that the social position of financiers and merchants is less ambiguous than that of industrialists, that time-honored codes exist for the one group which are absent for the other, and that entrepreneurs in finance and commerce can build upon acquired privileges which only slowly were extended to, and sometimes even had to be fought for by, industrialists.

On the basis of these reflections I think that Britain, in which independent industrial entrepreneurship developed earlier and throughout played a more forceful role, shows a more profound social-structural change away from medieval antecedents than France. In part this was probably due to the greater weakness of entrepreneurial institutions in medieval Britain than in France. But whatever the reasons, the victory of modern capitalism was more

[3] *American Journal of Economics and Sociology*, October 1952, pp. 97-110.

complete in Britain than in France, which continued until late in the nineteenth century to show features in its economic ideology which are reminiscent of a precapitalist system of values. An important aspect of this difference appears to me to be the more aggressive entrepreneurial spirit in Britain and with it the more successful exploitation of economic possibilities as they became available with the progress of science and technology.

In this paper, as well as at various places in my original essay, I have made reference to traditions in entrepreneurial behavior and norms. My second general proposition relates to this problem: Among the variables affecting entrepreneurial activity, past entrepreneurial performance and traditions of entrepreneurship occupy an important place. Though the proposition may sound tautological in this formulation, its full implication becomes clear if we consider its corollary: Since rigorous norms of entrepreneurial action often develop in a country with long traditions of entrepreneurship, any reorientation of entrepreneurial behavior must overcome not merely external obstacles (e.g. scarcity of capital, absence of a regular, disciplined industrial labor force, etc.) but also those intrinsic obstacles which may be imposed by the existing traditions among enterprisers. In order for new forms of entrepreneurial attitudes to develop, an overwhelming challenge must exist which the old forms are unable to meet. Industrial entrepreneurship, as distinct from entrepreneurship in trade and finance, demanded such new attitudes, and hence only rarely attained full-scale development. In fact, outside the Anglo-Saxon countries and possibly those regions of the Continent which came under the lasting influence of Calvinism or other dissenting Protestant sects, vigorous, independent industrial entrepreneurship hardly developed.

The relationship between Protestantism and the development of the "spirit of capitalism" was, of course, first explained by Max Weber. As is well known, a long controversy ensued in which some of Weber's opponents repeatedly emphasized the capitalist spirit and behavior of medieval merchants, notably in the cities of northern Italy. I believe that some of the disputes over points in Weber's thesis result from his failure to draw a sharp distinction between mercantile and financial capitalism, on the one hand, and industrial capitalism, on the other. If we make this distinction—and we should make it, simply because medieval commercial and financial "capitalism" encountered limitations in its growth potentialities which only modern industrialization overcame successfully—the importance of the Calvinist ethic appears to have been not in having created a "spirit of capitalism" as such, but rather in having contributed to its generalization among all classes and in having altered profoundly, in this manner, existing traditions and norms of entrepreneurial behavior. This process went furthest in Britain, Holland, and the countries colonized by British and Dutch settlers. It was much less conspicuous in France, and the persecution and final expulsion of the Huguenots were measures which enhanced the rigidities and relative "backwardness" of entrepreneurial thinking and action in France.

In the course of French economic development there were, of course, a number of turning points in which the old entrepreneurial traditions could have been broken and replaced by new ones. One such turning point was the beginning of the rule of Napoleon III. Another was the conclusion of the religious wars in the reign of Henry IV. At that time the hegemony of the financiers was reinforced; the industrialists were clearly pushed into the back seat, and, as if to impress upon them their political and social impotence, they were taken under the tutelage of the government. I began my account with the religious wars and their outcome because it appeared to me that the system created by Laffemas and Sully and their contemporaries constitutes an important factor influencing the traditions of French entrepreneurship.

This, then, in a sketchy and perhaps overly abbreviated form, is my "sociology," if it deserves that name. I thought that I could omit any extended discussion of this problem in my paper because I did not consider it my task to write an economic history of Britain and France within which the factor of entrepreneurship had to be "explained" and placed "into its proper perspective." I preferred to discuss, instead, the relationship between the forms of entrepreneurship actually realized in each country and the general impact of entrepreneurship on capital formation and economic growth.

For this reason I believe also that I need not discuss in detail the alternative explanation for the different growth rates of Britain and France tentatively suggested by Reubens. But I do wish to say that his interpretation appears to be impossible to prove and is stated in such general terms as to be of little use as an explanation. He says that Britain had a head start, that this head start was "stimulated by the profit inflations flowing from wars and monetary expansion," that France seems to have been "held back . . . by the difficulties of following closely behind the leader without an equally favorable geographical and cultural environment. . . ." But what matters, above all, is to explain why Britain had a head start, or rather why she got to the top in the course of the seventeenth and eighteenth centuries. I believe that the differences in entrepreneurship go a long way toward such an explanation. Moreover, France experienced a profit inflation from wars and monetary expansion, just as did Britain. And I can see no reason why France's following closely behind Britain should be a special handicap. It is significant, however, that as time went on, France fell more and more behind and in the nineteenth century was overtaken by Germany and the United States. Finally, I agree with Reubens that the geographical and cultural environments were of great importance in the slowness of France's development, especially the latter. But by drawing attention to these factors we have not really explained the difference in growth rates. In discussing entrepreneurship I have selected an aspect—and, as I believe, an important aspect—of the "cultural environment" and have attempted to trace its form and impact through the decisive periods of the economic development of the two countries.

PART IV

THE INFLUENCE OF ENTERPRISE AND BUSINESS ORGANIZATION IN UNDERDEVELOPED COUNTRIES

INVESTMENT DECISIONS IN UNDERDEVELOPED COUNTRIES

HENRY G. AUBREY
FEDERAL RESERVE BANK OF NEW YORK

1. *Introduction*

> "Just as peoples' outlook may affect their economy, so the nature of their economy influences their outlook."—*Report on Cuba,* Johns Hopkins Press for International Bank for Reconstruction and Development, 1951.

SCOPE OF THE STUDY

This paper is chiefly concerned with the economic, organizational, and institutional determinants of investment decisions in underdeveloped countries. Although the social and cultural determinants are discussed by another contributor, it will not be possible to maintain this distinction. To do so might even appear, at first sight, undesirable to those who favor a unified approach to problems of economic development. A sense of past neglect seems to impel economists to give, at present, more weight to "noneconomic" factors. This tendency, however laudable and indeed inevitable, threatens to lead to disregard of the economist's own field of investigation. Factors of undisputed importance, like the presence of traditional preferences or the absence of change-producing tendencies, are too easily accepted by the economist as noneconomic data, perhaps to be integrated into the economic system as somewhat shapeless propensities, difficult to define and still harder to measure. Having conveniently transferred the issue to the other social sciences, the economist is tempted to leave a basic question unasked or insufficiently answered: Are there economic determinants of such apparently noneconomic motivations?

Not infrequently, this issue is further obscured by a tendency to identify noneconomic with irrational motivation, whereby the impatient or zealous observer interprets as "irrationality" the subject's inability or unwillingness to undertake what is unquestionably deemed to be in his best interest in the long run. Transferred to

The author is an economist in the Research Department of the Federal Reserve Bank of New York. The views he expresses are his own and are not offered as representing in any way those of the Bank.

the field of economic preferences, this attitude—of the observer, not the observed!—induces another hazard, that of regarding as irrational those decisions and actions which are not considered socially desirable from a predetermined policy aim such as that of rapid or balanced economic development.[1] It would appear more appropriate to analyze the disincentives opposing the socially desirable action. It may then develop that there are distinct economic and institutional reasons for such decisions and actions. Other social sciences can fruitfully investigate the social and cultural continuity which characterizes the persistence of attitudes no longer deemed compatible with economic progress. The economist, however, can isolate, diagnose, and analyze the economic phenomena which induce expectations and, hence, "rational" actions favorable or inimical to economic development.

In focusing on investment, this study cannot escape an assumption which keeps close to the traditional concept of economic rationality: that of pecuniary motivation.[2] It is thus assumed that investment is not, or not primarily, undertaken for the enhancement of social status, for example, but for the purpose of acquiring assets apt to increase in value or to produce output whose sale is expected to result in assets exceeding the value of the original investment. A potentially controversial example will illustrate the point. The acquisition of real estate is often considered as evidence of sentimental attachment to land or of feudal patterns of unproductive investment. This explanation may be perfectly correct in some instances; in others, however, such "investment" may result from preferences well founded in the expectation of profit or, conversely, of security against a danger of depreciation that might face other forms of asset-holding.

This paper, therefore, starts from the assumption that a potential investor is willing to acquire other assets rather than hold idle hoards or cash balances. Each investment decision, however, still presupposes a choice of alternatives and, hence, a weighing of risks against security, of expected profits against potential losses. Assuming a desire for gain, a sizable range of investments of varying attractiveness usually exists: short-term or long-term, speculative or "solid," unproductive or productive. This relative attractiveness is the center of interest of this paper, which makes no claim of break-

[1] Cf. John H. Adler, "The Fiscal and Monetary Implementation of Development Programs," *American Economic Review*, May 1952, p. 592.

[2] Cf. Moses Abramovitz, "Economics of Growth," in *A Survey of Contemporary Economics*, B. F. Haley, editor, Irwin, 1952, Vol. II, p. 158.

ing new ground. An attempt is made, however, to present the scope of expectations and their factual background in underdeveloped countries in a more analytical and concentrated manner than that offered by the numerous country surveys and reports. Before proceeding in this direction, it appears proper to point to some topics of contemporary discussions which have a bearing on our handling of the problems of entrepreneurship in underdeveloped countries.

CHARACTERISTICS OF ENTERPRISE

The process of perceiving opportunities, evaluating them, and choosing between alternatives requires a number of qualities and attitudes which are subsumed in the concept of enterprise: intelligence and open-mindedness in discerning opportunities and appraising their various future possibilities; also perseverance in accepting sizable disutilities in the form of work and trouble in the execution of plans. In fact, the preliminary job of evaluation presupposes a series of steps rather than a single act of appraisal: forming judgments regarding the future course of yet-unexplored events, weighing the necessary adjustments to such a course, and devising and executing plans of adjustment.[3] While these steps require qualities which may be latent in a smaller or larger number of individuals, it may be well to recognize the importance of a suitable basis for the individual's confidence in his own judgment and his ability to carry out his plans. Past experience would seem to be the most favorable basis for such confidence. It may not be essential for this experience to be rooted in the individual's own past or to have been gained in precisely the same field of endeavor. If we talk of a "tradition" of entrepreneurship, its chief effective ingredient appears to be the degree of confidence provided by the subjective feeling of doing something that is new but not entirely so. It seems clear, without further elaboration at this point, that such a basis of subjective experience, or such easily accessible background for reference, is largely missing in early stages of development.[4] The gradual formation of such a framework of experience in the course of development may also help explain the emergence of native entrepreneurship within relatively short periods of time in

[3] Cf. *ibid.*, p. 157, and Frank H. Knight, *Risk, Uncertainty and Profit*, Houghton Mifflin, 1921, pp. 241 ff.

[4] Cf. H. W. Singer, "Obstacles to Economic Development," *Social Research*, Spring 1953, p. 23.

countries where it had been conspicuously scarce for long periods of the past.[5]

This stress on limited and gradual innovation appears to conflict with the more heroic concept usually associated with the name of Schumpeter. His prototype of the entrepreneur is a man who perceives new methods of production which deviate deliberately from the pattern of past performance. History provides relatively few examples of such sharp breaks in contrast to the frequent, perhaps "normal," case of novel features superimposed on familiar technology.[6] The degree of technological discontinuity has, however, some bearing on the extent of entrepreneurship which backward areas require for their economic development; in this context the discussion concerned is of interest to the present paper.

THE ROLE OF ENTERPRISE IN UNDERDEVELOPED COUNTRIES

At least two recent writers[7] have pointed out with great acumen that underdeveloped countries are not representative of a "Schumpeterian world." Their entrepreneurs are not original innovators because they obtain their technology ready-made from the industrial countries.[8] This process of adaptation would seem to rank lower in inventiveness than original innovation, but some comfort could be derived from the fact that the attribute of creativenesss is occasionally applied to this process, too.[9] Our present interest in this discussion lies in two different directions. A lesser degree of initiative is needed to apply existing technical knowledge than to initiate complete innovation; moreover, the process of developing a new technology and nursing it from the drawing board to commercial success is not only frustrating and time-consuming, but extremely costly. It requires capital and skills, both scarce in backward areas. Hence the "adaptive" type of enterprise ought to arise more easily in

[5] E.g. in Mexico in the past twenty-five years.

[6] Cf. Abramovitz, *op. cit.*, p. 142.

[7] Henry C. Wallich, "Some Notes towards a Theory of Derived Development," paper presented at the third meeting of Central Bank Technicians, Havana, 1952, mimeographed; and Singer, *op. cit.*

[8] Some implications of this fact will be discussed in section 3 of this paper. Cf. also Singer, *op. cit.*, pp. 24 ff.

[9] Cf. Fritz Redlich, "The Business Leader in Theory and Reality," *American Journal of Economics and Sociology*, April 1949, p. 226. He also coins the terms "creative capitalist" and "creative manager" for people responsible for new ways in their respective fields. The difference between passive acceptance of and active response to external stimulation is stressed by J. A. Schumpeter in "Creative Response in Economic History," *Journal of Economic History*, Supplement, 1947.

early stages of development than the more strictly Schumpeterian kind, however defined. In our context, then, the "adaptive" entrepreneur's task is finding and applying the most suitable known techniques; more will be said about this in the section devoted to the choice of technology.

The entrepreneurial activities required to start a new industrial enterprise in an underdeveloped country are not restricted to the choice of technology; different qualities are needed than those implied in the concept of an innovator who only once combines the factors of production in a new manner and at lesser cost. A "successful" entrepreneur under conditions of scarcity of entrepreneurship may turn out to be a man who does not permanently stay with the enterprise—a kind of professional promoter who withdraws when the new business is under way and starts another to which he applies his capital and both profits and experience acquired in his preceding promotional activities. This type of entrepreneur scouts for new opportunities, investigates them, and evaluates their potentialities. He has to define the nature of the product; assess the supply of materials, the scope of the market, and the proper organization to cover it; then decide on the size of the plant and the type of technology. Last mentioned, but often first in consideration, are schemes for financing, the distribution of risk, and remuneration for promotional services.[10]

Such professional promotion achieved considerable importance in the Indian system of managing agencies, which promoted some of India's most important industries. In their case the entrepreneurial function was somewhat institutionalized. Scarce private initiative may be supplemented by semipublic pioneering, in the form of development agencies or corporations not necessarily implying permanent public management. This tends to occur whenever the ability to conceive investment projects, plan them, and put them into operation becomes a more limiting factor than lack of capital. This is, indeed, the rule rather than the exception in those underdeveloped countries which have not yet developed that background of entrepreneurial experience mentioned above.

The purpose of drawing attention to the promoter type of enterprise in contrast to the owner-manager type with its permanent character was to emphasize a less publicized type of entrepreneurship. This may, incidentally, help to lay the ghost of the "Schum-

[10] A. A. I. El-Gritly, "The Structure of Modern Industry in Egypt," *L'Egypte Contemporaine*, November-December 1947, p. 377.

peterian entrepreneur," which still haunts discussions of contemporary enterprise under conditions far removed from the original theoretical model. This statement, however, should not be interpreted to mean that the "Western" type of entrepreneurship has no place in underdeveloped countries. It exists in many forms, in persons ranging from owners of humble shops to industrial tycoons like Francesco Matarazzo in Brazil, who started out with a small store in the interior and built an industrial empire comprising 286 separate enterprises.[11] Like most socio-economic phenomena, entrepreneurship is too complex to be cast into a single type or pattern.

CRITERIA FOR INVESTMENT PREFERENCES

Up to this point this paper has adopted the customary implicit assumption that entrepreneurship can be treated like a scarce commodity indispensable for economic development. Perhaps it should be regarded as a human catalyst which transforms, by the process called investment, potentially available resources into additions to the stock of national capital. A mere change of ownership of a piece of real estate, to give an example, could not be considered investment in this aggregative sense. In the mind of the potential investor, however, such acquisition of existing assets presents a real alternative competing with the type of investment which will eventually increase the output of goods and services. A study of investment choice cannot ignore such a realistic alternative on the ground that it cannot be considered "investment" in the aggregative sense. True, much depends on the use the seller of the asset makes of the proceeds of this sale; it is, however, evident that a continuous chain of such "unproductive" investments is not a negligible phenomenon but frequently presents a very potent distraction from the kind of investment that may be favorable to economic growth.

A conceptual restriction is revealed by the frequently used term "unproductive investment." Never clearly defined, it seems to refer sometimes to the creation of assets which will not directly increase productive capacity or average national productivity. At other times, the term appears to involve some kind of judgment about balanced development. The building of luxury housing is a favorite target of criticism for this school of thinking while the construction of housing per se is accepted as essential; in other words, this type of

[11] George Wythe, *Industry in Latin America*, 2nd ed., Columbia University Press, 1949, p. 163, and George Wythe, Royce A. Wight, and Harold M. Midkiff, *Brazil, an Expanding Economy*, Twentieth Century Fund, 1949, p. 177.

"unproductive investment" would seem to provide an opportunity for luxury consumption in whose absence, presumably, both the investment in question and the future unconsumed surpluses would be used in a better manner—that is, one which furthers development.

This kind of thinking implies a welfare judgment which does not conform to the profit-oriented investment criteria of the investing individual. Hence, some "unproductive" or "speculative" investment may be entirely logical and desirable for the individual investor while appearing undesirable from the standpoint of a policy aiming at rapid development of the economy as a whole; moreover, the time preference of the entrepreneur, being oriented toward profit, may differ from the socially determined time schedule of output increases of specific goods and services.[12] It is thus natural that critical attention is given to situations which favor a shift from investments of high social benefit to those of high private benefit, such as the diversion of investment into real estate or inventory accumulation induced by inflationary tendencies.[13] Conversely, policy discussions dwell on incentives, assistance, or controls by which governments may induce or compel a more "desirable" direction for investment.

For the purpose of this paper, however, a different course is adopted. Since we are concerned with the determinants of the entrepreneur's investment decision, we must attempt to view them from his point of view, assessing the subjective and objective factors that motivate his action in underdeveloped areas. Then only—and this paper does not claim to move more than a step in this direction—can we hope to assess objectively the relative strengths of forces which oppose or favor "desirable" types of investment. In referring to subjective factors first, no a priori judgment regarding rank of importance is intended. No matter how tangible the objective criteria, such as factor supply or size of demand, appear, the investment decision will be based on the perception of opportunities which, while pointing to the future, exist only in the present in the investor's mind. The process of evaluation which precedes decision and action is, essentially, one of sifting impressions, of matching observable factors with anticipated alternatives—in short, of assimilating events into the structure of expectations.[14] It therefore seems natural to

[12] Cf. Adler, *op. cit.*, p. 592.

[13] Cf. E. M. Bernstein and I. G. Patel, "Inflation in Relation to Economic Development," *Staff Papers*, International Monetary Fund, November 1952, p. 383.

[14] G. L. S. Shackle, *Expectations in Economics*, London, Cambridge University Press, 1949, pp. 70 and 75.

discuss first the place of expectations and their direction under conditions prevailing in underdeveloped areas—to place commensurate emphasis on uncertainty as a negative factor in investment decisions and to point to the entrepreneur's background as one element affecting this uncertainty. Then we shall consider the basic alternatives which are the objects of the investment decisions. And finally, the objective determinants of the investment decision will be discussed: conditions of entry; size of the market; availability of capital, labor, and skills; and costs, prices, and profits. Factual examples from underdeveloped countries will be used as much as possible to illustrate the points set out in a general fashion.

2. *Expectations and the Choice of Investments in Underdeveloped Countries*

INVESTMENT DECISION AND UNCERTAINTY

Any investment decision involves a weighing of profits and risks attending, or believed to attend, various alternatives of investment in the future. Leaving risk estimates aside for the time being, the evaluation of profit can be made the point of departure for our deliberations.

Since profits are the difference between prices and costs, the level and future course of both of the latter will have to be estimated. The expected volume of sales will enter into an estimate of gross revenue, both volume and prices depending on the size of the market, type and intensity of competition, customs protection, etc. Prime unit costs of materials and wages will have to be assessed, appraisals of the latter depending on estimates of productivity; these presuppose alternative hypotheses regarding technology and size of plant which are also influenced by the size of the expected market and the availability and cost of finance. All of these factors tie in with assumptions about both the internal and the marketing organization of the firm, assumptions which in turn determine overhead costs and affect profits, considering once more the volume of sales. These factors will be discussed in later chapters, but this list—which is far from exhaustive—will serve to illustrate the variety of interlocking considerations which can be ignored only at the investor's peril. It is one of the main propositions of this paper that an awareness of this peril, however dim it may be in any individual investor's mind, is one of the greatest obstacles to positive investment decisions.

In industrially advanced countries the basis for estimating the factors enumerated above is infinitely wider and the requisite skill more generally available. A "Schumpeterian entrepreneur" need not worry about the market because he will, by definition, produce his goods at lower cost and find an outlet for them by underselling others. The "imitator" among entrepreneurs has, as a rule, some direct knowledge of the product and its markets; otherwise, expert information and advice can be obtained at reasonable hire from individuals familiar with the trade or from experts in market analysis. Such outside technical advice is available to the little fellow, while larger firms can also draw on their own technical or research staffs.

In underdeveloped countries the situation is very different. Experts for exploratory investigation are rarely available locally; foreign experts are costly and their advice is not always suited to different conditions. Often the lack of or deficiencies in statistics make estimates of consumption and markets, of costs and capital requirements, very difficult if not totally impossible. Worse yet, since many preliminary services which come ready-made in industrial countries are absent, the initial capital outlay is increased and a risk of running short or "making do" with regard to skills, parts, and sometimes even power and transportation is incurred. Planning deficiencies, caused by lack of means to carry out the required scrutiny of new ventures, appear as an almost inevitable danger. Some of the factual country reports picture this situation.[15] The lack of economic and technical research facilities is sorely felt in underdeveloped countries and keeps even basic knowledge of opportunities from maturing. Government research is frequently recommended as a remedy, but it cannot alone build the bridge between an idea and its execution since ideas rarely arise where there is a vacuum with respect to knowledge or experience. It does not come as a surprise to hear from Indian observers that industrialists rarely base their estimates on scientific calculation. As a substitute, they tend to take as a model another firm they consider profitable and approximate its organization with regard to size of plant, equipment, etc. If no such comparison is available, the characteristics tend to be set in an arbitrary manner without proper consideration of cost.[16]

[15] E.g. El-Gritly, *op. cit.*, p. 377; *The Economic Development of Guatemala*, Johns Hopkins Press for International Bank for Reconstruction and Development, 1951, p. 97; and *The Economic Development of Iraq*, Johns Hopkins Press for International Bank for Reconstruction and Development, 1952, p. 40.

[16] D. R. Samant and M. A. Mulky, *Organization and Finance of Industries in India*, London, Longmans, 1937, p. 91.

It should be evident without further argument that the establishment of a new industrial enterprise in an underdeveloped country is fraught with great uncertainty, greater by far than that involved in the same kind of undertaking in a more advanced country. The greater the novelty of the enterprise in any one country, the slimmer the base of reference and experience in nearly all respects. The facts of such uncertainty will hardly be disputed; but is it possible to establish its degree and to discount it so as to leave sufficient incentive for a positive investment decision without depending entirely on a spirit of venture akin to that of the gambler? The theory of expectations seems to promise an answer to this question, and it appears desirable to investigate its relevance for our problem.

UNCERTAINTY AND PROBABILITY

Uncertainty is not identical with absence of knowledge. In practical contexts knowledge of some aspects may be combined with ignorance of others; it may be preferable to consider degrees of knowledge rather than its presence or absence.[17] Knowledge of future events is, of course, impossible and has to be replaced by a procedure of anticipation which consists of several elements: an expectation schedule of magnitudes assigned to each contingency or possibility for each future date, a probability weight for each such magnitude expressing the likelihood or range of probability that the anticipated contingency will actually occur, the degree of subjective confidence in the individual's ability to predict or to assign objective probability ranges to the several contingencies.[18]

Uncertainty is responsible for the lack of any unique future magnitude. Instead, there is a set of possible magnitudes of which one may be recognized as the most probable; the definiteness of this probable magnitude depends on the probability distribution and the width of the range which expresses this degree of uncertainty. After eliminating extreme values which lack high probability ranks, a practical range may be expected to emerge.[19]

Assuming for argument's sake that the above procedure of estimation can be carried out, how large can the expected practical range

[17] Knight, *op. cit.*, p. 199.

[18] *Ibid.*, pp. 236 ff.; Albert G. Hart, "Anticipations, Uncertainty and Dynamic Planning," *Studies in Business Administration*, University of Chicago Press, 1940, Vol. XI, No. 1, p. 52; and Sidney Weintraub, *Price Theory*, Pitman, 1949, p. 345.

[19] Oscar Lange, *Price Flexibility and Employment*, Cowles Commission, Monograph No. 8, 1945, pp. 29 ff.

be in underdeveloped countries? Where the base of experience is narrow, can any extreme values be assigned such low probability ranks as to eliminate them from practical consideration? Perhaps no outcome within a range from extreme success to complete failure is so improbable that it can be dismissed altogether; it would certainly be dangerous to apply to *unexplored* situations a belief that extreme values carry less probability weight, a notion than can be derived only from *known* frequency distributions. It seems reasonable to assume that the practical range of probability distribution would be very large in underdeveloped countries, commensurate with the prevailing lack of knowledge and the resulting degree of uncertainty.[20]

In any event, magnitudes in different future periods lack comparability unless they can be reduced to present values. According to theory, this may be achieved by discounting the future values by a factor equal to the difference between the most probable value actually expected and the equivalent value expected with certainty; this difference represents an uncertainty allowance or risk premium.[21] Obviously, uncertainty is also related to time and will be the greater the more distant the future event; the risk premium increases accordingly and may become so large that it would discount present values to a point too low to be acceptable. Planning beyond this limit, which Tinbergen called the "economic horizon," is no longer possible.[22]

Any critique of these theories need not rest on the manifest difficulty of carrying out such calculations in practice; this is a common shortcoming of economic theory. However, a difficulty of a different kind afflicts the concept of contingency or possibility which is implicitly based on the knowledge that similar occurrences have happened before under strictly comparable conditions. Applied to investment decisions, it is thus essential to ascertain the uniqueness or homogeneity of similar cases.[23] This brings us back to the factual base of reference and of experience, which is, almost by definition, extremely slim in underdeveloped countries. A new industry in a partly explored environment comes as close to "uniqueness" as any innovation in a world where few things are entirely new.

A related argument carries rather more weight. Is it possible to square the concept of probability distribution with a businessman's

[20] See also Shackle, *op. cit.*, p. 61.

[21] Cf. Lange, *op. cit.*, p. 32, and Weintraub, *op. cit.*, p. 345.

[22] Lange, *op. cit.*, p. 32.

[23] Cf. Knight, *op. cit.*, p. 247.

thinking about his potential future profits?[24] Is the probability approach, based on a precise concept of frequency distribution, its shape and skewness, really applicable to decisions which lack the requisite wide actuarial base? The basic concept of probability involves the idea of a large number of repeatable tests by which ranks are assigned to various possibilities, thus substituting actuarial risk for knowledge. There may be some entrepreneurial decisions of a routine character which are repeated frequently enough to provide a basis of experience. Investment decisions are not of that nature. As a rule, there are only a few of them in a lifetime, often just one. Comparable experiences of others are still limited in underdeveloped countries. No such decision is repeatable in the strict sense of the probability concept. Probability reckoning, as set forth by Hart and Lange, thus cannot be relied upon to facilitate investment decisions. Instead of "large numbers turning ignorance into knowledge," we are faced with a kind of uncertainty that is another form of ignorance.[25]

THE MOTIVATION OF "TRADITIONAL" INVESTMENT PREFERENCES

Having acknowledged the prevalence of uncertainty and the difficulty of reducing its impact in underdeveloped countries, it is now possible to visualize its effect on the choice of investment. The chief considerations would seem to be *degrees of risk*, i.e. the dangers of losses in various pursuits, and, conversely, the *chances of profits*. In both directions it will be well to distinguish between the objective base of experience in underdeveloped countries and the expectations to which it gives rise; whether these latter are called "traditional" or, as is sometimes the case, "irrational" is frequently determined by the observer's approach rather than by objective criteria.

Theory's contribution to the problem of investment choice is limited. Cases of complete aversion to risk will not concern us here, since willingness to assume risks is basic for enterprise. The degree of caution, however, may be related to the time dimension of the venture and the size of the investment relative to all assets owned by the individual. An element of diminishing utility may be responsible for lesser satisfaction from a larger average income with wider fluctuations over a long time than from a smaller average in-

[24] Moses Abramovitz, *An Approach to a Price Theory for a Changing Economy*, Columbia University Press, 1939, p. 77.

[25] Shackle, *op. cit.*, pp. 6 ff. and 115 ff.

come with smaller fluctuations. In terms of expectations, then, the choice would be between plans offering higher but less certain expectations of profit and plans promising lower but more certain profits. Moreover, the caution factor will probably become larger as the involvement increases. In other words, the estimated utility of potential additional profits becomes smaller as profits increase and, conversely, the estimated disutility of additional losses becomes larger as losses grow. Furthermore, a certain asymmetry may arise from time lags in assimilating new experiences into the base of experience; a new venture takes a long time to "prove itself" while an early failure is easily assimilated into an existing background of distrust toward new types of venture.[26]

Turning to the practical aspects of the problems discussed, there are three basic sets of reasons why industrial investment may not be undertaken: (1) Lack of knowledge or experience is responsible for inability to recognize opportunities, for failure to plan with sufficient accuracy, or for fear of not being able to execute plans properly. (2) Inherent uncertainties, partly related to lack of experience, cause the investor to consider industrial investment as more risky than other alternatives. (3) The chances of profit are less, or are deemed to be less, than in alternative investments.

The lack of experience and knowledge has been discussed and need hardly be documented further. More should be said, however, about the effects of awareness of risk. Industrial enterprise is inherently of a long-term nature, while the preference for short-term ventures in underdeveloped countries is notorious. This preference can be linked with considerations of security and profit.

Dealing first with *security* as related to stability, the volatility of the political atmosphere in many countries makes it imperative that investors understand that a change in regime is often not restricted to the political scene; such a change may involve shifts in administrative personnel and policies, which may affect commercial operations through means ranging from placing of government orders to tax practice, economic controls, monetary policy, and development plans. A short-term rhythm of operations makes it easier to adapt to new situations and, especially, in the present context, to avoid unforeseeable dangers. An industrial enterprise cannot be adapted so easily or quickly. It lacks the security that lies in liquidity and flexibility.

[26] Hart, *op. cit.*, p. 72; Abramovitz, *An Approach to a Price Theory for a Changing Economy*, as cited, p. 81; and Shackle, *op. cit.*, p. 75.

While fear of political instability implies fear of risks which cannot be foreseen concretely, other pessimistic expectations are based on ample experience.[27] The risk of devaluation may serve as an example of widespread factual significance. If the value of money declines year after year, distrust as to its future value favors investment which prevents loss. Hence, real estate becomes a favorite object of investment; this preference creates at the same time a highly active market, which confers greater liquidity on real estate than on other assets. This type of investment thus offers two elements of security: stability in real terms, and liquidity, a hedge against devaluation and also against unexpected contingencies. At the same time, it offers opportunities for quick and substantial profits. The conditions here described can be observed in a number of countries; they are mentioned most prominently in relation to Chile and Brazil.[28]

Another cause of instability, less frequently mentioned, is related to the economic structure of many underdeveloped countries and therefore is very serious. Countries depending on the export of a few primary products for a large part of their national income have, in the past, experienced vehement swings of an exogenous nature whose effects they could not control. They cut so deeply into income and consumption that they are, in many countries, the major factor responsible for prosperity or depression. Clearly, long-term planning in the shadow of such contingencies is both difficult and risky. Capacity of the plant and size of the investment are placed at the mercy of unforeseeable events. Short-term investment offers a better chance to "get out from under," with liquidity and flexibility again being the controlling factors.

In addition to such cyclical fluctuations, the seasonal cycle of such products causes chronic economic insecurity in some countries. In Cuba nearly the entire economy is geared to the rhythm of sugar production. Shortly after the season, which lasts only two to four months, economic activity tapers off. Such seasonal instability makes industrial production very difficult and planning for it still harder.

[27] It could be said that the former type is due to uncertainty, the latter to risk, in the sense in which Knight uses these terms; in Marschak's interpretation of Knight's terms "risk" is the known parameter of frequency distribution and "uncertainty" is lack of knowledge of this parameter. Cf. Jacob Marschak, "Lack of Confidence," *Social Research*, February 1941.

[28] Cf. *Report of the United Nations Mission to Chile 1949-1950*, United Nations, 1951, p. 3; *Report of the Joint Brazil-U.S. Technical Commission*, Dept. of State, June 1949, p. 151; and Bernstein and Patel, *op. cit., passim.*

Superimposed on this instability is the anxiety about the price of sugar, in which most persons in the economy have a direct or indirect stake, creating a kind of "boom mentality" conditioned by short-term fluctuations. Such a climate is most unfavorable to long-term ventures and favors activities where the turnover is quick and the profit high.[29]

Considerations of security affect not only the entrepreneur himself but the institutions or individuals to whom he may have to look for additional capital and credit. Banks will withhold credit if they consider the risk too high to be covered by normal interest charges; this, too, will be judged not by absolute standards but in relation to opportunities for lending funds for alternative investments. Lenders' risk is also determined by a desire to avoid such complications as litigation and foreclosure, which appear more likely in connection with untried ventures. In an unstable economy even "bankable" collateral is apt to become illiquid; banks prefer, therefore, to lend to trusted clients of old standing, and, unhappily, the innovators are less likely to be found among these members of the traditional commercial group.[30]

Before the discussion of risk and security is concluded, reference should be made to the belief that risk is gradually becoming less problematic to business because business is steadily working at reducing risks by auxiliary services, market research, and other devices.[31] Nothing could better illustrate the gulf between a developed country like the United States and an underdeveloped country, where, indeed, the absence of these facilities is one of the greatest obstacles to entrepreneurial initiative.

There are, of course, degrees of risk-taking in underdeveloped countries, too. Entrepreneurs entering existing trades find a stock of experience on which to draw, or they may be guided by reference to similar industries. It is being said that the cotton industry in India was not treading unknown paths because the raw materials and markets were at hand and the industry copied the jute industry.[32] Almost everywhere, however, industrial enterprise encounters a

[29] Cf. *Report on Cuba*, Johns Hopkins Press for International Bank for Reconstruction and Development, 1951, pp. 47 ff., 525 ff., and *passim*. A highly interesting analysis of the structure and course of the Cuban economy is provided by Henry C. Wallich, *Monetary Problems of an Export Economy*, Harvard University Press, 1950.

[30] Cf. *Report on Cuba*, as cited, p. 573.

[31] Arthur H. Cole, *Change and the Entrepreneur*, Research Center in Entrepreneurial History, 1949, p. 106.

[32] Samant and Mulky, *op. cit.*, p. 2.

powerful disincentive in the existence of other pursuits. Real estate investment, which is considered more secure and liquid than long-term industrial investment, requires less time and specialized knowledge for management of such investment and offers an opportunity for members of other professions to participate. Businessmen find inventory investment an attractive alternative to expansion of their own, or to investment in another, business. Inventories, too, are liquid and can be used as collateral for credit; their price is bound to rise in inflationary situations, when the supply of imports is likely to diminish as a result of balance of payment difficulties.[33]

Real estate and inventory speculation and short-term commercial transactions, as well as the policy of commercial banks favoring such transactions, are the greatest traditional deterrents to industrial enterprise in underdeveloped countries. In descriptions of this situation, we note sometimes a trace of righteous indignation that "solid" investment is not preferred to "speculation," with its connotation of levity. A reason for this attitude is that instability itself induces a gambling spirit when the economy is controlled by short-term fluctuations.[34] We have also seen that short-term transactions appear safer and more liquid than long-term ventures. Perhaps the best explanation of speculative preference for short-term transactions is found in the fact that "gambling" may actually appear safer than "solid" long-term investment, precisely because it is traditional and widespread. Moreover, a wide basis of reference and experience is the best antidote against fear or generally pessimistic expectations. The professional gambler could, if he cared, actually determine probability on the basis of actuarial risk. He has entered the market many times and has found that errors in judgment cancel out, to some extent, and leave a predictable return. The industrial investor lacks this kind of experience because he starts that particular industry only once.[35] Moreover, in inflationary situations created by development spending under conditions of inelastic supply, any expectation of price rises appears actually built into the economy. No wonder, then, that nearly all arguments of security militate *quite "rationally"* against long-term industrial investment and in favor of those traditional pursuits which the puritan mind places lowest on the scale of desirability.

From the point of view of security, *profit* expectations tend in the same directions as investment choice. Short-term transactions of the

[33] Bernstein and Patel, *op. cit.*, pp. 383 ff.

[34] *Report on Cuba,* as cited, pp. 58 ff.

[35] Knight, *op. cit.*, p. 247.

types described appear not only safer but often more profitable. There is a factual basis for this belief. One of the oldest pursuits, moneylending, is widespread and lucrative. Statistics are usually lacking, but there is evidence that rates run from 18 to 60 per cent per annum and often much higher. Estimates of yield in inventory speculation run up to 70 per cent in not unusual or strongly inflationary situations. Clearly, industrial enterprises need to expect much higher returns than the rates considered satisfactory in industrial countries if they are to compete for capital with such profitable alternatives.[36]

Although statistics of profits[37] in industries of underdeveloped countries are not plentiful, there is some evidence of high industrial profits. Dividends declared by the mills managed by five leading managing agencies in India averaged 24 to 100 per cent of share capital annually from 1914 to 1928 and 8.5 to 83 per cent from 1928 to 1932.[38] According to more recent figures from Chile, those for 1943, average profits of 222 industrial stock companies were 21 per cent of capital or 16 per cent of capital and reserves.[39] In Brazil 256 companies in the state of São Paulo had a median rate of profit to invested capital of 34.4 per cent in 1942. Among this group one-third had net profits of over 50 per cent and 25 companies had profits of over 100 per cent. In 1946, 222 firms in the same state showed an average profit of 19 per cent on capital plus surplus and in 1947 an average profit of 15.4 per cent. These average figures conceal large variations, from 4.4 to 30.9 per cent in 1946 and from 8.4 to 46.5 per cent in 1947. The 286 enterprises of the Matarazzo group showed profits of 90 per cent of paid-up capital and a chemical firm 123 per cent in 1946-1947.[40]

These scattered pieces of evidence can be interpreted to mean

[36] Cf., e.g., *The Economic Development of Nicaragua*, Johns Hopkins Press for International Bank for Reconstruction and Development, 1953, p. 10; *The Economic Development of Ceylon*, Johns Hopkins Press for International Bank for Reconstruction and Development, 1953, p. 515; and *The Economic Development of Iraq*, as cited, p. 278. Many other country sources report similar or higher figures.

[37] The available data refer often to dividends declared. Additions to reserves, an important item where undistributed profits are a prominent instrument of finance, are thus not covered.

[38] P. S. Lokanathan, *Industrial Organization in India*, London, G. Allen, 1935, pp. 291 ff.

[39] Wythe, *op. cit.*, p. 225. Figures of profits, not dividends, may be calculated with an eye on taxation.

[40] Wythe, Wight, and Midkiff, *op. cit.*, pp. 176 ff. It should be realized that profits in Brazil are subject to a risk premium for devaluation. The cost of

that there is a base of high profit expectations in industries and that only such industries as give promise of great yield are actually started, although the outcome, as may be expected, does not always justify the high hopes. In many instances industrial profits do not run so high that traditional forms of investment would not be expected to offer continued powerful competition in underdeveloped countries.

It would be interesting to find out what the expectations of profit and security were in comparable stages of industrialization in countries now far more advanced. It was not possible to undertake such specialized research for the purpose of this paper, but a few items of information relating to the early American cotton industry can be recorded. Offhand, it does not seem unreasonable to believe that a large increase of productivity which lowered costs so rapidly would have made for high profit expectations among the "imitators" who followed the pioneers. A very early report sets at 30 per cent the annual profit in making jeans from flax and cotton, spun on jennies;[41] it will be noted that this experience precedes the major innovations of the Industrial Revolution.

Profit expectations are reported to have been high in the early part of the nineteenth century because the Rhode Island spinners of cotton yarn, under the powerful leadership of Almy and Brown, the "pioneers" of the industry, kept the price steady while that of cotton dropped under the impact of the embargo. The experienced firms warned of accumulating stocks but the newcomers kept coming. Oddly, they survived, because new markets were opening under the influence of the embargo.[42] Uncertainty about the size of markets is relieved by manifest opportunities offered by wars and embargoes;[43] World Wars I and II were also powerful stimulants in underdeveloped countries.

With the founding of the Boston Manufacturing Co. in Lowell in 1813, the era of the modern, large-scale cotton industry in the United States began. This company paid its first dividend of 12.5 per cent in 1817 and paid 8 to 13 per cent semiannually thereafter;

living more than doubled between 1939 and 1946. Cf. Henry W. Spiegel, *The Brazilian Economy*, Blakiston, 1949, p. 98.

[41] J. Leander Bishop, *A History of American Manufactures from 1608 to 1860*, E. Young, 1868, Vol. I, pp. 407 ff.

[42] Caroline F. Ware, *The Early New England Cotton Manufacture*, Houghton Mifflin, 1931, p. 47.

[43] For other examples see Henry G. Aubrey, "Deliberate Industrialization," *Social Research*, June 1949, pp. 180 ff.

the sum of dividends paid between 1817 and 1822 was 104.5 per cent, presumably. In addition, there were accumulated reserves from plowed-back profits. In later years the dividends were less generous but averaged 9 per cent for large companies. Dividends of the Lowell companies were 6 to 11 per cent in 1830 and 18 to 24 per cent in 1831, and new capital for the cotton industry was easy to get. A contemporary letter to one of the companies read: "The rumor of your profits will make people delirious."[44] We would not expect to find similarly sanguine statements about profit expectations in the industries of underdeveloped countries today.

THE ORIGIN OF INDUSTRIAL ENTERPRISE IN UNDERDEVELOPED AREAS

The object of investment preference and the degree of industrial enterprise, then, are largely determined, in economic terms, by expectations of security and of profitability. The question now arises, To what extent are these expectations shaped by the individual's background in distinct national or occupational groups? It may be surmised that a man's experience and specialized skill will affect his outlook and trade preferences; moreover, the strength of his initiative may well be influenced by the degree of economic security which he has.

It has been said that early industrial entrepreneurs in Europe, as distinguished from the managers and moneylenders, were men with mechanical rather than financial skills; a climate favoring orientation in the direction of productivity and creative integration is, hence, considered essential for the successful industrial entrepreneur.[45] The question may well be asked whether this applies to the "imitators" among the entrepreneurs as much as to the relatively small number of "innovators" who led the field. Conversely, it is being said that profits, especially of the inflationary type, are not productively reinvested by plantation-owners, peasants, or speculators;[46] but all available evidence points to the prevalence of so many former traders among industrial entrepreneurs in many underdeveloped countries that the outlook on time preferences and profits must still reflect their "trading complex" even in the industrial

[44] Quoted in Ware, *op. cit.*, pp. 66-156.

[45] Bert F. Hoselitz, "Entrepreneurship and Economic Growth," *American Journal of Economics and Sociology*, October 1952, pp. 106 ff.

[46] "Some Financial Aspects of Development Programmes in Asian Countries," *Economic Bulletin for Asia and the Far East*, United Nations, January-June 1952, p. 9.

field.[47] A glance at the origin of indigenous industrial enterprise in India, the Middle East, and Latin America will bear this out.[48]

The managing agency system in India originated in British trading companies which expanded into market-related industries. Indian traders followed in their footsteps; merchants in Bombay who had made money in trade were pioneers in the textile industry, as had previously occurred in Lancashire. It is perhaps significant that the first successful cotton mill was established by a Parsi. A few wealthy merchants' communities, such as Parsis and Bhatias, were now prominent in industry.[49] It may, however, be premature to conclude from this fact that cultural characteristics are the prime determinant of such an attitude. Parsis and the Hindu merchant caste of Marwaris have different religious and social backgrounds. What they have in common is wealth and business experience acquired in related pursuits. The first is important as a source of capital and of credit; the second provides a major incentive unavailable to the uninitiated: these people had their market ready-made for them by their past trading activities.

Similarly, cotton merchants in Egypt invested some of their profits first in ginning and pressing cotton, later in spinning and weaving it. Industrial promotion was not always limited to closely related trades. Profits from the soft-drink and wine trades went into cigarette manufacturing and monopoly profits from the alcohol industry went into paper-making—examples of the self-propagating power of industrial enterprise. Initiative was also provided by retired British officials who remained in the country and went into business with local interests. A depression in agricultural prices and the proven profitability of industry under protection eased a transfer from investment preferences for land. The Bank Misr, under government auspices, introduced the middle class to security investment. Other promoters came from politics and the civil service.[50]

This experience is, in part, borne out in other countries of the Middle East. The first initiative, capital, and ability were usually provided by merchants and financiers, rarely by landlords or by craftsmen. An important characteristic element also entered the picture: immigrants from other countries. In Greece a number of

[47] *The Economy of Turkey*, Johns Hopkins Press for International Bank for Reconstruction and Development, 1951, p. 160.

[48] Foreign investment is not discussed in this context though its importance as a stimulant is fully recognized.

[49] Lokanathan, *op. cit.*, pp. 15 and 22.

[50] El-Gritly, *op. cit.*, pp. 374 ff.

refugees from Asia Minor established small industries after World War I. In Egypt, Syrians, Armenians, Jews, Greeks, and other Europeans played an initial role, with Egyptians later taking over as the most prominent group. In Turkey the expulsion of the Armenians and Greeks, traditional trading groups, was probably responsible for the lack of initiative, which had to be provided by strong government action. In Lebanon, Christian traders and returning emigrants were the source of industrial enterprise, while in Syria the Moslem traders were in the lead and the Christians turned to the professions. There is only one landlord among Syrian industrialists, hardly any in Iran.[51]

The importance of foreign immigrants for Latin American industry was, and still is, considerable. Lebanese and Syrians, starting as merchants and importers, today own about 500 large industrial enterprises in Brazil.[52] Itinerant traders, *mascates*, of Italian, later of Syrian, origin started small stores in the interior, progressing to stores in large cities and finally to industries. Syrian initiative is responsible for much of the textile industry in Brazil and Colombia.[53] An Argentinian syndicate which, in addition to manufacturing matches and explosives and establishing a bank, recently acquired exclusive rights for erecting a tin smelter in Bolivia is headed by a textile manufacturer of Syrian extraction.[54] Another instance of such "foreign investment" in Latin American countries is provided by a rayon-weaving plant established in Colombia by the Brazilian Matarazzo interests. The story of Matarazzo himself, referred to earlier in this paper, is an illustration of an immigrant's success in developing an industrial empire by expanding from one trade into lines related to it.[55]

The activities of Spanish and French investors in Mexico are another example of foreign investment's becoming national in character by virtue of the investor's settlement in the new country. The *Barcelonetas* of French origin contributed much to Mexican industrialization of the last quarter of the nineteenth century, and there are records of French families of earlier immigration periods who are still prominent in the country. Their path usually progressed

[51] Charles Issawi, "The Entrepreneur Class in the Middle East," paper in the volume for the Conference on the Near East, Social Science Research Council, October 1952, to be published by Cornell University Press in 1955. I am grateful to Mr. Issawi for making this paper and other material available to me, and for much other stimulation.

[52] *Ibid.*

[53] Wythe, *op. cit.*, pp. 164 and 271.

[54] *New York Times*, December 7, 1952, p. 36.

[55] Wythe, *op. cit.*, pp. 163 and 271.

from retail trade to wholesale trade, importing, and finally manufacturing. The Spanish were prominent in the cotton textile industry, contributing, in 1930, 26 per cent of the managers and 39 per cent of the capital. But this was not absentee investment. These people were residents of the country; they did not remit their profits but reinvested them in Mexico in business, which took on Mexican character.[56]

This material, however sketchy, seems relevant for our purpose. Did these foreign elements succeed because they were members of a distinct national group or because they brought with them, in addition to some capital, certain skills and experiences which were also finally responsible for dynamic expectations in the industrial field? The intensity of the dynamism may be explained by the necessity of "making good" in the new country.[57] This driving quality is always resented by the nationals, no matter whether it is possessed by *Turcos* in Latin America, Jews, Italians, Chinese, or Japanese. In spite of their different origins and cultures these immigrants appear to have had one thing in common: they were familiar with business, had acquired markets for specific merchandise they knew well, and had some capital, their own or borrowed from relatives or other members of their groups. Moreover, they possessed an international outlook and could look to friends in many foreign countries for technical advice, sources of equipment, and other pertinent data. In other words, in several important directions the immigrants' knowledge and skills were greater, the degree of their uncertainty smaller, and their economic horizons wider than was true of the "natives." This makes for more confidence and optimistic expectations and may thus explain more successfully than can cultural characteristics the entrepreneurial initiative encountered among these groups.

3. *Determinants of Investment Decisions in Underdeveloped Countries*

In this part of the paper the investment decision is divided according to the specific considerations which enter into it. A prospective entrepreneur will have to weigh the size of the market, the

[56] *Ibid.*, pp. 294 ff.

[57] Moreover, the ever-present fear of discrimination in which such groups live might make the risks of industrial investment appear smaller than they would appear to groups basically more secure. The author is indebted to H. W. Singer for this comment.

conditions of entry into a prospective industry, and the availability of resources—raw materials, power and transportation, capital, and labor, including degrees of skills—in order to estimate, or to form some kind of opinion about, productivity and costs, competition and prices, and, finally, the chances of profit. In the last resort, he will have to bring all these considerations to bear on his choice of alternatives regarding size of plant, type of technology, and organization. These latter elements, which form the object of the investment decision, will be briefly examined first to provide the focus for the following discussion of the determinants in their factual institutional framework.

OBJECTS OF INVESTMENT DECISIONS

The problem of size of firm and plant can be approached from various angles: Size is in part determined by the demand for the product and, in turn, determines the expected share of the market. The availability of resources, including capital, labor, and skills, is a major factor. These factors will have to be weighed against considerations of efficiency and cost, in relation to the expected price. The purpose of this section is to put these cross relations briefly into perspective,[58] while the underlying factual conditions will be set forth in the next section.

Limitations of the market effectively restrict the size of plant if year-round production in a large plant would exceed total annual consumption. Production will not be undertaken if the smallest efficient unit would produce more than visible demand justifies.[59] In other instances, the aim of least cost may conflict with the consideration of security. A plant with smaller capacity is less vulnerable if demand contracts, cyclically or otherwise, since smaller plants, using less specialized equipment, are more flexible in adapting themselves to changes in demand. Prevalence of small plants makes for greater elasticity of expansion since the added capacity of a large plant may exceed the growth potential of the market; an additional small plant, however, could be deemed to have a better chance of success.

In relation to capital, smallness may be a matter of choice or

[58] Many of these issues have been discussed in another paper of mine, "Small Industry in Economic Development," *Social Research*, September 1951, pp. 269 ff.

[59] Cf. *The Basis of a Development Program for Colombia*, Johns Hopkins Press for International Bank for Reconstruction and Development, 1950, p. 93, regarding the impossibility of starting the manufacture of electric light bulbs.

it may result from financial limitations. The latter do not necessarily prevent the establishment of an enterprise though experience shows that financial difficulties tend to persist. It is difficult for small firms to obtain additional capital.[60] On the other hand, under conditions of capital scarcity in underdeveloped countries, a decision in favor of a small plant is preferable to a negative one. If the only choice were between a large plant and none, it is all too likely that the capital would be used for traditional unproductive pursuits. Risk factors seem to favor a small commitment over a large one, and the greater flexibility of small plants may also increase confidence. Clearly, entrepreneurial initiative is related to the size of investment.

In discussing efficiency and size several criteria should be applied: technical, managerial, financial, and marketing.[61] These will be discussed in the next two sections.

The choice of technology is fraught with difficulties resulting in "technological uncertainty" about the quantitative relation between future inputs and future outputs, especially in planning beyond the range of the firm's engineering experience.[62] The knowledge of existing alternatives is not easily obtained in underdeveloped countries or is obtained only at considerable cost for foreign expert advice or travel; this situation favors large firms able to afford such additional initial expenditure. Moreover, shortage of capital and ample supply of labor militate in favor of less capital-intensive techniques in underdeveloped areas than in industrial countries.[63] It is a matter of argument whether the requisite techniques are available or have to be created anew after having become obsolete in industrial countries. In many industries the choice between practicable alternatives is much greater than is generally assumed. It should also be realized that the selection of proper productive equipment is no more important than plant organization: layout, material flow, integration of processes, process specialization, etc.[64]

[60] Cf. El-Gritly, *op. cit.*, p. 497, and Richard C. Osborn, "Efficiency and Profitability in Relation to Size," *Harvard Business Review*, March 1951, p. 91. In the United States the equity capital of small firms is only about one-half of total assets, compared with two-thirds to three-quarters in the case of large corporations. Credit-rationing makes additional borrowing also more difficult for small firms.

[61] E. A. G. Robinson, *The Structure of Competitive Industry*, rev. ed., London, Cambridge University Press, 1953, p. 17.

[62] Lange, *op. cit.*, p. 71, and Hart, *op. cit.*, p. 66.

[63] Cf. Singer, *op. cit.*, p. 25, and *Measures for the Economic Development of Underdeveloped Countries*, United Nations, 1951, p. 31.

[64] Cf. Corwin Edwards, "Brazil's Economy in the War and After," in *Economic Problems of Latin America*, Seymour E. Harris, editor, McGraw-Hill,

The choice of techniques and equipment has a bearing on problems set forth earlier in this paper. Smaller or less elaborate equipment costs less, and hence the capital requirements and risk involvement are smaller. Such equipment, as a rule, is easier to operate and requires less skilled labor than highly mechanized automatic machinery, which needs care and maintenance, involving additional capital and cost for spare part stocks and skilled mechanics. More elaborate equipment may have greater rated output, but this advantage is frequently voided by deficient skills and plant organization. Greater flexibility, inherent in less specialized equipment, may justify a sacrifice of efficiency in favor of a reduction of risk; thus it may pay to adopt devices, such as multiple-use design and shorter-life equipment, which increase flexibility or decrease risk involvement, in line with a foreshortened "economic horizon."[65] All these considerations apply not only to productive machinery but to auxiliary equipment as well.

The form of organization of the individual firm and that of the whole industry have considerable bearing on entrepreneurial initiative.[66] This section discusses the role of the corporation, aspects of centralization, integration, and marketing.

For the purpose of this paper, some features of the corporate form of business are of special interest. As a risk-reducing device it limits each investor's commitment to his share of the capital. On the other hand, unless his share is large, he forfeits the security of management control; protection of stockholders' interests has not reached a high level in many underdeveloped countries, and disregard of them in a number of instances obstructs the growth of security markets. Corporations, built upon the ability of managers rather than on the whim of individuals, can take the long view which industrial initiative and management require. On the other hand, the small number of potential investors in underdeveloped areas makes for close control of shares, often within families or groups of friends. This tendency and a desire for anonymity create diffidence in potential buyers of securities who lack basic information. The desire for anonymity also causes shares to be registered in the bearer's

---

1944, p. 279. Much factual material may be found in *Labour Productivity of the Cotton Textile Industry in Five Latin-American Countries*, United Nations, 1951.

[65] Cf. Abramovitz, *An Approach to Price Theory*, as cited, p. 81, and Yale Brozen, "Adapting to Technological Change," *The Journal of Business of the University of Chicago*, April 1951, p. 123.

[66] Cf. Abramovitz, "Economics of Growth," as cited, pp. 139 ff.

name in many underdeveloped countries, which makes tax evasion easier, thereby, perhaps, providing an investment incentive.

But the growth of the corporate form is slow in most countries. In Argentina, for example, the percentage of firms organized as stock and limited liability companies increased only from 6.3 per cent in 1935 to 8.1 per cent in 1943. In India, on the other hand, the joint stock company has been a feature of industry from the latter's beginning.[67]

Internal organization of the firm is related to size. Large firms can employ highly paid specialists, but increased specialization leads often to loss of coordination and, hence, of efficiency. Decisions are reached more easily and quickly in small firms, making for greater flexibility.[68] If ownership and management are combined in an individual, or in a small number of individuals, entrepreneurial initiative tends to be more immediate and personal than in a corporation with widely dispersed and anonymous holdings. Among individualistically minded people the lack of this close identification may well be a deterrent to corporate investment.

A large firm is plainly favored by its preferred position as a capital risk, as well as by the scarcity of entrepreneurial talent. But over and above the limited supply of very specialized talent other individuals can be used by smaller firms. A combination of activities in vertical or lateral integration, formal or informal, is favored by the scarcity of external economies. Difficulties in obtaining raw materials may compel a firm to expand in that direction or to build services taken for granted elsewhere. Thus a sugar-manufacturer in Egypt built his own railway and a river fleet. A new rayon mill had to install a complete mechanical workshop capable of making its own spare parts. Excess capacity in one direction, perhaps due to indivisibility, may lead to investment in successive stages.[69] It will, however, be realized that these factors contribute to a condition of quasi monopoly which makes the creation of other industries in the same field more difficult.

In the field of marketing, finally, advantages of large-scale organization are least pronounced. The larger the volume of sales needed to dispose of current production, the higher the sales ex-

[67] Bernstein and Patel, *op. cit.*, p. 391; *The Economic Development of Ceylon*, as cited, p. 82; Henry C. Wallich, "Fiscal Policy and the Budget," in *Economic Problems of Latin America*, as cited, p. 124; and Wythe, *op. cit.*, p. 105.

[68] Robinson, *op. cit.*, p. 38.

[69] Charles Issawi, *Egypt at Mid-Century*, London, Oxford University Press, 1954, Chap. 7. Information used with the author's permission.

penditure and other overhead costs. This trend is clearly visible in the United States, where a 1939 survey of corporations disclosed that sales per dollar of invested capital increased inversely with the size of total assets, from $.80 for corporations with more than $5,000,000 in assets to $5.42 for corporations with less than $50,000 in assets.[70] This trend is probably less pronounced in countries with less elaborate sales services, but the situation is in line with the observation that overhead capital and costs of small industries need not be relatively as large as those of large firms.[71] In other words, a less elaborate, cumbersome, and costly organization presents fewer deterrents to a positive investment decision. Incidentally, some of the benefits of large-scale organization can be made accessible to small operators by cooperative services in the fields of credit, buying, and marketing, as experience in the Far East demonstrates.

THE SIZE OF THE MARKET

Before making a final decision about the size of his commitment, technology, and organization, the prospective entrepreneur will have to consider the size of the market in two directions: the size of total demand for the product and the share of the total market which will be the target of the contemplated enterprise. Unless the new venture is to be the first of its kind in the country, the type and intensity of competition are important in calculating cost and prices. Estimation of the potential market is difficult in underdeveloped countries. Moreover, it requires assumptions as to whether the past level of incomes or its recent rate of growth will continue.[72]

These latter alternatives are very important because all observers are agreed that markets in underdeveloped countries are restricted by low incomes, which are due to generally low productivity. Thus the demand of the largest sector of the population is restricted to a few essentials, while that of the small wealthy group is oriented toward imports and is often too small to warrant domestic production. The inducement to invest in any individual industry is therefore restricted by generally low purchasing power.[73] Shifts in the

[70] Cf. *Private Capital Requirements*, Board of Governors of the Federal Reserve System, 1946.

[71] See Aubrey, "Small Industry in Economic Development," as cited, pp. 301 ff.

[72] Hart, *op. cit.*, p. 76.

[73] For a more elaborate theoretical treatment of the problem see Ragnar Nurkse, *Some Aspects of Capital Accumulation in Underdeveloped Countries*, Fiftieth Anniversary Commemoration Lectures, Cairo, National Bank of Egypt, 1952, pp. 4 ff.

distribution of income, brought about by inflationary trends, further depress the market in low-priced consumer goods industries on which demand concentrates when standards of living rise.[74] However, by raising the purchasing power of agriculture the base for industrial production could be increased, as industrialists in Mexico have realized.[75]

Among the palliatives sought to increase the domestic market, protection against foreign imports is almost universally adopted. High tariffs are supplemented by quantitative controls in the form of import or exchange restrictions, including a form of rationing in which a government may compel an importer to buy a standard ratio of domestic products. Such a law is on the books of Ceylon[76] and a similar practice has been used in Venezuela. While protection for industry is certainly necessary in its early stages, it also tends to raise prices, a problem left for more detailed discussion later. In the present context the question arises whether a policy of generally lower prices based on reduced markups would not be effective in increasing the volume of production, thereby raising aggregate incomes all around. Such an extension of markets would also offer greater opportunities for specialization and division of labor, thus increasing productivity and, indirectly, incomes.[77]

Low purchasing power and small markets have held the center of attention for so long that the frequent absence of industries to satisfy visible demand tends to be overlooked. In Nicaragua, for example, 4 to 5 million square yards of plain cotton goods which are now being imported could be made locally. In the absence of modern slaughtering and processing facilities the local price of crude lard is often higher than that of meat; hence, a large part of consumption is imported.[78] It may be concluded from these and other examples that the absolute size of the market is not necessarily the chief limiting factor; the difficulty of estimating demand in satisfactory fashion, for instance, may be more important.

[74] Bernstein and Patel, *op. cit.*, p. 384, and *The Economic Development of Iraq*, as cited, p. 279.

[75] Cf. Sanford A. Mosk, *Industrial Revolution in Mexico*, University of California Press, 1950, p. 49.

[76] *Basic Instruments and Selected Documents*, Geneva, General Agreement on Tariffs and Trade, 1952, Vol. II, pp. 66 ff.

[77] *The Economic Development of Guatemala*, as cited, p. 98, and *The Basis of a Development Program for Colombia*, as cited, p. 92.

[78] *The Economic Development of Nicaragua*, as cited, p. 120.

CONDITIONS OF ENTRY INTO THE INDUSTRY

The smallness of the market or uncertainty about the actual size of demand can be countered by a special kind of protection and inducement which actually guarantees a market to an entrepreneur willing to start a new industry. In many countries new industries cannot be established without the consent of the government, given either informally or through the issuance of licenses or privileges (*patentes*). On the ground that prospective competent newcomers will not be attracted unless they can operate without competition for a period of time, exclusive franchises are being granted to desirable new industries. This device is not new, of course, for it played a role in early European industry.

In Uruguay, for example, over 100 concessions with exclusive privileges for nine-year periods have been granted since 1921. In Panama, in 1937, exclusive rights to process milk were granted, along with prohibitions of the import of competing products. More recently, the Haitian government granted a twenty-five-year monopoly for the manufacture of soap. In Jamaica special protection amounting to a virtual monopoly was accorded to such industries as matches, condensed milk, and cement.[79]

These arrangements create a monopoly in order to attract new industry. Other measures are designed to protect existing industries against the competition of newcomers; their effect is static since no new industries are created. In Cuba government intervention in the cigarette industry, for example, takes the form of allocating production quotas, increasing them as demand increases but keeping new factories out. In Jamaica the government not only protected the copra industry from new competition in its own products but also guaranteed not to grant any licenses to manufacture substitutes or by-products, such as lard or margarine and soap, or to permit the import of additional machinery to make them. Several countries, including Chile and Mexico, have laws against overproduction born in the depression of the 1930's. In designated trades, like textiles, new industries can be established only with government approval.[80] In Argentina two companies received special privileges when establishing plants to make antibiotics and hormones while, so far, no similar concessions have been granted to competing companies.

[79] Wythe, *op. cit.*, pp. 73 ff., and *The Economic Development of Jamaica,* Johns Hopkins Press for International Bank for Reconstruction and Development, 1952, pp. 86 ff.

[80] *The Economic Development of Jamaica,* as cited, p. 236; Wythe, *op. cit.*, pp. 218 and 306; and Mosk, *op. cit.*, p. 97.

This method of attracting industry carries a danger of self-defeat by increasing output only, at the expense of future growth and through lowering real incomes by high prices.[81] Initially, the protection granted to new investors tends to eliminate a major element of doubt regarding the market, replacing it with the security of a *de facto* guarantee. Later, however, expansion and competition by new entrants are effectively negated; an inducement to a single new investor is thus turned into discouragement to others. Moreover, such *de facto* monopolies are more effective than monopolistic combinations in keeping prices high since there is no effective competitive mechanism to bring them down; this, in turn, keeps the market small and serves to justify further demands for protection. Finally, fundamentally the most dangerous effect is perhaps the disincentive to efficiency of operations. In the absence of competition and at a comfortable price level there is no apparent need to lower costs by improving productivity.

The risk of enterprise is also accentuated by rigidities affecting exit from the industry. For instance, Cuban law, anxious to protect workers against dismissal, does not permit liquidation of an enterprise without authorization by the secretary of labor, which can be obtained only with great difficulty. If the enterprise were sold, the labor contract would be binding on the successor, who would thereby be saddled with obligations beyond his control. Plainly, such a situation increases the risk of enterprise since the ultimate escape in case of failure leads to prolonged or costly agonies.[82]

AVAILABILITY AND MOBILITY OF RESOURCES

In underdeveloped countries the prospects of enterprise may be diminished by the lack of necessary resources other than raw materials and by government policies regarding resources. This is true, in particular, in the case of capital and credit. While common labor is usually plentiful, skilled labor and able technical and managerial personnel are often scarce.

Availability of Capital. Before discussing the supply side, which usually receives more attention, it is advisable to scrutinize demand in some detail. Comparing capital needs in underdeveloped areas with those for identical enterprises in industrial countries, substantial differences of two kinds are found: capital requirements are higher in underdeveloped countries, and it is, at the same time, more dif-

[81] Cf. *The Economic Development of Iraq*, as cited, p. 40.

[82] Cf. *Report on Cuba*, as cited, p. 140.

ficult to determine them with reasonable accuracy. Several factors combine to make such *capital requirements* high. In the first place, nearly all equipment has to be imported over long distances since underdeveloped countries are rarely equipped for such production. The cost of shipping and insurance is higher the greater the distance from the port of arrival and the less developed the intermediate transportation and unloading facilities are. Unfamiliarity with cheap sources of supply, the need to obtain costly foreign advice, and the profits of middlemen often add to the initial outlay.

The absence or the high cost of essential services, commonly known as external economies, quite frequently compels industrialists to provide their own power facilities, sometimes even their own transportation facilities, and such other services as those for repair. Large inventories are required because a network of industrial supplies is still lacking; raw materials have to be stored in the absence of efficient forward markets. Intermediate products like chemicals have to be imported, and, to meet emergencies, larger stocks need to be kept than would be required in more advanced economies. These shortcomings raise the requirements for working capital in addition to fixed capital. In other words, the lack of the Marshallian external economies of an industrial environment increases the capital cost of new industries, as is attested by many studies.[83]

As a result of these many shortcomings rooted in underdevelopment itself, it is crucially important, yet extremely difficult, for a new enterprise to estimate its capital requirements correctly. This calls for considerable advance knowledge of all ramifications of the problem and presupposes a degree of skill and experience rarely found in underdeveloped countries. Under these conditions correct estimation of capital needs is a major difficulty for a prospective industrialist, in addition to other uncertainties; by the same token, this difficulty adds to the risk of failure if the initial requirements are underestimated and more capital cannot be obtained after the inadequacy becomes evident. Initial mortality from this cause is often high. Additional capital, if secured, may be extremely costly. Undercapitalization is, in fact, a frequent phenomenon. Working capital, in particular, tends to be kept low, especially where other attractive investment possibilities exist; as long as the cost of construction is covered, working capital is supposed to take care of

[83] Cf. *The Economic Development of Guatemala*, as cited, p. 98, and *The Economic Development of Iraq*, as cited, p. 300.

itself somehow—by credit if necessary. Miscalculation is a more frequent cause of failure than actual shortage of capital, on which the blame is usually placed.[84]

A great deal can be done by government to lessen the extent to which the lack of essential services increases capital needs. This is realized in most developing countries, where high priority is given to transportation, communications, and power. These activities are so widely observed that specific documentation is hardly required. Attention should be drawn to a device less familiar in underdeveloped countries: the Industrial Development Co. of Puerto Rico went so far as to provide factory buildings for new industries from the mainland at favorable lease or purchase terms; this was a rather expensive measure for the government, its cost having been estimated at as high as $2,000 per worker employed.[85] It could be argued that this capital assistance goes too far if extended to all comers, irrespective of their own resources. On the other hand, such a contribution does more than relieve financial stringency. It removes one of the major elements of risk in investment decisions: by reducing capital needs it scales down the total capital involvement and does away with a major operation which must appear particularly irksome and risky to the uninitiated.

Prior to discussing specific sources of *capital supply* it may help to recapitulate the origin of savings, from which, in the last analysis, capital is formed. Private savings are highly concentrated in the hands of a comparatively small group of high-income-earners in underdeveloped countries. In line with population structure, a smaller proportion is of "saving age," roughly identified with the twenty- to sixty-five-year group. A part of savings are hoarded, invested abroad, or used directly by the savers for residential and commercial construction.[86] Inflationary pressures reinforce this tendency. Another large part of savings accrue as business savings and are used for reinvestment, again not contributing to free availability on the capital market.[87] It could be argued that reinvestment is not the

[84] Lokanathan, *op. cit.*, p. 150; Samant and Mulky, *op. cit.*, p. 97; *The Economic Development of Nicaragua*, as cited, p. 116; and El-Gritly, *op. cit.*, p. 377.

[85] Harvey S. Perloff, *Puerto Rico's Economic Future*, University of Chicago Press, 1950, p. 106, and *The Economic Development of Jamaica*, as cited, p. 84.

[86] An estimate for Brazil states that more than 60 per cent of savings were used for construction in 1947. *Report of the Joint Brazil-U.S. Technical Commission*, as cited, pp. 134 ff.

[87] "A Report on the Process of Inflation in Chile," mimeographed, Inter-

most desirable form of capital formation because it starves the capital markets of needed funds for new ventures while centering growth in existing industries. On the other hand, we cannot be sure that otherwise this capital would really flow into productive activities, considering the notorious preference of individual investors for other types of investment. Moreover, in Great Britain and also in the United States, historically self-financing has played an important part in capital formation; it was estimated that self-financing contributed nearly three-quarters of United States capital formation even in 1923-1929, when capital markets were also very active.[88]

Deficient channeling of savings into productive private investment remains the outstanding feature of capital formation in underdeveloped countries. To give only one example, it was estimated that in Guatemala not more than 20 per cent of total capital formation consisted of private productive investment, while about 40 per cent was public investment and the balance nonproductive private investment.[89] Regarding private investment, there is a relationship between investors' confidence and the weakness of capital markets. The success of certain managing agencies in India was due to the fact that their names rather than the soundness of the proposed schemes attracted capital; in fact, their guarantee was often a prerequisite for loans. A similar function is performed by private industrial banks, like the Bank Misr in Egypt, or by such public agencies as Mexico's Nacional Financiera; it consists of attracting funds and, in a way, acquainting the public with the bank's or agency's affiliated ventures.[90]

The weakness of security markets is too well known to require much elaboration. Among the reasons, partly mentioned before, are preference for the liquidity and security of real estate investment; unfamiliarity with securities, reinforced by the tendency of corporations to control existing stock closely (for instance, only sixteen

---

national Monetary Fund, 1950, p. 62, and *Report on Cuba*, as cited, p. 516. In regard to hoarding it is relevant to note that seasonal instability and frequent price swings are responsible for strong liquidity preference resulting in idle bank balances. On the other hand, this tendency cushions the economy against inflationary trends which would otherwise arise from large export proceeds received within short time periods. Cf. *ibid.*, p. 532.

[88] George Terborgh, *The Bogey of Economic Maturity*, Machinery and Allied Products Institute, 1945, p. 157.

[89] *The Economic Development of Guatemala*, as cited, p. 278.

[90] Lokanathan, *op. cit.*, p. 24; Samant and Mulky, *op. cit.*, p. 100; and El-Gritly, *op. cit.*, p. 455.

securities of those quoted on the Rio de Janeiro exchange were traded at least once a year from 1938 to 1944); lack of interest in security markets on the part of banks and other financial institutions; and disorganized bond markets, related to poor fiscal administration. In some countries, such as India and Egypt, British influence brought about early familiarity with the joint stock system, but the stock markets of many Latin American countries languished, registering only recently some sizable advances from low levels. The volume of transactions on the exchange of Mexico City increased sixfold from 1947 to 1951, and, what is more important, the share of stocks in the total grew from 12 to 22 per cent, that of industrial stocks from 7 to 17 per cent. In Colombia, only forty-nine corporations were registered on the stock exchange in 1939, compared with ninety-four in 1949; the capital secured by new issues increased, but only 20 per cent stemmed from new issues, the rest coming from retention of earnings. In Colombia, too, the turnover on the stock exchange concentrated on a very few well-known securities. In the first six months of 1949, six stocks accounted for 80 per cent of all transactions, two for 75 per cent.[91]

A factor contributing to the lag in capital markets is lack of interest on the part of institutional investors, e.g. insurance companies and autonomous government agencies, such as social security institutes. Their traditional preference for real estate finds justification in considerations of security against inflation. On the other hand, evidence is not lacking that the danger of inflation may cause flight into equities once the institutional framework exists.[92] By and large, however, financial initiative is restricted to a small number of wealthy families and individuals who take a large share of new issues by private placement, with preemptive rights to new issues in order to keep full control.[93]

Prevailing credit policies increase the tendency of investment to flow into unproductive activities. Commercial banks favor commercial transactions for a number of reasons related to considerations of security and profitability. By preference, credit is given to old and well-established firms, most of which are engaged in commercial and financial pursuits; a personal element also enters into this preference, for bankers and merchants belong frequently to the

[91] *Report of the Joint Brazil-U.S. Technical Commission*, as cited, p. 151, and *The Basis of a Development Program for Colombia*, as cited, p. 57.

[92] This was a factor in Egypt in World War II. El-Gritly, *op. cit.*, pp. 380 ff.

[93] *Ibid.*, p. 403.

same small group of men whose wealth was made in just these traditional types of business. As stated previously, the availability of collateral is also an important consideration of security; real estate and inventories are considered both liquid and secure, but they are typically related to traditional enterprise and not to new industries.

Security and profitability merge into motivations determining the length of the credit period. A short-term commitment offers the security inherent in mobility and flexibility. High rates of interest can be charged because short-term commercial and real estate transactions, including speculation, are notoriously profitable. Clearly, a new industrial venture, and many an established one as well, can ill afford to pay upwards of 12 per cent for its accommodation. Moreover, it is not healthy for industry to operate with short-term credit, since neither fixed nor working capital can be spared in times of stringency if the credits are not renewed.

Hence, commercial banks do not as a rule contribute very much to alleviate shortages of capital for industrial enterprise. Attempts at government direction of credit for productive purposes have been successful only to a limited extent, partly because a line is hard to draw and enforcement is difficult to achieve. Mexico experimented with a mixture of direction and credit restriction when increased reserves, required against inflated export proceeds, were relaxed in favor of desirable investment or credit. In practice, most underdeveloped countries have found it necessary to channel public credit into agricultural and industrial ventures which have been considered as being in the national interest.[94]

Availability and Mobility of Labor. Although a sufficient labor supply is usually taken for granted in densely populated countries, at some stage of industrialization obstacles may appear. Japanese industry experienced considerable trouble in securing sufficient labor and had to make elaborate and costly efforts at recruitment. Mobility of labor cannot be related solely to income differentials. No matter how poor living conditions may be in the village, the peasant or his family is frequently unwilling to leave the land. Fear of the unknown and of reduced security in alien surroundings looms large; if there is little to share in the village, it seems at least secure.

[94] Cf. *Report on Cuba*, as cited, pp. 136 and 597; Bernstein and Patel, *op. cit.*, p. 384; Adler, *op. cit.*, p. 596; *Review of the Economic Situation in Mexico*, Banco Nacional de Mexico, March 1953, pp. 3 ff.; and the many specific references contained in most country reports.

Such considerations of economic and emotional security, related to status system and social structure, impede the flow of workers to industry; they are also responsible for abandonment of industrial work and a return to the village, resulting in high labor turnover or at least in absenteeism. The creation of an industrial labor force, implying major changes of habits and attitudes, is a slow process, only partly related to wage incentives.[95]

When industry develops in underdeveloped areas new difficulties arise in labor relations, similar to those that arose in industrial countries not so long ago. A significant difference lies in the relative strengths of the contending elements and the alignments of political forces behind them. Labor unions had, and still have, a hard fight for recognition; in Latin America, for example, where industry has gained a position of importance, labor seeks the backing of the government. Affinity between labor and other political forces looking for change as an instrument of advancement led labor to positions of influence and power unknown in the early industrial history of other countries. The speed of this development and the rivalry of extremist movements are responsible for a lack of political sophistication on the side of labor; this it matched by a legalistic attitude toward labor problems on the part of employers and, often, of government administration, to the exclusion of economic and human aspects.[96]

These attitudes of labor can be explained by past abuses when governments tended to side with employers. Seasonal and cyclical instability makes for blind insistence on job security, sometimes ignoring economic reason or personal equity. Technological change is opposed, in the belief that reabsorption of displaced labor will be prevented by the lack of entrepreneurial initiative in a sluggish economy. This attitude results in make-work practices, overstrict seniority requirements, and excessively rigid job tenure. These difficulties are frequently stressed by employers, in addition to alleged bias in the administration of labor laws. There appears to be some evidence of the practical impossibility of discharging workers for any reason, no matter how sound, which results in the freezing of labor relationships to such an extent that mobility of labor is reduced

[95] For an elaborate treatment of the subject see Wilbert E. Moore, *Industrialization and Labor*, Cornell University Press, 1951; see also *The Economic Development of Ceylon*, as cited, p. 522.

[96] Cf. *Report on Cuba*, as cited, p. 361.

well below the minimum required for purposeful development.[97] Clearly, such rigidity greatly increases the uncertainty and risk of new enterprises by barring rapid adaptation to unforeseen difficulties. Knowledge of this difficulty is a deterrent to positive investment decisions, by adding rigidity to other risk factors and by reducing hope of high productivity. These conditions, it is hoped, will be gradually overcome inasmuch as some groups of employers have adopted more progressive attitudes, which in turn lead to a more understanding response by labor.[98]

Availability of Skills. The absence of skills on all levels is a symptom of underdevelopment and a deterrent to new ventures. If the importance of this human resource is not recognized from the outset, its absence is soon felt in the loss of efficiency and retardation of progress, decreasing the profit of existing enterprise and increasing the risk of those who venture forth in ignorance.

In most underdeveloped countries, even where common labor is plentiful and willing to join the labor market, there exists a lack of trained workers; moreover, such a shortage need not be general to handicap development as long as it persists in some vital occupations. The problem defies quick solution because its roots lie deep in the agrarian structure of backward economies; lack of general education is as important as failure to recognize the need for vocational training as a public responsibility. Rapid progress is now being made in understanding this problem, but its solution is a long and costly process. Hence, new industries have to train a great part of their own labor. This burden increases the cost of doing business and raises the capital outlay, creating an element of uncertainty and a risk of waste if the worker should leave his job after training. This risk becomes very real if pirating becomes an established practice because apprenticeship is discouraged by labor regulations; e.g. in Cuba apprentices have to be paid full wages while in training and cannot be discharged after six months' employment.[99]

[97] *Ibid.*, pp. 59, 149, and 366 ff., and *The Economic Development of Guatemala*, as cited, p. 98.

[98] *Report on Cuba*, as cited, p. 376, and Mosk, *op. cit.*, p. 28.

[99] *Report on Cuba*, as cited, p. 141; *The Economic Development of Ceylon*, as cited, p. 511; and Mosk, *op. cit.*, p. 264. A comprehensive picture of the need for vocational education, its preconditions, and the difficulties confronting it may be found in *Vocational Training in Latin America*, Geneva, International Labour Office, Studies and Reports, New Series, No. 28, 1951. The role of immigrants as a supply of skilled labor should not be underrated: Italians brought

In the higher and more specialized skills, the difficulty ceases to be one of large numbers and becomes one of a shortage of foremen or other supervisory personnel. Again the lack of general education proves to be a major handicap. Illiterates cannot receive written instructions, select repair parts, maintain material control, or attend advanced in-training classes. Dislike of manual labor among the educated is also a deterrent factor. Foreign companies are frequently successful in providing technical training on various levels in underdeveloped countries, thus forming a nucleus of skills for the economy.[100]

In the technical field another difficulty is added to the shortage of facilities for higher education: management lacks understanding of technical needs and how to fill them. A lack of comprehension of technical planning is not surprising, considering the background of entrepreneurship in underdeveloped countries and the disinclination to take a long view. It is not easy for a former merchant to see why he should pay large salaries for a technical expert, instead of buying some kind of machine offered to him and putting it into immediate operation; efficient plant management is thus rarely found. Regulations against foreign labor often make it difficult to hire or retain foreign technicians for a long enough period of time. Lack of confidence in technical management speaks for the establishment of advisory services and technical training facilities by governments.[101]

Industrial managerial skill is also short in underdeveloped countries. Alert and informed entrepreneurs are found, of course, but the requisite attitude of patient long-term planning is often stunted by lack of industrial experience. Perhaps industrial entrepreneurship need not be as specialized in underdeveloped countries as elsewhere, but even the basic techniques of business administration, scientific management, statistics, costing, and of personnel administration are frequently unknown. This results in difficulties of control and coordination, arising also from inability to delegate responsibility and authority. Differences in productivity can be traced to the quality of administration, initiative, and leadership in many fields, includ-

specialized skills to Latin America; so did the French in tanning, the English in textiles. Foreign technicians often remain and become a nucleus of skill diffusion (cf. Wythe, *op. cit.*, p. 53).

[100] *The Economic Development of Iraq*, as cited, p. 278; *The Basis of a Development Program for Colombia*, as cited, p. 92; and Mosk, *op. cit.*, p. 265.

[101] *Report on Cuba*, as cited, p. 156; *The Economic Development of Ceylon*, as cited, p. 511; Issawi, *op. cit.*, p. 8; Lokanathan, *op. cit.*, p. 315; and "Indianization for Foreign Firms," *The Economist*, May 16, 1953, p. 450.

ing marketing. Government can contribute expert appraisal and guidance, in some respects, but not the essential qualities of entrepreneurial skill.[102]

COSTS AND PRODUCTIVITY

The present section considers the needs for and supply of various resources once more, but from the point of view of cost. After reviewing his capital and labor requirements, a prospective entrepreneur can be expected to enter into a series of rational calculations designed to frame his profit expectations: the determination of costs of production and the formulation of a price policy. All the previous difficulties are compounded in this crucial process of estimation, for which the entrepreneur's own skill is often less than adequate.

Regarding costs, little more need be said about the lack of facilities and "external economies" discussed earlier from the standpoint of capital requirements: transportation, communications, power, repair facilities, supplies of raw materials and fuels, training for skills on all levels. If the industrialist has to provide all or any of these facilities, his cost structure will be doubly burdened: with the cost of additional capital and with the cost of its operation. This added cost is frequently permanent, but if these facilities are eventually provided by the community the industrialist's investment will be redundant and partly wasted, an expense which later entrants into the industry may not have to face. Clearly, such an addition to real costs affects the outlook for successful competition, in addition to increasing the over-all risk.

Although difficulties in obtaining finance for new ventures result in underestimation of needs and in subsequent dependence on unreliable and high-cost short-term accommodation, lack of foresight adds to the difficulty of cost estimation.

Labor cost is determined not only by wage rates but also by labor productivity, which is usually lower in underdeveloped countries than in the United States, even if the most modern machines are imported. Many reasons contribute to this effect: lack of skills and supervision, poor layout and material flow as well as other operational deficiencies, absence of ancillary services, etc. Sometimes such an elementary factor as poor nutrition is at fault. Low wages compensate in part for low productivity but fail in turn to provide in-

[102] *The Basis of a Development Program for Colombia*, as cited, p. 92; *The Economy of Turkey*, as cited, p. 160; *A Report on the Process of Inflation in Chile*, as cited, p. 62; El-Gritly, *op. cit.*, p. 498; and Samant and Mulky, *op. cit.*, p. 179.

centives for increased efficiency. The seemingly low cost of labor induces slack supervision and toleration of waste, resulting in still lower productivity.

The make-work tendencies of labor which arise from fear of unemployment are increased by insistence on low work norms and resistance to mechanization. Examples abound in the literature; only a few will be mentioned. In Syria strikers in the Aleppo cotton mills demanded that no worker should handle more than one loom, instead of three as in the past. In Mexico the unions resisted a norm in excess of four looms per worker, even where more efficient machinery would have permitted it; moreover, the modernization of the over-age equipment characteristic of the textile industry was delayed for years, in spite of earnest efforts by employers, unions, and the government to find a solution. Many specific instances of successful opposition to modernization in Cuba could be quoted.[103]

Such tendencies keep productivity low and give prospective employers a feeling of uncertainty regarding the difficulties they may encounter. The anticipation of productivity ratios in new industries meets many other obstacles. Some are related to the difficulties of transferring technology and selecting the most suitable technical installation and method. If we combine all this with the uncertainty afflicting the entire area of productivity and of labor relations, it becomes evident that a proper calculation of labor costs presents great difficulties.

PRICES AND COMPETITION

The analysis thus far permits an understanding of the tendency toward high prices in underdeveloped countries, usually noted with an undertone of disapproval. Costs are high because capital is scarce; many essential services must be obtained at private rather than public expense; labor productivity is low; direct costs are difficult to estimate, so prudence favors high prices in order to escape the penalties of underestimation. It is equally difficult to appraise the size of the market and hence a cautiously low estimate of sales increases the unit share of overhead costs; a tendency to keep unit profit high works in the same direction, but this last factor will be discussed in the next chapter.

[103] *The Basis of a Development Program for Colombia*, as cited, p. 92; *Report on Cuba*, as cited, pp. 60, 143 ff., 170 ff., and 185 ff.; Mosk, *op. cit.*, p. 126; and *Final Report of the U.N. Economic Survey Mission for the Middle East*, Conciliation Commission for Palestine, United Nations, December 29, 1949, Part I, p. 42.

All these considerations lead to a desire for high prices. But how can they be achieved in the face of competition? The answer is found in protective measures to keep out foreign competition and in quasi-monopolistic situations domestically.

In discussing protection, we are concerned not with the forms it takes in many countries but only with some of its effects. Sometimes a protective tariff is put on in order to attract industry, but, as in Latin America, although no industry may be started the tariff often remains, thus abortively increasing the level of domestic cost. In other cases high domestic costs or inflation encourage increased protection, but industry's response is apt to be not greater efficiency but higher prices and profits; these, in turn, make foreign competition possible again, which leads to new demands for protection. Such instances of overprotection should not detract from the merits of reasonable protection in raising the marginal productivity of capital as an incentive to investment. Duties on imports, however, should be made selective, and reducing them from year to year would be an incentive to improved efficiency; in Uruguay in 1931 and in El Salvador recently an increase of duty was canceled because the public did not benefit enough by the added protection![104]

Restrictions of domestic competition by outright cartel arrangements or by government price-fixing occur in any country, underdeveloped or advanced. Informal situations of monopoly or quasi-monopoly, however, arise more frequently in the former, and they are of greater interest for us. If a market is deemed so small that competition is effectively discouraged by fear of overcrowding, the established manufacturer has the market for himself and can set the price as high as he dares; a very small number of competitors does not have to resort to collusion to perceive the same advantage. In addition to the deliberate creation of a monopoly by governments, in order to attract new industry which is made immune against competition not only *de facto* but *de jure*, a profitable price may be actually guaranteed under a system of price control, as in the case of the cement industry in Jamaica.[105]

Scarcity of entrepreneurship and of capital limits the number of individuals in large industry to a small group; this may explain in part why large industry tends to be less competitive than small

[104] Wythe, *op. cit.*, p. 75; *The Economic Development of Nicaragua*, as cited, p. 100; *The Economic Development of Iraq*, as cited, p. 40; *Report on Cuba*, as cited, pp. 184 ff.; and El-Gritly, *op. cit.*, p. 569.

[105] *Report on Cuba*, as cited, p. 187, and *The Economic Development of Jamaica*, as cited, p. 236.

industry in countries like Egypt. Also, it takes a larger number of firms to saturate the market if the unit is small. In fact, it may be surmised that limitations inherent in demand would be less detrimental to growth where small-scale technology prevails because the addition of another small unit would not threaten the market with oversaturation.

Summing up, it can be said that estimation of future prices meets with less difficulty than that of future cost in underdeveloped countries. Protection and rigidities limit price competition in new industries. Thus the risk of competition is reduced, at the expense of flexibility and of efficiency. On the other hand, the ever-present awareness of economic instability, inherent in fluctuations of seasonal and cyclical character, tends to decrease the certainty which protection and monopoly give to price expectations. Elastic expectations resulting from inflation may bolster investment in some activities, but not, as we have seen, necessarily in the productive types; moreover, progressive distortions of the price structure are an inevitable concomitant of inflationary pressures.

PROFIT AND RISK

There is no basis of experience and information for complex considerations of profit maximization in underdeveloped countries; as a rule, profit will take the form of a fixed markup added to cost. It is often said that this markup is too high, in line with the customary high profit–low volume reasoning. As a result of the preceding analysis, the reasons can be summarized with some degree of precision.

It could be said, with some justification, that a policy of large volume at low unit profit is stressed in this country more than anywhere else because the United States market is so large; moreover, high incomes, equitably distributed, give a wide scope to consumer choice under competitive pricing conditions. It is quite true that some such improvement could often be achieved also in underdeveloped countries, but the limitations to such a policy should be equally understood. If incomes are low and the market small, large volume may not be attainable, no matter how low the price. To reduce profits drastically below customary levels would require optimistic expectations of a specific character: expectations that the market, or the obtainable share thereof, can be permanently expanded. Because the economies of underdeveloped countries tend to instability, seasonal or cyclical, including frequent small fluctuations related to world conditions, it seems natural not to gamble on permanently high demand but to take what the market will offer, as long as possible, and build up reserves against the time when the tide will turn with familiar rapidity. A bold price policy presupposes confidence in the future and ability to withstand the consequences of failure; neither of those preconditions is very common in underdeveloped countries. Hence, one reason for high profits is the inclusion of a risk premium against the effects of instability.

Another cause is found in the prevalence of inflationary trends. Profits seem high in money terms but may not be high in real terms. In fact, businessmen in countries where prices have risen steadily for years complain that profits are not high enough since wages anticipate future price rises. Moreover, there are indications that profit opportunities, initially stimulated by inflation, decline after some time while profits in less-favored activities have been squeezed by inflation from the outset. In any event, profits include a risk premium against continued shrinkage of working capital in real terms, a risk made virtually certain in the light of past experience.[106]

The pertinent question is, however, whether these profits are too high. If we divorce this problem from preconceived notions about "fair" profits, we ought to inquire whether lower profits could still be expected to attract investment to industry. The reply is found in two directions which we have already explored: the attraction of other investment, and the specific uncertainty and risks connected with industrial enterprise in underdeveloped countries.

The first of these points bears repeating without elaboration. In underdeveloped countries many opportunities exist for employing capital very profitably in commercial and financial ventures, or in real estate. A wide base of experience makes fairly certain high profit expectations in these traditional pursuits. Thus they appeal to the prospective investor not only as good investments but also as relatively safe ones, no matter how speculative they are.

In comparison with his position regarding this favorable balance sheet of profits and risks, the prospective investor has difficulty in appraising the prospective profits of industrial enterprise. As we saw, he finds it difficult, if not almost impossible, to determine his cost accurately in advance. The risk of miscalculation could be compensated only by a reserve added to cost or by a risk premium added to profit. The same calculation would apply to prices and

[106] Bernstein and Patel, *op. cit.*, pp. 377 ff., and *Report of the U.N. Economic Mission to Chile*, as cited, p. 2.

volume of sales, both difficult to forecast unless prices and market are guaranteed by monopolistic arrangements. To these risk premiums should be added the most weighty of all: that against loss of capital in new ventures.

The question then arises whether the expected profit will be deemed large enough to cover all these risk premiums and leave sufficient inducement to invest in industry rather than in other activities. Some incentives can be offered by governments. Exemption from duties on equipment and materials reduces capital outlay and cost. Exemption from taxes also reduces cost if such taxes are considered business expenses; otherwise a better ratio of profits before and after taxes results. Accelerated write-off for purpose of taxation operates in the same manner and, incidentally, reduces the period within which the investment can be recouped.[107] A virtual guarantee of profit, of course, eliminates several uncertainties at the same time. Thus in the last quarter of the nineteenth century the sugar industry in Brazil was guaranteed a return of 7 per cent on invested capital. Recently, prices were set for the copra industry in Jamaica so that profits would not be less than 5 per cent of sales.[108]

Doubtless, such measures tend to increase the margin of profit and also reduce some specific uncertainties. However, they are not sufficient to induce optimistic profit expectations large enough to balance a variety of risks. Risk premiums cannot be accurately calculated where a wide base of experience does not exist; degrees of confidence in approximate calculations must ultimately depend on faith that, in the long run, "the risk will pay." Economic development itself tends to bear out such expectations by a systematic upward shift of the schedule of marginal efficiency of capital in industry. Unfortunately, such a trend cannot be perceived in advance in the form of tangible signals to guide a prospective investor. Thus a rational weighing of risks against profit expectations, discounted by cautionary factors related to uncertainty, tends to turn investment decisions against industrial enterprise.

[107] It is often said that entrepreneurs in underdeveloped countries want to get their investment back within a few years, and this tendency is attributed to a get-rich-quick attitude. This may be the motivation in many instances, but another explanation presents itself: if the economic horizon is foreshortened, as a result of cumulative uncertainty, faster risk liquidation by amortization of capital may well be the condition which makes an investment at all acceptable.

[108] Wythe, *op. cit.*, p. 189; *The Economic Development of Jamaica*, as cited, p. 236; John H. Adler, E. R. Schlesinger, and E. C. Olson, *Public Finance and Economic Development in Guatemala*, Stanford University Press, 1952, pp. 109 ff.

SOME SOCIAL OBSTACLES TO "CAPITAL FORMATION" IN "UNDERDEVELOPED AREAS"

MARION J. LEVY, JR.

PRINCETON UNIVERSITY

THIS PAPER will examine some of the obstacles in the general social structure to the "formation of capital" in "underdeveloped areas." I do not believe that all such obstacles have been eliminated in highly industrialized areas or that even those that have been eliminated may not rise again (e.g. in cases in which highly authoritarian governments hold sway or in which general or nearly general social chaos exists). This paper is concerned with the general framework within which allocations of goods and services take place rather than with the solutions to such problems, assuming rational action within a particular (and usually implicitly) assumed framework. It is concerned not with whether these phenomena are good, bad, or indifferent, but instead with the effect on "capital formation" of the views of the members in the types of systems discussed as to what is good, bad, or indifferent.

By the term "economic" I shall mean "having to do with the allocation of goods and services." Both empirical and nonempirical goods and services are included. The latter category may be one about which the scientist can only be agnostic, but the people he studies often believe in it, and their beliefs have definite effects on their empirical actions and decisions. The term "economic" as defined here refers to an aspect of action and not to concrete acts or phenomena. There is no concrete action that does not involve some allocation of goods and services, but that is never by any means all that such actions involve.

I am deeply indebted to several persons in connection with this paper. Most notably I owe a debt to Gardner Patterson, who over a period of years has discussed and patiently criticized my attempts to handle these problems. He has always offered interdisciplinary cooperation of the most meaningful sort. In this specific paper he has helped me in many ways that defy identification, having, as he does, a great deal of practical experience with, as well as a theoretical interest in, these problems. I am also the beneficiary of many discussions of these questions with William J. Baumol, Klaus Knorr, Wilbert Moore, and Jacob Viner. None of these men can be held responsible for any shortcomings of this paper. If I have failed to learn from them, the fault is mine.

The "formation of capital," whatever we may mean by that phrase in this context, is a concrete action, as is its utilization. Our problem may be stated as follows: Are there patterns of social action (or, synonymously, social structures) such that operation in terms of them by the members of the systems in which they are found inhibits the "formation of capital"? If so, what are they? And are there such patterns that in general seem to characterize the social systems in so-called "underdeveloped areas" and that seem to have been either eliminated or greatly reduced in their inhibitory effects in so-called "highly developed areas"?

Finally a word is in order about the choice of "capital formation" as a focus for this paper. The original invitation to submit this paper spoke of "the influence of enterprise and business organization on the level and character of investment" as well as "economic motivation insofar as this rests on communal value schemes, culture, familial and extrafamilial relations, and so forth." Phrased in this way, no less than a sizable volume on the social structure of relatively nonindustrialized societies could satisfy the invitation. I have tried to narrow the subject to manageable size by the following series of assumptions. "Capital formation" is a necessary, though by no means sufficient, condition for "economic growth." "Capital formation" is a function of social action and (save for purely idiosyncratic cases) the result of the operation of identifiable social patterns. Social patterns inhibiting "capital formation" will either partially or completely inhibit "economic growth." Therefore, focusing the study on obstacles to "capital formation" will at least assure that all the matters we discuss are relevant to our problem.

This paper is divided into three parts. The first is concerned with an extremely brief examination of the concept of "capital" and a statement of the form of that concept used here and the reasons for the use of that form. The second is concerned with the obstacles to be discussed. The findings on these obstacles have been reached in terms of a more general systematic (and highly tentative) analysis of social structure, but they are presented as a list taken out of that context for purposes of brevity and communication. In this section of the paper, examples will be given largely in terms of hypotheses about the facts in China and Japan, with occasional references to other societies. These two countries have been chosen because (1) both were latecomers to the kind of development under discussion at this conference, (2) one of them was conspicuously successful in many respects in the attempt to "develop," while the other was conspicuously unsuccessful, and (3) my research in this field has been largely concerned with these two areas. There is the additional factor that, to the casual observer, the differences between them when such attempts started seemed to be negligible in relevant respects or else favorable to success in China. Although these societies have several unique features not shared by many "underdeveloped areas," I shall attempt to show that the specific types of obstacles discussed apply rather generally to other "underdeveloped areas."

The third part of this paper will be devoted to a brief statement of the problem of gathering data on the type of theories presented in the second section, or, more properly, to the question of seeking anything like relative confirmation of or disagreement with such theories. It would be misleading not to emphasize that what appear as statements of facts in the second section are actually hypotheses about the facts, just as the inductions and deductions drawn from these "facts" are hypotheses about their implications for the problem at hand.

1. *The Concept of Capital*

It is perhaps impertinent in a paper presented to an audience composed largely of economists for a sociologist to state that he finds a concept so central to their thinking as that of "capital" in an extremely confused state. Not only are many different referents of the concept of capital used, frequently without a statement of the explicit meaning, but there are also instances in which the general concept is defined in one fashion and thereafter used in another.[1]

I have no intention of getting involved in the general problems

[1] See, for example, Paul Samuelson's textbook *Economics, An Introductory Analysis*, McGraw-Hill, 1948, pp. 42-45. Samuelson defines "capital," quite usefully for his purposes, or states as a hypothesis about "capital," that "it has a *net productivity* over and above all necessary 'depreciation' costs." In discussing two subsidiary forms of this "capital," fixed and circulating "capital," he uses many examples, including among others residential housing and raw cotton in a textile mill. Empirically speaking, both of these examples may refer to things that by no means have a "net productivity. . . ." I have not picked this example merely to quibble with an outstanding economic theorist in an incautious textbook moment. By and large, this minor inconsistency will have little effect on an analysis (save for possibly increasing the difficulty of understanding economic failures) as long as the analysis is carried out within the type of social structure assumed as a framework in that volume, but it could give rise to serious problems outside such a framework. If Samuelson's concepts were followed strictly in their present form in societies with quite different patterns, a whole new set of concepts would have to be created or many relevant factors would be completely missed.

posed by the current state of the "capital" concept. I prefer merely to pick out the definitions of that concept and some of its subcategories that I shall use. For the sake of brevity, I shall not go into the reasons for choosing these referents of the concept and some of its subcategories, in the hope that they will be fairly obvious from the uses made of them. In any case, however unsatisfactory, elementary, or trite these definitions may be, they should make clear what is being discussed.

The term *goods* will be used to refer to all physical items in existence at any given point in time and space. The term *capital* will be used to refer to all goods that are not free goods in the classical economic sense.[2] The term *productive capital* will be used to refer to all capital the use of which can result in an output of goods valued at more than the cost and maintenance of the capital involved. The term *effective productive capital* will be used to refer to all productive capital the use of which in fact realizes more than its cost and maintenance. The term *nonproductive capital* will be used as a residual category of productive capital, the term *noneffective productive capital* as a residual category of effective productive capital. The prefixes *fixed* and *circulating* as applied to the various forms of the capital concept will have their conventional meanings.

The concept *money* will be used to refer to any generalized medium of exchange. This in itself poses many important problems for this paper. The general form of these problems has to do with the extent to which money is a generalized medium of exchange. For the sake of clarity in conceptual development, any unit of exchange will be considered *generalized* if it can be directly exchanged for two or more different types of units. In fact, however, most of the empirical systems considered have exchange units considerably more

[2] The definition of the term *capital* given here has been focused on the concept of goods in order to preserve greater continuity with its ordinary uses by economists. The problem of whether technical services should be included in this concept arises, particularly with regard to areas such as those in question. This problem has quite a practical basis, for today many foreign contracts and loans for building abroad specifically include an item of considerable proportions for technical services. In this paper the matter of technical services has been handled in other ways, but the problem is one that must be faced sooner or later. Unfortunately, the exploration of this problem immediately raises the question of a rather thoroughgoing renovation of the classic economic factors of land, labor, capital, and profits (or management). The resolution of the overlaps involved in those concepts in their classic statements may have rather far-reaching implications for economic theory as well as social theory in general, if a new set of concepts can be found which is capable of handling the empirical materials treated by the old concepts but which lacks their confusions.

generalized than this. Moreover, most of these systems have a single general type of unit that is accepted by the members of the system as the "correct" generalized medium of exchange in the system concerned. This acceptance is usually decreed and maintained by the predominantly politically oriented structures of the system, and the medium is called here the *official* or *legal money* of the system.

The use of official or legal money raises two central problems: (1) the extent to which nonofficial money (or moneys) exists in the systems concerned, and (2) the extent to which the money (or moneys), whether official or nonofficial, is a generalized medium of exchange (i.e. what sorts of things other than money can be exchanged for it and in what quantities). The term *monetary capital* will be used to refer to any money that may be exchanged for two or more goods that are not free goods. This is, of course, virtually equivalent to saying that it is defined as any money, given the definitions of money and capital used here. This verbal exercise is undertaken to get at the general form of the concept. The specific forms of the concept of monetary capital which will be of primary interest in this paper are those of *monetary productive capital*, along with its various residual and subsidiary forms, e.g. *monetary nonproductive capital, monetary effective productive capital*, and *monetary noneffective productive capital.* The combinations of these definitions are fairly obvious, e.g. monetary productive capital is money that can be exchanged for two or more types of productive capital. Attention will be concentrated on the implications of social structure for the two problems listed above insofar as these problems have a bearing on capital formation. The classic interest in the concept of money capital has lain largely in the fact that money capital makes possible the coordination of large amounts of small-scale savings for the purposes of development (or other purposes) and even makes possible savings that might not be technically feasible in a barter situation. The attendant difficulties, in the form of the implications of inflation, deflation, credit expansion, and the flight of money capital, will be left largely to the realm of more technical and strict economic treatment.

The term *formation* will be taken here as an undefined predicate, or at least as a term sufficiently well understood in its ordinary usage not to cause confusion here. This paper will be primarily concerned not with *capital formation* in general, but with *effective productive capital formation* (using the terms as defined here), which, I take it, is what students have generally had in mind in discussing "obstacles to capital formation" in both "developed" and "underdeveloped areas." This preoccupation involves us in many nasty problems. I feel that I must state my position on these problems lest a considerable part of what comes after be reduced to obvious question-begging. I shall make no real effort to justify this position. It is in part a question of judgment and in part one of empirical analysis. To argue the former would involve a lengthy missionary effort; to argue the latter would involve a full-scale comparative analysis of "developed" versus "underdeveloped" countries. I state my position on this problem because such a position is always either implicit or explicit in these discussions, and the position, however taken, may involve one in either a series of statements that are not conceivably falsifiable, and hence of no scientific relevance, or a highly controversial series of statements. I prefer the latter involvement, because one may learn something from agreement or disagreement with such statements. The position that I take involves, in addition to other problems, one of empirical measurement for which I must confess I have no solution. This may reduce the whole matter to something closely akin to the not conceivably falsifiable alternative.

These nasty problems center around the use of the term *valued* in the definition of *productive capital.* I shall judge value from the point of view of the members of the system concerned in general. If one judges value from the point of view only of those individuals making decisions, the argument tends to become circular unless one assumes that the category of self-consciously understood irrational action is possible, desired, empirically frequent, and not a contradiction in terms. It is generally to be expected that, in some psychic sense at least, those using capital will estimate their use as "capable of resulting in an output of goods valued at more than the cost and maintenance of the capital involved." The position that I take falls back upon some of Pareto's distinctions. I would judge a use as "valued at more . . ." if that use increases the ophelimity for a collectivity (or the membership of the system concerned in our case), the utility for a collectivity, or the utility of a collectivity. Furthermore, in reckoning these I would make an increase in net productivity per capita and net distribution per capita[3] of empirical goods and serv-

[3] By the term *increase in net distribution per capita* I mean that there has been an increase in average distribution that has in fact been accomplished so that either no person is worse off than before and some (preferably a majority for these purposes) are better off than before with regard to the things being distributed, or if anyone is worse off that worsening has resulted in more persons' having had their lots improved in these respects than having had their lots worsened.

ices always relevant and, for present purposes, the determining factor. This position involves certain evaluations on my part. Most notably, under this position a use is not "valued at more . . ." unless that use results in an increase in actual net distribution per capita as that has been defined in footnote 3 above. Pareto himself pointed out the problems of evaluation in general in his distinctions. I am only concerned with pointing out that the general criterion for evaluation that I have taken is by no means necessarily in conformity with the value structure of all societies. It does happen to be quite characteristic of most modern, so-called highly industrialized societies, whose members by and large seem to feel that the system to which they belong is better in general, and certainly better economically, to the degree that it keeps the per capita production and consumption of goods and services increasing and keeps widening the range of actual distribution of the increases in production and consumption.

This position involves one in certain evaluative controversies, for there are many who feel that the materialistic preoccupation of modern Western societies, which such a position reflects, is a source of major evil, and that the worst thing that we can do is to encourage others in this direction or base policy on it. I have taken the position for several reasons. First, however much societies may differ in the extent to which they value these standards, it is possible, I believe, to show that the members of every known society of any long-run stability have always had some such interests[4] and no society could be stable without these interests.[5] Second, such a standard does hold out the possibility of relatively useful and pre-

[4] I.e. people in general in such societies have recognized what it means to be "better off" in terms of material goods and services, and to some extent they have desired to be "better off" in these terms. Great differences have been and are present in what the members know about this condition or are willing to do to bring it about. It is conceivable and empirically possible that the members of a society have an interest in increasing net productivity and in increasing the amounts of material goods distributed to the members in general and that they still do not achieve such goals. It is highly unlikely, if not impossible, that the members of a society are completely lacking in such an interest if the society is to be stable. If a society were to be stable in the absence of such an interest, there would have to be in the society a level of productivity and distribution adequate for all the requisites of the society plus the capability of motivating production and distribution up to this level without motivating any increases or decreases in the level. Empirically speaking, I can think of no case of such precisely poised motivation, and analytically speaking, I cannot imagine how it could be realized in terms of general social structure.

[5] I.e. systems radically or completely ascetic in the material sense cannot long endure without change or destruction.

cise measurement, because whatever the difficulties involved, it is much more feasible to measure numbers of individuals and quantities of material goods and services than to measure attitudes and individual subjective values with our present measuring instruments. Thus it should be easier to tell whether a policy undertaken for such a reason had misfired or not, and negative results may well tell us as much in these circumstances as positive ones. Third, and this may be even more controversial, I believe that whatever the differences between "underdeveloped areas" and "developed" ones with respect to the degree of preoccupation of their members with material factors, if the "underdeveloped areas" "develop" in the sense that current social engineers seek to have them "develop" the resultant societies are far more likely to change in the direction of the general social structure of modern Western societies than to maintain their distinctive traditional patterns or combine them with the patterns characteristic of the "developed" societies. I think this will be true whether the engineers concerned are "natives" or "foreigners," whether they wish it so or not, whether they concentrate on "industrialization" in the sense of manufactures in modern, power-driven plants or "merely" modernize and improve agricultural and public health techniques and conditions. If this is correct, they will also develop in corresponding degree, if they lacked it before, the kind of preoccupation with material goods and services that characterizes the systems from which they are borrowing other patterns of behavior. I believe that, whether it be considered good, bad, or indifferent, such an emphasis on the material goods and services of this world is an integral part of the social structure of such systems.[6]

A word about the inclusion above of the phrase *net distribution per capita* is in order. Here again a value judgment has been made. I feel that the most penetrating discussion policy-wise that I have read in this field is that contained in Viner's recent volume.[7] In his discussion of definitions of the concept of an "underdeveloped country," I have found helpful the one that he finds more useful, and it seems to imply the phrase in question here. As Viner points out, in his use of the term a country may be "underdeveloped whether it is densely or sparsely populated, whether it is a capital-rich or a

[6] It would be out of place here to go into full-dress arguments about the requisites of these modern Western systems here. I have tried to raise these questions briefly and hypothetically elsewhere. See, for example, *The Structure of Society*, Princeton University Press, 1952, and *The Family Revolution in Modern China*, Harvard University Press, 1949.

[7] Jacob Viner, *International Trade and Economic Development*, Free Press, 1952.

capital-poor country, whether it is a high-income per capita or low-income per capita country, or whether it is an industrialized or an agricultural country."[8] The policy question discussed here seems to be oriented to the capital-poor, low-income per capita, relatively nonindustrial country. Viner's general concept is no less rewarding for such countries and has the advantage that, when our pressing concern with such areas has somewhat abated, the work done may have its cumulative implications for the more general problem to which he directs his concept.

Finally, a word about the use of such terms as "industrialization" and "modernization." By *industrialized* I shall mean the use of inanimate devices to multiply the effects of human effort and the use of inanimate sources of power in this multiplication. I shall call a system *modernized* to the degree that it approaches the type of system existing in the modern Western societies, taking quite arbitrarily the United States as the extreme so far reached in this respect. Since I shall use the latter term largely in connection with the technologies of communications, manufacturing, farming, public health, and the like, this should not cause serious trouble. This use is stated explicitly lest it contain relevant problems I have ignored that would be the more irritating if left hidden in an implicit concept. The real problem that bothers me about these terms, however, is their general connotation in the field of economics. Perhaps under these circumstances it is perverse to use these terms with altered meanings and implications. The altered meanings cluster about "industrialization," which tends to be taken to refer to modern manufacturing industries specifically, along with large-scale communications services and mining. As the term is used here, management, farming, public health, entertainment, education (even), etc., are all highly industrialized in the United States. I have defined the term in this manner because many of the "strictly economic" problems hinge on such considerations, regardless of whether it is manufacturing in the narrow sense that is being considered. Moreover, I think that there is no question but that the general implications for social structure of these sorts of activity have more in common than otherwise. This latter consideration is no less true of the referents of the term modernization. However "economic" in the narrow sense the examples of either of these terms may be, it is a basic assumption of this paper that such phenomena cannot exist without a whole host of necessary conditions in the general social structure (e.g.

[8] *Ibid.*, p. 125.

that the types of employment criteria necessary for highly industrialized production are likely to be quite incompatible with certain types of family structures). It is the essence of such an approach that any monistic theory of economic determinism is either true but empty or full but false.

2. *Obstacles to Capital Formation in Nonmodern, Relatively Nonindustrialized Underdeveloped Areas*

GENERAL OBSTACLES FOR LATECOMERS

It is a commonplace (but a very important one) of current discussion of issues such as this to point to the advantages enjoyed by latecomers to the process of modernization in general and industrialization specifically. The latecomers can take over the latest technologies without the costs of their development, though as many wise men have pointed out it is by no means always in their "best interests" to do so without careful discrimination. On the other hand, somewhat less has been said about the disadvantages of latecomers apart from their painfully obvious have-not status in these respects. I should like to consider here some of those disadvantages most obviously related to the question of the formation of effective productive capital.

The Problem of Conversion of Resources. In the first place, modern systems of production and consumption which developed more or less indigenously in countries such as England and the United States had one obvious advantage in converting their economic resources into new forms of effective productive capital. Here for a moment I would abstract from all the problems of the social patterns associated with such conversions and consider what might be called a more purely technological or engineering problem. In these terms those systems had a curve of development which was relatively smooth and continuous; that is to say, the technical problem of converting existing resources directly into new forms was not enormous and could be and was done. For example, the early machines could be built by currently available carpenters, wrights, etc., and with currently available goods in their existing forms. These workers and goods and subsequently the workers trained in the operation of the new machines and the goods produced by them produced still more modern ones, and so forth. There is serious question as to whether present levels could ever have been reached without some cases of this sort, if indeed such a statement is not banal. On the other hand, the latecomers (i.e. those in the non-modern, relatively nonindustrialized areas) can do this little if at all in any such direct fashion, and frequently neither they nor others regard such a process as in their best interest. This view has a sound basis since many of the interstitial stages of development of these forms of capital would be markedly uneconomic in the sense that they would cost more than their use could add even to aggregate output. This is especially true when more modern economies have outstripped this stage in a given field.

"Traditional" Chinese workers using "traditionally" available materials cannot produce a modern milling machine. Even if they could produce one such machine, it would be a "believe it or not" feat rather than an activity which was practical economically. These latecomers are therefore forced into interdependence with, if not dependence on, modern areas if they wish to take advantage of the latest in technologies. This is true not only of know-how but also of many physical materials. The latecomers may follow many courses in this process. They may get unilateral or multilateral aid from abroad such as straight transfers of productive capital in the form of gifts, grants, loans, or investments. The United States has been a source of such transfers on an unprecedented scale in recent years. Such aid is likely to raise many questions concerning the interdependence and responsibility of governments and individuals in foreign nations as well as questions of how far in advance or how reliably planning can proceed on such a basis. If aid from abroad is not to be the basis of economic growth, foreign trade in those traditional products in which the area has a comparative advantage becomes much more important, even if the earning of goods from abroad takes the form of general or forced saving locally and export of accumulated reserves. Japan chose such a course in the nineteenth century, fearing that foreign domination was likely to accompany gifts or loans from abroad.[9] Under such a course obstacles with far-reaching implications may arise at many points. It may, for example, mean radical reorientation and reallocation of domestic production and consumption even where traditional or semimodern techniques have such a comparative advantage for international trade that their use can make still more effective forms of productive capital formation possible. There has been some tendency

[9] Such fears are present today in many areas; without arguing the wisdom of these fears, past and present, it should be noted that foreign domination may be (and in some cases was) benevolent in these respects.

in national and international aid programs, now being corrected wherever possible by the sophisticated, for the underdeveloped areas to assume that the ends sought even for purposes like those suggested here, were best served by the immediate introduction of the latest possible technologies rather than by the use of intervening ones.

The implications of latecomer status for quite understandable reasons tend to run into one another. For this first one let it suffice to say that the fact that the curve of development is at least in part radically discontinuous for the latecomers poses purely physical obstacles to certain types of necessary effective productive capital formations. It cannot be done directly with what is at hand. Since, of course, comparative social phenomena are far more likely to show relative than absolute differences, it would be more correct to say that to the degree that a system is a latecomer it is less apt to be able to form much of its necessary effective productive capital as directly as earlier-comers or those present at the start.

Shifts in Self-Sufficiency. One characteristic of many, if not most, nonmodern, relatively nonindustrialized underdeveloped areas which tends to be overlooked or underestimated by those who are accustomed to thinking of modern Western societies as "natural" or "normal" in social history is the extraordinary (by modern standards) degree to which self-sufficiency with regard to both consumption and production is approximated and/or simulated by many of the social subsystems of these areas. Moreover, this approximation of self-sufficiency seems to be highly regarded by the members of such systems. There is, of course, no known society, whether modern or not, in which there are *no* interdependencies of subsystems in terms of allocations of goods and services, and there are some nonmodern, relatively nonindustrialized societies that depart markedly from the above-mentioned self-sufficiency (e.g. some of the major trading systems). On the whole, however, the contrast in these respects between the nonmodern and the modern society is marked. One need not remark at any length on the degree to which the tendency toward interdependence has gone in the United States. Here even most forms of housework, usually a stronghold of family self-sufficiency, involve an amazing network of interrelationships with public utilities, major manufacturers, sophisticated communications systems, and all sorts of nonfamilial business concerns. It is interesting to note that we not only do not characteristically regard these relationships as terribly complicated or delicate but are far more likely to point to such a state of affairs as greatly simplifying our problems—and so they do, given our type of system, in which, internally at least, self-sufficiency has probably been reduced to its lowest point in social history.

One of the earliest terms used in descriptions of production that involve effective productive capital is "roundabout." Whatever else it may imply, the process can progress little beyond the example of the use of sticks to knock down fruit before the question of the interdependence of more or less specialized units begins to arise. In the areas we are concerned with here, this interdependence begins to increase on a twofold basis. First, there is the universal increase in specialization that has so far accompanied virtually all increases in effective productive capital. But for the latecomers there is an added increase because of the gaps to be bridged. This does not follow as a matter of logical deduction. The added increase might not arise in the same degree if some foreign nation would provide all the capital necessary as a pure gift, or if capital of a nonproductive or noneffective productive nature within the system could be turned over to the new purposes. In these cases, only the increase in specialization everywhere attendant on increased uses of effective productive capital would be involved. The ordinary case, however, is far more likely to require at least some effort on the part of the members of the system to take advantage of their comparative advantages—the more so because of the difficulties of latecomers in making direct internal conversions to the new technologies, etc. This seems likely to involve considerable departures from the previous degree of self-sufficiency. Even if the degree of internal trading was high prior to this time, there are likely to be notable shifts because the changing emphasis on international trade is likely to involve either the production of new products or differing ratios of the old ones. Even if the system previously engaged in much international trade, there are likely to be shifts. The new requirements may involve new products or at least internal shifts in the domestic application of the income from the previous trade.

For present purposes I am concerned only with the implications for the degree of interdependency of the units internal to the system. In material to follow, I shall raise the question of international interdependency, but the likely increase in international interdependency has its reflection in decreases in internal self-sufficiency. Similarly, I must jump ahead to one other latecomer problem to be taken up below—scale. Given the line of development of technology in recent history, the latecomers can only utilize certain types of effective productive capital on a very large scale. This scale is likely to be large not only relative to the scales early involved in those countries in which modern systems developed on an indigenous basis, but also relative to the levels of savings which are practical in the country concerned. These questions will be taken up again. For the present suffice it to say that they imply other questions of large-scale organization of planning and execution of programs—including the programs designed both to form the relevant capital and to use it. Such organization must be carried out in terms of concrete units of some sort. These will have to be either adaptations of old units or newly created ones. In either case the question of their relationships with previously existing units is raised. Their interdependence with the old not only adds a new factor, but inescapably involves readjustments in previous interrelationships as well.

These shifts quite obviously involve changes in the actual organization of workers, administration, governments, etc. They also raise problems far beyond those of drawing up a new table of organization in the narrow sense. In many, if not most, of the nonmodern, relatively nonindustrialized underdeveloped social systems the type and degree of self-sufficiency of the subsystems have been intimately related to the general problem of control over deviance in the system, the sources of motivation, the techniques of locating and rewarding talent, the distribution of income, etc. Shifts in such self-sufficiency do not merely raise problems of teaching people to produce new or different things in new or different ways and not to produce others. They also involve considerable increases in sophistication about exchange and budgeting in terms of a generalized medium of exchange instead of in terms of goods and services directly. There are no concrete systems that are purely economic systems (i.e. concerned only with the allocation of goods and services), and nonmodern, relatively nonindustrialized systems are characteristically far less likely to have predominantly economically oriented concrete structures than are highly modernized ones. Even among relatively modern systems there are marked contrasts in these respects, as a comparison of the role of business organizations in the total social structure of France and the United States will show. Given shifts in the degree and types of self-sufficiency of the units in the nonmodern, relatively nonindustrialized systems, the changes in the purely economic aspects of the situation are likely to be considerable and of a kind about which we at present have little sound knowledge. But when these changes are considered in the context of the minimal changes in other aspects of these units, the real magnitude of this problem of social engineering begins to emerge. It is folly of the worst sort to assume that such programs can be confined to economic aspects. That folly is compounded if consideration is not given to whether or not the implications of a given program for the noneconomic aspects of the system will in turn raise contradictions for the changes sought in the economic aspects.

Even apart from the noneconomic aspects of the situation, the problems are thorny. In "traditional" China much of the allocation of goods and services was a function of jack-of-all-trades employment of family members in slack seasons. Shifts of some family members to nonfamily employment in relatively modern plants may greatly increase the individual productivity of a segment of the population while lowering that of the members of the system as a whole, if only because nonfamily organizations which supply what was previously handled in slack seasons are not forthcoming. Many other problems may also arise. In China the breakup of family units poses a critical problem of facilities to care for the aged. Capital expenditures on this sort of thing again must jump a gap covered gradually in other systems, and in such situations problems not only of allocation but also of motivation and control arise.

The problem of the increased interdependency of these nonmodern, relatively nonindustrialized areas with more modern areas, which is necessary if the former are to form effective productive capital, has been touched upon above as a problem of latecomers which has considerable implications for the type and degree of self-sufficiency of internal units. It is a well-known maxim of international trade theory that such trade, if pursued along the lines of the doctrine of comparative advantage, tends to increase the income of all systems concerned on the average in the long run but also tends to make them more vulnerable to fluctuations over which they have no control. The theory of this need not be elaborated here in its economic aspects. In its noneconomic aspects the question is relatively unexplored. As pointed out above, the shifts in self-sufficiency of subsystems of these countries have far-reaching noneconomic aspects. These are likely to become the basis for fundamentalist resistance in any event, but in the case of hard times resulting from such increased interrelationships the pressure can become extreme. Even in the absence of such fundamentalist reactions, the problems posed may be great. Fei Hsiao-T'ung tells of a Chinese village in which production for the international silk market brought boom times for a period, during which the role of women shifted markedly and the whole economy of the area was readjusted.[10] The 1929 crash then brought a readjustment far beyond the "traditional" Chinese readjustments to hard times. Such experiences may result in obstacles to the formation of effective productive capital from quite unexpected quarters.

There are other concomitants of the increased interdependency due to international trade. The underdeveloped areas concerned here not only become increasingly vulnerable to economic cycles abroad; they also become increasingly vulnerable to swings in foreign tastes. One or both of two problems may result. The units in terms of which production takes place in these areas are likely to be rather inflexible to change. This extends even to their types of products to a degree difficult for members of more modern systems to understand. If flexibility in production cannot be increased, they are vulnerable to shifts in allocation other than in the trade cycle narrowly considered. On the other hand, if this inflexibility is eliminated, quite striking changes in the social structure of the area must be brought about at the same time. While this argument may seem at first glance to contradict what has been said about necessary increases in specialization in circumstances like these, I believe that there is no contradiction here. Although modern technologies carry with them very high degrees of specialization, they tend over-all toward a specialization of operations rather than of products. There are tool and die machines and operators of many different types, but both can perform their operations in many different product contexts. The last war furnished hundreds of examples of this; for instance, typewriter plants converted to the production of machine guns with amazing rapidity and ease.

This sort of convertibility is interrelated with more than the specific character of our technology. It is almost certainly interrelated with many aspects of social life that seem to cry for reform from many points of view. In highly industrialized societies, social engineers are much concerned over the fact that workers today do not seem to have the same kind or degree of "ego investment" in their jobs as seems to have existed in the handicraft periods of the West. They feel that a man who tightens a single nut or fits a single type

[10] See his *Peasant Life in China*, Dutton, 1939, pp. 197-236 and 282.

of wheel all day, all week, all year, is bored with his work, has little creative feeling on the job, etc. They may well be correct, but they may also well be cautious before they try to "correct" this in any such obvious manner as having the worker identify himself with his specific output. The malintegration that this lack of positive identification with one's product may produce may be one of the major necessary prices paid for the minimal flexibility requirements of such systems. In any case, lack of flexibility may be a major obstacle to the formation of effective productive capital, and the creation of such flexibility inevitably raises questions of general social change.

The Problem of Scale for Latecomers. This problem has been alluded to above. The scale on which latecomers may have to operate in those respects in which they modernize is likely to be greater not only than those individual steps taken by the members of the areas in which these patterns of behavior developed indigenously, but also than the scale of current operations in the country carrying out the modernization. There are caveats on this score, of course. Centuries ago China carried out very large-scale projects—large-scale from almost any point of view. There was an inland canal over 1,000 miles in length and irrigation systems covering vast areas. But even so there were major differences from projects of today. The nature of the projects and the technologies involved were likely to be such that the crucial stage was that of planning; both execution and operation could be carried out on highly decentralized bases; and rates of obsolescence and depreciation were likely to be slow and gradual. This last feature was important because it meant that, if the levels of objectivity and ability necessary for original planning could not be easily maintained, the projects concerned would not suffer immediately and drastically. With most of the modern technologies, however, relatively slight deficiencies in maintenance can bring a major complex of activities to an effective halt.

Most of these large-scale efforts represented fairly direct conversions of relatively unskilled labor services into effective productive capital formation. Today the West probably does not have the ability to mobilize and operate efficiently large masses of relatively unskilled labor, while as recently as the last war one could see in China as many as 100,000 coolies mobilized to build roads and airfields two baskets of dirt at a time. As I have tried to point out above, however, much of the gap-jumping necessary for the nonmodern, relatively nonindustrialized underdeveloped areas cannot be made in this direct fashion, though maximum attention should be given to the development of whatever possibilities exist on this score.

The process involves either large-scale savings internally or large-scale gifts, investments, etc., from abroad. The problems about the latter need not detain us here. One of the troublesome problems about the former is that most of the areas with which we are as a practical matter most concerned are characterized by populations living on what is by standards of modernization the margin of subsistence (or well below it). The problem of increasing their savings therefore raises very difficult issues. This is further complicated by the public health issue. Whatever the implications may be for population increase, public health conditions in these areas must be improved if development of the sort sought is to take place. Here we are obviously involved in humanitarian considerations, but we are also involved in matters a great deal less sentimental. The question of motivation for various kinds of efforts is certainly connected with mortality and health conditions.

There is another question, however, that is more often overlooked. The kinds of interdependency created by the lines of development sought place a progressively increasing emphasis on interstitial adjustments between and among different activities. In highly industrialized areas these reach a fineness of adjustment often overlooked. These levels of adjustment cannot be maintained on anything like a practicable economic basis in the face of high rates of absenteeism and low rates of human operation. It is not a question of sentiment. A peasant farmer may take an hour or two out to shake with a malarial chill and make it up by toiling further into the night, but the absence of a worker from a modern assembly line for such a period cannot be tolerated. There must be provisions for his immediate replacement. These are, of course, relative matters; I have deliberately chosen extreme examples.

Perhaps more relevant than the mortality rates in these areas with which we are concerned are those of endemic and partially debilitating diseases. These make for high absentee rates in more modern forms of production, as well as for low rates of performance while on the job. Therefore, whatever reliance is to be placed on internal savings must be planned so that the savings will be accumulated in such a way as not to depress public health standards further, as might happen if food consumption were lowered.

The improvement of public health is related to the question of scale in another sense. If one admits that it is a necessity, for any or some combination of reasons of sentiment, motivation, and efficiency (let alone such reasons as public appeal, etc.), one must realize that these public health programs tend to be huge. Modern medical technologies have made attacks on many of these endemic diseases relatively cheap and effective, but they inevitably raise problems of the general ecology of the areas concerned. It may be necessary, for example, to clean out bromeliads in a whole area in order to stop the malaria problem. To get a reliably healthy pool of a thousand people, it may be necessary to improve the health of several hundred thousand, or even several millions, in some of the densely populated areas. These public health programs are likely to be large in other senses too. Most obviously they are concerned with sources of water supply, and it is a short step from the question of uncontaminated wells to that of dams and large reservoirs.[11]

Going back to the problems of scale in general and the attendant problems of saving, there are other questions no less thorny. Many if not most of these areas lack the kind of agencies necessary to coordinate and utilize such savings as are being or can easily be accumulated. The members of the population with large personal incomes are not accustomed to putting their incomes to use in the formation of effective productive capital; they are far more accustomed to hoarding them or to applying them to other forms of nonproductive or noneffective productive capital. Furthermore, attempts to change such habits are likely to run into resistance from the most powerfully mobilized quarters in the society. Japan, for reasons to be referred to later, was a notable exception, and her experience should be studied carefully, if only for this reason. The Japanese feudal lords accepted debentures for their landholdings without a murmur. Since they knew nothing of how to handle or manipulate debentures, their use came into the hands of the zaibatsu, who owned or controlled the banks. Quite peacefully, land reform was carried out, and the effective control of much of the financial resources of the society was turned over to people who did not own them but who could use them for the developmental purposes sought. This has not happened in most of the other areas with which we are concerned.

In order for the necessary saving to be effective, or in some cases to be done at all, entirely new social units must be created. If these are to operate effectively, they must be interrelated with

[11] These latter are likely to raise international complications, since hydraulic systems are notorious disregarders of national boundaries.

other social units in the area. For limited purposes, governments can resort to forced saving based on considerable physical coercion, but this is always an extreme and raises its own special problems. Most notably, perhaps, it raises the eternal political problem of "Who is to guard the guards themselves?" and thus it opens up the whole question of the general maintenance of stability in the system concerned.

One may ask about the ready convertibility of the indigenous entrepreneurs and financial investors in these societies. Japan is one of the few cases that offers any hope. In general, on a private basis these individuals are not only used to asking and expecting interest rates so high as to make impossible the necessary programs,[12] but they are also not trained or accustomed to look for the most relevant forms of investment for growth purposes. Most notably and most generally in these areas, they have turned to land as offering greatest returns, security, and general social prestige. This has had far-reaching social implications in terms of tenancy, etc., but it has not generally facilitated the formation of effective productive capital. It has tended to redivide rather than to increase the shares in production of the members of a system.

While the scale problem is difficult enough in individual productive enterprises and in the public health field for latecomers, it is probably even greater in the fields of public utilities, communications, and education. I have pointed out above that it is a great mistake to think of industrialization solely in terms of individual mechanized operations. As a minimum, one may hold that the requisites and necessary correlates of such operations are widespread special forms of social patterns. It is difficult to make isolated stabs at modernization except for demonstration purposes. It is possible to put a team of agricultural experts in a single Indian village, have them concentrate on improving yields by showing the farmers technically better procedures for utilizing the means at hand, and get encouraging results. It is not possible to do this on a scale that will have substantial effect on India as a whole without improving roads, setting up agricultural stations, improving both amounts and character of education available, etc.

Doing these things simultaneously on the scale necessary has in-

[12] One must be wary about interpreting the interest rates frequently quoted as high in a relative sense. When one takes account of the chronic inflation in some of these areas, the real interest rate may not be abnormally high, and the absolute rate charged may be necessary to get selection of effective productive investments.

triguing ramifications which there is only space to indicate here. Improved communications systems, for example, might be loosely called a generalized necessity for development in these areas. Furthermore, these are fields in which the interstitial stages of development are almost everywhere out of the question. In many of these areas it may make very good sense to set up some operations in terms of household industry and others in terms of modern manufacturing plants. It may, for example, be better to have fishing done by hand from dories rather than by fleets of modern trawlers. I doubt, however, that in any case it will make sense to set up a railroad system as in the nineteenth century or a road system that will handle animal-powered vehicles but not motor-driven ones.[13] This doubt has many bases, but one of them is the costliness of *expertise* and the extent to which inefficient communications can fritter away this commodity.

Public versus Private Development for Latecomers. As a teasing introduction to this question, one may say that it is extremely unlikely that the highly modernized systems of the world today could have developed indigenously on the basis of any systems other than ones that relied very heavily indeed on private individual operations, and that it is extremely unlikely that latecomers can carry out such development without relying very heavily on public operations. One may relate such a hypothesis to many different aspects of social structure, but for the present it may be related to the general problem of latecomers, and most especially perhaps to the particular problem of scale. The most obvious difficulty in this connection is the collection and utilization of large amounts of productive capital in such a way as to make it effective. Even given some huge private fortunes in these areas, many of the necessary projects require investment on a scale far beyond the private means of a single wealthy individual or groups of such individuals.[14] The problem is further

[13] This is not the equivalent, of course, of maintaining that a road system is not effective productive capital unless it is a four-lane superhighway. Effective productive capital may in fact be reduced if an area goes further in this direction than is necessary for other simultaneous lines of development, or if it goes to such lengths at the expense of other developments that would, in combination with less ambitious highways, add more to effective productive capital.

[14] On the other hand, it should be kept in mind that there are at least two general considerations that often favor smaller projects. In the first place, in the absence of certainty about the outcome of any investments, especially since other economies are not static, a series of small projects may have the effect of spreading risks. Second, a series of small projects privately financed may afford many

complicated by the fact that many of these private accumulations may take the form of either nonproductive capital or noneffective productive capital because of the habits and motivations of those who control them. In general, the mechanism for collecting and making available savings in small individual amounts from members of the population at large have not developed indigenously either. Here again the habits and motivations of the population at large may also interfere.

Such areas are likely to lack both the motivations and the mechanisms for gathering the amounts of productive capital necessary and for transferring control of it readily from one group to another in such a manner as to make it and keep it effective. These problems are present quite apart from the lack of such amounts and the problems of getting them from abroad or building them up at home. But even if these problems were absent, it would be difficult to utilize such productive capital as could be gathered. Here again the scale is relevant, because it is germane to the scale on which one must train experts to handle the programs that can make effective productive capital out of productive capital. In these areas private sources can hardly be expected to provide both the capital needed for specific purposes and that necessary to educate the individuals who will have to administer and use it.

Moreover, many of the uses to which capital must be put in these efforts at development cannot well be taken care of on a private basis, except on a private philanthropic basis. Private philanthropy can do no more than scratch the surface. Some of the largest-scale requirements are ones that cannot well be linked to any private earning system without creating at least as many problems as they are designed to eliminate. Here one might leave out communications as a possibly controversial case and stick to such things as public health and education. The income of the largest private philanthropic foundation in the world could not crack China's public health or education problems even if it devoted all of its income to that effort. In effective productive capital formation in nonmodern, relatively nonindustrialized underdeveloped areas, the difficulty is probably never one of setting up a single productive operation alone, if it ever is in any area. It is rather one of preparing the peoples of a whole area to operate in these new terms. In no highly developed, modern countries are these necessary background expenditures

---

fewer difficulties in terminating noneffective ventures before losses have become unduly great.

borne privately, and in the latecomer countries the problem of setting up, as well as maintaining, such facilities has to be faced. These background investments may pay off handsomely to the system as a whole, but they are unlikely to be linked to a form of financial reward that will enable them to be handled by private enterprise. This means that in some respects at least the mechanism of the market cannot be relied upon.

There are other reasons too. The question of scale raises in a radical form the problem of control. If the job could be done largely on a small-scale, private basis, the market situation might take care of small-scale individual failures, but the very large ones are crucial for the system. In these areas one has the difficult problem of coordinating different efforts, even if the members of the area concerned are agreed upon the goals they seek. Roads must be coordinated with agrarian as well as commercial and manufacturing developments. All of them must go with public health and education. Given the standards of living of these areas, the sums and materials involved in failures are likely to be seen in starkly tragic terms. These problems were not so acute in the Western systems, which developed gradually and were nowhere faced with jumping gaps comparable to those that confront the latecomers. Probably none of these areas will achieve the development sought unless a major part of the planning and operation of the process is carried out on a public basis.

Surprisingly, perhaps, the level of private operations will itself rest heavily on public planning. That is to say, there will have to be large and sophisticated public programs in most of these areas to get private operations under way. Private operations as they are understood in the West are often not understood in these areas at all. In addition, the necessary social patterns for the operation of such private efforts are largely lacking.[15] In "traditional" China, for example, one was adequately protected in private dealings if one had established either directly or through a carefully chosen go-between a personal bond with those with whom one dealt. Strangers, however, were fair game in a radically *caveat emptor* fashion that would horrify the most rapt laissez-faire idealists of the modern West. But in the new situations, if these enterprises are to operate

[15] The necessary social patterns for *public* efforts in these directions are also frequently lacking, but it is somewhat easier for a government, if it is strong and if it is so inclined, to create the necessary patterns than it would be for private individuals to do so.

successfully, the old, highly personalized basis for conducting affairs will have to be abandoned and be replaced by something more stable and predictable than "individualism by default."

This is not to argue, of course, that there is no role for private initiative in these areas; quite the contrary is the case. But initiative must be subject to some limits if matters are to proceed smoothly, and some developments cannot be handled on this private basis. One of the biggest problems in these areas is how the projects that must be carried out on a public basis can be best coordinated with the sphere left open to private initiative. For reasons too complicated to go into here, the Japanese seem to have had an unbelievably felicitous situation in these respects, for the public planners and the major figures in the sphere of private initiative either were the same or acted as one.

One could follow the problems of latecomers throughout the social structure in much greater detail than has been done here, but this discussion will serve to raise questions about some of the social implications of being a latecomer and either wanting to modernize or being forced in that direction. In addition to the fact that such systems need effective productive capital in amounts and types not needed before, they have special problems. There are obstacles to the formation and use of such capital that can be traced in considerable part to their desire to jump a gap. Here they and we are faced with a dilemma. These processes of development ordinarily treated in terms of their economic aspects alone have highly restricted but nonetheless requisite noneconomic aspects. The most highly modernized and highly industrialized systems, in which these patterns developed indigenously and gradually, seem to have these requisite patterns developed in very high degrees, but these are not necessarily the patterns that are prerequisites for the latecomers.

The first level of naïveté in these matters is to believe that one can take over the latest technology and leave what one wishes of its social setting behind—that one can combine the "best of East and West," to quote a popular nostrum of our times. The first level of sophistication is to understand that patterns of behavior go with those technologies and that those patterns are by no means restricted merely to the persons in direct physical contact with the technologies.[16] This first level of sophistication is likely to lead to attempts to import the whole thing in full flower at once or to pose

[16] This is by no means equivalent to saying that the technology is an independent variable and all these other factors dependent variables.

that as an ideal to be aimed at. The full extent of the problem has not been approached, however, until it is realized that these latecomers, who may want to change or are forced to change, face a problem of transition and that the requisites of a given state of affairs are by no means necessarily the same as the prerequisites of bringing that state of affairs about. In some cases the prerequisites and requisites may be identical, but whether they are and in what respects they are cannot be reckoned without taking into consideration the social basis from which the change takes place. It may be, for example, that the French Revolution, including the Terror, was a state of affairs which was a prerequisite of modern France, but many of the aspects of that situation are certainly not requisites of France as she is today and in fact would destroy her.

THE SOCIAL BASIS FROM WHICH CHANGE TAKES PLACE

The General Problem of Control. The foregoing discussion about the general problem of latecomers has laid the basis for a discussion of the problem of control from one particular point of view. Assuming that high degrees of control are necessary for latecomers, why should they be so difficult to achieve? Many of these latecomers have highly authoritarian societies with a great deal of centralized power and responsibility, and many others (or even the same ones) are systems in which the members have long been accustomed to agree on highly traditionalized forms of action in general and expression of disagreements in particular. There are many problems to be solved before this can be fully answered, but for present purposes some central considerations can be stated briefly. In the first place, even though the systems may have highly developed degrees of control, the types of control may be different from those necessary for the new ends. Even if the members of the system approve of the new ends in general, they may not approve of the specific requirements placed upon them. The fact, for example, that a system can control and coordinate large amounts of unskilled labor does not mean that it can control new allocations of capital either on a private or on a public basis.

Perhaps a more formidable problem on the whole is posed by our second consideration. How are systems of control affected by the new patterns that must be introduced if the new forms of productive capital are to be effective? In many of these areas the new forces undercut the old system of control. This is particularly apt to happen in those systems in which control is primarily a function of the continued stability of units in terms of which action is expected to be predominantly traditional rather than critically rational, in which membership is determined by who one is rather than what one can do, and in which the relations among members are vaguely rather than precisely defined and delimited.[17] The new patterns are likely to put great pressure on such units, and in some cases the effects may be startling even with only limited introduction of the new patterns.

"Traditional" Chinese society is an excellent example. Here one can make out an excellent case for the facts that the whole system of control in the society rested upon family stability, that the family in the "traditional" setting created many strains but was capable of containing them, and that the new patterns undercut that capability for containment. In Japan, on the other hand, we find a contrary case, but a very special one. In Tokugawa Japan there was a great dependency on the family but a clear recognition of overriding loyalties to the feudal hierarchy. There was also a clear tradition of concentration of this loyalty on a single individual, the emperor. This permitted a rather easy transfer of these loyalties back to the emperor and hence directly to the national state. Virtually without bloodshed and in extremely rapid and dramatic steps, the daimyo and the shogun, the top power- and property-holders of a genuinely feudal society, were shorn of their power and their property, and control over what was left to them was rather effectively placed in the hands of those who could put such resources to work for the formation of effective productive capital. On the basis of general social analysis I feel that there is reason to believe that China is more typical than Japan of the problems of control to be encountered. In any case, the world has seen only three cases of latecomers who have been highly successful in modernization (i.e. Japan, Germany, and Russia), and all of them have shown serious tendencies to get into trouble with their neighbors, even though they were highly successful in the process of modernization itself.[18]

[17] This whole question can be handled with much greater precision than is attempted here, but it is likely to involve jargon and analysis that would lead us astray for present purposes. A brief treatment of some of these questions is to be found in my paper "Some Sources of the Vulnerability of the Structures of Relatively Nonindustrialized Societies to Those of Highly Industrialized Societies," in *The Progress of Underdeveloped Areas*, Bert F. Hoselitz, editor, University of Chicago Press, 1952, pp. 113-125.

[18] I would suggest, as perhaps a far-fetched hypothesis, that the very factors that were relevant to their initial successes also played a part, in the world

It may be true in some sense that systems with a long-run prospect for stability accompanied by high rates of formation of effective productive capital (assuming that any of them can be stable) will have to have what we consider to be relatively democratic and permissive allocations of power and responsibility, but it certainly does not follow that such systems are the best bases from which to accomplish the transition swiftly and peaceably to such a stage. It also does not follow that any and all forms of authoritarianism and the like are equally more efficient bases. What does follow from this argument is that the formation of large amounts of effective productive capital, which will have to be done largely on the new bases, cannot be carried out without substantial alterations in the existing social structure of those systems. The very use, for these purposes, of their indigenous patterns of control may radically alter those patterns and other features of the society. It is, perhaps, not too much to say that all attempts to increase modern effective productive capital formation are subversive of the social structure of relatively nonmodern, nonindustrialized societies. At least it would be better to assume so than to be totally unprepared for the problems raised by such well-intentioned changes.

So far two types of questions have been raised, directly or indirectly, about the problem of control in a period of transition: they relate to (1) the importance of control and (2) the possibility that the old forms of control may be broken down with great rapidity while new ones may be created only very slowly. In the discussion, examples have been taken largely from the field of what is commonly considered production rather than consumption. This is largely a matter of conforming to conventions in these respects. It may be that some day we shall find that these two concepts fall into the category of concepts such as anabolism and catabolism, which apply to processes or aspects of processes that are classified under one or the other concept depending on the point in the more general process from which they are viewed. Conventional usage is a bit mixed on this score. At one and the same time, we speak of General Motors Corp. and United States Steel Corp. as producers in some absolute sense and then speak of the importance

context in which they found themselves, in the subsequent problems they posed for themselves and others. Here we are not concerned with that stage of aftermath but with the processes of modernization themselves. Nevertheless, we should probably keep in mind that the process of modernization on a smooth basis may well not be worth the effort if its price is to be a repetition of the history of the last four decades.

of the position of the former as a consumer of the products of the latter. Our mixed usage might be straightened out by abandoning the pretense of an absolute distinction in these respects and stating the point of view from which we speak in labeling a given aspect of action as production or consumption. Whether or not this is done, consumption in either sense poses no fewer problems of control than production. If development is to be planned and coordinated at all, there will have to be some basis of control over what individuals in the system are permitted to buy—certainly with respect to amounts and in many cases with respect to composition as well. If the members of the system are motivated without overt forms of control or via their own volition to demand commodities and services that do not block the formation of effective productive capital, so much the better, perhaps; if they cannot be, then either controls must be present or the programs will be ineffectual. The problem is magnified to the extent that the areas concerned are dependent upon international trade for the financing of their development.

Here again, the Japanese case is instructive. The Japanese not only demonstrated an ability to organize and coordinate effective productive capital formation; they also played on public tastes in such a way as to prevent certain of their comparative advantages from being wiped out or radically altered. Within the limits of changes necessary to improve public health and communications systems, the Japanese government was unbelievably skillful in getting its citizens to work in very modern ways and with very modern tools and to go home and live in the old or "true" Japanese way. They did not eliminate the effects of industrialization on the general social structure. Family patterns and many other patterns did change. But the Japanese seem to have directed and controlled many of the changes to a degree unequalled elsewhere. Furthermore, although elements of coercion were by no means lacking, the degree of voluntary cooperation must have been extremely high for the system to have operated as it did.

To summarize, these systems must either be able to generate considerable control over deviance or have such patterns of motivation that deviance is relatively unlikely to arise. They must do this with rather strict limits on the use of purely coercive forms of control. These limits are the stricter because the transitions call for the increased use of imagination and initiative either on a public or on a private basis, and many of these forms of imagination and initiative must contradict the traditional sense of fitness and propriety in the system. This delicate balance must be achieved, given the ends sought, where the process of development that is being sought is extremely likely to undermine the general allocation of power and responsibility. Moreover, in some cases these underminings are likely to be explosive in their rapidity. With our present knowledge of comparative social structure we have just begun to state the problem that we face, and no convincing solutions suited to our ends are available.

The Security of Investment. In these areas there are many specific problems of control that are strategic. One of the easiest to illustrate is the implications of the method of allocation of power and responsibility for the security of investment. Here the problem is somewhat different if we distinguish between private and public investment. In addition to the fact that these systems can hardly escape a large element of public investment, there is little doubt that the interests of transition would be well served if considerable room were left for private initiative. This has been true in most of these areas, primarily through private influence on public affairs, if in no other way. Moreover, it is likely to continue to be the case. This raises two types of problems. In the first place, in many if not most of these systems the relevant entrepreneurs have had, ideally speaking, a low social status. These people, generally called merchants, have frequently been extremely powerful in the same way that gangsters and political bosses have sometimes been the powers behind the thrones of individuals of high social prestige in our society. However much "protection" some merchants may have built up in these systems, the general power structure is likely to be capricious from any single individual's point of view. In the second place, the very process of development in these areas is likely to make the positions of power-holders unstable in such a way that the systems of power may well take on a capricious aspect with regard to public as well as private ventures. In recent history, for example, some of these leaders have—rather self-consciously, it would seem—attempted to rule by use of mobs. Mobs can be an extremely effective means of bringing pressure to bear on either public or private individuals, but in the nature of the case it is almost impossible to hold mobs responsible for their actions and hence to put a stop to what one has started.

These systems are also likely to be characterized by extreme differences in income, with a relatively small but very wealthy group widely separated from the population in general. Such a group is likely, however, to be large enough to provide a considerable market for luxury items produced by other systems. Expenditures of this type result in nonproductive capital formation or, what is more likely, in transformations of productive capital to nonproductive capital. The problem is more far-reaching when one considers that (1) the foreign exchange resources of these areas are likely to be small in relation to their requirements for development, (2) many of the forms of effective productive capital must be purchased abroad, and (3) many of the forms of nonproductive capital desired must also be purchased abroad.

The wealthy group furnishes a ready source of demand for such forms of nonproductive capital, but in a system in which the power-holders are likely to treat individual entrepreneurs capriciously (at least from the point of view of those entrepreneurs) the entrepreneurs may well have a very powerful motivation for what may here be called in a loose sense "commercialization" rather than industrialization. Speaking more accurately, these entrepreneurs may seek their incomes primarily through exchange that involves no increase in effective productive capital formation (or even a decrease) instead of through such formation.

Let us take automobiles as an example. The importation of automotive products can certainly increase effective productive capital in these areas, in which communication difficulties are likely to be great and transport costs to be high. Many of these areas need improved and expanded road networks if automobiles and trucks are to be used effectively, but few if any of these areas are so deficient as to make all uses of these products noneffective capital formation. But if the imports of such products consist largely of luxury models from the West for the purposes of heightening the enjoyment of private leisure, effective productive capital has been diminished by at least the amounts involved. The same would be true if plants were built for the production of such automobiles, although the loss would not be as great, because of the convertibility of such plants to other uses. Luxury automobiles themselves are not highly convertible, and even plants set up for such production may have extremely limited prospects if the comparative advantage situation of the area concerned puts these plants in the category of noneffective productive capital formation.

In such situations, profit from the furnishing of exchange services is much safer and surer than profit from production of goods plus the services of exchange. The entrepreneur who concentrates on the former runs the risk of having his inventory confiscated, but the one who concentrates on the latter runs the risk of having his inventory plus his plants confiscated. In addition, inventories are a great deal easier to hide than are plants plus inventories. To the extent that an emphasis is placed on "commercialization," the entrepreneur is likely to be forced to seek his greatest market in the luxury realm or in markets closely dependent thereon, for this realm is already in existence and does not have to wait to be keyed into a general program of development. Not only is the risk of loss less, but the turnover is likely to be much greater and to be effected in a much shorter period. Moreover, it is far easier to shift such investments with shifts in demand. It is not a matter of chance that at the height of many transportation shortages in China, the wealthy and those holding public office or related to officeholders had luxury automobiles that represented nonproductive capital, that consumed vitally needed foreign exchange, and that added to the problems thus created by siphoning off still further resources for the fuelling and care of such automobiles.

If this sort of motivation is to be kept to a minimum, the government must be stable and must not be capricious with regard to property rights. In those areas where control is great, there is likely to be a government that cannot easily be held responsible for capriciousness with respect to property rights. The role of foreign settlements in China and of colonial governments in general might well be re-examined from this point of view. Even though those inventions of foreigners for their own convenience became the symbol par excellence of the worst in the relations between the more and less modern areas, they probably did much to foster some forms of effective productive capital accumulation. Through their banks the foreign settlements often made monetary capital secure, and the colonial governments were less likely to confiscate property. In both cases there were prices to be paid. The base for luxury demands was widened, and much of the development that took place was in the hands of foreigners rather than of those who regarded themselves as the true members of these systems. This latter point has had several repercussions. The most obvious has been that the developments themselves have sometimes become the objects of the same sorts of hatreds as the colonial visitors. Thus in North Africa the local inhabitants destroyed something like a million trees (a vital factor in land reclamation) planted by direction of now-deposed foreign rulers. Social history is replete with such semisuicidal cases of babies throwing themselves out with their own dirty bath water. When public sentiments have been inflamed to rid the area of its foreigners, these forays are the more difficult to control. Hardly less obvious is the fact that such patterns of development have left the members of an area quite unprepared to take over management of developments made by colonial powers now departed. For all the criticism of Great Britain's behavior in India, much was accomplished by the British, though undoubtedly if a great deal more that was possible had been accomplished it would have served the needs of India even more.

The problem is perhaps subtler with regard to projects to be carried out publicly. The implications of the question of general stability are obvious enough. If the groups in power are likely to shift frequently, many projects will certainly be wiped out, many will be stopped while under way, etc. But capriciousness may still remain even when such stability problems do not arise. Many of these areas have governments by crony and by nepotism which are considered not only not evil but even virtuous. Under these circumstances a change in favorites may introduce elements of caprice, and even stability may lead to many expenditures on noneffective productive or nonproductive capital. When such governments use mobs for the attainment of their ends, they are gravely limited not only in what they can plan, but also in what they can preserve. Here the problem is further complicated by the fact that these limitations are extremely difficult if not impossible to predict in advance. Finally, the efforts of these governments to remain in power may also undercut economic development. In the Middle East, we now have an example of a potentate who wishes economic development with little or no increase in public education and the like. Within limits, based as his economy is on the production of oil for export, much development has taken place from his point of view, but certainly most of the income from that source has so far gone into relatively nonproductive capital formation.

Motivation for Effective Productive Capital Formation. One of the major obstacles to the formation of effective productive capital is the formation of capital of other sorts. The social structure of these areas has not generally been highly productive of motivation for effective productive capital formation. In the first place, in many if not most of these areas the entrepreneurial role has had low prestige. As will be suggested below, this can operate in more than one way, but ideally speaking such roles have frequently been roles to be gotten out of rather than the reverse. In the second place, such systems have placed heavy emphasis on the maintenance of the *status quo* with regard to social patterns, and the kind of capital formation relevant here can move forward hardly at all without being subversive of the *status quo.* In the third place, these societies have generally been characterized by populations which as a whole have been split up into units (such as family units) in which self-sufficiency of the units is highly prized. This means that a good part of the motivation for capital formation has been directed at supplying the directly and indirectly generated needs of the restricted wealthy groups, in which the family units are not self-sufficient. Such motivation has therefore been highly susceptible to the appeal of "commercialization" as contrasted with industrialization. In the fourth place, the radically ascetic orientations of these areas have tended to focus on other-worldly asceticism rather than radical mastery over the physical facts of the empirical world. In the fifth place, the concepts of the public good in these areas have been oriented to renovations of the *status quo* and not to revolutions of the social system; the concern of the ruling groups with such things as public education, public health, and the like, if present at all, has been primarily impelled by a desire to avoid trouble. This has meant that motivation for the general background formations of effective productive capital has not been great. There are undoubtedly many other factors of this order that a more systematic study of these questions would produce.

I would suggest as a hypothesis that in most of these areas the motivation for such capital formation as is assumed here to be most desired either has been negatively produced (i.e. that it is either an unintended but recognized function of the operation of these systems or an unintended and unrecognized function of their operation) or is a function of the operation of opportunism or "individualism by default" in the somewhat undefined context of the conditions of transition under the impact of contacts with more modern systems. This hypothesis is in no sense tested or proved. It is presented merely because its exploration may prove illuminating in some cases, even if its application is not as general as the hypothesis states. The implications of the differences between the two sources of such motivation seem interesting. The first sort offers the easier possibility of planned transition despite its negative source in the systems from which change takes place. The line of concentration of effort of the second sort is likely to be far more difficult to predict and is far more likely to reflect short-run private interests that are not coordinated with those of the system as a whole.

In the cases of China and Japan we have an illuminating comparative example of this sort. One of the social patterns associated with highly industrialized, modern systems is the so-called open-class type of stratification as opposed to a closed-class type. The former involves the possibility of social mobility of individuals and their families with regard to class position. The latter refers to a system in which, ideally and actually speaking, it is expected that an individual will remain in the class position which he is given at birth. Usually this position is the one occupied by his parents. The distinction between ideal and actual patterns has been brought into the discussion here because class systems that are, ideally speaking, open are frequently in actuality clogged to a high degree. That is to say, in actuality the possibilities of social mobility in an ideally open-class system may be very restricted. This is a case, however, in which an ideal pattern that is not in fact lived up to may nevertheless be of great importance as a feature of the social structure. It is reasonably safe to say that most of the areas with which we are concerned have either highly clogged open-class systems or closed-class systems. It might also be pointed out that societies with class systems that are, ideally speaking, closed may actually have social mobility. It may be suggested as a useful hypothesis that societies that have, ideally speaking, open-class systems are more likely to have a single ideal class type, whereas those with ideally closed-class systems are likely to have a specific ideal class type corresponding to each of the closed class distinctions.

There are marked examples of these distinctions. The caste system in India, insofar as it remains, is an extreme form of a closed-class system, and there are ideal expectations for each of its many distinctions. For those who believe in the caste system there and the system of religious orientations that goes along with it, the religious sanctions for these variegated ideal types are rather clear-cut. These people believe in reincarnation and that one's role in the next incarnation is a function of how well one has fulfilled the expectations of the previous roles. If an Indian is born a member of the Sudra caste, his chance for advancement is believed to be improved to the extent that he performs the Sudra role well. The Brahmin role has much higher prestige than the Sudra role, but for a member of the Sudra to act like a Brahmin, however virtuous he may be in all other respects, is to assure that his next incarnation will be lower in the scale rather than higher. For those who hold such beliefs, the effects on their actions are considerable. It is difficult if not impossible to understand or to analyze what they do without taking this into account. By no means all societies have such neatly "internalized" methods of maintaining such structures. In Tokugawa Japan a samurai had full authority to cut down with his sword a merchant or peasant who dared to act as though he were of higher status.

In "traditional" China there was both ideally and actually an open-class system, though actually the system got highly clogged especially toward the end of dynasties. In some cases elements of closure, ideally speaking, were also introduced, but they seem never to have caught on fully or to have been well maintained. Despite much careless recent writing, China has not been a feudal society for 2,000 years, unless one uses the term feudal in its purely invidious sense, meaning a society in which many people are poorly off and a few are very well off by our standards, and which is not "modern." For 2,000 years China certainly has not had the closed-class system so characteristic of those European systems that we are accustomed to call feudal. The path of social mobility was through the acquisition of a classical Chinese education and the attainment of public office through competition in the examination system or some subversion of that system. Officeholding, scholarly attainments, and income from either office or the absentee ownership of land (or both) were the requirements of gentry status. A man who acquired these raised his family in general to that level in Chinese eyes. In theory the examination system was open to all, and, though occasional bits of closure were introduced by barring some from these competitions (e.g. the sons of merchants or actors), these barriers were never well maintained. Those with money enough to educate their sons could usually ignore or get others to ignore these restrictions.

In this society, merchants had very low prestige, ideally speaking, and the wealthiest merchant was inferior to any member of the gentry, the peasantry, or the artisans, in that order. Actually, of course, the merchants were frequently very powerful and very much respected, just as gangsters and political bosses in our society sometimes circumvent ideal expectations. To put the matter briefly, this setting furnished powerful motivation to take both capital and talent out of entrepreneurial roles and put them into roles that were either simply not germane or even obstacles to the type of development in which we are interested. Able sons of merchants were to be educated in the classical Chinese manner as soon as the family could afford it. That education had many appealing features, but it was by no means suited to roles concerned with effective productive capital formation. Capital was absorbed in the education of these sons and in the purchase of land rather than in reinvestment in entrepreneurial roles. Ideally speaking, gentry were not supposed to be concerned directly with production but were expected to live as devoted scholars or as public functionaries. The test par excellence of success in entrepreneurial roles in "traditional" China was how long the pursuit of these roles had to be followed before the family could be transferred to gentry roles and types of investment. These types of investment tended to involve either nonproductive capital formation or noneffective productive capital formation. Although there were exceptions, this was the general pattern. There were also even further implications of this setting for the problem with which we are concerned here, but those given will have to suffice for present purposes.

In Japan, on the other hand, there was both ideally and actually a closed-class system with very few exceptions (and probably without any, ideally speaking). Here too the merchants, ideally speaking, had low social status, and persons of high social status were not expected to contaminate themselves with entrepreneurial roles. Landholding and certain types of education and habits irrelevant to or subversive of modernization were characteristic of the high status groups. Moreover, the merchants, though ideally of low status, became in fact very powerful. Unlike the Chinese, however, merchants in Japan could take neither talent nor capital out of merchant roles on any large scale. Much was spent on luxury consumer goods, but patterns of social abstemiousness in the society placed a brake on this sort of obstacle to effective productive capital formation. The merchants could not buy land in any substantial quantities, if at all. This was a feudal system in the ordinary historical sense, and landownership went with the positions in the feudal hierarchy.[19] The merchants had to be constantly on the lookout for new enterprises to absorb the talents of the next generation and the profits from their past operations. They were aided and abetted in the opening up of new avenues by a factor also present to some extent in China. In many ideal respects, to pay attention to the merchants

[19] Even the samurai did not "own" land but had certain rights to rice income from the lands of the daimyo to whom they were attached.

was so beneath the dignity of their superiors that the merchants' behavior was not regulated in the same detail by either law or custom as was the behavior of those holding more important roles in the society.

The analysis of the distinctions between China and Japan here is too brief for any save illustrative purposes. Suffice it to say that the merchants of Tokugawa Japan were themselves the leaders of their country's modernization, which went ahead with remarkable facility. Most of the zaibatsu of modern Japan became powerful members of the new government as well as the industrial, financial, and commercial leaders of the new state. From the start of the modern period the great family enterprises of Japan were highly diversified. The Mitsui and Mitsubishi were in everything from fishing through manufacturing to banking and insurance. This diversification shows some marked contrast to the family fortunes of the West, which originally seem to have been based largely on a single line of endeavor, such as railroads, steel, chemicals, or banking. Here again the Japanese reflect their background, for the same sort of diversification characterized the interests of the Tokugawa merchants. Early in the development of Japan the Tokugawa merchants, faced with limitations characteristic of a feudal economy, had been forced to seek many different ways of investing their incomes.

The contrast with the Chinese merchants of the "traditional" period is marked. With the introduction of the new forces in China the old merchants occupied the roles of middlemen or went in heavily for "commercialization," although they still continued to take their talents and their capital out of such roles as quickly as possible. The banks of China gravitated into the hands of such men and of large landholders, who quickly became one and the same. These banks made land loans to a much greater extent than those of Japan. The new businessmen of China seem really to have awaited a whole generation's training in schools abroad, and even those so trained were continually being drained off into administration of landholdings and into "commercialized" efforts from which large and quick profits could be made. Government office was exploited for private advantage, as it no doubt was in Japan. But in Japan private advantage was conceived to lie in the direction of the formation of effective productive capital, and this was not the case in China. One of the few convertible elements in the Chinese situation was, curiously enough, the high prestige of education for gentry status. With the wiping out of the examination system and, even before that, with demonstrations of the power of those with new ways, many of the merchants and many of the gentry explored the idea of Western educations as a path of prestige for their sons. These were the sons who tried to do what the Japanese did, but they ran into immediate problems. In the first place, they picked up many things in their new education that alarmed the older generation. These were new ideas about marriage and the family, etc., which shook the faith of their elders in their judgment. Furthermore, it was their elders, without such education, who had control of the capital assets of the area. Land was a rock of security, and the employment of relatives was a minimal manifestation of humanity. Finally, in the 1930's, when some headway was being made by the differently educated young, the Japanese dealt China what may in the long run prove to have been her most serious blow. The Japanese took over just those areas in which new plants and projects were struggling to operate in new ways. In so doing, they wiped out the basis for power of the young, progressive businessmen in the Kuomintang and left power in the hands of the most "traditionally minded" and correspondingly the most "land-oriented" men in China.

One other factor may be mentioned here to illustrate the rather strange way in which the transformation of social factors may have results different from those expected. China had a civil service system with methods of seeking out talent via the examination system. Japan did not. Both China and Japan were societies in which nepotism not only was not a sin but was in fact a virtue. In the Chinese bureaucracy no effort was made to teach the point of view that nepotism was evil; an effort was simply made to insulate people against it—to make it impossible for nepotism to operate. It may be taken as an assumption here that the operation of nepotism in either the public or the private sphere is likely to interfere with the formation of effective productive capital. In the Chinese case the fatal flaw was the type of civil service system. It was based on achievement in a type of education almost certain to be an obstacle to the new requirements. In Japan, however, the saving grace was a little-studied system of "civil service by adoption." Japanese family heads who lacked an able son to succeed them could and sometimes did deliberately seek out a young man who had already demonstrated considerable ability of the type sought and adopt him. Unlike the Chinese system, this meant that people were picked for criteria relevant to the tasks they would perform. What is perhaps even more important from the motivational point of view, this procedure united the family interests and the occupational-role interests of the person picked rather than leaving a possible conflict between them. It was a system not unlike that in this country of giving conspicuously able managerial personnel stock in the company to assure their undivided interest. The zaibatsu of Japan seem to have raised this practice of civil service by adoption to the point of explicit family policy.

Formation of Other Types of Capital. One of the most obvious obstacles to the formation of effective productive capital is the formation of other types of capital. This does not imply a sort of "wage-fund" doctrine of capital in any absolute sense, but it seems reasonable to maintain that the formation of nonproductive capital represents a diversion from the formation of effective productive capital. It is an obstacle in two other senses as well. In the first place, any nonproductive or noneffective productive capital requires some type of conversion if it is to become effective productive capital, and in some cases it may be impossible to make such conversions.[20] In the second place, the formation of these other types of capital may interfere positively with the formation of effective productive capital.

In our discussion we shall not be concerned with the formation of noneffective productive capital because of the idiosyncrasies of individual judgment. There are going to be such failures in all types of systems from the most to the least modern. Our interest lies in such capital when there is a good possibility that it is noneffective for reasons rather systematically related to social structure on a rather general level.[21] Our first concern here is with the formation of nonproductive capital, and in this connection it is well to keep in mind the evaluations built into the concepts used here.

As mentioned above, most of the areas that we have discussed are ones with a comparatively small number of very wealthy people and a vast majority with very low incomes and living on the bare margin of subsistence, neither in good health nor for long, by modern standards. With incomes of that type, the vast majority can do little to change this picture through their own efforts alone. We are not concerned here with whether any of these people at either extreme of the income scale are good or evil, but merely with

[20] Such capital might be called *absolutely nonproductive capital.*

[21] We simply tease ourselves if we believe that any science will accurately predict the idiosyncratic; the state of development of the social sciences as compared with the natural sciences is such that what appears to be idiosyncratic is encountered on a far more general level in the former than in the latter.

how they do or can behave and with some of the implications of their behavior. Cannot the income of the wealthy be taken over directly and turned to new purposes? Regardless of what one thinks about state interference in these matters, the problem is not simple. In the first place, the wealthy people usually have a great deal to say about their governments and are strategic to the system's traditional mode of operation. This means that steps taken in violation of their wishes must face the question of revolutionizing the social structure, as has been done to some extent in Turkey and Japan. In the second place, the wealthy have not customarily used their wealth in a manner relevant for the new purposes.

Much of the income of the wealthy has gone into nonproductive capital or into capital that is productive only indirectly and hence is a form of noneffective productive capital. Nonproductive capital takes many forms, which can be classified in part under Veblen's rubric of conspicuous consumption. Many of the wealthy maintain extremely elaborate households. While they have performed a service in preserving much of the art of the various areas, such capital is not convertible on the whole into productive forms. They have also employed much of their wealth to reallocate the various resources of the community, primarily by investing in land. This has had profound effects on the social structure by increasing tenancy and the like, but these reallocations have had little if anything to do with improving the productivity of the resources. In some cases, however, such concentration of control over resources may be useful for purposes of conversion, because it may make possible use of large units of resources for modernization. In some types of agrarian production, this may be crucial, since the alternative usually consists of small, highly cut-up landholdings on which economies of largescale production are difficult to achieve. While it has been hard to dispossess large landholders it has been even harder to dispossess small ones.

The expenditures of the wealthy on conspicuous consumption are for the most part down the drain as far as present purposes are concerned. The far-reaching effects of this are more obvious if one realizes that most of the production of the artisans in these areas goes to satisfy the demands of the wealthy and their retainers. The basic support of these economies rests largely on agrarian production in highly self-sufficient units to which the artisans have contributed little. The convertibility of these artisans to other occupations may be extremely difficult, especially to the extent to which these occupations are highly traditionalized, as they generally are.

In addition, in many if not most of these areas there has been a complex of motives leading to the amassment of "hard goods" such as jewels and precious metals. To some extent, this has been motivated by their display value, but there is probably no small element of concern over security involved. Resources in this form do not produce an income, but in societies in which the governments can be capricious from the point of view of the individual (whether because of authoritarianism or instability matters little here), these forms of wealth are difficult to destroy and relatively easy to hide and transport. Furthermore, in most cases their value has been surprisingly stable throughout history. (Aluminum, once regarded as a precious metal, has been an exception.) While hoarded, these forms of capital remain unproductive, but the savings they represent are at least productive at the second remove as long as the general world demand for such items holds up. Japan is a case in point. In her development, hoards of specie were systematically used to get effective productive capital from abroad.

It is comparatively simple to say that for modernization to take place one must inhibit these nonproductive capital formations, confiscate hoards, exchange them for effective productive capital, etc. But like so many things simply said, this is not simply done. The nonproductive capital frequently is involved in the income of large groups such as the artisans. Furthermore, one cannot stop these modes of expenditures without having some plan for handling the consequent dislocations—or without facing the results thereof. When one turns from the wealthy to the populace at large, the problem turns into the whole problem of modernization. Even the little the populace has may be expended in relatively nonproductive forms; correction of this involves nothing less than a revolution in social structure. The economic allocation of an area is not a concretely separable set of factors. It is only one way of looking at the system in general.

The bases for noneffective productive capital formation promise to cause even greater difficulties. If the motivation to abandon the old is strong enough, many of the problems of nonproductive capital formation may be rather easy to handle, although many of them are functions of the desire to change itself. One of the most notable of these is what has already been dubbed "conspicuous industrialization." Some of the most progressive reformers in "backward" areas are sometimes the most difficult to handle. The modernization involved in setting up agrarian cooperatives lacks the obvious features of a modern steel mill, a cellophane plant, or an assembly depot for automobiles, but these latter may be more than a simple waste of short resources. In areas lacking a comparative advantage for such production and unable to utilize the output of such plants, their running costs in terms of scarce foreign exchange may be a more significant obstacle to the formation of effective productive capital than their initial cost or their maintenance in idleness. There is more than naïve emulation involved here. There is the relevance of heavy production facilities to the maintenance of armies and fleets, a matter to be discussed briefly below. There is also the problem of modern nationalism, which seems to go along with these transformations. Under these conditions, counsel from abroad to the effect that the most modern plants are by no means those most suited to modernize an area in all respects may be and is often regarded as a form of imperialism.

"Conspicuous industrialization" is a function of pride, folly, and uncritical hope on the part of local inhabitants and foreigners alike. There are other problems that are less obviously a function of human fallibility. These areas in general lack experts, and foreign areas have not supplied them as easily as some assumed would be the case. Only education and development of a sort that is costly and not easily motivated on a private basis can correct this lack. Here one is faced with questions of the type of *expertise* needed, the ability of the experts to communicate and get along with the nonexperts, a stable continuity of experts if they must come from abroad, etc. The social systems in these areas have not generally provided the kind of education necessary for the development of such experts. There is even a further difficulty in that neither we nor they have the experts needed to train such experts.

Another feature related to the new nationalism is suspicion of foreigners in general and of those of the modern West in particular. One need not review the basis for this. There are sins on both sides, if one must pass judgment; the record of the West has by no means always shown a high concern for the prosperity and human dignity of the inhabitants of these areas. In addition, the new leaders have in many cases deliberately played on these feelings of resentment as a method of gaining or holding power. This has in some cases resulted in keeping major elements of productive capital noneffective. Although one may not wish to assess blame in the recent historical developments in Iran, there is no doubt that it exemplifies the immediate transfer of a major resource into a noneffective state. Rational arguments in purely economic terms are relatively ineffective in solving problems of this order.

The use of capital for armies, fleets, and air forces raises another problem. Whatever such items may mean in terms of sovereignty and international prestige, they are a waste from the point of view of effective productive capital unless it can be shown that the multiplier effects of such expenditures more than offset the expenditures themselves. Even this would raise the question of whether or not other sources of stimulus could not be found which would themselves be effectively productive. Japan, Germany, and Russia all carried out their transformations despite such formations of capital, and it would be useless to raise the question here as to how many of their international problems were a function of such expenditures. However, it is not fruitless to ask what would have happened if capital expenditures had been consumed in other directions. This, unfortunately, raises the whole question of the relevance of world peace and security to the formation of effective productive capital. Solutions to such questions are probably utopian.

Expenditures of capital in the name of nationalism either directly or indirectly do not often result in effective productive capital formation. It is important to note this, but lest this observation seem to support the notion of crusades against nationalism in the "backward areas" (and such crusades are likely to be ineffective) a word should be said on the other side. Whatever its shortcomings, intense nationalism is a general sort of faith in terms of which individuals may be motivated in many diverse ways. I have tried to show in other connections above that, because of the impact of the new forces, the traditional patterns in these areas are likely to be under heavy and effective assault—and this through no one's malevolence or plotting. Intense nationalistic sentiment, growing either with or without explicit encouragement, may well be the major new and unspecified general form of faith in terms of which the new values may be integrated into the life of the members of the traditional society. There is always some pride and faith in the identity of the traditional system to serve as a basis for nationalistic identification. In the future we may look back and see that nationalism, for all its costs to men in terms of lives, treasures, and accomplishments lost, has played a necessary role in these developments.[22]

[22] In addition to the factors mentioned above, nationalism may play a vital role in stimulating internal investment.

There is one highly general reason for believing this. The conversions seem to require that considerations of personal identification such as one's family, village, class, school, and circle of friends be progressively ignored in one's selection for different sorts of treatment. These "particularistic criteria" (in the jargon of sociology) are utilized in all societies for some purposes, but their role is sharply limited in highly modernized societies by contrast with relatively nonmodernized ones for reasons that need not detain us here. These modernized societies place heavy emphasis, especially in the roles most vital to the operation of the new technologies, on generalized qualities and performances (i.e. "universalistic criteria," in sociological jargon). At the same time, although we know relatively little in any precise sense about motivation in general, it would seem that personal identification with a cause is of great importance in creating and maintaining such motivation as is necessary for the sort of effort involved in the developments sought here. The traditional bases of such identifications may well interfere with effective productive capital formation by raising such problems as that of nepotism. Nationalism is also an identification of the particularistic sort that can and does interfere with the process of effective productive capital formation; but it bases its personal identification on a sufficiently large group so that within the group an exceedingly broad basis remains for the selection of individuals in terms of what they can do rather than who they are.

The problem of nationalism as both an aid and an obstacle in this process points up one other extremely general consideration. It is not difficult to persuade researchers and even the general public that some of the features of the traditional basis are obstacles to change, that some may aid it, and that some may act in both ways. It is, however, no less necessary to realize that some of the factors that may be prerequisites for the process or even requisites of the maintenance of the desired goals may also in part inhibit the attainment of those goals. One of the major policy problems posed in these areas is that of neutralizing the inhibitory effects of patterns that are unavoidable if the changes sought are to be achieved. This is another of the fundamentals in the naïveté of the assumption that clever social engineering will be able to achieve a combination of the "best of the East and the West."

The Demographic Problem. The demographic problem has received so much attention from thoroughly qualified experts that I intend here merely to point up some of its implications for the present discussion. The elements of the problem are well known. Most of the so-called underdeveloped areas are characterized by very high and steady birth rates and high but fluctuating death rates. The net rate of increase is thus usually small. The absolute size of these populations relative to their present incomes is such that considerable portions of the populations involved live close to or well below the margin of subsistence by Western standards. The death rates in these areas, as well as the rates of debilitating diseases, arise from sources such that modern medical technology can with comparative ease greatly reduce them and make them relatively stable at lower points. It would be extremely expensive to cut them to the rates considered endurable in the most modern societies, but comparatively cheap and easy cuts would still have dramatic effects for the nonmodern, relatively nonindustrialized underdeveloped areas. In addition, because of the size of populations and the traditional modes of occupation, the introduction of modern forms of capital will encounter no shortage of manpower in general, though there will probably be acute shortages of properly trained and educated persons. Under such circumstances the pressures to take advantage of medical technologies available are likely to be great; if for no other reason than the problem of absenteeism, reductions in the death rate and the rates of endemic diseases are likely to be requirements for the changes sought. Heretofore, efforts to reduce the birth rate rapidly have not been successful. Some Westerners believe such efforts to be ethically bad, and the vast majority of those in the areas concerned are for one reason or another much preoccupied with keeping it high. We know, however, that in the past those societies that have industrialized have, whether they wished to or not, been characterized by falling birth rates for a whole series of reasons (about which our knowledge is by no means certain). But these birth rates have not fallen without very considerable population increases taking place in the interval. In the course of the process in the West, most of the areas concerned had considerable untapped resources in the form of land, etc., available. That is not the case with the areas concerned here, pending rather radical developments that seem to be nowhere in the making. With a 1 per cent net increase in population per year an area's population will double in 69.7 years, with a net increase of 2 per cent it will require 35 years, and with a net increase of 3 per cent 23.4 years will do the trick. Given the height of birth rates, the type of death rates, and the available medical technology, net rates of increase of

1 per cent on a temporary basis should be simply achieved, and ones of 2 or 3 per cent are by no means out of the question. I say "on a temporary basis" because, barring quite radical rates of development, the death rates would soon rise again from starvation, and the attendant social unrest (nowhere do even the most backward peoples cherish high death rates from such sources) would surely not be conducive to high rates of development.

All this means that for capital formation to be effective and productive, the rate of increased productivity that it brings must be geared to the increases in the net rate of growth of population that seem certain to accompany it. Moreover, the distributive system must get these increases to the population on a corresponding basis. If the net rate increases 1 per cent per year, the increase in capital formation must be such as to allow increased production of 1 per cent per year at a minimum. When one considers that some of these areas have base populations today in the neighborhood of 400 million and that several tens of millions is by no means uncommon, the implications of the demographic problem for that of the scale of the programs mentioned above are not difficult to visualize. Furthermore, the relationship will probably have to be more than a one-to-one correspondence to be effective, because some of the increases in production will of necessity be such that their distributive implications will not be immediate. The comparative advantage situation of the particular area will be important for this problem, and such things as "conspicuous industrialization" will have large effects.

Thus there can be little doubt that a major problem in social engineering is to bring about unprecedented drops in the birth rate. Study may show us what factors in industrialization are most important, and such knowledge may make it possible to attempt to maximize these effects. Currently, however, we have no major source of assurance that this is possible, much less that it is practicable. The implications of what we seem to know are stark. If declines in the birth rate can be achieved, there is little doubt that their implications will be revolutionary for the social structure. They will certainly require radical alterations in family structure, and in many areas they are sure to raise large-scale problems about the care of the aged. In those societies in which the major sources of control are highly dependent upon family patterns, the whole problem of a new basis for control will be opened up. One could go on. The problem in terms of goods and gold may be large enough, but its solution cannot even be begun solely in those terms. Radical increases in the net rate of population growth could make current rates of capital formation noneffective in any area, and in the nonmodern, relatively nonindustrialized areas it is difficult to see how this is to be avoided.

One of the knottiest problems in connection with this grim demographic picture is its implications for the general state of motivation in the areas concerned. We know little enough about motivation, but in a common-sense way we feel (and such scientific findings as we have do not seem to contradict this feeling) that in all of these areas there is an interest in the material improvement of the way of life in terms of better health, more food, better housing, and a larger per capita income of goods and services. This is enough to make certain aspects of the new forces from the West appealing for one reason or another to one group or another in these areas. However, the introduction of these new ways has implications not appealing to these peoples. In some cases it is realized in advance that many undesired patterns and conditions will accompany the desired changes; in most cases, however, this is not fully realized. These peoples always seem to want to maintain many of their traditional patterns and many that inhibit the formation of effective productive capital. As suggested above, nationalistic sentiments are important in this connection. Furthermore, the expectations of accomplishment via the new ways are likely to be grandiose. Expectations of precipitate results are the order of the day. These expectations are fostered by the attitude of many of the experts from the West. These experts come from societies which could not have the systems they have without this element of confidence in the ability of their ways to conquer such obstacles quickly and easily. Almost everywhere in the areas to be developed, the increased survival of children, dramatic improvements in public health, and increased life expectancy are publicly viewed as blessings. The implications of these blessings are not likely to be immediately grasped as flowing from the same source. The sense of sacrifice of traditional ways is likely to be acute. The failure of productive capital to be effective because of these factors is likely to result in serious undermining of hope and motivation. Initial successes are more apt to be complicated by subsequent disillusionment. The most difficult problem of all, however, is that the motivation (such as that in terms of nationalism) which permits certain unpopular features to be put into effect is likely to turn into substantial motivation for their elimination, despite the fact that many of the features so attacked are likely to be requisites for any long-run success of the program. Productive capital may, of course, be rendered noneffective by irrational action economically oriented. It may also be rendered noneffective by quite rational action or irrational action oriented to the maintenance of traditional patterns. The motivation of the latter is the more likely in cases of disillusionment flowing from the demographic problem of these areas.

The problems connected with the demographic situation will require large-scale planning and coordination, which in turn are likely to require the participation of some major public body in addition to or apart from private initiative. Public control is also necessary if the private interests and the public controlling bodies in the area are not identically composed or do not see eye to eye. If the demographic problem is not to hinder the formation of effective productive capital, such formation must take into consideration the demographic problem as well as more orthodox questions of the marginal productivity of capital. For example, it may "pay" in this sense to try deliberately to urbanize and industrialize certain areas, because shifts from rural to modern urban settings and shifts from traditional to modern occupational roles have quite frequently been associated with the breakup of traditional families and with falling birth rates. It may also pay early in the game to seek to increase the production of, and the ability to purchase, heavy consumer goods, because the availability of such goods, along with birth-control techniques, may be accompanied by an attitude of choosing between more children and more such goods. Such considerations cannot, of course, be admitted to the exclusion of more orthodox questions of the productivity of alternative employments of capital, but neither can they be ignored in areas in which the demographic problems are so different from those now generally faced by the more highly modernized and industrialized areas. The fact that many of our demographers are also highly trained economists should be an asset in this problem of social engineering.

Foreign and Domestic Action Not Oriented to Internal Balance. In this field there has been a great deal of discussion of the role of imperialism in area developments. Like many highly charged controversies, this problem will probably turn out to have been characterized by more heat than light and by more failures to communicate than actual differences over points raised. As indicated above, foreign "interference," even when narrowly motivated by self-interest, has by no means been devoid of positive significance in the formation of effective productive capital. There are still, no doubt, groups in the world who, consciously or unconsciously, would prefer to see developments in the nonmodern, relatively nonindustrialized areas serve to increase effective productive capital in their own countries or in any conflict of interests prefer to serve themselves rather than others. The implications of this, whether termed exploitation or not, for the formation of noneffective productive capital are fairly obvious. This problem may always be with us, but in the current world situation I think that it is not the main source of difficulty with regard to foreign participation in the areas discussed here. It is certainly not in any *overt*, announced sense the motivation of the major powers on either side of the iron curtain, and both sides have reason to stand in much fear of giving world opinion grounds for such an accusation.

On the domestic side there is likely to be more ground for such fear. Individual initiative is likely to be very important for the development of effective productive capital in all of these areas, but such initiative raises difficult questions of control. The tendency of individual initiative to use capital-forming as a way station in escaping from lesser roles into more traditionally evaluated ones, the motivation for "commercialization" rather than the formation of effective productive capital, and the problem of "individualism by default" have all been mentioned above. The last of these three may be particularly troublesome. The other two are, after all, functions of highly structured social situations, and to that extent the possibility of operating in terms of those structures to negate their effects is opened up. The third, however, is more likely to be a function of the breakdown of social structures and the absence of new ones which would place limits on opportunism without physical coercion. This may have nothing whatever to do with the problem of the "evils of human nature." It may be a function of the fact, for example, that persons used to making decisions in terms of the implications of their actions for their families now no longer have such families or cannot calculate effects in these terms.

In the West, where the virtues of individualism are so much appreciated by the general public, we have lost sight of what a highly stylized individualism it is. One has only to look at some of the nineteenth and eighteenth century arguments against publicly supported education, post offices, etc., to see how much this situation has changed. Moreover, the most conservative of our organizations representing private business would hardly now advocate permitting the kind of financial manipulations and deals that characterized the extremely rapid development in the United States in the late nineteenth and early twentieth centuries. This is not the place to go into the structural ramifications of "individualism by default." Suffice it to say that any substantial amount of such individualism would greatly complicate the problem of planning and coordination necessary for the formation of effective productive capital in these underdeveloped areas.

It is, perhaps, going much too far if one maintains that the "it's a plot" theory of social problems in either international or domestic affairs is never tenable, but over the centuries efforts to analyze social problems predominantly in such terms have had such modest success that it might be desirable for the present to regard such an approach with skepticism. Whatever the history of the past may have been, the great present danger in the nonmodern, underdeveloped areas, without considering the iron curtain countries for the moment, is not that one nation or group of nations will urge another to develop for its own betterment without any genuine interest in the betterment of the nation being developed. Even if one or more nations should do so, our problem would not be one of obstacles to the formation of effective productive capital in the "backward areas" but would be one of the formation of effective productive capital in the relatively modern and highly industrialized areas. The effectiveness and productivity of the capital for the more "advanced areas" in this case would be predicated on the use of resources of all sorts in the less "advanced areas" with no concern for the formation of effective productive capital there save as it may serve foreign interests. Even if one assumes the best intentions on the part of the foreign powers, however, there will still be enough factors that will impede the process.

Our ignorance is likely to be a greater enemy than any evil machinations. In both foreign and domestic cases we are likely not to have any real basis for knowing what the direct and indirect effects of given attempts to increase the formation of effective productive capital will be. In addition to the fact that some of the factors themselves vital to this end will have inhibitory effects, many factors not vital to such an end will also be introduced and may have inhibitory effects. We are by no means clear about how the parts of these modern, highly industrialized areas interrelate; we are no more clear about the relatively nonmodern, nonindustrialized underdeveloped areas; and we are correspondingly unclear about what must be done to develop the latter and what the effects of such actions may be. It is not going too far to say that one of the major difficulties in the formation of such capital is this ignorance. Few of our current experts are of much help to those responsible for policy decisions in these fields. We need a great deal of research on these problems, but at all times we are likely to have to operate with less knowledge than would be desirable. This is not a counsel of despair, but it indicates that those concerned with such programs must have an ability to recognize failures and a willingness to write them off without throwing further "good" capital after "bad."

The question of handling Machiavellian intents domestically is part of the general problem of control touched on above; that of handling international Machiavellianism is still, alas, a problem of balances of power, with some assistance toward a solution coming from the United Nations Organization.

Conservation of Resources. One of the most persistent notes of explicit warning on the modern scene is that struck by the conservationists, who have pointed with alarm to the manner in which natural resources such as timber, land, minerals, etc., have been exploited in the most modern, highly industrialized areas as well as in the more "backward areas." I do not intend to deny those arguments; I merely want to raise questions about them in connection with the problem posed here.[23] There is little reason to question the fact that, by some standards, we have been prodigal in our use of these resources, and perhaps there is nothing but good to be gained from trying to prevent a repetition of such experiences. The same solicitude is no less germane to the question of capital in general.[24] The cutting of forests without plans or investment in reforestation has its analogue in the use of machinery by labor skilled enough to operate it but not to maintain it in such a way as to prevent rapid depreciation, etc. The problem raised here is whether the conservationists' position does or does not involve an absolute (and usually implicit) standard of waste. It may well be that certain "ruthless" exploitations of resources, quite uneconomic at other times and by other standards, are quite necessary for these developments. If these resources are directly absorbed in uses that do not have impli-

[23] Much of the material presented on this point is based on discussions of this matter with Jacob Viner. He cannot, of course, be held responsible for the shortcomings of its use here.

[24] However, it may even pay in some cases to engage in what may be shoddy investment by modern Western standards, especially if this permits an area to get some benefits more quickly and at the same time spread risks.

cations for maintaining or raising current rates of productivity, the conservationists are on extremely sound ground, and failure to heed their warnings will certainly impede the formation of effective productive capital or dissipate at a greater rate than otherwise that which is already in existence. In the nature of the case the argument of the conservationists envisages the future. The question that must be raised in this connection is that of the productivity of the employment of these resources. Has, in effect, the compound interest on the barns and houses built in the deforestation of the United States amounted to more than those forests would be worth had they been left standing? One may add to this the question of the income from the land thus cleared. This is not to say that the conservationists are wrong; but in any particular case one must estimate whether they have made the necessary allowances mentioned above as well as allowances for risks to the capital left better preserved but less used, for obsolescence of such capital, for changing evaluations of it, etc.

What may in some respects be very wasteful employments of capital, by current standards, may in some of the underdeveloped areas concerned provide a sort of bunched stimulus to development of effective productive capital that may far outweigh its waste by these other standards. The demographic problem is relevant to these considerations. If such prodigal uses of resources can quickly reduce birth rates, they might be well worth the future problems they would pose.

The solution to this question may vary widely depending on the resources of the area concerned. In some areas forest may simply be burned off to get arable land, and in others forests may have to be planted. But all underdeveloped areas are likely to face this problem in some form because it is an inescapable aspect of the problem of alternative possible employments for scarce resources. Certainly all these areas face it with regard to the employment of machinery, for all of them have a general dearth of skilled labor to combine with machinery. One can always defer the use of machinery until a higher level of training has been reached. But overconservation of various forms of capital may well be a major obstacle to the formation of effective productive capital in some places. This possibility is increased by the fact that outsiders in trying to help these areas and local inhabitants in trying to improve their situations are likely to be much concerned with avoiding the mistakes made before. Even if they have correctly calculated the extent of the wastes in the more "advanced areas," counsel against such practices in South America, for example, may not be warranted. Here one is faced not only with the usual problem of lack of necessary information, but also with the problem of the potential nontransferability of information that may be quite adequate in some contexts.

Separation of Ownership and Control. The pattern of separation of ownership and control through such modern devices as stock companies and debentures of all sorts has become a commonplace in the West, but it is not familiar in all areas, especially in the relatively nonmodern, nonindustrialized areas, for a number of reasons. One of these may well be the much more limited extent to which money is a generalized medium of exchange. A second is the question of security of investment in general. A third, closely related in some senses to the second, may be the fact that in most of these areas individuals must either handle their own affairs directly or have them handled by someone with whom they have a strong personal bond. A fourth factor may be that in most of these areas productive enterprises are generally expected to be handled in terms of some specifically traditionalized unit such as the family or the village. A fifth may be the frequent emphasis on a high degree of self-sufficiency of the productive units. There are, no doubt, many other considerations that could be added to this list. Those given here should serve to open up the question and consist of observations that can probably be quite widely documented.

The limitations suggested above on the separation of ownership and control by the technique conventional in the West for accomplishing this on a private enterprise basis handicap the extent to which private initiative can operate in these areas. They raise serious problems of amassing capital for the enterprising person who is not at the time in command of a private fortune. To some extent this will cut down on the range of enterprise and initiative available to the system. This will be the more serious if one does not know in advance exactly what forms of initiative are most likely to pay off, and of course there is never such perfect prescience.

The limitations on separation of ownership and control on a private basis have other implications as well. They are likely to mean that much of the saving necessary for economic development will have to be carried out on a forced basis. Savings thus made can, according to the system, be used for different types of capital formation by either private or public agencies. In any case forced saving as compared with voluntary saving is likely to have social repercussions in the form of various types of discontent. Systems in which these savings are utilized by private individuals may make them a focus of aggression, and those in which they are used by public agencies may have the same effect with regard to public sources of control.

The separation of ownership and control by virtue of general public control of ventures, even when they are nominally owned by the government, also raises problems. Here there is little if any possibility of accumulating the capital necessary except via forced savings, taxes, etc. This is more likely if the general public is not accustomed to the depersonalized separation of ownership and control. Even in the most modern Western countries, government bond issues in which participation has been based on purely private initiative seem to have been successful on a large scale only under quite dramatic circumstances in which general sentiments of loyalty and the like as well as economic interest in the narrow sense have been appealed to. It may well be that people in the nonmodern, relatively nonindustrialized underdeveloped areas will calmly become habituated to such operations only if the public agencies take on general responsibility for the economic aspects of the life of the areas. This will, of course, pose all of the usual problems of a planned economy plus those of general development.

One other problem is worth pointing up in this connection.[25] This problem has to do with what has come to be referred to as the "circulation of the elites" in common-sense language. This is the problem of the role of experts and the difficulty of making them available and using them. The separation of ownership and control, especially when it carries with it depersonalized, relatively objective administration, may greatly stimulate the circulation of relevant experts in the system. This is true of at least two types of experts. In the first place, it is true of what one might call "business experts," those innovators especially skilled at detecting new avenues for effective productive capital formation, who may operate in terms of far vaster resources than they can command as individuals. This, of course, poses a corresponding problem of their individual mistakes in judgment. In this connection, motivations in the direction of "commercialization" would have to be carefully watched. In the second place, such separation should increase the sphere and ease

[25] I am indebted in considerable part to Klaus Knorr for private discussion of this question. He is in no way to be held responsible for any inadequacies of the discussion here.

of operation of what might be called "staff experts," those experts with a generalized command over technical know-how. The larger amassments of capital and the greater fluidity with regard to alternative employments of capital made possible by such separation are likely to provide new fields for such experts. These are fields that would not in general be uncovered by the mass of individual savers, who might lack either the imagination to see such opportunities[26] or the ability to save enough to put such imagination and initiative to work. This is the more likely if such separation also serves as an important step in freeing control of such enterprises from the highly personalized basis so common in these areas. In China, for example, where family obligations are so strong in "traditionally" oriented individuals that it is very difficult to resist the pressures of nepotism, such separation may be an important technique for avoiding these problems. It will never suffice alone as a technique for negating such pressures. But it is the essence of all of the problems on this score that no single technique by itself has any real probability of success.

SUMMARY

In what has been said above a division has been maintained between the special problems posed by the position of latecomers in this process of modernization and the general problems inherent in the basis from which change takes place in these underdeveloped areas. The former are problems that are in some sense common to all these areas; the latter are problems that will vary considerably with the special features of the areas concerned. Nevertheless, in the latter an attempt has been made here to focus attention on a series of difficulties that are likely to be rather widely distributed, with occasional digressions to point out major lines of differentiation.

As stated early in this paper, what has been presented here should be regarded as a set of tentative hypotheses rather than as scientifically established results. In my own work these hypotheses have been generated by analysis on a considerably more systematic, technical, and general basis than would be practicable here, but that work is also at a relatively untested stage of development. The intention throughout this paper has been to open up problems relevant to the framework in terms of which the allocation of goods

[26] Such imagination is not likely to be generalized throughout the population, and the general traditional orientations of the public in these areas are likely to inhibit it.

and services takes place. The generalized interest in the theory of allocation that has been a feature of the more strictly defined field of economics has, as is well known, operated in terms of a fairly constant (for the areas concerned in that theoretical development) set of assumptions (often implicit) about the framework in terms of which this allocation takes place. While there have been notable differences in the areas of primary concern in the theoretical development (e.g. the forms of business in France as contrasted with the United States), it has to a considerable degree been practicable to proceed in this fashion, since a large number of theorists have been willing and able to avoid the fallacies of overgeneralization and of reification. In the relatively nonmodern and relatively nonindustrialized underdeveloped areas even this degree of practicability is strictly limited. The different social patterns in these areas set different limits within which allocation takes place, and the changes in allocations occasioned by the shifts in the new directions result in more than reallocations of goods and services. In other words, these changes in allocations cannot be made except as parts of general structural changes in the social systems themselves. This is not some form of economic determinism. All of the new allocations involve allocations of roles, power and responsibility, integration and expression, solidarities, and the like, as well as allocations of goods and services. Only the fact that we have been able to take these factors more or less as constants in the modern Western countries has obscured their relevance. The noneconomic aspects of the social systems in underdeveloped areas do not always support, and often contradict, the patterns necessary if allocations of goods and services are to be brought more into conformity with those of more modern areas. The higher material productivity of the more modern areas will not be available to other areas unless such changes take place.

On the other hand, this does not make the general body of economic theory a matter of no concern to the people interested in relatively nonmodern, relatively nonindustrialized underdeveloped areas. Many of the existing theories will hold, although within a different setting than generally exists in the West, and many others will serve to set limits on what can be accomplished by certain types of internal social changes. The doctrine of comparative advantage will, for example, continue to point up the folly, from the point of view taken here, of internal pressures in the direction of "conspicuous industrialization." The question that must be faced in these areas is not that of abandoning one form of analysis and substituting another. It is rather a question of using the two or more forms together. In the course of this type of analysis, the perspective gained may sharpen the tools for purposes for which they have hitherto proved themselves highly useful but by no means fully adequate.

3. *Problems about Data*

Here again one is faced by a question in regard to which it will serve no one to ignore a parlous state of affairs. The kind of questions opened up in this paper have not been adequately explored in general and have been pursued in few if any cases in specific areas in the detail necessary. Even on questions that can be answered by data conventional for economists, such as prices, incomes, outputs, and the like, we have few figures for these underdeveloped areas, and not all of those we have are reliable or adequate for present purposes. Even the demographic data is chaotic; in the case of China, for example, it is easy to get into an argument about where, within 50 million one side or the other of 400 million, the population of China lies. Estimates of birth and death rates pose no fewer difficulties. Need for these conventional forms of data is obvious enough, but it must be borne in mind that their collection may involve very substantial outlays of capital with no very obvious and immediate return in terms of increased productivity. Some efforts are, however, being made in these directions.

But what of the more general questions such as the readier convertibility of certain types of class structures as compared with others? Data on these can, perhaps, be gathered by attitude questionnaires, but here one is faced with two problems. In the first place, even in their most expert applications these techniques are primarily in the stage of instruments being tested. In all of the areas concerned here, however, there exist these problems plus very substantial additional ones of communication posed by differences in language, values, etc. The problem is further complicated by the time factor. Policy decisions in these areas are not likely to await the completion of detailed, statistically precise studies by social scientists.

Moreover, the availability of records in these areas varies widely. While the historical records of the "traditional" period in China are voluminous, there are fewer records for the modern period. And our knowledge of the pitfalls of the data for the modern period is a great deal less reliable than that of the sinologists relative to the more classical materials. In addition, in some areas very few records of either sort exist. Most of these areas have not been studied on the scale or in the manner essential to produce the needed materials. Many of the available studies are on discrete questions and contain little general information about the social structure of these areas. We are likely to know a great deal about a particular village in India, for example, and have little knowledge of how far these results can be generalized for the area as a whole.

In studying these problems, there is no alternative to "sinning bravely" unless we decide not to attempt it at all and to learn what we can, if we can, from *ad hoc* experiences. This latter procedure has not been very fruitful in the past. I would propose three general lines of procedure in these respects. All are unsatisfactory in terms of an ideal of scientific thoroughness and reliability of findings. All three are, I believe, better than nothing, if one is careful to keep in mind their shortcomings and is prepared to use failures to increase the prospects of future successes.

The first of these is to concentrate on the gathering of types of data with which scholars have had the most experience and which seem to offer minimum problems of collection because of such difficulties as language differences. Demographic data and conventional economic data are good examples of this type. Although there are enough problems in gathering this sort of data, it is easier to obtain interobserver reliability in the reporting of the number of deaths and births and marriages or the value of foreign trade in different commodities or of bank deposits (if these exist) than it is to find out with precision whether individuals are more oriented to their families than to the state. These data will serve a dual purpose. Even if they are not relevant for many of the types of questions raised here, they will fulfill the purposes for which they are ordinarily designed. At the same time it should be possible to attain some confirmation of some of the kinds of hypotheses presented here via a double process of hypothesis formation. One may raise questions of the following sort: If it is true that the introduction of certain new bases of employment into a system like that of China (in which, according to our hypothesis, general control over deviance is maintained through the family and family solidarity) tends to undermine the family structure, can implications of this for the birth rate (or perhaps for family size) be deduced? One may then check the deductions by data on the birth rate (or on family size), and the confirmation or disproof of the deductions by these data will throw light on the hypotheses from which the deductions were made, if the process of deduction has not been faulty. In other words, a systematic effort can be made to link quite involved hypotheses to the data which are simplest to collect and with which we are most experienced. This is by no means visionary or without precedent. Irene Taeuber in her work on Japan for the Office of Population Research at Princeton has for some time been making extensive attempts of this sort. This may not be as good a procedure as more direct tests of many of these propositions would be. It obviously involves an extra step of deduction, and perhaps one of induction as well. Errors may crop up in these extra steps. But with our present linguistic training, the present state of our methodologies for confirming these hypotheses more directly, and the urgent need for increased knowledge about these areas, it is by no means a stratagem that we can afford to overlook. Already, responsible spokesmen both within and without these areas have helped us by advocating increased collection of such data. Furthermore, from our extensive experience with such data we are likely to be good judges of the respects in which they are unreliable. In the absence of highly reliable data, we shall still be the better off for knowing in what specific respects our data are unreliable. Finally, the process of double hypothesizing may well lead to new and fruitful suggestions for data-gathering within the more orthodox procedures now known.

The second line of procedure places the researcher on even thinner ice. In China, for the present, as far as members of the non-Communist world are concerned, the gathering of any kind of reliable data on the current state of affairs is virtually impossible, and this may be equally true in other areas for different reasons. Lacking something better, our hypotheses about the Chinese situation may be used in conjunction with our hypotheses or theorems about social phenomena in general to predict likely developments. To the extent that these predictions can be verified or disproved, our hypotheses about the facts and our more general theorems receive some form of test. Without going into the details of the analysis, on this basis one can predict that without quite radical changes from what seem to be the present preoccupations of the Communist regime, that regime cannot long remain stable, for many but by no means all of the reasons that brought disaster to its predecessors. On this score one can make even more specific predictions of where and why discontent and difficulties are likely to crop up. These can to some extent be confirmed by news releases from the Communist regime itself.

Closely related to the second line of procedure is the third and perhaps the most risky. This is essentially a line of procedure that has often been used more or less self-consciously by anthropologists, sociologists, and many amateur observers in the past. Many past observations on many different social systems, although not assembled in any highly precise form, give us a fairly good sense of adequacy. Such senses are always to be viewed by scientists with suspicion lest one lose sight of the very real possibility of error involved in any procedure as tenuous as this and as dependent upon one's estimate of the reliability of the person who did the research. With this sort of caveat well in mind, however, research like that of Malinowski on the Trobriand Islanders should by no means be ignored because of lack of replication or because it is not in such a form that degrees of variance and the like can be computed from it. I think that the feeling of adequacy that skilled critics frequently have in the presence of such studies arises from the fact that many of the generalizations in these studies tend to reinforce one another. To put the matter another way, many of the generalizations drawn about such systems in this way and from many different starting points (i.e. many different inductions) converge, as it were, in their implications. As stated above, this is a risky business, but we have one general sort of test for reliability here. If such convergence can be shown to be purely tautological, we are faced with a case of logical exercise based usually on implicit assumptions and concepts which, if made explicit, quickly reduce our converging hypotheses either to statements that are not conceivably falsifiable or to statements that are true but empty. If this cannot be done, one may take comfort in the position that such convergence on the basis of pure chance is highly unlikely. If anything like reliability can be claimed for some of the hypotheses, the confirmation of the analysis is improved to that degree.

At the very least, these three lines of procedure furnish alternatives to inaction on these problems of research and can be used to bring to bear what social scientists have learned in the past in other connections. They will have two other effects as well. They will result in the more explicit statement of our reasoning about these problems so that we shall be better able to seek out errors when results indicate that our analyses have been faulty. They will also provide a systematic set of hypotheses in terms of which we can gather better data when that becomes possible. They will simultaneously provide a systematic set of hypotheses to be checked by the gathering of these data. While the disproof by these data of many of these hypotheses may be hard on the sensitivities of individual researchers, disproof no less than verification will add to our general knowledge.

COMMENT

R. RICHARD WOHL, Research Center in Economic Development and Cultural Change, University of Chicago

In his very challenging essay Aubrey examines the "economic, organizational, and institutional determinants of investment decisions in underdeveloped countries." For present purposes he prefers to divorce these considerations, as much as he can, from related social and cultural variables. ". . . it will not be possible," he warns us at the outset, "to maintain this distinction." On the whole, however, he keeps very steadily to the main question: Are there economic determinants which can account for the apparently uneconomic behavior with which entrepreneurs in underdeveloped countries are commonly credited?

Throughout his discussion Aubrey draws a sharp line between the kind of behavior that may be expected, or sought, by outside observers on the basis of what are thought to be desirable social policies for rapid, or balanced, economic growth; and the kind of investment decisions made by entrepreneurs acting out of a decent regard for their own self-interest, prudently weighing the safety of their capital and the possibilities of profit before they commit their resources. From the vantage point of this distinction, he shows how (considering the conditions under which they operate) their preferences are sensible and, by their standards, quite sound. Such opprobrious terms as "unproductive," "sterile," or "speculative" when applied to investment decisions turn out to be little more than invidious epithets evoked from those who do not understand or approve of the manner in which such entrepreneurs register their preferences.

Aubrey then proceeds to sift a great mass of reports describing, and attempting to explain, entrepreneurial behavior in industrial investments in underdeveloped countries. At this point, incidentally, he renders students in this field a great service. He has thoroughly ransacked the literature, and his verdict on its unsatisfactory character is conclusive. He trenchantly argues that entrepreneurs in these countries have ample reason to regard industrial investments as especially hazardous and unrewarding as compared with other alternatives which are open to them. In most cases, and except under greatly favoring conditions, the discrepancy between what is regarded as socially desirable and what is individually prudent is too great to expect that businessmen will freely invest their capital in the former.

This point is so persuasively argued, in so many different and relevant contexts, that it sometimes becomes difficult to visualize just how entrepreneurship ever breaks through the careful and cautious hesitation of these businessmen. Several observations are offered to suggest how this takes place.

Aubrey remarks that the promoter may be an important agent in fostering industrial investment. The "successful" entrepreneur in a less advanced economy, he points out, may well be the one who makes a practice of starting new industrial enterprises and getting rid of them quickly. The chief function of such a promoter is to scent opportunity and to dramatize its possibilities for fellow businessmen who lack his insight and initiative. He defines the product, gauges its possible market, investigates the availability of labor, raw materials, and the like, "packages" the project; and then ducks out to sponsor a new promotion. His efforts are rewarded by payments for promotional services and by such incidental profits as he can pick up along the way.

Such promotional pacemakers, no doubt, are to be found frequently in underdeveloped countries. Their very success, however, raises more questions than it helps to answer. Such promoters surely depend on an audience of investors who will take industrial enterprises off their hands once they are established. Where does this group of investors come from? Aubrey often and amply demonstrates that industrial investments, by their very nature, are unattractive to the typical entrepreneur in an underdeveloped country. Such investments threaten illiquidity, are troublesome to manage, often demand knowledge and techniques which are unfamiliar and relatively difficult to muster. All these features are repeatedly shown to be distasteful to entrepreneurs in underdeveloped countries.

This suggestion is nonetheless one which may be greatly improved by future research. What kinds of enterprises and what kinds of appeals are effectively used by such promoters? Why can entrepreneurs in underdeveloped countries be induced to accept "enterprise" at one remove? And what kinds of obstacles do they feel have been overcome by the promoter in establishing the firm? The continuing success of promoters of this kind depends on disposing of viable enterprises. There is probably as much chicane associated with the launching of new businesses in underdeveloped countries as there has been elsewhere; but, at all events, such promoters cannot go on indefinitely disposing of "gold bricks." How do they choose the projects they sponsor?

Similar queries are raised by another of Aubrey's comments, which at first sight appears cryptic. Aubrey argues, very convincingly, that there is a significant relation between the willingness to invest in industrial enterprises and a stock of previous experience on the basis of which the entrepreneur can base judgments of risk and potential profit. Typically, he says, the background of relevant experience is shallow in underdeveloped countries. He then goes on to point out that such experience may be built up gradually, and that once accumulated it "may also help explain the emergence of native entrepreneurship within relatively short periods of time in countries where it had been conspicuously scarce for long periods of the past" (page 399). In support of this contention he cites Mexico's experience during the last quarter century. As before, it would be interesting to know by what means such headway is made.

Throughout the paper several tantalizing hints are thrown out in reply. All of them raise questions to which further research may be addressed:

1. Must there first be, for instance, a group of "pioneers" who attempt industrial enterprises before they have enough know-how and who fail, and on the basis of whose failures secure knowledge of what is feasible and profitable is built up? What induces such pioneers to make their attempts in the first place, if in fact they do so?

2. Or, as is suggested elsewhere (page 405), does a spectacularly successful venture breed a host of imitators to follow in its wake?

3. Is a principle of analogy followed by investing entrepreneurs? Is there a spread of entrepreneurship between roughly similar kinds of undertakings, businessmen going forward on the assumption that what made for success in one line will do so in another which resembles it somewhat? (See the examples drawn from the Indian experience in cotton and jute, page 411.)

4. Or, as remarked in another place (page 415), is there a drift from trading ventures and commercial business of one kind or another to industrial enterprise?

We have reason to be very grateful to Aubrey for sorting out the rather confusing evidence so far collected on these points. The questions raised above are addressed, in effect, to all past and future students of entrepreneurial behavior in underdeveloped countries. What Aubrey has shown is that past work has often been based on a confusion of the standards used in evaluating the ways in which available capital is disposed of in these countries. As a polemic against naïve and unreflective observation of such behavior, his paper is effective and conclusive beyond any qualification. He shows, incontrovertibly, that many of the diagnoses which have been made and many of the policies which have been offered in remedy proceed from incomplete or wrong assumptions. Having made this point so effectively, Aubrey does not, however, venture to draw what seem to me to be some rather obvious conclusions suggested by the evidence he has collected.

For one thing, he has shown beyond cavil that there is urgent need for some sort of typology of entrepreneurs in underdeveloped countries even if only one that is tentatively stated. Following the available literature, Aubrey tends to speak of "entrepreneurs" and "entrepreneurial behavior" as if these were roughly homogeneous in these countries. He is, of course, aware that this is not the case; and he richly documents the variation that exists in the many different examples cited throughout his discussion. Since we are all interested in economic change and how such change affects economic growth, it may be that in working out a classification of entrepreneurial types we shall be able better to locate groups which are more receptive of, or vulnerable to, change and innovation than it has been possible to do in the past.

Aubrey himself makes a notable contribution in this direction by stressing the importance of experience and special knowledge in fostering economic development. In one place (pages 416-418) he considers the entrepreneurial significance of foreign immigrants, who, in so many places, have shown much more initiative and enterprise than the natives of the countries to which they have come. The nature of the entrepreneurial impulse in these groups has for long appeared to be a vexing paradox to students in the field. Time after time it has been discussed in terms of differences in national character or by means of an unrevealing and unprovable set of psychological determinants which have done little more than compound the original paradox. Aubrey suggests that such immigrants may well have had superior knowledge and past experience and, by reason of their social marginality, may have been in a better position to detect and capitalize on opportunities which seemed unappealing to less experienced, more socially integrated native entrepreneurs. This is an extremely suggestive insight and, potentially, very fruitful, because it can be improved and tested by empirical study.

A further profitable inference is suggested by the relatively bland outcome of Aubrey's exhaustive inquiries. Considered in the light of past investigations, his study of entrepreneurial behavior in underdeveloped countries seems to have drawn only some rather feeble conclusions. We know little, as Aubrey shows, of the process by which changes in entrepreneurial attitudes and behavior take place. As was mentioned earlier in discussing some of the questions raised, the key problem for scholars in this field is to discover how industrial investment decisions change over time. At any given moment a clear-headed and unbiased observer can produce justifications for prevailing practices. How, in the course of time, can an entrepreneurial environment be created which will overcome what presently seem to be insuperable obstacles to native entrepreneurs in underdeveloped countries? Are there necessary preconditions which must be fulfilled before private venturesomeness can be counted on for significant industrial investments? These questions still await answers. It is much to Aubrey's credit that he has surveyed a field in which ambiguities abound and has managed to suggest, openly and by implication, the directions for promising research in the future.

J. J. Spengler, Duke University

Before I consider certain specific points made in these two very interesting papers, I should like to raise a question of the sort Edwin Cannan raised many years ago when he pleaded for a simpler economics. Do we not need a simpler economics of development? Are not some of the concepts and the models that are being proposed for the analysis of problems of underdevelopment too complicated? Is it not the part of wisdom to concentrate attention only upon the dominant components of those factors which are deemed of major importance in accounting for underdevelopment?

Is not this approach admirably suited both to ease the task of analysis and to simplify the formulation of a strategy and a set of tactics adapted to getting development underway?

I believe that Aubrey's analysis bears out what has just been said. He reports that Faustian character, the Schumpeterian entrepreneur, to be conspicuous by his absence from underdeveloped economies. Should we not, therefore, give up discussion of entrepreneurship in terms of this not very well-defined concept? Should we not instead identify the characteristics of entrepreneurs found in underdeveloped countries, specify the additional (if any) characteristics likely to be acquired by these entrepreneurs under probable circumstances, discover the modes of interaction connecting the entrepreneur with his relevant environment in underdeveloped countries, etc.? Given such information, entrepreneurs might be classified in ways that would facilitate statistical analysis of entrepreneurial behavior, or at least we would have a suggestion as to which of the characteristics associated with this behavior are important.

Aubrey's attempt to apply the theory of uncertainty as it has been developed with respect to advanced economies indicates, as he himself discloses, the limited applicability of this concept for the analysis of entrepreneurial behavior in underdeveloped countries. He is arguing, if I read him correctly, that *objective* (or actually existing) uncertainty tends to be greater in underdeveloped than in developed countries; that, in consequence, *subjective* uncertainty (i.e. uncertainty as it exists in the mind of the decision-maker) is greater; and that, because the disposition of entrepreneurs to initiate and/or develop enterprise is inversely associated with subjective uncertainty, such uncertainty constitutes more of a block to the expansion of enterprise and economic activities in underdeveloped than in developed countries. Now this may be the case; but we do not actually know that it is. We must first ascertain the relationship that actually obtains between objective and subjective uncertainty in various cultures through study of entrepreneurial and managerial behavior and through analysis of the influence of occupational backgrounds upon the response of entrepreneurs to variations in objective and subjective uncertainty. At present, therefore, it is information much more than recondite models that is needed, and it is this need that Aubrey is attempting to satisfy.

(*1*) It would seem advisable to determine the influence of balance in growth upon profit expectations as these are viewed by entrepreneurs producing for a domestic as distinguished from a foreign market. If a number of complementary activities are developing simultaneously, each expanding entrepreneur is helping to provide a market for increments in output that other expanding entrepreneurs are bringing into being, with the result that a situation of the sort contemplated in Say's law is approximated. When, on the contrary, one or a few but not most of the complementary entrepreneurs are expanding, it is much less likely that the expanding entrepreneurs can satisfactorily dispose of their increments in output. Accordingly, balanced growth operates to reduce objective and subjective risk and uncertainty; lack of balance has a contrary effect.

It is regrettable that only average profit rates appear to be available. When these averages are low it is likely, of course, that the influx of capital from advanced countries will be deterred and that, if as a result aggregate profit is relatively small, capital formation will not be greatly augmented by the reinvestment of earnings. It were better if we had marginal profit rates and if we could estimate with some degree of confidence how they were likely to vary, by industry and by capital use, as more and more capital was invested in particular industries under varying conditions. It is often said that nonindustrial employments of capital unduly divert capital from industrial employments; yet there are not at hand data to determine whether such diversion, if it takes place, is economically unwarranted. (We should be even more handicapped if there were grounds for supposing that the marginal social benefit of investment exceeded its marginal private benefit.) Concerning the employment of capital in general, it may be said that when nonvoluntary means are employed to augment the rate of capital formation, similar means are likely to be employed to absorb this capital and thereby prevent manifestations of the sort consequential upon *ex ante* oversaving.

One's appetite is whetted for more information concerning the origins of entrepreneurs in underdeveloped countries than Aubrey and Levy give us, even with respect to the entrepreneurial role of immigrants possessing certain skills. One gets a general impression that industrial entrepreneurs originate in trading and mercantile backgrounds, but insufficient information is provided concerning the evolution of this process. Levy's account suggests (as did Hoselitz's) that a merchant class is likely to generate an industrial entrepreneurial class if the former, though reasonably secure in its property holdings, is denied access to class memberships that remove merchants and members of their families from the pursuit of commerce and/or industry; for under these circumstances merchant families cannot easily give up business, and some of the accumulating capital and offspring are likely to seek opportunity outside commerce and in industry if falling returns in commerce threaten. Even so, we need much more information concerning what becomes of the sons of merchants in various societies, and how the movements of these sons affect the movements of family capital and the reinvestment of earnings.

Aubrey implies that restriction upon freedom of entry into an industry may initially stimulate investment by reducing uncertainty, whilst recognizing that such restriction may in the end restrict investment. It may well be, however, that even in the short run such restriction, by excluding various entrepreneurs who have some capital they would risk, serves to restrict rather than to promote investment. In general, it would appear to be difficult to make out a case for a policy of restriction of freedom of entry even in the short run, given its probable consequences.

Presumably, the increasing pressure of the masses for additional income and consumption (noted by Levy and others) is more likely to reduce the supply of capital available for private investment (such as Aubrey is concerned with) than for investment in social overhead (urban improvements, housing, education, and the like), transport, communications, public utilities, etc. The latter kinds of investment must normally be underwritten or subsidized in large part by the state in underdeveloped countries, since the marginal private return on such investment falls short of its marginal social benefit and private entrepreneurs usually cannot afford to undertake such investment without subsidy. (This was the case in the nineteenth century in the United States, for example.) Therefore, investment of this sort needs to be viewed as public or quasi-public investment and susceptible of increasing support by the state. Even so, if there were too little capital formed voluntarily to meet the direct needs of industrial and commercial entrepreneurs, and this appears to be the case in prospect in many countries, the shortage could be made up out of governmentally enforced saving, accomplished through taxation, wage controls, and a slowly rising price level.

Respecting prices and costs, it is preferable to speak of a country's price and cost structure, since some prices and costs are relatively high whereas others are relatively low. Concerning the investment-retarding influence of labor bottlenecks, more information than is now available is needed regarding how long it takes workers to learn new skills in an underdeveloped country and how much (if any) overpricing of labor is produced by contemporary trade-unionism.

It would appear that, given the market imperfections and the probable lowness of demand elasticity in underdeveloped countries, the maximization of short-run profits calls for high percentage profit margins; and that percentage profit margins will tend to be higher in small than in large cities and in interior than in coastal towns. Changes in income, production costs, and marketing techniques, however, may increase demand elasticity or extend entrepreneurial time horizons and thereby reduce profit margins.

It is commonly suggested that overinvestment in land and real estate diverts capital from industrial employments and retards economic development. This argument, though conceivably valid, needs much more amplification than it has had. For overinvestment in lands tends to produce reactions in the factor-price structure that partially counterbalance the initial output-reducing effect. (a) If too many entrepreneurs, or too many other agents of production, are combined with land, the spread between the rates of return on these various agents and those on land will increase, and land will become relatively less attractive to investors. This spread may become so great that land loses much of its appeal as a source of investment. (Insofar as the desire to invest in land occasions saving that otherwise would not take place, the adverse effect of overinvestment in land is offset by the resulting greater amount of saving.) (b) If overinvestment in land means that land is upgraded in the hierarchy of assets held by men, it must be accompanied by a compensatory redistribution of nonlanded assets, some of which were initially surrendered to land-sellers by land-buyers. What becomes of these nonlanded assets? If they are consumed or wasted, they are not added to the nation's stock of capital, with the process of consumption or waste rather than overinvestment in land responsible. If, on the contrary, the nonlanded assets are added to the nation's capital stock and set to work, the nation's gross national product is increased and much of the adverse effect of overinvestment in land is offset. (A presumptive rationale of landed investment might be established in terms of asset theory.)

(2) The burden of Levy's paper appears to be that, because the disparity between backward and advanced countries is so much

greater today than a century or so ago, a backward country, wanting to catch up, is more dependent upon foreign sources for certain skills, materials, etc., than once was the case; and that the task of catching up is made even harder by the relative lack of entrepreneurs and capital, by difficulties of integrating private and public enterprise, and by the great disparity existing between the localized self-sufficiency of underdeveloped economies and the generalized interdependency characteristic of advanced economies. Because of the nature of the problem, the interventionist role of the state must at first be very great if an underdeveloped economy is to be transformed. Moreover, the role of the state cannot be relaxed until after a built-in developmental process has been set going.

Levy's analysis calls attention to a number of problems associated with economic development that economists tend to overlook: how to maintain sufficient social control in a society while the initiation of development is dissolving the older, hitherto effective modes of social control; how to convert a low-status, proto-entrepreneurial class into a high-status, expanding entrepreneurial class; how to make the motivational structure foster capital formation; how the rise of nationalism may be made to stimulate the transformation of particularistic into more universalistic social criteria; how to render sociological circumstances favorable to the separation of ownership and management; how to optimize resource conservation; how to make systems of family organization favorable to economic expansion; etc.

Among the matters I found open to objection in Levy's paper are these: his use of a much more cumbersome set of notions pertaining to capital than is required; his failure to indicate whether the age of cultures affects in any way their susceptibility to change; and his failure to describe in greater detail the sociological nexus between output of effort and its remuneration, between remuneration and proportion of income saved, between the profitability of technological improvements and their adoption, and so on.

Among the checks to natality proposed by Levy are the stimulation of urbanization and the introduction of patterns of consumption unfavorable to natality. He does not, however, discuss a thesis stated in very primitive form by J. S. Mill and developed recently by Harvey Leibenstein and others. According to this view, demographic and related obstacles to economic development can be surmounted most effectively if an economy forms capital at a very high annual rate (say, one increasing the capital stock 4.5 to 6.5

per cent per year) over a short period (say, 10 to 15 years). For so high a rate of capital formation (a growth rate of 4.5 per cent) in about 11 years might transform the aspirations of men and lead them to regulate their numbers effectively enough to permit per capita income to rise continuously. Can a sufficiently high rate of saving be maintained? (E.g. if population grows 1 per cent per year, a 4.5 per cent rate of growth in per capita output probably would entail the saving of something like one-fifth of a nation's income.) Supposing that it can be maintained, will the sustaining of such a growth rate undermine many of the circumstances presently responsible for the continuance of Malthusian situations? If the answer is in the affirmative, a quite different sort of domestic and foreign investment policy is called for in many underdeveloped countries than is now being pursued.

WILBERT E. MOORE, Princeton University

Although Aubrey and Levy start from different theoretical concerns, there is a remarkable consistency in their analysis of economic behavior in underdeveloped countries.

Several general virtues of these papers should be noted. First, both authors avoid a naïve distinction between "economic" and "noneconomic" elements in a social system, and deal with the production and distribution of goods and services and the decisions relating to the factors of production within an institutional framework. Neither author neglects "culture," and neither exaggerates its importance. Second, both authors indicate the relevance of formal economic analysis to underdeveloped areas, a point of view that I believe some economists have abandoned too readily.

On this latter point a word of caution may be appropriate. The standard assumptions and categories of economic theory apply most readily to that sector of any underdeveloped area where market mechanisms or some reasonable facsimile operate. Such a sector exists in all contemporary societies, however limited it may be. Failure to recognize the existence of partial modernization probably accounts in part for the dispute over both the applicability of economic theory in non-Western economies and the importance of the obstacles to growth implied by the premodern social structures of primitive and agrarian economies. However, there are genuine differences in social systems, including the degree to which archaic forms of organization and conduct have been shattered. To speak meaningfully of investment decisions within the framework of Aubrey's analysis, for example, requires at a minimum that the social structure has been sufficiently loosened to permit us to think of the person with capital as having a genuine choice. A system of entailed property rights managed and transferred within the family structure would make standard economic analysis formal to the point of pure exercise.

How, then, are "institutional" factors relevant to the analysis of underdeveloped economies? In principle, in the same ways that they are relevant everywhere—namely, in forms of organization and patterns of behavior, and in variations in norms and motives. One or two illustrations of each of these relevant points may suffice.

Every society has some form of family and kinship system, but these vary markedly along a number of dimensions. The variations affect the production and consumption of goods and services in a number of ways. One form of relationship of considerable importance for the possibilities of economic growth is the incompatibility between an extended family and kinship structure, on the one hand, and a mobile, merit-placed work force, on the other. This functional incompatibility is noted by Levy in his paper and elsewhere. To the degree that industrialization in a broad sense does take place, preservation of the "best" features of the traditional order is likely to be pious nonsense. To the extent that the traditional structure is deliberately or indirectly shored up, new enterprise is likely to be isolated, limited in growth potential, or actually stillborn.

The organization of productive units is also of considerable importance. Quite apart from such questions as the economic advantages and costs of scale, which seem to me to be too little studied, there are several speculative points of considerable interest with regard to economic growth. One of these points is the possibility that large units gain greater immunity from traditional pressures and restraints than do small "family" enterprises, both in investment decisions and in personnel policies. Another and related hypothesis is that contrary to common-sense notions about inflexible bureaucracies, the possibilities of adapting to existing supplies of skills and developing new skills and increased supplies through training may be greater in large organizations than in small ones. Aubrey's work on small units and the summary in his paper are indeed valuable. I believe, however, that the issues are still complex and that their solution will require, sooner or later, modification of the individual entrepreneur as the model for analysis of economic decisions and practices.

On the relevance of norms and motives—a subject provocative of many senseless debates between economists and other social scientists—one or two illustrations of significant differences may be noted. The evidence seems to me to be quite overwhelming that aspirations differ in different times and places, and that the notion that the "cake of custom" serves only to hold in check universal aspirations represents a hopelessly distorted view of human motivation and its predominant source in social learning. Concretely, there are differences in the value placed upon change, whether of individual position through mobility or of processes and products. Emphasis on the innovating role of the entrepreneur tends to blind us to the very considerable and deliberate organization and institutionalization of change in industrial societies, in marked contrast to what must be regarded as the more "normal" set of social values and individual goals. That modern forms of economic enterprise have had some degree of successful penetration into all sorts of traditional systems does not demonstrate that they have done so by releasing previously frustrated passions.

Finally, there are one or two notes of a somewhat different sort that may be added to Levy's discussion of the population problem in underdeveloped areas. Not only is the problem of the relation between total economic and demographic growth troublesome, but the age structure of a population with high fertility and high mortality implies a very heavy "dependency burden" of the young—many of whom will not live to become producers. This youthful dependency makes educational improvements especially difficult precisely where they are most needed. Moreover, mortality reduction is initially likely to have the greatest impact on infant and child mortality, so that for a transitional period the dependency burden is likely to increase in the process of modernization.

HARRY OSHIMA, National Bureau of Economic Research

These comments apply principally to the numerous references made by Levy to Japanese economic and social history. The composite picture of Japanese economic development that emerges from Levy's references appears quite different from the picture I have formed from studying the history of Japanese development. Since I am not a specialist in Japanese history, my interpretation may be somewhat inconsistent with the most recent results of the intensive historical research now going on in Japan.

On page 459 Levy states that the wealthy members of under-developed countries are not likely to invest in the "formation of effective productive capital" and that "attempts to change such habits are likely to run into resistance. . . ." He then points out that Japan "was a notable exception. . . ." "The Japanese feudal lords accepted debentures for their landholdings without a murmur. Since they knew nothing of how to handle or manipulate debentures, their use came into the hands of the zaibatsu, who owned or controlled the banks. Quite peacefully, land reform was carried out, and the effective control of much of the financial resources of the society was turned over to people who did not own them but who could use them for the developmental purposes sought."

These statements raise several points at issue. First of all, the debentures given to the feudal lords in 1876 were in exchange not for landholdings but for the right to collect taxes from the peasants. Before this the cultivators were required to turn over a certain proportion of their crops as taxes to the feudal lords, who in turn distributed part of this to their retainers, the samurai. With the coming of the new regime, i.e. from 1873 on, land taxes were paid to the Meiji government instead of to the feudal lords and samurai. In recognition of the former feudal prerogative, the Meiji government offered to capitalize the annual tax in the form of debentures to the lords and samurai. The land reform alluded to by Levy is generally referred to as the land tax reform of 1873; that is, with the acquisition of the right to tax the peasants, the new regime realized from the outset that a modern land tax system required each piece of land to have a clearly recognizable legal owner upon whom the taxes could be levied. Since the feudal concept of holdings and tenure did not meet this requirement, each cultivator was given a certificate of ownership to the land that he and his families had tilled and held from time immemorial. This distribution of certificates of legal recognition to landownership should not be confused with land distribution.

Second, if the feudal lords accepted these debentures "without a murmur," it is because some of them knew that it was utterly futile to resist the armed strength of the new government, which made it sufficiently clear what the consequences of such action would be. To be precise, however, it should be noted that the debentures distributed to each individual differed in amount: those who received large amounts probably accepted without a murmur; but most of the recipients got relatively small amounts. The resentment of the latter was one of the causes of the numerous samurai uprisings in various localities throughout Japan which finally culminated in the great Satsuma Rebellion of 1877. Also the distribution of certificates of landownership conferring legal recognition to the holders of land was accompanied by demonstrations and riots over various claims and counterclaims.[1]

On the subject of the "ready convertibility of the indigenous entrepreneurs and financial investors" into accumulators of effective productive capital, Levy observes on page 460 that "Japan is one of the few cases that offers any hope." In most underdeveloped countries local merchants demand exorbitantly high interest rates and tend to invest their funds in the purchase of land and other nonproductive sources. This passage, together with similar references to feudal lords as entrepreneurs cited in the first quotation, appears erroneous.

First, while a small portion of the debentures were invested in railroads and banks, most of them were used for the purchase of land, for loans at usury rates, and for trading.[2] Moreover, the indigenous entrepreneurs and financial investors in general also preferred investments in land and loans to peasants at usury rates during the formative years of Japanese development, namely, the first few decades of the Meiji era. While no doubt there were some cases of "ready convertibility," these were the exception, and in general the "indigenous entrepreneurs" preferred the extremely high rent (50 per cent or more of the crop) obtainable from land purchases and the high interest rates from usury loans to very risky investment in modern plant and equipment with low returns. It was because of the reluctance of both small and large investors that the Meiji regime found it necessary to embark on a vast program for the construction of government factories, mines, railways, shipyards, etc.

In the coordination of developmental projects carried out on a

[1] See E. Herbert Norman, *Japan's Emergence as a Modern State*, International Secretariat, Institute of Pacific Relations, 1940, p. 139 and other parts of this book, for various points covered in the above discussion. See also Takao Tsuchiya and S. Okazaki, *Nihon Shihonshugi Hattatsuchi Gaisetsu* (*Outline of the Development of Japanese Capitalism*), pp. 26-53 and 77-78, and W. W. McLaren, *A Political History of Japan during the Meiji Era, 1867-1912*, Scribner, 1916, pp. 82-90.

[2] See H. Ouchi, *Nihon Zaisei Ron, Kosai Hen* (*Treatise on Japanese Public Finance, Volume on the Public Debt*), pp. 35-38; Norman, *op. cit.*, pp. 110-114; and Tsuchiya and Okazaki, *op. cit.*, pp. 26-46.

public and private base, Levy feels that "For reasons too complicated to go into here, the Japanese seem to have had an unbelievably felicitous situation in these respects, for the public planners and the major figures in the sphere of private initiative either were the same or acted as one" (page 464). It is not clear precisely what situation is referred to here. Read in the context of this section, it seems to relate to the government practice of building modern factories, mines, shipyards, vessels, etc., and turning them over to private groups at extremely low prices or without compensation.[3] This may have been felicitous for the recipients of these properties, but hardly for the economy as a whole. Since the recipients were usually the few large financial houses (the zaibatsu), this policy was in part responsible for the concentration of production in Japanese industry in a small number of firms.

Levy's description (pages 476-479) of the role of the merchant near the end of the Tokugawa period and in the early Meiji period seems unsatisfactory at many points. Since a point-by-point refutation of the description will take up too much space, it may suffice to say that the picture one gets from his discussion differs from that presented by recent historical research. My basic disagreement is with Levy's assumption that in the formative years of the Meiji period the merchant class was responsible for "effective productive" capital formation. (And because of this assumption he goes into a description of the social habits of this group both before and after the Restoration.) My views are more in accord with the statement by E. H. Norman that "big private capital preferred to remain in trade, banking and credit operations, particularly in the safe and lucrative field of government loans, while small capital had no inducement to leave the countryside where trade, usury and, above all, high rent—averaging almost sixty per cent of the tenant's crop—prevented capital invested in agriculture from flowing into industrial channels."[4]

[3] Only rarely were industrial plant and equipment sold by auction, as in the case of the silk factory in Tomioka. T. Fujita, *Nihon Shihonshugi to Zaisei* (*Japanese Capitalism and Public Finance*), pp. 166-169.

[4] Norman, *op. cit.*, p. 111. It might be added that the problem of entrepreneurship in the late Tokugawa period has been the subject of a lively controversy and intensive research among economic historians in Japan during recent years. One school of thought holds that a nonfeudalistic type of entrepreneurship (the putting-out system and large-shop production) had developed on a considerable scale, while another group denies its widespread existence. A third group argues that while there was a fairly extensive development of the putting-out system and large-shop production, these were essentially feudalistic in character.

Japan is again singled out as "very special" in the discussion of the ability of nations to maintain systems of control in the new system. "There was also a clear tradition of concentration of this loyalty on a single individual, the emperor. This permitted a rather easy transfer of these loyalties back to the emperor and hence directly to the national state. Virtually without bloodshed and in extremely rapid and dramatic steps, the daimyo and the shogun, the top power- and property-holders of a genuinely feudal society, were shorn of their power and their property . . ." (page 466).

While there is some truth in the first part of the quotation, it is well to keep in mind the following problem: If the Meiji Restoration had brought about as thoroughgoing a change as the French Revolution, would the tradition of loyalty to the emperor have survived? The change to the Meiji era from the shogunate system was limited and, as Honjô points out repeatedly, "Power simply passed from the upper grade to the lower grade samurai."[5] In this situation, as far as the large majority of the population was concerned, the new forces which might have strained the tradition of loyalty were kept in check.

On the other hand, it is misleading to describe the Meiji Restoration as taking place "virtually without bloodshed." Even if one takes into account military battles alone, the shift of power from one group of samurai to another involved intermittent fighting from 1844 to 1869.[6] And if a larger perspective is taken, one must surely include the hundreds of peasant revolts which, though abortive in most cases, sapped the inner strength of the Tokugawa shogunate.[7]

There are other references to which we are inclined to take exception. But the foregoing remarks are sufficient to indicate that, though Japanese development is one of the most fascinating in the world, it is not quite as exceptional as Levy would have it. No doubt, when compared with development in other countries, there are many interesting contrasts in the behavior of Japanese entrepreneurs, landlords, peasants, and workers in the developmental

[5] Eijirô Honjô, *Social and Economic History of Japan*, Kyoto, Institute for Research in Economic History of Japan, 1935, p. 141. Also see Norman, *op. cit.*

[6] See James Murdoch, *A History of Japan*, Yokohama, Kelley and Walsh, 1903, Vol. 3, last two chapters, and S. Toyama, *Meiji Ishin* (*Meiji Restoration*), Tokyo, 1951.

[7] See Hugh Borton, *Peasant Uprisings in Japan of the Tokugawa Period*, Tokyo, Asiatic Society of Japan, 1938, and Takao Tsuchiya, *An Economic History of Japan*, Tokyo, Asiatic Society of Japan, 1937, p. 165.

process as it unfolded in the total milieu of the early Meiji era, but there are also equally interesting similarities.

Last, it is difficult to say to what extent the comments above, if correct, would modify or invalidate the various hypotheses and policies advanced by the author in the paper. Some of them would probably be affected, because the author states that "examples will be given largely in terms of hypotheses about the facts in China and Japan . . ." (page 442). But it is difficult to be precise about this, since the author may have had other nations in mind even though no explicit references are made to them in framing the hypotheses.

Reply by Henry G. Aubrey

Since I have no quarrel with the comments made by the discussants, no rejoinder is needed. I propose, therefore, to use some of the comments and others I received from nonparticipants[1] in order to sharpen the focus on some issues which perhaps were not made sufficiently explicit in my paper.

It appears desirable to make a distinction between "objective" obstacles and "subjective" uncertainty, a point made very properly by Spengler. It is, of course, true that uncertainty is essentially a subjective criterion, and, from this angle, it would not seem to matter whether the objective data fully justify the doubt which manifests itself in a feeling of uncertainty. What matters for our purpose is the observed frequency or the inferred likelihood of certain data's evoking such an uncertainty response in a number of individuals who may be deemed willing to consider a concrete possibility of industrial investment in underdeveloped countries. In this respect the most useful distinction may be that between "objective" difficulties rooted in the economic institutional and political framework of underdeveloped countries, and the "subjective" difficulty of assimilating such data into a framework of experience.

Objective difficulties include, among other things, instability of the economic system due to the overwhelming strength of external factors in an export economy. Political instability belongs in the same category, and both factors are responsible for a foreshortened economic horizon which makes long-term, illiquid investments appear hazardous. Another objective factor is the difficulty and the cost of raising sufficient capital and the resulting danger of under-

[1] I am greatly indebted to L. M. Dominguez and H. W. Singer for their lucid and probing criticisms.

capitalization. Yet another is the difficulty of proper cost calculation in new ventures.

The enumeration and discussion of a fairly long list of such factors in my paper may have created the impression of a cumulation of nearly insuperable difficulties, which makes it appear a near-miracle that investment in underdeveloped countries does, after all, take place. Such was not my intention. I should perhaps state unequivocally that some investments in such countries can be decided on positively or negatively with as great assurance as in developed areas. My analysis was largely directed toward the area of indeterminacy which exists between the least controversial extremes of "good or bad risks." I had not planned to venture a distinction between developed and underdeveloped countries in this respect; but if the data I submitted suggest any differentiation, it lies in the greater area of "indeterminacy," and this term would perhaps be the best substitute for the self-contradictory concept of "objective uncertainty."

I only regret Spengler's lack of interest in my attempted application of expectational theory because the subjective factors tend thereby to be underrated. I discounted the expectational approach merely with regard to the use of actuarial probability. I feel quite strongly, however, that the concept of uncertainty can be used to great advantage as one of the instruments by which the economist can introduce noneconomic factors into his analytical framework. Vague concepts like "resistance to change," "speculative preferences," etc., acquire operational meaning for the economist if they can be integrated into his system as determinants of specialized entrepreneurial experience and skill, or the lack thereof, or as the entrepreneur's ability to appraise elements of cost and profit in some kind of rational calculation based on precedents. Awareness of limits to such appraisal are registered subjectively in the form of uncertainty. The influence of uncertainty on risk-taking in investment decisions is a complex matter of which we ought to know more in detail, as Spengler says. I pointed to concrete situations in underdeveloped countries in order to make the relevance of uncertainty at least plausible; how great it is under specific conditions cannot be stated with assurance, nor can we generalize on the extent of differences between underdeveloped and other countries. If, however, my paper used an imperfect tool with less than due caution, further research will doubtless provide correction and refinement.

REPLY BY MARION J. LEVY, JR.

I do not feel that it is appropriate in this volume to make a detailed reply to Oshima's questions. I feel that on several of the points he has raised we are either speaking past one another or merely using somewhat different vocabularies. On other points I feel that there is genuine disagreement between us. On these points I must confess that I should prefer to await the outcome of a fairly extensive program of research on Japan. This research in which I am presently engaged touches on several of the points raised by Oshima. The findings of the research may persuade me to reject my present hypotheses and embrace his, or, what is more likely, lead to modifications of both positions or to new ones altogether. To pursue these questions via a reply here would take us into substantive issues very far afield from the interest of this volume. It would require considerable space and involve questions about which neither Oshima nor I have at present much more than hypotheses about the facts to offer. As for the relevance of his comments for the general concerns of my paper, I can only remind the reader—and this with no invidious implications for the validity of Oshima's remarks—that I pointed out early in the paper that the "empirical" materials presented would consist largely of "hypotheses about the facts in China and Japan," that these materials were presented merely as examples or illustrations, and that the generalizations presented in the paper were themselves more properly to be viewed as hypotheses than in any other light at the present stage of their development.

PART V

TECHNOLOGICAL PROGRESS AND INVESTMENT

TECHNICAL CHANGE AND CAPITAL FORMATION

ABBOTT PAYSON USHER

HARVARD UNIVERSITY

1. *Acts of Skill and Insight*

THE STUDY of technical change in the economy has been hindered by the failure of students to treat effectively the kinds of novelty that are a normal and continuous consequence of the skilled activities of engineers and technicians and those that are related to acts of insight and the process of invention. In the history of the sciences and technology, primary emphasis has fallen upon the process of invention and, all too frequently, upon selected items in the process as a whole. In the administration of the economy, however, acts of skill have played a commanding part in the diffusion of new technical processes both by fields and by geographic areas.

Many presume that the diffusion of technical knowledge and the applications of known techniques are imitative acts devoid of novelty. Tarde's sharp distinction between imitation and invention is hardly more than a broad generalization of attitudes that have been widely held over long periods of time.[1] But these interpretations rest upon concepts of knowledge, skill, and invention that fail to recognize the pervasiveness of novelty in our behavior. They are inconsistent with the concept of emergent novelty that is rapidly developing in the biological and psychological fields.

The distinction between acts of skill and inventions is suggestively drawn by Gestalt psychology. Novelty is to be found in the more complex acts of skill, but it is of a lower order than at the level of invention. As long as action remains within the limits of an act of skill, the insight required is within the capacity of a trained individual and can be performed at will at any time. At the level of invention, however, the act of insight can be achieved only by superior persons under special constellations of circumstance. Such acts of insight frequently emerge in the course of performing acts of skill, though characteristically the act of insight is induced by the conscious perception of an unsatisfactory gap in knowledge or mode

[1] Michael M. Davis, "Gabriel Tarde: An Essay in Sociological Theory," thesis, Columbia University, 1906, pp. 52 and 56-61.

of action.[2] The principles underlying the distinction are clear, but application to particular cases is difficult, because it is not easy to know whether even a specific individual actually performed the act as and when he chose. Common usage reflects the difficulty of making rigorous classifications of activities that involve any elements of novelty.

This problem of boundaries between acts of skill and inventions has a long history and is an underlying feature of the laws granting monopoly privileges for the introduction of new industries and new processes. Special privileges were at first granted to favorites of the rulers in nearly all European states, but opposition developed and it became customary to base the privileges on some element of novelty. Despite emphasis upon the idea of invention, privileges were given for introducing new trades and processes that were admittedly not inventions. Although this development followed similar lines in several major jurisdictions, it will be enough for our present purpose to confine our attention to English law. A principle first stated by counsel in 1598 was embodied in the important section of the Statute of Monopolies (1624) which became the basis of the patent system in England. This authorized the issue of "letters patents and grants of privilege for the term of fourteen years, or under, to be made of the sole working or making of any manner of new manufactures within this realm, to the true and first inventor or inventors of such manufactures."[3] Until the middle of the nineteenth century, judicial decisions emphasized the phrase "new manufactures within this realm." The device or process needed only to be new in England; and it did not have to be an invention. As late as 1803 Lord Ellenborough stated the issue sharply. "There are common elementary materials to work with in machinery, but it is the adoption of those materials to the execution of any particular purpose, that constitutes the invention; and if the application of them be new, if the combination in its nature be essentially new, if it be productive of a new end, and beneficial to the public, it is that species of invention which, protected by the King's Patent, ought to continue to the person the sole right of vending."[4]

[2] Wolfgang Köhler, *Gestalt Psychology*, Horace Liveright, 1929, pp. 371-394; Kurt Koffka, *Principles of Gestalt Psychology*, London, Routledge, 1935, pp. 382, 628-631, and 641-646; and A. T. Welford, *Skill and Age: An Experimental Approach*, Oxford, 1951, pp. 11-27.

[3] Harold G. Fox, *Monopolies and Patents*, University of Toronto Press, 1947, p. 219.

[4] *Ibid.*, p. 229.

The Constitution of the United States did not permit the issue of a patent for the introduction of a device or process developed abroad by a person other than the person introducing the process in the United States. But improvements that should be classed as the work of a skilled mechanic were not excluded either by the statute or by the earlier case decisions. This trend was reversed in 1850 by the decision in *Hotchkiss* v. *Greenwood.* The doctrine was laid down that "unless more ingenuity and skill in applying the old method . . . were required . . . than were possessed by an ordinary mechanic acquainted with the business, there was an absence of that degree of skill and ingenuity which constitute essential elements of every invention."[5] This doctrine was adopted both in the United States and in England. The British statute of 1932 explicitly excluded any obvious development of existing knowledge; and the Supreme Court of the United States in 1941 took the position that the new device "must reveal the flash of creative genius, not merely the skill of the calling."[6]

It is tempting to fill in the literary background for this identification of invention with the work of genius. As early as the seventeenth century many scientists and inventors were becoming self-conscious about the recognition of the priority of their achievement, for they felt that this constituted their claim to fame. Huygens took pains to state very carefully the relation of his work on the pendulum to the work of Galileo. Newton was offended by Leibnitz's publications on the calculus without the acknowledgements that he felt to be due him.[7]

We cannot give space to this problem, but it is important to recognize the danger of this identification of invention with an act of genius. It leads toward an undue emphasis upon a relatively small number of acts which are presented without due regard to the conditions which made them possible, and to a concept of change at infrequent intervals in units of great magnitude, although the simplest effort of analysis makes it clear that acts of insight are numerous, pervasive, and of very small magnitudes. The analysis of behavior, and most particularly of social action, becomes confused and misleading if the transcendental point of view is not carefully and consistently distinguished from the empirical.

[5] *Ibid.*, p. 245. [6] *Ibid.*, pp. 239-240 and 247.

[7] Edgar Zilsel, *Die Entstehung des Geniebegriffes*, Tübingen, J. C. B. Mohr, 1926; Nathaniel D. M. Hirsh, *Genius and Creative Intelligence*, Sci-Art Publishers, 1931, esp. pp. 277-317; and Wilhelm Lange-Eichbaum, *The Problem of Genius*, London, Routledge, 1931, pp. 6-7.

All modes of action can be reduced to three categories: innate activities, acts of skill, and inventive acts of insight. The broader descriptions of these categories are clearly formulated in recent research in biology and Gestalt psychology, but so much work remains to be done that definitions of boundaries must be treated tentatively and the interweaving of different types of activity sketched with caution.

Innate activities are unlearned modes of action that develop as responses to the structure of the organism or the biochemical processes that control its functions. Current research and analysis present interpretations of these activities that differ in many important respects from the older concepts of instinct.[8] Acts of skill include all learned activities whether the process of learning is an achievement of an isolated adult individual or a response to instruction by other individuals of the same or different species of organisms. Inventive acts of insight are unlearned activities that result in new organizations of prior knowledge and experience. In this meaning the concept was introduced by Köhler in his study of apes (1917). It has been further developed by Koffka, but it is still incompletely generalized. It is not recognized by those who do not accept the general positions of Gestalt psychology.

Biologists now find grounds for presuming the existence of learning and acts of skill among wide arrays of subhuman organisms, especially among the social insects and many higher mammals. Psychologists recognize the presence of some acts of insight among subhuman organisms, but the basis of inference presents many special problems and results are uncertain. The importance of this new analysis for the social sciences lies in the superiority of these techniques for the study of the boundary between acts of skill and acts of insight at the higher levels in technology and economic administration.

Generalization of the concept of an act of skill leads to its extension to fields of conceptual activity involving interpretations of codes, rules for group behavior, and the execution of policies for individual or group activity. Inventive acts of insight occur in all these conceptual fields. Social activity involves an interweaving of acts of skill with interspersed acts of insight. No particular field

[8] Nikolaas Tinbergen, *The Study of Instinct*, Oxford, Clarendon Press, 1951; *Comparative Psychology*, Calvin P. Stone, editor, 3rd ed., Prentice-Hall, 1951; William Morton Wheeler, *The Social Insects*, London, Routledge, 1928; and Conroy Lloyd Morgan, *The Criminal Mind*, Longmans, 1930.

should be presumed to involve a single type of action. The term "innovator," as applied by Schumpeter to the entrepreneur, suggests a kind of differentiation from inventors in the technical fields that is likely to be misleading. Executives, like technicians, must be presumed to perform many acts of skill, and likewise to achieve many acts of insight and invention.

Legal doctrines in the field of patent law suggest the more important gradations of novelty that may be found in administration and engineering. The concept of the act of skill presents three choices for testing the relation of existing knowledge to an improvement. We may take as a measure the achievement of any person trained in the field, that of a superior person with general interests and training, or that of a superior person with special interests and training. The inventive act of insight emerges only under special conditions of a different kind. These conditions cannot be controlled at will. The new perception or novel synthesis is produced by some special constellation of circumstances that invites or requires a special response. Although in a particular instance the act of insight may not involve an essentially different response to circumstance from what we find in an act of skill, the conditions which precipitate the act of insight are not regularly recurrent. In the act of skill there are forms of recurring action which fall within a definable range of variation; and, over time, it is presumed that action will be necessary throughout the whole range of variables. Novelties emerge, but within limits which are defined by the possible changes in conditions. From time to time the performance of an act of skill may result in a new observation of the properties of materials or a new perception of relationships or a new mode of action. Acts of insight thus occur in the normal course of the exercise of skills.

Since acts of skill are so directly related to an established technique of action and to organized systems of knowledge, the individual act of novelty is often ignored. Acts of insight, especially at high levels, are likely to become the focus of all our attention, so that we are prone to ignore individual acts of novelty in long sequences of action which can best be described as processes of invention. Uncritical observation of behavior is likely to give too little stress to elements of novelty in acts of skill, and to present inventive acts of insight as completely unconditioned, isolated actions.

In a formal theory of invention, according to the general principles of Gestalt analysis, it is possible to recognize four distinctive steps in the process of invention: the perception of an unsatisfactory pattern, the setting of the stage, the primary act of insight, and critical revision and development. Acts of insight occur at each step if major elements of novelty are involved.[9] The first and last steps in the process commonly involve close relationships with acts of skill. New problems emerge, because some inadequacy of existing knowledge or of current modes of action is perceived. Existing skills are seen to be inadequate. Some measure of failure in the performance of an act of skill touches off a sequence of invention. If stage-setting is deliberately undertaken by systematic experimentation, acts of skill enter at this stage also, but not too clearly. After the major act of insight has occurred, critical revision and development involve a very intimate interweaving of minor acts of insight and acts of skill performed at high levels by persons of special training.

The work of Frank Julian Sprague upon electric traction affords two striking illustrations of the development of new techniques which at the final stages were performed under contracts with sharply restricted terminal dates. Both contracts were designed to demonstrate the possibility of extending to allied fields equipment that was already in use in narrower fields. At that time they were incidental to the activities of an established business, and costs were treated as promotional expenses.[10] The trolley system at Richmond, Virginia had to submit to rigorous tests before a fixed date, as did the multiple-unit system for rapid transit service, first installed at Chicago. Neither dateline was actually met. By making financial concessions, an extension of time was obtained for the Richmond contract. A preliminary test for the system of multiple control was carried out one day after the date specified, and a full test made ten days later. The delays were due partly to illness and partly to mechanical problems and not to new acts of insight or inventions which occurred after the contracts were signed. The substantive inventions preceded the making of the contracts. In terms of the process of invention, the work that held up the contract was work of critical revision. In professional terminology, it was engineering work; the psychologist would classify it as the exercise of a series of acts of skill. They involved a combination of activities in the fields of technology and entrepreneurship.

These instances also serve to demonstrate the need of much in-

[9] Abbott Payson Usher, *A History of Mechanical Inventions*, McGraw-Hill, 1929, Chap. II; rev. ed., 1954, Chap. IV.

[10] Harold C. Passer, *The Electrical Manufacturers, 1875-1900*, Harvard University Press, 1953, pp. 241-243 and 271-273.

vention after the decisive demonstration of a new technique. Supplementary inventions of tertiary rank were necessary to secure full efficiency, and further secondary inventions were ultimately made. The quality of this work is usually ignored in descriptions of the application of the technique, except in accounts dominated by professional interest in technical detail. Practical application of a new technique does not mean that the process of invention has come to an end. But, in general, it is true that, as development proceeds, acts of skill become increasingly important.

There is no difference in the general character of the behavior of entrepreneurs and technologists. Entrepreneurs and executive directors invent new concepts of social ends and new procedures in social action. They discover new meanings in motivations and new modes of reconciling authority with individual freedom. But these acts of insight are dispersed through a highly diversified array of acts of skill which are often incorrectly classified because they are generalized to a greater degree than acts of skill in the fields commonly regarded as skilled and professional.

In considering the history of science and technology, the acts of insight and the processes of cumulative synthesis that can best be identified with invention are obviously more important than the acts of skill which are performed in the current applications of knowledge to individual and social needs. It is dangerous, however, to presume that the performance of acts of skill does not require abilities of a high order. At lower levels of action mere competence may suffice for much of the activity in the field. At higher levels—in the fields of art and the professions, and in leadership of large groups—mere competence has a narrowly limited value. Virtuosity in performance becames an essential requirement. Accomplishment with such distinction is possible only to small numbers of individuals, and, even if no major acts of insight are involved in their activity, their achievements are no less important to the social life of the group than the achievements of inventors. At the higher levels, however, acts of skill and insight are so completely interwoven that we cannot easily distinguish them.

2. *Primary Inventions and Discoveries*

The concept of a process of invention requires a notion of a sequence of acts of insight which leads to a cumulative synthesis of many items which were originally independent. Strictly speaking, each act of insight is an achievement of novelty of the highest order. Practically, we characterize as an invention only some concept or device that represents a substantial synthesis of old knowledge with new acts of insight. Common usage, however, does not require us to assume that an invention is practical. In fact, there has been a strong tendency to stress the outstanding importance of discoveries of new properties and relationships, and of new devices for producing motion when they are merely laboratory models or small devices for entertainment or mystification. These attitudes are well grounded, and this distinction between the working model or demonstration and the commercially useful machine is especially important for the history of technology since 1600. New scientific concepts have emerged, new devices have been invented, but practical application has been long deferred.

Transcendentalists and romantic individualists have commonly sought a single inventor in each sequence of achievement. Insofar as emphasis has been placed on sheer priority, the scientist is ranked ahead of the engineer, the achievement of a new principle counted as the true invention, and the practical application of the principle treated as a mere unimpeded act of skill achievable by any competent technician. There has been, thus, a large group who wish to credit Galileo with the "invention" of the pendulum clock because he perceived the bare principles involved, though no complete clock movement was produced during his lifetime. The work of Huygens has been treated as the explicit achievement of the discoveries and inventions of Galileo. In general, there has been a tendency to emphasize the scientific achievement if there is any single principle definite enough to seem to imply all the subsequent steps in the sequence. In the history of the steam engine the attempts to give primary credit to the early work have not successfully challenged the common appraisal of Watt's work.

This search for the unique inventor is naïve and ill grounded. All the items specified and many other acts of insight are an integral part of the history of the steam engine. Even if we accept the unduly restricted common meaning of the word invention, there were many inventions and a large number of acts of insight which are entirely ignored by the lay public though fully appreciated by engineers who have any interest in history. Emphasis upon the achievements below the level of practical use must not lead to an underestimate of the high degree of originality involved in practical applications of the general principle.

The scientific and technical achievements below the level of practical commercial use fall into several broad categories that do not lend themselves to comprehensive enumeration in detail. In the field of pure science we can recognize easily the discoveries of new properties of materials, the perception of new relationships expressed as principles or laws, the invention of apparatus for the observation and measurement of natural phenomena. Above this level of generality we find laboratory models and demonstrations which lead directly from primary principles to applications. Otto von Guericke's work on air pressure affords a conspicuous illustration of this phase of scientific work. The primary principles had been worked out by Torricelli and Pascal, but Guericke invented an air pump by which he could produce a significant vacuum. Guericke's work was important both for the development of the atmospheric engine of Newcomen and for the establishment of a technique of experimentation which, with improvements, enabled Boyle to carry the analysis of pressure in gases to the formulation of the famous laws.[11]

If we wish to complete the survey of work below the level of general commercial use, we must include the production of new objects of luxurious consumption. The development of technology has been profoundly influenced by the desire to produce articles of superior quality and special character for ritualistic use and for consumption by dignitaries of church and state outside the limits of explicit ceremonial use. Under such circumstances considerations of cost have been ignored and processes and products developed to gratify the desire to achieve distinction. In the early history of metallurgy, glass-making, and textile production, the development of luxury items was an important factor in invention. In the modern period the development of clocks and watches illustrates the importance of ritualistic and luxury demand. The mechanical clock was clearly developed in response to the ritualistic needs of the larger ecclesiastical establishments. Water clocks were not a convenient means of maintaining the schedule of services. Even a crude mechanical clock was superior; it was more accurate and required less attention. With improvements in craftsmanship, clocks and watches became an outstanding item of luxury consumption. In

[11] Blaise Pascal, *The Physical Treatises of Pascal: The Equilibrium of Liquids and the Weight of the Mass of the Air*, trans. I. H. B. and A. G. H. Spiers, Columbia University Press, 1937, pp. xv-xx, survey of whole episode. The appendices contain selections from the works of Galileo and Torricelli. Hans Schimank, *Otto von Guericke, Burgermeister von Magdeburg*, Magdeburg, Stadt Magdeburg, 1936, pp. 37-55.

many instances the accuracy of the movement was subordinated to the decoration of the case. But these crafts became the basis of work in light engineering which laid a secure foundation for the heavy-duty power engineering that became important in the eighteenth century.

There is thus a broad field of activity in which costs have been subordinated to the achievement of novelties in science and in the production of luxuries. Activities in this field have fallen somewhat outside any economic calculus. In the early modern period much of the work of scientist-inventors was associated with gainful professional work, especially in the fields of art and engineering. Painting, sculpture, architecture, and general engineering were not sharply specialized occupations. Much experimental work was done in the shops or studios, so that science, invention, and practice of the arts went hand in hand. The universities also created opportunities for science and invention. In the seventeenth century Galileo and Newton were the most distinguished representatives of the universities, though they were not alone. Boyle, Huygens, and Otto von Guericke were the most distinguished men who had personal wealth to use for their work. Patronage of the wealthy and of chiefs of state was of course a further source of finance for work in primary science and invention.

The sixteenth, seventeenth, and early eighteenth centuries were more notable for the accomplishments in science and primary invention than for achievements that added conspicuously to the productivity of industry and agriculture. However, the foundations were laid for the great technical achievments that followed directly upon the development of power engineering that stems from Watt. In the nineteenth century, basic work in the field of electricity was accomplished in a period in which practical achievements lay in the fields of mechanical and civil engineering. It is, therefore, important to recognize the necessity of this underlying work in science and primary invention. In general, the financing of such work came from sources which were essentially the same as in the sixteenth and seventeenth centuries; but the external features were somewhat different.

Since the beginning of the nineteenth century the research programs of the major universities have undergone a remarkable development. The private laboratory has given place to organized laboratory instruction in the universities, and research has become a recognized duty. General university functions have been expanded by the establishment of special research centers in the universities supported by public funds or private endowment, or both. Direct governmental support of basic research has a longer history in the agricultural field than elsewhere, but the importance of public provision for primary research is increasing in other fields. Even if political pressures require state-supported research to give much time to secondary research of immediate interest, the larger organizations will doubtless contribute much to basic research and primary invention.

The research organizations of many corporations today provide a certain amount of free time for the personal projects and interests of the research worker. In some corporations, too, the general program of the staff includes many basic or primary problems not expected to yield immediate commercial results.[12]

3. *Secondary Inventions and New Investment*

In order to clarify distinctions between different types of invention, they may be classified as primary, secondary, and tertiary. Underlying inventions not carried to a stage of general commercial use may be classified as primary inventions. Inventions which open up a new practical use may best be considered as secondary inventions, whatever their importance. Any invention which extends a known principle to a new field of use should be so classified. The noncondensing engine and the locomotive should thus be treated as distinct secondary inventions, despite the utilization of some of the principles of the Watt condensing engine. Improvements in a given device which do not clearly extend the field of use can be classed as tertiary inventions. They are not to be ignored, but they stand in a different position in the sequence of technical change, and they have different consequences for the economy. Such inventions may increase the efficiency of the secondary invention or add to its convenience and safe operation; but they remain subordinate in importance if they do not extend the field of use.

In the field of secondary invention the associations and problems of the inventor are profoundly changed. Contacts with science are weakened and contacts with business assume commanding importance. When functions are not fully specialized, the inventor acts as

[12] J. D. Bernal, *The Social Function of Science*, London, Routledge, 1939, pp. 35-70, 126-154 and 261-291; Charles E. K. Mees, *The Organization of Industrial Scientific Research*, McGraw-Hill, 1950, pp. 5-16 and 51-149; and Paul Freedman, *The Principles of Scientific Research*, Public Affairs Press, 1950.

an entrepreneur; this stage is characterized by the inventor-entrepreneur just as the first stage is characterized by the scientist-inventor. These differences in the activities of inventive types were clearly present in Schumpeter's mind, but the problems cannot be adequately analyzed in terms of his categories of invention and innovation. All activities at the stage of secondary invention involve close interweaving of acts of skill, acts of insight, and inventions. In enterprises which take a lead in the introduction of new inventions and processes, both inventors and administrators are engaged in inventive work of commanding importance. They also achieve great virtuosity in the performance of the associated acts of skill. Schumpeter underestimated the degree of novelty involved in these acts of skill—of both the engineers and technicians and the administrative staff of the enterprise.

The character of the choices to be made and their relation to the financing of the enterprise can be appreciated best if we concentrate attention on particular examples. Three cases are especially significant: the development of the locomotive, the development of interchangeable-part processes of manufacture, and the introduction of the Bessemer process in the iron and steel industry. All three cases exhibit the importance of a period in which technical achievements were imperfect. The early locomotives did not compete decisively with horsepower. Whitney's methods of production were at first limited in scope and used elementary techniques; but though not fully developed for thirty or more years they were commandingly successful from the start. The Bessemer process, in its early form, was restricted to particular ores. The failure to understand these limitations at the outset led to such great disappointment that the whole procedure for the introduction of the process had to be changed.

In histories of these inventions these critical periods of difficulty are frequently ignored or underemphasized. Full analysis is clearly necessary in order to understand the process of investment in new industries. If good judgment is exercised, risks of loss do not exceed the risks in established industries. The beginnings of commercial application precede the full accomplishment of the secondary invention. In many instances even the major invention remains to be achieved; in other cases the process of critical revision is conspicuously incomplete. The implications of Schumpeter's analysis suggest the opposite order of development: the completion of the secondary invention is represented as preceding the entrepreneurial work on application.

If we study the history of the locomotive with a dominant interest in engineering detail, we find three important steps in the achievement: the Pen-y-darran locomotive of Trevithick, 1804; the *Royal George*, built by Timothy Hackworth in 1826; and the *Rocket*, built by Robert Stephenson & Co. in 1829. Trevithick's engine was impractical because its steam capacity was low and it was too heavy for the cast iron rails then in use. Hackworth's *Royal George* was an effective heavy-duty freight locomotive decisively superior to horses, but it was not suitable for passenger service and needed much improvement in details. The *Rocket* was the first locomotive in which all essential features were incorporated in a mature form, and definitely the first locomotive designed to operate at high speeds on rails. It is an oversimplification to stress any single one of these steps as the controlling secondary invention. The vocabulary of common speech does not supply convenient words to express an achievement spread over time in a number of steps. The best we can do is to use the plural form "secondary inventions."

The problems of new investment have been dominated by the multiplicity of steps involved at this stage and by the relatively small magnitudes of improvements necessary to justify the expenditures. Trevithick's locomotives were incidental to his work on the high-pressure engine as a stationary source of power. The expenses incurred in making the model and in demonstrations of the road locomotive (1798-1802) were covered by the income from the engineering work that was Trevithick's primary concern. The demonstration at Pen-y-darran was financed by Homfray, the mine-owner for whom Trevithick had built a number of stationary engines. The engine itself was built to work a hammer, so that the special expenditure was restricted to the adaptation of the engine to operation on the tram line at the mine. The test was not intended to open up an application of steam power to the transport work of the mine.[13] Although demonstrations of the locomotive on rails were made at London in 1808, Trevithick did not himself, or through associates, develop any project for the systematic operation of a tram line by steam locomotives. His work, however, inspired the projects in the northeastern coal fields which began with Blenkinsop's work at the Middleton Colliery, three miles south of Leeds (1812).

[13] H. W. Dickinson and Arthur Tetley, *Richard Trevithick: The Engineer and the Man*, Cambridge University Press, 1934, pp. 42-65.

These locomotives were largely the work of Matthew Murray, but royalties were paid to Trevithick for the use of his patents. Blenkinsop added a rack rail, so that this application of steam has been frequently regarded as a diversion of attention from the basic pattern of steam traction. The toothed wheel, however, was not intended to make up for lack of adhesion in a smooth rail; it was a naïve and relatively simple driving mechanism which was good enough to remain in operation for many years around the collieries.[14] These applications, therefore, were in no sense failures.

A locomotive sent to the Royal Iron Foundry in Berlin for the mines at Gleiwitz could not be put into operation because of the opposition of the local engineers and workers. There was similar resistance to the use of a locomotive in the colliery at Saarbrücken.[15] It may be that these engines failed to achieve all the potentialities that other inventors realized, but they were good enough to compete directly with horses. There are a few statements about the costs and the performances of these engines, but they are not detailed enough to inspire much confidence. Fully loaded, speeds were about 2.5 miles per hour. With light loads, 10 miles per hour was claimed.

The development of the mature type of locomotive and of the civil engineering work on the line was accomplished by Hedley and George Stephenson on the tram lines operated by the Wylam, Killingworth, and Hetton Collieries and the famous Stockton & Darlington Railroad, which was a colliery line with supplemental common-carrier functions. All this highly novel work was accomplished in the course of the systematic operation of transport service at these collieries. Use on a restricted scale, but with success, led to a great enlargement of the scale of operation and to a commanding technical superiority over alternative modes of transportation. It is easy to overlook the fact that the early achievements in the restricted field were of material value.

The Stockton & Darlington and the Liverpool & Manchester Railroad represent two successive enlargements of the application of the locomotive. The Stockton & Darlington was an alternative to a canal. It offered common-carrier service, but the company leased the right to operate passenger service to contractors who put horse-drawn coaches on the line. Freight service was operated by locomo-

[14] C. F. Dendy Marshall, *Early British Locomotives,* London, Locomotive Publishing, 1939, pp. 19-30.

[15] *Ibid.,* p. 34, and C. F. Dendy Marshall, *Two Essays,* London, Locomotive Publishing, 1928, pp. 19-21.

tives on level stretches and by cable haulage on two inclines. No feature of the project was at that time new, though it did involve a longer line than the colliery tram lines. The Liverpool & Manchester project was an alternative to a line operated by cables and stationary engines. It was planned to offer both freight and passenger service. Passenger service had not previously been attempted on rails, but a number of steam coaches were in operation on highways out of London and the potentialities of the locomotive were understood though still underestimated. Speeds of 15 to 20 miles per hour were presumed to be achievable. The conditions for the Rainhill competition prescribed a speed of not less than 10 miles per hour. The *Rocket* averaged 15 miles per hour, and ran for a time at a rate of 29 miles per hour. After the accident to Huskisson, the *Northumbrian* of similar design ran 15 miles at a rate of 36 miles per hour. Fifteen or sixteen years later the *Rocket* ran 4 miles in four and one-half minutes, or at a rate of 53 miles per hour.[16]

The Liverpool & Manchester project marked the culmination of eighteen years of work in the application of the steam locomotive to tram lines. Under progressively exacting conditions of use, both the locomotive and the civil engineering work were greatly improved. Wrought iron rails of improved design replaced the cast iron rails used at Pen-y-darran for Trevithick's demonstration. The locomotive had greater steam capacity, and the differentiation between the freight and the passenger locomotive was understood. The technique had been carried to a point at which it could be used for a generalized system of inland transport. The work of these critical years involved the cooperation of engineers as skilled technicians and as inventors, and of businessmen as colliery managers seeking means of expanding transport services for which the supply of horses was becoming a limiting factor. Novelties were emerging at many levels and in many forms but under conditions which made losses unlikely, though the magnitude of the gains was uncertain. The new technique could be used if it was not less productive than the current alternative. As long as the scale of operations remained small, the dangers of losses were also small. Overoptimism was not likely to develop until the whole group of secondary inventions had been completed, and work began for the generalization of the new

[16] Samuel Smiles, *The Life of George Stephenson and of His Son Robert Stephenson*, Harper, 1868, pp. 325 and 327n.; and Clement E. Stretton, *The Locomotive Engine and Its Development*, London, Lockwood, 1896, p. 36.

technique in the economy as a whole. The railway crisis started in England in 1845.

The general pattern observed in the development of the locomotive and the railroad may be seen also in the history of Eli Whitney's manufacture of muskets on the principle of interchangeable parts. The idea itself was not new. The Swedish engineer Christopher Polhem had perceived the general elements of such a system of manufacture, though he had not attempted to work within the field of precision mechanisms. Work on firearms on such a system had been tried in France but had not been pushed to conspicuous and decisive accomplishment.

The significance of Whitney's work lay not only in the bare idea, but also in the progressive mechanization of the process with machine tools capable of great precision. The actual manufacture of muskets passed through several stages. The first contracts were executed by filing the parts of the lock to conform to patterns or jigs. The parts were worked out in soft metal, subsequently tempered and hardened. At first, only the locks were made on an interchangeable-part system. Later the stocks were shaped on pattern-turning lathes which reduced the amount of hand labor to a minor fraction of the prior requirements. The lock mechanism, too, was manufactured by methods which reduced handwork and increased the degree of precision achieved. This was accomplished by developing the technique of die stamping for some parts, and by the development of the milling machine to supplant the laborious processes of filing. These activities covered about twenty years. There was thus a group of interrelated secondary inventions, all of which were essential to the mature accomplishment, though commercial success was assured when the new procedure had not been carried beyond its most elementary form.[17]

The array of machine tools ultimately developed were not implicit in or even suggested by the system of jig filing that was first used. The new tools were independent inventions of great merit and importance whose earlier history and background lay in the field of lathes, which worked originally in wood and soft metals below the level of precision required by the system of interchangeable-parts manufacture.

The complexity of the stage of early secondary invention is illustrated also by the history of the refining processes in the iron and

[17] Jeanette Mirsky and Allan Nevins, *The World of Eli Whitney*, Macmillan, 1952, pp. 128-146 and 177-205.

steel industries. The transition from an industry dominated by malleable iron to one dominated by steel was brought about by the improvement of refining processes, so that a larger scale of production could be achieved at lower costs. The development was begun by the introduction of the Bessemer converter. By means of intense internal combustion, this device decarburized the cast iron coming from the blast furnace. The treatment of the charge of the converter required about twenty minutes. Puddling, the process then in use, required eight or ten hours to treat a much smaller charge and used highly skilled labor.

When Bessemer's process was announced it was immediately recognized as a potentially controlling factor in the industry. Bessemer proposed to lease the right to use the process on a royalty basis. As soon as attempts were made to apply the process, however, serious difficulties appeared. Much of the iron produced was brittle and poor, its quality far below any standard required in the industry. Bessemer was convinced of the truth of his claims, but careful analysis finally revealed the fact that the process could be used only in the treatment of iron that was free from phosphorus. Many of the ores then in use contained more phosphorus than was allowable if the new process was to be used. Bessemer now found it necessary to join some ironmasters in the organization of a company to apply the process to suitable ores.[18]

Conditions in the iron and steel trades became very complex. The new process was directed to new fields in the market, and the older firms and older processes of production were able to maintain themselves for an interval; but conditions were very unstable, and the value of ores was profoundly affected by the selectivity of the Bessemer process. Balanced use of ores was ultimately made possible by two new secondary inventions: the open hearth process provided a method of refining that was effectively competitive with the Bessemer process commercially and happily suited to an array of ores that could not be treated by the Bessemer process. Neither of these processes was adapted to ores containing much phosphorus, though the open hearth was more tolerant of phosphorus than the Bessemer process. This difficulty was overcome by two chemists, Thomas and Gilchrist. They devised a basic lining for the refining furnaces which removed the phosphorus by a chemical reaction. With the two refining processes and the use of basic linings when

[18] Sir Henry Bessemer, *Autobiography*, London, Offices of *Engineering*, 1905, pp. 155-177.

required by the ores, it became possible to treat the whole array of commercially important ores. The transformation of the industry thus required all three of these secondary inventions. The full accomplishment took place between 1854, when the Bessemer process was announced, and 1878, when the basic lining of the furnaces was achieved by Thomas and Gilchrist.

The introduction of secondary inventions is profitable from a very early stage once capitalist methods of production have reached a point at which monopoly power can be achieved even for short periods of time. The inventor-entrepreneur cannot secure profit unless the introduction of the device or process can be controlled through patent privileges, secrecy, or dependence upon small numbers of specially trained workmen. The textile inventions of the eighteenth century, Whitney's cotton gin, and Oliver Evans' mechanization of flour-milling afford characteristic illustrations of the weakness of the position of the inventor when the machines can be built by any craftsman without drawings or detailed specifications. When machine-building becomes a fully specialized occupation in any given field, new devices can be controlled and protected even without a patent system, though patent privileges are of undoubted social value in creating property rights to invention.

The development of the use of power in transport and manufacture is also an important condition. Increases in the scale of manufacture through the use of power or through the opening of wider markets give new significance to monopoly. The great watchmakers of France and England in the eighteenth century made outstanding contributions to their craft and to the whole field of mechanical engineering. But their most distinguished inventions merely gave them prestige in a craft which at best enabled them to sell their products to distinguished customers willing to ignore the costs of objects of luxury and ostentation. The work of the Dollands in the optical field is perhaps even more striking, because telescopes and microscopes appealed almost exclusively to wealthy amateurs with little serious interest in science. Work on the chronometer was stimulated by the prizes offered in France and England for a means of determining longitude at sea.

The characteristic phenomena of capital formation as we know them since 1800 are clearly attributable to the precision working of iron and steel and the developments in the related field of general power engineering. The textile inventions of the eighteenth century would have had a different and more restricted application if it had not become possible to supplant the machines of wood and soft metals with well-designed machines of iron and steel.

4. *The Spatial Diffusion of New Techniques*

When the first cycle of secondary inventions is complete, or even well launched, the diffusion of the new technique throughout the economy presents a new set of problems. At this stage new acts of insight and new inventions are somewhat obscured because such a large part of the total task can be achieved by acts of skill. Furthermore, no particular invention is necessary at any given time to make the process or activity commercially effective. Delays incidental to positive invention cease to be of immediate consequence; improvements that are achievable are desirable, but they merely increase the profit derived from a process that is already profitable. There is thus some justification for the overemphasis so commonly placed upon particular inventions in the first cycle of secondary invention; but, though understandable, these judgments are misleading.

The usual treatment of Watt's inventions gives too little credit to Newcomen and to the engineers who developed the high-pressure engine. In the textile series the stress on the earliest forms of the inventions is excessive. With the caprice characteristic of incomplete analysis, the importance of the work of the Darbys in the iron industry is ordinarily understated, but the emphasis upon puddling and rolling and upon the steel-making processes in the nineteenth century is sound. The history of the iron industry is perhaps the clearest instance of a succession of secondary inventions whose independence and importance are rarely questioned.

The acts of skill which dominate the spatial diffusion of new techniques appear both in the field of technology and in the field of economic administration. The process of development discloses new characteristics which are most effectively described if we distinguish between meliorative effects and the cumulative accumulation of knowledge, on the one hand, and growth as a quantitative and adaptive phenomenon, on the other. Once the point of secondary invention is reached the scale of the economy and its productivity are affected. These results can be observed in the growth of population and in the changes and net increases in consumption.

Approached from this point of view, the process of growth in the economy is a resultant of the array of accelerating factors represented by technical changes and the decelerating or limiting factors of scarcity of resources. Older concepts of change assumed the intermittent occurrence of particular changes in an essentially stable economy. A mature concept of the process of invention requires us to conceive of changes as essentially continuous in units of small magnitude. Discontinuities are not felt as such because the magnitudes are small. The substantial continuity of the process of growth is clear in the records of the iron and steel industry and in the field of power engineering. When products of specialized use are involved, the case is not as clear. Illustrative material is afforded by the history of the petroleum industry and by the development of heavier-than-air flight. The statistics of the production of illuminating oils are interesting when the whale oils and mineral oils are combined in one series for a substantial period. Adequate analysis of the records, however, would require more space than is here available.

There is enough statistical material to show that growth in the economy proceeds at varying rates: at accelerating rates up to the inflection point; at decelerating rates beyond it. In some fields growth may occur as a continuous process of deceleration, as presumed by Raymond Pearl, but such rigorous conditions are not characteristic of the biological processes in individual organisms or of human economies. It is not possible at this time, with the data available, to identify a specific mathematical formula with the process of social growth. The records we have now, however, are consistent with the suggestions made by R. A. Lehfeldt in 1916. He pointed out that the integral of the normal curve affords a satisfactory formula for much statistical material if we use the logarithms of the items. The formula expresses a cycle of orderly growth between two limiting magnitudes at varying rates of change.[19] The framework of the curve does not quite fit the facts of social life, because major technical changes displace the upper asymptote and release new potentialities of growth. The upper asymptote of the preceding cycle is passed and becomes the lower asymptote of the next cycle. Even with good statistical material, the records of actual growth would not conform to the formula in portions of the curve close to the asymptotes implicit in the major portion of the record.

The production of pig iron in Great Britain in the eighteenth and nineteenth centuries exhibits as much conformity to the integral

[19] R. A. Lehfeldt, "The Normal Law of Progress," *Journal of the Royal Statistical Society*, Vol. LXXIX, 1916, pp. 329-332.

of the normal curve as the quality of our statistical material would warrant us to expect. The magnitude of the growth is most vividly reflected in the figures for per capita consumption: 1735, 15 pounds; 1800, 26 pounds; 1830, 77 pounds; 1890, 303 pounds. The record discloses a relatively smooth curve despite the major inventions that were required to make this development possible.[20] It seems strange that there is no evidence of more discontinuity. Some might take the position that the whole development was implicit in the application of coal and coke to iron-making. A better explanation is that the occurrence of inventions and acts of insight does not stand outside the formula of probability. Favorable constellations of events occur as a matter of chance. Over a large field and long periods of time, the emergence of novelty may well conform to the formula of probability. The normal curve may thus be related to all the arrays of phenomena involved in the process of growth.

If these inferences are justifiable, we have means of studying the rate of capital formation in economies undergoing technical change. Even if the statistical record of capital is inadequate, sampling methods will give an indication of the changing relations between product and capital, so that inferences can be drawn from the records of production.

The organic quality of the process of growth has important bearings upon the financial operations underlying new investment. It is not necessary to assume that the funds are deflected from older channels by the higher bids in new industries and undertakings. The credit resources available are sufficient to make the new investments largely dependent upon the expectations of gain in the new activity. New techniques of production affect the value of resources so directly that technological change is reflected in increases in the physical quantity and in the value of basic resources. New techniques of transportation affect site values and the values of agricultural and mineral lands that would otherwise be inaccessible to markets. These facts are obvious, but the timing of these changes in values is sometimes inadequately analyzed.

Analysis must be considered from two points of view: that of the statistician and that of the entrepreneur. The statistician may legitimately regard the change in value as implicit in the substantial accomplishment of the secondary inventions. Changes in the coal and iron resources of Great Britain would, therefore, date from the

[20] Witt Bowden, Michael Karpovich, and Abbott Payson Usher, *An Economic History of Europe since 1750*, American Book, 1937, pp. 384-385.

successful work of the Darbys with coke. All these resources would have been revalued at least after 1735. Any survey of physical resources may legitimately distinguish between potential and actual resources. If technical and market conditions do not justify current utilization, particular deposits should be classified as potential. If workable at current costs, resources are actual. In a region whose resources are significantly known, the stocks available from the statistical point of view commonly provide for long periods. Primary minerals are available as "actual" resources for intervals of 300 to 500 years; and potential resources in mineralized areas extend in many instances to 1,000 years.

The entrepreneur must deal with shorter time spans and more immediate market relationships. He is primarily concerned with close analysis of actual resources, though potential resources may be of great moment if the technical or transportation problems admit of some change in technique that would bring the resources into the current cost structure in the industry. The entrepreneur considers three categories of resources: resources that are actual but not proven by detailed surveys, proven resources, and currently developed resources. The time span for entrepreneurial activity would rarely exceed twenty-five years, though acquisitions of title to prospective ores may well be carried further. The essential feature of the situation lies in the emergence of material values well in advance of current exploitation. These values can properly support a structure of long-time loans, and with good judgment should involve no greater risk than in a supposedly established industry. The long-time value structure in the old industry is not insulated against change. The development of petroleum as a primary fuel, for example, has had an adverse effect on the values of coal properties.

The influence of new techniques of transport upon land values is more complex than the effects of technical change on particular fixed resources. Changes in transportation affect site values for all classes of sites, but most particularly for the first-, second-, and third-class urban units. These sites increase in size proportionately to the population within a given area and an expansion of their market areas.[21] The internal structure of the urban units is effected both by local facilities for transport and by techniques of house construction.

[21] George Kingsley Zipf, *Human Behavior and the Principle of Least Effort*, Addison-Wesley, 1949, pp. 374-383.

Both mineral lands and agricultural land are sensitive to the market connections that are a function of transport costs. Improvements in transportation, therefore, affect all the values of the land and fixed resources of the economy. The application of power to land transport has completely transformed the world economy. Before the development of the railroad the world economy was in effect the maritime fringe of the great continents. The interiors were open only to the extent that some form of water transport was available, and, as a consequence, contacts with the deeper interiors were very restricted. The railroad opened all these interiors to world markets, and today the emergence of a truly global economy is painfully evident. Its substantial emergence can perhaps be dated as early as 1878, when wheat from the prairies of the United States entered the European markets with such devastating effect.

No problems of technical diffusion and expansion are as complex as the agrarian dislocations created by the introduction of new transport facilities extending the areas devoted to particular crops. Such areas of cultivation bear no significant relation to the development of demand for the product. The extension of the sugar culture to the New World presents a complex episode of this type that cannot be accurately analyzed because of the inadequacy of our statistical material. On the other hand, the expansion of wheat culture in the prairie regions of the United States, Russia, and Australia can be studied in detail. Large portions of these areas were suitable only to wheat culture, as the rainfall pattern was unfavorable to general farming. Beyond the margins of wheat culture, specialized grazing became important.

Competition with these frontier producing areas was disastrous to the established agricultural areas in Europe dependent upon general farming; both mixed and cereal farming areas suffered, though the latter were more severely affected than the former. Wheat prices fell, even in relation to other commodities. Since nonhuman uses could be brought into the market only at prices that were unremunerative to growers, primary reliance lay in the expansion of human consumption. Over the period of fifty-five years studied by Malenbaum, acreage expanded in excess of the requirements for human consumption. In the decade 1929-1939, this excess acreage averaged 35 million acres per year.[22]

[22] Wilfred Malenbaum, "Equilibrating Tendencies in the World Wheat Market," thesis, Harvard University, 1941. Cf. especially the author's summary of conclusions. Substantially the same analysis was published subsequently by

The problem of maintaining equilibrium in the spatial economy appears in a special form in the construction of the railroad network. In Great Britain, public policy became committed at an early date to a principle of requiring presumptive evidence of cost recovery as a condition for the grant of a charter. In France and in the United States it was recognized that some railroad construction could advisedly be authorized even if there were no prospect of recovering all the costs immediately—or perhaps even ultimately. The grounds for this position are different in different circumstances. Some areas of France were provided with more service than they could themselves support in order to avoid losses from major displacement of population in such areas. In the United States it was presumed that losses would be temporary, but this optimism has not always been justified, though the operation of the network in the United States has been affected by a pattern of ownership that results in the segregation of strong and weak lines.

The diffusion of new techniques throughout the world economy is certainly not a smooth process that admits of the continuous maintenance of equilibrium conditions. The difficulties come from many sources: the magnitude of the units of investment, the length of the time intervals needed to produce effective responses in the economy, the number of different regions affected by a single change in technology, and the divergent influences upon particular kinds of resources or activities. Coal deposits and coal-mining have been profoundly affected by the development of petroleum as a major fuel and by large-scale hydroelectric installations. Furthermore, the demand for coal in transportation has been influenced by the development of pipeline transport of oil and gas, and by long-distance transmission of electricity. Economy in the use of coal was recognized as an undoubted necessity as late as 1920; but when the changes came, the magnitudes of the reductions in demand could not be absorbed without drastic reorganization of the industry.

For all these reasons it is desirable to think of these spatial problems as growth problems. All such changes are not necessarily positive and advantageous. Even the most important technical advances affect adversely many activities and even entire regions.

The time intervals involved in the general process of technical advance are certainly much longer than current economic literature

---

him as *The World Wheat Economy, 1885-1939*, Harvard University Press, 1953.

is ready to recognize. Some broad entrepreneurial policy decisions most certainly recognize intervals of twenty-five to thirty years, but the technical changes themselves do not disclose all their influence within such intervals. The development of the mineral economy reaches maturity with the development of petroleum and a generalized system for the distribution and use of energy in the form of electricity. The beginning of the change can be dated from the Newcomen engine and Darby's use of coal and coke, in the years 1708-1712. A period of more than 200 years must, therefore, be considered. With long time intervals the achievement of equilibrium becomes more difficult.

5. *Technology and Centralized Administration*

It is tempting to presume that centralized administration might achieve a more adequate equilibrium in the economy than has been achieved in the past. Analysis of technical change certainly creates the presumption that important increases in the size of administrative units are likely to emerge as a consequence of changes in the techniques of communication. Increased speed of communication, new techniques of collecting and organizing information, and larger-scale units of production all lead us to presume that administrative units will become larger both in private and in public administration. Comprehensive control of the economy from some highly centralized policy committee raises a different issue. The precise form of the central authority is perhaps less important than the concept of the direction of investment in terms of statistical aggregates. If we assume that these aggregates can become the sole basis of primary economic policy, the economy must be a closed organic system.

The organic concept of the state and of the economy has exerted a powerful influence upon the social sciences since the early nineteenth century. No problem presents more sharply the issues between idealistic and empirical interpretations of history and of social structure. Idealists assert that the social structure is a closely knit and comprehensive whole. Empiricists hold that society consists of a loosely related array of structures, none of which is comprehensive. Individual elements may belong to more than one structure, and the parts may be combined in different ways in different periods of history. To the empiricist the wholes possess less vitality than their parts—though the parts cannot function except in some broader structure.

We therefore face a significant issue of analysis when we consider the aggregative records of an economy: Do these aggregates indicate the presence of an organic whole that can be directly administered as a comprehensive entity? The idealist assumes that society is such a monolithic whole. However, a concept of emergent novelty and a theory of invention presented as cumulative synthesis are inconsistent with such a position. We should think of the events in our social life as a relatively large number of systems of events, some of which have contacts with each other; some of them, however, are positively opposed to each other. It is possible to show readily that many of these systems of events have no genetic relationship; though, over long periods of time, events which have not been related in the past converge toward a new synthesis. This pluralistic concept does not exclude the concept of organic structure, but it attributes organic relationships to smaller units and presumes that these relationships are created by social process. The organic wholes recognized by the empiricist are never comprehensive.

The statistical universes which are found in social life disclose systems of order that can be analyzed in terms of probability. We must think of these aggregates merely as representations of arrays of events disclosing a multiplicity of causes which afford no clues to the degrees or degree of interdependence or independence. The empiricist thinks of them as statistical aggregates which reflect large numbers of individual items. In the field of investment, multiplicity is manifested as a large number of separate judgments—judgments about the values of resources and new materials, about costs of production and of marketing, and about consumer responses to different price policies. Even in fields dominated by well-organized markets, values are not independent of individual judgments; they do not come to the entrepreneur from the outside as a final fact. He is concerned with a future that is not fully calculable, so that even in the best market economy individual judgment must be exercised. The market registers an array of judgments; it does not make judgments.

Centralization of fiscal and monetary authority can serve usefully in guiding many of the value judgments to be made, but fiscal and monetary policies do not make independent judgments unnecessary. Wise policies can direct the process of investment, but they cannot change the primary character of the process as a summation of individual items proceeding upward from a large number of separate decisions. It is not necessary to assume that all decisions are made by entrepreneurs charged with the administration of independent corporations operated on a profit basis. Government corporations or departments may also be making judgments about investment in which cost factors may be given primary importance or subordinated to other social interests. The form of the process would not be altered by the introduction of new criteria for decisions as long as it is recognized that many independent decisions are being made.

The fully administered economy may seem to achieve unity, but this is not necessarily the case. Are the totals for the comprehensive plan aggregates of items that have been added together or are they allocations of funds that are divided after the total has been determined by a judgment of a central executive officer? No final answer can safely be given to such a question. In the past, concentration of authority has frequently been carried beyond the limits of the actual and effective making of executive decisions. Orders that emanate from the highest levels of authority are actually based on information and texts that are collected and prepared by lower levels of the bureaucratic hierarchy. Since the operation of bureaucracies is capricious, it is dangerous to generalize about the effective limits of the authority of central executive officers. Practical limits of centralization are determined by techniques of communication. We may now recognize the desirability of a much greater concentration of administrative power than was possible before the introduction of the telegraph and telephone, but even after all these developments, and with ancillary inventions in electrical tabulation, it is probable that important limitations to centralization should be recognized. If there is to be any innovation, there must be opportunity for independent judgments about the use of time and of uncommitted funds. Novel achievements emerge most freely beyond the limits of the pressures of convention and authority. The existence of many different authorities is the ultimate safeguard of the individual and the basis for the continuity of the process of invention in all its forms and fields. Major innovations in technology would probably encounter more resistance in an authoritarian society than in a society without full concentration of control over property and choice of occupation.

The adaptation of social and economic administration to changing circumstances will probably be quicker and more successful in a society without full centralization. But social and economic structures will undoubtedly function even if centralization is carried beyond the point of full efficiency.

INNOVATION AND CAPITAL FORMATION IN SOME AMERICAN INDUSTRIES

W. RUPERT MACLAURIN

MASSACHUSETTS INSTITUTE OF TECHNOLOGY

ECONOMIC growth is so broad a subject that in one sense almost every specialty can be included in it without any effort; yet it does seem fruitful to make a *major effort* to focus the relevant specialties on the factors influencing growth as such. The most serious difficulty is to provide a framework in which the various contributions can be additive.

Since my assignment was as a companion speaker to Usher, I should like to stress my belief that our respective approaches are complementary rather than conflicting.

1. *The Process of Invention and Innovation*

Usher's distinguished book on *The History of Mechanical Inventions*[1] has greatly helped us to understand the process of invention by showing the nature of the continuous stream of new techniques making for evolutionary change. Viewed from a high perspective, the dams and waterfalls in this stream disappear and all that confronts us is a ribbon of water descending steadily toward the ocean.

The process of invention *can* be fruitfully studied from the standpoint of a continuous flow of ideas. Yet it is equally valid to think of the process in terms of discontinuity. In the last 100 years many major inventions have been applications of somewhat earlier breakthroughs in fundamental science. One way of looking at the history of science is to recognize that new conceptual schemes are exceedingly difficult to create,[2] that men capable of creating them are rare, and that there is a random element in the timing of the appearance of such men. It is true, of course, that the introduction of major new conceptual apparatus has frequently been preceded by a substantial whittling away at older concepts. But I do not believe that the process is automatic. An intellectual field may remain dormant for a long period because no man of exceptional vision rises to offer a new and challenging approach.

[1] Abbott Payson Usher, *The History of Mechanical Inventions*, McGraw-Hill, 1929.

[2] Cf. J. B. Conant, *On Understanding Science*, Yale University Press, 1946.

This paper will discuss some case studies of innovation, in order to bring out sharply the nature of technological discontinuities and some of the reasons for them. The material will be examined in an essentially Schumpeterian framework. My main concern is with the pulsating character of innovation and with the entrepreneurial and technological factors leading in particular sectors of the economy to growth, maturity, decay, and regeneration.

I am aware that the term "innovation" lacks precise definition. Yet I prefer it to Usher's "emergent novelty," primarily because I am impressed by the importance of the entrepreneur as a key figure in innovative change and wish to stress the distinction between invention and innovation. The entrepreneurial skill required to introduce a major innovation is rare. Economists have too often concluded that, granted an advance in technology and a strong economic incentive, innovators will automatically appear. On the contrary, as in science, significant opportunities frequently lie available for years, awaiting the right combination of creative vision and action. Then, once the initial difficulties have been overcome, the imitative process can be carried out much more rapidly by men of lesser stature. Later, when the original idea has been fully exploited, there may again be a long wait for new men and new money to advance to another stage.

To my thinking, the Schumpeterian hypothesis linking innovation to long (Kondratieff) cycles in business activity is fruitful for an analysis of economic growth. While we lack adequate statistical data for a long enough period of time to arrive at any proven conclusions, we can say that there have been waves of high investment activity associated with particular fields; and there are factors in the process of invention and innovation that might lead us to expect the wavelike movement to persist.

Thus if fundamental new concepts occur only at intervals, such a basic scientific fact may well affect the pace of technological change. We need to know more concerning the relationship between the propensity to develop pure science, the propensity to invent, and the propensity to innovate[3] before we can conclude that any wavelike force exists;[4] but in the meantime the hypothesis deserves further testing.

[3] See W. W. Rostow, *The Process of Economic Growth*, Norton, 1952, and my article "The Sequence from Invention to Innovation and Its Relation to Economic Growth," *Quarterly Journal of Economics*, February 1953, pp. 97-111.

[4] The reader who wishes to pursue this point further is referred to my *Invention and Innovation in the Radio Industry* (Macmillan, 1949), in which con-

Any analysis of technological change and economic growth needs also to take account of certain shifts in the demand for innovations that occur as the more obvious material needs of society are satisfied and we advance to higher standards of living.

In a mature economy, like that of the United States, opportunities for investment are likely to become increasingly concerned with tertiary industries rather than with primary or secondary industries.[5] By tertiary industries I mean *all types of service industries,*[6] including transportation, community services, education, and recreation. In the last 150 years the proportion of our population engaged in agriculture has steadily declined while the percentage engaged in manufacturing has increased. But we have reached a stage where the manufacturing *proportion* can be expected to diminish.

Today the demand for new technology is distorted by military considerations. But the potential growth of services intensifies the need for organizational innovation and for a technology applicable to the service industries. Successful organization innovations will require the application of human relations skills of a high order. It seems not unlikely, therefore, that in America in the second half of the twentieth century innovating entrepreneurs will be drawn more from the group of men trained as social engineers than, as in the first half of the century, from those with a background in physical engineering.[7]

2. *Some Examples*

Whether or not we accept the concept of long waves of business expansion bearing some approximate relation to a forty-year cycle, the period from the depression of the 1890's to the outbreak of World War II had certain distinguishing characteristics that can be usefully analyzed. In the Western economic world, and particularly in America, this was an era dominated by the growth of the automobile industry, of electric utilities, and of the chemical industries.

---

siderable attention is given to the relationship between innovative and imitative entrepreneurship and to the problem of the "cluster effect."

[5] See A. G. B. Fisher, *Clash of Progress and Security*, London, Macmillan, 1935.

[6] Considerably more work could be usefully done to clarify industrial definitions. I include newspapers, television broadcasting, hospitals, helicopter buses, ski tows, theatres, and community swimming pools as "service industries."

[7] Is it too much to hope, as a corollary, that the second half of the twentieth century will also witness the coming of age of the social sciences?

THE AUTOMOBILE INDUSTRY

The automobile industry has certainly been one of the most vigorous new industries in America. Yet by the late 1920's the innovative characteristics of the industry began to change. There can be no simple explanation of this fact. But a partial answer lies in the quality of entrepreneurial leadership, the absence of a research conception, the explosive rate of previous growth, and the success of the established oligopoly.

More than any other figure, Henry Ford typified the automobile industry in its first innovative phase. His principal contribution was in pressing aggressively for cost-price reductions to achieve a mass market. He weighed all technological changes against this objective. A skilled mechanic without professional training, Ford never included fundamental research as part of his program. Nor was it part of the program of his competitors. Therefore, while the automobile industry could perhaps have been preparing during the 1920's for basic innovations, it was in fact not doing so. Henry Ford himself was aging, though maintaining firm control of the helm. Thus he did not see the limitations of planetary transmission until a very costly shift in production was forced on him by his competitors.

More important than the character of entrepreneurial leadership was the fact that there was no strong incentive for radical technological change in the automobile industry in the late 1920's. A sound, efficient, durable car had been produced by the industry and a vast market demand had materialized. Low-cost mass assembly plants had been constructed; a smoothly working network of dealer outlets had been established throughout the country; special credit institutions had been created to finance installment purchases; and the used-car market was well organized. The automobile industry had grown up; the major *new investment* phase was over for the time being.

What was done next could be broadly described as extensions and refinements. More cars required, first and foremost, better roads; and these were provided. Greater riding comfort in the lower-priced cars was added as automobiles were used increasingly by the masses for pleasure, and higher speeds were offered for the wide new roads of the West.

During the 1930's and 1940's, advances continued to take place in mechanical and chemical engineering which made it technically possible to obtain more powerful fuel, more miles per gallon (if one wanted this, and many who turned to European cars did), and longer and more economical use of tires; and there was the possibility, not yet introduced commercially, of a jet engine.

In a dynamic society, technology does not stand still. From this point of view Usher is certainly correct in stressing the continuity of technological change. The creative urge is widespread and the demand for novelty great. But an industry may choose to stress the novelty of style changes, the recreational use of a radio in a car, the comfort of a heater, better springs, and other improvements not requiring a major new investment in capital equipment. By 1930 the American automobile was established as a satisfactory product in terms of mass demand.

Twenty-three years later one can say that there has been comparatively little innovative change. And it is interesting to speculate on what *might* have happened if Henry Ford had died, say, in 1929 and left in control a son with a strong innovative flair. I think that, if he had been as shrewd as his father, such a son would have been torn between a desire to do something fresh and important with the automobile and a realization that the more prudent and sensible policy was to consolidate past gains. Had the desire for "emergent novelty" been compelling, he might well have turned the company over to his associates and devoted his energies to some other field. As a possible parallel, after Paul Hoffman had succeeded in re-establishing the position of the Studebaker Corp. in the automobile oligopoly, he shifted his interests to the Economic Cooperation Administration and the Ford Foundation. It is perfectly possible to lose interest temporarily in the generalship of an enterprise simply because it is running well on its established momentum.

There is in fact an important difference between the life of an inventor and the life of an innovator. An inventor—like Thomas Edison or Lee De Forest or, in modern America, Edwin Land—granted some access to sources of capital, can spend his life moving from one invention to another in a broad field without a major wrench every time he shifts. Thus Land can work successively on polarized light and sun glasses, headlight glare, three-dimensional movies, and a picture-a-minute camera so long as his creative energies are concerned with the inventive rather than the innovative phases. Such activities can be financed by royalty returns on patents or by small-scale manufacturing so long as *some* of the inventions are translated into action. Inaction, as in the case of Land, who was not able to interest the automobile industry in the headlight glare problem,[8] does not need to be frustrating if the inventor feels that he has solved the basic technical problem. But the innovator must succeed through obtaining action; this is much more time-consuming, given the resistances to change which are built into our institutional environment.

I cannot see, therefore, how we can escape from stressing discontinuities when we are discussing innovations. It is not indulging in a "great-man theory" of history to conclude that innovators like Henry Ford are unusual. If the economic environment is propitious, such men may have an opportunity to participate in the creation of an important new field. But when they have done so successfully, they are not *likely* to move into another entirely new field with equal success. More probably they will exploit and develop what they have created.

When, therefore, an innovative breakthrough takes place, it tends to run its course. In modern American industry, dominant innovators do not usually perpetuate themselves.[9] In the early days of a growing enterprise, it is much more feasible to run a one-man show. The dominant figure can be in on all decisions. But with growth and success, men of lesser imagination are required to carry out the original goals. Frequently, control passes to those men who have devoted their lives to straightening things out. Such people get tired of too much change. Even if there is no such delegation of control, efficient management requires consultation, which is more time-consuming as the business becomes more complex and which inevitably slows up bold decisions. If, as occasionally happens, there is a struggle for power, the loyalties of the organization tend to group around the mediators rather than the disruptive forces. The wise innovator, therefore, frequently finds that after a certain stage of successful achievement he will get more satisfaction from devoting his major creative energies to outside activities. This is perhaps an explanation of many of the extracurricular activities taken on in middle and later life by successful businessmen. As another type of reaction, C. F. Kettering, on retiring from General Motors, became far more active in research than he had been for years.

There are thus several reasons to expect that a major innovation

[8] An example, incidentally, of the lack of research-consciousness in this industry.

[9] Nepotism is frowned upon, and there are rules against it in many large enterprises.

like the automobile will have an explosive expansionary effect that will later taper off.[10] A research conception which was not part of the intellectual scheme of the automobile industry might help to maintain the volume of new investment. If the automobile pioneers had believed in and understood research, they could have provided a more interesting innovative record since 1930. But I do not believe that research would have provided a major change in the investment pattern simply because the automobile was such a success without much real research.[11] More light, however, can be thrown on the possibilities for continuous innovation if we examine the record of an industry that sprang from science and that has placed important emphasis on research from the beginning—namely, the electrical manufacturing industry.

ELECTRICAL MANUFACTURING

The development of central power stations and the invention of the telephone have had as profound an effect on industrial development as has the automobile's rise. Partly because the technological discoveries involved were more recent and more complex than in the case of the internal combustion engine, the electrical manufacturing industry[12] and the telephone industry have maintained a much closer link to science than the automobile industry has. These ties also developed partly in response to the interest of some of the scientists who joined the first two industries. Professor Elihu Thomson founded the Thomson-Houston Electric Manufacturing Co. in Lynn, Massachusetts in the 1880's. This concern became a key element in the General Electric Co. when it was founded in

[10] Concerning Siegel's comments on this point at the conference, I do not wish to imply that there is no future for the automobile industry. A giant corporation has great power to perpetuate itself, especially if it uses creative research as a method of regeneration. But for the reasons that I have stated, I believe that a pulsating force in its investment growth is much more probable than straight-line growth.

[11] To date, the research undertaken by the automobile companies has been aimed at the engineering improvement of existing products rather than the creation of new products. For classification purposes I prefer to call this type of work "advanced engineering development," reserving the term "research" for more fundamental inquiry without such immediate, practical results in mind. There is some evidence that the automobile industry is very slowly reaching a comparable assessment of its research role and that important changes in this respect will occur in the next decade.

[12] For reasons that remain somewhat obscure, the *electric power companies* and the *telegraph companies* did not keep nearly as close to science. An exception today is the active research interest of the Detroit Edison Co. in atomic energy.

1892. Thomson remained as a consultant of the new company. In 1900 General Electric decided to establish a research laboratory at Schenectady devoted to "fundamental scientific inquiry," and Professor Willis R. Whitney was appointed the first director. It has become one of the leading scientific laboratories in the United States, with many distinctions, including that of having a Nobel prize winner—Irving Langmuir—as one of its full-time staff members.[13]

General Electric was responsible for many of the advances that took place in the electric lamp from 1900 to 1940. The patents acquired from these advances, plus outside patents which were purchased, gave the company undisputed control of the electric lamp industry. With decreasing costs through mass production and steady improvement in machine design, General Electric was able to make very comfortable profits on the incandescent lamp throughout this period. In fact, the lamp division was probably the most profitable division of the entire enterprise and carried a considerable proportion of the total research expenditures for the company.

With this background and with the acquisition for its laboratories of such notable figures as Irving Langmuir and W. A. Coolidge, one might have expected General Electric to be ready in the late 1920's with a new form of lighting which would capture the public imagination. Technically this was possible, for the fundamental work on the fluorescent lamp had already been done in Europe by that time. But the propensity to innovate was not there. General Electric was making profits in incandescent lamps; the lamp was satisfactory; the company had patent control; everyone in the industry paid royalties. This scarcely provided the environment out of which one would expect a rapid change.

Possibly, also, one might have expected General Electric or Westinghouse, both of which were supporting fundamental scientific research, to pioneer in atomic energy development. Both companies had a major stake in the manufacturing of power equipment for central stations. Might they not have invited a Niels Bohr or a Fermi to work in their laboratories on atomic power?

But the commercial prospects for atomic energy seemed and were still a long way off in the 1920's and 1930's. The leaders of General Electric, Owen Young and Gerard Swope, who had been responsible for the recent growth of the company and who were in control

[13] The only industrial laboratory in the United States sharing this honor is that of the Telephone Co.—through C. J. Davisson.

in this period, had made their mark and acquired comfortable fortunes. They were, quite properly, more concerned with the future stability of the enterprise than with taking major risks. It is probably too much to expect a highly successful business concern producing satisfactory products to jump way into the future, even though the company is research-minded. The business philosophy of General Electric and Westinghouse was to keep close enough to science to be somewhat ahead of the times.

In the words of Owen Young: "Fifteen years is about the average period of probation, and during that time the inventor, the promoter and the investor, who see a great future for the invention, generally lose their shirts. . . . This is why the wise capitalist keeps out of exploiting new inventions and comes in only when the public is ready for mass demand."[14]

Even with far-sighted management, which I believe General Electric had in the 1920's and 1930's, one has to expect a certain myopia. It is hard to take such a broad view of one's field that you anticipate its being undermined.[15] In my own institution, the Massachusetts Institute of Technology, no major contributions were made during the 1930's to the exploration of nuclear physics (apart from developments in instrumentation).

In the General Electric case a research conception did not lead to any major innovative change in lighting until the fluorescent lamp was introduced at the end of the 1930's. This was about the time when the last of the basic incandescent lamp patents were expiring. Competitively, General Electric had been in a position to take its time about such a development. Each concern in the industry operated under a quota. Patent control was so complete that it was virtually impossible for any *new* concern to enter the industry. The one lighting company which eventually broke away from General Electric and did some independent work on the fluorescent lamp (but not the original work) was Sylvania Electric, whose growth was slow and took place initially under the General Electric umbrella. By merger and by acquisition, Sylvania eventually obtained a 6 per cent quota of the total incandescent lamp business; after that there was nobody else to absorb. It was only

[14] Maclaurin, *Invention and Innovation in the Radio Industry*, as cited, p. 88.

[15] For example, Western Union, in the period when it was the most powerful communications company of its day, turned down the opportunity to purchase the telephone patents of Alexander Graham Bell.

through the assistance of the Department of Justice that Sylvania was able to break out from the quota system in about 1940.

It is, of course, impossible to *prove* that a new development such as fluorescent lighting could in fact have been introduced in the late 1920's instead of the late 1930's. But the basic technology was known, and it is my own belief that, if the entrepreneurs in control of the industry had had their full competitive vigor at the end of the 1920's, there was no reason why they could not have "ordered" a new type of lighting. We have reached such an advanced stage of engineering that, if the basic research has been done, many inventions *can* be made to order.[16] In this sense the process of invention is no longer subject to the caprices of the lone inventor. Research teams can be assembled from professional engineers, and, with some reasonable leadership and adequate budgets, a limited objective such as a change from incandescent lighting to fluorescent lighting is largely a function of management. My conviction is, therefore, that the petering out in the process of creation that was evident in the General Electric and Westinghouse laboratories beginning in the late 1920's was due partly to the fact that, as in the automobile industry, the companies had had a long run of successful years and their established leaders were more immediately concerned with the protection of past gains than with rushing into new developments.

I do not wish to imply that the petering out which I think I have observed is likely to be permanent. There are too many dynamic forces in the lower layers of a great enterprise to make this probable. Nor do I believe that a wavelike movement is *inevitable*. A full discussion of this point would lead us into the difficult realm of "succession of management"—a problem to which comparatively little articulate thought has been given. In specific terms, the question of why the quite exceptional top-management team of Young and Swope did not replace itself would have to be answered.

One other point that should be stressed here is the increasingly high cost of new technical developments in well-established fields. When technology becomes more advanced, it is normally no longer possible to make pioneering inventions with simple technical equipment and inexpensive apparatus. Edison was able to invent and develop to a commercial stage the original incandescent lamp with equipment that, by present standards, would be considered exceed-

[16] The wartime developments of radar and the atomic bomb are cases in point.

ingly crude. But the work of Coolidge and Langmuir in perfecting the lamp through improved filaments and gas-filling required much more elaborate experiments and much costlier and more precise equipment.

Moreover, in order for the fluorescent lamp to compete with an existing product that had already been perfected, it was essential that the new lamp work well. Large sums of money had to be spent on painstaking experiments with fluorescent powders, on the problem of end-blackening, on the elimination of flicker, and on instantaneous starting before the lamp was an assured commercial success. This meant that the propensity to innovate was dependent on the possession of a large research budget. What eventually happened was that Sylvania used the fluorescent lamp as a means of breaking out from under General Electric leadership, although General Electric did the major development work on the fluorescent lamp. And General Electric easily won its suit against Sylvania on fluorescent lamp patents. In fact, with the exception of Westinghouse, none of the licensees in the lamp industry had the resources or the basic technical skill to undertake a pioneering breakthrough of this type *on its own.*

Moreover, to help spread the use of higher-powered incandescent lamps and fluorescent lamps, General Electric and Westinghouse found it necessary to spend very substantial sums of money over the years in institutional advertising of the "better light—better sight" variety.

To summarize, then, from the General Electric experience, research, as one would expect, gave the company an opportunity to maintain a higher level of new investment than would otherwise have occurred. But from the standpoint of the economy as a whole, the most significant new investment opportunity lay in a fundamental change of energy source from steam power stations to atomic power. Since such a development is *not yet ready,* it is easy to see why a business enterprise would not attempt to push too far ahead of commercial prospects. The sums of money required for atomic energy development are so vast and the military applications so direct that government sponsorship is essential. In retrospect, it seems unlikely that the power companies and the electrical manufacturing concerns, even had they wanted to, could have pushed atomic energy development sufficiently to provide a continuous innovative investment stream.

On the more limited basis of providing investment in new types of lighting, there were better prospects for continuity. But the patent position of the dominant concern—General Electric—and the personal goals of the key entrepreneurs in the firm did not induce such a change until the time was fully ripe.

We are thus faced with an economic dilemma. Patents and monopolistic position are essential ingredients in providing financial support and incentives for large-scale resarch on and development of complex new products. A research-minded company has to work exceedingly hard during the rapid growth period of a new art to build up a watertight patent structure. Having done so, it is not consistent with normal economic motivation for it to throw away the advantages of the monopoly by forcing a very rapid rate of obsolescence.

We can see this same problem in another example taken from the electrical revolution—the radio and television industry.

RADIO AND TELEVISION

In the radio industry there were more competitors than in the electric lamp industry. But by 1927 the Radio Corporation of America had obtained undisputed patent control, and thereafter every radio-manufacturer in the United States had to obtain a license from and pay royalties to this concern. RCA conceived of itself as performing the centralized research function for the entire industry. Substantial license fees were charged, and the announced plan was to plow back these royalties into further research.

A somewhat younger industry than lighting, commercial radio in this country nonetheless dates back to the formation of the American Marconi Co. in 1899. This concern, which was controlled from England, was bought and absorbed by the newly formed Radio Corporation of America in 1919. Owen D. Young of General Electric was the principal entrepreneurial figure behind this organizational innovation, with the stock being shared originally by General Electric, Westinghouse, and the Telephone Co., all of which in effect pooled their radio patents in RCA. And since the concerns which dominated radio research were these same three, the key entrepreneurial figures were men who had made their marks by the late 1920's. There has since been a revolt against this domination, involving new men and newly made money. This revolt, however, led by such concerns as Philco, Zenith, and Admiral, has taken over twenty years to develop. During this period, from about 1930 to 1950, these newer concerns were primarily concentrating on methods of breaking down the RCA licensing procedures; their innovative activities were focused on sales and distribution methods or, as in the case of Sylvania, on low-cost manufacturing of tubes rather than on research and invention. The fact remains, however, that the history of the most important invention and innovation in the radio industry in the last twenty years, television, is primarily a history of research by the large established concerns—the Telephone Co., General Electric, Westinghouse, and RCA.

The most significant aspect of television research was the high expenditure for technical development required before *any commercial returns* were received. The Radio Corporation of America spent $10 million for research and development in the precommercial stage. The role of government regulation was very significant here. New channels had to be obtained; and regulatory commissions were gravely concerned over their responsibility to protect people from finding their sets obsolete because of later developments. The budget for television development had to come from the royalty receipts from the licensees, from the profits from broadcasting, and from the direct manufacture of sets and tubes. In such a situation, until an established product has been fully exploited—and this takes a good many years—it may very well not be to the economic interest of a concern with a dominant position to push too aggressively with a new product which renders its current products obsolete. Technologically, commercial television could have been introduced in 1930, but management was not ready then to provide the necessary support.

The paradox of technological change and investment lies in the fact that the basic shift toward service-type industries is requiring increasingly expensive preparatory work with government agencies. Second, research and development are becoming big business in themselves, and require ample budgets. Under these conditions, the concern which has not achieved a monopolistic position through a differentiated product or through patents finds it difficult to pioneer in innovations. Though many of our great modern corporations do "create what they later exploit," I have found no evidence yet of any large concern which consciously attempts to use research and innovation as a means of maintaining an *even flow of new investment.* Nor can I see any reason why new firms can be counted on to emerge at the right historical moment.

3. *The Next Long Cycle*

Though we may be straying into the realm of prophecy, it may help our analysis if we speculate about the long cycle in which we are now living in America. Let us assume for the purposes of discussion that the main upward thrust of the present cycle began about 1940 and was greatly stimulated by the rush of new technical developments emerging from the war. What industries can we expect to carry us during the 1950's and the 1960's? And what part is technology likely to play in such an upward phase?

While we could expect some continuation of technological change and new investment in the industries that carried the last major investment wave—electric power, chemicals, and the automobile—it does not seem probable that these industries will provide new outlets for investment on anything like the scale that they created in the last cycle. In a broad sense, these fields would appear to be somewhat exhausted. Although the most important new development in electric power is atomic energy, a great deal more work will have to be done in reducing costs before atomic energy is likely to displace our existing electric power stations. Servomechanisms, on the other hand, may result in an important new investment in automatic electrical machinery in our factories.

The revolution in chemistry and the rise of the chemical industries contributed to the last upsurge and can be counted on again in the next two decades. We have still not exploited all the possibilities for creating new products which represent chemical substitutes for natural processes.

More promising from the standpoint of capital consumption is the provision of better community services. Our metropolitan areas today are mostly obsolete. I should like, therefore, to discuss the investment opportunities provided by urban redevelopment in the light of modern technology. Since transportation is a key feature in such development and commuting distances are reaching the breaking point, let us also examine the prospects arising from the technology of the aviation industry. The *logical* next step in transportation from the city to the country lies in aviation rather than in the automobile, though we can certainly expect the continuation of a major investment in new construction of roads. But revolutionary change would come with the development of large-scale private flying. So let us consider the investment opportunities provided by the airplane.

THE AVIATION INDUSTRY

Is technology the principal factor inhibiting the growth of private airplane use? From what I have been able to learn from scientists and engineers in this industry, I believe not. The basic scientific work has been completed, making it possible to fly with safety under most weather conditions in either a helicopter or a helioplane requiring a short take-off space. But much work still needs to be done on reducing instrumentation costs, making piloting easier (especially in a helicopter), and providing landing fields before a mass market can develop. Without the possibility of a mass market, assembly line economies are not possible.

What, then, are the bottlenecks? The aviation industry is now controlled by men who have made their fortunes and built up substantial enterprises manufacturing large commercial transport planes and military planes. These markets have very different requirements from that for the private plane. High speed and durability are essential; original cost is comparatively unimportant. In consequence, there has been very little development work by the large, established manufacturers[17] on low-cost private planes. In fact, because of a cost-plus approach and the rapid change of military models, it is questionable whether the background of the main aviation industry provides a suitable environment for such work.

A secondary factor is that since aviation is closely regulated and since there is opposition to every new landing strip, large sums of money need eventually to be spent in building feeder airports, creating parking facilities for private planes at such airports, and getting public acceptance of the private plane in the surburban backyard.

It is my own belief, therefore, that whether or not this type of development comes in the next twenty years is primarily a function of innovative leadership. From the group of small, obscure concerns now producing helicopters or light planes, one or two entrepreneurs may emerge with the vision and energy of a Henry Ford. Such entrepreneurs could take advantage of the vast sums that have been spent on military research in aviation, but their principal difficulty will be in building an organization and overcoming resistance to change. The large capital resources of the well-established company would be a great advantage, but the new risk-taking approach probably requires new ventures.

[17] Such as Douglas, Boeing, Lockheed, and United.

If we accept the probability that new men and new money will be needed for this new type of industry, we must also recognize the fact that the launching of such ventures is more difficult today and the obstacles to be overcome are more persistent than they were forty years ago. One of the prices of SEC regulations, public safety measures, etc., is that entrepreneurial innovation becomes much more difficult. Perhaps it would be more accurate, however, to say that the process becomes different and that different skills are necessary. In complicated fields which are tinged with the public interest, organizational innovation is the most serious bottleneck in holding up the process of translating technological change into significant new products.

METROPOLITAN REDEVELOPMENT AND HOUSING

Similar obstacles beset one of the other major industries which might carry our next long wave—the housing industry.

The automobile, supplemented soon perhaps by the airplane, makes it *technologically possible* now for most Americans to live in a functional house which is well engineered for a servantless society and which provides the beauty and restfulness of the country. The basic research has all been done. The first requisite was to break down the traditional approach to housing and re-examine dwellings in the light of modern technology. Such men as Le Corbusier and Frank Lloyd Wright were among the pioneers. With the development of electric household devices, of lower-cost automatic heating facilities, of new methods of inexpensive glass production, and of new materials for interior wall construction, an inexpensive housing product became technologically possible and the general acceptance of it would represent a very significant improvement in mass living habits.

But the missing link again, I believe, is organizational innovation. Let us examine some of the obstacles that have to be overcome.

Companies specializing in prefabricated houses are not likely to solve the problem. A very small proportion of the cost of housing is in the shell; the economies obtained by mass production of panels not only are negligible but are often outweighed by the diseconomies of transportation and high overhead costs. A house, far more than most products, is very much at the mercy of local influences—local planning commissions, zoning ordinances, and building codes are key factors.

The large, established enterprises in building are component manufacturers such as Johns Manville, Revere Copper & Brass, American Radiator, and United States Gypsum. These concerns are in oligopolistic positions where they make comfortable profits, and because no one of them contributes more than a very small proportion of the total cost of the house, the demand for many of their particular products is inelastic. One cannot count on very much from such companies, therefore, in the way of radical cost-cutting improvements.

The organizational innovation that appears necessary is the emergence of some house-assembling companies of national stature who will in time develop sufficient power to control and direct community development wherever they operate. There have already emerged from the chaos of the individual-house-building industry a few enterprises of regional stature—such as Levitt & Sons. But it is very uncertain whether these essentially local concerns—successful in serving their particular communities—can grow beyond this. Most house-building concerns lack the capital resources or the management skills to serve more than a local area. American industries have characteristically grown through branch plants. But this growth has not normally had to contend with the exceptional strength of local influences in housing. Housing enterprises also have had to weather the high degree of seasonality and cyclicality of the industry, which has meant that many attempts at mass production have led to bankruptcy through high overhead costs and inadequate capital.

It may well be that the housing industry will have to grow very slowly, first through the emergence of a few local innovators with vision and then by merger of the more vigorous elements on a regional and national scale. I believe, however, that to develop the full investment potentialities of the industry, an organizational innovation not now in existence and different from that in most other industries will be required. The men who are to provide the leadership for such an innovation will have to understand the nature of the challenge. If they do so, the necessary technology for significant reduction in costs will be at their command.

4. *Conclusions*

By discussing the process of invention and innovation in particular firms and particular industries, I have tried in this paper to indicate that:

1. Invention and innovation do not go hand in hand, and there is no predictable time lag between them.

2. Basic breakthroughs in the physical sciences leading later to revolutionary changes in technology are discontinuous.

3. Due to the infrequency of the appearance of innovators, the comparative ease of imitation, and the resulting tendency for entrepreneurial activity to come in clusters, innovations are likely to peter out when the key figures associated with them have carried their original ideas to their logical conclusion.

4. The emergence of the large corporation with a research organization suggests that regeneration is more probable in corporations today than it was 100 years ago.

5. The initiation of major innovations usually requires new men and new money—a requirement which is likely to be met by new firms. I believe that the "new men" are much the most troublesome part of this sequence. In completely new fields it is relatively easy to launch a small new firm; and, while new methods are necessary to obtain capital for new ventures, the right man can usually find the money.

6. For the last 100 years at least, technology has had a tendency to outrun innovation, so that at any given point of time the possibility of applying technology to the introduction of new products has greatly outdistanced the actual performance. In fields dominated by large, established corporations the problem of succession of management is to place new men at the top with innovative vigor equal to that of their immediate predecessors.

7. As higher standards of living bring about a shift from primary and secondary manufacturing to tertiary or service-type industries, organizational innovations become increasingly important.

8. Since it is apparent that innovating entrepreneurs are rare and that needed skills are changing in character, much more careful study could profitably be given to the nature of those skills and the proper environment in which to train men in them.

COMMENT

Walter Isard, Massachusetts Institute of Technology

In discussing Usher's paper I shall dwell upon its implications (and those of his works in general) for the study of economic growth. For I believe that he points up a basic set of considerations which thus far has not received adequate attention.

Usher views the historical record as a basic interaction of technology and resources. The advance of technology, and more specifically its introduction into our society in the form of innovation, have proceeded not randomly but continuously, at times at accelerating rates, at times at decelerating rates, and even at times at rates approaching zero which have presented plateau periods.

At any given point of time an innovation occurs at one place, or at least at a relatively few places, in the world. Its spatial diffusion over wide areas of the world proceeds also at accelerating, decelerating, and even zero rates. Any advance in technology constantly revalues the resources of any particular area, so technological progress over time constantly changes both the absolute and the relative *productivity potential* of each area, since each has a unique resource endowment.

However, technological progress is a social process. It is not divorced from society; in fact, it is much influenced by the values of any given society. The direction and rate of technological progress in any given area and the rate at which innovation successful elsewhere is accepted are significantly affected by the cultural traits and patterns of the people of that area. Among those cultural traits and patterns, the economic institutions, institutions regarding property ownership, monetary and financial institutions, and practices of business organizations are of major significance in their effect on technological progress and the acceptance of progress. Hence, in studying economic growth and capital formation, we confront a complex interaction of social, political, economic, and geographical factors, as Kuznets has so neatly argued.

But no matter how much we emphasize entrepreneurial attitudes, community relations, financial institutions, saving habits, and the like, there is still a basic play of technology upon resources—resources which differ from area to area and which give these areas different productivity potentials at any given point of time.

Let us now leave this world of generalities and become more concrete. Let us consider the papers by Kuznets and Goldsmith. A wealth of interesting, though tenuous, statistical material was presented. A number of interesting hypotheses emerged. But it seems to me that before one can reach any meaningful conclusions about economic growth from these materials one must build around them a perspective in both time and space. One must put these data against a background which for key points of time in the past, given the state of technology, yields the different productivity potentials existing in the various areas of the world. One cannot escape the fact that the existence of different productivity potentials greatly influences the rate at which the areas can accumulate capital, or their ratios of capital formation to national output, and so forth. I wish we had before us a table on the resource endowment of different parts of the world—a table such as Usher has developed or such as that in A. J. Brown's pamphlet on *Industrialization and Trade*.[1] It would show very striking inequalities in the current resource positions of the various areas. No one, I am sure, would deny that these major differentials, given our existing technology, greatly influence the rates at which the various nations can accumulate and invest capital today. And so it has been at every point of time in the past. My point is that in order to utilize efficiently the data which Kuznets and Goldsmith have developed one must consider the historical impact of changing technology upon different resource potentials, along the lines that Usher suggests in his paper and in some of his other writings.

Let me proceed to another concrete illustration. The discussion earlier in this conference centered around the entrepreneur and the conditions which influence entrepreneurial action. There was much talk about comparing social conditions and organizations of various kinds and their associated national rates of growth—comparing those in France with those in Germany, or with those in England or Japan. I heartily endorse comparative analysis—but only of the right kind. Once in a while one heard at the conference the word "resources," in the general context of "mineral resources." But there did not seem to be any recognition of what I would consider a rather elementary fact, namely: *A given difference in social conditions* (assuming that we can isolate and agree upon that difference) *will yield one set of discrepancies in growth rates among nations when resource or productivity potentials are the same, and a significantly different set of discrepancies when resource or productivity potentials are significantly different.*

Let me be more specific by referring to Hoselitz's paper. He states: "Compared with Britain, France exhibits a pattern of retarded economic growth and industrialization. Yet in the history of the two countries there was a time when there were few apparent differences in the over-all productivity of the various factors, and

[1] London, Royal Institute of International Affairs, 1943.

when technological procedures and general economic organization appear to have been on a fairly even level" (page 294). After considering differences in raw materials endowment and geographical position, he concludes that to explain the differences in rates of growth between Britain and France, "the decisive factors have to be sought rather in their respective social environments" (page 295). I may be misinterpreting Hoselitz, but I feel that at least this is the viewpoint of many who have joined in the discussion at the conference.

In attempting to prove that the French resource position for the basic iron and steel industry was as good as the British, Hoselitz presents some materials on ores and imports of iron into both Britain and France. I do not wish to quibble about the data for they are not the important ones. With respect to the iron and steel industry during the eighteenth and the first half of the nineteenth century, *coal resources, not ore resources,* were the most strategic. This is obvious when one considers that from 7 to 10 tons of coal and only 2 to 3 tons of ore were required for 1 ton of malleable iron or steel. The importance of coal emerges conclusively from the actual figures on malleable iron and steel production, which show that modern iron and steel furnaces have been oriented to coal sites rather than ore sites.

To repeat, coal was the most strategic factor in iron and steel location. And with respect to coal, given the techniques of the eighteenth and nineteenth centuries, the British position was far superior to the French. One cannot deny that this was an important factor in the differences in their rates of growth.

I do not want to be misunderstood and accused of being a geographical determinist. I do not wish to minimize the entrepreneurial and general cultural factors; they are very important. If French entrepreneurship had been more vigorous, techniques of blending coal and of treating inferior coals to make them more useful could have been worked out so as to improve France's inferior coal position. Nonetheless, to some extent at least, the difference would have persisted.

To conclude, what I am urging is that we should not underestimate study of the impact of changing technology upon resource patterns, much along the lines that Usher has pioneered. If the economic historian or economic development theorist is to make headway in attacking the entrepreneurial or the capital formation problem, he must develop a framework which recognizes that the historical data for diverse regions reflect the compounding and interaction of numerous social, cultural, and institutional differences as well as differences in resources and productivity potentials.

IRVING H. SIEGEL, The Twentieth Century Fund

1. The Possibility of a Framework. In his opening paragraph Maclaurin makes a passing reference to the fact that "The most serious difficulty" in the study of factors influencing economic growth "is to provide a framework in which the various contributions can be additive." I want to comment on this important subject first.

Since the study of economic growth is in a significant sense a branch of history, a search for a unique framework (or for alternative frameworks really congruent with each other) seems destined to fail. The history of history further suggests that a word like "progressive" is preferable to "additive." Earlier contributions sufficiently prove their worth when they stimulate the formulation or facilitate the testing of new hypotheses, when they encourage or aid the reinterpretation of given data from new vantage points.

Historians have never agreed upon a unique framework, and students of growth likewise approach their own many-faceted subject with a proper variety of preconceptions and interests. Investigators of growth are bound to have different preferences concerning (1) the unit of observation or the level of inquiry, (2) the system of categories for which data should be accumulated or hypotheses formulated, and (3) the amount of data which ought to be collected prior to the design and testing of hypotheses.

As for the first point, growth obviously has its "micro" and "macro" levels. Thus a researcher may wish to concentrate on the origin and vicissitudes of a *principle, process,* or *product*; or on the life and work of a key *individual*; or on the evolution of a *firm* or *industry* as a quasi-organism; or on the changing role of *government*; or on the economic development of one or more *countries.*

As for the second point, opinions will naturally differ on the categories which are most convenient, relevant, or fruitful for the analysis of growth. Thus the selected categories may emphasize the critical role of certain human bents or modes of possible behavior—like the so-called "propensities" of Rostow[1] and Maclaurin.[2] More

[1] W. W. Rostow, *The Process of Economic Growth,* Norton, 1952.

[2] W. Rupert Maclaurin, "The Sequence from Invention to Innovation and Its Relation to Economic Growth," *Quarterly Journal of Economics,* February 1953, pp. 97-111.

often, the lists of growth determinants also explicitly include significant nonhuman categories. Abramovitz, for example, mentions five broad categories—the supplies of the factors, the attributes of the population, economic organization, legal and political institutions, and provisions for acquiring and using knowledge.[3] Many other students, like J. M. Clark, Clough, and Moulton, offer somewhat similar lists; and Spengler presents a much more detailed one.[4] Still another approach is exemplified by the mathematical-model-builders, who are satisfied with a small number of quantifiable aggregative variables for studying the behavior of the whole economy or of a major sector. A much more popular quantitative approach emphasizes trends and relationships among time series. This one is typified by the work of most government and private research organizations and of such academic students as Colin Clark.

As for the third point, the inseparability of fact and theory should be obvious, whatever the tactical emphasis at the outset of any investigation. Nevertheless, debates on this matter still erupt. The recent controversy between representatives of the Cowles Commission and the National Bureau of Economic Research on the roles of empiricism and hypothesis covered essentially the same territory as an exchange almost a generation earlier between Lowe and Mitchell.[5]

While no pseudo-Kepler is likely to arise and persuade us to adopt a unique framework, we must nevertheless recognize that modern conditions favor the revival of "laws of history," of agreeable evolutionary or dialectical "stage" theories of development, of streamlined versions of the "historicism" against which the Poppers and Hayeks still declaim. In a tense world well wired for sound, in which deliberate growth is the order of the day, more attention is likely to be paid to the originator or propagator of a bold, grand, oversimple, mathematically grounded hypothesis than to the scholar who is content to "chronicle small beer."

Maclaurin's paper, like his well-known earlier work, deals essentially with "micro" phenomena, with the role of key individuals or pivotal firms in the growth of particular industries. From studies

[3] Moses Abramovitz, "Economics of Growth," in *A Survey of Contemporary Economics*, Bernard F. Haley, editor, Irwin, 1952, pp. 132-178.

[4] Joseph J. Spengler, in *Problems in the Study of Economic Growth*, National Bureau of Economic Research, 1949.

[5] *Business Cycles: The Problem and Its Setting*, National Bureau of Economic Research, 1927, pp. 59-60.

of such cases he seeks to distill ideas concerning the determinants and the character of growth in general. His categories are non-quantitative. Elsewhere I have had occasion to endorse his literary case-study approach as a necessary element of an eclectic research program.[6]

2. Discreteness of Innovation. Maclaurin prefers to emphasize the discrete nature of innovation on the "micro" and "macro" levels. He observes a tendency for the innovating entrepreneur (unlike the inventor) and his vehicle, the firm, to pursue the exploitation of only one basic technological idea. He is also impressed with the appearance of innovating entrepreneurs and firms in bunches, in many industries at one time, as though marshalled by the "wave-like force" of a Kondratieff cycle.

While change may be viewed on the "micro" level in terms of unitary ideas, it is important not to overlook the familiar fact of diversification, of coexistence within a firm of many such ideas in different phases of evolution. The innovating *entrepreneur* may come, exploit his great idea, and go; but the innovating *entrepreneurship* of a firm (especially of a corporation) may still survive, finding new champions and new avenues of expression. Numerous firms may be named—especially in the chemicals industry, unfortunately not discussed by Maclaurin, but even in the industries he does consider—which are continually diversifying their processes and products, growing in new technological directions from within, through merger, or through cooperative undertaking with other companies. The overlapping of discrete pulses of innovation could form a fairly continuous whole, even as short fibers make a long thread.

I do not share Maclaurin's belief in the fruitfulness of the Schumpeterian thesis linking innovation to the long cycle of business activity. In so saying, I do not mean to deny various important points Maclaurin makes—for example, that innovation does not necessarily follow invention, that skillful innovating entrepreneurship is rare, that imitation is easier than innovation, that scientific breakthroughs occur only occasionally, that successful individuals and firms could lose their zest for novelty in the course of exploiting one idea. I mean rather that an adequate "macro" theory of innovation must explain more than the clustering of new investment opportunities, inasmuch as new unitary ideas actually are being introduced and developed continually. The long cycle, moreover, is obscure. It

[6] I. H. Siegel, "Technological Change and Long-Range Forecasting," *Journal of Business*, July 1953, pp. 155-156.

requires more concrete definition than as a "wavelike force" if it is to explain anything. Besides, such a cycle might better be regarded as only a manifestation, a consequence rather than a cause, of the phenomenon of clustering.

To explain clustering, we should look for significant historical conjunctures, for transitory circumstances of potent, pervasive influence. For example, war and preparation for war, which have no explicit part in Maclaurin's scheme (except, perhaps, as retardants of the anticipated shift in economic activity toward the tertiary industries), provide occasions and conditions for broad innovational breakthroughs. Might not the technological history of our country be convincingly rewritten in terms of the "waves" of investment in novelty "generated" by Korea–World War II, World War I, the Spanish-American War, the Civil War, etc? The result would of course be a caricature, but a likeness nevertheless. In short, Kondratieff could be dispatched with Occam's razor.

3. *Three Cases.* Maclaurin's brief sketches of the automobile, electrical manufacturing, and radio and television industries are instructive moral tales. These industries presumably took at the flood a Kondratieff wave that led on to fortune. The automobile industry achieved success without benefit of research-minded leaders or of sustained innovation in the large sense. The other industries have a strong research tradition, but innovation there has been slowed by past profitable investment, monopoly power of the dominant firms, and cost and patent restraints on would-be challengers.

Diversification is conspicuously neglected in Maclaurin's treatment of the three industries. The electrical manufacturing industry is discussed in terms of lamps—one unitary idea—only. Nothing is said of the numerous other product lines of Westinghouse or General Electric; or of their wide range of research activities.[7] The discussion of the automobile industry might have mentioned the ventures of Ford into tractors and, briefly, into aircraft; or General Motors' tie-up with Du Pont, its production of diesel-electric locomotives, its quasi-public status as a munitions contractor.

Maclaurin's sketches suggest gaps in the theory of economic decision-making which need consciously to be filled. First, the behavior of the innovating entrepreneur should be brought within the same formal calculus that includes the entrepreneur who ac-

[7] C. G. Suits, "Seventy-five Years of Research in General Electric," *Science*, October 23, 1953, pp. 451-456.

cepts the existing boundaries of economic space. Second, innovation and all other alternatives open to the entrepreneur (including research, rounding out of product lines, market expansion through advertising, and organizational innovation to save taxes) should be brought under the sway of a common principle like "marginalism" or game theory. As usual, such a treatment of decision-making would be instructive even though it would mean an idealization of actual behavior.

Finally, I wish Maclaurin had more explicitly related his conclusions of the three case studies to his anticipations of the "next long cycle." The "paradox of technological change and investment" to which he refers has often been interpreted as an omen of stagnation or as an argument for strong antitrust or other measures to foster competition. Yet in Maclaurin's treatment this paradox does not seem to pose special obstacles to the future growth of existing industries or to the expansion of a company into new fields. Presumably, the flow of nongovernment investment funds will somehow remain adequate for a vigorous, growing economy. The only real worry, it seems, is the availability of the entrepreneurial talent to, say, solve the problems of organizational innovation besetting tertiary industries like private aviation and prefabricated housing. But there are some fundamental questions here which should not be obscured by the confident (and largely plausible) proposition that "the right man can usually find the money."

4. Growing Points of the Economy. It would be idle to match prophecies concerning the "next long cycle" in view of the hazards and the melancholy history of technological forecasting.[8] I wish instead to make some remarks on the methodology of inquiries into technological prospects.[9]

The Twentieth Century Fund study of such prospects, which has been in progress for more than two years, suggests that the growing points in the economy are numberless and almost everywhere (even in existing monopolistic firms). The sites of new growth are to be found in the primary and secondary as well as in the tertiary industries. The directions of growth are shaped by the research and development activities pursued competitively or with government funds throughout the *private production sector*; by the demands of *government*, especially for security purposes; and by the

[8] See my article in the *Journal of Business*, cited above.

[9] See also I. H. Siegel, "Conditions of Technological Progress," *American Economic Review*, May 1954, pp. 161-177.

demands of the *household sector* as it seeks a higher standard of material welfare and an upgrading of the quality of "leisure." The pervasive circumstance of cold war, with its "distorted" incentives and its emphasis on the technical training of manpower, spurs the discovery and development of new principles, processes, and products which today are directed toward military ends but tomorrow will be convertible to civilian needs. (Maclaurin's private helicopters—or, more probably, "helibuses"—will be reckoned among the progeny of the Korean affair, even as peacetime atomic energy should be counted with the technological offspring of World War II. In these instances, as in so many others, government is at least the midwife if not the father.)

To investigate systematically the technological prospects of the economy, it would seem desirable to give explicit recognition to research and development in the primary and secondary as well as the tertiary industries. We may emphasize the limitations of Colin Clark's Procrustean triple classification by designating such industry-creating activity as itself a *quaternary* industry. Second, explicit attention should be given to government entrepreneurship—to leadership in organizational and institutional innovation, in the conception of and demand for new munitions prototypes, in the training of the military and civilian personnel who will eventually facilitate the peacetime use of military ideas, in setting up new industries (like atomic energy), in effecting substantial resource improvements, etc. Again, for purposes of dramatization, we may call such activities *quinary* or fifth-order. Finally, note should be taken of the increasing variety and volume of appliances, gadgets, amusements, etc., demanded for leisure-time activities. The totality of consumers may be imagined to form a *sixth-order* industry, especially insofar as they demand and use goods and services beyond the level of subsistence. (A *seventh-order* category, based on specialized foreign demand—which could become significant in the next few decades—may also be defined.)

In short, a triple classification appears too gross for the study of long-term growth. The tertiary category, especially, is too broad and heterogeneous. To assert the shift of activity in the direction of this category is not very illuminating. Besides, this sort of proposition tends, like the nonstatistical "stage" theories, to confuse what Clapham designated as logical succession and historical succession. While Maclaurin stresses organizational innovation in the "next long cycle," the importance of such activity throughout our history should not be overlooked. For example, the Constitution, the National Banking Act, the Morrill Act, and the Federal Reserve Act were triumphs of organizational innovation within the tertiary category (government) even while the primary or secondary industries were in the ascendant. The development of the commercial corporation and the growth of consumer credit (to which Maclaurin alludes in his discussion of the automobile industry) are other early organizational landmarks.

PART VI

GENERAL THEORETICAL APPROACHES

STRUCTURAL ANALYSIS OF REAL CAPITAL FORMATION

ADOLPH LOWE

GRADUATE FACULTY, NEW SCHOOL FOR SOCIAL RESEARCH

Introduction

1. The following observations are intended to supplement in a limited way the investigations, which are the center of discussion at this conference. The observations are limited in three respects. They concentrate on certain issues of real capital formation and completely disregard those of "finance" and "business organization," which are the major theme of most of the other papers. Furthermore, they are concerned with purely analytical problems of "model-building" and have no direct relationship to statistical and descriptive data. Finally, this paper deals with only one aspect of the theory of capital formation, which I call "structural." Since this term has acquired rather diverse meanings in recent writings, I had better explain what it is to signify in the context of this paper.

2. The course, persistence, or change of economic processes can be studied under two different aspects. On the one hand, there exist certain objective-quantitative relations among the components of the system—say, between effective demand and aggregate employment or between the depreciation of existing equipment and the output of capital goods. On the other hand, there are the motivations and behavior patterns of householders, firms, and productive factors, which shape the prevailing objective relations and are shaped by them. No economic analysis is complete that does not take into account the events occurring in both fields and, in particular, their interaction. But if this requirement of "total analysis" is in principle admitted, no harm arises from provisionally studying the phenomena in each field separately.

Much of the distinction between these two fields of inquiry is customarily expressed by the contrast between macroeconomics and microeconomics. But the particular point of difference—namely, between the "impersonal order" and the "personal forces"—which is

I wish to express my gratitude to Julius Wyler for a number of critical suggestions, pertaining in particular to Part 2. Moreover, his own work in the field of structural analysis, still unpublished, has provided a valuable check for some of the propositions established below.

stressed here, has little to do with the degree of aggregation, by which the microeconomic study of firm and industry is traditionally separated from the macroeconomic study of the system as a whole. It is for this reason that I prefer the terms "structural" and "functional." They are neutral to the level of aggregation, and permit the input-output relations among different industries to be considered a "structural" order, just as Leontief considers them, while the motive-behavior complex of the Soviet planning authorities appears as a "functional" problem, even though the ensuing decisions concern the system at large.

3. Among the structural problems thus defined, those which relate to the money flow (income-expenditure-saving, etc.) can be distinguished from those which relate to the physical flow of goods and services (consumer goods–capital goods; natural resources–intermediate goods–finished goods) occurring in and between different "sectors" of the economy. Whereas the former structural relations can be fully described in value terms, the latter have, in addition to the value dimension, a physical-technical dimension.

For both types of structural relations another distinction is important. Interest may be directed to the actual relations between effective demand and the level of aggregate employment, or between the output of capital goods and the level of investment, as these magnitudes appear in an empirical system in historical time. Or attention can be focused on a hypothetical order of either the money flow or the physical flow, which is required to attain a postulated state of the system, such as a certain level of employment or a particular order of distribution, or simply stationary or dynamic equilibrium. According to the viewpoint taken, structural analysis results then either in a number of empirical-statistical relations supplementing the information contained in national income accounts, or in a set of "consistency conditions."

This paper deals almost exclusively with the *physical-technical structure* of industrial systems, insofar as it affects the process of capital formation. And it interprets structural analysis in the "normative" sense, as being concerned with physical-technical *consistency conditions.* These conditions are related, on the one hand, to the sectorial order of stationary and dynamic equilibrium and, on the other hand, to the sectorial adjustment paths required for an industrial system to accomplish, under the impact of economic growth, the formation of real capital in the most "economical" manner. It hardly needs stressing that structural problems of this nature arise under any form of economic organization, individualist or collectivist. It is mainly for reasons of space that the following observations confine themselves to capital formation in a free market system. Moreover, the difference in economic organization affects the results of functional rather than of structural analysis.

4. This line of investigation has been chosen for two reasons. First, the problems encountered in its pursuit touch upon important practical issues pertaining to economic growth in both advanced and backward countries. The specific contribution that "normative" structural analysis can make to the clarification of such practical issues will be discussed at the end of this paper. Second, in contradistinction to its money flows, the physical-technical structure of an industrial economy is still largely unexplored. This is especially true of the manner in which more or less fixed coefficients of production affect the adjustment processes in such a system.

The assumption of fixed technical coefficients is basic for the subsequent exposition. Its practical importance lies in the fact that it reflects the degree of specificity of inputs and outputs. It thus describes the limits set in an industrial system to short-run aggregate expansion as well as to short-run sectorial adjustment. While the former issue is especially relevant in the early stages of industrialization, the latter bears upon the stability of fully industrialized systems. A few cursory remarks must suffice to support this view.

Originally a product of the Industrial Revolution, with its emphasis upon large-scale specialized equipment and differentiated skills, specificity of real capital and labor has varied considerably during the historical stages of industrialization. During the nineteenth century the prevailing tendency was undoubtedly in the direction of increasing specificity. This has somewhat changed during the last generation, and we may well assume that, under purely technical aspects, standardization of equipment parts, further automation, and novel methods of labor training will in the future promote greater flexibility of the industrial structure. But a new trend in economic policy seems to counteract this technological tendency. Paradoxically, during the nineteenth century the instability of a rigid structure provided its own cure, by periodically creating large pools of idle resources that facilitated adjustment and growth. An effective full employment policy is now likely to make for new rigidities. Its very success in stabilizing the structure of money flows may well aggravate the adjustment problems that the physical-technical structure poses. Thus, with all due regard to the dangers arising from insufficient demand, which are now generally admitted, inelasticity of supply owing to technical rigidities stands as another threat to the stability of advanced economic systems. At the same time, in the different "climate" in which economic development is pursued today, the physical-technical bottlenecks that hamper rapid expansion in backward regions will be felt much more strongly than under the earlier conditions of slow initial growth.

The emphasis placed here upon fixed coefficients of production and the ensuing technical rigidity of the system may not, at first sight, seem appropriate to the main topic of this paper. In the Marshallian tradition, changes in real capital are regarded as a problem for long-period or even secular-period analysis, referring to a time span over which the technical coefficients must be treated as perfectly variable. If this is admitted, are we not going to miss our very problem if we argue on the basis of fixed technical coefficients? Brief reflection will show that this apparent concentration on short-run problems, far from conflicting with the study of long-run economic growth, is an indispensable condition for understanding the latter.

Long-run analysis of economic growth describes a sequence of states of the system, which differ with respect to the quantity and/or quality of real capital. But it must be kept in mind that this sequence, except in the limiting and quite unrealistic case of steady exponential growth, is essentially discontinuous. In analogy with comparative statics it depicts successive levels of capital "formed" without regard to the intervening processes by which capital is "being formed." Now it is precisely these intermediary processes that are in the foreground of this investigation. Their systematic place in the larger context of growth analysis can easily be clarified.

First of all, these adjustment processes, through which capital formation occurs, are indeed of a short-period nature in the strict Marshallian meaning of the term. Through them, additional and possibly qualitatively different real capital is created; but this is done with the help of the initially given quantity and quality of real capital. In other words, given full utilization of the available equipment as a typical modern condition in advanced as well as underdeveloped regions in accord with what was stated above, the prevailing technical coefficients can be varied only by a process of production which is conditioned by the existing coefficients.

Second, since the technical structure of the given stock of real capital is unalterable in the short period, the degree of its specificity, and of the prevailing factor specificity generally, has a decisive influence upon the path of the adjustment process as well as upon its duration. Finally, while themselves short-run phenomena, these processes of capital formation are the links between successive stages of growth and thus transform the sequence of discontinuous states into a continuous long-run process.

5. From these considerations one cannot help concluding that the technical structure is a fundamental determinant of the behavior, and especially of the mode of change, of any economic system. Therefore, it is rather surprising that, until quite recently, the whole issue received little attention in academic economics. It is to Leontief's lasting credit that he not only devised a theoretical model for the analysis of these structural relations, but also initiated a comprehensive empirical-statistical test for his matrix, which has greatly deepened our insight into the operation of the productive mechanism. Leontief traces his own work back to Walras's model of general equilibrium. As far as the multiplicity of variables is concerned, Walras's parentage is undeniable. But to the extent to which the input-output matrix concentrates upon the interrelationship of "industries"—that is, aggregates larger than individual firms but smaller than the customary components of macroeconomics—the prototype was established by Marx in his laborious attempts to describe the processes of "simple" and "expanded" reproduction by a quantitative schema. Marx's schema is much more highly aggregated than Leontief's matrix; it distinguishes only between one group producing consumer goods and another producing means of production. But as in modern input-output analysis, Marx's interest was focused upon physical-technical interrelations in and between these two groups rather than upon the value structure of the total process, which was Walras's ultimate concern.

My further observations will be based upon a modified version of the Marxian schema. In view of the much more extensive disaggregation of the input-output model this decision might, at first sight, be likened to the use of a shovel when a bulldozer is available. And this all the more so since the Leontief model is built upon the same technological assumption of constant input coefficients that has been postulated above. If, nevertheless, the simpler model has been employed, this has been done for two reasons. The first is purely pragmatic. For the practical purpose of planning, one can hardly go too far in disaggregating an interindustry model. But this advantage of Leontief's model in all empirical concerns turns into an obstacle when it is applied to the solution of theoretical problems of a general dynamic nature. It proves just too difficult to trace analytically the path of such a large number of variables, especially if they are exposed to several stimuli simultaneously.

The second reason is substantive and more basic. All subdivisions of the productive structure are not equally important for the study of particular dynamic processes. One can, in principle, conceive of different patterns of disaggregation, each one appropriate to a specific problem. Now, with certain modifications to be explained presently, Marx's schema seems to be suited especially well to the study of real capital formation. There is an a priori presumption that the theoretical problems associated with the building up and wearing down of the capital stock, with the relation between capital stock and output flow, with the processes of "widening" and "deepening," and with the effects of innovations upon capital formation are basically the same in every industry. But their solution is bound to differ according to whether we study "capital-producing" or "capital-using" processes, a distinction which is central for the Marxian schema. I speak of an "attempt," because in its original form the schema is defective in at least three respects.

The first defect refers to the relation between capital stock and output flow. In spite of his continuous preoccupation with "capital," the equations that Marx presents in his structural analysis are meaningful only if understood as describing flows. Appropriate stock variables must be added to make the schema an analytical tool for the study of capital formation.

Another defect is that Marx's distinction between two industrial groups focuses upon fixed capital goods only. If the schema is to apply also to working capital goods as goods in process, each of the groups must be disaggregated into "vertical" stages, depicting the process by which natural resources are technically transformed into finished consumer or equipment goods.

Finally, certain essential "circular" processes can be clearly described only if the equipment goods group is further disaggregated into one subgroup which produces the equipment for the consumer goods group, and another subgroup which produces the equipment for both subgroups of the equipment goods group.

This is, in its most general features, the model I shall use as a tool for the study of real capital formation under the impact of growth.[1] I shall begin with a brief analysis of the structural conditions that determine stationary equilibrium. Then follows an exposition of certain dynamic relations: first, as they arise under the impact of once-over changes; second, as they take shape under continuous change. In the latter category the structural conditions of a constant rate of change, viz. dynamic equilibrium, are distinguished from those of varying rates of change with more complicated adjustment paths, as they emanate, for example, from non-neutral technical changes. During the exposition itself little will be said about the practical relevance for advanced and backward countries of the problems discussed. A brief conclusion will suggest possible applications of this analytical technique.

1. *Structural Conditions of Stationary Equilibrium*

GROUP MODEL AND STAGE MODEL

6. We start out from an elementary set of relations describing the flow of production over the period t:

$$(1) \qquad \begin{aligned} (F_a \cdot d_a \equiv f_{at}) \times n_{at} \times r_{at} &\longrightarrow a_t \\ (F_b \cdot d_b \equiv f_{bt}) \times n_{bt} \times r_{bt} &\longrightarrow b_t. \\ (F_z \cdot d_z \equiv f_{zt}) \times n_{zt} \times r_{zt} &\longrightarrow z_t \end{aligned}$$

At this stage of the argument we deal only with physical magnitudes. Therefore, the relationship between inputs and outputs is expressed as no more than a causal nexus, symbolized by arrows. Similarly, the multiplication signs stand for the technical combination of the input factors in fixed proportions.

To the right of the arrows, a signifies the output of a units of equipment goods which are intended to make equipment goods, henceforth called "primary equipment," whereas b signifies the output of b units of equipment goods intended to make consumer

[1] The model has been described in greater detail in my paper "A Structural Model of Production," *Social Research*, June 1952, pp. 135-176. There reference is also made to the earlier literature on the subject, including a critical comparison between the Marxian concept and the so-called Austrian concept of a "linear" structure of production that underlies much of modern theoretical reasoning in economic dynamics. In view of the subsequent application of the model to dynamic problems, Hans Neisser's *Some International Aspects of the Business Cycle* (University of Pennsylvania Press, 1936), Appendix to Chapter I, deserves special mention.

goods, henceforth called "secondary equipment"; z denotes the aggregate output of z units of consumer goods.[2]

To the left of the arrows are the corresponding inputs for each of the three groups, the relevant group being specified by a subscript. These inputs are subdivided into the basic factors of production: fixed capital goods, f; labor, n; and natural resources, r. For the input of fixed capital goods two expressions are given: one, denoted by f, is a direct expression of the input flow entering the corresponding output flow; the other expresses the same magnitude in terms of the existing stock of fixed capital goods, F, multiplied by the prevailing rate of depreciation, d. In principle, similar stock magnitudes could be added to the flow expressions for the other two factors, and they are quite useful for the study of certain dynamic problems. In a study of the dynamics of capital formation they can be disregarded. (Whenever stocks appear in our models and equations, they are symbolized by capital letters, whereas flows are described in lower-case letters.)

7. In the above form the group relations are the result of a far-reaching aggregation. Each group describes the output of a given period in terms of *finished* goods, ready for use either as means of consumption in the households or as means of production in the firms. These outputs of finished goods are the technical result of the productive process, which transforms natural resources with the help of labor and equipment goods. This process of transformation can, and for the solution of certain problems must, be disaggregated into a number of "vertical stages." A second set of relations describes such a stage model for the group of consumer goods:

$$
\begin{array}{lll}
(2) & (F_{z_1} \cdot d_{z_1} \equiv f_{z_1t}) \times n_{z_1t} \times r_{z_1t} & \longrightarrow w_{z_1t} \\
& (F_{z_2} \cdot d_{z_2} \equiv f_{z_2t}) \times n_{z_2t} \times r_{z_2t} \times w_{z_1t} & \longrightarrow w_{z_2t} \\
& (F_{z_3} \cdot d_{z_3} \equiv f_{z_3t}) \times n_{z_3t} \times r_{z_3t} \times w_{z_2t} & \longrightarrow w_{z_3t} \\
& (F_{z_4} \cdot d_{z_4} \equiv f_{z_4t}) \times n_{z_4t} \times r_{z_4t} \times w_{z_3t} & \longrightarrow z_t \\
\hline
& (F_z \cdot d_z \equiv f_{zt}) \times n_{zt} \times r_{zt} & \longrightarrow z_t
\end{array}
$$

[2] In order to simplify the subsequent exposition the physical distinction among the outputs of the three groups is treated as absolute. This is, of course, not so in reality. Certain products, and the industries producing them, belong in more than one group (e.g. coal, steel, even certain machine tools), though in every concrete instance one can always determine where a specific commodity should be placed. For a more refined exposition see my paper, *op. cit.*, pp. 144-146.

This model is based on the assumption, to be examined more closely, that the technical process of production by which the natural resource r_{z_1} is transformed into the finished consumer good z can be subdivided into four stages. The outputs w (working capital goods) of each stage appear as inputs in the subsequent stage, down to the "stage of completion," whose output is the finished good. The total for the inputs of each factor in all stages must be equal to the consolidated expression that appears in model 1 and is restated at the bottom of model 2.

8. What precise meaning can be attached to the notion of a *technical* sequence of stages of production? There is no doubt that, from the point of view of business organization, a number of successive interfirm exchanges can be distinguished where the buying firm uses its purchases for further manufacturing. Though useful as an indicator of business differentiation and also important for the solution of the "transaction problems" in the theory of money, from the technical point of view separate stages of production are arbitrary. Only for the first stage, where the "gifts of nature" are "seized," and for the last stage, when the finished product is handed over to the prospective user (or speculator), can a definite meaning be attached to such a distinction.

The fact that from a technical point of view the production flow is indivisible has always been recognized in attempts to find a quantitative expression for the stock and the flow of working capital goods. The total of all "stage outputs," which can be derived from any given order of business differentiation, cannot be used for this purpose, since it contains unavoidable double counting. Therefore, proper measures for working capital can be established only by referring to factor inputs.[3] But if we are interested in the manner

[3] Any such measure presupposes a genuine summation of all inputs, which itself is conditional upon the comparability of physically different inputs in a homogeneous value dimension. A simple measure can be devised if we assume that the inputs of fixed capital goods, labor, and natural resources are evenly distributed over all stages as given by the state of business differentiation. Denoting aggregate input of all factors over a stated period by i, the *flow* of working capital goods which move during that period in the vertical direction toward completion equals $i/2$, since under the conditions assumed half the factor input must serve the replacement of the working capital used in each stage. If the inputs are unevenly distributed over the stages, the fraction $i/2$ changes to i/q, where $0 < q < 1$. The *stock* of working capital goods, on the other hand, which must be maintained in the interest of continuous production is then im/qp, where p records the period of observation over which we measure i, and m expresses the "period of maturation," that is, the time it takes with given technology to transform a unit of natural resources into a finished good.

in which a *given* order of business differentiation is affected by vertical shifts of factors—because of, for example, alterations in physical returns or nonneutral technical changes—a stage model of the kind described in model 2 is a useful analytical tool. The particular problems of capital formation discussed below refer to fixed capital only, so that the stage model can be disregarded in favor of the consolidated group as formulated in model 1 (see, however, section 19 below).

9. This conclusion is likely to meet with strong objections from those who conceive of the whole productive process in "linear" fashion. A schema like that described in model 2 underlies the so-called Austrian concept of the structure of production. Originally devised by Eugen v. Boehm-Bawerk, it was introduced into the Anglo-American tool chest by Wicksell and his followers, especially Hayek, eclipsing the much sounder notions of J. B. Clark.[4] The discussion ended in stalemate with the well-known controversy between F. H. Knight and Nicholas Kaldor,[5] to the complete disregard of the work of F. A. Burchardt,[6] in which a happy synthesis between a "circular" and a "linear" model had been achieved.

The point at issue is the place of fixed capital goods in the structure of production. Because they are the result of the productive process, they cannot be treated as data side by side with labor and natural resources. On the other hand, the attempt to "dissolve" their contribution into inputs of labor and natural resources fails since, to make fixed capital goods, other fixed capital goods are needed in addition to labor and natural resources. Therefore it is not possible to treat fixed capital goods as the output of some intermediary stage in the vertical model, as Boehm-Bawerk and his followers have suggested. In other words, all attempts to describe the process of production in purely linear fashion, tracing all finished

---

In particular, the last concept will prove useful when the process of capital formation is studied more closely. For a generalization of the above results see Julius Wyler, "Working Capital and Output," *Social Research*, Spring 1953, pp. 91-99.

[4] See his *Distribution of Wealth*, Macmillan, 1926, Chaps. XVIII-XX.

[5] Nicolas Kaldor, "Annual Survey of Economic Theory: The Recent Controversy on the Theory of Capital," *Econometrica*, July 1937, pp. 201-233; F. H. Knight, "On the Theory of Capital: In Reply to Mr. Kaldor," *Econometrica*, January 1938, pp. 63-82; and Nicholas Kaldor, "On the Theory of Capital: A Rejoinder to Professor Knight," *Econometrica*, April 1938, pp. 163-176.

[6] "Die Schemata des stationaeren Kreislaufs bei Boehm-Bawerk und Marx," *Weltwirtschaftliches Archiv*, Kiel, Vol. 34, 1931, pp. 525-564, and Vol. 35, 1932, pp. 116-176.

goods technically back to nothing but man and nature, not only are unrealistic but involve an infinite regress.

A solution of this apparent paradox that is in accordance with both facts and logic is possible only if it is recognized, as Marx and J. B. Clark did many decades ago, that fixed capital goods are replaced and multiplied by a process of physical self-reproduction analogous to the maintenance and increase of the stock of the organic factors of production: men, animals, and plants. Not all fixed capital goods have this technical capacity. It is the characteristic of a particular group, called machine tools. In conjunction with one another and with labor and natural resources (in the form of special working capital goods), these tools are capable of making other equipment as well as their own kind. This circular process raises group a to a strategic position in the technical structure of every industrial economy, whatever its social organization. In other words, group a is the bottleneck which any process of rapid expansion must overcome, a problem which a linear concept of the structure of production cannot even locate, let alone study, in substantive terms.

10. Returning now to the original group schema described in model 1, we can transform it into a set of equations by interpreting its variables (with the exception of d) as price-sum magnitudes pertaining to the output of three physically distinct aggregates. Such a "two-dimensional" determination enables us to establish certain equilibrium conditions of a continuing stationary process, and to express them in marketing terms as well as in physical-technical terms.

For the system to continue in stationary equilibrium, the outputs of period t_1 must become the inputs of period t_2. Thus we have

$$
\begin{aligned}
(3) \qquad & a_{t_1} = f_{at_2} + f_{bt_2} \\
& b_{t_1} = f_{zt_2} \\
& z_{t_1} = n_{at_2} + n_{bt_2} + n_{zt_2} + r_{at_2} + r_{bt_2} + r_{zt_2}
\end{aligned}
$$

In words, the primary machinery produced during period t_1 reappears physically in period t_2 as the fixed capital goods operating in the two equipment goods groups, whereas the secondary machinery b_{t_1} becomes the fixed capital goods operating during period t_2 in the consumer goods group. By this physical application, the outputs of both primary and secondary machinery replace the wear and tear of equipment which occurred in the act of their own production as well as of the simultaneous production of consumer goods. In the same manner, the consumer goods output during period t_1 can be said to "replace" the "wear and tear" of the prime factors N and R—in our context a helpful interpretation of the stationary income claims of their owners—and to serve their maintenance over the period t_2.

To bring about the proper physical "relocation" the three groups must behave in the manner of countries involved in a triangular exchange relationship. The whole output of secondary machinery of group b moves to group z in exchange for an equivalent amount of consumer goods. Part of these "imports" into group b are used to feed the prime factors employed there, whereas the rest are "re-exported" to group a for primary equipment required to replace f_{bt_1}. The "imports" of consumer goods into group a go to the prime factors of this group, whereas the wear and tear of its equipment f_{at_1} is replaced from its own output at_1. In the same manner the prime factors employed in group z are fed out of their own output of consumer goods.

The fact that, as in international trade, these exchanges of non-substitutable goods occur through the marketing actions of individual firms and households in no way reduces the importance of the structural relations among the groups at large. Their significance for macroeconomic analysis is analogous to that of balances of payments in international exchange. The equilibrium conditions of a stationary flow can then be expressed in the following, more comprehensive form:

$$(4) \qquad f_{zt_2} = b_{t_1}$$
$$= z_{t_1} - n_{zt_2} - r_{zt_2}$$
$$= n_{at_2} + n_{bt_2} + r_{at_2} + r_{bt_2}$$

and

$$(5) \qquad f_{bt_2} = a_{t_1} - f_{at_2}$$
$$= z_{t_1} - n_{bt_2} - n_{zt_2} - r_{bt_2} - r_{zt_2}$$
$$= n_{at_2} + r_{at_2}$$

In words, the secondary machinery required per period in group z must equal, physically and in value terms, the output of such equipment produced previously in group b. But it must also equal in value terms a definite amount of consumer goods, namely, the total previous output in group z minus that group's present requirements, a difference which must equal the amount presently demanded by all income-receivers in groups a and b. Furthermore, the primary machinery required per period in group b must equal, physically and in value terms, the surplus of such equipment produced previously in group a over and above that group's own present requirements, and must also equal the value of consumer goods at present demanded by the income-receivers in group a. This latter magnitude, in turn, must equal the total previous output in group z minus the present requirements of consumer goods in both group z and group b.

From these relations a simple inequality can be derived which defines in structural terms the nature of all dynamic processes in the sense of growth or decline of the system. In such a situation there is for any period during which aggregate change occurs:

$$f_z \lesseqgtr n_a + n_b + r_a + r_b$$

$$f_b \lesseqgtr n_a + r_a$$

Model 1 and equations 3 to 5 tell us all that is relevant for the group structure in a continuing stationary process. Not only do they describe the physical transformation of inputs into outputs and conversely, but they also express the changing meaning of the corresponding money flows in subsequent periods. In model 1 interpreted as equality between input values and output values, the n, r, and f variables must be understood not only as costs to the firms, but also as the money receipts that accrue, in the form of income and amortization, to the holders of the respective stocks. In equations 3 to 5 the same symbols represent the expenditures on consumer and equipment goods respectively. On the other hand, the a, b, and z variables in model 1 denote receipts from sales, while they measure aggregates of expenditure in the later equations.

This "ambiguity" has a parallel in the Keynesian model, which also has a "supply" as well as a "demand" meaning. In the first interpretation Keynes deals with aggregate output, consumer goods output, and investment goods output. His second interpretation refers to aggregate income, divided into one part spent on consumer goods and another part called savings, which is spent on investment goods. Far from prejudicing analytical clarity, this change of meaning of the basic variables in successive transactions only emphasizes the circular nature of the exchange process.

STATIONARY GROUP RELATIONS IN TERMS OF CAPITAL COEFFICIENTS

11. Our next step is to derive some analytical tools, with the help of which the "group ratios"—that is, the relative size of the three groups and their components in any given state of the system—can be expressed. For this purpose certain concepts relating to a system's capital structure must be defined.

a. "Total value productivity" is defined as the unit cost of a given output:

$$\epsilon = \frac{o_v}{i_v}$$

that is, output value over input value. "Labor productivity" is then consistently defined as

$$\epsilon_n = \frac{o_v}{n_v}$$

that is, output value over payrolls; and "capital productivity" as

$$\epsilon_c = \frac{o_v}{f_v}$$

that is, output value over replacement value.

For problems other than those discussed in this paper, the relation of input value to output *quantity* is a preferable measure. This is especially true of all investigations having to do with the effect of technical changes on physical productivity, a problem with which we are not concerned here. With technology constant, the two measures are, of course, identical.

In recent studies it has become customary to express capital productivity by the ratio o/F—that is, output (quantity or value) over the value of the capital *stock*—or the reciprocal measure. However convenient these measures are for practical purposes, three objections must be raised against the use of a stock magnitude in the definition of productivity. First, while there is a corresponding measure for labor productivity (o/L, that is, output over the number of workers in man-hours), there is obviously no symmetrical measure for total productivity. Second, the same capital stock may yield different outputs according to the prevailing rate of depreciation. This is the reason why the above measure o_v/f_v explicitly introduces the rate of depreciation, f_v being equal to $F \cdot d$. Third, by combining a flow magnitude with a stock magnitude, we introduce a time dimension into the measure of productivity, a dimension which is happily absent when two flow magnitudes with the same time coefficient are combined.

b. Our second concept is "capital depth" in the sense in which the term was first used by Hawtrey. This concept we define by the ratio

$$k = \frac{F_v}{o_v}$$

that is, the value of the capital stock over the value of output.[7] The measure has a time dimension and can therefore be applied only to clearly defined periods of observation. As in the definition of productivity, it is possible to relate the quantity, rather than the value, of output to the value of capital stock. Accordingly, "value capital depth" can be distinguished from "quantity capital depth." Throughout this paper k refers to value capital depth.

Combining the measure for capital depth with the rate of depreciation, we have the reciprocal of the measure proposed above for capital productivity:

$$kd = \frac{F}{o}d = \frac{f}{do}d = \frac{f}{o}$$

This coefficient kd will be a principal tool in the subsequent structural analyses.

c. Our third concept is "capital intensity," which is the ratio

$$c = \frac{F_v}{n_v}$$

[7] If we were to add to the value of the capital stock the value of the *working* capital stock, the above measure would change to

$$k_{f+w} = \frac{F_v}{o_v} + \frac{W_v}{o_v}$$

Since, as shown in footnote 3 above,

$$W_v = \frac{im}{qp}$$

we obtain by equating the period of observation with the period of maturation

$$k_{f+w} = k_f + \frac{1}{q}$$

or the value of the capital stock over the value of payrolls of the workers operating it over a stated period. Having also a time dimension, the measure is formally analogous with capital depth. It will prove important in the analysis of labor-displacing and labor-attracting technical changes.

12. The coefficient kd, the reciprocal of capital productivity, will now be used for a reformulation of the structural relations which prevail among the three strategic groups in a stationary process. To simplify the exposition, I shall from now on drop the variable r from the set of input factors, assuming either that natural resources are "free gifts" or that the factor n stands for all income-receiving factors. The latter assumption disposes also of any discussion of how to treat interest in a stationary system.

As a first approximation, capital depth coefficients and depreciation rates are taken to be the same in all groups. The sum of outputs $a + b + z$ over the given period is denoted by o. The total capital stock of the system can then be expressed by ok, and the flow of depreciation over the stated period by okd, to which the condition attaches that $k < 1/d$; okd is equal to $a + b$, that is, the output of equipment goods in the given period. This yields

$$z = o - (a + b) = o(1 - kd)$$

$$b = f_z = F_z d = o(1 - kd)kd$$

$$a = o - (z + b) = ok^2d^2$$

Therefore,

$$z : b : a = 1 : kd : \frac{k^2d^2}{1 - kd} \tag{6}$$

which also measures the ratio of the three capital stocks

$$F_z : F_b : F_a$$

With unequal k's and d's for the three groups, the expression changes to

$$z : b : a = 1 : k_z d_z : \frac{k_z d_z k_b d_b}{1 - k_a d_a} \tag{7}$$

and

$$F_z : F_b : F_a = 1 : k_b d_z : \frac{k_a d_z k_b d_b}{1 - k_a d_a} \tag{7a}$$

Thus once the capital depth coefficients and depreciation rates for the respective groups are known, the relative share of the output of the groups in the gross national product and the relative size of net national income, which under stationary conditions coincides with the output of consumer goods, are determined. So is the ratio of the capital stocks, and the distribution of prime and supplementary factors over the groups.

If a stationary process is studied, all capital problems are reduced to replacement problems, that is, to the maintenance of the existing ratios among the three groups. When we turn to the analysis of certain dynamic processes, the notions of both "group ratios" and "intergroup equilibrium conditions" will prove useful in dealing with the concomitant problems of capital formation.

2. *The Dynamics of Once-Over Changes*

13. This is not the place to undertake a critical review of all the definitions of economic "dynamics" that have been put forth in recent years (Frisch, Hicks, Samuelson, Harrod). In what follows the term includes any economic process which is exposed to change, whether bipolar as in the case of a shift in tastes, or aggregate as under conditions of growth or decline of the system as a whole. For the purpose of this paper bipolar changes are disregarded. Among aggregate changes it is convenient to distinguish between once-over and continuous changes.

Harrod defines a once-over change as a single act of change in one or more of the data of the system, such as an increase in labor supply owing to the influx of a certain number of immigrants at a given point of time, or the introduction of a particular technical improvement.[8] After the absorption of such a once-over change the system is supposed to operate again under the previously prevailing (zero or constant) rate of data changes. Unlike Harrod I regard such once-over changes as legitimate problems for dynamic analysis. In the first place, far from dealing with "trivial matter" "satisfactorily to be handled by the apparatus of static theory" (*ibid*, p. 7), all the practically relevant cases of once-over changes occur in the framework of otherwise continuous change, and the interplay between the two types of change can hardly be studied in terms of comparative statics. Second, and more important, a description of the adjustment path that the system pursues under the impact of once-over changes

[8] R. F. Harrod, *Toward a Dynamic Economics*, Macmillan, 1948, Lecture One.

points up particularly well the structural problems of capital formation, which beset all dynamic processes operating under any rate of change other than constant.

I shall concentrate upon one particular type of once-over change, since the basic problems can best be thrown into relief by an isolating analysis. For this purpose a change in labor supply will be selected and the results of the analysis supplemented by a few remarks on "neutral" changes in productivity.

To highlight the issues relating to capital formation, severely restrictive assumptions have been made. The system is assumed to move initially in stationary equilibrium under conditions of pure competition, with firms of equal size operating in continuous production under minimum average costs. Constant returns are to prevail on all natural resources, which are treated as free goods, and the capital depth coefficients and rates of depreciation are to be equal in all groups.

All these conditions can easily be relaxed. There is also no difficulty in analyzing a simultaneous change in labor supply and productivity, as will be indicated below. It is even more important to realize from the outset that the results, though gained within a stationary framework, are fully applicable to a dynamic framework. In other words, changes in a positive rate of change can be analyzed by "superimposing" our results upon a process in dynamic equilibrium with a steady rate of growth.

A ONCE-OVER CHANGE IN LABOR SUPPLY

14. Our stationary equilibrium is supposed to be disturbed by an increment α of labor supply, expressing the potential increment Δn_v in the value of labor effort as a fraction of the value of the stationary labor effort n_v per period of observation. Our problem, then, concerns those aggregate changes of, and structural shifts among, the three groups which describe the "optimal" path for the absorption of the increment or, what amounts to the same thing, restore in the most economical manner stationary equilibrium on a higher level of input and output.

It may be advisable to emphasize once more that the concomitant "functional" problems—namely, the particular behavior patterns and motivations of the actors in the market that are the condition for the realization of the structural adjustment—are not discussed in this paper. One fundamental functional assumption referring to savings and investment will be stated below. For the rest little can be said about the functional aspects of dynamic processes before the structural conditions have been clarified.[9]

There are, in principle, two ways in which a labor increment can be absorbed: either by utilizing the existing equipment at more than its optimum intensity—in other words, by expanding output all through the system beyond the point of minimum average costs through a change in factor proportions in favor of labor—or by building new equipment. In accordance with my basic assumption of fixed technical coefficients, I shall concentrate upon the second alternative.[10]

15. In order to provide the labor increment with working places and real income, the stationary factors must perform a temporary act of net saving and net investment. Its monetary aspect, in which we are not interested here, consists in the transfer of appropriate purchasing power from the stationary income-receivers to the entrepreneurs, by an act of voluntary saving, by credit inflation, or even by a general fall in wages resulting from the increased competition in the labor market.[11] Its real aspect, in which alone we are interested, consists in all three cases in the displacement of factors in the consumer goods group, factors which—given the required mobility—can be transferred to the equipment goods groups for the purpose of expanding the output of equipment. As a first approximation, it is assumed that such mobility exists for labor, so that a weaver can in the very short run be used as, say, a steel worker. However, the whole problem to be studied would be eliminated if the same notion of mobility were applied to fixed capital goods. I therefore assume that the displaced looms cannot be used in steel-

[9] The ultimate reason for the dependence of functional analysis upon structural analysis lies in the fact that all dynamic behavior patterns are shaped by expectations, which in their turn are related to the prevailing structure. For a more detailed exposition see my paper "On the Mechanistic Approach in Economics," *Social Research*, December 1951, pp. 403-434.

[10] Even if some short-period variability of factor proportions is admitted, the concomitant rise in user costs provides "a motive for increasing the stock of equipment." See J. R. Hicks, *A Contribution to the Theory of the Trade Cycle*, Oxford, Clarendon Press, 1950, pp. 39-40. Therefore, for all but very small increments in labor supply the alternative chosen above seems the only realistic one.

[11] Whether, and under what conditions, such a decrease in wages frees business funds and thus provides the equivalent of savings, or rather leads to a proportional price fall that leaves real incomes unchanged, is a functional problem whose answer clearly depends on prevailing expectations. The same is true of the effect that such a fall in wages has upon the capital depth of the subsequent investment.

making, the expansion of which forms part of the process of real capital formation.

16. This process of equipment-building requires closer examination in accord with what was said above about the technical relationship between primary and secondary machinery. Obviously, once the total labor increment has been finally absorbed, all three groups will have expanded by a rate equal to α under our assumption of unchanged factor proportions. But since under the same assumptions there is no reserve capacity in the field of primary machinery, the addition to secondary machinery presupposes the prior expansion of the output of primary machinery. We saw above that it is the circular nature of production in group *a* which makes such expansion possible. The fall in output of consumer goods has freed capacity not only in the respective group *z*, but also in group *b*, which supplies the replacement of secondary machinery, and in group *a* itself, which provides the replacement of capacity in group *b*.

It is this freed capacity in groups *a* and *b*[12] which forms the nucleus for the "self-expansion" of primary machinery and thus for the "widening" of productive capacity in all three groups. And it is in the gradual self-expansion of group *a* that the prime factors initially displaced in groups *b* and *z* will have to find employment during this first phase of adjustment. The second phase—namely, the process of net absorption—begins when output in group *a* has risen to a point that permits aggregate employment to rise above the stationary level. This then induces the gradual expansion of groups *b* and *z* beyond the level of employment and output to which saving on the part of the stationary factors had reduced them originally, to the new equilibrium level.[13]

[12] Since the physical goods used as primary machinery operate in some instances also as secondary machinery (e.g. extracting machinery and steel mills providing the material for certain household articles or transportation services, and even machine tools "shaping" the final consumer good), the fall in real consumption also "frees" some capacity in group *z* which can be utilized for the expansion of group *a*. We shall soon see that the size of the freed capacity in groups *a* and *b* can be easily determined. To do so for group *z* presupposes a detailed knowledge of the income elasticities of demand. For this reason the issue is disregarded in what follows, an omission that gives the subsequent conclusions as to "waste" and as to the length of the construction period a slightly "pessimistic" bias.

[13] To clinch the argument I would have to demonstrate the complementary functional processes in a step-by-step analysis. These processes refer, above all, to the mechanism that transfers aggregate savings to the entrepreneurs in group *a*; to the consequent attraction of idle prime factors to that group; to

This sketchy description of the process of real capital formation under the conditions assumed forms the background for the structural analysis to follow. More specifically, it will now be our task to formulate, in terms of a minimum number of independent variables, certain strategic relationships which characterize the process of capital formation. They refer to the dynamic group ratios, to the danger of "overbuilding" the capital stock, and, above all, to the length of the "period of construction."

The independent variables, which are to serve as data for our analysis, are four. Two of them—namely, k (capital depth) and d (depreciation)—are directly related to the size of the capital stock. The other two are α, the rate of growth of the labor increment, and s, the ratio of aggregate planned savings to aggregate income in the various phases of the adjustment process. Since in our "normative" model, planned savings always equal planned investment, s also measures realized savings and investment.

Group Ratios

17. The structural shifts occurring during the process of capital formation can best be read in the variation of the group ratios. Not all the possible variations will be discussed at this point. There is, however, one intermediate phase in the adjustment process that requires closer examination. It concerns that stage of expansion when an amount of prime factors, equal to the amount originally displaced in groups b and z, has found re-employment in group a. Or, as we can also say, it describes the maximum expansion

---

the "multiplier" process by which groups b and z gradually expand, once expansion of group a begins to raise aggregate employment and income above the stationary level; and, last but not least, to the expectational conditions, upon which the postulated behavior patterns depend.

Moreover, a definite pattern of saving and investment must be postulated. The pattern assumed here requires constant (ex ante) ratios equal for savings and investment up to the point where the stationary level of employment is again reached; from there on, as absorption proceeds, the savings ratio must fall in proportion to the fall in investment demand, which, with the completion of absorption, reaches zero. It has been stated above that groups b and z will not expand before employment in group a has been increased to the point where aggregate employment equals again the stationary level. This conclusion follows from the premise that the (ex ante) savings and investment ratios are equal and constant during the first phase of the adjustment process.

If some of these postulates appear rather unrealistic, the reader should remember that we are not concerned here with the description of empirical processes, but with the analysis of the conditions for "optimum" adjustment within the framework of a free market system.

of group a which, with a given savings ratio, can be achieved with the available amount of stationary prime factors. Output at this stage, denoted by the subscript $_{00}$, compares with the stationary magnitudes denoted by $_0$ as follows:

$$(8)\qquad \begin{aligned} z_{00} &= z_0(1-s) = o_0(1-s)(1-kd) \\ b_{00} &= f_{z_{00}} = z_0(1-s)kd = o_0(1-s)(1-kd)kd \\ a_{00} &= o_0 - (z_{00}+b_{00}) = o_0[1-(1-s)(1-k^2d^2)] \end{aligned}$$

Therefore,

$$(9)\qquad z_{00} : b_{00} : a_{00} = 1 : kd : \frac{k^2d^2(1-s)+s}{(1-s)(1-kd)}$$

It agrees with common sense that group a expands with the size of the savings ratio and the capital depth coefficient and rate of depreciation of the original capital stock. We saw above that expansion of group a presupposes that savings "free" part of the available capacity of primary equipment for the purpose of self-reproduction. The variables k and d determine the potential range within which capacity can be "freed," and s determines the size of capacity actually freed within that range. In this manner it is the savings ratio which fixes, within the limit of the technical variables k and d, the point of maximum expansion of group a in the sense defined, that is, before net absorption starts. In an empirical free market, in which the (ex ante) savings ratio is the result of many independent decisions, this may lead to the overbuilding of the capital stock and subsequent waste of part of the addition to primary equipment which is produced during the phase of expansion. We encounter here a possible conflict between the goal of economizing resources and the institutional order of a free market system.

The Overbuilding of Primary Equipment

18. The problem referred to is customarily dealt with under the heading of the acceleration principle. In particular, the older "accelerationists" (Aftalion, J. M. Clark) felt troubled about the "waste" of equipment stock, which seemed to them bound up with any decline in the rate of increase in consumption. Our example of an isolated, once-over change provides a good test for this proposition, since after a single act of expansion the rate of growth of consumption falls back to zero.

The foregoing analysis supplies all the necessary tools for such a test. First of all, it tells exactly where the alleged overbuilding will occur. Since, as the above group ratios show, the demand for secondary equipment always moves in proportion to the demand for consumer goods, the critical sector can only be group *a*, the current output of which, after the expansion, may indeed exceed the final *replacement* demand in both group *a* and group *b*. Second, we can calculate in terms of our independent variables the size of the additional primary equipment required in the new state of equilibrium, as well as the size of the actual supply of such equipment at the point of maximum expansion described by equation 8.

The first magnitude, primary equipment stock required (StR_{a+b}), can be ascertained in the following manner. *Total* additional investment—that is, the increment of both primary and secondary equipment—must amount to

$$StR_{a+b+z} = \alpha ko \quad (10)$$

Of this addition to total capital stock an amount of

$$StR_{a+b} = \alpha k^2 do \quad (10a)$$

must consist of primary equipment, equivalent to the replacement demand for both primary and secondary equipment.

The second magnitude, net addition to primary equipment stock actually supplied in advance of absorption (StS_a), can be calculated on the basis of equation 8. It amounts to the total stock of primary equipment in operation at the maximum point of expansion as defined above, minus the stationary stock of primary equipment. Or in symbolic language:

$$\begin{aligned} StS_a &= (a_{00} + b_{00} - a_0 - b_0)k \\ &= sk(1 - kd)o \end{aligned} \quad (11)$$

Potential waste W of primary equipment built during the process of expansion then amounts to

$$\begin{aligned} W &= StS_a - StR_{a+b} \\ &= [s(1 - kd) - \alpha kd]o \end{aligned} \quad (12)$$

We can generalize this result by dropping the assumption that the coefficients of capital depth and depreciation valid for the new capital stock are equal to those of the stationary stock. By denoting the new coefficients as k' and d', we obtain

$$W = [sk(1 - kd) - \alpha k'^2 d']o \quad (12a)$$

It is obvious that the expression within the brackets can, but need not, be positive. The result depends on the relative size of the variables s, k, and d, on the one hand, and α, k', and d', on the other. A high ex ante savings ratio, which under our assumptions is identical with a high "investment ratio," and a high capital depth coefficient of the original equipment make for waste, whereas a high rate of growth coupled with a high capital depth coefficient of the equipment increment counteract it. Depreciation rates for both original and additional capital stock affect waste inversely.

Assuming a savings-investment ratio of 10 per cent, and on both sides capital depth coefficients of 3 and depreciation rates of 10 per cent, a rate of once-over growth in the neighborhood of 25 per cent would avoid any waste. This example assumes, in accord with our model, that all planned savings are actually invested in the service of a *change* in the rate of growth. In any empirical market system observed over the last century, a large part of s has always been needed to sustain a positive *constant* rate of growth, and it is hardly surprising that Kuznets and Tinbergen have found little empirical evidence for any investment waste.

This is not the place to dwell upon the flaws which mar the conventional exposition of the process of "overbuilding."[14] Apart from faulty notions about the structure of production, which obscure the process of expansion, the pessimistic conclusions arise from the assumption that the entire addition to equipment must be built in one arbitrarily chosen period of construction, an assumption that implies a fantastically high savings ratio. In reality the independent variable is not the construction period, but the savings-investment ratio in conjunction with the coefficients of capital depth and depreciation and the period of maturation of the capital increment (see section 19 below). In other words, in principle the choice is between speedy adjustment by means of a high savings-investment ratio involving the danger of waste, and slow adjustment by a low savings-investment ratio. The latter alternative keeps the building of capital stock in line with subsequent replacement demands, though at the price of making the consumer "wait" longer for the fruits of investment. Of course, in practice the choice between these two alternatives

[14] See, e.g., Gottfried Haberler's *Prosperity and Depression*, Columbia University Press, 1946, Chap. 3, pars. 17-24, esp. par. 19.

is open only to a planned system, which can manipulate s in such a manner that, with given k, k', d, and d', it just satisfies the requirements of α. In a free market system, in which none of these variables is subject to over-all control, overbuilding, though by no means inevitable, is a possible danger.

The Period of Construction

19. The assertion that the appearance or nonappearance of waste is related to the size of the savings ratio, deserves further investigation, which will also supply us with an exact measure of the minimum period of construction for the capital increment.

Given a system in which labor and equipment are fully utilized, how long will it take to produce an additional unit of a consumer good? Under the assumption of full utilization of the available capital stock, a prior increase in the output of primary and secondary equipment is the condition for an increase in the output of consumer goods. Thus in all three groups some units of natural resources must undergo the process of transformation into a finished good described in our stage schema (model 2). The total construction period that must elapse before the additional consumer good is available consists then of the sum of the "maturation periods," m_a, m_b, and m_z, required in the three groups to move the respective natural resources down to the stage of completion.

The notion of a "period of maturation" was introduced in discussion of the concept of a stock of working capital goods (section 8). With a given technology, m is an empirical constant which of course differs not only from group to group but from industry to industry. Therefore, if we want to apply this concept to a general process of expansion rather than to the increase in output of a single consumer good, it seems that we must introduce the notion of an "average" period of maturation, a concept that would be difficult to establish empirically. In fact, however, what is needed in order to measure the period of construction is the *longest* rather than the *average* period of maturation in each group, because the new equilibrium cannot be attained before the good with the longest period of maturation reaches the state of completion. It does not appear impossible to ascertain empirically such "maximum" m's.

These considerations seem to yield a measure for the period of construction (PC) required to expand the output of consumer goods in a system in which initially all resources are fully utilized. We obtain[15]

$$PC = m_a \text{ max.} + m_b \text{ max.} + m_z \text{ max.}$$

This measure is based entirely upon empirical technical constants without any reference to economic variables such as s. However, if examined more closely, the expression is defective in two respects.

First of all, we have so far implicitly assumed that the initial stock of primary equipment necessary to expand such output is fully available from the outset. Our exposition of the expansion process (section 16) indicated that this is not so. The initial stock of primary equipment must be "freed," and, as was shown above, the amount "freed" depends upon the fall in replacement demand, which in its turn is determined by the prevailing savings ratio. Thus under the conditions assumed—with real capital formation throughout the system—the actual period of maturation in group a exceeds m_a max. as defined above. It is a multiple of m_a max., the multiplicand g measuring the number of maturation periods required to expand the equipment stock "freed" (StF) to the size of the equipment "required" for the subsequent over-all increase in output (StR).

Secondly, a multiplicand has also to be added to m_b max. Once the required addition to the stock of primary equipment is available, it has to be used for maintaining itself and, above all, for raising the stock of secondary equipment to the required level. The latter aim could be achieved in *one* maturation period only if the size of the additional primary equipment were geared to the continuous *increase* rather than to the current maintenance of the additional secondary equipment. For any size of the additional primary equipment smaller than indicated, a period of $j \cdot m_b$ max. is required to construct the addition to secondary equipment.

The true value for the period of construction is then

$$PC = g \cdot m_a \text{ max.} + j \cdot m_b \text{ max.} + m_z \text{ max.} \tag{13}$$

and we have now to determine the magnitudes of g and j.

[15] Since small variations of the initially available capacity are in practice possible, the measure yields the upper limit for the construction period necessary to accommodate a *small* rate of growth. For *large* rates of growth the result gives the lower limit.

It may be objected that to increase consumer goods output, the system need not "wait" until the last piece of primary and secondary equipment comes from the assembly line. This is certainly true of a partial expansion of group z. But such "staggering" obviously cannot affect the length of the adjustment period for aggregate expansion. We can get *some* consumer goods earlier, but only at the price of having to wait longer for the remainder.

Whereas the three m's are technical constants, g is a variable. To determine it, we need a measure for StF, for StR, and for the rate of growth of StF. It will now be shown that all these variables are related to the independent variables of our system.

Primary equipment freed, StF, consists of capacity freed in both group b and group a. The size of capacity freed in group b is determined by the fall of replacement demand on the part of group z. The latter being equal to $skdz_0$, the stock of primary equipment freed in group b amounts to sk^2dz_0.

On the same principle, an additional stock amounting to $\frac{sk^3d^2}{1-kd}z_0$ is freed in group a.[16] And the total stock of primary equipment freed equals

$$StF_{a+b} = \frac{sk^2d}{1-kd}z_0 = sk^2do_0 \tag{14}$$

StR, the aggregate size of the primary equipment stock *required* (stock freed plus increment) can be determined in accord with equation 10a above:

$$StR = (s + a)k^2do$$

Finally, the rate of growth of StF is a function of k. Each unit of stock freed produces an output equal to StF/k, which itself is added to the equipment stock and, allowing for its own depreciation, is ready to produce additional equipment in the next maturation period. Thus the rate of growth of StF equals[17]

$$\frac{k(1-d)+1}{k}$$

Thus we obtain

$$StF\left[\frac{k(1-d)+1}{k}\right]^g = StR$$

[16] The stock freed in group a equals aks. Since, according to equation 6 above,

$$a = \frac{k^2d^2}{1-kd}z$$

then

$$aks = \frac{sk^3d^2}{1-kd}z_0$$

[17] Since g refers to m_a max., all variables such as k, k', d, and d', which have a time dimension, must be related to this period.

and

(15)
$$g = \frac{\log \frac{s + a}{s}}{\log \frac{k(1 - d) + 1}{k}}$$ [18]

We have finally to determine the magnitude of j, which measures the number of maturation periods required for the addition to secondary equipment. From equation 10a we can derive the size of the secondary equipment stock required as

$$StR_b = ak(1 - kd)o_0$$

The amount of primary equipment additionally available for the production of secondary equipment (over and above replacement of primary equipment) follows from equation 12 as

$$StS_{a \text{ for } b} = sk(1 - kd)(1 - kd)o_0$$

which produces per period of maturation m_b max. an output of secondary equipment

$$\Delta o_b = \frac{sk(1 - kd)(1 - kd)}{k} o_0 = s(1 - kd)^2 o_0$$

Therefore,

(15a)
$$j = \frac{StR_b}{\Delta o_0} = \frac{ak(1 - kd)}{s(1 - kd)^2} = \frac{ak}{s(1 - kd)}$$

The upshot of all this is that, given the three periods of maturation as technical constants, the minimum period of construction of the total additional equipment stock required can be calculated on the basis of our independent variables. As one would expect on common sense grounds, both g and j, and thus the construction period in its entirety, are directly related to the rate of growth and the depth

[18] The term g measures the number of maturation periods necessary to build the additional stock of primary equipment. Assuming $k = 2$, $d = 1/10$, $s = 1/10$, and $a = 1/5$, equation 15 yields $g =$ circa 3.3. How are we to interpret the decimal .3? It can mean either that, after the lapse of three maturation periods, the then-available capacity need be employed only over another three-tenths of one period to reach the desired aggregate output, or that only three-tenths of the capacity available after three periods need be utilized for another full period. Since with a given technology the maturation period is fixed, only the second interpretation makes economic sense. From this it follows that g must always be rounded upward to the next highest integer before the minimum period of construction can be established.

and depreciation rate of the additional capital stock, and inversely related to the savings ratio and the depth and depreciation rate of the original capital stock.

We saw above that the savings ratio may well prove excessive in view of the goal of optimum utilization of resources. We now have it confirmed by quantitative analysis that the higher the savings ratio the shorter is the minimum period of construction. Thus, as was indicated above, a conflict of goals may arise in a free market system between "maximum speed of adjustment" and "minimum waste of resources." Considering their low savings ratio, the economies of underdeveloped countries are unlikely to be caught in this dilemma.

SOME REMARKS ON "NEUTRAL" CHANGES IN PRODUCTIVITY

20. Besides a change in labor supply it is, above all, a change in technology that may induce a once-over change in capital formation. Since the most important type of technical change—namely, factor-displacing and factor-attracting innovations—will be discussed in the context of continuous change, only "neutral" changes in productivity will be discussed here. Harrod defines a neutral advance as one that does not alter the coefficients of capital depth.[19] In other words, output rises in the same proportion as capital stock, so that the group ratios in the new equilibrium do not differ from those in the original equilibrium.

As an analogy to the growth rate α of the labor force, a measure for the once-over rise in productivity is needed. This measure, π, is best defined as the difference between the coefficient of total productivity prevailing in the original equilibrium and that prevailing in the final equilibrium:

$$\pi = \frac{\epsilon_1}{\epsilon_0} - 1$$

where both ϵ's are related to i_0, that is, the unit input of the stationary process (see section 11). Equations 10, 10a, 12, 12a, 15, and 15a can then be rewritten by substituting π for α. By inserting $\alpha + \pi$ in the respective terms, we obtain expressions for the required capital stocks, for waste, and for the period of construction under conditions of a simultaneous once-over change in both labor supply and productivity.

[19] *Op. cit.*, p. 23.

3. *The Dynamics of Continuous Change*

21. Turning now to the capital problems related to continuous change, we have first to make a convenient breakdown of this large topic. To explore all structurally relevant cases, from the conditions for dynamic equilibrium to the multitude of dynamic disequilibria and the conditions for re-equilibration, would require a book. Therefore, it seems advisable to subdivide this part according to a formal principle which is applicable to all cases and can serve as a sort of "cadre," into which the reader may fit those other problems which cannot be discussed in this paper.

The distinction between "constant" and "varying" rates of change supplies such a principle. It restates, in a manner, the criterion for distinguishing between a stationary process and a once-over change, but now introducing this criterion into a framework of continuous change. The "equilibrium norm" of a constant rate of change, which in a stationary process implies a *zero* rate of change, now implies a *positive* rate of change. And, as has already been stated (section 13), processes involving varying rates of change can then be analyzed by the technique applied to once-over changes.

THE DYNAMICS OF A CONSTANT RATE OF CHANGE (DYNAMIC EQUILIBRIUM)

22. Certain structural conditions for dynamic equilibrium have received wide attention during the last decade. Considering the Keynesian origin of most of this work, it is not surprising that all the representative formulations (Harrod, Domar, Hicks) are in aggregate terms. Therefore, they describe the conditions which relate to the structure of the income-expenditure flow (section 3 above) rather than those which concern the physical structure of production. One of our tasks will be to show that, within the frame of reference assumed by the originators, the Harrod-Domar conditions, though necessary, are not sufficient to assure dynamic equilibrium.

For this purpose these conditions themselves must be formulated in terms of our independent variables. Dynamic equilibrium can prevail only if, for any given period, the supply of real capital equals the demand for real capital. Assuming a savings (investment) ratio of s, supply of real capital in terms of aggregate output equals $s(1 - kd)o$. Demand for real capital can be determined with the help of equation 10 by interpreting a as a constant rate of growth. Adding to the constant growth in labor supply a constant increase in neutral technical advances, $(\alpha + \pi)ko$ measures the aggregate demand for real capital.

Therefore, in dynamic equilibrium

$$s(1 - kd) = (\alpha + \pi)k$$

or

$$\frac{(\alpha + \pi)k}{1 - kd} = s \tag{16}$$

This condition for dynamic equilibrium differs from the "no waste" condition formulated in equation 12 only by the absence of the variable d in the expression for the stock required. The modification indicates what, with respect to capital formation, is the difference between the two types of growth. In "wasteless" once-over growth, stock-building is precisely geared to subsequent replacement demand, whereas in continuous growth the demands of both stock replacement and stock expansion must be satisfied.

It is immediately clear that equation 16 is equivalent to both

$$G_n C_r = s \qquad \text{(Harrod's condition)}$$

and

$$\frac{\Delta I}{I\sigma} = s \qquad \text{(Domar's condition)}$$

The terms $\alpha + \pi$ in equation 16 have the same meaning as Harrod's G_n ("natural rate of growth") and Domar's addition to investment, $\Delta I/I$, whereas our k is identical with Harrod's C_r ("required capital coefficient") and is the inverse of Domar's σ ("investment productivity"). The only difference is that Harrod and Domar relate s to net output or income, whereas equation 16 relates s to gross output.

Thus there is general agreement that dynamic equilibrium cannot persist unless income and investment change at a rate equal to the product of the prevailing savings ratio and Domar's coefficient of investment productivity. But for dynamic equilibrium to be assured in an industrial system with factor specificity, the rate of growth of net output and investment, that is, $\alpha + \pi$, not only must equal the critical product, but must remain constant. Furthermore, given such a constant rate of growth, not only the critical product itself, but also the factors composing it, will have to remain constant. If the rate of growth changes, persistence of dynamic equilibrium will be conditional upon complicated shifts among the groups of production, *even if the product of the savings ratio and the investment productivity ratio spontaneously and simultaneously adjusts itself to the new rate of growth.* Similar shifts will be required if s or $1/k$ change, *even if their product remains constant.* The fact that, and the manner in which, such shifts are likely to destabilize the system will be demonstrated below.[20] In preparation for this discussion the more restrictive conditions, which are both necessary and sufficient for the maintenance of dynamic equilibrium, will now be established.

23. For this purpose we must, first of all, formulate structural equations of production, equivalent to the set of stationary equations formulated in model 1, but now appropriate to dynamic equilibrium:

(17)

$$[(1+a)^{t_n} + (1+\pi)^{t_n}][(F_{at_0}d \equiv f_{at_0}) + n_{at_0} + \sigma_{at_0}] = a_{t_n}$$

$$[(1+a)^{t_n} + (1+\pi)^{t_n}][(F_{bt_0}d \equiv f_{bt_0}) + n_{bt_0} + \sigma_{bt_0}] = b_{t_n}$$

$$[(1+a)^{t_n} + (1+\pi)^{t_n}][(F_{zt_0}d \equiv f_{zt_0}) + n_{zt_0} + \sigma_{zt_0}] = z_{t_n}$$

The set of equations in 17 differs from the stationary equations in two respects. First, the number of input items, contained in the right-hand brackets, is increased by the factor σ, representing savings over the chosen period. Second, the left-hand brackets contain a multiplicand, namely, the rate of growth by which the system expands from period to period as a result of increase in labor supply and of neutral advances. Therefore, the equations describe the level of *real* output attained in period t_n, expressed as the compounded level of real output in period t_0.

From set 17 we can derive the structural conditions of dynamic equilibrium, equivalent to those described for stationary equilibrium in equations 4 and 5:

(18)
$$\begin{aligned} f_{zt_2} + \sigma_{zt_2} &= b_{t_1} \\ &= z_{t_1} - n_{zt_2} \\ &= n_{at_2} + n_{bt_2} \end{aligned}$$

[20] It is true that both Harrod and Domar regard dynamic equilibrium as described by their equations as extremely unstable. But the initiating shock is always seen in a discrepancy between planned savings and the rate of growth times capital depth, whereas the above propositions include the case of parallel movement and even some cases of constancy of these two rates.

$$(19) \qquad f_{bt_2} + \sigma_{bt_2} = a_{t_1} - f_{at_2} - \sigma_{at_2} = z_{t_1} - n_{bt_2} - n_{zt_2} = n_{at_2}$$

These equilibrium conditions contain implicitly also the condition formulated in equation 16, that is, the Harrod-Domar condition for aggregate dynamic equilibrium. But they point up, above all, the physical-technical relations that must persist among certain strategic components of the three groups if today's outputs are to serve as tomorrow's inputs in a steadily expanding process. The underlying principle is that the Harrod-Domar conditions must apply not only to aggregate output and investment, but also to output and investment in each of the three groups.[21]

In this respect a comment is in order with regard to the variable σ. As is the case with all the other variables, σ has a twofold meaning, one monetary, one real (see section 10 above), that is, it measures both savings and investment. As measures of investment σ_a, σ_b, and σ_z express that distribution of total investment over the three groups on which persistence of dynamic equilibrium depends. As measures of savings they express the relative amounts of funds *available* for investment in each group rather than the relative amounts *accumulated* there. In other words, for the maintenance of dynamic equilibrium it does not matter how much of the income of each group is saved by the respective income-receivers, so long as the aggregate savings ratio remains constant and the "oversavings" of one or more groups are transferred to the "undersaving" group(s) for investment there.

[21] It may well be asked whether the above revision of the Harrod-Domar equilibrium conditions goes far enough. Factor specificity is likely to obstruct short-run shifts not only *among* the equipment goods and consumer goods groups, but also *within* each one of these groups. From this consideration the ultimate conclusion can be drawn: to assure stability, the structure of demand as well as the rate of growth must remain constant.

Indeed, this conclusion eliminates large and sudden changes in demand. This, incidentally, is a type of change which as a rule involves also some change in the system's total capital structure, that is, a shift *among* the groups. For small and slow changes in demand the less severe conditions as formulated in equations 18 and 19 remain valid, since such changes would seem to fall within the range of tolerance for frictions that exists even in an industrial economy.

For a related problem see Robert M. Solow and Paul A. Samuelson, "Balanced Growth under Constant Returns to Scale," *Econometrica*, July 1953, pp. 412-424. Hans Neisser's criticism of their paper in *Econometrica*, October 1954, pp. 501-503, does not affect the above conclusions, which are based on the assumption of fixed input proportions.

24. In order to explore fully the structure of dynamic equilibrium, we must now determine the prevailing group ratios. Starting from the group ratios that characterize stationary equilibrium (equation 6), it is easy to see that output of consumer goods in dynamic equilibrium (z_{dy}) is reduced below the stationary level by the amount of net savings. Therefore,

$$\begin{aligned} z_{dy} &= z_0(1-s) \\ &= (1-s)(1-kd)o_0 \end{aligned}$$

It will be apparent that this expression is identical with the one given in section 17 for the initial change in output of consumer goods under the impact of a once-over change. The difference is that in dynamic equilibrium with constant money supply, only the *money* expression for z_{dy} lies permanently below the money expression for z_0, but real output rises continuously.

In establishing the size of b_{dy}, a certain complication must be considered. During the first phase of a once-over change, b_{00} simply serves as replacement of f_{z00}. In dynamic equilibrium, b_{dy} must fulfill the same function but must also provide for an additional stock of secondary equipment in accord with the prevailing rate of growth. Thus

$$\begin{aligned} b_{dy} &= f_{zdy} + F_{zdy}(a+\pi) \\ &= \left[(1-s)(1-kd)kd + (1-s)(1-kd)\frac{kd}{d}(a+\pi) \right] o_0 \end{aligned}$$

From equation 16 we know that $s(1-kd)/k$ can be substituted for $a+\pi$. This yields

$$b_{dy} = (1-s)(1-kd)[kd(1-s)+s]o_0$$

Finally,

$$a_{dy} = o_0 - (b_{dy} + z_{dy}) = [kd(1-s)+s]^2 o_0$$

so that

$$\begin{aligned} (20) \qquad z_{dy} : b_{dy} : a_{dy} &= 1 : kd(1-s) + s : \frac{[kd(1-s)+s]^2}{(1-s)(1-kd)} \\ &= F_{zdy} : F_{bdy} : F_{ady} \end{aligned}$$

Introducing different capital depth coefficients, different rates of depreciation, and different savings ratios, the three group ratios become

$$(20a)\quad z_{dy} : b_{dy} : a_{dy} = 1 : (1 - s_z)k_z d_z + s_z : \frac{[(1 - s_z)k_z d_z + s_z][(1 - s_b)k_b d_b + s_b]}{(1 - s_a)(1 - k_a d_a)}$$

The ratio $F_{zdy} : F_{bdy} : F_{ady}$ can be obtained by multiplying the members on the right side of equation 20a with k_z, k_b, and k_a, respectively.

25. It may be appropriate at this point to demonstrate how, with the help of equation 20 (or 20a), the actual structure of the system can be derived if the values of *o, s, k,* and *d* are given. The group ratios and capital stock ratios appropriate to the given values of *s, k,* and *d* follow from equation 20. The absolute values of the group outputs can then be derived by subdividing the value of *o* accordingly. The absolute values for the capital stocks equal the absolute values of the respective group outputs multiplied by the respective *k*'s. The absolute values of the inputs f_z, f_b, and f_a follow from the respective group outputs multiplied by *kd*. The income magnitudes $(n + \sigma)$ equal the residual of $o - f$ in each group, and with the help of *s* we can divide the respective sums of $n + \sigma$ into their components. The equilibrium conditions, equations 18 and 19, provide a final check.

THE DYNAMICS OF A VARYING RATE OF CHANGE

26. Once we admit variations in the rate of change, any one of our independent variables, α, π, *k, d,* and *s*, and any combination of these variables can undergo such a change. A complete survey might have to include also shifts in taste, at least to the extent to which the bi-polar changes in capital stock bound up with such shifts do not fully balance, and also changes in the supply of natural resources, especially diminishing returns on land.

This discussion will be confined to two examples, which illustrate some of the structural problems of capital formation that arise in the context of varying rates of change. One deals with shifts in the demand and supply functions for investment; the other is concerned with nonneutral—that is, factor-displacing—technical changes.

Shifts in the Investment Functions

27. What is at stake here can best be understood in terms of the Harrod-Domar conditions as formulated in equation 16:

$$\frac{(a+\pi)k}{1-kd}=s$$

A shift relating to the variables of this equation can mean two things. On the one hand, and this is the usual interpretation, it can refer to a shift of the demand for investment relative to the supply of investment—in popular language, to either undersaving or oversaving. But it can also mean a proportionate change on both sides of the equation by a simultaneous parallel change in the savings ratio and the output of capital goods. This alternative has greater realistic significance than may appear at first sight. It covers, for example, the case of a mature economy in which the community responds to a falling rate of population increase with a rise in the average propensity to consume. Even more important is the case of an over-investment boom in Hayek's sense, in which rising real wages cut into savings and enforce a reduction of aggregate investment.

It is interesting to note that Harrod, Domar, and all their critics are exclusively concerned with the first alternative, that is, a relative change between the two functions. Parallel shifts do not seem to pose any problems to them, though these are the real test for any equilibrium condition which is formulated in aggregate terms only.[22] The analysis of such shifts will now serve to complete the argument about the conditions of dynamic equilibrium, which was started in section 22 above.

28. The case of a parallel shift in the demand and supply functions for investment can be expressed in the following modification of equation 16:

$$h\frac{(a+\pi)k}{1-kd}=hs \qquad \text{(16a)}$$

where h measures the change in the rate of growth and in the savings ratio as the ratio between the new and the old level of these two magnitudes. If interpreted as an "ex post" relationship, the above equation is of course a truism. The problem to which I want to draw attention is posed by the structural shifts within the aggregate, which are enforced by the transition from the state described in equation 16 to that described in equation 16a.

22 "All that is required for the argument immediately to follow is that any changes in s, i.e. savings expressed as a fraction of income, should be small by comparison with experimental changes in G" (Harrod, *op. cit.*, p. 79). The same position is taken by E. D. Domar, "The Problem of Capital Accumulation," *American Economic Review*, December 1948, p. 779, though the inherent assumption of factor mobility is realized.

To follow up these shifts I assume that, with a constant coefficient of capital depth, the rate of population growth falls and that the savings ratio adjusts itself immediately. Even though these shifts are simultaneous, the structure of production is now in disequilibrium. To regain equilibrium, the output of consumer goods and of secondary equipment must rise (in accord with the rise in the average propensity to consume) relative to the output of primary equipment. This change in the output ratio between groups z and b, on the one hand, and group a, on the other hand, depends upon a corresponding reshuffling of factors. Some primary equipment and labor, which under the previous higher rate of absorption produced additional primary machinery, will now have to produce more secondary machinery. This, however, will not keep the total previous stock of primary equipment fully employed. It is true that, once the new dynamic equilibrium has been reached, the *aggregate* stock of primary and secondary equipment equals the aggregate stock that would exist had the rate of growth not fallen. But the share of the secondary equipment stock in the aggregate is now higher, and the share of the primary equipment stock is reduced correspondingly. Therefore, some primary equipment must be scrapped or at least kept idle until the system grows into the existing capacity, always assuming that, for reasons of specificity, it cannot be used as secondary equipment.

A similar though less drastic friction arises in the labor market. More labor is now needed to mind machines in group z, whereas some labor formerly employed in making machines in group a will be displaced. Labor is never so specialized that gradual transfer cannot take place. But whether and when such adjustment, and with it the approach to a new equilibrium, will occur depends upon what effect capital devaluation and temporary unemployment in group a will have on entrepreneurs' expectations and behavior.

Here the limits of structural analysis have been reached and functional analysis, the study of behavior patterns, must take over if the actual stability conditions are to be established. In a general way one may venture the guess that adjustment hangs in the balance, to say the least, if the magnitude of h is considerable and the shift occurs suddenly. The coincidence of both circumstances in a "strong" boom makes this phase of the cycle highly unstable.[23]

[23] In this context see my critique of Hicks in "A Structural Model of Production," *Social Research*, June 1952, pp. 168-173. Though I still maintain my objections to Hicks' explanation of the downturn, in the light of the above

Thus dynamic equilibrium through time is assured only if major shifts among the groups can be excluded. This is equivalent to saying that the Harrod-Domar conditions must be fulfilled for each one of the three groups—the postulate contained in the above formulation of the equilibrium conditions in equations 18 and 19.

A measure for the waste in primary equipment, which a parallel downward shift of the savings and the investment functions creates, can easily be ascertained by comparing the size of the stock necessary to sustain the higher rate of growth with that required to sustain the lower one. The former equals

$$St\,A(\text{vailable})_{a+b} = (a_{dy} + b_{dy})k$$

Using equation 20, we can transform this into

$$St\,A_{a+b} = [(1-s)kd + s]ko$$

If the change in the rate of growth, expressed as the ratio between the new and the old rate of growth, equals h, the new stock of primary equipment required equals

$$St\,R_{a+b} = [(1-sh)kd + sh]ko$$

Waste, which is equal to the difference between the two expressions, then is

$$W' = sk(1-h)(1-kd)o \tag{21}$$

W' varies directly with the size of the capital coefficient and the original savings ratio, and inversely with the change in the rate of growth. If h is positive—that is, if the rate of growth increases—waste is "negative." Then equation 21 measures the additional amount of primary equipment required for the system to adjust to the new rate.

A comment is in order on the relationship between the two kinds of waste, which are determined by equations 12 and 21 respectively. They refer to quite different phenomena. The term W, waste due to "overbuilding," indicates that actual investment overshoots the fixed target of required investment. The term W', waste due to a parallel shift in the demand and supply functions for investment, indicates that the investment target itself changes in the downward direction. If it changes in the upward direction, W' is

considerations my own conclusions as stated in the article seem to me now in need of some more "pessimistic" modification.

negative. But there is then no positive W either, since no "overbuilding" can occur so long as the new, higher rate of growth is maintained.

It may well be asked whether the functional obstacles which obstruct adjustment to a falling rate of growth interfere also with adjustment to a rising rate of growth. At the beginning of such a change some secondary equipment and the labor operating it will certainly be displaced. Absolute specificity completely prevents the former from being shifted to group a, and the latter can at best be shifted with some delay. One might argue that the effect of structural frictions upon expectations is less destabilizing in an expanding than in a contracting system. But in the former case an investment decision must be made, while in the latter case output can follow the price signals of a rising consumer demand. Whatever the ultimate conclusion may be, a parallel shift of the savings and investment functions establishes an interesting mechanism. It brings about a change in the income-expenditure structure which as such does not distort the structure itself. This lack of distortion is probably the reason why Harrod and Domar pay no attention to such parallel shifts. However, the change in the income-expenditure structure indirectly causes a distortion of the technical structure. This secondary distortion may in its turn destabilize the income-expenditure structure after all.

29. The second alternative—namely, a relative change in the investment demand and the investment supply functions—can be expressed by the following inequality:

$$s \gtrless \frac{(a + \pi)k}{1 - kd}$$

The s refers of course to planned savings, whereas the right side defines planned investment. With regard to the effect that such an inequality is likely to have upon the stability of dynamic equilibrium, I have little to add to the insights which the discussion of Harrod's and Domar's work has brought to light during the last few years.[24] Since, as in the previous case, the conclusions must ultimately be derived from behavioral premises, they are again a task for functional rather than for structural analysis. But a brief digression into this area may be of value at this point. It will bring to light the special contribution that structural analysis makes to

[24] See in particular the writings of Sidney Alexander, W. J. Baumol, Joan Robinson, and T. C. Schelling.

"total" analysis. I choose for this purpose the case of potential oversaving, which, in the wake of the Keynesian challenge, was long the center of attention, and which still forms a subject of controversy between Keynesians and certain neoclassicists.[25] The reader will easily be able to apply the argument to potential undersaving.

According to the traditional neoclassical position, an excess of planned savings over planned investment will be adjusted either by a rise in the average capital depth of the system or by a harmless *numéraire* deflation. The link is the depressing effect which potential oversaving is supposed to exert upon the rate of interest, which in its turn is supposed to induce an increase in the demand for capital goods per unit of labor.

The objections to this harmonistic solution concern both links of the argument. First of all, the rate of interest may not fall at all. The initial excess of planned savings over investment must reduce demand for and prices of consumer goods. This is likely to create elastic price expectations all around and increase the demand for cash. But even if the rate of interest were to fall, the situation in the consumer goods market just described would hardly be conducive to an expansion of investment. Thus in either case the result will be a fall in aggregate employment with all the latent dangers of a general "real" deflation.

So far everybody has won and all must have prizes. But this is so only because the two parties argue at cross purposes, implicitly assuming different types of technical structure. The neoclassical argument is correct for a perfectly mobile structure, where absence of specificity reduces the period of constructing additional capital goods to an insignificant length. In this structure the fall in consumer goods output can at once be balanced by a rise in the output of producers goods, leaving the elasticity of price expectations unchanged. Far from obstructing adjustment, the fall in consumer goods output is the very condition for an equilibrating shift of factors from groups z and b to group a. Even if the rate of interest should not fall sufficiently, or the investment elasticity of such a fall should be small, the ensuing general fall of commodity and factor prices (as a result of the "hoarding" of savings, to use old-

[25] See, e.g., the controversy between Domar and E. H. Stern in *American Economic Review*, December 1949, pp. 1160-1172, and, more recently, Harold Pilvin, "Full Capacity vs. Full Employment Growth," *Quarterly Journal of Economics*, November 1953, pp. 545-552, together with R. F. Harrod's "Comment," *ibid.*, pp. 553-559.

fashioned language) need not affect the real magnitudes of the system. When perfect mobility prevails, the downward adjustment of the *numéraire* can take place simultaneously and in the very short run all over the system, leaving expectations again unaffected. The maximum permissible length of this "short run" can be determined. It must not exceed the shortest of the various income periods in the system (i.e. one week, under present institutional arrangements). If it is longer, factor unemployment cumulates and the monetary deflation deteriorates into a depression.

One has only to spell out its implicit conditions to realize that the neoclassical argument is completely unrealistic in an industrial system. But it is equally clear that it is the lags in the adjustment process due to specificity, especially of equipment goods, and the consequent *longue durée* of the construction period that create cumulative unemployment with its detrimental effect upon the elasticity of price expectations. Whatever justification there is for the Harrod-Domar pessimism with regard to the stability of dynamic equilibrium—and there is a good deal—it rests ultimately upon the technical rigidity of an industrial order of production.

This result is not accidental. Though the proposition cannot be proven in the context of the present paper, it can be stated as a general rule that to endanger the stability of the system, distortions of the income-expenditure structure must influence expectations in a particular manner. Whether they do so or not is largely dependent on the length of the potential adjustment period, which in its turn is directly related to the prevailing technical structure.[26]

In summarizing this discussion of the consequences that possible changes in the strategic variables can have for the stability of dynamic equilibrium, we can distinguish between three levels of progressively restrictive conditions. The optimistic extreme is represented by the traditional neoclassical approach, which disregards all aspects of specificity. There capital depth is treated as a variable, which changes inversely with a highly sensitive rate of interest. Since any shock arising from a change in either the rate of growth or the savings ratio can be absorbed without delay by a change in k, dynamic equilibrium is stable.

An intermediate position is taken by Harrod and Domar. They treat k as a constant; therefore, changes in the rate of growth relative to the savings ratio cannot be absorbed without frictions and pre-

[26] For a more detailed exposition see my paper "On the Mechanistic Approach in Economics," as cited.

carious consequences for expectations. But so long as $s/(a + \pi)$ and therefore k remain constant, dynamic equilibrium once existing is stable, though it may shift from one level of activity to another one.

The most restrictive conditions for dynamic equilibrium have been postulated above. Not only the fraction $s/(a + \pi)$ and thus capital depth, but both the numerator and the denominator of the fraction, that is, the savings ratio as well as the rate of growth, must remain constant in order to prevent destabilizing structural shifts among the groups of production.

Nonneutral Technical Changes

30. The theory of technical change is still a stepchild of economic analysis. The sweeping generalizations of Marx and Schumpeter have not been followed by more detailed macroeconomic investigations. In Keynesian economics technical change figures as no more than one investment variable among others. More recent work, e.g. the writings of Yale Brozen or William Fellner, has by and large taken a microeconomic turn. Therefore, I shall have to introduce my structural analysis with some more general remarks, to determine, first of all, the context in which macroeconomic problems of capital formation arise when technical changes disturb dynamic equilibrium.

In order to narrow the field, the following observations will be confined to *cost-reducing* technical changes, to the exclusion of *want-creating* innovations, or, to use the customary term, "new products." If I read the literature correctly, the latter have so far proved refractory to exact analysis, due mainly to two complications. First, they introduce a simultaneous change in both the supply and the demand function; second, since the product is "new," the change in the supply function cannot be related to any previously existing supply function—the main difference from cost-reducing changes. Thus what follows refers only to "technical progress" in the narrower sense.

In contradistinction to what was discussed earlier, in section 20, here only "nonneutral" technical changes will be considered. Harrod's definition of neutrality, which was adopted above, refers to a proportional rise of output and capital stock, leaving k unchanged. Harrod is fully aware that this definition implies an assumption about the relative demand for factors in the new state as compared with the old. By a neutral advance "the productivity of labor embodied in machines is raised in equal measure with that of those engaged in minding machines."[27] In other words, neutral advances are neither labor-displacing nor capital-displacing.

These considerations yield a convenient definition of nonneutral technical changes. They comprise all changes that cause at least temporary displacement of one or more factors somewhere in the system, though not necessarily in the industry which introduces the change. It is the kind and size of such displacement, and the manner in which the displaced factors can be reabsorbed (what Continental economists have called the "compensation" problem), that are in the center of the structural analysis of nonneutral technical changes, so far as capital formation is concerned.

In the conventional manner I distinguish between labor-displacing and capital-displacing changes. Within each of these two subgroups there are three different types, according to whether, per unit of output, units of both factors are displaced or, whether, with units of one factor displaced, the employment of the other remains constant or even increases. It is highly desirable to find an economic indicator for distinguishing the five possible cases (one case appears in both subgroups). For this purpose, I list in the following table the manner in which each type modifies capital depth, capital intensity, capital productivity, and labor productivity, in the sense in which these terms have been defined in section 11 above.

Types of Technical Change	*Capital Depth*	*Capital Intensity*	*Capital Productivity*	*Labor Productivity*
1. Pure labor-displacing	constant	rising	constant	rising
2. Labor-displacing, capital-displacing	falling	?	rising	rising
3. Labor-displacing, capital-attracting	rising	rising	falling	rising
4. Pure capital-displacing	falling	falling	rising	constant
(5. Capital-displacing, labor-displacing)	falling	?	rising	rising
6. Capital-displacing, labor-attracting	falling	falling	rising	falling

It is at once clear that neither capital depth nor capital intensity is a good criterion, because quite different types of change affect these coefficients in the same manner. This is also true of the two productivity coefficients if only one of them is taken as indicator. If, however, capital productivity is used to characterize the types of labor-displacing changes, and labor productivity to characterize the types of capital-displacing changes, a clear distinction can be

[27] Harrod, *op. cit.*, p. 23.

established.[28] All five cases have empirical significance. Because each type can materialize simultaneously in all three groups, or in any two or in only one, because different types can materialize simultaneously in different groups, and furthermore because capital displacement can refer to fixed as well as to working capital goods, the number of possible models exceeds any manageable range. But in each case the same structural principle is at work, so that the selection of a few simple cases will suffice to formulate the basic problems and to indicate their solution.

I shall concentrate upon pure labor-displacing changes and supplement the results with only brief comments upon type 3, labor-displacing and capital-attracting changes, and type 4, pure capital-displacing changes. The capital change in both cases will be confined to changes in fixed capital. In accord with the general tenor of this paper, only problems related to capital formation will be discussed, to the exclusion of the productivity effects, private or social, and the distributive effects of technical changes.

31. As indicated above, structural problems of capital formation arise in two phases of the innovation process: one at the beginning if the introduction of the new device requires a change in the fixed capital applied; the other when the operation of the new device has displaced some factors of production, the reabsorption of which requires additional real capital. In trying to design models for these problems we are confronted with two alternatives. We can choose as our general frame of reference an economic process in equilibrium, stationary or dynamic, or—an alternative more appropriate for the past history of capitalism—a process in which part of the available resources are idle. Obviously the task of "capital construction" is greatly facilitated in both phases of adjustment if idle capacity exists in the two equipment goods groups. On the other hand, such a frame of reference inevitably involves the whole complex of business cycle analysis. Pursuing this line not only would take us far afield, but would also prevent us from studying the structural issues in isolation. The analysis will therefore be continued within the framework of dynamic equilibrium. Considering the bottlenecks referred to earlier, which nowadays obstruct smooth adjustment to large changes

[28] If depreciation rates should vary inversely with the change in capital stock, new complications would be introduced. They could be taken care of only by explicit reference to the behavior of the depreciation rate. In order not to complicate our analysis, I shall, during the subsequent exposition, assume an unchanged rate of depreciation.

in the rate of change in both developed and underdeveloped countries, the alternative chosen recommends itself also on practical grounds.

These assumptions yield a simple solution of the "construction" problem. It does not arise in a pure labor-displacing technical change because the value—that is, the claim upon factors though not necessarily the physical form of the equipment stock—remains unchanged by definition. This presupposes, of course, that the change-over to the new technique takes place after the old equipment is fully amortized. On the other hand, a construction problem does arise in capital-attracting changes, as does a problem of capital liquidation in capital-displacing changes. For either case the preceding analysis of once-over changes and of a downward shift of the investment function can be used. What was said, for example, about the "construction period" (section 19) and the two types of waste (sections 18 and 28) is fully applicable here.

The problem of "compensation" is more complex. There is, above all, no general agreement that compensation is a "secular-period" problem in the Marshallian sense, or, in other words, that the reabsorption of technologically displaced labor really requires prior capital formation. It is not possible to pursue this question through all its ramifications at this time, and a few remarks must suffice to justify the position taken below.[29]

Starting from a pure labor-displacing device, three short-period solutions of the compensation problem have been suggested since the days when Ricardo deserted the harmonist camp in the chapter "On Machinery." One points to compensating "demand," arising either from the profits of the technical pioneer or, if the improvement is generalized over the whole industry, from the rise in consumer real income resulting from the fall in price of the improved output. Whatever one may think about the cogency of this argument,[30] it certainly implies capital formation in those fields toward which the alleged increase in aggregate demand turns.

[29] For a more systematic treatment see my paper on "Technological Unemployment Reexamined," in *Wirtschaft und Kultursystem*, G. Eisermann, editor, Erlenbach-Zuerich, Eugen Rentsch Verlag, 1955, pp. 229-254.

[30] The proposition that aggregate demand for commodities rises, in the manner postulated, above aggregate supply and thus raises demand for labor to the equilibrium level is highly dubious. Since the displacement of workers also initially reduces demand, a compensating demand of pioneers or consumers seems required to restore equilibrium between supply and demand within the smaller flow of production from which the displaced workers are eliminated.

The second solution hinges upon the variability of factor proportions. In its most extreme version the argument asserts that any amount of idle labor can always be employed on the *existing* capital stock, if only wages adjust to the declining marginal productivity. Now under conditions of factor specificity, as they prevail in an industrial system, the argument cannot refer to the physical form of the existing capital stock, but only to its value. In other words, compensation is then a long-period problem, depending upon the prior transformation of the existing stock of capital goods into a physically different one. Such transformation will not by itself create any friction if the change-over coincides with the moment when the old equipment must be replaced anyhow. But while firms can plan "construction" in this manner, there is no mechanism which assures such a happy coincidence in the case of compensation. If the two points of time differ, compensation is again conditional upon the formation of new real capital.

The third solution is Ricardo's own: employment of displaced workers in occupations which do not require fixed capital, such as menial services and—happy age!—warfare. The wide range of "services" offered in any depression is an indication that this solution is not without practical relevance. The general trend of modern industrialism toward "tertiary" occupations at the expense of "secondary" ones may indeed provide a safety valve for *secular* technological unemployment of a steady nature. But it is unlikely to absorb the shocks which arise from large discontinuous innovations of a labor-displacing character.

However, the adherents of short-period compensation may point to the fact that many of these discontinuous innovations are at the same time capital-attracting. In this case the compensation issue, far from creating an adjustment problem, seems to alleviate the difficulties bound up with the initial construction phase. By creating another need for capital formation, compensation of technological unemployment offers work to the additional stock of primary equipment which had to be built to make the initial capital expansion possible, and may thus preclude "waste." The argument certainly deserves consideration. But it is decisive only when the capital depth of the initial investment approximates that of the compensation investment, and even then only over the period during which the compensating equipment must be built. After this second construction period the waste problem again appears, though somewhat mitigated by the need for larger replacements, which have now to maintain two capital stocks.

From all these observations it appears that large, sudden, and highly productive innovations of a labor-displacing nature do pose a problem of capital formation (as capital-displacing changes pose a problem of capital liquidation). Therefore, the results obtained above for the length of the construction period and for waste can again be utilized. But they now require an important modification, because nonneutral technical changes alter permanently the relative scarcity of labor and equipment. This is equivalent to saying that the factors have to be reshuffled among the three groups before the new equilibrium can be attained. This new shift in the group ratios is much more complicated than the adjustment to changes in the over-all rate of growth, discussed above (sections 22-29).

32. Limitations of space permit the detailed exposition of such a shift for only the simplest case, namely, a pure labor-displacing improvement occurring in the consumer goods group. Given a system in dynamic equilibrium as described in equation 20, and also the ratio of workers displaced in group z to workers originally employed there, how will the group ratios, which describe the new equilibrium after compensation, differ from the original? To aid the comparison it is assumed that the supply of money is kept constant, so that output prices adjust to the fall in unit costs which results from the reduction of labor costs.

The principal link between the two equilibria is a systematic rise in the capital depth of the critical group z. This rise in capital depth can be derived from the more obvious rise in capital intensity, which is only another way of saying that less labor is now applied per unit of capital.[31]

The general relationship between capital intensity c (see section 11) and k can be established as follows:

$$c = \frac{F}{n_v} = \frac{ok}{o - f} = \frac{ok}{o - kdo} = \frac{k}{1 - kd}$$

or

$$k = \frac{c}{1 + cd}$$

[31] It may be appropriate to stress once more the fact that both capital depth and capital intensity are understood here in value terms.

Denoting the displacement ratio as defined above by δ_z, we have

$$c_{z_1} = \frac{c_{z_0}}{1 - \delta_z}$$

where the subscripts 0 and 1 refer to the original and subsequent equilibrium respectively. Therefore,

$$(22) \qquad k_{z_1} = \frac{c_{z_0}}{1 - \delta_z + c_{z_0} d_{z_0}} = \frac{k_{z_0}}{1 - \delta_z(1 - k_{z_0} d_{z_0})}$$

Since the technical change is confined to group z, no change in capital depth occurs in groups a and b, so that $k_{b_1} = k_{b_0}$ and $k_{a_1} = k_{a_0}$. By simply substituting $k_{z_1} = k_{z_0}$ in equation 20, the group ratios in the new equilibrium can be established.

It is now possible to determine the capital requirements upon which compensation depends. The new group ratios in combination with the respective capital depth coefficients yield the new ratios among the capital stocks of the three groups, from which the absolute capital increments can be calculated for any given absolute level of the original output. Our previous investigations supply the tools for determining the length of the construction period required for compensation and the size of capital waste occurring, if any. As a matter of fact, since innovations are the prime cause of uneven changes in the rate of growth, it is in this context that these tools prove their usefulness.

There is, however, an additional obstacle to short-run compensation. It is immediately clear that, in view of the change in capital intensity and capital depth in group z, all workers originally displaced cannot be re-employed there. Some of them must be shifted to groups a and b to produce, and subsequently to replace, the addition to the capital stock required in group z. A measure can be devised for the required shift which at the same time expresses the resistance that labor specificity offers to short-run adjustment. Such a measure is the shift ratio γ_z, that is, the number of workers displaced in group z that must be shifted to groups a and b relative to the total number of workers originally displaced in group z. It can be determined as follows:[32]

[32] The term N symbolizes here the number of workers, labor being treated in the interest of simplification as the sole income-receiving factor. This term is supposed to be uniquely related in all groups to the value input of labor per period. In this interpretation N is a stock magnitude equivalent to F, with a depreciation rate equal to N_v/n_v. (For this interpretation see section 6).

$$\gamma_z = \frac{N_{z_0} - N_{z_1}}{N_{z_0}\delta_z} = \frac{n_{z_0} - n_{z_1}}{n_{z_0}\delta_z}$$

since $n_z = z - f_z = (1 - k_z d_z)z$, we obtain

$$\gamma_z = \left[1 - \frac{1 - k_{z_1}d_{z_1}}{1 - k_{z_0}d_{z_0}}\right]\frac{1}{\delta_z}$$

According to our previous assumption (footnote 28), the rates of depreciation are not supposed to change. Therefore, by substituting for k_{z_1} the expression obtained in equation 22, we have

(23) $$\gamma_z = \frac{k_{z_0}d_{z_0}}{1 - \delta_z(1 - k_{z_0}d_{z_0})}$$

If instead of being purely labor-displacing, the technical change is at the same time capital-attracting, then

(24) $$k_{z_1} = \frac{k_{z_0}(1 + \beta_z)}{1 - \delta_z(1 - k_{z_0}d_{z_0}) + \beta_z k_{z_0}d_{z_0}}$$

where β_z expresses the increase of the capital stock in group z as the ratio of the increment to the original value of the stock. From this we obtain

(25) $$\gamma_z(\beta_z) = \frac{k_{z_0}d_{z_0}(\delta_z + \beta_z)}{[1 - \delta_z + k_{z_0}d_{z_0}(\delta_z + \beta_z)]\delta_z}$$

33. The general principle expounded in the foregoing section is applicable to all cases of factor-displacing innovations. However, in most cases additional considerations must be taken into account, of which two are briefly indicated here.

First, whenever labor-displacing innovations are introduced in one or both equipment goods groups, technology in the consumer goods group remaining unchanged, one might expect that the value capital depth coefficients would change in the innovating groups. In fact this is not so, because the value of the *input* "equipment" adjusts itself in the new equilibrium to the increased productivity—that is, to the value of its *output*, which itself is equipment. Therefore, both the value of the capital stock and that of output must fall in the same proportion, leaving the quotient k unchanged. On the other hand, the price fall of secondary equipment because of the technical change in group *a* and/or group *b* must affect the value of the capital stock in group *z*, reducing there the value capital depth coefficient although the physical-technical combination of the factors has not itself changed.

Second, in applying our procedure to capital-displacing improvements, we must remember that such changes *reduce* both value capital intensity and value capital depth in the innovating groups. Thus the effect is just the opposite of that which arises from labor-displacing changes. This enables us to treat capital-displacing changes as labor-attracting changes. To give an example, for a pure capital-displacing change in the consumer goods group we have only to substitute $1/(1-\delta)$ for $1-\delta$ in equation 22. We then obtain the critical coefficient k_z, with the help of which the shift ratio and the new group ratios can be derived in the manner described.

5. *Application: "Ideal" and "Real" Models*

34. As stated in the Introduction, this paper is concerned only with the structural part of the theory of dynamic processes. Within this area two main problems have been studied: (1) the minimum capital requirements for various types of economic growth, and (2) the optimum paths that the system must follow in order to readjust the dislocations that different types of growth inflict upon a pre-existing state of stationary or dynamic equilibrium, "minimum" and "optimum" to be related to minimum waste of resources and/or maximum speed of adjustment. A final question remains to be answered: Are the results of such structural analysis useful in helping to solve the empirical growth problems which arise in advanced as well as in backward economic systems?

From the outset it is readily admitted that, in an empirical science, the effort spent upon the construction of "models" can be ultimately justified only by what they contribute to the understanding of real phenomena. In order to pass this test our structural models need elaboration in at least two directions. First, the level of abstraction will have to be reduced below the one chosen in the foregoing exposition, which is appropriate to pure theory only. Second, and more important, we have so far been concerned almost exclusively with "structural" relations and movements, that is, with the impersonal conditions for the absorption of dynamic shocks. But, as was stressed in the beginning, no practical economic problem can even be posed, not to say solved, without due regard to the personal forces as manifested in the motivations and behavior patterns of the actors. To formulate the general principle in the terminology established above: Only when combined with functional analysis can structural analysis be "applied."

However, even when supplemented by a study of the appropriate motivations and behavior patterns, structural analysis of the type performed above will never yield a "real" model, that is, a simplified image of any actual growth process. We have to remember that we have not been concerned with the *descriptive* analysis of structural relations and movements as they occur in empirical systems in historical time, but with *normative* analysis, that is, with the structural requirements for the optimal achievement of a postulated goal, say, equilibrating growth. Were we to extend our analysis to the functional conditions required to hold the system to the structurally required path, we should be able to fill the lacunae in our "ideal" models, but reality, that is, actual behavior and the real structure that emanates from it, would still escape us.

This gulf between "ideal" and "real" models is perhaps less wide in a collectivist system. There the actual dispositions of the planning authority reflect what, under the aspect of the chosen "holistic" goal, are regarded as required structure and required behavior. Any deviation of the "real" from the "ideal" behavior is then treated as illegitimate, and as a subject for the penal code rather than for economic study. No such concurrence prevails in a free market system, where the real order of the whole is not based on holistic decisions but is the result of the independent decisions of the "particles." If we want to construct models of the ensuing real processes, we have to study the actual motivations and behavior patterns that prevail in the actual structure under observation, and to derive from them the actual paths of adjustment to change. Obviously this task is beyond the reach of the purely deductive method with the help of which our "ideal" models are established; it can be accomplished only with the help of inductive procedures which, in particular, should tell us what the actual behavior patterns are in a given situation.

Thus our results have, in principle, nothing to contribute to the description of actual growth processes, and even less to the prediction of their future course. However, by establishing what, relative to certain postulated goals, are the most economical forms of growth, they yield the "efficiency norms" by which the performance of empirical growth processes must be judged. They present an image of "perfect" growth, and thus point up and locate the structural and functional deficiencies of any empirical system under observation. By disclosing at the same time the structural relations and functional forces most appropriate to optimum performance, our "ideal" models offer guidance for the improvement of the real processes, and are thus the scientific foundation for economic policy. A few remarks on some practical issues to which our findings can be applied in this manner are to bring these observations to a close.

35. It is not claimed that the models of once-over and continuous growth described above exhaust the possible range of dynamic processes. Above all, they are concerned only with "exogenous" shocks, to the exclusion of those endogenous changes which, following Frisch's example, modern econometrics has placed in the center of its dynamic investigations. But the number of practically relevant dynamic processes is few, if attention is focused upon the formal properties of rise and fall, continuity and discontinuity, proportionality and disproportionality.

Each of the models discussed above can be associated with one or more characteristic growth phenomena which have appeared during the era of world-wide industrialization. Our "ideal" model of once-over growth has some sort of empirical replica in the processes by which a "stationary" preindustrial system moves off dead center into "development." It is hardly necessary to stress the essential difference between the model underlying the analysis in Part 2 and the real structure of any underdeveloped country: the almost complete absence in the latter of groups *b* and *a*. But this very difference emphasizes the strategic position of real capital formation, that is, the nature and duration of the processes by which real capital is built.

How easily this aspect of the developmental process can be lost sight of is apparent in an otherwise most interesting attempt at utilizing structural analysis for practical purposes. I refer to H. W. Singer's essay on "The Mechanics of Economic Development."[33] There the Harrod-Domar formula for dynamic equilibrium is used to determine for certain parametric values the relationship between the rate of development, the rate of population increase, capital productivity, and savings. On the basis of what he regards as plausible parameters, Singer concludes that autonomous development not supported by capital imports is practically impossible.

I come to the same conclusion, but for different reasons. For

[33] *Indian Economic Review*, Vol. 1, No. 2, 1952, esp. pp. 15-18.

Singer the main obstacle lies in the size of the capital depth coefficient for developmental investment, which he puts at 5. With this assumption, a savings ratio of more than 16 per cent would be required to sustain a population increase of 1.25 per cent per year and an annual increase of real income of 2 per cent. But unless most of the new investment consists of "social overhead capital" like transportation, irrigation, etc., a capital depth coefficient of 5 seems much too high. If development were to concentrate on manufacturing projects with an average depth coefficient of slightly under 2, the developmental goal might be reached with a savings ratio of only 6 per cent, which Singer regards as a feasible level. In other words, with this one change in the empirical parameters, autonomous development does not seem to encounter any obstacles.

It is against such optimism that our structural analysis guards. The Harrod-Domar formula (equation 16) tells us what rate of growth can be sustained with a given savings ratio, *once the primary real capital necessary for such growth has been formed.* It does not reveal anything about the period of construction, which separates the moment when consumption shrinks because of saving from the moment when real capital has expanded sufficiently for additional consumer goods to reach the market. We saw above that this period of construction is positively correlated with the period of maturation in the field of equipment goods production, and negatively correlated with the originally available stock of real capital. In both respects the typical underdeveloped country is placed most unfavorably, and the "waiting period" during which savings depress the standard of living may extend over many years, unless capital imports alleviate the situation. Therefore, a savings ratio that can be regarded as tolerable once development has actually started, may prove far too high to move the system off dead center.

The next step would then lead to an analysis of the structural consequences of importing real capital from abroad. They obviously differ according to whether the imports consist of primary equipment or secondary equipment. The latter case seems typical for the early stages of industrialization. But there is at least one example—the Soviet Union—in which emphasis was placed from the beginning upon primary equipment. In either case the construction period is drastically reduced. The short-run benefits to the consumer are greatest with imports consisting of secondary equipment. They are pure gains, which do not require even temporary sacrifices in the standard of living, if the real capital can be borrowed under such conditions that the current productivity increase exceeds interest and amortization, and if an equivalent of the current service on the foreign debt is physically adapted to the demand for exports. But even if the equipment imports have to be paid for by consumer goods exports, foreign trade is a much speedier method of physical transformation than domestic investment.

36. Scattered remarks about the "maturity" issue have already pointed to the potential use of our structural models for the secular growth problems of developed countries. As was stated before, whereas capital formation creates a difficult *bottleneck* in the early stages of industrialization, in the later stages it is the need for interindustry *shifts of resources* and the threat of *capital waste* that, in addition to the bottlenecks related to compensation, delay and deflect the "ideal" adjustment. From this it follows that real growth in developed countries is so closely interrelated with fluctuations that, at least for the past, secular and cyclical problems cannot be studied fruitfully in isolation.

This impression is strengthened by some earlier considerations (section 28) which suggest that the model of once-over growth, superimposed upon the model of continuous growth, might be usefully applied to the analysis of a "strong" boom. To build a structural framework for cyclical analysis one must of course go further. The model of a discontinuous change in a positive rate of growth must be refined on the basis of what can be known of models of nonneutral technical changes. An even more complicated superimposition of change processes—introducing analysis of noncompensated factor displacement—seems required for the study of "weak" booms.

SOME GENERAL REFLECTIONS ON CAPITAL FORMATION AND ECONOMIC GROWTH

W. W. ROSTOW

MASSACHUSETTS INSTITUTE OF TECHNOLOGY

1. *The Theme: Organized Disaggregation*

THE relation between capital formation and economic growth is a large part of the total problem of economic growth. Taking the rate of change of output to be a function of the rate of change in the size and quality of the working force and of the capital stock, this conference is analyzing the total growth problem, leaving the working force aside. And even then, in Levy's paper and elsewhere, the relation of capital formation to the size of the population—and even to the size and quality of the working force (Grossman)—has come into the discussion. We have taken on, then, a considerable and ramified set of issues.

Further, these issues are distinctly revolutionary. There appears to be complete unanimity—reflected in the substance of the papers as well as in the program of the conference—that the relation of capital formation to growth cannot be treated by the conventional tools of short-run economics. We appear to agree that, by definition, we are dealing with problems of rates of change over time rather than with short-period equilibrium; and that continuing changes in capacity, technique, and taste—normally treated exogenously in modern economic theory, or in once-over change exercises—must somehow be introduced endogenously. More than that, we all appear to believe that an understanding of the relation between capital formation and economic growth demands that somehow, at some stage of the analysis, we bring to bear on the relevant economic variables social, political, and cultural forces which affect their net movement.

Because we agree about the range of the relevant variables, we come at this problem from many directions—in academic terms, from many different disciplines. The contributions here range from Lowe's austere theory through a spectrum of generalized but limited insights, based on empirical situations and data, back to that developing branch of social theory represented by Levy's contribution. At the present, early stage of concerted thought on growth, our contributions necessarily must be partial. All the papers presented at the conference discuss one or another of the sub-determinants of the relation between capital formation and economic growth, rather than the relation itself, in its full complexity and grandeur.

We are, then, trying to make diverse bodies of data and diverse social science techniques effectively converge. On this view of our common problem, the present group of papers represent a major stride forward. There is an emergent area of common understanding—sometimes implicit, often explicit—as to how the various pieces of the puzzle fit together. There is more here than mere courteous acknowledgment that each has a right to his private line of approach. Not only is there agreement that we each have hold of a piece of the elephant; a consensus on the elephant's shape is also beginning to emerge. It is evident that we have been reading each other's articles and books. Before this conference I was inclined to the view that little actual work of synthesis had been done, beyond laudable programmatic statements. The noneconomic variables had not been satisfactorily related to the economics of the growth process. I think we can agree that this conference has made important progress toward this kind of synthesis. Although none of the studies presented for this conference pretend to meet the workmanlike vision of orderly growth analysis that Lowe holds up as a goal, a number of them go an important distance toward linking coherently the disparate variables that determine the relation of capital formation to economic growth.

There is, for example, Aubrey's systematic consideration of the manner in which the conventional profit maximization analysis of capital formation must be modified to fit the context of industrial enterprise in underdeveloped countries. This exercise goes well beyond empirical description. Hoselitz's reflections on British and French entrepreneurship since 1700 are explicitly linked to the relative scale of capital formation and over-all growth rates in the two countries; and Cochran seeks to make American entrepreneurial history illuminate Kuznets' American growth statistics. These papers are not merely summaries of odd institutional evidence. Similarly, Maclaurin's reflections on innovation pose questions of the first order of importance concerning the productivity of different kinds of investment and innovations. There are many other indications throughout these papers that the concerted study of a commonly understood problem is replacing methodological exhortation.

Under these circumstances the evident function of a commentator is to heighten a little our awareness of the links among the various approaches to growth analysis and to open up for general discussion the question of useful next steps. I shall simplify my task by elaborating a single arbitrary theme: the importance of organized disaggregation in growth analysis. This theme is relevant whether we are primarily concerned with making formal theoretical models of the growth process (Lowe); organizing rigorous statistical measures of historical patterns (Kuznets); examining functionally such sub-determinants of growth as the flows of loanable funds (Goldsmith) or the flows of science, invention, and innovation (Usher, Maclaurin, Cochran, and Hoselitz); defining current growth problems in particular settings (Aubrey, Grossman, and Holzman); or examining systematically the noneconomic motives and institutions which help determine the economic outcome (Levy). In all these tasks we must try increasingly to link the aggregate variables to organized knowledge of the components and sectors of which they are composed.

2. *Disaggregation and Growth Models*

It follows from this central theme that I have found the argument of Lowe generally sympathetic and suggestive. Although couched in the language of growth, the theoretical exercises of Harrod, Domar, Hicks, and Goodwin (and others) have not been concerned with the variables determining differences in the rate and structure of growth. Their primary purpose has been to demonstrate that the growth process is likely to proceed in unstable cycles of unemployment. By introducing a degree of disaggregation and by setting in motion some of the variables usually frozen in growth models, Lowe has linked income analysis to the problems of changing economic structure. He opens for formal examination the relations between over-all growth and the changing levels of sectorial capacity within the economy; and he makes clear the significance of the timing and sequence of structural change for cyclical and other disturbances.

The principal exercises on which Lowe concentrates are a once-over change in labor supply, the relation between changes in the consumption function and the structure of the economy, and the problem of factor displacement in technical change. These are all important cases. They permit Lowe to bring within the scope of rigorous formal treatment those problems in economic growth which are generally dealt with *ad hoc*, if at all.

At the end of his paper Lowe speculates on two major issues which belong high on the agenda for further analysis: first, the question of the capital-output ratio;[1] second, the manner in which formal theoretical analysis can be related systematically to psychological, sociological, political, legal, and other variables which shape the growth process in real life.

I am convinced that we require far more extensive empirical analysis of the relation between changes in the capital stock and its total consequences for the level of output than we now have available.[2] An improved understanding of the past and of relative growth rates among contemporary industrialized societies hinges on a clarification of the determinants of the productivity of different kinds of investment at different stages in the growth sequence. Our ability to prescribe appropriate patterns of investment for underdeveloped areas will also depend on the refinement of such knowledge.

We will have to go behind such global estimates of the capital-output ratio as those used by Lowe in his discussion of Singer's estimates (pages 632-633). The capital-output ratio as currently used is, after all, a kind of index number. Its level (and especially the interpretation of changes in it, or of differences in its level as among different areas) can only be understood in the light of an understanding of its components. Those who are now attempting to plan the pattern of investment outlays in underdeveloped countries make more or less explicit assumptions not merely about the total capital-output ratio but also about the short- and long-period effects on the level of output of investment in particular sectors; and they take into account not only sectoral differences but the cost of noncapital inputs as well. I would suggest that there is a weaker case for using over-all capital-output ratios than there ever was for focusing attention on over-all price or production indexes.

The lines of thought suggested in Lowe's paper which link savings-consumption balances to the structural problems of growth deserve to be pursued. But without losing touch with the aggregates which make up his (or other possible) growth equations, we might

[1] The imperfections and ambiguities of the capital-output ratio as a general measure of capital productivity are being examined by others and will not be discussed in the present paper.

[2] The author developed this theme at length in his unpublished paper presented before the 1953 conference of the International Economic Association at Santa Marguerita, Italy, "Trends in the Allocation of Resources in Secular Growth."

usefully disaggregate our analyses beyond the level of his theoretical structure.

Over any particular period, in any national or regional economy which is growing, the growth process is carried forward by a relatively few major sectors. These may incorporate new technical possibilities, like the early British textile factories; they may reflect fundamental political decisions of the society, like the post-1945 boom in the armament industries of the world; they may reflect a newly indulged taste, as real income rises, like American suburban housing. These leading sectors set in motion behind them a whole train of secondary effective demands as, for example, suburbanization elevates the demand for automobiles and new commercial construction. Historically these leading sectors create external economies which facilitated the development of new leading sectors as the momentum of the old ones decreased. Thus, for example, the textile engineering firms moved into locomotives; and a steel industry built on rails turned easily to machine tools. In the end, the structural categories suggested by old-fashioned capital theory or by the categories of modern income analysis will have to be pierced to the point where the structural characteristics of growth can be examined with an intimacy and particularity Lowe does not attempt.

3. *Disaggregation and Statistical Analyses of Growth*

My observations on Kuznets' statistical essay relate closely to those I have made on Lowe's theoretical paper. Kuznets' work has produced an orderly body of data on the relation of capital formation to national product. In particular, he makes possible a quantitative assessment of the historical role of international capital movements in modern economic development.

Those who contribute statistical clarity to the murky field of economic growth put us especially in their debt. They have a right as well as a need to work within narrow analytic boundaries. The particular limitation that Kuznets accepts at the present stage is to postpone the measurement of the relation of capital formation to the rate of growth (as opposed to the relation between capital formation and the level of national income). I have no doubt that he has on hand, or ready at hand, systematic information on this central quantitative relationship. In fact, in his equally valuable statistical study, Goldsmith gives us (page 115) a table of growth rates which might be directly linked to Kuznets' figures on the proportion of national income invested at various stages in the growth process of Western nations. A portion of Kuznets' subject is, of course, narrower and more sharply focused than the over-all relation between capital formation and growth rates. He is concerned to measure roughly the quantitative importance of international capital flows, and to speculate on the meaning of the proportions that emerge.

When, as will surely happen, other analysts exploit this statistical breakthrough, they will have to proceed in terms not merely of the over-all scale (or proportion) of capital flows but of the particular directions in which they were used by the capital-importing nation. The story of international capital investment is tied up with particular stages in the growth of particular economies, and even with the situation in particular sectors. The capital exports from Britain in the 1830's, for example, can be understood substantially in terms of the world cotton market and the extension of cotton lands in the American South which proceeded in response to current and prospective cotton prices. At later stages in Anglo-American history, substantial British flows are intimately associated with wheat and railroads. In the late 1880's the major flows from London result from the emergence of the Argentine into some kind of political stability, which permitted it to bid for resources to finance basic port, railroad, and other facilities. To understand and to interpret fully the aggregate data Kuznets has supplied, we will have to study the components and examine the recognizable process which led to the ebb and flow of international funds.

I would suggest that Kuznets' generalization that "the volume of international capital exports was restricted primarily because the *supply* of savings available was limited" (page 43) may be modified when the evidence has been examined in the light of his calculations. Although the United States of the 1840's, for example, had immense if not unlimited long-run capital-absorptive capacity, it also had just passed through a land and public works boom in which the British investor lost a substantial part of his shirt. Americans could appear in the City of London in 1840 only at some personal risk; and the British at this stage turned their flows of investment inward to the development of their own railways. The limitation on international capital flows resulted from a changing balance between the attractiveness and the believed degree of risk in various rapidly developing parts of the world, and the attractiveness of home investment. Moreover, the expected (private) rate of return over cost could be high in domestic sectors where demand pressed against capacity, even when no dramatic technological innovations were being introduced or rich new resources were being developed. The determinants of maximum short-run private profitability are not identical with the determinants of a maximum rate of growth.

In the end, of course, the limitation was, as Kuznets says, one of capital supply; for there were usually, in the nineteenth century, claimants on the international capital markets who were turned away. But international capital flows were the result of a somewhat more complex and shifting balance of market incentives and restraints than Kuznets' conclusion might indicate.

Speculating, for a moment, on what would happen if Kuznets' calculations were combined with data (for comparable periods) of the kind presented in Goldsmith's growth rate table, I suspect that we would find significant differences between the proportion of national income invested and the rate of growth, even among advanced countries, as well as differences within countries at different stages in their economic history.[3] Kuznets' pioneering study (1930) on secular movements in production has demonstrated the universality of deceleration in particular sectors of the economy. There seems little doubt that among the forces which determine deceleration in particular industries is a kind of diminishing returns to particular forms of innovation. The capital-output ratio in the British cotton industry in 1790 was almost certainly quite different from that in 1840, 1890, or 1930. The relative long-term stability of the over-all capital-output ratio in certain advanced countries may well emerge as the result of the balancing out of differing rates among different industries at the same period of time, some young, others old. It will only be when we have quantitative knowledge of the capital-output ratio in different sectors of an economy, at different historical stages, that we will be able to understand differing over-all levels, or even relative long-term stability in the over-all level.

Turning now to the other contribution of solid statistical substance (that of Goldsmith) I should like to make one comment in passing, strictly as an economic historian. My field has been bedeviled by a tendency to lapse into institutional description leading virtually nowhere from the economist's point of view. There is hardly a textbook in economic history which does not have its chapters or section devoted to the evolution of financial institutions. Occasionally thrown into these sections are brief and inadequate stories of

[3] See, for example, Brinley Thomas's discussion "Migration and the Rhythm of Economic Growth," *The Manchester School*, September 1951.

financial crises, odd price data, and random reflections on the business cycle. So far as I know, Goldsmith's is the first effort to treat quantitatively the accumulated mass of data on the historical pattern of financial institutions in various countries, and the first effort to link such institutional analysis with the problem of capital supply and economic growth. Aside from its contribution to growth analysis, Goldsmith's paper is an important essay in economic history.

Like those of Kuznets and any others who deal with growth in orderly quantitative terms, Goldsmith's conclusions are limited by the nature and character of his data and the limited distance that he can go quantitatively in coping with the growth process as a whole. Nevertheless, his fundamentally agnostic interim conclusion (pages 158-160) conforms closely to the instinctive answer of an economic historian: namely, that men have made their economic purposes effective in an enormous variety of ways, and one would not expect a simple correspondence between particular kinds of institutions for mobilizing savings and the rate of growth. Modern economic history suggests a certain suspicion of firm correlations between particular institutional patterns (political, cultural, and social, as well as economic) and rates of growth.

One further comment on Goldsmith's paper. I am reasonably doubtful that, even after we have pursued the analysis of growth for several further decades, we will emerge with what a modern economic theorist would regard as a theory of economic growth. There are too many variables to be disciplined into forms where the number of equations are equal to the number of unknowns; and, even more important, the kinds of variables we would all wish to see introduced from the side of politics, social structure, and culture do not lend themselves to a Newtonian kind of theory, elaborated from clear, minimum arbitrary hypotheses. However, the technique of comparative morphology, of which Goldsmith's paper is a distinguished example, and for which there are important precedents in certain of the natural sciences, may prove highly appropriate to our problem.

4. *Invention, Innovation, and Entrepreneurship*

I turn now to four related papers presented to the conference by Usher, Maclaurin, Cochran, and Hoselitz. As Lowe says (page 622), "The theory of technical change is still a stepchild of economic analysis." In one part of our minds and in the ritualistic listing of the determinants of the level of investment and of the rate of growth, the state of technology has always had its formal place in economics. Moreover, Schumpeter and others have produced important and stimulating generalized observations on the process which lies between fundamental science and the productivity of investment inputs. What is lacking is a systematic view of invention, innovation, and the diffusion of innovation which might be effectively woven into a total analysis of the scale and productivity of capital investment.

If the Keynesian curve of marginal efficiency of capital has any operative meaning, it has always contained implicit assumptions about these variables. The level of effective demand for investment, in terms of expected rates of return over cost, has always depended not merely on the state of technology in some generalized sense but on the extent to which entrepreneurs were prepared to apply known innovations.[4] Behind the level of capital demand, even in the short-run Keynesian sense, lie processes analyzed by Usher and Maclaurin and the qualities of entrepreneurship treated by Cochran and Hoselitz.

Usher's paper presents, in heightened form, the thesis with which his name has long been associated: namely, that invention is to be regarded as a continuous flow, representing the product of the more or less purposeful investment of a society in that peculiar creative sector, applied science. Against the background of evidence that Usher has amassed over the years, it is no longer tenable to treat invention and technical innovation as an exogenous force striking from time to time against the productive system through the medium of some Hegelian hero. Despite its peculiarities, invention is a normal part of the investment process, directed, like other forms of investment, toward believed areas of high rate of return over cost. Although Usher himself does not discuss this form of investment—the investment of resources in the generation of productive technical possibilities—in terms of a general theory of capital formation, it is time for economists to weave this variable into their analyses in a quite formal way. This demands that they include, among the sectors of the economy, that sector representing the current capacity to produce new technical improvements, and that they examine the order of magnitude of the investment input and its productivity in different societies at different periods.

[4] For an effort to link growth analysis to the Keynesian analysis of the determination of the level of investment see the present author's *The Process of Economic Growth*, Norton, 1952, pp. 65-69.

Maclaurin's further observations on this theme indicate that to treat innovation in any kind of strict relation to capital formation, we must engage, again, in an important degree of disaggregation. Maclaurin has built up, from his examination of the innovation process in particular industries, persuasive evidence both for the changing productivity of innovation at various stages of an industry's history and for differences in the productivity of innovation as among sectors of the economy. His evidence reinforces the view that the capital-output ratio must be examined in terms of sectors of an economy. Maclaurin dramatizes the argument by exploring the prospects for investment productivity in advanced countries, where an increasing proportion of total output, and especially of new investment, goes into service and other nonmanufacturing industries. Here the natural sciences may not help the growth process as much as in periods when the heavy and engineering industries lead the way. Maclaurin's general argument comes to rest on prospects for the housing industry, which, apparently throughout the world, has resisted innovation with remarkable tenacity. He suggests that the maintenance of high investment productivity in advanced countries may depend on the generation and acceptance of housing innovations, to which the social scientist as well as the engineer will have to contribute.

Taken together, Usher's and Maclaurin's arguments add up to a strong case for including the scale and productivity of the flow of innovations as an important determinant of the capital-output ratio, and for alertness to the possibility of variations in that ratio arising from the historical stage of the innovation process in particular industries and sectors of the economy.

The arguments of Cochran and Hoselitz take us a step further. They are concerned to indicate, in the context of three countries (the United States, Britain, and France) the conditions under which men have been willing to undertake the risks of capital formation. While it is convenient and important in many analyses to distinguish the kind of risk-taking which goes into the lending of money from that associated with its borrowing or with the willingness to initiate or diffuse innovations, these various determinants of the scale and productivity of investment outlays tend to merge under certain institutional circumstances. The papers by Cochran and Hoselitz relate to both sides of the market for loanable funds. The early stages of British and American capitalism saw these separable elements in capital formation focused in the same institutions or even in the same persons. This identity remains partially with us in the current role of retained earnings in corporate finance, as well as in the role of governments as both entrepreneur and supplier of loanable funds on a substantial scale.

It is an important virtue of Cochran's essay that this issue and other analytical problems of general interest come clearly through his effort to take stock of the present position of American entrepreneurial study. His paper is heartening for those who have watched the development of the sprawling field of entrepreneurial research. It seemed for a time that we would be confronted by an endless series of histories of firms drawn up in implicit analytical terms derived simply from the firms' own records, without any link to the main body of thought and research on capital formation and economic growth. Although entrepreneurial study received an enormous impetus from the theoretical insights of Schumpeter, its first phase took the form of the amassing of empirical data, with little attention to its generalization or to its relationship with other bodies of thought. These individual studies varied, of course, in their general interest and quality; but they were characterized by a failure to relate the role of the entrepreneur to the other factors determining the firm's capital formation. The firm's history was often inadequately linked to the region of which it was a part and to more general aspects of the nation's economic history, as reflected in quantitative and other evidence of growth and fluctuations.

It is clear that Cochran is seeking to make this body of historical data illuminate the statistics, such as they are, and help explain changes in rates of capital formation in the United States. The links that are made by Cochran (for example, page 341 and especially pages 363-364) are certainly not as fine as the statisticians would desire or as Cochran would like to make. Nevertheless, it is evident that we have turned a corner in the field of entrepreneurial history. Cochran's paper is an indication that this field has begun to justify itself as a central part of the study of capital formation at its most generalized level.

Much the same kind of intellectual progress is represented in Hoselitz's paper on the comparative economic performances of Britain and France as they relate to the character and quality of entrepreneurship since 1700. Again we find a purposeful effort to link the conclusions on entrepreneurship to the over-all rates and patterns of growth. Although the number of entrepreneurial studies available on France is less than on the United States, the influence of the unique social, political, and cultural structure of France as it operated through its entrepreneurs on the growth process has attracted some of the ablest men working in economic history. Hoselitz's extremely interesting effort at synthesis has excellent foundations.

These two essays in entrepreneurship illustrate once again the central theme of this commentary. When we deal with entrepreneurs, we are dealing with men who made decisions within individual firms and allocated the resources of individual firms. Our evidence is, by definition, micro- rather than macroevidence. We are in a Marshallian world of partial equilibrium when we examine the records of a firm, even a highly monopolistic firm. We are examining the supply of loanable funds, demand expectations, and the risks of innovation in the precise but limited settings of particular capital formation decisions. Our generalizations must be built up, therefore, from knowledge of firms to sectors of the economy; and, ultimately, as Cochran and Hoselitz have tried to do, these intermediate generalizations must be linked with over-all evidence on the rates and patterns of national growth. There is, however, an enormous jump from the microdata of the historian to the over-all, long-period growth rates to which Cochran and Hoselitz relate their entrepreneurial findings. As a result, their evidence can at the moment be brought to bear only in the form of broad generalizations and insights concerning the forces determining high or low, accelerating or decelerating, rates of growth. If, however, they had available systematic data on the growth rates of particular sectors of the economy, their evidence on entrepreneurship in particular industries at particular periods could be much more fully used. Qualities of entrepreneurship have always varied widely among the various sectors of an economy, and the data available to the expert on entrepreneurial history could illuminate the stories of sectors much more precisely than they can aggregate national statistics.

Moreover, in order to explore the meaning of aggregate growth statistics, we must, as noted earlier, examine them in the light of the differing growth rates in different sectors of the economy. Since entrepreneurial qualities are not uniform as among the sectors, we must bring our knowledge of entrepreneurial history to focus at the sectorial level. This will not preclude coming back again to the larger issues which Cochran and Hoselitz approach directly. It will mean that they will be able to approach these larger issues having moved up within a more systematic structure of analysis and a more systematic structure of statistical evidence than is now available to them.

5. *The Partial Equilibrium Analysis of Investment*

Although Aubrey's paper belongs, in subject matter, with the growing literature on problems of growth in underdeveloped areas, intellectually it stands with the essays of Cochran and Hoselitz. Like them, Aubrey has organized a vast amount of empirical data at an intermediate level of abstraction, thus rendering our knowledge of the facts more accessible and, especially, more susceptible of manipulation. Whereas Cochran and Hoselitz seek to make their data illuminate the relations between entrepreneurial quality and over-all rates of growth in three major countries, Aubrey's contribution is of a more general, theoretical nature. He systematically explains, in terms of a partial equilibrium analytic structure focused on the determinants of individual investment decisions, the differences between the profit maximization model which governs our thought about investment in the Western world and the shape of the investment problem in underdeveloped areas. He demonstrates forcibly the manner in which the context of underdeveloped areas demands a relaxation or change in many of the implicit and explicit assumptions carried over from knowledge of the capital formation process in Western capitalist societies.

Within its narrow limits Aubrey's paper presents an orderly analysis of noneconomic variables. The social, political, cultural, and technical determinants of economic growth are carefully and precisely linked to the strictly economic variables which govern individual investment decisions. In the end we emerge with a heightened understanding of the clash, from the point of view of the individual investor, between profit maximization and security, and of the cross purposes which may develop between the interests of the individual investor and society as a whole.

Nevertheless, a key problem for growth analysis remains. How can Aubrey's evidence and analysis be translated into terms which would bear on the aggregate categories of such theoretical structures as Lowe's or which would illuminate aggregate data on underdeveloped areas of the kind Kuznets has mobilized on more advanced countries? The answer lies, again, I believe, in building up the study of sectors. At the level of a particular industry we can link the wealth of partial equilibrium data available to the aggregates and seize on the full determinants of the scale and productivity of investment. The leap is too great for systematic analysis without the sectorial substructure; and we are likely to shift from one side of the moon to the other, as we now tend to do, assisted merely by intuitive speculation.[5]

6. *The Soviet Case*

The two papers available on the Soviet Union, like many of the others, help clarify factors which determine the relation between capital formation and economic growth, without directly assaulting that key relationship.

The student of growth within a single economy has important prima-facie advantages over the general theorist or the functional specialist in one or another variable affecting the growth rate. The examination of a given country makes it vastly easier to bring into focus the full range of forces, economic and noneconomic, at work in the growth process. The unity of the area and the society under examination directly facilitates the unification of various strands in the analysis. It is quite natural for Holzman, for example, to weave into his treatment of Soviet inflation (page 261) the peculiar Soviet organization of the firm, brilliantly depicted in the various studies of Berliner. Although Holzman is concerned with a relatively narrow and clear-cut issue of public finance, he moves easily between his statistical data and the ideological, institutional, and other forces which determined the outcome for the price level.

Similarly, the analyst of a single national economy finds it easy, if not unavoidable, to treat the aggregates determining capital formation and growth in terms of sectors. There is a quality of intimacy in Grossman's analysis of current trends in Soviet capital formation. His insights into the meaning and problems of the Fifth Five-Year Plan, and the aggregate growth rate it incorporates, come alive for the reason that he is, by definition, examining over-all objectives in terms of their principal sectorial components. Capital-intensity ceases to be a remote antiseptic variable in an equation (pages 182 ff.). It is tied in ways that are quantitative in conception —if not exactly measurable—to the position in Soviet agriculture,

[5] For pioneering examples of the kind of sectorial analysis I have in mind see Paul G. Clark, "The Telephone Industry: A Study in Private Investment," and Anne P. Grosse, "The Technological Structure of the Cotton Textile Industry," in W. W. Leontief and others, *Studies in the Structure of the American Economy*, Oxford, 1953.

housing, and even education, as well as to other sectors of the economy about which we can amass useful, if partial, evidence.

It is not accidental that some of the most original current work on capital formation and economic growth has arisen from speculation on the comparative economic performances of the United States and the U.S.S.R. We may or may not, over the years, be able to organize exact statistical evidence on the productivity of different kinds of investment outlays. But we should certainly be able to develop propositions, quantitative in character, which permit us to compare the growth patterns in different economies, and to isolate the reasons for differences among them. In his essay on "Capital Formation and Allocation" this is precisely what Kaplan did; and he concludes: "Thus, if the data can be believed, and if the analysis has been correct, the greater rate of increase of industrial output in the USSR [than in the United States] has been due, basically, *not* to differences in the USSR—United States rates of investment, but rather to differences in the *direction* of investment."[6]

It has been my experience as a historian that neither the business cycle nor trend periods (in prices, interest rates, etc.) could be understood as historical phenomena until changing sectorial patterns of investment in the past had been examined. I am reasonably confident that the same body of data will emerge as central to the historical understanding of long-term growth rates and their determinants.

7. *The Contribution of Sociology*

We come, finally, to Levy's study of "Some Social Obstacles to Capital Formation in Underdeveloped Areas." This is a remarkable paper in several respects. First, Levy has taken care to clarify the economic determinants of capital formation before bringing to bear on them the insights of social theory. He has entered into the economist's problem, in terms recognizable to the economist. Second, he has chosen to state his preliminary hypotheses mainly in terms of a comparative analysis of two societies, those of Japan and China. In combination these qualities make possible a more detailed linkage of economic theory and social theory than one usually finds in interdisciplinary efforts. There is no quick generalization here, associating particular social systems with the conditions for rapid growth.

[6] In *Soviet Economic Growth*, Abram Bergson, editor, Row, Peterson, 1953, p. 80.

Levy has begun to examine the components of social systems in relation to components of the economic process.

My sympathy for his approach derives from the agnosticism of the historian. Men have worked hard and imaginatively in the past out of a variety of motives. Economic progress has been achieved by societies as different in structure, institutions, and prevailing value systems as Britain and Japan, the United States and the Soviet Union. Neither Marxist theory nor any other general theory of society now available satisfactorily accounts for the diversities in pattern which societies have exhibited in general, and in their economic performance.

In contrasting the response of Japan and that of China to the challenge of Western industrial and military strength, Levy has chosen good illustrative material. They differ from the West, and they differ from one another. He has demonstrated how diverse the relations can be between the elements in an old culture and the requirements of industrial capital formation. On the whole, the inherited structure of Japan, as of the mid-nineteenth century, lent itself more easily to economic growth than did that of China; but this net conclusion arises from a complicated set of circumstances, not susceptible of easy generalization. Moreover (as Levy suggests, page 478), the comparison is incomplete unless we embrace in our analysis unique historical circumstances—e.g. the chronic military pressure on China, which Japan was spared, including the disastrous effects of the Japanese invasion (from 1931) on the social and economic structure of the Nationalist China which began to emerge in the 1920's.

8. *Comparative Morphology and a Non-Newtonian Theory of Growth*

If it is true that we are unlikely to find simple associations between types of social structures (or cultures) and the conditions for economic progress, what becomes of the prospects for a general theory of economic growth? It is, of course, possible that in the fullness of time we shall develop an accepted general theory of society of which economics is one facet. Given the nature of the growth problem, nothing less is implied by the concept of a theory of economic growth. For the foreseeable future, however, our aim might well be more modest: to array the patterns of growth known to us in terms which permit systematic comparison. After all, the number of societies which have passed through the transition to industrialization is limited. It should not be beyond the capacity of the social sciences to array the quantitative information available on them, in roughly uniform categories; and to explore the reasons for similarity and difference of pattern, in the light of the full determinants of economic performance. From such a grand exercise in comparative morphology, higher-order generalizations will surely emerge, relating both to the strict economics of growth and to the general social determinants of economic performance.

I believe that some such intermediate goal is implicit in most of the papers presented to this conference. The method of comparison of national patterns is used explicitly by Kuznets, Goldsmith, Hoselitz, and Levy; on a functional basis, the morphologist's technique is used by Aubrey, Maclaurin, and Usher; and, as indicated earlier, the general significance of the Soviet economic performance is increasingly being examined by means of international comparison.

I have tried in this paper to suggest the importance of sectorial analysis in furthering our understanding of economic growth. I believe it important for the refinement of theory; in the collection and interpretation of statistics; and, especially, as a means of linking systematically bodies of partial empirical evidence to aggregative concepts and data. Finally, meaningful international comparisons of growth patterns and processes require the building up of this intermediate level of analysis. The degree and kind of disaggregation appropriate will vary, as indicated in this paper, with the nature of the problem chosen for analysis and the nature of the data available.

In concluding I would make a further proposal: we might well attempt to codify, in a rough way, the measure of our theoretical agreement. Theory is a way of looking at things. Whether or not our various particular contributions will be susceptible of aggregation and cross comparison depends in part on whether we look at the growth process in similar ways. More technically, the usefulness of national growth studies will depend in part on whether or not we use comparable statistical categories and introduce into our analyses similar bodies of noneconomic data.

I am aware of the attachment that grows up between a social scientist and his private vocabulary, and of the dangers that inhere in the encouragement of abstract discussion in murky fields. Nevertheless, there may be some use in it for us, seeking to understand a many-sided problem, trying to use, in our own work, the results achieved by colleagues whose training, vocabulary, and data are often unfamiliar.

COMMENT

WILLIAM J. FELLNER, Yale University

My interpretation of Lowe's position will be based exclusively on the paper which he has submitted to this conference. On the other hand, in my interpretation of Rostow's position, I will also take account of his previous work. It seems to me that the essential characteristic of Rostow's position is his primary concern with the beginnings of growth processes in specific sectors of the economy, and their propagation through interrelations among the many sectors of our complex systems.

Rostow's and Lowe's analyses may be said to relate to two different aspects of the same problem—the relationship between long-run and short-run growth requirements. Both Rostow and Lowe place great emphasis on the necessity of analyzing the structure of resource specialization in connection with growth conditions.

I believe that the connections as well as the differences between these two contributions can be made clear by first distinguishing two types of structural analysis from each other, a long-run variety and a short-run variety, and by subsequently pointing out that both authors warn us effectively against relying on the long-run type of analysis without taking cognizance of certain results that can be obtained only by engaging in so-called short-run theorizing. The characteristic of short-run theorizing in this sense is that it deals with specialized resources—with different kinds of equipment rather than with "capital," and with different sorts of workers rather than with "labor."

In the aggregative models of recent years a basic condition of economic growth has been developed in terms of the rate of growth of output, the marginal capital-output requirement, the ex ante average propensity to save, and the rate of output itself. The aggregative condition is that the product of the first two of these four magnitudes should equal the product of the last two. In a continuously growing economy, this condition would have to be continuously satisfied. In an economy which shows merely long-run growth trends, there must be a long-run tendency toward satisfying this condition; that is to say, the violations of this condition must not permanently stop the growth process. Such aggregative theorizing must be supplemented by structural investigation, because by merely looking at the aggregative condition we cannot arrive at meaningful propositions as to the circumstances under which it is likely to be satisfied. Let us now distinguish between a long-run and a short-run variety of structural analysis, and then turn to the connecting links.

The long-run type of structural analysis directs attention to proportions between various broad categories of factors of production, in the unspecialized sense. On this level of analysis the fact that stands out most is that, in industrial economies, the capital stock is growing more rapidly than the supply of factors cooperating with capital. It would be unrealistic to assume that the growth process could continue against a lasting and substantial pressure of diminishing returns to capital. Consequently, we need improvements (innovations) to offset such a tendency. Furthermore, these improvements must have the effect of raising the marginal productivity schedule of capital, not just that of any factor of production. If improvements fail to raise the marginal productivity schedule of capital sufficiently, the growth process will be interrupted, excess capacity will develop, output will contract, and labor will become unemployed. While the improvements must be primarily capital-productivity-raising (or labor-saving), they must not treat the productivity schedule of labor too badly, because if they do so, there will have to be a continuous decrease in the share of labor or a continuous increase in chronic unemployment. It is difficult to tell what the limits of tolerance of the system were in early times to a decrease in the share of labor. Today these limits of tolerance would be small; and we have reason to believe that, in fact, there has been no long-run tendency in this direction for many decades. The limits of tolerance to increasing chronic unemployment are nil, nor has there been a tendency toward this condition, although for a while the depression of the 1930's made some economists very pessimistic about this.

To repeat: improvements must raise the productivity schedule of capital sufficiently to offset the tendency toward diminishing returns to capital; at the same time, their relatively labor-saving character must not be so great as to turn the long-run labor scarcity into chronic superabundance of labor. In the long run, the character of improvements must tend to adjust to relative factor scarcities. This is the main problem which we detect on the first level of structural analysis.

On the second or short-run level of structural analysis, we take account of the existence of specialized resources. Here another growth requirement meets the eye. Changes in the demand structure must be gradual enough not to overtax the mobility of resources; or, alternatively expressed, the mobility of resources must be sufficient to permit the specialized resource structure to adjust to the changing structure of demand. In a continuously growing economy this condition would have to be continuously satisfied. In an economy which shows merely long-run growth trends, each successive violation of the condition must be eliminated within a reasonable period of time. No individual violation must permanently arrest the growth process. This is the problem to which our attention is called on the second level of disaggregation.

It seems to me that the contributions of both Rostow and Lowe have the merit of warning us against forgetting about one level of structural analysis while we are moving on the other level. While it is methodologically convenient to distinguish the long run from the short run, we must recognize that the two interact, and that therefore resource specialization—commonly conceived of as a short-run phenomenon—requires attention even in the interpretation of long-run tendencies. In other words, both papers prove that interactions make it necessary to keep one eye on one level while we engage in detailed analysis on the other level. Let us see how Rostow and Lowe accomplish this.

Rostow shows very clearly the significance of two circumstances of which it is easy to lose sight when an oversimplified account is given of innovational requirements.

One of these circumstances has to do with the phenomena of total effective demand, external economies, and technical complementarisms. Improvements in one industry or in one sector usually give rise to growth in other sectors—in supplementary sectors, to use Rostow's terminology—quite aside from the likelihood of further innovations in these supplementary sectors. Even along given production functions, it becomes more profitable to produce iron and steel if a railroad network has been constructed, and to build railroads if there exists a ferrous metal industry of appreciable capacity. For somewhat different reasons, it is more profitable to build suburban houses if there exists an automobile industry, and more profitable to manufacture automobiles if much of the population is suburban. Rostow's analysis confirms the impression that these demand interactions, external economies, and technical complementarisms must have been quite significant. In the early German protectionist literature, tariff arguments were based on considerations of this sort. Recently, it has become more usual to base an argument for over-all planning on these same considerations. Such tariff arguments or planning arguments are logically not without justification—the difficulty here of course is that tariffs, on the one hand, and over-all planning, on the other, possess disadvantages of a different kind. Rostow's paper is not concerned with the policy aspects of the problem, nor will I dwell upon them. However, I would like to draw an inference which relates to the innovational requirements of the economic system. On what I called the first, or long-run, level of structural analysis, I concluded that in each period new improvements are needed to prevent a pressure of diminishing returns from developing. The interrelations with which Rostow is concerned should make us think that the periods in which further new improvements are needed are considerably longer than the periods for which conventional marginal efficiency schedules are drawn. When the investments which equate the marginal efficiency with the rate of interest have been completed, the growth of total effective demand, external economies, and technical complementarisms may very well raise the marginal efficiency schedule for the next short period, even if there are no further improvements; and it may take many years before the next innovations of great significance are needed to offset diminishing returns. Of course, it would be very unrealistic to think that the growth of supplementary sectors is unconnected with further innovations. But the point here is that, as a consequence of demand interactions, external economies, and technical complementarisms, further innovational activity will not have to carry the entire burden.

However, Rostow's approach also proves that for another reason the proper adjustment of innovational activity to relative resource scarcities may become difficult in some periods. It is not unreasonable to expect a tendency toward more labor-saving innovations when the increase in the labor supply is especially small in relation to that of the capital supply, and to expect a tendency toward less labor-saving innovations when the discrepancy between the two is smaller. It is not unreasonable to expect an adjustment of the character of innovations to relative resource scarcities. But Rostow makes it clear that innovational activity must adjust to something else too. At different levels of the national income, there occur relative demand shifts of different kinds, and innovational activity will be directed to opening up sectors which at that stage have potential for relative growth. Consumers become interested in automobiles when they are reasonably well-fed and -clothed, and not in the reverse sequence. The requirement that innovational activity should adjust to income elasticities of demand may be in conflict with the requirement that it should adjust to relative resource scarcities. Or rather, the adjustment to relative resource requirements may have to occur under considerable strain if other adjustments are also needed. For example, if labor is a relatively scarce factor and demand shifts call for developing a strongly labor-using sector—a sector with small capital-intensity—the labor-saving character of innovations will have to become all the more pronounced. Innovations will have to raise the capital-productivity schedules to a correspondingly larger extent.

In summary, I would like to suggest that Rostow's approach leads to certain conclusions with respect to the innovational requirements of growth, conclusions which prove that we have to keep an eye on the existing resource specialization even when we engage in long-run analysis and are primarily concerned with relative scarcities in broad factor categories. Innovations are needed because factor supplies in the broad, unspecialized sense do not grow at equal rates. But demand interdependence and external economies in specific industries and technical complementarism, which connects specific sectors of the economy, have a marked influence on the timing of the required innovational activity; and shifts in demand between different specialized sectors have exerted an important influence on existing degrees of relative factor scarcity.

It seems to me that Lowe's paper relates mainly to problems which develop on what I called the second level of structural analysis or disaggregation, where our attention is directed to the mobility or immobility of specialized resources. Lowe draws a useful distinction between investment goods industries producing equipment for other investment goods industries, investment goods industries producing equipment for consumer goods industries, and consumer goods industries. To any given demand structure there must correspond a pattern of resource specialization which is compatible with the required level of activity in these sectors. Starting from here, we may further disaggregate to any extent that seems methodologically desirable, but the general character of the specialization requirements can be made sufficiently clear in Lowe's initial three-sector model. It is clear that in a growing economy, or for that matter in any economy with changing demand structures, the pattern of specialization will never be in equilibrium with the demand structure. There will always be some amount of wrong specialization. Sufficiently small maladjustments may be overcome simply by changes in inventories or by some degree of excess capacity or overutilization, while major maladjustments will interrupt the growth process. Whether these interruptions will be short or long (or will possibly degenerate into a permanent stoppage) should be expected to depend on the outcome of a race between mobility and the rate of recurrence of such maladjustments.

From Lowe's paper we may conclude that the limited mobility of specialized resources may interfere with innovational activity and with the growth process in general, even if the innovational process does meet the so-called long-run requirements. In this connection I would like to refer to Lowe's illustration of difficulties which may arise if ex ante savings and ex ante investment change in the same proportion, but change substantially. In terms of long-run analysis, one might expect continued smooth growth. But the structure of production would have to be rearranged to such a substantial extent that the pattern of specialization would be out of gear with the requirements of the situation. The question is not whether we *call* disturbances of this sort "short-run." It is whether in the clock-time long run they prove to be episodic. We are here faced with a race between mobility and wrong specialization. This is not the same as the classical race between diminishing returns and improvement, but the two "races" become interrelated with each other.

These are effective warnings against overlooking resource specialization with the excuse that our interest is in the "long run." Perhaps both authors are somewhat inclined to go too far in rejecting the traditional type of long-run theorizing. I am convinced that there are significant problems that are discernible by analysis that deals with broad, unspecialized categories of factors of production. In my comments I have explained what, in my opinion, these problems are. I don't know whether either Rostow or Lowe means to suggest that nothing essential becomes visible in theoretical frameworks that deal with "capital" and "labor" in general. At any rate, I would not go along with that proposition. But I fully agree that a useful theory of economic growth must pay a great deal of attention to problems which cannot even be posed before we take account of the specialized character of resources.

MOSES ABRAMOVITZ, National Bureau of Economic Research and Stanford University

When I undertook the assignment of commenting on Rostow's paper, I did not realize that his contribution would consist so largely of a review and systematization of the other papers presented at this conference. A discussion of Rostow's paper would, therefore, impose on me an uncomfortable degree of detachment from the original material. Under the circumstances I feel impelled to join more directly in the discussion of theoretical approaches to the economics of growth.

(*1*) My point of departure is the well-known fact that studies of long-term changes or persistent international differences in the level of economic activity inevitably bring into prominence a number of factors which have been understandably neglected in studies of short-term changes. These are factors which differ markedly from country to country but change only slowly over time. In studies of short-term economic movements in single countries, such factors are well treated as constants. But they are of the greatest importance for an explanation of continuing differences in levels of activity and rates of growth.

Among these neglected factors are such human qualities as enterprise, industry, mobility, adaptability, and thrift; and such aspects of economic and social organization as the effectiveness of a country's financial and business organization and the legal and traditional sanctions protecting property, contract, and person. Economists have been impressed with the probable importance of variation in such factors as these for explaining international differences and secular change in income, and have concentrated attention upon them, tried to assess their significance, and tried to trace their roots. In doing so, they have explored very bravely, but no doubt very awkwardly, territory which is quite strange and difficult for them. Instead of following the familiar paths traced by private pecuniary interest, they have stumbled among problems in which the influence of pecuniary interest seems remote: family organization in relation to enterprise and efficiency; the social prestige attaching to industry and trade compared with other occupations or no occupation; nonpecuniary attachments to locality, product, or method of work; the degree of habituation to abstract financial instruments; and so on through a great variety of factors which influence the energy and effectiveness with which people, as individuals or groups, pursue their material advantage. In short, in this area economists pay the other social sciences the solid compliment of trying to be practitioners of their disciplines. And I suspect that, in addition to making a sociological or psychological contribution here and there, we are also going to discover how difficult the problems of the other social sciences are compared with those of traditional economics.

All this effort by economists outside the bounds of ordinary economics is right and proper. Like many other students, I have urged its necessity in connection with studies of economic growth.[1] But the fact that our eyes are now fully opened to the importance of extra-economic considerations should not cause us to close them to the contribution which traditional economic considerations can make. I suspect there is some danger of this. Moreover, there is evidence that others feel the presence of this danger too. For example, Aubrey in his paper writes: "A sense of past neglect seems to impel economists to give, at present, more weight to 'noneconomic' factors. This tendency, however laudable and indeed inevitable, threatens to lead to disregard of the economist's own field of investigation" (page 397).

However this may be, there *is* surely a wide range of insights into long-term changes and international differences in economic development to be derived from traditional economics. I should like, therefore, to present—or, better, simply to recall—some ten theoretical propositions, or hypotheses, derived from orthodox economic reasoning, which should help to interpret the secular trends and international differences observable in capital formation measures. Just as in the case of the noneconomic factors, their range of application and their relative importance are still unknown. But they are plausible; they are subject to verification; and they deserve close study by economists interested in economic growth.

(2) The first two hypotheses are quite commonplace derivatives from the theory of production.

1. *Capital formation, as a proportion of net national product, varies directly with the ratio of the labor force to the capital stock.*

2. *Capital formation, as a proportion of net national product, varies directly with the ratio of natural (i.e. "nonhuman" natural) resources to the stock of capital.*

[1] For example, in "Economics of Growth," in *A Survey of Contemporary Economics*, Bernard F. Haley, editor, Irwin, 1952, Vol. II, pp. 132-178.

The reasoning behind these two propositions is that, as among countries (or times) otherwise similar, the marginal productivity of capital will tend to be relatively high where (or when) the quantity of other resources is large relative to the stock of capital. Where the marginal productivity of capital is relatively high, it may be assumed that the backlog of unexploited opportunities to use additional capital profitably is relatively large. And the rate at which unexploited opportunities are seized—that is, the level of capital formation—is presumably related to the size of the existing backlog of such opportunities.

Some qualifications on the significance of these hypotheses must be made immediately. They assume diminishing returns to the factors of production, a tendency which may be defeated for many years by the economies of scale in the early development of "empty" countries. As between advanced and backward countries, it is doubtful whether the difference in the opportunities for gain, which these propositions express, will emerge from the welter of opposing forces. On the other hand, the propositions are consistent with the available evidence indicating that capital formation ratios in advanced countries fall in the course of economic development, at least after the early decades of industrialization.

3. *Capital formation, as a proportion of net national product, varies positively with the rate of population growth.* This proposition is evidently related to the first, but whereas the first expressed the effect of the cumulative backlog of investment opportunities, this expresses the effect of current additions to the backlog created by population increase. It may be presumed that current additions are of little significance if the cumulative backlog of unexploited opportunities is very large. On this reasoning, the proposition may be expected to be of importance only in relatively well-developed countries.

There is already a certain amount of empirical support for the hypothesis, but it needs further refinement. In particular, the effects which operate through the size of the population at large should be distinguished from those which operate through the number of families, and from those which operate through the size of the labor force. It would be interesting, too, to discover whether population growth stimulates investment enough to cause capital stock to grow as fast as the number of people, and whether the investment so stimulated is disproportionately concentrated upon residential housing and community facilities.

4. *Capital formation, as a proportion of net national product, varies positively with the relative size of a country's capital goods industry.* Keynes' treatment of the marginal efficiency of capital expresses the rationale of this hypothesis. The reasoning is that the rate of profit depends not only on the expected absolute yield from given additions to our physical equipment but also on their cost. The cost of capital goods varies positively with the level of investment because the capital goods industry, including the labor attached to it, cannot quickly be expanded. Thus the size attained by the capital goods industry at any time acts to limit the level of investment for considerable periods.

But not necessarily consistent w/ propositions #1 and #2

The significance of the hypothesis is somewhat limited by the fact that, to some extent, capital goods are produced by the same industries that produce consumer goods. To some extent, then, the distinction between capital formation and consumption is merely a matter of intent. Automobiles are an example.

More important is the fact that in some situations productive capital requires no special industrial outfit or organization for its production. The leading illustration is perhaps the capital embodied in cleared farm land wrested from a wilderness. The facts that this was the prime form of capital required by this and other new countries in their early development, and that for this purpose each pioneer farmer constituted his own capital goods industry, presumably help explain the rapid growth of some originally empty countries.

In all strictness, the argument applies only to a closed economy. For individual countries, capital equipment can be purchased as well as produced. Foreign purchases are, however, limited by a country's borrowing capacity, by the capacity of its export industries, by the elasticity of foreign demand for its products, and by the home demand for imported consumer goods. If, therefore, home-produced investment is limited by supply conditions in the domestic capital goods industries, imports of capital goods are limited by conditions controlling the balance and composition of international trade.

5. *A rising supply of money tends to raise the level of capital formation, and a falling supply tends to reduce it.* The problem envisaged here arises when there is a secularly rising demand for goods which is made possible, not by prior increases in production in the manner contemplated by Say's law, but rather by increases in money demand. If such a rise in the demand for goods persists

over many years, we may neglect the possibility of excess capacity and infer that prices will be rising. In this process a number of factors operate to encourage capital formation either singly or in combination. The new money may appear as an addition to liquid assets in the hands of individuals or firms. In that event, spending will be stimulated, and part of it is likely to be for capital goods. Alternatively, the additional money demand may arise in government spending based on new money or in foreign demand. In either case, there will be a strain on existing productive capacity, and the resulting profits will stimulate investment. Finally, the new money may appear as a result of the purchase of securities and loans with newly created bank money, and the consequent ease of financing will cause investment to rise. In all these cases, a general rise of prices eventuates which raises the general level of profits since, for well-known reasons, the prices at which goods are sold are likely to rise more rapidly than the prices which represent costs, at least so long as the pace of inflation is accelerating. The generally high level of profits stimulates investment partly because of the glow it casts on the future, partly because it encourages new investors to seek a share in existing markets, and partly because realized profits constitute an easy source of self-financing and an encouragement to lenders. It is this impact of general commodity inflation on investment which Keynes stressed in the historical analyses in the second volume of the *Treatise on Money*.

The range of application of this hypothesis is, of course, in doubt. Hayek and indeed most of the neoclassical writers seem to deny its validity altogether. They stress the fact that increasing injections of money are required to maintain investment booms based on forced saving. This, they maintain, produces recurrent collapses in which capital formation is discouraged. And since many investments stimulated by rising prices prove unprofitable when prices finally cease rising, let alone when they begin dropping, at least a portion of the capital produced during the boom goes to waste. It has also been urged, particularly in connection with backward economies, that chronic inflation diverts entrepreneurial energies from real capital formation to speculative trading in land, securities, and commodities, to the prejudice of productive investment. Since a priori speculation and common knowledge are incapable of settling the relation between the trends of money supply, prices, and the level of investment, the question deserves close study.

6. *Private investment, as a proportion of national product, varies directly with public investment.* The argument which leads to this hypothesis is that there exists in every country a considerable range of valuable uses for capital which private business finds it difficult or impossible to exploit, because either the projects are too risky or the returns too long deferred or the venture too large or the benefits too diffuse to form the basis for private sale and profit. Examples of such social capital are familiar, and it is obvious that, once installed, they give rise to numerous opportunities for profitable private investment.

Attempts to verify and measure the strength of the relation between public and private investment will presumably have to allow for a lag of uncertain and variable length. They will also have to take into account the fact that public investment need not be direct; it can be indirect as in the cases of subsidy, loan, or guarantee of credit. Moreover, they will have to recognize that public investment in spheres in which profitable private operation is possible competes with private investment and so may have a negative net effect.

7. *The international distribution of economic activity, and therefore of investment, shifts over time as a result of the impact of developing technology upon the distribution of locational advantages.* The relation between technological advance and economic growth is, on the noneconomic side, still a mysterious process, involving the psychology and sociology of scientific progress, a theory of the translation of new knowledge into economically productive technology, and an understanding of the diffusion of the novel product or process within and between countries. Usher and Maclaurin have contributed to this aspect of the problem in their papers submitted to this conference—to say nothing of earlier work by them and others.

On the economic side, corresponding to any given "state of the arts," to use the old-fashioned phrase, there is, *certeris paribus*, a certain distribution of production throughout the world which maximizes total output or minimizes the total cost of a given output. This ideal international distribution of production is determined by the distribution of geographically fixed resources (including existing capital equipment and population insofar as they are immobile) taken in conjunction with the techniques available for exploiting resources and for transporting the resulting products to places of further manufacture and eventual consumption. The static theory of location asserts, either explicitly or implicitly, that there is a tendency for the actual distribution of economic activity to approximate the ideal geographical pattern.

As technology progresses, however, shifts occur in the advantages that localities possess for production. The resources of some regions, which were of little importance before, become very valuable, while regions previously highly favored may lose some of their advantages. In the process of adapting economic activity to the changing pull of locational advantage, investment is stimulated in the former regions and discouraged in the latter.

Some of the very broad results of these shifts during recent centuries are clear: for example, the opening of continental interiors, the shift of activity from centers of surplus food supply to places rich in sources of power and industrial raw materials, and the trend toward spatial concentration of productive activity. But neither the empirical study of the impact of changing technology on the geography of production nor the adaptation of static location theory to the problem of differential rates of growth is yet far advanced. Both, it seems to me, deserve heavy stress in the near future.

I now add two hypotheses concerned with savings as a determinant of capital formation.

8. *Capital formation per capita tends to rise with income per capita.*

9. *Capital formation per capita tends to decline as the distribution of income approaches equality.*

The basis for the eighth proposition is Marshall's dictum that savings per capita vary directly with the "excess of income over necessary expenses."[2] The ninth requires additional support from the plausible but far from obvious notion that, as between income classes, absolute differences in saving increase more rapidly than absolute differences in income.

The eighth proposition implies no commitment to the questionable view that the ratio of savings to national income tends to increase as per capita income rises. However, both the eighth and ninth propositions assume that capital formation varies directly with the propensity to save. It will be recognized that this assumption may not be justified if investment demand at various levels of income is insufficient to absorb the available savings. Such in-

[2] *Principles of Economics*, 8th ed., London, Macmillan, 1920, p. 229.

vestment insufficiency may be due to causes independent of saving, but it may also be due to saving itself when the profit from increasing output through investment depends on how much of an increment of real income tends to be spent.

A final proposition completes this decalogue of orthodox hypotheses:

10. *Capital formation, as a proportion of national product, tends to increase as the proportion of income going to profits rises.* In classical economics this proposition was implicit in the view that profits were the almost exclusive source of savings and that saving might be treated as identical with capital formation. In more modern writing the theory is supported by a variety of arguments. Unless the profit ratio is high because competition is restricted, the incentive to invest is stronger the larger the volume of profits. Next, the level of business saving presumably varies with the volume of profits. And business saving, since it constitutes self-financing, bypasses all the obstacles involved in bringing together the supply of saving and the demand for additional money capital.

(3) The purpose of these comments is merely to recall the insights which orthodox economic theory affords into the problems of economic growth. Since I do not wish to exaggerate the probable usefulness of such hypotheses as guides to an understanding of experience, a few additional remarks seem essential.

I have presented these ten propositions as derived from orthodox economic thought for two reasons. In the first place, the validity of each depends upon the effective operation of the profit motive. This implies that the propositions are likely to prove of greatest use in interpreting the course of events in those areas of the world and in those periods in which money income is highly valued and in which commerce is firmly established as an approved way of life. Orthodox economic theory, by its nature, is likely to be most useful in connection with developed countries or with the foreign activities of their nationals. But even in primitive economies the drive for gain is not wholly absent, and until a more systematic effort is made no one can tell how far orthodox reasoning can take us.

Second, the propositions attribute differences in the profitability of investment to the range of variables to which the older economists paid most attention—that is, the quantity of human and nonhuman resources, tastes, technology, and monetary conditions and policy. The profits to be earned by investment are, however, also influenced by a wide variety of factors connected with economic and financial organization and with governmental policy. These presumably will have to be invoked to explain differences in capital formation not only between advanced and backward economies, but also among the countries in each group and in each country over time.

The study of the implications of economic organization, of law, and of governmental policy is a familiar branch of economics, though not perhaps of the orthodox variety. We may take Aubrey's paper to be a good example of this type of work. The study of variations in economic growth due to differences in the strength of pecuniary drives and to the degree of rationality with which income is pursued, and the investigation of the origins of economic institutions—here are the true happy hunting grounds of economic sociology, as Levy's paper suggests.

Granted the importance of orthodox theory, therefore, we can also easily see that it will have its limits. But even *within* the area in which such theory will best apply, the process of exploiting its insights will not be easy. This is likely to prove true in part because of the considerable number of variables which even orthodox reasoning suggests are important, in part because of the scarcity of reliable data, and in part because of the statistical problems of identifying the significant variables in the face of rampant covariation. Finally, part of the difficulty arises because the model of the secular trend of capital formation which the various orthodox hypotheses combine to form is unlikely to be one in which each factor exercises an independent influence in accordance with a simple mechanical analogy. Interrelations can already be discerned on the basis of our present scant knowledge. The contribution of savings to capital formation may be either positive or negative according to the strength of the inducement to invest and the behavioral characteristics of the money markets. The rate of population growth affects the inducement to invest through its influence upon the size of the labor force; but it also affects the supply of savings through its influence upon the ratio of workers to dependents and through the fact that the various income classes reproduce at different rates.[3] The rate of population growth itself is presumably a function of the growth of income and, therefore, of capital formation. All this suggests that the application of orthodox reasoning to growth problems will involve not merely strenuous empirical investigation, but the solution of a variety of sticky theo-

[3] See Kuznets' paper, esp. Appendix C.

retical riddles. It also suggests that the attempt, exemplified in this paper, to recognize a dichotomy between economic and extra-economic considerations can at best represent only a stage of work. The two sets of causes are too closely interwoven for either to be kept impounded during the stretches of time relevant to the problems of economic growth.

AUTHOR INDEX

SUBJECT INDEX

Recent and Forthcoming National Bureau Books

NATIONAL BUREAU BOOKS *are available from bookstores or Princeton University Press, Princeton, New Jersey, except that contributors and subscribers to the National Bureau should order directly from the National Bureau of Economic Research, 261 Madison Avenue, New York 16, New York.*

The Pattern of Financial Asset Ownership: Wisconsin Individuals, 1949 (in press) Thomas R. Atkinson	175 pp.	$4.00
Problems of Capital Formation: Concepts, Measurement, and Controlling Factors (in press) Studies in Income and Wealth, Volume Nineteen	400 pp.	7.50
Capital Formation in Residential Real Estate (in press) Leo Grebler, David M. Blank, and Louis Winnick	484 pp.	10.00
The Measurement and Behavior of Unemployment (in press) Special Conference 8	575 pp.	10.00
Consumption and Business Fluctuations: The Shoe, Leather, Hide Sequence (in press) Ruth P. Mack	8½ x 11 in., 304 pp.	7.50
Urban Mortgage Lending: Comparative Markets and Experience (in press) J. E. Morton	200 pp.	4.00
Policies to Combat Depression (in press) Special Conference 7	432 pp.	8.50
Personal Income during Business Cycles (in press) Daniel Creamer	212 pp.	4.00
Input-Output Analysis: An Appraisal (1955) Studies in Income and Wealth, Volume Eighteen	384 pp.	7.50
Short-Term Economic Forecasting (1955) Studies in Income and Wealth, Volume Seventeen	520 pp.	7.50
Minimum Price Fixing in the Bituminous Coal Industry (1955) Waldo E. Fisher and Charles M. James	556 pp.	10.00
Business Concentration and Price Policy (1955) Special Conference 5	524 pp.	9.00
Long-Range Economic Projection (1954) Studies in Income and Wealth, Volume Sixteen	488 pp.	9.00
Mortgage Lending Experience in Agriculture (1954) Lawrence A. Jones and David Durand	256 pp.	5.00
The Frontiers of Economic Knowledge (1954) Arthur F. Burns	376 pp.	5.00
Regularization of Business Investment (1954) Special Conference 4	538 pp.	8.00